THE PUBLIC PAPERS AND ADDRESSES

OF FRANKLIN D. ROOSEVELT

THE PRESIDENT AND HIS CABINET, 1938

THE PUBLIC PAPERS
AND ADDRESSES OF
FRANKLIN D. ROOSEVELT

WITH A SPECIAL INTRODUCTION
AND EXPLANATORY NOTES BY
PRESIDENT ROOSEVELT

Volume Seven

THE CONTINUING STRUGGLE
FOR LIBERALISM
1938

NEW YORK / RUSSELL & RUSSELL

The material in these volumes has been

compiled and collated by

S A M U E L   I .   R O S E N M A N

Counsel to the Governor during the ad-

ministration of Franklin D. Roosevelt

as Governor of the State of New York

1929-1932

Contents

Contents

Contents

Contents

Contents

Contents

Contents

Contents

Contents

Contents

Contents

Contents

The Continuing Struggle for Liberalism

Introduction

IT HAS frequently been said that eternal vigilance is necessary to preserve our liberties. It is equally true that eternal vigilance is necessary to keep democracies and their governments truly liberal. We in the United States have had first hand experience with that truism since the end of 1933, when, for the first time, the full effects of our program of recovery and reform began to be felt. For, as soon as the clear action of the new administration in 1933 had started the wheels of industry turning, there came the demand from some sources to stop all of the reforms, and to let things begin again to run on as they had during the previous decade.

Of course, the people of the United States have always understood that the new administration never intended to be a mere rescue party — organized to save the economic system and turn it back to the small, powerful group which had formerly controlled it through their concentrated economic power. The Government in 1933 was determined not only to save the system, but also to remove from it the abuses, evils, and widespread maladjustments which had brought it to the very brink of destruction. The Government was determined that the system, thus preserved and reformed, should no longer be subject to the control of the handful of men and corporations that had dominated it in the false boom days before 1929.

To carry out that determination was to resist, from 1933 down to date, all the efforts of mighty forces — day by day, year by year. These forces had tremendous interests at stake — wealth, privilege, economic power, political power. Although few in number, they had the resources which enabled them to make the most noise, and to become the most vociferous in the press, over the radio, through newspaper and outdoor advertising, by floods of telegrams and letters to the Congress, by employment of professional lobbyists, by all the many means of propaganda and public pressure which have been developed in recent years.

In 1938 the efforts of this minority, consistent in its opposition since 1933, rose to new heights. They had tried stubbornly at the polls in 1936 to stop our program of reform. They had failed. They had tried in 1937 to stop it in the courts, where they had been so successful during 1935 and 1936. Here, too, they had failed. Therefore, through the years of 1937 and 1938, their activities to impede progress and to bring about a repeal or emasculation of the New Deal measures of reform were redoubled.

There were several reasons for this particular burst of effort this year. First, the Supreme Court fight, although it had been finally successful in obtaining its objective, had been defeated in the Congress. The enemies of liberal government tried to hail that loss of a single battle as a defeat of the entire progressive program of the administration. A strong "putsch" was organized to try to make it appear as though the representatives of the people in the Congress had, by failing to pass the Supreme Court bill, repudiated the principles and conduct of the New Deal.

Second, there had come a substantial business recession— commencing in the fall of 1937, and continuing through the first half of 1938. That recession has been discussed at length in various items and notes in these volumes.[1] These same minority groups sought at once to take advantage of it by blaming it exclusively on the attitude and legislation of the Government, claiming that the administration was "strangling business" and "ruining confidence," and preventing "full recovery."

In 1932, the national income had fallen as low as $38,000,000,000 from a high in 1929 of about $80,000,000,000. Since 1932, and for each and every year thereafter, up to and including 1937, the national income had gradually risen until it reached the figure of $68,000,000,000.

This consistent and continuous recovery was stopped short in 1937 by several factors. First, the production and specula-

[1] See Items 152 (pages 490-492) and 156 (pages 519-520), 1937 volume; and Items 26, 49 and 50, this volume.

tive buying of heavy and consumer goods had been increased by industry at such a rapid pace that they had completely outstripped the ability of the people of the country to buy such goods. The same thing happened in 1937 on a small scale, that had happened in 1929 on a prodigious scale, namely, the purchasing power of the consumers of goods had been exceeded too quickly and too greatly by the amount of merchandise manufactured. The result was that large inventories of stocks had accumulated, which could not be sold.

In addition, the prices of merchandise had been forced up by business too drastically during the year 1937, in spite of all the efforts of the Government to discourage such inordinate increases. The mounting prices, in turn, contributed also to the inability to sell the goods manufactured, and helped to create a large excess of goods which could not be sold.

At the same time, with the steady rise of business through 1936 and early 1937, the Government had begun to cut down its own expenditures for relief and work relief. It did so with the reasonable expectation that private industry, with its increased markets and output, would take up some of the slack, and provide some of the employment which had previously been furnished by the Government through public works projects. In this the Government miscalculated.

It soon became obvious that 1937 was too early to begin to cut down drastically on the expenditure of public funds which had been furnishing the necessary purchasing power for those who could not otherwise get it. The Government's expectations that industry would take up the process of giving employment were not fulfilled. Industry failed to supply jobs to replace those which had been lost by curtailment of Federal work relief.

At the same time, it is also undoubtedly true that, in some quarters, labor had gone too far in its demands and in its conduct, especially with respect to sit-down strikes.[1]

The explanation for the recession may, therefore, legitimately be placed at the door of all three — Government, capital,

[1] See note to Item 72, 1937 volume.

and labor. It should be remembered that at no time did this recession ever reach alarming proportions. There was never any semblance of the panic or stagnation or hopelessness which had developed in 1932. Our Government had been adequately prepared to deal with it—and did deal with it quickly and effectively. However, the recession, such as it was, was seized upon by the opponents of reform and liberal government, as a great talking point from which to urge that, unless the whole business of reform and progress were stopped right away, the industrial system of America would collapse, and the Government itself would become bankrupt.

All of the big guns and resources of pressure politics and modern propaganda were brought into play in late 1937 and 1938, to try to strike down liberalism in the Congress and in the executive branch of the Government.

The policy of the Federal Government, however, continued to follow the only path of true recovery and the only assurance of preservation of our system of private profit and free enterprise —the continuance and strengthening of social reform and progressive legislation.

When I called the Congress into extraordinary session in 1937, I pointed this out; and I announced the determination of the Federal Government to proceed with its program on all fronts with full speed.[1]

Accordingly, I recommended the enactment of new farm legislation. I called for a comprehensive farm program—not only to replace the old measures which had been declared unconstitutional by the Supreme Court, but one which would go forward. I called for legislation for soil conservation and for regulation of crop production so as to furnish an ever-normal granary which would give the farmer a fair share of the national income, and at the same time, would also assure the consumer a steady supply of food and textile fibre at reasonable prices.

I also recommended to this extraordinary session of the Congress the enactment of legislation providing for minimum wages

[1] See Item 152, 1937 volume.

and maximum hours and the abolition of child labor in all interstate occupations. Only in this way could sweatshop conditions be eliminated and workers receive a reasonable purchasing power — to enable them to live with some degree of decency, and to provide a market for the products of the farms and factories of the nation.

And, in order to make government more efficient in planning and in executing its duties and responsibilities, I recommended a comprehensive plan of reorganization of the administrative branch of the Federal Government and a great expansion of the planning functions of government.

These recommendations were renewed by me when the Congress reassembled in regular session in January, 1938. In addition, I made other recommendations showing that the New Deal was determined not to stop in its tracks, but to press forward in its program of progress. I recommended, for example, that new tax legislation was necessary — first, to prevent continued tax evasion by some few individuals and corporations; and, second, to make sure that the principle of ability to pay was not violated by the tax structure.

I also called attention to some of the grave social abuses which had grown up in the use of capital — not all capital, but in a limited portion thereof. In other words, I made it clear that what I was attacking was not business in general or all business practices, but certain clearly wrongful business practices which were ruinous to the rest of the economic system of the country. I pointed out that, in addition to tax avoidance, these practices included: excessive capitalization, continued write-ups of investment values, security manipulations, collusive bidding and price rigging, high-pressure salesmanship which creates cycles of overproduction and recessions in production, the use of patent laws for monopolistic purposes, and unfair competition. I also called attention to the unfortunate practice of industry to move from one locality or region of the country to another — in an effort to find the cheapest possible wage scales, or in order to try to intimidate local and state governments from the passage of progressive legislation for the protection of labor.

Above all, I stressed the grave danger and serious problems which had arisen, and which always arise, out of the growing concentration of economic power, involving, as it did, the control by a relatively few men of other people's money, other people's labor, and other people's lives.

In a special message to the Congress on April 29, 1938, I pointed out that this concentration was seriously impairing the economic effectiveness of private enterprise as a way of providing employment for labor and capital, and as a way of assuring a more equitable distribution of income and earnings among the people of the nation as a whole. To meet this situation I recommended a thorough study of the concentration of economic power in American industry and the effect of that concentration upon the decline of competition. I suggested that this investigation should include an examination of the existing price system and price policies of industry to determine their effect upon the general level of trade, upon employment, upon long term profits and upon consumption. Such a survey, I pointed out, should not be confined to the traditional anti-trust field, but should review critically the social and economic effects of tax, patent and other government policies.

Much of the legislation which I recommended was passed during 1938. For example, a new farm program was adopted;[1] legislation establishing minimum wages and maximum hours and outlawing child labor was finally passed;[2] additional funds were provided for the construction of public works to furnish employment; and a congressional and administrative committee was set up to study the whole subject of monopolies and the concentration of economic power.[3] Administrative reorganization was delayed until 1939.[4]

[1] See Item 24, this volume.
[2] See note to Item 57, 1937 volume.
[3] See Item 59, this volume.
[4] See note to Item 41, this volume.

Introduction

Many of the great measures debated in 1937 and 1938 — farm legislation, reorganization of government, minimum wages and maximum hours, increased public works, monopoly controls, judicial reforms, water power development, low-cost housing — have, by now, become more or less accepted as part of our economic life. It is a little difficult, therefore, to look back even across the short period to 1938 and remember how bitter and how difficult was the struggle — in the Congress and out of the Congress — which was necessary in order to have some of these laws adopted. The opposition to them — chiefly from the same sources which had opposed the whole program of reform since 1933 — developed into "blitzkrieg" proportions. Misrepresentation as to motives, and falsehoods as to objectives and results, became common practice, especially in the columns of some of the large newspapers.

In that struggle, a few Democratic members of the House and Senate — who had been elected in 1936 and in earlier years on liberal platforms, and who had pledged themselves to support the great objectives and social measures enunciated in those platforms — had definitely allied themselves with the opponents of the program. I do not mean merely that these members had disagreed with one or two or more items in the program, and had suggested other measures which they thought more likely to obtain the same results. Obviously, no fault could have been found in any respect with legislators who thought that the liberal principles of the Democratic platform of 1936 could be carried out by other measures, and who proposed and fought for such other measures. But that was not what was happening. The blunt fact is that these men were deliberately repudiating the very principles of progress which they had espoused in order to be elected — and which were, in some cases, the only reason that they had been elected.

It became quite obvious that this kind of conduct was not only a renunciation of platform pledges, but was actually endangering the successful accomplishment of the Federal Government's determination to preserve a liberal, progressive administration.

The primary obligation and responsibility for determining the general objectives and direction of any administration naturally lie with the President himself. However, he can do little alone, without the cooperation of the Congress. In this particular instance the vast majority of the Congress were members of my own party. The number of Democrats in the Congress had been increased during each and every Congressional election commencing with 1932. They had each time been elected on a platform which expressly called for the adoption of liberal legislation. But, in spite of this, that type of legislation had begun to be repudiated by several of them; so that if the process were not checked, the whole liberal program might eventually become jeopardized.

I believe it to be my sworn duty, as President, to take all steps necessary to insure the continuance of liberalism in our government. I believe, at the same time, that it is my duty as the head of the Democratic party to see to it that my party remains the truly liberal party in the political life of America.

There had been many periods in American history, unfortunately, when one major political party was no different from the other major party—except only in name. In a system of party government such as ours, however, elections become meaningless when the two major parties have no differences other than their labels. For such elections do not give the people of the United States an opportunity to decide upon the type of government which they prefer for themselves for the next two or the next four years, as the case may be. I do not mean necessarily that expression of choice at the polls should concern itself with details, or with particular methods. But it is essential that the general trend and direction of government should be left to the determination of a majority of the people; and the only way that they can express their will is by voting for the candidates of that party which espouses the particular trend in government which they prefer.

Introduction

Generally speaking, in a representative form of government there are usually two general schools of political belief — liberal and conservative. The system of party responsibility in America requires that one of its parties be the liberal party and the other be the conservative party. This has been the division by which the major parties in American history have identified themselves whenever crises have developed which required definite choice of direction. In Jefferson's day, in Jackson's day, and in Lincoln's, and Theodore Roosevelt's, and Wilson's day, one group emerged clearly as liberals, opposed to the other — the conservatives.

One great difference which has characterized this division has been that the liberal party — no matter what its particular name was at the time — believed in the wisdom and efficacy of the will of the great majority of the people, as distinguished from the judgment of a small minority of either education or wealth. The liberal group has always believed that control by a few — political control or economic control — if exercised for a long period of time, would be destructive of a sound representative democracy. For this reason, for example, it has always advocated the extension of the right of suffrage to as many people as possible, trusting the combined judgment of all the people in political matters rather than the judgment of a small minority.

The other great difference between the two parties has been this: The liberal party is a party which believes that, as new conditions and problems arise beyond the power of men and women to meet as individuals, it becomes the duty of the Government itself to find new remedies with which to meet them. The liberal party insists that the Government has the definite duty to use all its power and resources to meet new social problems with new social controls — to insure to the average person the right to his own economic and political life, liberty, and the pursuit of happiness. That theory of the role of government was expressed by Abraham Lincoln when he said, "the legitimate object of government is to do for a community of people whatever they need to have done, but cannot do at all, or cannot do so well, for themselves, in their separate and individual capacities."

The conservative party in government honestly and conscientiously believes the contrary. It believes that there is no necessity for the Government to step in, even when new conditions and new problems arise. It believes that, in the long run, individual initiative and private philanthropy can take care of all situations. The test of allegiance to one or the other of these schools of political and economic thought cannot be based on a person's views with respect to one particular measure or policy or even several of them. The test is rather whether a person adheres to the broad general objectives of the particular party as expressed in its fundamental principles.

The clear and undisputed fact is that in these later years, at least since 1932, the Democratic party has been the liberal party, and the Republican party has been the conservative party.

There can, of course, be no quarrel by anybody with anyone who sincerely subscribes either to the principles of liberalism or conservatism. The quarrel in 1938 was with those who said they were liberals, but who, nevertheless, proceeded to stand in the way of all social progress by objecting to any measure to carry out liberal objectives. The usual procedure of this type of liberal is to say that he believes in the objective, but that he does not like the details of the particular method proposed to carry out the objective. He says, *"Yes"* — that he is in favor of the end; *but* he objects to the means — at the same time offering no alternative method, and seldom, if ever, raising a finger of his own to try to obtain the ultimate objective. I have frequently referred to this type of individual as a "yes, but —" fellow.

The true liberal does not claim, of course, that the remedies with which he proposes to attain his objectives are perfect. But he is willing to start with something less than perfect in this imperfect world. The conservative, on the other hand, believes generally that all remedies proposed by the Government itself are usually unnecessary, and that perfection can be obtained more readily and more quickly through private initiative.

Introduction

It is a comparatively simple thing for a nation to determine, by its votes, whether it chooses the liberal or the conservative form of government. On the other hand, a nation can never intelligently determine its policy, if it has to go through the confusion of voting for candidates who pretend to be one thing but who act the other.

I have always believed, and I have frequently stated, that my own party can succeed at the polls only so long as it continues to be the party of militant liberalism. I do not mean to imply that only enrolled Democrats are liberal voters, or even that all enrolled Democrats are liberal voters. I do not mean to imply, on the other hand, that only enrolled Republicans are conservative voters, or that all enrolled Republicans are conservative voters. There is a vast number of independent voters who are unwilling to become affiliated with either party, but whose social and political outlook is definitely liberal, and whose votes have been cast for liberal candidates. On the other hand, millions of enrolled Republican voters — affiliated under the conservative Republican leadership for one reason or another — have nevertheless consistently voted for the type of government and candidates who appear under the liberal banner.

But, as the head of the Democratic party, I think that it is nothing more nor less than political consistency for the candidates standing for election on the liberal program of my party to act like liberals after the election is over.

It was that belief, and the complete realization of the fact that some Democratic candidates had acted in repudiation of progressive and liberal government, that I took an active part in some of the primary elections of 1938 — in an effort to keep liberalism in the foreground in the councils of my own party, as well as in the legislative and executive branches of the Government itself.

My participation in these primary campaigns was slurringly referred to, by those who were opposed to liberalism, as a "purge." The word became a slogan for those who tried to misrepresent my conduct to make it appear to be an effort to defeat certain Senators and Representatives who had voted against one measure or another recommended by me — particularly those who had voted against the Supreme Court bill of 1937. Nothing could be further from the truth. I was not interested in personalities. Nor was I interested in particular measures — because most of the liberal measures I had recommended had already been passed. I was, however, primarily interested in seeing to it that the Democratic party and the Republican party should not be merely Tweedledum and Tweedledee to each other. I was chiefly interested in continuing the Democratic party as the liberal, forward-looking, progressive party in the United States.

The primary campaigns in which I actively spoke, consisted of one congressional campaign in my own home State, one senatorial campaign in my other home State of Georgia, one in Kentucky (where the choice was not between a conservative and a liberal, but between two liberals, one of whom was the experienced Democratic leader of the Senate), and one senatorial campaign in the State of Maryland, where I was accompanied by the chairman of the Democratic National Committee. It must be remembered, also, that in some of these States, and in some other States, a definite misuse was being made of my name by one candidate or the other, falsely claiming that I favored his election. Under such circumstances I exercised my clear right to speak out in the interest of truth.[1]

In these primary campaign speeches, I made it clear that I was not trying to dictate to the people of any State as to how they should vote. What I was trying to do was to impress upon them the necessity of voting for liberal candidates — if they wanted a continuation of the liberal kind of government which they had had since 1933.

Looking back on the domestic issues of 1937 and 1938, there is much satisfaction in realizing that the American people, as a whole, were not taken in by the bitter accusations and dire predictions of those who cried "dictatorship," "imminent bank-

[1] See Items 80, 90, 100, 113, and 132, this volume.

ruptcy," or "strangulation of business." The determination of the people to continue the same liberal program of progressive reform was clearly expressed at the polls in 1938. As was to be expected, after the steady and continued increase in Democratic representation in the Congress in 1932, 1934, and 1936, the Democratic majority fell off somewhat in 1938. But the fact that, after the elections of 1938, there were 69 Democratic Senators and 262 Democratic Representatives, as against 23 Republican Senators and 169 Republican Representatives, shows that the cause of progressive government had found definite approval with the people, and that the people were determined that it be continued.

The political struggle of 1938 had not been in vain. Liberalism in Government was still triumphant.

Franklin D. Roosevelt

White House,
Washington, D. C.,
June 16, 1941.

1 ⟨ Annual Message to the Congress.

January 3, 1938

Mr. President, Mr. Speaker, Members of the Senate and of the House of Representatives:

IN ADDRESSING the Congress on the state of the Union present facts and future hazards demand that I speak clearly and earnestly of the causes which underlie events of profound concern to all.

In spite of the determination of this Nation for peace, it has become clear that acts and policies of nations in other parts of the world have far-reaching effects not only upon their immediate neighbors but also on us.

I am thankful that I can tell you that our Nation is at peace. It has been kept at peace despite provocations which in other days, because of their seriousness, could well have engendered war. The people of the United States and the Government of the United States have shown capacity for restraint and a civilized approach to the purposes of peace, while at the same time we maintain the integrity inherent in the sovereignty of 130,000,000 people, lest we weaken or destroy our influence for peace and jeopardize the sovereignty itself.

It is our traditional policy to live at peace with other nations. More than that, we have been among the leaders in advocating the use of pacific methods of discussion and conciliation in international differences. We have striven for the reduction of military forces.

But in a world of high tension and disorder, in a world where stable civilization is actually threatened, it becomes the responsibility of each nation which strives for peace at home and peace with and among others to be strong enough to assure the observance of those fundamentals of peaceful solution of conflicts which are the only ultimate basis for orderly existence.

Resolute in our determination to respect the rights of others, and to command respect for the rights of ourselves, we must keep ourselves adequately strong in self-defense.

1

1. Annual Message

There is a trend in the world away from the observance both of the letter and the spirit of treaties. We propose to observe, as we have in the past, our own treaty obligations to the limit; but we cannot be certain of reciprocity on the part of others.

Disregard for treaty obligations seems to have followed the surface trend away from the democratic representative form of government. It would seem, therefore, that world peace through international agreements is most safe in the hands of democratic representative governments — or, in other words, peace is most greatly jeopardized in and by those nations where democracy has been discarded or has never developed.

I have used the words "surface trend," for I still believe that civilized man increasingly insists and in the long run will insist on genuine participation in his own government. Our people believe that over the years democracies of the world will survive, and that democracy will be restored or established in those nations which today know it not. In that faith lies the future peace of mankind.

At home, conditions call for my equal candor. Events of recent months are new proof that we cannot conduct a national government after the practice of 1787, or 1837 or 1887, for the obvious reason that human needs and human desires are infinitely greater, infinitely more difficult to meet than in any previous period in the life of our Republic. Hitherto it has been an acknowledged duty of government to meet these desires and needs: nothing has occurred of late to absolve the Congress, the Courts or the President from that task. It faces us as squarely, as insistently, as in March, 1933.

Much of trouble in our own lifetime has sprung from a long period of inaction — from ignoring what fundamentally was happening to us, and from a time-serving unwillingness to face facts as they forced themselves upon us.

Our national life rests on two nearly equal producing forces, agriculture and industry, each employing about one-third of our citizens. The other third transports and distributes the products of the first two, or performs special services for the whole.

The first great force, agriculture—and with it the production of timber, minerals and other natural resources—went forward feverishly and thoughtlessly until nature rebelled and we saw deserts encroach, floods destroy, trees disappear and soil exhausted.

At the same time we have been discovering that vast numbers of our farming population live in a poverty more abject than that of many of the farmers of Europe whom we are wont to call peasants; that the prices of our products of agriculture are too often dependent on speculation by non-farming groups; and that foreign nations, eager to become self-sustaining or ready to put virgin land under the plough are no longer buying our surpluses of cotton and wheat and lard and tobacco and fruit as they had before.

Since 1933 we have knowingly faced a choice of three remedies. First, to cut our cost of farm production below that of other nations—an obvious impossibility in many crops today unless we revert to human slavery or its equivalent.

Second, to make the government the guarantor of farm prices and the underwriter of excess farm production without limit— a course which would bankrupt the strongest government in the world in a decade.

Third, to place the primary responsibility directly on the farmers themselves, under the principle of majority rule, so that they may decide, with full knowledge of the facts of surpluses, scarcities, world markets and domestic needs, what the planting of each crop should be in order to maintain a reasonably adequate supply which will assure a minimum adequate price under the normal processes of the law of supply and demand.

That means adequacy of supply but not glut. It means adequate reserves against the day of drought. It is shameless misrepresentation to call this a policy of scarcity. It is in truth insurance before the fact, instead of government subsidy after the fact.

Any such plan for the control of excessive surpluses and the speculation they bring has two enemies. There are those well-meaning theorists who harp on the inherent right of every free born American to do with his land what he wants — to cultivate it well — or badly; to conserve his timber by cutting only the annual increment thereof — or to strip it clean, let fire burn the slash, and erosion complete the ruin; to raise only one crop — and if that crop fails, to look for food and support from his neighbors or his government.

That, I assert is not an inherent right of citizenship. For if a man farms his land to the waste of the soil or the trees, he destroys not only his own assets but the Nation's assets as well. Or if by his methods he makes himself, year after year, a financial hazard of the community and the government, he becomes not only a social problem but an economic menace. The day has gone by when it could be claimed that government has no interest in such ill-considered practices and no right through representative methods to stop them.

The other group of enemies is perhaps less well-meaning. It includes those who for partisan purposes oppose each and every practical effort to help the situation, and also those who make money from undue fluctuations in crop prices.

I gladly note that measures which seek to initiate a government program for a balanced agriculture are now in conference between the two Houses of the Congress. In their final consideration, I hope for a sound consistent measure which will keep the cost of its administration within the figure of current government expenditures in aid of agriculture. The farmers of this Nation know that a balanced output can be put into effect without excessive cost and with the cooperation of the great majority of them.

If this balance can be created by an all-weather farm program, our farm population will soon be assured of relatively constant purchasing power. From this will flow two other practical results: the consuming public will be protected against excessive food and textile prices, and the industries of the Nation

4

and their workers will find a steadier demand for wares sold to the agricultural third of our people.

To raise the purchasing power of the farmer is, however, not enough. It will not stay raised if we do not also raise the purchasing power of that third of the Nation which receives its income from industrial employment. Millions of industrial workers receive pay so low that they have little buying power. Aside from the undoubted fact that they thereby suffer great human hardship, they are unable to buy adequate food and shelter, to maintain health or to buy their share of manufactured goods.

We have not only seen minimum wage and maximum hour provisions prove their worth economically and socially under government auspices in 1933, 1934 and 1935, but the people of this country, by an overwhelming vote, are in favor of having the Congress—this Congress—put a floor below which industrial wages shall not fall, and a ceiling beyond which the hours of industrial labor shall not rise.

Here again let us analyze the opposition. A part of it is sincere in believing that an effort thus to raise the purchasing power of lowest paid industrial workers is not the business of the Federal Government. Others give "lip service" to a general objective, but do not like any specific measure that is proposed. In both cases it is worth our while to wonder whether some of these opponents are not at heart opposed to any program for raising the wages of the underpaid or reducing the hours of the overworked.

Another group opposes legislation of this type on the ground that cheap labor will help their locality to acquire industries and outside capital, or to retain industries which today are surviving only because of existing low wages and long hours. It has been my thought that, especially during these past five years, this Nation has grown away from local or sectional selfishness and toward national patriotism and unity. I am disappointed by some recent actions and by some recent utterances which sound like the philosophy of half a century ago.

1. Annual Message

There are many communities in the United States where the average family income is pitifully low. It is in those communities that we find the poorest educational facilities and the worst conditions of health. Why? It is not because they are satisfied to live as they do. It is because those communities have the lowest per capita wealth and income; therefore, the lowest ability to pay taxes; and, therefore, inadequate functioning of local government.

Such communities exist in the East, in the Middle West, in the Far West, and in the South. Those who represent such areas in every part of the country do their constituents ill-service by blocking efforts to raise their incomes, their property values and, therefore, their whole scale of living. In the long run, the profits from child labor, low pay and overwork enure not to the locality or region where they exist but to the absentee owners who have sent their capital into these exploited communities to gather larger profits for themselves. Indeed, new enterprises and new industries which bring permanent wealth will come more readily to those communities which insist on good pay and reasonable hours, for the simple reason that there they will find a greater industrial efficiency and happier workers.

No reasonable person seeks a complete uniformity in wages in every part of the United States; nor does any reasonable person seek an immediate and drastic change from the lowest pay to the highest pay. We are seeking, of course, only legislation to end starvation wages and intolerable hours; more desirable wages are and should continue to be the product of collective bargaining.

Many of those who represent great cities have shown their understanding of the necessity of helping the agricultural third of the Nation. I hope that those who represent constituencies primarily agricultural will not underestimate the importance of extending like aid to the industrial third.

Wage and hour legislation, therefore, is a problem which is definitely before this Congress for action. It is an essential part of economic recovery. It has the support of an overwhelming majority of our people in every walk of life. They have expressed themselves through the ballot box.

Again I revert to the increase of national purchasing power as an underlying necessity of the day. If you increase that purchasing power for the farmers and for the industrial workers, especially for those in both groups who have least of it today, you will increase the purchasing power of the final third of our population — those who transport and distribute the products of farm and factory, and those of the professions who serve all groups. I have tried to make clear to you, and through you to the people of the United States, that this is an urgency which must be met by complete and not by partial action.

If it is met, if the purchasing power of the Nation as a whole — in other words, the total of the Nation's income — can be still further increased, other happy results will flow from such increase.

We have raised the Nation's income from thirty-eight billion dollars in the year 1932 to about sixty-eight billion dollars in the year 1937. Our goal, our objective is to raise it to ninety or one hundred billion dollars.

We have heard much about a balanced budget, and it is interesting to note that many of those who have pleaded for a balanced budget as the sole need now come to me to plead for additional government expenditures at the expense of unbalancing the budget. As the Congress is fully aware, the annual deficit, large for several years, has been declining the last fiscal year and this. The proposed budget for 1939, which I shall shortly send to the Congress, will exhibit a further decrease in the deficit, though not a balance between income and outgo.

To many who have pleaded with me for an immediate balancing of the budget, by a sharp curtailment or even elimination of government functions, I have asked the question: "What present expenditures would you reduce or eliminate?" And the invariable answer has been "that is not my business — I know nothing of the details, but I am sure that it could be done." That is not what you or I would call helpful citizenship.

7

On only one point do most of them have a suggestion. They think that relief for the unemployed by the giving of work is wasteful, and when I pin them down I discover that at heart they are actually in favor of substituting a dole in place of useful work. To that neither I nor, I am confident, the Senators and Representatives in the Congress will ever consent.

I am as anxious as any banker or industrialist or business man or investor or economist that the budget of the United States Government be brought into balance as quickly as possible. But I lay down certain conditions which seem reasonable and which I believe all should accept.

The first condition is that we continue the policy of not permitting any needy American who can and is willing to work to starve because the Federal Government does not provide the work.

The second is that the Congress and the Executive join hands in eliminating or curtailing any Federal activity which can be eliminated or curtailed or even postponed without harming necessary government functions or the safety of the Nation from a national point of view.

The third is to raise the purchasing power of the Nation to the point that the taxes on this purchasing power — or, in other words, on the Nation's income — will be sufficient to meet the necessary expenditures of the national government.

I have hitherto stated that, in my judgment, the expenditures of the national government cannot be cut much below seven billion dollars a year without destroying essential functions or letting people starve. That sum can be raised and will be cheerfully provided by the American people, if we can increase the Nation's income to a point well beyond the present level.

This does not mean that as the Nation's income goes up the Federal expenditures should rise in proportion. On the contrary, the Congress and the Executive should use every effort to hold the normal Federal expenditures to approximately the present level, thus making it possible, with an increase in the

Nation's income and the resulting increase in tax receipts, not only to balance future budgets but to reduce the debt.

In line with this policy fall my former recommendations for the reorganization and improvement of the administrative structure of the government, both for immediate Executive needs and for the planning of future national needs. I renew those recommendations.

In relation to tax changes, three things should be kept in mind. First, the total sum to be derived by the Federal Treasury must not be decreased as a result of any changes in schedules. Second, abuses by individuals or corporations designed to escape tax-paying by using various methods of doing business, corporate and otherwise — abuses which we have sought, with great success, to end — must not be restored. Third, we should rightly change certain provisions where they are proven to work definite hardship, especially on the small business men of the Nation. But, speculative income should not be favored over earned income.

It is human nature to argue that this or that tax is responsible for every ill. It is human nature on the part of those who pay graduated taxes to attack all taxes based on the principle of ability to pay. These are the same complainants who for a generation blocked the imposition of a graduated income tax. They are the same complainants who would impose the type of flat sales tax which places the burden of government more on those least able to pay and less on those most able to pay.

Our conclusion must be that while proven hardships should be corrected, they should not be corrected in such a way as to restore abuses already terminated or to shift a greater burden to the less fortunate.

This subject leads naturally into the wider field of the public attitude toward business. The objective of increasing the purchasing power of the farming third, the industrial third and the service third of our population presupposes the cooperation of what we call capital and labor.

Capital is essential; reasonable earnings on capital are essential; but misuse of the powers of capital or selfish suspension of the employment of capital must be ended, or the capitalistic system will destroy itself through its own abuses.

The overwhelming majority of business men and bankers intend to be good citizens. Only a small minority have displayed poor citizenship by engaging in practices which are dishonest or definitely harmful to society. This statement is straightforward and true. No person in any responsible place in the Government of the United States today has ever taken any position contrary to it.

But, unfortunately for the country, when attention is called to, or attack is made on specific misuses of capital, there has been a deliberate purpose on the part of the condemned minority to distort the criticism into an attack on all capital. That is wilful deception but it does not long deceive.

If attention is called to, or attack made on, certain wrongful business practices, there are those who are eager to call it "an attack on all business." That, too, is wilful deception that will not long deceive.

Let us consider certain facts:

There are practices today which most people believe should be ended. They include tax avoidance through corporate and other methods, which I have previously mentioned; excessive capitalization, investment write-ups and security manipulations; price rigging and collusive bidding in defiance of the spirit of the antitrust laws by methods which baffle prosecution under the present statutes. They include high-pressure salesmanship which creates cycles of overproduction within given industries and consequent recessions in production until such time as the surplus is consumed; the use of patent laws to enable larger corporations to maintain high prices and withhold from the public the advantages of the progress of science; unfair competition which drives the smaller producer out of business locally, regionally or even on a national scale; intimidation of local or state government to prevent the enactment of laws for the protection of labor by threatening to move elsewhere; the shifting of actual production from one locality or region to another in pursuit of the cheapest wage scale.

The enumeration of these abuses does not mean that business as a whole is guilty of them. Again, it is deception that will not long deceive to tell the country that an attack on these abuses is an attack on business.

Another group of problems affecting business, which cannot be termed specific abuses, gives us food for grave thought about the future. Generically such problems arise out of the concentration of economic control to the detriment of the body politic — control of other people's money, other people's labor, other people's lives.

In many instances such concentrations cannot be justified on the ground of operating efficiency, but have been created for the sake of securities profits, financial control, the suppression of competition and the ambition for power over others. In some lines of industry a very small numerical group is in such a position of influence that its actions are of necessity followed by the other units operating in the same field.

That such influences operate to control banking and finance is equally true, in spite of the many efforts, through Federal legislation, to take such control out of the hands of a small group. We have but to talk with hundreds of small bankers throughout the United States to realize that irrespective of local conditions, they are compelled in practice to accept the policies laid down by a small number of the larger banks in the Nation. The work undertaken by Andrew Jackson and Woodrow Wilson is not finished yet.

The ownership of vast properties or the organization of thousands of workers creates a heavy obligation of public service. The power should not be sought or sanctioned unless the responsibility is accepted as well. The man who seeks freedom from such responsibility in the name of individual liberty is either fooling himself or trying to cheat his fellow men. He wants to eat the fruits of orderly society without paying for them.

As a Nation we have rejected any radical revolutionary program. For a permanent correction of grave weaknesses in our economic system we have relied on new applications of old democratic processes. It is not necessary to recount what has been accomplished in preserving the homes and livelihood of millions of workers on farms and in cities, in reconstructing a sound banking and credit system, in reviving trade and industry, in reestablishing security of life and property. All we need today is to look upon the fundamental, sound economic conditions to know that this business recession causes more perplexity than fear on the part of most people and to contrast our prevailing mental attitude with the terror and despair of five years ago.

Furthermore, we have a new moral climate in America. That means that we ask business and finance to recognize that fact, to cure such inequalities as they can cure without legislation but to join their government in the enactment of legislation where the ending of abuses and the steady functioning of our economic system calls for government assistance. The Nation has no obligation to make America safe either for incompetent business men or for business men who fail to note the trend of the times and continue the use of machinery of economics and practices of finance as outworn as the cotton spindle of 1870.

Government can be expected to cooperate in every way with the business of the Nation provided the component parts of business abandon practices which do not belong to this day and age, and adopt price and production policies appropriate to the times.

In regard to the relationship of government to certain processes of business, to which I have referred, it seems clear to me that existing laws undoubtedly require reconstruction. I expect, therefore, to address the Congress in a special message on this subject, and I hope to have the help of business in the efforts of government to help business.

I have spoken of labor as another essential in the three great groups of the population in raising the Nation's income. Definite strides in collective bargaining have been made and the right of labor to organize has been nationally accepted. Nevertheless in the evolution of the process difficult situations have arisen in localities and among groups. Unfortunate divisions relating to jurisdiction among the workers themselves have retarded production within given industries and have, therefore, affected related industries. The construction of homes and other buildings has been hindered in some localities not only by unnecessarily high prices for materials but also by certain hourly wage scales.

For economic and social reasons our principal interest for the near future lies along two lines: first, the immediate desirability of increasing the wages of the lowest paid groups in all industry; and, second, in thinking in terms of regularizing the work of the individual worker more greatly through the year — in other words, in thinking more in terms of the worker's total pay for a period of a whole year rather than in terms of his remuneration by the hour or by the day.

In the case of labor as in the case of capital, misrepresentation of the policy of the government of the United States is deception which will not long deceive. In both cases we seek cooperation. In every case power and responsibility must go hand in hand.

I have spoken of economic causes which throw the Nation's income out of balance; I have spoken of practices and abuses which demand correction through the cooperation of capital and labor with the government. But no government can help the destinies of people who insist in putting sectional and class-consciousness ahead of general weal. There must be proof that sectional and class interests are prepared more greatly than they are today to be national in outlook.

A government can punish specific acts of spoliation; but no government can conscript cooperation. We have improved some matters by way of remedial legislation. But where in some particulars that legislation has failed we cannot be sure whether it fails because some of its details are unwise or because it is being sabotaged. At any rate, we hold our objectives and our principles to be sound. We will never go back on them.

Government has a final responsibility for the well-being of its citizenship. If private cooperative endeavor fails to provide work for willing hands and relief for the unfortunate, those suffering hardship from no fault of their own have a right to call upon the Government for aid; and a government worthy of its name must make fitting response.

It is the opportunity and the duty of all those who have faith in democratic methods as applied in industry, in agriculture and in business, as well as in the field of politics, to do their utmost to cooperate with government — without regard to political affiliation, special interests or economic prejudices — in whatever program may be sanctioned by the chosen representatives of the people.

That presupposes on the part of the representatives of the people, a program, its enactment and its administration.

Not because of the pledges of party programs alone, not because of the clear policies of the past five years, but chiefly because of the need of national unity in ending mistakes of the past and meeting the necessities of today, we must carry on.

I do not propose to let the people down.

I am sure the Congress of the United States will not let the people down.

2 ⊄ The Annual Budget Message.

January 3, 1938

To the Congress:

PURSUANT to provisions of law I transmit herewith the Budget of the United States Government for the fiscal year ending June 30, 1939, together with this message, which is a part thereof. The estimates have been developed after analysis of the revenues, obligations, and reasonable needs of the Government, and I recommend appropriations for the purposes specifically detailed herein.

In simple fairness to the Treasury of the United States I am confident that the Congress and the public will bear in mind certain fundamentals relating to the making of the National Budget.

The first step calls for the presentation, before the 15th of September, by every department and agency head, of estimates of appropriations for the fiscal year beginning the first day of the following July—in other words at least nine months before the spending of the money can begin. These estimates, carefully prepared by the budget officers and other officials of each department and agency, are intended to represent what they consider the minimum needs of the work assigned to them by law.

Thereupon the Director of the Budget presents these totals to the President who without taking up the thousands of separate items asks the Secretary of the Treasury for estimates of the total amount of tax receipts which the Government may obtain during the twelve months beginning nine months later. This estimate by the Secretary of the Treasury is furnished him by civil-service experts who have long-standing experience with the whole subject of forecasting economic conditions in what may well be called the remote future. These experts properly call attention to the fact that they are asked to guess what the economic status—and therefore the tax receipts—will be during the fiscal year beginning the first of the following July.

If the forecast of tax receipts made by these experts, who are at least of equal competence with the experts of the largest banks and industrial corporations of the United States, show that the departmental estimates of expenditures will exceed the estimated tax receipts, the President instructs the Director of the Budget to make every possible effort as a result of his hearings to pare the departmental estimates in order to reduce the total.

During the months of November and December and after the hearings have been held by the Director of the Budget, he

presents to the President the total estimates with his recommendations.

Again the President obtains from the Treasury Department
a check-up on estimated revenue during the year beginning the
following 1st of July. If the new report shows a probable falling
off of revenue, he makes every effort with the assistance of the
Director of the Budget to make further reductions before approving the final department and agency budgets.

It should be remembered that the laws provide that the departments and agencies shall carry out certain duties. By these
laws, the President and the Director of the Budget are, in effect,
prohibited from eliminating Government functions or curtailing them to the point of ineffectiveness.

The result is that the President and the Director of the
Budget arrive at a figure for each department and agency which
they believe to be the proper amount under which the functions
required by law can be carried out with reasonable efficiency.

During the final two weeks of the calendar year, the President
obtains once more from the Treasury Department its final estimates of tax revenues during the fiscal year which begins more
than six months later.

Since the tax revenues from practically every major source depend on business conditions during that future fiscal year the
Treasury's figures of necessity are based on a prophecy of business conditions beginning six months later and ending eighteen
months later.

Business concerns are more fortunate. They also lay out programs months and even a year and a half in advance. But their
programs are flexible. They are controlled currently by the
condition of business, which permits the making of necessary
changes from month to month and even from week to week.

The affairs of the Government are not so flexible. The Budget
reports are the administration's fiscal plan; and in the form
adopted by the Congress during the winter and spring, it becomes practically a fixed program of expenditure which cannot

be changed for many months even though economic conditions radically change the receipt side of the ledger.

While I re-emphasize the difficulty of estimating the revenue of the Federal Government from six to eighteen months before that revenue flows in, there is satisfaction in knowing that during the past 4 years the estimates of tax receipts thus made far in advance, have been infinitely more accurate as proven by the final result than in the preceding years. Estimates remain a prophecy; but our prophecies have been far better borne out by later events than prophecies of earlier years.

It is also worth while to call the attention of the Congress and the public to the fact that a very large proportion of our total expenditures represent fixed charges which cannot be reduced by Executive action. These charges are obligatory on the President and the Treasury, and include interest on the public debt, military and naval pensions, contributions to retirement funds and to the old-age reserve account, and many grants in aid to States.

Another class of expenditures, which, though subject to some measure of administrative control, does not afford opportunity for large reductions, is made up of those which carry on the normal, everyday operations of the Government. For example, the major part of the appropriations for the State Department is required to pay the reasonable salaries of consuls, diplomatic agents, secretarial staffs, and ministers who represent American interests in every part of the world.

The third type of expenditure is represented by the major effort of the Government to help the economic security of large groups of citizens in every part of the country who, for many reasons, definitely require some form of Government assistance. This includes various kinds of aid to save farms and homes from foreclosure, to furnish work relief for needy able-bodied unemployed, and to provide old-age pensions, unemployment insurance and other assistance under the social-security program. Obligations such as these, though large in amount, can be reduced only by depriving a very large proportion of our population of benefits which modern civilization insists on.

The final category includes items of public expenditure for capital improvements—such as new highways, new river and harbor projects, new flood control, new public buildings, new reclamation projects, and other new public works. All of these items can be contracted or expanded to conform with the contraction or expansion of Government income.

This year I recommend that such items be curtailed. First, because expected Government income will be less, and second, because it has been amply demonstrated that they do not provide as much work as do other methods of taking care of the unemployed.

For example, we have appropriated as Federal aid to new permanent State highways almost $1,500,000,000 during the past five years; and an equal sum has been spent during the same period for constructing, repairing, and improving roads and streets by Federal agencies administering unemployment relief. These vast expenditures have put our highway systems far in advance of what would have been normal expansion. I do not propose eliminating Federal aid to highways, but I do ask that such aid be restored to approximately the predepression figures.

We have a great accumulation of unliquidated "matching" authorizations for aid to States running into the year 1940— but the States also should be encouraged to bring their highway budgets back to a more normal figure. Therefore I hope that the Congress will start at this session to cut down the actual appropriations used to match State funds.

For the ten years up to June 30, 1933, the Federal Government spent an average of $40,000,000 a year for river and harbor improvements. During the past five years we have spent an average of over $100,000,000 a year. Meanwhile, a justified demand for greater protection against floods has developed. Flood protection is necessary and in this Budget I am curtailing the estimates for new river and harbor improvements in order to provide more money for flood emergencies.

Reclamation projects have been started which will call for future appropriations of nearly $600,000,000. It seems obvious to me, and I hope it will be to the Congress, that no further projects should be authorized until projects now under construction have reached a substantial stage of completion.

During the past five years we have built more than 1,100 new Federal buildings — almost doubling the number of such buildings throughout the country. It is true that this saves the renting of buildings, but to offset that saving we are paying in many cases far more for maintenance of these new buildings than we formerly paid for leasing private quarters. Except for meeting the problem of adequate housing for Government departments and agencies in the District of Columbia, I am strongly of the opinion that the public-building program should be restricted to the comparatively small number of projects where the capital investment will be returned through savings in annual operating costs.

Expenditures. — The most important fact of this Budget is the reduction of $539,000,000 in the estimated expenditures for the fiscal year 1939. They amount to $6,869,000,000, compared with estimated expenditures during the current fiscal year of 1938 of $7,408,000,000.

It is hoped that this fact will not be overlooked. It is fair to say that this estimated reduction may, by force of circumstances, become smaller because of future events which today cannot definitely be foretold. I refer specifically to the possibility that due to world conditions over which this Nation has no control, I may find it necessary to request additional appropriations for national defense. Furthermore, the economic situation may not improve — and if it does not, I expect the approval of Congress and the public for additional appropriations if they become necessary to save thousands of American families from dire need.

Revenues. — During the first ten months of the calendar year

Actual and estimated receipts and expenditures of the Government for the fiscal years 1931–39
(Classifications include expenditures from both general and emergency funds)

[In millions of dollars]

	Estimated			Actual					
	1939	1938	1937	1936	1935	1934	1933	1932	1931
RECEIPTS									
Internal revenue:									
Income tax	2,414.2	2,692.9	2,157.5	1,426.6	1,099.1	818.0	746.2	1,057.3	1,860.4
Miscellaneous internal revenue	2,190.1	2,279.5	2,181.2	2,009.6	1,657.2	1,469.6	858.2	503.7	569.4
Unjust enrichment tax	10.0	5.0	5.9						
Taxes under Social Security Act	598.8	571.0	252.2						
Taxes upon carriers and their employees	116.9	150.3	.3						
Processing tax on farm products				76.6	521.4	353.0			
Customs	390.4	415.3	486.4	386.8	343.4	313.4	250.8	327.7	376.6
Miscellaneous receipts	199.0	206.5	210.3	216.3	179.4	161.6	224.5	117.0	383.2
Total receipts	5,919.4	6,320.5	5,293.8	4,115.9	3,800.5	3,115.6	2,079.7	2,005.7	3,189.6
EXPENDITURES									
Regular operating expenditures:									
Legislative, judicial, and civil establishments:									
Legislative establishment	20.8	21.1	20.7	21.7	19.6	16.6	17.7	21.9	21.4
Department of Agriculture	124.9	150.0	176.1	122.9	71.1	62.7	72.2	98.0	71.5
Department of Commerce	44.5	41.2	40.3	44.3	39.0	30.8	41.7	48.1	56.9
Department of the Interior	95.2	122.6	112.4	78.5	74.4	49.9	55.8	63.4	60.6
Department of Justice	40.7	39.8	38.6	38.5	32.8	31.7	44.1	51.7	44.4
Department of Labor	17.5	24.5	30.7	26.9	18.6	12.7	13.7	14.7	12.2
Post Office Department (deficiency)	18.2	29.6	39.3	85.9	64.0	64.2	117.4	203.0	145.7
Department of State	16.3	17.6	17.1	17.2	18.7	12.0	13.8	16.7	15.3
Treasury Department	157.1	178.0	184.6	164.1	123.0	111.8	133.9	161.0	136.1
War Department (nonmilitary)	48.2	47.5	53.1	46.2	44.1	41.1	43.1	47.9	46.9
District of Columbia (United States share)	5.0	5.0	5.0	5.7	4.5	5.7	7.8	9.5	9.5
Independent offices and commissions	171.6	150.4	96.8	81.7	45.1	36.1	76.6	108.8	89.4
Subtotal	760.0	827.3	814.7	733.6	554.9	475.3	637.8	844.7	709.9
National defense	991.3	957.0	888.6	870.5	656.5	499.9	633.6	664.5	667.3

Veterans' pensions and benefits	538.6	573.7	1,128.2	2,348.6	605.9	554.1	848.9	972.8	942.6
Interest on the public debt	976.0	927.0	866.4	749.4	820.9	756.6	689.4	599.3	611.6
Other (refunds of receipts, settlement of war claims, etc.)	50.8	47.9	48.1	41.1	38.7	62.8	69.7	150.0	97.0
Total	3,316.7	3,332.9	3,746.0	4,743.2	2,676.9	2,348.7	2,879.4	3,231.3	3,028.4
Public works:									
Public highways	140.1	280.1	350.6	243.9	317.4	267.9	178.2	209.9	173.8
Tennessee Valley Authority	41.0	46.0	41.2	48.8	36.2	11.0	.....	.....	.....
Reclamation	60.4	69.5	52.3	49.9	40.9	24.8	25.2	26.3	13.9
Rivers and harbors, improvement	60.0	81.2	142.4	137.8	132.9	76.4	50.5	55.4	51.4
Flood control	63.9	71.2	54.6	52.3	38.7	48.1	39.7	29.2	37.8
Public buildings	53.2	74.4	76.3	71.9	58.1	78.7	105.7	86.2	67.6
Grants to public bodies, including administration	153.8	189.5	272.9	233.9	48.9	18.8	.....	.....	.....
Other	47.1	66.2	89.1	74.0	89.6	87.4	59.4	71.7	59.6
Total	619.5	878.1	1,079.4	912.5	762.7	613.1	458.7	478.7	404.1
Unemployment relief:									
Direct relief	35.9	126.8	184.3	591.7	1,914.1	715.8	350.7	.....	.....
Work relief (W.P.A. and C.W.A.)	1,000.1	1,322.2	1,896.7	1,264.4	11.3	805.1	.....	.....	.....
Civilian Conservation Corps	230.0	310.0	385.8	486.3	435.5	331.9	8.8	.....	.....
Total	1,266.0	1,759.0	2,466.8	2,342.4	2,360.9	1,852.8	359.5	.....	.....
Loans (net)	68.0	a 47.9	a 307.1	a 180.8	102.1	819.5	911.8	404.0	235.4
Subscriptions to stock and surplus	5.0	45.6	47.1	88.9	156.7	820.9	71.9	627.0	3.0
Agricultural Adjustment Program	586.1	442.5	515.8	541.6	743.0	290.2	.....	.....	.....
Social security	813.2	658.7	447.7	28.4	.....	.....	.....	.....	.....
Railroad retirement	119.5	139.7	5.5	.3	.....	.....	.....	.....	.....
Supplemental items	75.0	200.0	.....	.....	.....	.....	.....	.....	.....
Total expenditures, exclusive of debt retirement	6,869.0	7,408.6	8,001.2	8,476.5	6,802.3	6,745.2	4,681.3	4,741.0	3,670.9
Net deficit	949.6	1,088.1	2,707.4	4,360.6	3,001.8	3,629.6	2,601.6	2,735.3	481.3
Gross public debt at the end of each fiscal year	38,528.2	37,603.6	36,424.6	33,778.5	28,700.9	27,053.1	22,538.7	19,487.0	16,801.3

a Excess of credits, deduct.

21

1937 business conditions improved materially and it was the consensus of opinion in Government and in business circles that the improvement would be maintained in 1938. There was every reason to expect that the revenues for the fiscal year 1939 would be greater than the expected revenues for 1938 and that with a reduction in the cost of relief, the total expenditures for 1939 would greatly decline. That was the basis for our expectation of a balanced Budget for the fiscal year 1939.

The recent recession in business has changed that outlook. Today it is necessary to revise the estimates of revenues. They will be less than we had anticipated. They will, as far as we can tell, remain below our estimated necessary expenditures.

We hope that the calendar year 1938 will bring an improvement in business conditions and, therefore, in tax receipts. The Treasury, leaning to the conservative side, predicts some improvement over the present level but does not assume in its figures that business in the calendar year 1938 will reach as high a level as in the calendar year 1937.

The present estimate of revenue for the fiscal year 1939 is $5,919,000,000 compared with the present estimate of receipts for the fiscal year 1938 of $6,320,000,000 — or, in other words, a falling off of $401,000,000.

Balance. — The net result of these estimates of expenditures and receipts shows for the fiscal year 1939 a net deficit of $950,000,000, but it is fair to state at the same time that this deficit will be $138,000,000 less than the expected deficit in the current fiscal year. In other words, for the third year in succession we would continue to decrease the deficit.

It will be of interest to compare the major classes of receipts and expenditures for the fiscal years 1931 to 1939 as set forth in the accompanying table:

RECOMMENDATIONS

Appropriation item veto. — An important feature of the fiscal procedure in the majority of our States is the authority given to the executive to withhold approval of individual items in an appropriation bill, and, while approving the remainder of the bill, to return such rejected items for the further consideration of the legislature. This grant of power has been considered a consistent corollary of the power of the legislature to withhold approval of items in the budget of the executive; and the system meets with general approval in the many States which have adopted it. A respectable difference of opinion exists as to whether a similar item veto power could be given to the President by legislation or whether a constitutional amendment would be necessary. I strongly recommend that the present Congress adopt whichever course it may deem to be the correct one.

Commodity Credit Corporation. — At present the funds for the operations of the Commodity Credit Corporation are provided through allocations from the Reconstruction Finance Corporation. Such losses as the Commodity Credit Corporation may sustain upon its commodity loans remain an indefinite charge against the Treasury until the liquidation of the Reconstruction Finance Corporation. In order to provide for an annual review of the operations of the Commodity Credit Corporation and of its annual net cost to the Government, I recommend the enactment by the Congress of legislation which will require an annual appraisal of the assets of the Corporation, and, as a means of providing funds to make and guarantee its loans, provide the Corporation with adequate capital and authorize the issuance by it of obligations guaranteed by the United States. Congress would be advised annually of the Corporation's net profit or loss and be in a position to make such appropriations as might be necessary to meet any annual impairment of the capital of the Corporation that would result from losses sustained upon its loans.

REVIEW OF THE FISCAL YEARS 1937 AND 1938, AND THE FISCAL PROGRAM FOR 1939

This review concerns itself with the cash actually received and paid out by the Treasury in the fiscal year 1937, with the estimates of receipts and expenditures for the fiscal year 1938, and with the fiscal program for 1939.

Fiscal Year 1937

Receipts. — Total general fund receipts for the fiscal year 1937 amounted to $5,293,840,237 which was $534,000,000 less than was estimated one year ago but a gain over 1936 of $1,178,000,000. The receipts from income taxes were $215,-000,000 less than the estimate contained in the 1938 Budget, while miscellaneous internal-revenue taxes were $94,000,000 less.

It was believed last January that taxes on carriers and their employees would produce $134,552,000, but litigation delayed collection of these taxes and only $345,088 was received in 1937. The tax on unjust enrichment produced only $5,886,836 as against Budget estimates of $82,000,000 a year ago, while the receipts from social-security taxes were $72,000,000 less than was estimated at that time. Customs and miscellaneous receipts, however, exceeded the amount anticipated a year ago by $40,000,000 and $18,000,000, respectively.

As pointed out in my message of April 20 last, the March 1937 tax returns brought to light certain defects in the present revenue law. As a result of these disclosures, committees of Congress have been considering corrective tax legislation; and I hope that there may be enacted at an early date such amendments to the revenue law as will maintain the revenue producing power of the present tax structure while correcting at the same time existing proven inequities.

Expenditures. — The total expenditures for the fiscal year ended June 30, 1937 (exclusive of expenditures from postal revenues), amounted to $8,105,158,547 as compared with an estimate of $8,480,804,493 in the Budget submitted a year ago. This latter estimate included an amount of $404,525,000 for statutory debt retirement while the actual expenditures for this purpose were $103,971,200. Thus, excluding debt retirement, the expenditures for the fiscal year 1937 were $75,092,146 less than the estimate for that year contained in the 1938 Budget. The total expenditures for recovery and relief were $3,014,589,-913 as against an estimate of $3,144,689,700. Revolving funds showed a net credit of $243,569,165, which was $84,963,435 less than the previous Budget estimate of $328,532,600. Transfers to trust accounts totaled $872,386,048, while the estimates for this purpose amounted to $842,235,300. For the operation and maintenance of the regular departments and establishments of the Government, including interest on the public debt, there was expended $4,357,780,551, while the amounts estimated for these purposes totaled $4,417,887,093.

Deficit and public debt. — The gross deficit for the fiscal year 1937 amounted to $2,811,318,311. Excluding $103,971,200 for statutory debt retirement, the net deficit was $2,707,347,111. The estimated net deficit, as contained in the Budget submitted a year ago, was $2,248,128,774. The increase in the net deficit is more than accounted for by the decline in receipts.

The increase in the gross public debt during the year amounted to $2,646,070,239, bringing the total gross debt on June 30, 1937, to $36,424,613,732.

Fiscal Year 1938

Receipts. — The income of the Federal Government during the fiscal year 1938 is expected to increase $1,026,673,000 over that of 1937, the increase of $1,101,573,000 in internal-revenue collections being partially offset by a reduction of $74,900,000 in other classes of receipts. The total revenues from all sources (exclusive of postal revenues) will amount to $6,320,513,000. This figure, however, is less by $973,100,000 than the estimate of revenues for 1938 contained in the Budget last year.

Income taxes are expected to produce $2,692,900,000 as compared with 1937 receipts of $2,157,526,981. Miscellaneous internal-revenue taxes will amount to $2,279,511,000 as compared with actual collections in 1937 of $2,181,217,856. The re-enactment of legislation levying taxes upon carriers and their employees will produce $150,300,000 in 1938, whereas last year's receipts amounted to only $345,088. Taxes under the Social Security Act, levied on a six-month basis in 1937, produced $252,160,840, and in 1938, on a full-year basis, will produce $571,002,000. The tax on unjust enrichment is estimated at $5,000,000, or $886,836 less than the receipts from this source in 1937. Customs duties are expected to yield $415,300,000 in 1938, whereas in 1937 they produced $486,-356,599. Miscellaneous revenues are $2,411,030 less than last year, the estimate for the current year being $165,409,083; and from realization upon assets there will be derived a total of $41,090,917, or $1,432,505 less than in 1937.

Expenditures. — The total expenditures (exclusive of expenditures from postal revenues) for the fiscal year 1938 are now estimated at $7,614,858,300. Included in this amount, however, are statutory debt retirements of $206,215,700. Eliminating debt retirement and the non-recurring item of adjusted compensation payments, the 1938 expenditures are expected to be about $35,900,000 less than last year. There is a decrease of $1,185,600,000 in expenditures for recovery and relief, the agricultural adjustment program, the Civilian Conservation Corps, and refunds of taxes, and an increase of $1,149,700,000 for the following purposes: $52,500,000 for the legislative, executive, and judicial offices and the civil departments and agencies; $167,800,000 for the general public works program; $89,700,000 for national defense; $2,300,000 for veterans' pensions and benefits; $90,900,000, principally for grants to States, under the Social Security Act; $60,600,000 for interest on the public debt; $280,100,000 for payments into the old-age reserve account and the railroad and Government employees' retirement funds; $200,000,000 for supplemental items; and $205,800,000 representing a reduction in revolving fund credits.

Deficit and public debt. — Excluding public-debt retirements, the net deficit for 1938 is now estimated at $1,088,129,600 as against an actual deficit in 1937 of $2,707,347,111. The gross public debt on June 30, 1938, is estimated at $37,603,646,918. This, of course, does not take into account any future changes in the debt which may occur as a result of the Treasury policy with respect to the sterilization of gold.

Fiscal Program for 1939

Receipts. — The estimates of revenues for the fiscal year 1939, which are necessarily based on existing tax laws, amount to $5,919,437,000. This is $401,076,000 less than the anticipated receipts for 1938. With the exception of social-security taxes and realization upon assets, each major class of revenue shows a decline below the 1938 level. Income taxes are estimated at $2,414,200,000, or $278,700,000 less than for 1938. Total miscellaneous internal revenue will be $2,190,072,000, which is $89,439,000 less than 1938. The taxes upon carriers and their employees are expected to total $116,900,000, a decline of $33,400,000 from 1938, which is due largely to the fact that the 1938 collections included 1937 accruals deferred by litigation. Social-security taxes will be $598,865,000, an increase of $27,863,000 over 1938. The tax on unjust enrichment will produce $10,000,000, as compared with $5,000,000 for 1938. Miscellaneous revenues show a total of $148,882,320, or less than the current year by $16,526,763. Realization upon assets is estimated at $50,117,680, an increase of $9,026,763 over 1938.

Expenditures. — The expenditures contemplated for the fiscal year 1939 (exclusive of those from postal revenues) total $7,070,558,000. This includes $201,515,000 for statutory debt retirement, leaving $6,869,043,000 for other purposes, which is $539,600,000 less than the amount estimated for 1938. There are net increases of $52,917,000 in the regular activities of the civil departments and agencies which are more than accounted for by increases of $62,000,000 under the Rural Electrification Administration and the United States Maritime Commission. The general public works program will require $404,026,500, or $73,957,000 less than for 1938. Expenditures for national defense are expected to be $54,847,000 greater than for 1938, reaching a total of $988,623,400 in the fiscal year 1939. On the other hand, the expenditures for veterans' pensions and benefits will decline from $573,682,800 for 1938 to $538,610,000 for 1939, because of the completion of payments of insurance claims on account of deaths occurring during the World War. Expenditures under the agricultural adjustment program will increase $143,573,000 in 1939, due principally to the legislation enacted during the last regular session of Congress providing for subsidy payments to cotton producers.

The Civilian Conservation Corps, because of a contemplated reduction in the number of camps and reduced expenditures for cooperating agencies, will require $230,000,000, or $80,000,000 less than for 1938. Expenditures for administration and grants to States under the Social Security Act will reach a total of $338,230,000, which represents an increase of $66,525,000 in grants to States and a decrease of $1,991,000 in administrative expenses. The interest payments on the public debt will amount to $976,000,000, or $49,000,000 more than for 1938.

Expenditures for recovery and relief are estimated at $1,138,-304,000, or $841,356,600 less than for 1938. The operations of the Social Security Act and the unemployment-compensation laws of the States have the effect of materially reducing our program for work relief. Moreover, operations under the new Housing Act will greatly assist in providing employment. We can also look to the regular public works program to provide a certain amount of employment. With these aids and the assistance confidently expected from private industry, I hope that the foregoing amount for expenditure will be sufficient to meet the needs for 1939. An estimate of appropriation of $1,000,000,000 for this purpose is contained in the 1939 Budget.

Expenditures from revolving funds are expected to amount to $141,961,000, which represents, because of an excess of receipts of $37,778,200 in 1938, an increase in total expenditures of $179,739,200. For the old-age reserve account the estimate

2. The Annual Budget Message

is $475,000,000, an increase of $90,000,000 over 1938. For the railroad retirement account $177,250,000 will be required, $20,286,000 less than for 1938. An accumulation of payments due in 1937 had to be met in 1938, whereas there will be no accumulation to be carried over into 1939. The amount for supplemental items is $75,000,000, which is $125,000,000 less than the amount now indicated for 1938.

Deficit and public debt. — The net deficit for the fiscal year 1939 is $949,606,000, or $138,523,600 less than the deficit for the current year. The gross public debt on June 30, 1939, is estimated at $38,528,252,918. This does not take into account any changes in the debt which may occur as a result of the Treasury policy with respect to the sterilization of gold.

It should be pointed out, however, that the increase in the debt by reason of the deficit does not mean that the Treasury will borrow that additional sum on the market. There will be available during the fiscal year for investment in special issues of Government obligations, the net sum of approximately $1,163,000,000, which represents investments of $600,000,000 from the old-age reserve account and the railroad and Government employees' retirement funds and $573,000,000 from the unemployment trust fund, and a reduction of $10,000,000 in investments held for account of the adjusted service certificate fund. As a result of these investment operations the Treasury financing for the fiscal year 1939 would be confined to refunding maturing obligations.

The accompanying table shows the gross public debt at the end of the fiscal years 1936 and 1937 and the estimated gross debt at the end of the fiscal years 1938 and 1939.

Appropriations. — The appropriations and reappropriations recommended in this Budget, including those for the Postal Service, the District of Columbia, and probable supplemental items, total $7,973,843,219. The appropriations and reappropriations already made and prospective supplemental items for the fiscal year 1938 for the same purposes total $8,629,921,393. This is a decrease of $656,078,174.

29

[In millions of dollars]

	June 30, 1939 (estimated)	June 30, 1938 (estimated)	June 30, 1937	June 30, 1936
Market operations:				
Held by—				
Public (banks, insurance companies, trust companies, corporations, individuals, etc.).................	30,240	30,519	30,677	29,408
Federal Reserve System..............	2,564	[1] 2,564	2,526	2,430
Government agencies................	509	[1] 509	451	381
Government trust funds.............	1,300	1,260	1,212	933
	34,613	34,852	34,866	33,152
Special issues:				
Held by—				
Old age reserve account.............	1,143	661	267	....
Unemployment trust fund...........	1,538	965	312	19
Railroad retirement account.........	137	80	....	....
Employees' retirement funds.........	432	371	316	280
Veterans' funds....................	515	525	538	127
Other...........................	150	150	125	200
	3,915	2,752	1,558	626
Gross debt......................	38,528	37,604	36,424	33,778

[1] As of Dec. 1, 1937, and it is assumed for the purpose of this statement only that they will remain at these amounts throughout the fiscal years 1938 and 1939.

3 ❡ The Four Hundred and Twenty-second Press Conference. January 4, 1938

(Need for industrial planning to ascertain demand and purchasing power — The responsibilities of labor unions — Jurisdictional strikes.)

THE PRESIDENT: Well, having talked to the bankers [referring to Budget Press Conference] for the last hour, I am glad to welcome the medical profession. I don't think there is any particular news.

Q. Mr. President, in Detroit today the Hudson Motor Car

Company announced a new small automobile to compete with Chevrolet and Ford. They announced also that they would put six thousand men to work in a few weeks in addition to the six thousand men already at work, that they were going to spend eleven million dollars, and that their payroll would be increased by over a million dollars more than it is. The news is rather good for this season, and I was wondering if you would care to comment.

THE PRESIDENT: Excellent, excellent, perfectly fine. I wish we had more of it. That reminds me — I will tell you a story. Last August, the last week of August, I was in a little village, and I happened to know the fellow who runs the garage, and who is also the agent for one of the larger automobile companies. We used to play on the same ball team together.

I said, "Bill, how are you getting on?" He said, "I am getting on too well."

I said, "What do you mean?"

He said, "It is this way: You know, people in this vicinity to whom we cater, own a total of about one hundred automobiles — pleasure cars — which they use. Well, these people are not rich and they do not get a new car every year. They get their cars every three years or four years or five years or six years. I figure the average turnover is about one car — one new car — every three years, perhaps a little bit more. I figure they ought to buy about thirty new cars every year." Then he said, "This year, in this community, they have bought sixty-two new cars. Well, I have sold a lot of them myself. I have sold over half of them myself. I had no right to and they had no business buying sixty-two new cars. That means that next year I am going to have an awful year. Sixty-two families out of a hundred have new cars, and I don't think next year I will sell more than ten or fifteen cars. That is why I say I am doing much too well."

I just use this by way of example of one of the evils I mentioned yesterday in my message to the Congress. I said,

"How do you account for it?" He said, "There are two reasons: The first is that all of us fellows who sell cars have been pushed to sell more cars, and we have been told to hand out a line of talk."

I said, "What kind?" He said, "We have been handing out a line of talk that next year the cost of an automobile will go up a hundred dollars, that you had better buy one now, that next year it will cost a hundred dollars more. You have no idea how that word has been spread out in this country: 'Buy now or you will have to pay more next year.' A lot of people bought on that statement who would not have bought otherwise. Another reason is that they did something I thought was awfully foolish. We have been selling cars on an 18-months' paying basis, and they told us that we should adopt a new policy of selling on a 24-months' paying basis. Well, what does that mean? I used to go and say, 'Buy a new car and pay for it at forty dollars a month.' I can now go to them and say, 'You can get a new car for thirty dollars a month and pay for it in twenty-four months instead of eighteen months.' They say, 'That is pretty good; I guess I will buy.'" In other words, they have been budgeting cars too fast.

That is one illustration. Another one is this: I said to a very large steel manufacturer the other day, "How is it that you suddenly dropped from 90 per cent to around 28 per cent?" "Oh," he said, "a lot of factors entered into it. One was automobile steel. Then there was another curious thing that happened: The railroads in the country last spring suddenly came to us and gave us orders for all the steel rails that they needed for a full year and they said, 'We want them now.' So all through the summer we were working seven days a week, turning out steel rails, to fill these orders, and they got all their steel rails in the course of the summer months. Now they do not need, or want, any more for another nine months."

I said, "What do you think of it?" He said, "I call it highly unintelligent."

That is another illustration.

Q. Is that another parable?

THE PRESIDENT: No, it is a straight story—actual illustrations.

Q. Stories about sixty-two families?

THE PRESIDENT: Oh, no; it has nothing to do with individual people. It was just an unintelligent way of handling business; and it is so admitted by the people today who were responsible for it.

Now, we want to help them so they won't do that sort of thing in the future. If there is any way in which the Government can help, we will help.

Q. Why did the railroads want the rails right away?

THE PRESIDENT: Because they thought the price of rails might go up. I think that was the chief reason.

Q. Would you say it is a good business idea for a firm at this time to expand as this firm is doing?

THE PRESIDENT: I don't think I can go into that because this, after all, is a selling campaign. If we can put men to work building cheap cars for the people of this country, that would be pretty good, with emphasis on the word "cheap."

Q. How can the Government do anything to prevent this type of unintelligent business operation? Can you give us any idea of how you would go about it, what can be done?

THE PRESIDENT: Oh, yes; I think so. Let us take an example: Don't write the story that I am advocating the immediate reenactment of NRA. But the fact remains that in quite a number of the code industries under NRA it was perfectly legal for the heads of all the companies in a given industry to sit down around a table with the Government, and, from their own statistics and the statistics of their own trade associations and the statistics given them by the Government, figure out much more clearly than they ever had before, as an industry, what the probable demand of the country would be for a period of six months or a year ahead. In

33

other words, they could make a more intelligent group estimate as to the purchasing power of the country and the inventories of the particular article necessary for the immediate future.

Now, done that way, it is a perfectly legitimate thing for them to do — sitting there, with the Government, and trying honestly to find out what the needs are going to be for the next six months or a year, so that they won't overproduce. It is legitimate just so long as it is done without any attempts at price-fixing or driving competitors out of business or things like that as a result of the conference.

There is a question today whether a meeting of that kind, around a table, is legal under the anti-trust laws. A lot of people are afraid of it. I would very much favor making it a completely legal thing to do: to meet around a table to find out, with the help of the Government, what the demands are, what the purchasing power of the country is, what the inventories are.

Q. How would the estimated annual production be allocated among the units of the industry?

THE PRESIDENT: Don't do that — keep competition. . . .

Q. In your message yesterday, you mentioned the need for responsibility on the part of labor organizations which should grow commensurately with their own power. I wonder if you think there is a need for further responsibility on the part of labor unions at the present time?

THE PRESIDENT: Yes — I think it is growing too. For example, among labor unions there has been a distinct increase in willingness to make public their accounts of receipts and disbursements. Isn't it the Garment Workers Union in New York that makes public its receipts and disbursements?

Q. Yes, sir.

THE PRESIDENT: That is a growing tendency, and it is a good thing.

Q. I think his question referred to the need and your answer implied —

THE PRESIDENT: Oh, no; I meant there was a growing assumption of responsibility.

Q. You said it was a good thing that this trend is now evident. Could you explain that a little further?

THE PRESIDENT: The trouble is when you come down to specific things. I suppose the easiest way of putting it is this: In England there is a great deal more responsibility on the part of labor unions than there is here. They went through the growing pains there that we are going through here now; they went through them ten or fifteen years ago; and we are now heading in the same direction that they have been going.

Q. There is an idea that has been growing among some members on the Hill—an idea of having labor unions made responsible by legislation, responsible for their contracts, mutually responsible with employers.

THE PRESIDENT: It is difficult to answer that specifically. All we can point out is a series of cases where we have to devise ways and means to prevent them from going on in the same way. Just for example, there is a very difficult situation at the present time out in Portland, Oregon, where they have those lumber mills where they saw up the logs. A good many years ago they organized a union among the workers in those mills which became an affiliate of the A.F. of L. and which was placed under the jurisdiction of Hutcheson of the Carpenters Union. Later on, the C.I.O. went into the same plants and organized. As I remember it, the Federal Government held an election there, and the C.I.O. organization won a majority, whereupon the minority refused to accept, pulled out the teamsters, and tied up everything "tighter than a drum." Later on the Governor of Oregon held another election. He thought it would go the other way. It didn't. They still went C.I.O. by a bigger majority. The entire works were still tied up.

That would seem to be a local situation, but it isn't. It extends back to the East Coast. The carpenters on the East

Coast are told that they cannot build a house out of red wood that is shipped out of Portland, Oregon. That is a pretty impossible situation, to tie up building construction in the East because there is a jurisdictional fight in the West.

That happened to be between the A.F of L. and the C.I.O. You get the same thing in building trades. You want to put a garbage chute into a new apartment house or a dumb-waiter chute, and one particular union might start to go ahead with it when the elevator shaft men would say, "No, that is an elevator shaft," and then the whole building is tied up. That is the kind of thing I was referring to. We need definite improvement to end jurisdictional disputes.

Q. Do you expect to get it done with Federal legislation?

THE PRESIDENT: I don't know.

Q. Do you think it should be done with Federal legislation?

THE PRESIDENT: I think the first thing is to give them a chance to do it themselves, the same way we gave capital a chance to cure some of its ills; do it, so far as possible, without legislation.

Q. Does that imply that if capital does not do it that legislation may be had?

THE PRESIDENT: If neither side cures its ills, something will have to be done.

(See also Items 26, 49 and 50, this volume, for discussion of industrial prices and business conditions.)

4 (The President States His Views on the Proposed Referendum to Declare War. January 6, 1938

My dear Mr. Speaker:

IN RESPONSE to your request for an expression of my views respecting the proposed resolution calling for a referendum vote as a prerequisite for a declaration of war, I must frankly state that I consider that the proposed amendment would be impracticable in its application and incompatible with our representative form of government.

Our government is conducted by the people through representatives of their own choosing. It was with singular unanimity that the founders of the republic agreed upon such free and representative form of government as the only practical means of government by the people.

Such an amendment to the Constitution as that proposed would cripple any President in his conduct of our foreign relations, and it would encourage other nations to believe that they could violate American rights with impunity.

I fully realize that the sponsors of this proposal sincerely believe that it would be helpful in keeping the United States out of war. I am convinced it would have the opposite effect.

Yours very sincerely,

The Honorable
William B. Bankhead,
Speaker of the
House of Representatives

NOTE: Several constitutional amendments have been introduced from time to time in the Congress, requiring a referendum to declare war; but none of them has ever been passed.

5 ("We in Turn Are Striving to Uphold the Integrity of the Morals of Our Democracy." Address at the Jackson Day Dinner, Washington, D.C. January 8, 1938

Mr. Vice President, Mr. Speaker, Mr. Farley, Ladies and Gentlemen:

WHEN speaking before a party gathering in these modern days, I am happy to realize that the audience is not confined to active members of my own party, and that there is less of unthinking partisanship in this country today than at any time since the Administration of George Washington.

In the last campaign, in 1936, a very charming lady wrote me a letter. She said: "I believe in you and in what you are trying to do for the Nation, I do wish I could vote for you — but you see my parents were Republicans and I was brought up as a Republican and so I have to vote for your opponent."

My reply to her ran as follows: "My father and grandfather were Democrats and I was born and brought up as a Democrat, but in 1904, when I cast my first vote for a President, I voted for the Republican candidate, Theodore Roosevelt, because I thought he was a better Democrat than the Democratic candidate."

I have told that story many times, and if I had to do it over again I would not alter that vote.

Conditions and parties change, as we know, with every generation. Nevertheless, I cannot help but feel pride in the fact that the Democratic Party, as it exists today, is a national party representing the essential unity of our country. As we move forward under our present momentum, it is not only necessary but it is right that the Party should slough off any remains of sectionalism and class consciousness. Party progress cannot stop just because some public officials and private or local groups fail to move along with the times. Their places will be amply filled by the arriving generation. That is on the principle that "Nature abhors a vacuum."

In these recent years the average American seldom thinks of Jefferson and Jackson as Democrats or of Lincoln and Theodore Roosevelt as Republicans; he labels each one of them according to his attitude toward the fundamental problems that confronted him as President, when he was active in the affairs of government.

These men stand out because of the constructive battles they waged, not merely battles against things temporarily evil but battles for things permanently good — battles for the basic morals of democracy, which rest on respect for the right of self-government and faith in majority rule.

They knew, with the wisdom of experience, that the majority often makes mistakes. But they believed passionately that rule by a small minority class unfailingly makes worse mistakes — for rule by class takes counsel from itself and fails to heed the problems and, therefore, the good of all kinds and conditions of men. In the long run the instincts of the common man, willing to live and let live, work out the best and safest balance for the common good. And that is what I mean by the battle to restore and maintain the moral integrity of democracy.

At heart some of the small minority on the other side seek and use power to make themselves masters instead of servants of mankind. At heart they oppose our American form of government.

That is the cause of the great struggle that we are engaged in today — a struggle for the maintenance of the integrity of the morals of democracy. And we are in the process of winning it.

Let me talk history. President Washington, feeling his way through the organizing years of the infant Republic, questioned whether government would not be most safely conducted by the minority of education and of wealth.

But Jefferson saw that this control, if long exercised by a minority, would be destructive of a sound, representative, democratic system. He preached the extension of the franchise and government more responsive to the public will.

Against Jefferson were almost all the newspapers and magazines of the day. And so, to disseminate his policies in every hamlet and town his associates resorted to printing simple leaflets and pamphlets.

We know that the handful of printers and editors who helped them were harried and arrested under the sedition law with the full approval of the great papers and magazines of that time. That, my friends, was the first effort, with the cooperation of the owners of the press, to curb the essential freedom of the press. It failed just as any similar effort would fail today.

Time went by. Men were not eternally vigilant and once more the control of national affairs was maneuvered into the hands of a group of citizens small in number. The government's face was turned toward the handful of citizens of the seaboard—that small group that owned the Bank of the United States and the great merchant and shipping companies. The government's back was turned on the tens of thousands of pioneers who were settling the mountain regions and spreading over into the new country that lay westward to the Mississippi.

Jackson took up the battle of these pioneers of the West and South, and the battle of the inarticulate poor of the great cities. For that, like Jefferson, he was called a rabble rouser.

He had to fight the same evil Jefferson fought—the control of government by a small minority instead of by a popular opinion duly heeded by the Congress, the Courts and the President.

The Bank of the United States was the purse and sword of the opposition, and with it were aligned all those who, like the early Federalists in Jefferson's time, were at heart in favor of control by the few.

With it were aligned all the nationally known press of the day, with the exception of three newspapers. The Bank sought to array all the money in the country against him.

No one who reads the history of that period can allege that either Jefferson or Jackson attacked all of the bankers, all of the merchants or all of those of wealth. Nor can anyone say that even a majority of these elements of the population were opposed to either one of them.

The fight was won—as all such fights are won in the long run—because Jackson was fighting on the side of the people, whose instincts did not fail him. He was fighting for the integrity of the morals of democracy.

Another generation went by. Lincoln emerged—and was scorned for his uncouthness, his simplicity, his homely stories and his solicitude for the little man. He faced opposition far behind his battle lines from those who thought first and last of their own selfish aims — gold speculators in Wall Street who cheered defeats of their own armies because thereby the price of their gold would rise; army contractors who founded fortunes at the expense of the boys at the front — a minority unwilling to support their people and their government unless the government would leave them free to pursue their private gains.

Lincoln, too, fought for the morals of democracy — and had he lived the south would have been allowed to rehabilitate itself on the basis of those morals instead of being "reconstructed" by martial law and carpetbaggers.

There followed, as we remember, after 1865, and lasting for many years, an uninspired commercialized era in our national life, lighted briefly by the stubborn integrity of Grover Cleveland.

Then came Theodore Roosevelt and resurgence of the morals of democracy. He, too, preached majority rule to end the autocracy of the same old type of opposition. He pleaded for decency — strenuous decency — in public as well as in private life. He laughed at those who called him unprintable names, and challenged again the small minority that claimed vested rights to power.

You and I, in our day and generation, know how Wilson carried on his fight. If the cataclysm of the World War had not stopped his hand, neither you nor I would today be facing such a difficult task of reconstruction and reform.

On the eighth of every January we honor Andrew Jackson for his unending contribution to the vitality of our democracy. We look back on his amazing personality, we review his battles because the struggles he went through, the enemies he encountered, the defeats he suffered and the victories he won are part and parcel of the struggles, the enmities, the defeats and the victories of those who have lived in all the generations that have followed.

In our Nation today we have still the continuing menace of

a comparatively small number of people who honestly believe in their superior right to influence and direct government, and who are unable to see or unwilling to admit that the practices by which they maintain their privileges are harmful to the body politic.

After Jefferson's election in 1800, an election over their violent opposition, such people came to him and said: "Let us alone — do not destroy confidence." After Jackson had won his fight against the Bank of the United States, they said the same thing. They said it to Lincoln, they said it to Theodore Roosevelt, and they said it to Wilson. Strangely enough, although they had no confidence in a people's government, they demanded that a people's government have confidence in them.

In my Message to the Congress on Monday last, I made it abundantly clear that this Administration seeks to serve the needs, and to make effective the will, of the overwhelming majority of our citizens and seeks to curb only abuses of power and privilege by small minorities. Thus we in turn are striving to uphold the integrity of the morals of our democracy.

There is an ancient strategy, recently used, whereby those who would exploit or dominate a people, seek to delude their victims into fighting their battles for them. And in these days of organized nation-wide publicity, the strategy for undermining a government move against minority abuses is to make this appear to be an attack upon the exploited majority itself. Thus during the past few months attacks on the misuse of concentrated power have been distorted into attacks upon all business big and little and upon our whole system of private profit and private enterprise. During the past few days I have been happy to note a definite improvement of understanding on the part of many who have been led to follow this false guidance.

The source and influence of such misguidance of public opinion can be easily located.

I was interested the other day to read the report of a correspondent of a London financial magazine who had recently surveyed conditions in our Middle West and other parts of the Nation. He found a point of view in other parts of the country wholly different from that of the principal financial centers such as New York and Philadelphia and Chicago. And he found this other interesting development. Wherever an enterprise is controlled locally its managers have a local independent point of view. But when the business is controlled from great financial centers, the local manager takes his cue from what his bosses are saying hundreds of miles away.

That, from an outsider, confirms our traditional democratic antagonism to concentration of control over large areas of industry beyond the needs of operating efficiency, and it strengthens our resolve to outlaw the methods by which such control is achieved and to reestablish the independence of local and regional enterprise.

Let me give you an example. As you know, I have been discussing the problem of the electric utilities with business men and lawyers and public officials during the past month or so.

I am convinced that the great majority of local or regional operating utility companies can come to an understanding with the government, Federal and state and local, and with the people of the territories which they serve. That would enable them to obtain, within their own localities or regions, all of the new capital necessary for the extension or improvement of their services.

But most of these operating companies are owned by distant holding companies — pyramided holding companies — which are finance companies and not operating companies. Very few investors in this country who invested in the operating companies have lost money. But thousands of investors have lost their money in buying holding company securities which had Blue Sky above them instead of tangible assets behind them.

That evil of utility holding company control is not going to grow in the days to come because this government has now passed laws to prevent similar occurrences in the future. But we have not yet corrected the existing evils that flow from mistakes of prior administrations. We cannot condone their continuance.

It has been estimated, I think fairly accurately, that there are outstanding some $13,000,000,000 worth of electric utility securities and that the substantial control of this total is vested in the hands of the owners of less than $600,000,000 of the total. That means that the ownership of about four per cent of the securities controls the other ninety-six per cent.

There, my friends, is the case of a ninety-six inch dog being wagged by a four-inch tail. If you work it out in feet and inches it is an amazing dog. But think of the power of that four inches.

I have recently described other things that cannot be reduced to terms of natural history — other activities which ought not to be tolerated in our democracy — price-rigging, unfair competition directed against the little man, and monopolistic practices of many kinds. Call them evils, call them abuses, call them unfortunate facts. It makes no difference. Give to me and give to your government the credit for a definite intention to eradicate them. Give to me and give to your government the credit for believing that in so doing we are helping and not hurting the overwhelming majority of business men and industrialists throughout the United States.

We hope and believe that these evils and abuses and unfortunate actions will in greater part be eliminated by the co-operative action of that overwhelming majority.

The White House door is open — I am forgetting about that famous key just now — the White House door is open to all our citizens who come offering to help eradicate the evils that flow from that undue concentration of economic power or unfair business practices — who offer to do all that is possible by co-operative endeavor and to aid in corrective and helpful legislation where that is necessary.

We know that there will be a few — a mere handful of the total of business men and bankers and industrialists — who will fight to the last ditch to retain such autocratic control over the

44

industry and the finances of the country as they now possess. With this handful it is going to be a fight — a cheerful fight on my part, but a fight in which there will be no compromise with evil — no letup until the inevitable day of victory.

Once more the head of the Nation is working with all his might and main to restore and to uphold the integrity of the morals of democracy — our heritage from the long line of national leadership — from Jefferson to Wilson — and preeminently from old Andrew Jackson himself.

6 ❡ A Greeting to the Conference on Better Care for Mothers and Babies. January 10, 1938

Dear Madam Secretary:

WILL YOU convey to the delegates to the Conference on Better Care for Mothers and Babies my appreciation of their interest in the problems that will come before the conference. I rejoice that the responsible officials of the Federal Government and the States will have the benefit of their counsel in developing practical ways of providing more adequate care for mothers and infants.

The Interdepartmental Committee to Coordinate Health and Welfare Activities is at the present time considering the many questions involved in conserving the health of the people and will soon present a report in which will be outlined its recommendations with respect to the next steps to be taken. Clearly, preserving the lives and health of mothers and their newborn babies is of first importance in safeguarding family life and the welfare of the whole people. I look forward with interest to the findings of the conference.

Very sincerely yours,

The Honorable,
The Secretary of Labor,
Washington, D. C.

7 ❨ The Four Hundred and Twenty-fifth Press Conference (Excerpts). January 14, 1938

(Elimination of water from capital structure of utility companies — Utility valuation — Grants to cities for municipal power plants — Elimination of holding companies — National defense — Trend of business.)

THE PRESIDENT: I don't think I have any news in particular. I found the memorandum [Wendell L. Willkie memorandum]. I guess it was Pete who was asking about it.

Of course we have been working on the subject since this memorandum was left. That was away back in November — November 23rd — and there has been a lot of water which has gone over the dam since then. This whole memorandum, of course, is based on treating the utilities as a whole, not differentiating between the four inches and the ninety-six, and we have got a new definition now in the minds of the public. It is the same old story about trying to lump all business together. We have got away from it now, but this memo was based on the old-fashioned idea of lumping all the utilities into the same category. There is nothing particularly new about it. It is marked, "Confidential," so I cannot give you the thing textually.

Q. Will you work on this one now? [Giving the President a newspaper clipping containing the memorandum referred to.]

THE PRESIDENT: Sure; I did not know it had come out. That is fine. I had no objection to its coming out, but the darned thing is marked "Confidential," so I did not know.

Q. It came out while we were in Florida.

THE PRESIDENT: In the first place, this memorandum indicates that it expresses his own personal views and proposals, acting on behalf of The Commonwealth & Southern Corporation. It does not speak for anyone else.

It goes on to say, "In my judgment, the greatest immediate requirement of the utility industry is a large inflow of com-

mon capital indispensable for much needed additional construction."

I think that is perfectly true in regard to the operating
companies — a great majority of the operating companies.

[Reading] "I have certain suggestions which I believe will
immediately stimulate such investment and make possible
a large construction program with a considerable increase
in employment.

"One of the factors of great importance to the investor
in the utility industry is a stable method of property valuation. You have recently recommended what I understand to be the 'prudent investment' method. The utilities
of the country have issued most of their securities . . .
under court rulings which have required that in fixing the
value of utility properties, the reproduction cost must be
one of the elements considered."

Of course, that immediately brings up one subject which
he does not mention in this, and that is the amortization of
securities. If, as a practical purpose, the securities of the operating companies which had been issued under the former
rulings of the Supreme Court had been amortized, you would
not have very much difficulty with the capital structure at
the present time.

[Reading] "I think the chief objective is to find a method
that will induce the investment of capital in the industry.
I am fearful that the retroactive application of any new
method would be disturbing to the capital market."

Again speaking of the operating companies, if an amortization or sinking fund had been set up on the senior securities when they were issued which, of course, we think now
is a sound thing, you would not have any trouble in the way
of disturbing the capital market.

[Reading] "On the other hand, the utilities, if informed
in advance, can adjust themselves to a new method to be
applied in the future.

"In order to reconcile conflicting ideas, therefore, while

47

at the same time avoiding such disturbance, I have to suggest the following formula:

1. That the utilities immediately eliminate from their capital structures all write-ups heretofore claimed by the Federal Trade Commission."

Again you have to differentiate between the operating company and the holding company and, frankly, I don't know enough of that particular Federal Trade Commission report—it was not on all of them, it was on some of them—to give an intelligent answer to that particular suggestion. Some of it may be all right and some may not. Of course it would have to be gone over again before you would get to a final decision.

[Reading]

"2. That the utility valuation under the rule established by the courts apply either up to this date or to the date of the commencement of your first term as President and that after such date and for the future the prudent investment method be adopted."

Of course that is impossible, because if the thing is wrong now or has been wrong since the 4th of March in 1933, I cannot see where you have any right morally to compound a felony by law, with the Government saying that the crimes of the past will be entirely forgotten and forgiven and that we will leave the water or the wind in the existing capital. Two wrongs do not make a right. I think that is perfectly obvious.

[Reading] "But an understanding as to the method of valuation is, in my judgment, only one of the clarifications necessary in order to establish a relationship between the government and the utilities which will restore investment confidence in the industry. There are certain questions in the mind of the prospective utility investor—"

Again the question of the utility investor

[Reading] "—with reference to such things as the action to be taken under Section 11 of the Public Utility Act of

1935; the procedure of selling power to be practiced by federal agencies such as the Tennessee Valley Authority, and the accounting practices to be followed by those agencies; the future policy of the Federal Government with regard to the making of gifts and loans to municipalities to build duplicate utility systems.

"In order to answer these questions in the public mind, may I suggest the consideration of the following program:

1. Clarification of the Public Utility Act of 1935 as follows:

   (a) Retention of all its regulatory provisions over financing and accounting practices, issuance of securities, relationship between operating companies and holding companies, etc.

   (b) Modification of . . . the . . . 'death sentence.'"

Of course, there you come right down to the heart of it. In other words, he wants the four-inch tail to be legalized for all time to come. We cannot agree on that, ever.

[Reading] "2. Determination of the following policies for the Tennessee Valley Authority and other similar federal projects."

Well, there are a whole lot of them, six of them, in this memorandum and the answer is two-fold: In the first place, we are all agreed that the percentage of territory, population and power affected by Government projects is somewhere between 12 and 15 per cent of the total, and the other 85 per cent is not affected by any Federal power manufactured at the present time. That is an old story.

In those areas, the 12 to 15 per cent of the Nation, we are trying to work out — for instance, Mr. Ross, out on the Columbia, is trying to work out a satisfactory arrangement with the local utilities.

The other point raised is as to the loan and grant methods to municipalities that want to put in their own power plants. The very simple answer on that is the Government recognizes the right of any municipality to put in its own power plant if the vote is so determined. That is just plain American form of government. You cannot get away from it and they do not pretend they can. Even Mr. Willkie said, "Of course not; they have the right to do it if the state gives them the right." It is not a Federal problem at all.

Q. What they say is that you are subsidizing them with that 45 per cent grant?

THE PRESIDENT: All right; if they want to complete a new highway, we give them WPA labor; if they want a new sewer system built, we give them WPA labor; if they want a new water works, we give them WPA labor. I think the Supreme Court has made it fairly clear that there is not very much difference. You cannot draw the line in one place and not draw it in the other.

Q. Isn't there a difference in the sewers and the highways? They do not compete with private industry from the practical standpoint.

THE PRESIDENT: Well, I am talking about constitutional law. That is plain constitutional law.

Q. Yes, I realize that, but you are also talking about a very practical —

THE PRESIDENT: Well, on the practical end, of course the ideal is this: That if a municipality wants to build its own power plant, it will offer a fair price for the existing private utility, and if the utility turns it down, its facilities have got to be paralleled. That is perfectly simple.

Q. Mr. President, to go back to your phrase of a moment ago, "water and wind in the capital structure of these corporations," do you know of any device, short of a wringer, that can reduce that at the present time?

THE PRESIDENT: In the case of operating companies or holding companies?

Q. Either. Either is in the same condition.

THE PRESIDENT: Of course there isn't a universal rule but, in the case of the operating companies, the amount of wind or water is comparatively small. In talking with operating company executives, in the cases we have talked about, the individual cases, we have come to the conclusion that the amount of wind or water is so comparatively small that some method can be found for forcing it out without hurting the operating company. Now, in the case of the holding companies, you have an entirely different picture, because there is such a very large percentage of water.

Q. Do any of the holding companies amortize?

THE PRESIDENT: That I don't know. I would say, offhand, that a great majority of them do not.

Q. I believe there are something like twenty-five municipal plants that may be created now by following the Supreme Court decision on the PWA case. Is it the intention to allow grants to those municipalities where they already have existing private facilities?

THE PRESIDENT: Under the old law — I think this goes back to 1934 — their applications were treated just like all other applications, and where it looked as if the bonds were sound, the thing went through just like any other local improvement. Then the thing was taken to the courts and the money was hung up on a peg for them. In other words, we had a moral obligation to go through with the original allotment if the courts said we should. Now the courts have said that we should, that it is the constitutional thing to do. So, we are taking the money off the peg and giving it to them under the original allotment, in good faith.

Q. Doesn't that in each case, or in most cases at least, permit competition with private capital?

THE PRESIDENT: I don't know. They may be buying out in a great many cases. I think you will find that probably in a great many of these cases of municipalities building their own plants, that they will not duplicate lines, that they will work out some form of purchase from the local private company.

If you remember, in the case of Knoxville, they worked out in that case with the Electric Bond & Share subsidiary a price, and the price was approved by 98 per cent of the bond-holders, 97 per cent of the preferred stockholders and 95 per cent of the common stock holders. The thing was all ready to work, all ready to go through, whereupon, although there was full knowledge that they had spent months on this, and with the full knowledge of the Electric Bond & Share officials in New York City, they got the local ice company and some of the minority two per cent of the stockholders to throw the thing into the Court, where it has been tied up ever since.

There was a substantial agreement on the price in that case and you will find a good many other cases where there was substantial agreement on the price.

Q. You were making a contrast between operating and holding companies and you said that in the case of holding companies there is an entirely different situation and then somebody asked you a question. Have you concluded your statement about that?

THE PRESIDENT: Except this: I suppose the easiest way of putting it, of putting the holding company case, is this: What we are trying to do, frankly, is to eliminate the power in the four per cent tail. I have had these people come in to me, heads of operating companies, and say, "We are ready to shoot."

"Can you raise the money locally?"

"Sure we can."

"Well, why don't you?"

"Because the holding company in New York does not let it go through; they want to do the financing there."

You will find lots of cases there where the president of the operating company is in good shape to go ahead and the holding company is holding it up. That is another reason for the term, "holding company."

Q. To hold up. (*Laughter*)

THE PRESIDENT: Now, of course, you cannot have a generic statement about all holding companies, because they all differ, each one, from the other. Some of them have quite a lot of equity, without any question, and others have very little equity, as in the case where about six hundred million dollars' worth controls thirteen billion dollars' worth of utility capital. That just can't go on. I think they all recognize it.

Q. Is bankruptcy the way to eliminate the power?

THE PRESIDENT: No; oh, no! There are various ways out.

Q. Sir, are you leading up to eliminating holding companies entirely?

THE PRESIDENT: Yes.

Q. Is that a fair question?

THE PRESIDENT: Yes. Now, an investment trust is a different thing from a holding company. I give you that as a suggestion — as long as the investment trust does not vote its stock.

Q. You said all holding companies. Is that even of the first degree?

THE PRESIDENT: Why have any at all?

Q. Does that extend to other lines of industry?

THE PRESIDENT: Yes.

Q. How could that be done, Mr. President?

THE PRESIDENT: You take on the question of banking holding companies, that is another very good illustration. You find a situation in a good many parts of the country where in a very large geographical area practically all of the banks are controlled by some holding company. The little local bank is going. It is a bad thing. Why can't a bank in a community, that is able to support a bank, run itself under proper supervision by the Federal Government, which we give today? It has depositors' insurance and a careful checkup at all times.

Q. Will legislation be proposed, Mr. President?

THE PRESIDENT: I don't know; I haven't got to that yet.

Q. Will it be by the taxing power, Mr. President?

THE PRESIDENT: I don't know; I haven't got to that yet.

Q. You suggested that in your message of June, 1935?

THE PRESIDENT: Yes.

Q. Mr. President, does that mean the branch banks?

THE PRESIDENT: No.

Q. You know there are chain banks?

THE PRESIDENT: That is a very different thing.

Q. Mr. President, is this what you call docking the dog's tail?

THE PRESIDENT: I would not call it that. I'd say, "cutting the muscle in the dog's tail."

Q. It might be a case of cutting the tail off right back of the ears, Mr. President.

THE PRESIDENT: I would hate to destroy his looks, you know; he could have a perfectly good tail if you cut the muscle in it.

Q. Mr. President, you said a few minutes ago that money had been hung on the peg for some of the municipal plants. Do you intend to appropriate any more money for the same purpose?

THE PRESIDENT: No.

Q. No more?

THE PRESIDENT: I have nothing in the Budget at all on it.

Q. Have you made any decision with regard to your supplemental national defense program?

THE PRESIDENT: I have been too busy. I am going back to the House now, as soon as the Conference is over, to write it.

Q. Can you tell us whether that will include items for the Army as well as for the Navy, or simply Navy?

THE PRESIDENT: You are ahead of the game; wait until Monday or Tuesday. . . .

Q. Mr. President, have you had any reports indicating any change in the business situation?

THE PRESIDENT: That is too general a statement. You had better go and ask the Central Statistical Board about that. It is a mighty long subject. Some places are picking up, in others they are standing still and in one or two they are still going down. The general trend is a good deal better than it was before Christmas. . . .

(Note: References in this Press Conference to a four-inch tail are allusions to the statement made by the President in his Jackson Day Dinner Speech, Item 5 of this volume, at page 44 with respect to concentration of control of voting power in utility holding companies. For a discussion of the Public Utility Holding Company Act of 1935, see Item 110, 1935 volume.)

8 ⟨ Presidential Appeal for Red Cross Aid for Civilian Chinese. January 17, 1938

My dear Admiral Grayson:

THERE IS, I am confident, a widespread desire on the part of our citizens in every section of the country to contribute to a fund to aid in meeting the extreme distress of millions of civilian people in China. I feel that our people are deeply sympathetic with those in need in this situation and will wish by their voluntary contributions to take some larger part in aiding in this humanitarian task in which the peoples of many countries are participating. The need of the Chinese is evidenced by the fact that when the International Red Cross Committee made inquiry of both the Japanese and Chinese Red Cross Societies the Japanese Society replied that their resources were adequate to deal with their situation and the Chinese stated that they very much needed outside assistance.

In order to give effect to this desire to aid the people of China it is necessary that some organization be designated to supervise the collection and distribution of the funds and for such a task we naturally turn to the Red Cross.

I should like to request, therefore, that the Red Cross take such steps as it may deem appropriate to afford the American people an opportunity to respond by their contributions to the need of our suffering fellow-beings and I trust that their response will result in a good-will offering of as much as perhaps one million dollars. In response to such an appeal I urge that all our citizens give promptly and generously.

Very sincerely yours,

Rear Admiral Cary T. Grayson,
American Red Cross,
Washington, D.C.

(Similar appeals were made for Spanish civilians and the victims of the Nazi invasion of the lowlands; see Item 160, this volume, and Item 41, 1940 volume.)

9 ⟨ A Greeting to the United Methodist Council. January 17, 1938

My dear Bishop Waldorf:

I CONGRATULATE the Methodist Council upon its thoughtful and reverent approach to the momentous questions which are to command its attention during the forthcoming meetings to be held in Chicago.

In a world perplexed by doubt and fear and uncertainty, there is need for a return to religion, religion as exemplified in the Sermon on the Mount. We need more and more a consciousness of the fact that in the highest and the noblest sense we are our brother's keeper and I want to reiterate the belief I have already affirmed many times that there is not a problem, social, political or economic, that would not find full solution in the fire of a religious awakening.

So it seems to me that your purpose in making a study of the needs, privileges and opportunities of the day in which we live in order that religion may have its rightful place in the solution of our problems, points a way fruitful in promise of effective results. Today when we see religion challenged in wide areas of the earth we who hold to old ideals of the Fatherhood of God and the Brotherhood of Man must be steadfast and united in bearing unceasing witness to our faith in things of the spirit.

In that faith I wish you and your co-workers Godspeed. You are the sowers of the seed. May God bless the harvest.

Very sincerely yours,

Bishop Ernest Lynn Waldorf,
United Methodist Council on the Future
   of Faith and Service,
Chicago, Illinois.

10 ❧ Presidential Statement on the Merit System in Federal Civil Service. January 19, 1938

IN RECOGNITION of National Civil Service Week and the Fifty-fifth Anniversary of the enactment of the Federal Civil Service Act of 1883, I am glad to state once more my convictions with regard to the merit system for the federal government.

I have recommended and I support legislation for the extension of classified civil service upward, outward, and downward.

I have recommended and I support the policy for extension of the Classification Act to insure equal pay for equal work in the field services.

I have recommended and I support legislation to perfect the merit system in the central agency and in departments with ample safeguards to insure the proper use of discretionary powers needed by those who shall administer the system.

I conceive the establishment of a sound national personnel program to be one of the most important constructive steps in the improvement of government administration today.

(See also Item 74, 1937 volume, and references cited.)

11 ❧ The Four Hundred and Twenty-seventh Press Conference (Excerpts). January 21, 1938

(*Suggestions of Business Advisory Council — Conference of labor and capital — Agriculture — Price level — Holding companies — Conference of small business men.*)

Q. Mr. President, the Business Advisory Council had some specific suggestions the other day as to what you might do. Can you give us any comment on any of the suggestions made?

THE PRESIDENT: I think only this: I think we are clearing the atmosphere very, very well and the whole thing is most helpful. They are, for example, learning that the whole question is one that just does not involve business alone, that it is all of those other things that I mentioned the other day, agriculture, labor, transportation — the whole list of them. We are trying to see things from a national point of view, and we are making very distinct progress.

Q. Is there a proposal to appoint some new committee of some sort, sir, to discuss those things, as a sort of advisory committee, to take in agriculture and labor and other factors?

THE PRESIDENT: There again, we cannot, any of us, be factual. In other words, we cannot say that there is going to be a special body set up. What we are trying to do is to work out ways and means by which, without legislation, we shall be able to have these different groups in the Nation come together and exchange information among themselves.

It was, for example, helpful the other day in that conference in the White House to have John Lewis and Phil Murray sitting at the same table with Tom Lamont and Owen Young. Well, that was only two groups. Agriculture was not there. Transportation was not there. Credit was not there.

In this conference the other day with the fifty people, in addition to the list of things that they brought up on their memorandum, we talked about quite a number of other things that fit into the entire picture which they had not discussed among themselves. There was, for instance, the question of the expansion of credit facilities and investment facilities. Those things were not down on their particular agenda and they were very much interested. Also there was the clearing up in their minds of a great many things where they had completely false impressions. It is the old story. Most of these things are due to politics, we know, like the crowd who said, "What is the use in curtailing acreage and at the same time in improving acreage?" Well, of course we all know because I have talked about it so often that the two are not in any way inconsistent. If you prevent soil erosion, you improve land and, at the same time, you are taking certain lands out of cultivation. The two things go hand in hand and are not inconsistent. That requires stressing.

Another thing that some of them are not clear on is — well, for instance, the editorial I happened to pick up saying that it is frightfully inconsistent for the President to say, as he did in 1933 and 1934, that we have got to raise the price level in the country and then, in the spring of 1937, to say that prices are too high. Well, of course the President never said anything like that at all. The objective is exactly what it was in 1933. The price level at that time was about 68 or 69 in comparison with the 1924-1926 period which was 100, and our objective was to get it up to somewhere around that 100, and we did pretty well. Obviously, however, it was perfectly proper to object to certain rises in commodity prices which threw the whole picture out of balance. Go back in your own minds to last April, when I cited the 18- and 19-cent copper. There is the illustration. That was bringing, on the same scale, it was bringing copper not to 90 or 100 but to about 180. That is getting just as much out of line in the particular instance on the particular commodity on the upside as it had been on the downside during the depression. So there is, again, no inconsistency.

Take the question of our old friend, the holding company, which we have been talking about lately. Last week, in the conference, we were talking about public utility operating companies and that type of holding company. Obviously we were not talking about, let us say, the Pennsylvania Railroad which is an operating unit but which operates, because it is in a great many states, through a dozen different corporations. That is not a holding company. Nobody ever accused the Pennsylvania Railroad Company, as such, of being a holding company. We talked about certain bank stock holding companies which are not management companies. Immediately some of our Wall Street write-up friends tried to confuse that — I hope mistakenly — with the question of branch banking. They are two entirely different subjects.

It is things like that that are being clarified in the minds of all those people. They are also getting the point of view of a great many of these problems, such as the failure to get legislation, or to stop legislation — failures which are not due entirely to the administrative end of the Government — that Congress fits into the picture too. One of them suggested the other day that this business group was not getting sufficient cooperation from the Administration on the crop control bill. I pointed out that the Administration last January, at the request of the Congressional leaders, did not draw the bill. We very carefully kept our hands off. These people said, "Well, we do not know that." So it is an educational process, but it has been working out very satisfactorily.

Q. Have you noticed any disposition on the part of the 10 per cent, so-called, to eliminate the abuses complained of in your State of the Union message?

THE PRESIDENT: I think they are understanding that better. There will be some irreconcilables, of course, but taking it by and large the cooperation is good.

Q. Do you expect, as a result of these conferences, to issue a statement that will clear the air for everybody, including the Press?

THE PRESIDENT: No. You will have to use your own brains.

Q. Can you tell us anything about your plans to see the small business men?

THE PRESIDENT: They are coming in some time next week. We are going over the names because there are so many. I think we have probably had about four or five hundred letters from small business men.

Q. What sort of small business men?

THE PRESIDENT: Well, everything below the big business men.

Q. True, but where does that begin?

THE PRESIDENT: I cannot define it any more than that. Some fellow may be employing twenty-five men and another twenty-five hundred men.

Q. And still be small?

THE PRESIDENT: Yes.

(See also Items 26, 49 and 50, this volume, for further discussion of industrial prices.)

12 ❨A Letter of Greeting for Senator Alben Barkley of Kentucky. January 21, 1938

My dear Mac:

I UNDERSTAND that friends of Alben Barkley are giving a dinner in his honor in Louisville tomorrow night and since you are also a Kentuckian I wish you would go down to Louisville and tell the home folks how much we in Washington think of their senior Senator.

Alben Barkley, during his twenty-five years in Congress — first as a member of the House of Representatives and now for more than a decade as a member of the Senate — has rendered distinguished service. Kentuckians have always borne a conspicuous part in our national affairs and the present senior Senator is not only the inheritor of a great tradition of public service but the exemplar in modern terms of that tradition.

These are critical times, times which demand all that a public man can command of resources and experience. Senator Barkley's long familiarity with national affairs, his integrity, his patriotic zeal, his courage, and loyalty and his eloquence in enunciating and elucidating problems and principles give him exceptional equipment as a legislator and as a leader.

For all that he has done in his country's service, his countrymen owe him a debt of gratitude which it is difficult to estimate but which I embrace this opportunity to acknowledge. I send him and all who gather in his honor my hearty good wishes.

Very sincerely yours,

Honorable Marvin H. McIntyre,
The White House,
Washington, D.C.

13 ⟪The Four Hundred and Twenty-eighth Press Conference (Excerpts). January 25, 1938

(National defense needs — Conference of small business men — Prices and wages in the steel industry.)

THE PRESIDENT: I have got a lot of news today. I suppose I might as well forestall questions — a number of them. That would be the easiest way.

First, on this conference that is just over, I think Chairman Taylor gave you the gist of it. We discussed the needs on national defense, Army and Navy, from many angles and the message will go up to the Congress as soon as I get it written. I cannot give you the date yet. If I get it written by Thursday next it will go up then and, if not, then on Friday. I want to get it up Friday at the latest. No details.

On the question of these small business men that we defined so carefully the other day, I find there are about 500 requests which have already come in. Of course it is physically impossible for me to see all 500 of them, so we are arranging for Secretary of Commerce Roper and Assistant Secretary Draper to see them, probably next Monday although the date has not been finally set. That will be over in the Department of Commerce and they will talk things over. I suppose they will probably elect their own chairman to preside over them with the assistance of Assistant Secretary Draper and the Secretary, if they can both be there. When they finish their discussions, it is my hope that they will send, of their own choosing, about ten or twelve of the people who have been there around here to see me. I will see them when they come, at the conclusion of their discussions over there.

That seems to be the only practical way of handling it.

I got word that I was to be asked a question. I have been thinking that question over and I have written out the answer so that there won't be any question as to the answer.

The question was this — I think it was Fred's, but I don't know.

MR. STORM: I had a question for you on steel prices, Mr. President.

THE PRESIDENT: Fred's question was, "Do you agree with Mr. Fairless that steel prices can't be reduced without cutting wages?"

You will all get copies of this. The answer is this:

(Reading from a Press statement, released in mimeographed form.)

"I'm afraid it won't help for me to answer that question again.

"I have said so frequently — and I do not know how to say more clearly and unequivocally than I have already said — that I am opposed to wage reductions.

"I am opposed to wage reductions because the markets of American industry depend on the purchasing power of our working population. And if we want to restore prosperity we must *increase,* not *decrease,* that purchasing power."

Now, those are words of one syllable.

"There may be a special *hourly* wage situation in some building trades —"

That is what I referred to in the Message.

"— in some localities which so far as the total yearly earnings are concerned may call for different treatment, but even there our primary purpose is to increase and not decrease the total of the *annual* pay of the workers."

Is that clear?

Q. Yes, sir.

THE PRESIDENT: [Reading] "Now as to prices.

"A mass production industry depends on volume for profits."

That is why it is a mass production industry.

"No mass production industry can expect to make a profit when the volume is small. The steel industry cannot make a profit at 30 per cent capacity but it can at 50 per cent or 55 per cent of capacity."

And remember, of course, that in the case of the steel industry — on the figures I am using — 100 per cent of capacity means three shifts, 24 hours a day operation, and, I think, six days anyway and maybe seven days a week. So a hundred per cent means running everything they have wide open, 24 hours a day.

"The only way to get volume up is to produce goods for a price the public will pay. A mass production industry in its own interest should ask for its production what the people can afford to pay.

"But that does not mean that such price reductions can come out of wages. Those who believe in the profit system must recognize that those who get the profits when business is good must bear the losses when business temporarily is slack. Those who get the profits when industry gets the volume are the ones to bear the risk of such price reductions as may be necessary to stimulate and restore volume.

"Those in charge of a well-managed and solvent industry should no more consider casting the burden of a temporary business recession upon their workers than upon their bondholders. To cast such burden on bondholders is financial bankruptcy. To cast such burden on its workers is not only moral bankruptcy, but the bankruptcy of sound business judgment.

"Industrialists kill the goose which lays the golden egg when they keep prices up at the expense of employment and purchasing power. Industrialists kill the goose which lays the golden egg when they cut wages and thereby reduce purchasing power. Either policy is self-defeating and suicidal.

"If industries reduce wages this winter and spring, they will be deliberately encouraging the withholding of buying — they will be fostering a downward spiral and they will make it necessary for their Government to consider other means of creating purchasing power."

Now, the reason for that is two things: First, from the statistics we find that a number of businesses in a few sections of the country — not many, for it has not receded to any length at the present time — are in the process of reducing wages. The other reason is that there have been whisperings of a further effort on the part of a few industries in those sections and other parts of the country to reduce wages, hence this statement today.

It is all in words of one syllable. It answers every question that can possibly be asked, and there we are.

Q. Mr. President, if the Steel Corporation persists in its stand —

THE PRESIDENT: What is that?

Q. If Mr. Fairless and his colleagues in the Steel Corporation persist in their stand that wages must be reduced if prices are to be reduced, what is the next step?

THE PRESIDENT: Well, the step was this statement. That was the next step.

Q. What is the step beyond that?

THE PRESIDENT: Now you are becoming "iffy."

Q. Mr. President, John L. Lewis told the Mine Workers Convention this morning that labor will resist any downward cut in prices as well as wages, meaning — well, of course he won't object to price cuts if they do not affect the wage scale, but they will fight price cuts if they mean wage cuts. Have you any comment on that?

THE PRESIDENT: I said exactly the same thing here. If price cuts are based on wage cuts, they are wrong. I have also said that in some industries we all know that price cuts may be made without reducing wages. . . .

(See Items 26, 49 and 50, this volume, for more extended discussion of industrial prices.)

14 ❲ The Four Hundred and Twenty-ninth Press Conference (Excerpts).

January 28, 1938

(Message to the Congress on national defense — 1939 appropriations — Equalization of burdens in time of war.)

THE PRESIDENT: The National Defense Message is going up today at eleven o'clock, and Steve will have copies for you as soon as you get out. There are seven specific recommendations and one general recommendation:

First, the authorization for the Army of additions to anti-aircraft matériel in the sum of $8,800,000. Of that sum, $6,800,000 is for the fiscal year 1939.

Second, for the better establishment of an Enlisted Reserve for the Army, to make it correspond to the Fleet Naval Reserve, $450,000.

Third, for the manufacture of gauges, dies, and other aids to manufacture of Army matériel, $6,080,000, of which $5,000,000 is for the fiscal year 1939.

Fourth, $2,000,000 for making up deficiencies — toward making up deficiencies in ammunition for the Army.

Fifth, that the existing authorized building program for increases and replacements in the Navy be increased by 20 per cent.

Sixth, that Congress authorize and appropriate for the laying down of two additional battleships and two additional cruisers during the calendar year 1938. This will call for the expenditure of a small amount of Government funds during the fiscal year 1939.

Seventh, that the Congress authorize and appropriate a sum not to exceed $15,000,000 for the construction of a number of new types of small vessels, such construction to be regarded as experimental in the light of new developments among navies, and to include the preparation of plans for

66

other types of ships in the event that it may be necessary to construct such ships in the future.

Those are the seven specific recommendations; then there is one general recommendation:

I believe also the time has come for the Congress to enact legislation aimed at the prevention of profiteering in time of war and the equalization of the burdens of possible war. Such legislation has been the subject for many years of full study in this and previous Congresses.

Q. Mr. President, is there anything about the size of battleships there?

THE PRESIDENT: Oh, no!

Q. About the size of guns?

THE PRESIDENT: No — oh, no!

Q. Or as to the character, Mr. President, of those small vessels?

THE PRESIDENT: No — oh, no!

Q. Mr. President, what do you figure this steps the appropriation up for in 1939?

THE PRESIDENT: I don't know — oh, in 1939 — 15, 16, 17, 22, 28 — about $29,200,000.

Q. Mr. President, what do you mean by the "equalization of burdens in time of war"?

THE PRESIDENT: What?

Q. What do you mean by "equalization of burdens in time of war"? Do you want to explain that?

THE PRESIDENT: Well, so that the whole nation will engage in war if we unfortunately have one. . . .

Q. Mr. President, the terms of this Message — of course we haven't seen it yet — is it the intention that Congress shall determine the size of vessels, or is that to be authorized and left to the Navy staff?

THE PRESIDENT: Well, it is done sometimes both ways. Sometimes the Congress appropriates the money and the Navy fits the money to the ship; other times the Congress directs the actual tonnage of the ship.

Q. It is the intent here that there shall be that sort of cooperation?

THE PRESIDENT: Those are technical details that it is a great deal better to say nothing about. Otherwise you will get out on a limb. . . .

Q. Mr. President, if we may get back to the general proposition of war, when and if one comes — that is, the proposal that has been talked by a good many groups of persons of drafting manpower, capital, and manufactures; in other words, making all subject to national defense requirements.

THE PRESIDENT: In one sense, I don't quite like the word drafting.

Q. That is the word that has been used.

THE PRESIDENT: Yes, but I think we ought to have a better word than drafting.

Q. Mobilization?

THE PRESIDENT: That's it — mobilization.

(See following item for the national defense message to which reference is made.)

15 ❨ The President Recommends Increased Armaments for Defense. January 28, 1938

To the Congress:

THE CONGRESS knows that for many years this Government has sought in many Capitals with the leaders of many Governments to find a way to limit and reduce armaments and to establish at least the probability of world peace.

The Congress is aware also that while these efforts, supported by the hopes of the American people, continue and will continue they have nevertheless failed up to the present time.

We, as a peaceful Nation, cannot and will not abandon active search for an agreement among the nations to limit armaments and end aggression. But it is clear that until such agreement is reached — and I have not given up hope of it — we are compelled to think of our own national safety.

It is with the deepest regret that I report to you that armaments increase today at an unprecedented and alarming rate. It is an ominous fact that at least one-fourth of the world's population is involved in merciless devastating conflict in spite of the fact that most people in most countries, including those where conflict rages, wish to live at peace. Armies are fighting in the Far East and in Europe; thousands of civilians are being driven from their homes and bombed from the air. Tension throughout the world is high.

As Commander-in-Chief of the Army and Navy of the United States it is my constitutional duty to report to the Congress that our national defense is, in the light of the increasing armaments of other Nations, inadequate for purposes of national security and requires increase for that reason.

In spite of the well-known fact that the American standard of living makes our ships, our guns and our planes cost more for construction than in any other Nation and that the maintenance of them and of our Army and Navy personnel is more expensive than in any other Nation, it is also true that the proportion of the cost of our military and naval forces to the total income of our citizens or to the total cost of our Government is far lower than in the case of any other great Nation.

Specifically and solely because of the piling up of additional land and sea armaments in other countries, in such manner as to involve a threat to world peace and security, I make the following recommendations to the Congress:

(1) That there be authorized for the Army of the United States additions to anti-aircraft matériel in the sum of $8,800,000 and that of this sum $6,800,000 be appropriated for the fiscal year 1939.

(2) That there be authorized and appropriated for the bet-

ter establishment of an Enlisted Reserve for the Army the sum of $450,000.

(3) That there be authorized the expenditure of $6,080,000 for the manufacture of gauges, dies and other aids to manufacture of Army matériel, the sum of $5,000,000 thereof to be expended during the fiscal year 1939.

(4) That the sum of $2,000,000 be authorized and appropriated toward the making up of deficiencies in ammunition for the Army.

(5) That the existing authorized building program for increases and replacements in the Navy be increased by 20 per cent.

(6) That this Congress authorize and appropriate for the laying down of two additional battleships and two additional cruisers during the calendar year 1938. This will call for the expenditure of a very small amount of Government funds during the fiscal year 1939.

(7) That the Congress authorize and appropriate a sum not to exceed $15,000,000 for the construction of a number of new types of small vessels, such construction to be regarded as experimental in the light of new developments among Navies; and to include the preparation of plans for other types of ships in event that it may be necessary to construct such ships in the future.

I believe also that the time has come for the Congress to enact legislation aimed at the prevention of profiteering in time of war and the equalization of the burdens of possible war. Such legislation has been the subject for many years of full study in this and previous Congresses.

It is necessary for all of us to realize that the unfortunate world conditions of today have resulted too often in the discarding of those principles and treaties which underlie international law and order; and in the entrance of many new factors into the actual conduct of war.

Adequate defense means that for the protection not only of

our coasts but also of our communities far removed from the coast, we must keep any potential enemy many hundred miles away from our continental limits.

We cannot assume that our defense would be limited to one ocean and one coast and that the other ocean and the other coast would with certainty be safe. We cannot be certain that the connecting link, the Panama Canal, would be safe. Adequate defense affects therefore the simultaneous defense of every part of the United States of America.

It is our clear duty to further every effort toward peace but at the same time to protect our Nation. That is the purpose of these recommendations. Such protection is and will be based not on aggression but on defense.

NOTE: The recommendations made by me in the foregoing message were but the beginning of a vast program of rearmament.

With respect to the army, I included only those items which had been recommended by the War Department as immediately necessary. It was obviously impossible to do everything at once, and these were the first steps. Practically all the requests for appropriations made by me were adopted by the Congress in the Military Appropriation Act for the next fiscal year.

The recommendations with respect to the Navy are all itemized in the message; and were adopted by the Congress substantially as recommended.

See also press conference discussion of this message, Item 14, pages 66-68, this volume; for other messages recommending increased appropriations for national defense, see Items 1, pages 1-4, 8, 21, 37, 72, 1939 volume; Items 1, pages 1-4, 48, 54, 68 and 152, 1940 volume.

16 ❡ Radio Address on the Occasion of the President's Fifth Birthday Ball for the Benefit of Crippled Children. January 29, 1938

My Friends:

MY HEART goes out in gratitude to the whole American people tonight — for we have found common cause in presenting a solid front against an insidious but deadly enemy, the scourge of Infantile Paralysis.

It is a very glorious thing for us to think of what has been accomplished in our own lifetime to cure epidemic diseases, to relieve human suffering and to save lives. It was by united effort on a national scale that tuberculosis has been brought under control; it was by united effort on a national scale that smallpox and diphtheria have been almost eliminated as dread diseases.

Today the major fight of medicine and science is being directed against two other scourges, the toll of which is unthinkably great — cancer and infantile paralysis. In both fields the fight is again being conducted with national unity — and we believe with growing success.

Tonight, because of your splendid help, we are making it possible to unite all the forces against one of these plagues by starting the work of the new National Foundation for Infantile Paralysis. The dollars and dimes contributed tonight and in the continuing campaign will be turned over to this new Foundation, which will marshal its forces for the amelioration of suffering and crippling among infantile paralysis victims wherever they are found. The whole country remains the field of work. We expect through scientific research, through epidemic first aid, through dissemination of knowledge of care and treatment, through the provision of funds to centers where the disease may be combated through the most enlightened method and practice to help men and women and especially children in every part of the land.

Since the first birthday celebrations in 1934, many splendid results have been accomplished so that in literally hundreds of localities facilities for combating the disease have been created where none existed before.

We have learned much during these years and when, therefore, I was told by the doctors and scientists that much could be gained by the establishment of this new National Foundation for Infantile Paralysis, I was happy, indeed, to lend my birthday to this united effort.

During the past few days bags of mail have been coming, literally by the truck load, to the White House. Yesterday between forty and fifty thousand letters came to the mail room of the White House. Today an even greater number — how many I cannot tell you, for we can only estimate the actual count by counting the mail bags. In all the envelopes are dimes and quarters and even dollar bills — gifts from grown-ups and children — mostly from children who want to help other children to get well.

Literally, by the countless thousands, they are pouring in, and I have figured that if the White House Staff and I were to work on nothing else for two or three months to come we could not possibly thank the donors. Therefore, because it is a physical impossibility to do it, I must take this opportunity of thanking all of those who have given, to thank them for the messages that have come with their gifts, and to thank all who have aided and cooperated in the splendid work we are doing. Especially am I grateful to those good people who have spread the news of these birthday parties throughout the land in every part of all the big cities and the smaller cities and towns and villages and farms.

It is glorious to have one's birthday associated with a work like this. One touch of nature makes the whole world kin. And that kinship, which human suffering evokes, is perhaps the closest of all, for we know that those who work to help the suffering find true spiritual fellowship in that labor of love.

So, although no word of mine can add to the happiness we share in this great service in which we are all engaged, I do want to tell you all how deeply I appreciate everything you have done. Thank you all and God bless you all.

17 ❨ Informal, Extemporaneous Remarks to a Number of Visiting Protestant Ministers. Washington, D.C. January 31, 1938

(Dr. Oscar F. Blackwelder of the Lutheran Church of the Reformation, President of the Washington Ministerial Union, made the following statement [excerpts only are printed] today when he, in company with more than two hundred Protestant ministers, was received by the President in his offices at the White House.)

Mr. President:

By vote of the Ministerial Union of Washington, I pray the privilege of presenting this message for our body to you.

In accepting your hospitality we are confident that we come into the presence not only of our Chief Executive but of our friend and brother in the Christian Faith. . . .

Mr. President, conscious of the historical contribution of Christianity to human betterment, both personal and social, we are anxious as a group of ministers to do our part today and we believe we speak in the spirit of the clergy of America.

In your address before the Federal Council of Churches in Constitution Hall in 1934, you declared, "No greater thing could come to our land today than a revival of the spirit of religion — a revival that would seep through the homes of the nation and set the hearts of men and women of all faiths to a reassertion of their belief in God and their dedication to His will for themselves and for their world. I doubt if there is any problem — social, political or economic — that would not melt away before the fire of such a spiritual awakening." That word of yours we have used nationwide. It has brought courage to the church life of America.

We pastors of the Protestant Churches of Washington, although holding many different political opinions, wish to pay our respects to you as our fellow Church man as well as Chief Executive. We desire to pledge through you our thought, our prayer, our useful service to our country in these difficult days and to request you to make any suggestion of ways and means by which we and our brethren in the ministry can be of the highest value to our day and generation.

17. Remarks to Protestant Ministers

(The President replied, speaking extemporaneously.)

I am grateful to you for this wonderful expression of faith— of faith and works. I am glad that you referred to what I said in 1934 about the need of spiritual reawakening in the country. I do not know how you gentlemen feel, but I cannot help feeling myself, from the testimony that comes to me day by day, that there has been definite and distinct progress towards a spiritual reawakening in the four years which have passed since I spoke in 1934. I receive evidences of this from all our Protestant Churches; I get it from Catholic priests and from Jewish rabbis, as well.

It is a very significant thing that this awakening has come about in America. It makes me realize more fully that we do have, in addition to the duty we owe to our own people, an additional duty to the rest of the world. Things have been going on in other countries—things which are not spiritual in any sense of the word—and that is putting it mildly.

I must make a confession: I did not realize until the last few years how much influence America has in the world. I did not really, deep down in my heart, believe very much in church missions in other lands. Today I do. I have seen what the American church missions have accomplished in many countries, not only on the religious side but on the side of health and of education. After all, the three of them tie in very definitely together. We call what we have been doing "human security" and "social justice." In the last analysis all of those terms can be described by one word; and that is "Christianity."

We have made great progress at home. I believe, in making that progress, we have had a great influence in other nations of the world. We have gone far in these years toward a greater human security and a greater social justice. We don't want to stop that progress. We want to keep on. We have a task, not only for four years or eight years or twenty years to come—but a task that lasts through all eternity. As long as we continue to make the progress we are making, we can look for a safer and better America in our own lifetime.

You good people have been working toward that end. You have been rendering a great service to your Government.

We still have a long way to go. Whether we like it or not, we have to think about the average man, woman and child in the United States. We are doing just that; and they appreciate it. That is one reason why the Churches are stronger today than they were four years ago. If we can continue to make the same progress in the next several years as we have in the past, we can feel we have been good and faithful servants.

I appreciate your coming here and all I can say is God bless you; keep up the good work.

18 ❮ A Memorandum on Petroleum Reserves in the United States. February 3, 1938

Memorandum for
   Chairman Doughton
   Representative Vinson

I AM sending you herewith for your information a copy of estimate of Petroleum Reserves in the United States which has just been prepared by the Petroleum Conservation Division of the Department of the Interior. This report was prepared for the Conference of Governors of oil-producing States, held at Hot Springs, Arkansas, January 24, 1938.

I am also enclosing copy of report on this Oil Conservation Conference made by Mr. E. B. Swanson, the Associate Director of the Petroleum Conservation Division of the Department of the Interior.

This is sent to your Committee because there has been raised the question of placing a small tax on crude petroleum, not only for the purpose of producing revenue but also for the purpose of conserving our oil resources, both for the use of industry and for national defense.

The report in regard to reserves is somewhat more alarming

than I had previously believed. For instance, present drilled reserves are estimated to be capable of supplying demand only until November, 1941, and to meet expected demand during twenty years to come it would be necessary, in addition to production from known reserves, to discover twenty-eight billion barrels of new oil. Such new discoveries would have to be made at a rate of discovery greatly exceeding discoveries made during the past seven years.

NOTE: The purpose of the analysis submitted in the foregoing letter was to emphasize the need for maintaining an adequate rate of discovery and development of new oil reserves in the United States. The figures show that our present reserve is an adequate back-log, which would afford some protection against an unanticipated and extraordinary demand, or against some temporary slack in new discoveries. It is not sufficient, however, in itself, to rely upon with confidence for filling our greatly increasing demand for oil for a great many more years, unless the rate of discovery and development is increased.

While the reserves have increased quantitatively for the past seven years, the demand for oil in the United States has increased more rapidly. As a result, our present proved reserves, when measured in terms of demand, are no larger relatively than those of 1934. During the last seven years crude oil demand in the United States has increased 54 per cent, which is an average annual increase of nearly 8 per cent. It is estimated that the present proved reserves are adequate to take care of about thirteen years of demand; and in order to keep up with this ratio it has been necessary for the oil industry to discover or develop nearly twice as much crude oil per year as is consumed per year.

Furthermore, there must be taken into consideration not only the proved reserves, but also the ability of such reserves to produce oil as needed. For example, although it has been calculated that there are current proved reserves of about 20 billion barrels, which is about thirteen times the present annual consumption, it would not be physically possible to produce that much in thirteen years. It would require a much longer time to do so. Therefore, even with unrestricted production, if there were no more discoveries, while there might be enough produced to equal the whole demand for the first five years, that production would subsequently decline over a period of years, during which time the output would not equal the current demand.

Therefore, there is this pressing need continually to discover and develop new reserves; and this warrants recognition as a national policy of the necessity of maintaining a reasonable field price for crude oil and a limitation of overproduction, in order to protect our proved reserves. To maintain such a reasonable price, there should be uniformity and efficiency in the administrative policies and practices of all the State regulatory agencies engaged in regulating oil productions; and there should be a discontinuance of any wholesale or retail

marketing practices, such as price cutting in petroleum products, which work to the detriment of refiners and producers.

For further measures taken to conserve oil and regulate its production, see Items 30, 62, 95, 95A, 1933 volume; Item 90, 1934 volume; Items 21, 68 (pages 232-233), 103, 1935 volume; Items 18 and 90, 1937 volume; Items 32, 88 and 97, 1939 volume; Item 49 (page 217), 1940 volume; and accompanying notes.

19 ❡ The Four Hundred and Thirty-first Press Conference (Excerpts). February 4, 1938

(Conference of small business men — The fixing of wages.)

Q. Was not the small business men's conference held at the request of the small business men?

THE PRESIDENT: Yes, and no. The origin, of course, is perfectly simple. We got in the White House, beginning about two months ago, a large number of letters saying, "Please, can we come down to Washington? Why don't you pay the same attention to us?" There were hundreds of them that wanted some kind of a conference in Washington. It was perfectly vague, but they wanted to be here. Of course, to a good many of them we wrote back and said it was impossible to see everybody individually and would they write their views. They still kept coming back and saying, "We would like to come to Washington." There were a good many hundreds of them. We were confused, quite frankly, with the dilemma. If we said "No" to them, certain agencies in the country would say that we were turning them down. If we invited them down here, it would be very difficult to handle a group of that kind. But I do not think it is a fair thing to ridicule either them or their efforts.

Q. How were they invited? Were those who wrote the letters, were they the ones?

THE PRESIDENT: Yes, largely. I think entirely. They were all people who had written letters.

Q. Mr. President, a great many of the delegates expressed the belief that the conference has been a flop. Do you share in that view?

THE PRESIDENT: I don't know. I have not heard from them.

Q. Mr. President, have you asked any Federal agency to study the possibility of extending financial aid to small business men?

THE PRESIDENT: Well, that matter is under study, as I said last week.

Q. Mr. President, may I read one sentence from Senator Wagner's speech on the Housing Bill, when he subscribed to the idea of taking out the prevailing wage amendment? He said:

> If we ever come to the time when we in this body pass laws saying how much a bricklayer shall receive per day, how much a carpenter shall receive, how much a clerk working in private industry of any kind shall receive, and begin to fix all those wages, we will destroy unionism and freedom of collective bargaining and advance on the road toward fascism. [Page 1266, Cong. Record, 75th Congress, 3rd Session.]

Would you mind telling us whether that is your thought, too?

THE PRESIDENT: It goes in line with everything I have always said, always. Now, do not misinterpret that. There are lots of ways of misinterpreting it.

Q. His idea was that if you go beyond fixing, you get into this realm of doubt and danger.

THE PRESIDENT: I will just give you one thought on it. You know we talked a good deal about a floor for Agriculture. Well, just use the analogy on wages. The Agricultural bill does not attempt, in any way, to set the price on corn or the price on anything else. All it does is sets a floor. Use the same analogy on wages and you will about hit it right. . . .

(See note to Item 57, 1937 volume, for an account of the Fair Labor Standards Act, which, among other things, placed a floor under wages.)

20 ❨ Radio Greeting to the Boy Scouts of America from the White House, Washington, D.C. February 7, 1938

Fellow Scouts:

I AM happy to receive this report from Mr. Head on the accomplishments of our organization. On this twenty-eighth birthday of the Boy Scouts of America we should be especially thankful for a youth movement which seeks merely to preserve such simple fundamentals as physical strength, mental alertness and moral straightness — a movement to support the ideals of peace.

I congratulate our leaders and especially our Scoutmasters who have made an outstanding record possible. We have increased in numbers and I am confident on the basis of what I, myself, have observed that we also are improving in the quality of Scouting. Last summer I had the opportunity to visit with thousands of you, from all parts of the country, in your great Jamboree camp here in Washington. I am really sorry that every citizen of the country did not see, as I did, the great national encampment of Scouts here along the Potomac River. I have seen no more cheering sight from the standpoint of the national future.

The theme chosen for our Boy Scout Week Observance — "Building a Stronger Generation" — is thoroughly worth while. I have always believed that scout training does help to build health for boys and young men. It encourages them to get out into the open, to develop good health habits. It helps to make them hardy and vigorous. Of course, we all recognize that

"Building a Stronger Generation" involves more than good health. It involves strong character, initiative, resourcefulness and ideals of service — qualities that you practice in your scouting experiences.

But it involves, also, learning all about other people — your neighbors and their problems, the people who live in the other end of town and their problems, the people who live in the next town and their problems, those who live in the next State and their problems — in other words, the problems of every part of the United States. When you have accomplished that you will realize, also, that there are problems outside the United States which affect you and your family and friends. Thus, the ideals of scouting include not only character and service but also knowledge. They will be as real and vital to you in your manhood as they are to you today in your boyhood.

It is my conviction that, through work with our youth, we shall secure the greatest assurance of maintaining our democracy in the face of those forces which advocate forms of government not consistent with our cherished American traditions. And the strength of this youth movement will develop in exact proportion to the support accorded it by communities who are interested in preserving our democracy.

I extend to you my best wishes for the year to come. Boy Scouts today — you will be the citizens tomorrow, with a nation's keeping in your charge. I believe that you will be worthy of the trust.

21 ⟨ A Recommendation Extending Financial Assistance for Home Builders. February 7, 1938

Dear Jesse:

IN ORDER that the benefits of the new Federal Housing Act may be made immediately available to all who wish to build and to those who wish to invest in the debentures of national mortgage associations, I wish the Reconstruction Finance Corporation to organize a national mortgage association in Washington with a paid-in capital stock of $10,000,000, and provide it with management. I should also like the Corporation to reserve $40,000,000 more for capital in other national mortgage associations, or as additional capital for the National Mortgage Association of Washington.

It is my hope that builders, material and supply people, working men, prospective home owners, and those who may desire to build private or multiple dwellings for rent or sale will cooperate in taking advantage of this new law.

The obvious effect of such whole-hearted cooperation will stimulate business and provide employment for hundreds of thousands.

Inasmuch as the debentures of national mortgage associations can only be issued against first mortgages that are insured by the Federal Housing Administration, they are backed indirectly, but nevertheless effectively, by the credit of the United States Government.

These debentures will be exempt both as to principal and interest from all taxation (except surtaxes, estate, inheritance, and gift taxes) now or hereafter imposed by the United States, by any Territory, dependency, or possession thereof, or by any State, county, municipality, or local taxing authority. They will afford an attractive and absolutely safe investment for people of small or large means, and should be issued with this in view so as not to be a drain on the Federal Treasury.

Very sincerely yours,

Mr. Jesse H. Jones,
Reconstruction Finance Corporation,
Washington, D. C.

NOTE: Pursuant to my request contained in the foregoing letter, the Reconstruction Finance Corporation organized the Federal National Mortgage Association with capital of $10,000,000 and surplus of $1,000,000. This Association is owned and operated by the Reconstruction Finance Corporation and deals exclusively with mortgages insured by the Federal Housing Administration (see Item 82, 1934 volume; Item 157 of 1937 volume, and notes).

As of January 1, 1941, it has authorized the purchase of 53,700 mortgages, aggregating about $223,000,000; and purchases have actually been completed on more than 50,000 of these mortgages, aggre-

gating more than $200,000,000. Of these, only 392 mortgages, aggregating about $1,700,000, have been foreclosed.

The Federal National Mortgage Association purchases at par and accrued interest any mortgages insured by the Federal Housing Administration on new homes, including large size housing projects.

22 ⟨A Request for Supplemental Appropriations for Unemployment Relief.

February 10, 1938

To the Speaker of the House of Representatives:

I HAVE the honor to submit herewith for your consideration a supplemental estimate of appropriation of $250,000,000, for relief of the unemployed.

> Emergency and Work Relief: To continue to provide relief and work relief as authorized in the Emergency Relief Appropriation Act of 1937, and subject to all the provisions thereof, $250,000,000, which amount shall be added to, and proportionately increase the specified amounts of the limitations prescribed under the appropriation made in such Act [50 Stat. 352].

According to the best estimate available at this time it appears that, during the past three months, approximately three million persons have lost their jobs with private employers. This increase in unemployment could not, of course, have been foreseen at the time the last relief appropriation was under consideration. Hundreds of thousands of needy unemployed persons have recently applied for relief work which could not be provided for them with the funds on hand. It has become increasingly clear that these needs cannot be met unless employment by the Works Progress Administration is increased immediately.

The funds available on January 1, 1938, would permit employment of an average of only 1,700,000 persons for the six months ending June 30, 1938. The number of persons on the Works Progress Administration rolls today is 1,950,000. Funds available at this time will not only not take care of the additional burden caused by the recent increase in unemployment but will require a sharp reduction in the near future of the number on the Works Progress Administration rolls. This estimate of $250,000,000 will permit the continued employment for the next five months of the number now on such rolls, and will provide a reasonable measure of relief for those who have recently become unemployed and are in need.

NOTE: The Emergency Relief Appropriation Act of 1937 had appropriated $1,500,000,000 for the Works program for the fiscal year 1938 (50 Stat. 352).

Until the early fall of 1937 business conditions had been improving rapidly and unemployment had been decreasing. This recovery stopped abruptly, however, in September of 1937 (see Item 49, this volume). Unemployment began to rise very quickly; and, as a result, welfare offices in cities and towns throughout the United States were flooded with requests for relief.

During the first six months of the fiscal year ending June 30, 1938, employment on the WPA program was on a fairly constant level, averaging 1,527,000 people. During these months, however, several millions of people were thrown out of private employment; therefore, the WPA Administrator authorized an increase in the WPA employment rolls of about 300,000 persons for the month of January, 1938. By February 5, 1938, WPA employment had reached 1,945,000 people.

As I pointed out in the foregoing message, unless additional funds had been appropriated it would have been necessary to reduce that amount about 100,000 men each additional month to the end of the fiscal year, in order to average approximately 1,700,000 men during that period.

This message was therefore sent by me asking for an additional appropriation of $250,000,000 in order to provide the funds for the WPA to employ an average of 2,191,000 people during the second half of the fiscal year. Even this would provide work for only a portion of the persons who had been thrown out of employment by the recession.

The requested appropriation was made by the Congress (Public Resolution No. 80, 75th Congress). As a result thereof the employment rolls continued to rise, and by June, 1938, they had reached 2,743,000. The average employment for the second half of the fiscal year was 2,342,000, or 151,000 more than was predicted.

By September, 1938, the number of unemployed began to decrease very appreciably.

For a discussion of the activities of the WPA, see Items 54, 86A, 89, 116, 1935 volume; Items 36, 37, 41, 42, 47, 90, 176, 219, 240, 1936 volume; Items 45, 71 (pages 264-268), 1937 volume; Item 69, this volume; Items 5, 10, 27, 42, 1939 volume; Items 7, 34, 50, 1940 volume.

23 ⟪A Greeting to the Radio Broadcasting Industry. February 12, 1938

My dear Chairman McNinch:

IT IS a pleasure through you to extend greetings and good wishes to the radio broadcasting industry on the occasion of the Sixteenth Annual Convention of the National Association of Broadcasters to be held in the Capital of the Nation.

During the past year we have witnessed basic developments and progress in radio which will have a profound effect upon the application of broadcasting in this country as well as on the North American Continent.

One of the greatest advantages of the system of licensing broadcasting is that it is sufficiently flexible to lend itself readily to adjustment to meet our changing social and economic needs. In a new field of public service such as that of broadcasting we may and should expect rapid progress in both the development of the art and in meeting the public requirements that this national resource shall increasingly contribute toward our social as well as our economic advancement. The broadcasting industry has, indeed, a very great opportunity to serve the public, but along with this opportunity goes an important responsibility to see that this means of communication is made to serve the high purposes of a democracy. I have the high hope that the industry under the guidance of and in cooperation with the Federal Communications Commission will prove itself to be worthy of the great public trust reposed in it.

I hope the forthcoming deliberations will be fruitful of wise judgments in dealing with the many and diverse problems that enter into the broadcasting industry.

Very sincerely yours,

Honorable Frank R. McNinch,
Federal Communications Commission,
Washington, D. C.

24 ⟪ Presidential Statement on Signing the Agricultural Adjustment Act of 1938.

February 16, 1938

TODAY as I sign the Agricultural Adjustment Act of 1938 my mind goes back five years to the day in March, 1933, when I recommended to the Congress the passage of the original Adjustment Act to rescue farmers from the intolerable plight of the depression. At that time I recognized frankly we were taking "a new and untrod path." But events have shown that in rejecting inaction at that time and in determining to face the problem and meet it directly with a farm program which could be improved as circumstances required, we chose wisely. Great progress has been made since the Agricultural Adjustment Act of 1933 went into effect.

Gradually, through these years, the basic principles of national farm policy have become clear. By experience we have learned what must be done to assure to agriculture a fair share of an increasing national income, to provide consumers with abundant supplies of food and fiber, to stop waste of soil, and to reduce the gap between huge surpluses and disastrous shortages. The Nation is now agreed that we must have greater reserves of food and feed to use in years of damaging weather and to help iron out extreme ups and downs of price. We are agreed that the real and lasting progress of the people of farm and city alike will come, not from the old familiar cycle of glut and scarcity, not from the succession of boom and collapse, but from the steady and sustained increases in production and fair exchange of things that human beings need.

A year ago, a national conference of farm leaders in Washington advocated federal legislation to serve these ends. During the recess of the Congress, committees were at work. The task was complex and difficult. In order that the Congress might have opportunity to complete legislation in time to meet this year's farm problems, I summoned the special session last November. This Act is the result.

The Agricultural Adjustment Act of 1938 represents the winning of one more battle for an underlying farm policy that will endure. Therefore it is historic legislation. It is not perfection, but it is the constructive product of the able and sincere work of many men. I believe the overwhelming majority of the people will commend members of Congress and others who have devoted themselves to the making of this law. As we go ahead under the new Act, let us resolve to make it an effective instrument to serve the welfare of agriculture and all our people.

It will be put into operation as quickly as possible, and in the meantime I ask that all those who are doing or will do spring planting govern their operations in the light of this new law.

While the new Act makes many important changes in the existing plan for the benefit of agriculture, it is to be noted that, with one exception — the provision for "parity" payments — the improved plan for agricultural adjustment does not entail any greater annual cost than the sum authorized under the present one, which is known as the Soil Conservation and Domestic Allotment Act. Parity payments would increase the present authorized cost, and in order to make such payments it would be necessary to provide additional revenue needed to finance them.

24. Agricultural Adjustment Act of 1938

NOTE: The Agricultural Adjustment Act of 1938, which I signed in connection with the foregoing statement, marks the beginning of the third general period in the history of our agricultural adjustment program.

The original Agricultural Adjustment Act was approved by me on May 12, 1933; and, with it, began the first period of our program. The necessity for the adoption of that statute, the history of the conditions and steps leading up to it, and the results of its adoption in improving the economic conditions of the farmers of the country are set forth in Items 20 and 54 of the 1933 volume.

That statute provided for adjusted production of seven basic commodities: wheat, corn, cotton, hogs, rice, tobacco, and dairy products. Later, nine other commodities were added to this group. Benefit payments were made on voluntary contracts between the government and each producer who cooperated in the program. The money for these payments was raised from taxes on the processing of the commodities involved.

The primary objective of the original statute of 1933 was to bring about an increase in farm income by reducing the surpluses which had dragged prices down.

This statute was declared unconstitutional by the Supreme Court on January 6, 1936, with respect to its acreage control and processing tax provisions, which were, of course, the very foundation upon which the Act was based (U. S. vs. Butler, 297 U. S. 1).

The second period of agricultural adjustment was the passage of the Soil Conservation and Domestic Allotment Act on February 29, 1936, following as quickly as possible the Supreme Court decision invalidating the original Agricultural Adjustment Act of 1933. The basic principle of this second statute was that of voluntary soil conservation by farmers and the payment of money to them for cooperation in this soil conservation program.

Under this Act, payments were made to farmers who consented to shift parts of their farms from raising soil-depleting crops, such as corn, wheat, cotton, tobacco, and rice, to raising soil-conserving crops instead, such as grasses and legumes; and who cooperated by adopting and carrying out regularly prescribed soil-building practices.

An annual appropriation of $500,000,000 per year was made to carry out this program. The practices and results of the program are described in the note to Item 28 of the 1936 volume.

It became obvious in 1937 that this soil conservation program would not be sufficient to adjust the supply of crops to the demand for them in such a way as to give the farmer a fair return on his products or a fair share of the national income. Accordingly, steps were taken to adopt a more comprehensive and broader program. My recommendations for such a program are set forth in Items 87, 139, and 158 of the 1937 volume. One of the chief reasons for calling the extraordinary session of the Congress in the fall of 1937 was to adopt such a program.

The third phase in the history of agricultural adjustment was the adoption by the Congress of this new suggested program in the Agricultural Adjustment Act of 1938, which was signed by me on February 16, 1938 (52 Stat. 31). It went much further than the two preceding statutes.

Briefly, this statute and the other statutes later enacted to carry out the present farm program provide: (1) conservation payments for farmers who plant their products within certain acreage allotments and who carry out prescribed soil-building practices; (2) payments of money, called parity payments, to producers of corn, wheat, cotton, tobacco, and rice who plant these commodities within the limit of certain allotments made to them; (3) the making of loans by the government on certain farm commodities, with the two-fold purpose of forming a support to prevent the collapse of farm prices when the surpluses are too big, and also of storing excess reserves of commodities as an ever-normal granary with which to make up for bad crops in drought or other unproductive years; (4) federal crop insurance on

wheat so as to insure wheat growers against losses on bad crops; and (5) artificial marketing control of surplus crops raised, providing that such control is first approved in a formal referendum by two-thirds of the farmers producing such commodity.

There are also several other minor activities authorized under this statute and related legislation, such as: freight rate investigations and studies; purchases of surplus farm products for distribution to persons on relief; attempts at marketing expansion through research on new possible uses for farm products; and allocation of funds for the purpose of helping to maintain a fair share of foreign markets for American farm products.

Taking up the conservation payment feature first, it is divided into two principal parts: the allotments of acreage among farmers, and the promotion of soil-building practices. Under the program, which is democratically administered by the farmers themselves as will be hereinafter described, a national acreage goal is figured out for each of the soil-depleting crops, such as corn, wheat, cotton, tobacco, potatoes, rice, etc. These figures are arrived at on the basis of careful estimates of market requirements and good soil practices, and are figured at amounts which are adequate to provide abundant supplies for domestic needs, export needs, and reserve requirements. These goals are then divided first among the States, then among the counties, and then among the many individual farms in each county actually raising these commodities.

Before planting time, each farmer is notified of the amount of his acreage allotment and of the specific soil-building practices and goals which have been recommended by the local county committees of farmers for his particular farm. He is also informed by his local committeemen as to how much money he will be paid for limiting his planting to these allotments, and for using the kind of soil-building practices which have been prescribed for him.

The farmer can thereupon decide whether to cooperate in the program or not. Cooperation is entirely voluntary. If the farmer decides to cooperate, he limits his planting to the amount of his own particular acreage allotment, and carries out the approved soil-building practices within the goal established for his farm. The farmer's intention to participate in the program is indicated by his signing an agreement to do so, called a "Farm Plan for Participation." Some time later during the summer or fall, a representative of the county association makes a visit to the farmer to measure the acreage which has been planted with soil-depleting crops, and to inspect the soil-building practices which the farmer has carried out. This is known as the performance check. This check determines whether or not the farmer has fully performed his agreement, and what the amount of his payment will be.

These payments are known as "conservation payments," and are made for specific accomplishments under the provisions of the conservation part of the farm program. An annual appropriation of not to exceed $500,000,000 is authorized for these conservation payments.

The second type of payments, known as parity payments, is made in order to give the farmers a fairer share of the national income, and is meant to take the place of the payments made under the old Agricultural Adjustment Act of 1933. The Agricultural Adjustment Act of 1938 provided that when appropriations are made therefor, the Secretary of Agriculture, shall make payments to the producers of the major crops — corn, wheat, cotton, rice, and to-bacco — on their normal production of such commodities in amounts which, together with the proceeds of the sale of their crops, will provide money to such farmers in an amount as nearly equal to "parity price" as the funds appropriated will permit. This "parity price" is defined in the statute as that price which will give to the particular commodity a purchasing power in relation to articles that farmers buy for themselves, equivalent to the purchasing power of such commodity during the five years before the beginning of the last World War, which is considered a normal base period (August, 1909–July, 1914). These parity payments are supposed to be in addition to, and not in substitution for, payments otherwise authorized.

Funds available for parity payments are apportioned to these various commodities in proportion to the amount by which each fails to reach the parity income. In order to receive parity payments on any crop, a farmer must limit his planting of that particular crop within the acreage allotment for his particular farm, and must not have offset this by overplanting on any other farm in which he has an interest.

Parity payments have been appropriated by the Congress each year since the agricultural adjustment program became fully effective; but, in spite of my repeated protests and the protests of the Department of Agriculture, the Congress has failed to provide any taxes or sources of revenue for these appropriations (see Item 158, 1937 volume; Item 91, 1939 volume). This failure is referred to also in the last paragraph of my statement printed as Item 24 above.

The next item of the present program, as enumerated above, is commonly referred to as the "ever-normal granary." This name is generally applied to a system of farming adapted to maintaining a continuous and fairly stable supply of farm products at prices fair to both the farmers and the consumers. In other words, it seeks to obviate

periods of glut when farm prices fall below a level which is fair to farmers, and also to obviate periods of scarcity when prices for farm products rise to a level which is unfair to consumers.

The other parts of the AAA program, such as acreage allotments, conservation payments, and marketing quotas (described later), all do their share to help regulate and determine the amount of the supply of the commodity. The granary itself, however, is built up through loans made by the Commodity Credit Corporation on agricultural commodities stored up as reserves. A farmer, for example, who is cooperating in the AAA program may obtain a loan on any part of his crop which he does not sell, and he may store it either on his own farm or in a licensed warehouse. He furnishes security for his loan by giving a chattel mortgage to the Commodity Credit Corporation on this part of his crop. In this way reserves are stored up in years of abundance which can be released in years of crop failures or when unexpected national demands arise. The loans enable farmers to take surpluses out of the market in years of heavy production and low prices, and to dispose of these supplies in years of low production at fairer price levels. At the same time consumers, of course, are protected against excessive prices which might come in bad crop years, because there are always these stored-up reserves ready to be sold in years of scarcity.

These loans may be made on any agricultural commodity. They are, however, mandatory on corn, wheat, and cotton, whenever the supply of the crop rises above certain specified levels or when prices fall below certain specified levels.

Although the commodity loan rates vary from time to time, the legislation in effect most recently provided rates to farmers cooperating in the AAA program ranging from 52 to 75 per cent of parity for loans on cotton, corn, and wheat. On May 14, 1941, however, these rates were increased by the Congress up to a maximum of 85 per cent of parity prices. Loans may also be made to non-cooperators in years when marketing quotas (described later) are in effect, at 60 per cent of the rate available to cooperators, on that part of their crop which would be subject to penalty if marketed.

In order to safeguard the government against accumulation of unwieldy surpluses, glutted markets, and extreme price collapse, it is provided that if the use of a marketing quota for any crop is opposed by more than one-third of the producers voting in a referendum, no loan should be made on that commodity until the beginning of the next marketing year.

Another feature of the ever-normal granary program is crop insurance. At the present time crop insurance is limited to wheat (see Item 20 and note, 1937 volume). Crop insurance again offers protection to both producers and consumers, because the premiums, which are paid by farmers in kind in order to insure their crops against bad years, are held in reserve in the same way, to be paid out in time of crop failures.

The next item of the program concerns marketing quotas. These are intended to be used only in years of unusually large supplies. Their purpose is to regulate the marketing of the commodity, and to assure a fair share of the market to those farmers who adjust their production in an attempt to balance supply and demand. As provided in the Agricultural Adjustment Act of 1938, quotas may be applied to cotton, corn, wheat, rice, tobacco, and peanuts. In any year when the production of any one of these basic crops rises above a certain specified level, the Secretary of Agriculture is directed to proclaim a marketing quota on that commodity. Within a prescribed period thereafter, a referendum is held among the producers of that commodity on the question of whether or not they wish to use such quotas in marketing their crop. Such quotas become effective only if two-thirds of the farmers voting in the referendum approve them. If they are approved they apply to all farmers — AAA cooperators and non-cooperators alike.

If a marketing quota has been approved, it means that the farmer must keep the amount of his marketing within his quota. This quota, for most of the crops, is the actual production on his own acreage allotment. On all marketing in excess of this quota he must pay a penalty. Consequently, a farmer who has planted within his acreage allotment is able to market his entire production without penalty. Marketing quotas were established for cotton and for some types of tobacco in 1940.

The AAA program is administered in great part by the farmers themselves through elected representatives. All farmers who cooperate in the AAA program are members of the county agricultural conservation association in their particular county. This association is the local administrative unit of the Agricultural Adjustment Administration. The operating expenses of the association are paid by its members out of their AAA payments. The business of the association is carried out through committees elected by the members — one for each community and one for the county as a whole.

The community committee is composed of three farmers elected annually by their major farmers. There are approximately 73,000 community committeemen who administer the program in their communities or townships.

Delegates elected from all the communities in the county choose three farmers to serve as the county committee of the AAA. This committee distributes county acreage allotments equitably among the farmers of the county, approves the soil-building practices for which farmers may earn payments, and in general adapts the national program to local conditions. There are approximately 9,000 county committeemen.

In each state there is a state committee known as the state agricultural conservation committee. The state committee is composed of the director of the state agricultural extension service and three to five farmer members, appointed by the Secretary of Agriculture on the basis of local recommendations. These committees' duties are much the same as those of the county committees, but on a state-wide basis.

The administration of the program in Washington is handled on a regional basis, with one director for each of the six regions into which the country is divided.

In this way the administration of the program is completely decentralized, and is conducted as a fully democratic process by farmers themselves through their own elected farmer representatives.

The program is now financed entirely out of the Treasury of the United States, since the processing taxes by which the original AAA program was financed have been declared unconstitutional. In connection with sugar, however, payments are offset by collections of an excise tax on refined sugar.

The average-sized conservation payment earned by the five and three-quarters million farmers who cooperated in the 1939 program, for example, was only $86.40, and the average parity payment was only $38.67. More than 77 per cent of all farmers participating in the 1939 program earned conservation payments of less than $100, and about 92 per cent earned payments of less than $200.

As for the results of this AAA program over the eight years from 1933, I shall quote the following excerpts from a report of the Agricultural Adjustment Administration of the United States Department of Agriculture, made public in January, 1941:

"During the last eight years, the AAA farm program has faced a variety of emergency problems. They have successively included staggering surpluses, drought of an unprecedented degree, the recasting of the farm program following the Supreme Court decision of 1936, the accumulation of new surpluses under the 1936 and 1937 programs, the administration of new legislation in 1938, and, at present, war in Europe. Then, too, because the 1938 winter wheat crop had been seeded months before the 1938 legislation was enacted, the present farm program was in complete operation for the first time in 1939. Yet American agriculture has made a tremendous recovery during this period.

"*Income.* Cash farm income in 1939, including Government payments, amounted to an estimated 8.5 billion dollars as compared with 4.7 billion dollars in 1932. From 1929 to 1932, farm income had declined to a point where farmers were able to buy only about 58 per cent as much city goods as in 1929. In 1939 they were able to buy about the same amount of goods as in 1929. Likewise, the value of farm real estate increased by about 5 billion dollars from 1932 to 1939. The nation's farm mortgage debt has been reduced more than 2 billion dollars, or 23 per cent, since 1932. Farm bankruptcies have decreased 71 per cent. . . .

"*Conservation.* In 1939, the last year for which complete figures are available, new seedings of alfalfa, clover, and other soil-conserving crops by farmers cooperating under the AAA totaled more than 41 million acres; trees were planted and other forestry improvement practices were carried out on about 350,000 acres; nearly 6 1/2 million tons of fertilizer and lime were applied; other erosion-control practices, such as strip-cropping and contour-farming, were carried out on approximately 26 million acres, and nearly 355 million feet of terraces were constructed during the year.

"Ranchmen cooperating in the range conservation program carried out natural reseeding of their range land through deferred grazing practices on 25 1/2 million acres, and artificial reseeding through the

94

use of 3,184,000 pounds of grass seed. They built 21,000 earthen tanks and reservoirs — new watering places for stock — on 19,400 ranches, moving nearly 39 million cubic yards of material, which more equitably distribute grazing throughout the range. They made contour ridges and furrows, and used spreader dams to hold the water on the grass.

"*Consumer protection.* Through the reserves of corn and wheat built up in the AAA Ever-Normal Granary, consumers are protected against the scarcity and high prices which regularly have accompanied periods of drought and short crops in the past. Reserves of corn — the raw material from which our meats, eggs, milk, and other dairy products are produced — in the past have amounted to only seven per cent of a normal year's production. In each of the drought years, 1934 and 1936, corn production was about 40 per cent below normal. Meat prices sky-rocketed and consumers suffered great hardships. Now, with the help of loans, farmers have created an Ever-Normal Granary of corn reserves amounting to more than 25 per cent of a normal year's crop. Wheat farmers, with the help of the wheat loan and the crop insurance program, are doing the same. Moreover, the Sugar Act of 1937 specifically provides for the protection of consumers against excessive prices for sugar.

"In the 1940 Ever-Normal Granary reserves, the nation finds a bulwark of protection against whatever circumstances may arise from the European conflict. Our granaries contain one of the greatest supplies of food and fiber in our history. Over and above our expected domestic consumption and exports, we have on hand 14 million bales of cotton, 700 million bushels of corn, 390 million bushels of wheat, and 2½ million barrels of rice. Our stocks of poultry and dairy products, fruits and vegetables, meats and lard, and other commodities are just as plentiful. Through the Ever-Normal Granary and the loan programs, farmers have obtained better prices for their crops and at the same time have maintained reserves adequate to meet any emergency.

"*Wheat.* Cash income of the nation's wheat producers was 167 per cent larger in 1939 than in 1932, rising from 200 million dollars to 534 million dollars, including an estimated 138 million dollars in government payments. In the fall of 1939, United States wheat prices were around 30 to 35 cents above their usual relationship to world levels. Farmers who put their wheat under loans were also able to take advantage of the 25- to 30-cent-per-bushel price rise which occurred during the winter. The 1939 seeded acreage of wheat was 63.7 million acres, compared with 67.2 million acres for the 1928-32 period.

"*Cotton.* Cotton producers' cash returns from seed and lint increased from 461 million dollars in 1932 to 844 million dollars in 1939, including estimated government payments of 215 million dollars. Cultivated acreage of cotton in 1939 amounted to 24.7 million acres, compared with 41.4 million during the 1928-32 period. On this acreage shifted out of soil-depleting crops, Southern farmers produced soil-improving crops and badly needed food and feed crops for home use which appreciably increased their standard of living.

"*Corn*. Planted acreage of corn in 1939 was 91.5 million acres, approximately 13 million acres less than were being planted during the five-year period before the AAA. Yet cash income from corn increased from 110 million dollars in 1932 to 476 million dollars in 1939, including an estimated 150 million dollars in government payments.

"*Tobacco*. Even though tobacco producers did not take full advantage of the AAA program in 1939 and produced one of the largest crops on record, their 1939 cash income was still more than double what it was in 1932. The increase was from 115 million dollars to 271 million dollars including estimated government payments of 7 million dollars. Now tobacco farmers are using all features of the program in cushioning the effects of the European war which has so sharply curtailed tobacco exports.

"*Sugar*. The income of continental United States sugar-beet and sugarcane producers rose from an average of $63,000,000 in the period 1928-33, which preceded the sugar programs, to $84,000,000, including government payments, in the period 1934-39, during which such programs were in effect — an increase of more than 33 per cent. The income from sugar production in Hawaii and Puerto Rico has also improved during the period sugar legislation has been in effect.

"*Dairy*. Dairy farmers' income in 1939 was 37 per cent greater than in 1932, having risen from 991 million dollars to 1,355 million dollars.

"*Meat animals*. Cash income from meat animals rose 97 per cent from 1,158 million dollars to 2,276 million dollars."

The entire AAA program has been perhaps the outstanding example of how the initiative, the planning, the management, and the resources of government can be used to help millions of its citizens acquire a fairer share of the national income. And it has done this in a way which is not only equitable to the rest of the nation, but actually helps every other group and section of the country by providing additional markets for their goods and by furnishing protection for them against high prices.

For additional measures designed to aid the farmer, see Items 18, 22, 22A, 29, 73, 83, 84, 92, 106, 125, 130, 151, 179, 1933 volume; Items 6, 21, 27, 29, 62, 76, 80, 1934 volume; Items 18, 50, 51, 59, 84, 113, 135, 151, 152, 177, 181, 1935 volume; Items 4, 6, 11, 39, 131, 133, 218, 1936 volume; Items 19, 25, 53 (pages 196-200), 91 (pages 313-314), 93 (pages 317-319), 1937 volume; Items 26 (pages 102-110), 42 (pages 194-196), 64, 93, 95, this volume; Item 47, 1939 volume; and Items 8, 18, and 31, 1940 volume.

25 ⟮ Recommending Credit for Borrowers to Help Employment. February 18, 1938

Dear Jesse:

WHILE the modifications we have heretofore made in your lending authority since my letter to you of October 18th permit emergency loans of various character, it is my wish that you make credit available to all deserving borrowers to which you are authorized to lend, especially loans that will maintain or increase employment.

Very sincerely yours,

Mr. Jesse Jones,
Reconstruction Finance Corporation,
Washington, D. C.

NOTE: As will be seen from an examination of the note to Item 49 of this volume, business activity had been on the steady increase up to 1937. With it had come an increase in credit facilities. It began to look as though the stagnation of business and industrial credit had been overcome, and that private capital would thereafter be willing to do the necessary financing of the business of the nation.

As a result, in early 1937, I authorized the Reconstruction Finance Corporation to suspend the exercise of its lending authority.

As the recession of 1937 and 1938 became more acute, however, and when it became apparent that private capital was not willing or able to furnish the necessary credit facilities to carry on the business processes of the nation, I sent the foregoing letter to the Reconstruction Finance Corporation requesting it to resume the extension of credit to "all deserving borrowers to which they are authorized to lend." I emphasized the desirability of making loans in the places where they would help maintain or increase employment.

Since the foregoing request, the Corporation has authorized loans aggregating about $3,250,000,000, making its total authorization through December 31, 1940, about $15,000,000,000. Of these authorizations the loans actually disbursed since my request of February 18 were $1,385,000,000.

Since the organization of the Corporation in February, 1932, the loans actually disbursed out of the total authorizations up to December 31, 1940, have been about $11,-000,000,000, of which about $9,000,-000,000, or 82 per cent, has been repaid.

The loans authorized and disbursed by the Reconstruction Finance Corporation have recently been devoted to many and varied purposes. For examples, loans have been made in aid of agriculture; to help carry out the provisions of the Farm Tenancy Act; to the Federal Surplus Commodities Corporation; Disaster Loan Corporation; Cotton Export Corporation; Joint Stock Land Banks; Commodity Credit Corporation.

Loans have been made to assist the opening of banks or to accelerate distribution to the depositors of closed institutions. Investments have been made in private banks and in the Export-Import Bank.

Loans have been made to States, municipalities, and political subdivisions of States to help construct useful self-liquidating public facilities. Loans have been made to railroads. In cooperation with the banks of the United States, many millions were loaned to business

and industry, most of which have been in smaller amounts. Since my foregoing request, and pursuant to an amendment of the Reconstruction Finance Corporation Act on June 25, 1940 (Public No. 664, 76th Congress), the Corporation has participated in the defense program by making loans on a more liberal basis to, and making purchases of the capital stock of, private industries engaged in defense activities.

It has also made loans to mortgage loan companies, building and loan associations, public school districts, drainage districts, mining and smelting companies, rural electrification projects, and mortgage loans on real estate. This statement of loans refers chiefly to the period between February 18, 1938, and January 1, 1941.

A general statement of the work of the Reconstruction Finance Corporation during the first term of my Administration is set forth at pages 398-404 of the 1933 volume.

The following tables show the general work of the Reconstruction Finance Corporation during the first and second terms of my Administration (March 4, 1933–January 19, 1941), indicating the amount actually loaned and the amount actually repaid.

It will be seen that the fears were not well founded of those who believed in "letting-well-enough-alone," and who opposed extending credit with public funds to anybody except railroads, banks, and other financial institutions. The amount of loans already repaid to date indicates the care and judgment with which these loans were made; and shows that only a negligible part of the capital of these loans will become uncollectible.

I think that the record of good loans made by the RFC will compare most favorably with private banking operations in general, especially in view of the fact that the lending has been conducted on a scale far beyond the ability or willingness of private capital to emulate.

RECONSTRUCTION FINANCE CORPORATION
LOANS, INVESTMENTS, AND ALLOCATIONS DISBURSED AND REPAID FROM MARCH 4, 1933 TO JANUARY 19, 1941, INCLUSIVE

	Amount Disbursed[1]	Amount Repaid and Other Reductions[2]
Loans on cotton, corn, tobacco, and other commodities	$ 836,412,758.86	$ 837,168,949.52
Loans for distribution to depositors in closed banks	951,180,069.78	937,650,836.34
Loans to receivers of building and loan associations	2,954,564.27	2,649,386.89
Loans to railroads (including receivers)	470,251,730.59	295,409,540.53
Loans to drainage, levee, and irrigation districts	91,121,841.88	7,756,650.94
Loans to Public School Authorities	22,865,175.00	22,310,000.00
Loans to business enterprises, except to aid in National Defense (including fishing, mining, milling, and smelting)	241,125,588.58	117,928,060.94
Loans to banks and trust companies	186,907,783.35	802,692,326.88
Loans to Federal Land Banks	368,436,000.00	387,236,000.00
Loans to mortgage loan companies	428,309,981.03[3]	348,470,336.87[5]
Loans to aid in financing self-liquidating construction projects	321,107,641.28	320,446,607.76
Loans for the repair and reconstruction of property damaged by earthquake, fire, tornado, flood and other catastrophes	12,003,055.32	10,780,523.33
Loans to regional agricultural credit corporations	131,808,191.11	170,969,088.44
Loans to building and loan associations	18,179,085.65	101,939,542.86
Loans to insurance companies	10,169,729.62	82,369,307.15
Loans to joint-stock land banks	19,769,670.82	21,853,723.75
Loans to livestock credit corporations	721,425.03	6,230,893.90
Loans to Federal intermediate credit banks	9,250,000.00	9,250,000.00
Loans to State funds created to insure deposits of public moneys	13,064,631.18	13,064,631.18
Loans to agricultural credit corporations	2,028,390.94	4,180,038.75
Loans to credit unions	150,442.79	578,157.21
Loans to processors or distributors for payment of processing taxes	14,718.06	14,718.06

	Amount Disbursed[1]	Amount Repaid and Other Reductions[2]
Loans to Rural Electrification Administration $	150,500,000.00	$ 2,425.46
Loans on preferred stock in banks..........	45,449,300.76	17,416,477.57
Loans on preferred stock in insurance companies.............................	34,375,000.00	12,304,881.37
Purchase of capital stock in The RFC Mortgage Company......................	25,000,000.00	—
Purchase of preferred stock in one insurance company............................	100,000.00	—
Purchases of preferred stock, capital notes and and debentures in 6,079 banks...........	1,197,835,905.80[4]	674,858,696.66[5]
Purchases of securities from P. W. A.	640,552,546.16	526,323,470.32
Loans and purchases of stock to aid in National Defense.............................	62,072,268.80	691,821.15
Loan to Export-Import Bank.............	25,000,000.00	—
Loans to public agencies for self-liquidating projects.............................	123,299,816.57	98,866,816.57
Purchase of capital stock in the Federal National Mortgage Association.............	11,000,000.00	—
Loans to Secretary of Agriculture..........	37,000,000.00	—
	$6,490,017,313.23	$5,831,413,910.40
Allocations to other governmental agencies and for direct relief...................	2,486,916,799.05	2,782,446,055.33
Total..........................	$8,976,934,112.28	$8,613,859,965.73

[1] Including amounts disbursed on authorizations made prior to March 4, 1933.
[2] Including amounts repaid on disbursements made prior to March 4, 1933.
[3] Includes $146,636,421.81 to The RFC Mortgage Company and $119,553,134.85 to the Federal National Mortgage Association.
[4] Includes $76,500,000.00 for stock of Export-Import Banks.
[5] Includes $104,277,887.21 by The RFC Mortgage Company and $38,834,237.65 by the Federal National Mortgage Association.
[6] Includes $2,500,000.00 by the Second Export-Import Bank of Washington.

26 ❨ The Four Hundred and Thirty-fifth Press Conference. February 18, 1938

(Achieving a balanced price structure — Labor costs — Price-fixing in the coal industry — Farm prices — Relief — Foreign debts — Credit policy — Shipbuilding costs — Alliance with other American countries.)

Q. Good morning, Mr. President.

THE PRESIDENT: How's the class? [referring to charts on the desk in front of him, which are to be explained to the correspondents and some of which are printed at the end of this press conference].

Q. Back to school — going to school again.

THE PRESIDENT: Yes, we are all accustomed to it.

Q. Mac is going to explain it to us.

THE PRESIDENT: Yes. (*Laughter*) The dotted line [referring to charts in front of him] represents the high cost of liquor.

Q. Well, we are going up to where we can get it a little cheaper. The Nelson House bar is always —

THE PRESIDENT: [interposing] Yes, they do not have the same overhead.

Q. I don't think they will be able to get in today, it is a big crowd.

THE PRESIDENT: Really?

Q. Charge a buck a head and we would make some dough out of it.

Q. Yes.

THE PRESIDENT: I am requested by Mr. Wile [Frederic William Wile] to file a plea in avoidance. He sent me the following this morning and it calls for an answer on the part of Mr. Sullivan. Wile says:

> I would make an observation
> For your private information
>   Re a subject on which
>   You're somewhat in the dark.
> I am filled with high elation.
> When you tune in the wrong station
>   And mistake *me*
>   For a man who's made his Mark.
>
> Though he's no New Deal supporter,
> On behalf of a reporter
>   I venture upon a prayer to embark.
>   Sullivan's got the reputation
>   Which deserves perpetuation,
> So I humbly rise to plead,
>   God save the Mark!"   (*Laughter*)

Q. [Mr. Sullivan] That is about all I have to rely on. (*Laughter*)

THE PRESIDENT: Well, as you know, I talked with various agen-

cies of the Government the past week in an effort to clarify
for you certain economic problems and they worked up for
me yesterday a statement on which they are all agreed. That
is pretty good, to get six or eight different agencies of the
Government to agree. It might be called noteworthy. So, I
think the best thing I can do is to read what they have all
agreed on. It is not very long and Mac [Mr. McIntyre] — it
is only three and a half pages — has mimeographed copies
of this so you won't have to take it down.

(The President then read to the correspondents the statement
printed at the end of this press conference.)

Well, that is what they all agreed on. Then they had some
charts, and I threw out all the charts I could not understand
and I kept the ones I could understand and they are here
behind me.

This chart [indicating chart "Wholesale Prices and Employment"] shows that wide disparities between rigid and
sensitive prices, between finished goods and raw materials,
are closely related to low levels of employment shown on
the lower curve, and that high levels of employment accompany balanced prices. The last two years are shown in
more detail at the right of the chart. These [indicating] on
the left are from 1929 through 1937. These will be taken
out to the Press Room and you can look at them and
memorize them.

This chart [indicating chart headed "Per Capita Farm and
Nonagricultural Income Available for Living and Living
Costs, 1924-38"] shows incomes of farm and city workers
compared with the living costs from 1924 through 1937. It
shows first that living costs are relatively stable as compared
with farm and city workers' incomes. The top dotted line is
living costs. The dash line is per capita non-farm income, and
the black line at the bottom is the per capita farm income. It
shows also that a rise in prices and incomes can be achieved
without a corresponding increase in the cost of living. You

see, things were going along pretty well at that stage of employment through 1929, but here [indicating a point midway through 1929] this discrepancy between the dotted line and the black line is beginning to widen.

This chart [indicating chart entitled "Wholesale Prices of Selected Agricultural Products, 1929-38"] shows index numbers of selected farm products from 1929 through 1937. Taking the 1929 prices as 100, this chart shows the movement of the four major farm commodities since that time. The first is cotton, 10 spot markets. The next one is wheat. The dotted line on the chart on the bottom shows hogs and the other, the black line, shows corn. As you know, corn and hogs go together.

The 1929 prices, which are taken as a base, were themselves not very high in several cases, due to falling off in export demands, which had already begun to occur. Those averages were wheat 117, corn 93, hogs and cotton 18.25.

The chart also shows that, even with Triple A operations, the prices of farm commodities continuously varied up and down and have not shown the rigidity shown by administratively determined prices. Here [indicating] there is a sharp fall.

This chart [indicating chart entitled "Wholesale Prices of Selected Building Materials"] is, I think, one of the most significant ones. It shows the price trends of certain building materials. The top dotted line is cement. It shows that it started at about 105 in 1929, went down to nearly 80, came back in 1934 to just where it was before and has continued on the same level of around 105. On the other hand, structural steel, starting at 100, went down to 80, and in 1934 came back to 98, and since then has gone to nearly 120.

Then you come to two other building materials, wall board and house paint, that today are both below the 1929 level. They took a big drop, of course, in 1932, but they have come back and have leveled out pretty well and are running along lower than what they were in 1929.

Now, the next line is plaster. In 1929 it was 90. It has gone up by a series of leaps and bounds until it is now nearly 180.

Prepared strip shingles did somewhat the same thing. They started below 90, went down to 80, and went clear up to 150, and are now back to 120, which is still 30 points above what it was in 1929.

Q. You said that was a significant chart. What is the particular significance?

THE PRESIDENT: It is the breaking down of raw materials in one industry, building, and it shows that you cannot make one general rule. You see, plaster is way up, prepared shingles are way up, and wall board and paint are still a little down.

Q. The point is in the divergence?

THE PRESIDENT: Yes, and also the fact that, taking it by and large, there are some pretty important materials there that are way up above the 1929 level. Now, this is going to save time and then if you have any more questions it is all to the good. I worked out some questions I thought you might ask. This is not to preclude you from asking others. Somebody will say, with a mind full of generalities, "What is to be done?" The problem is being talked on a good many fronts. There are many elements in the recovery program that have already been directed toward a better balance of prices. For example, the new farm bill will help, and we hope also that the new housing program, when it gets under way, will help.

Q. Will you give us a copy of that?

THE PRESIDENT: On the question of what is to be done: The problem is being talked on a good many fronts. There are many elements in the recovery program which have already been directed toward a better balance of prices. That phrase, "better balance of prices," is the key to the whole thing. For example, the new farm bill will help, we hope the new housing program will help, and the expanding relief program will help.

Somebody else with a mind full of generalities will ask

the second question: "Does this mean inflation?" No, the policy is to help restore balance in the price structure.

Somebody will say, "Are we going to have a further deflation of the dollar?" The answer is, "No."

Then, along the same line, is the action that was taken on Monday in regard to the sterilization of gold. Is it a part of the plan to increase prices? Yes, that was one of the considerations for doing it, but not the only one; there were a lot of others.

Then somebody will say, "How do you reconcile this with what you said last April, nearly a year ago?" I jotted down this note, "A question like that is a good deal like saying that a man who warns you to go slow on the curve is responsible if you run off the road."

Q. Will you read that over again, Mr. President?

THE PRESIDENT: It is like saying that a man who warns you to go slow on the curve is responsible if you run off the road.

We all agree that price dislocations were one of the major causes of the recession. They included price maladjustments and speculative buying, which had been developing through the end of 1936 and the first four months in 1937, before I issued the warning that some prices were going too high. And the only question in my mind, from the point of view of hind sight, is, "Ought I not to have issued that warning before I did?"

Q. The warning in this case, Mr. President, was your observation in April?

THE PRESIDENT: Yes.

Then, more on finance is the credit policy of the Government: We expect to continue to maintain easy credit conditions. The Treasury and the Federal Reserve Board are both cooperating toward that end.

We talked in the past a good deal about the 1926 price level. Are we aiming at the 1926 price level? Yes and no. In other words, it is not a question of restoring the level definitely to a given year. We are seeking to balance the relationship among different groups of prices that will promote full employment.

Q. Will you repeat that?

THE PRESIDENT: We are seeking to balance the relationship among different groups of prices that will promote full employment. In other words, suppose I put it this way: Away back in 1933, as you remember, we did a lot of talking in 1933 and 1934 about bringing the price level up from around 68 or 69 to somewhere around 90 or 100. We took 1926 as a criterion. Why? Because that year represented what might be called the average of the loaned dollar; it was the average of the dollar which was owed by people. Now, since 1933 or 1934, there has been a great deal of new loaning and new borrowing in terms of the dollar of 1935, 1936 and 1937. That has to be taken into consideration as a modifying factor on the 1926 dollar. Do you understand that?

Q. Which way does the modification go, up or down?

THE PRESIDENT: Down, in that case. In other words, I cannot say that we are going to try to get the price level back to 90 or 95, as compared with 1926. It is a varying thing by which you take, originally, a norm, a figure. Now, subsequent happenings have some relationship on that original figure you take and the effect in the last few years has been downward from that figure of 100.

Q. What is the difference between the 1926 price and the 1935 price level? That is, how much spread is there between the two?

THE PRESIDENT: Well, if 1926 was 100 — I do not know, I would have to ask Henry Morgenthau.

MR. EARLY: We can give them that afterwards.

THE PRESIDENT: Don't use this: We got it up somewhere between 90 and 92 in the beginning of 1936 and 1937.

Q. Then the price to be aimed at would be somewhere between 92 and 100?

THE PRESIDENT: But what you write today would not be followed six months from now.

Q. It is somewhere below 1926, but somewhat above what it is today?

THE PRESIDENT: Yes.

Q. It is easy to see how the new farm bill would bring about the balance in agricultural prices, but not so easy to see how the relief program and housing program would bring about a balance in the industrial prices. Can you explain that further?

THE PRESIDENT: Well, of course on both housing and relief it tends to increase production and it is very largely in industries that there is need to increase production.

Q. Mr. President, do you contemplate using relief for any new activity other than it has been used for?

THE PRESIDENT: No.

Q. In the case of the housing program, do you not think, sir, that the wage levels are also a factor?

THE PRESIDENT: That is the very next question. You are a mind reader. Are labor costs too high? The real answer to lower costs of production is to be found in increased volume rather than lower wages. That is in spite of the fact that earnings per hour in manufacturing were 24 per cent higher in 1936 than in 1932.

Q. The only one who can get it is Kannee [Henry Kannee, stenographer at press conferences]. (*Laughter*)

Q. Would you mind repeating it?

THE PRESIDENT: The real answer to lower costs of production is to be found in increased volume rather than in lower wages.

Now, here is the illustration: Despite the fact that earnings per hour in the manufacturing groups were 24 per cent higher in 1936 than in 1932, the labor costs per unit of output were only 6 per cent higher. This was due in part to the fact that the productivity of labor increased. To put that in plain English, the efficiency of labor increased, but it was primarily due to the fact that labor can be used more efficiently in mass production industries when those mass production industries operate at the high level of output. It is further demonstrated by what happened in the last five months. Despite the fact that wages have not increased in the last five months, the shrinking volume of output has forced up labor costs per unit of production as much as they had risen in the previous four years.

Q. The shrinking output at what time?

THE PRESIDENT: In 1932 to 1937. The shrinking output forced up the labor costs per unit of output as much as they had risen in the last four years. . . .

Then, further on wages because I have not completely covered that yet, did the wages rise too fast last spring, that is, in the spring of 1937? There were very few wage increases between 1934 and October, 1936, very few; but in the following nine months — that is to say, from October, 1936, through to July, 1937 — hourly earnings in manufacturing plants rose from 57 cents to 65 cents. In other words, it was a sudden rise. There had been very little rise in the past few years.

We know that many firms were in a position to increase wage rates in the two previous years, 1935 and 1936, and therefore it was probably not healthy for business to have postponed for so long their wage increases with the result of having to absorb wage increases in a large lump in those nine months from October, 1936, to the summer of 1937.

Then, just by way of commenting further on that, I notice that during the downswings, recessions, people speak of the need of flexible wages and feel that wages should fall. Then, during recovery, as the figures prove, they seem to forget that wages should also be flexible and should rise. They delay wage increases until the last possible moment and then, at the peak of a boom, grant wage increases that are small when measured against current profits of industry.

Q. Take that last sentence slower.

THE PRESIDENT: They delay wage increases until the last possible moment and then, at the peak of a boom, grant wage increases that are small in comparison with their profits, but which, at the same time, are difficult to maintain when their volume falls off. The automobile industry is the prize example of that.

Q. Mr. President, then, in the case of the automobile industry, do you say that if they increase production to full capacity and prices were reduced, there would be a material increase in sales?

THE PRESIDENT: No, no. There is such a thing as increasing production to the point where the country cannot swallow it — gets indigestion. If the wage increases were not so long delayed but were made as business improved, managers of business would have a longer period of activity in which to adjust themselves to changes. It means, if the AP would give you a few small raises, twice a year, it would be better for the AP than if they gave you a 50 per cent raise all in one lump sum.

Q. [Mr. Storm] I will take mine either way, Mr. President. (*Laughter*)

Q. On that subject, have you any thought of the sliding wage scale in connection with variations in prices?

THE PRESIDENT: No.

The next question I asked myself —

Q. [interposing] On that question, Mr. President, what do you think of a system of profit sharing in that connection?

THE PRESIDENT: Well, of course that is being introduced in a good many industries, I think very successfully, taking it by and large.

The next question is, "How about coal price fixing?" Well, there you get your specific industry question. The prices of bituminous coal are not high; that is, the price at the mine. I am talking about the price at the mine, not the prices you have to pay in your own houses. Cutthroat competition at the mines has always dominated this particular industry and has made it impossible for the industry to pay decent wages and give a profit. Of course we all know that. The purpose of the Guffey Act is to help establish the bituminous coal industry on a sound basis. That means that prices must not be set so high as to transfer business from efficient coal mines to other types of fuel — competitive types of fuel — or to give monopoly profits to coal producers.

Then Mark's [Mr. Sullivan's] little red hen asks about the new farm bill. The farm prices are glaring examples of prices that are now too low. The farm bill is intended to prevent extreme declines in farm prices and to maintain income of farmers in years of excessive yields caused by nature. At the same time, by carrying over excessive supplies from years of large crops to years of lean crops, the bill is intended to prevent such rapid rises in farm prices due to short crops as occurred in the winter of 1936-1937, and which added to speculation at that time. Of course we know that when a commodity starts going up it seems to be human nature that the faster it goes up the faster the speculative element enters the picture and tends to speed up the rise and drive it too high.

The effect of this agricultural, industrial and monetary policy on foreign trade ought to be good in that foreign trade always improves when business activity improves. That is a fact that we seem to have discovered nowadays. Any measure that helps to bring about recovery in the United States also helps in world recovery and serves to increase both purchases from foreign countries — in other words, imports — and sales to foreign countries — in other words, exports.

Q. How about sugar prices?

THE PRESIDENT: Somebody wanted to know about sugar prices. That, of course, is a different subject and falls into a different category, because the sugar act of 1937 established the sugar policy definitely and there is no reason to expect any change.

Well, I think that is all I have got here.

Q. Mr. President, how about the expanded relief program?

THE PRESIDENT: Yes, that is $250,000,000.

Q. Is that the expansion?

THE PRESIDENT: Yes.

Q. No more than that?

THE PRESIDENT: No, we hope not.

Q. Earlier in your statement you referred to the relation of of the debt burden to the general behaviour of prices. I wondered if you considered the war debt or foreign debt burden?

THE PRESIDENT: No, exclusively the domestic debt.

Q. Has the foreign debt question been considered in any other connection in the past twenty-four hours?

THE PRESIDENT: No, not any more than in the last forty-eight days or the last four hundred and eighty days.

Q. You said that the Treasury Department and the Federal Reserve are going to adopt a policy designed to furnish freer credit. Can you be more specific on that?

THE PRESIDENT: Not policies, measures.

Q. What measures?

THE PRESIDENT: Whatever measures are needed to carry out a policy. I did not say they were going to — wait a minute until I get this: We expect to continue to maintain easy credit conditions, and the policies of the Treasury and the Federal Reserve Board are definitely along that line.

Q. Most of the things you said have related to stiffening up the fluid prices. Have you said anything about methods to give fluidity or flexibility to the rigid prices?

THE PRESIDENT: Now you are asking about the industries that are more monopolistic. We hope so, but are not ready to "shoot on it." It is a big problem.

Q. What about the excessive prices of the shipbuilders? It seems more or less to apply to both Merchant Marine and Naval.

THE PRESIDENT: We are very much concerned. I have been talking to Joe Kennedy for the last two weeks, ever since the bids came in. They are far and away above the cost of building ships during the war period when the materials that entered into ships were a great deal lower — no, they were higher than they are today. Today they are lower, but the price of the ship has gone up and, frankly, the whole problem of shipbuilding in this country is a headache under present conditions.

Q. On that point, again, Mr. Kennedy went before the Committee on the labor provisions of the Merchant Marine Act and, I think —

THE PRESIDENT: [interposing] Not on that. I am going to talk to him about it in ten minutes, when he is sworn in.

Q. He suggested, as an alternative, that they might build a few Merchant Marine ships in the Navy Yards. Is there any civil or legal inhibition against it?

THE PRESIDENT: The chief problem is that the Government Navy Yards are about as full of construction work as they ought to be.

Q. If you are going to have a continuing program, is it possible to have Navy Yards —

THE PRESIDENT: [interposing] If the Government is going to build them, there are three ways: One is to finance a new yard, put in new equipment, new ways, supervise it, and have the work done under what might be called private management. If you remember, during the war we built a good deal and bought a good deal on the fixed fee basis.

Q. "Cost plus"?

THE PRESIDENT: No, not "cost plus" but "fixed fee," which is all the difference in the world.

Another method would be to build our own yards and build them ourselves. The third would be to put new equipment and new ways in Navy yards and have the Navy build them. All of those are very, very slow methods of getting a Merchant Marine.

Q. How about building them abroad?

THE PRESIDENT: That is one of the suggestions made by Mr. Kennedy and the interesting thing is that almost every Congressman and Senator says: "That is the practical way of doing it, but I could not vote for it." (*Laughter*)

Q. How do you explain why they are able to build them cheaper in foreign ports?

THE PRESIDENT: I don't know. I don't think anybody knows.

Q. Was your remark on war debts meant to imply that the subject was mentioned?

THE PRESIDENT: Oh, no. It was mentioned, but it is mentioned about once a week and we don't seem to be any further than we were two years ago.

Q. There was a story published this morning that one of the Latin American countries has or is about to present a proposal for a military and naval alliance of all the Americas to guard against aggression by Europe or Asia?

THE PRESIDENT: Yes, I read the story and I never heard of it until I read the story. You will have to ask the Secretary of State. Maybe he has heard something about it. I doubt it.

Q. Would such alliance, if it came up, be contrary to our policy?

THE PRESIDENT: That is a very "iffy" question.

Statement and chart read and displayed to correspondents during foregoing Press Conference.

THIS ADMINISTRATION has from the beginning pursued a policy designed to promote full employment of our human and material resources. That continues to be our policy. The productive power of our workers and our resources, if fully utilized, can provide and maintain a national income far above any levels we have yet reached.

An important factor that determines whether we shall succeed or be blocked in our endeavor to attain full employment and a high level of income is the behavior of prices. In this connection careful attention must be given to: (1) the relations of the prices of various groups of commodities to each other; (2) the relations between commodity price levels and the levels of debt burdens and costs; (3) the direction and rate of movement of the general price level. To further its broad objective the Administration has, therefore, in its agricultural, industrial, and monetary programs necessarily been concerned both with the relation of the prices of groups of specific commodities to each other and with the movement of the general price level.

The measures employed at any given time to further this policy must fit the needs of that time. A year ago there was ground for concern that a too rapid rise in the prices of some commodities was encouraging a speculative boom. During the past six months, on the other hand, the general price level and industrial activity have been declining. Government policy must be directed to reversing this deflationary trend.

This does not mean that all prices should advance, nor that the rise should be rapid. Prices of different groups of products must be brought into balanced relation to one another. Some prices and some costs are still too high to promote that balanced relationship between prices that is necessary for sustained recovery. Continued high prices of many of the commodities not subject to highly competitive market forces intensify the downward pressure on all other prices. Those industries that have maintained prices and curtailed output should seek the restoration of profits through increased rather than through restricted output.

The prices of some items are still at the highest levels reached in 1937; some are even higher than in 1929. When high prices sharply curtail sales there is real danger. This is shown by our recent experience with housing. A year ago there was a serious shortage. We had unused productive resources ample to overcome the shortage. Yet all the major elements in housing costs advanced so sharply by the spring of 1937 as to kill a promising expansion of activity in an industry whose restoration is vital to continued recovery.

WHOLESALE PRICES OF SELECTED BUILDING MATERIALS
1929 = 100

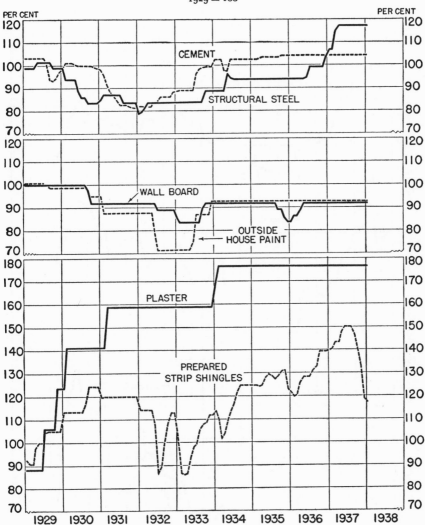

WHOLESALE PRICES OF SELECTED AGRICULTURAL PRODUCTS, 1929-38
Index Numbers (1929 = 100)

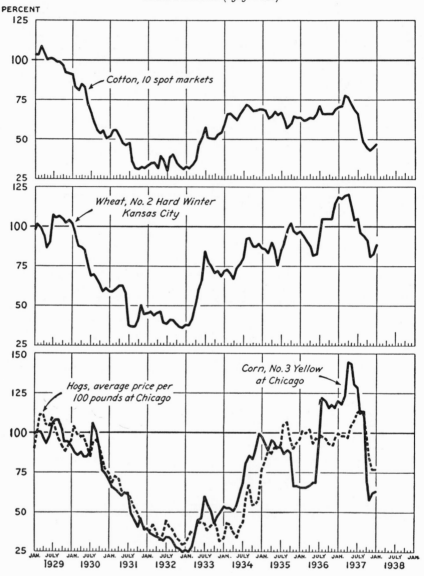

PER CAPITA FARM AND NONAGRICULTURAL INCOME AVAILABLE FOR LIVING AND LIVING COSTS, 1924-38

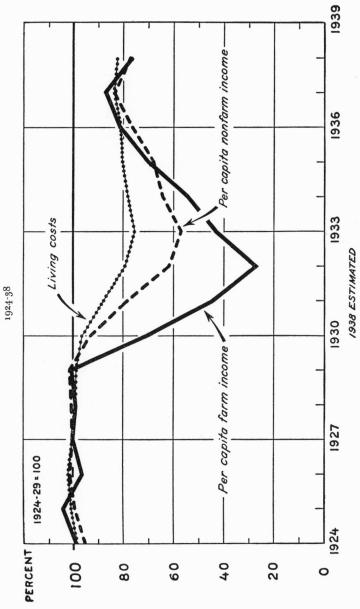

117

WHOLESALE PRICES AND EMPLOYMENT

Monthly, 1929 to Date

Monthly, 1936 to Date

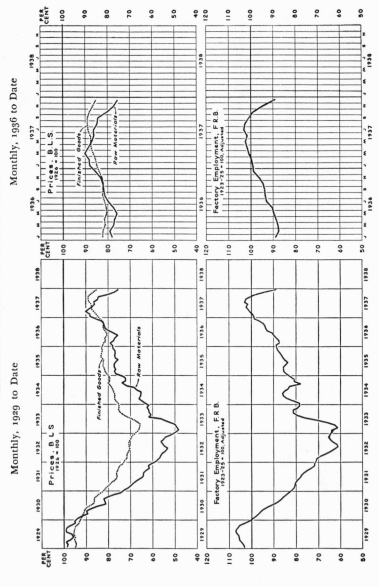

For industries, such as agriculture, that operate at a high level of capacity even when business activity is at low levels, the restoration of profits must come primarily through higher prices. Higher prices in such industries and increased output in other industries will, by increasing profits, encourage new investment in replacement and expansion of equipment. This is necessary to full recovery.

The average family will benefit from the business recovery which a balanced price structure will foster. Increased employment and more continuous income should much more than offset any increase in the cost of living. Recently wholesale prices have declined markedly, yet that decline has been reflected in the cost of living only to a very slight degree. A moderate rise in wholesale prices at this time should only slightly affect living costs. Incomes of most families will increase while the cost of what the housewife buys should show little change. The average family will enjoy a higher standard of living.

It is clear that in the present situation a moderate rise in the general price level is desirable, and that this rise need not and should not extend to all prices. The rise should take place in and must be mainly confined to classes of commodities whose prices are too low. These include most of those raw materials and finished products which are produced and sold under highly competitive conditions. Such rise must not be so sharp or continue so long as to lead to a repetition of the unhealthy speculative conditions of a year ago. That sharp rise in prices encouraged speculative inventory buying which, combined with the decline in housing construction, laid much of the ground for the present recession. We must do everything we can to prevent this from happening again.

Our program seeks a balanced system of prices such as will promote a balanced expansion in production. Our goal is a constantly increasing national income through increasing production and employment. This is the way to increase the real income of consumers.

This is not a policy of restriction; it is a policy of abundance.

Our agricultural, industrial, housing and monetary programs have been and will be directed toward this end.

(This statement was prepared at the President's request by Henry Morgenthau, Jr., Secretary of the Treasury; Henry A. Wallace, Secretary of Agriculture; Frances Perkins, Secretary of Labor; Marriner Eccles, Chairman of the Board of Governors of the Federal Reserve System; and economists of various executive departments.)

NOTE: The foregoing statement and charts were discussed by me at the Press Conference printed immediately preceding the statement. For a further discussion of the economic conditions prompting the Press Conference and statement, see Item 49, this volume. As will appear in the note attached to said item, commodity prices and business activity had declined seriously during the latter half of 1937, and the business and industrial outlook in early 1938 seemed confused and uncertain.

Many critics of the Administration were accusing it of pursuing an intentional price deflation policy which was retarding business recovery.

In the foregoing statement I sought to assure the public that a rise in the general price level at that time was desired by the Administration, and that the policies of the Administration would be directed toward that end. I pointed out that this was not at all inconsistent with the efforts of the Administration to prevent unwarranted price increases to dangerous levels, particularly for those products subject to monopoly control.

The purpose of the statement and charts was to show the importance of keeping a balanced system of prices which promotes a balanced expansion in production. The economy of a nation can get out of joint by abnormally high prices, and by abnormally low prices. The important thing is to keep employment and income ahead of increases in the cost of living.

For a statement of the effects of the national policy on the improvement of financial and business conditions see note to Item 49, this volume, and also Introduction to this volume.

27 ❡ The President Transmits to the Congress the Report of the Advisory Committee on Education. February 23, 1938

To the Congress:

I TRANSMIT herewith, for the information of the Congress, report of the Advisory Committee on Education appointed by me in September 1936, to study the experience under the existing program of Federal aid for vocational education, the relation of such training to general education and to prevailing economic and social conditions, and the extent of the need for an expanded program.

NOTE: The Advisory Committee on Education was appointed by me on September 19, 1936. Whereas its initial studies were confined to vocational education, the committee, pursuant to a letter of April 19, 1937, from me to Chairman Floyd W. Reeves, undertook later a study of the entire subject of the federal relationship to the state and local conduct of education (see Item 62, 1936 volume; Item 44 and note, 1937 volume).

The report which was transmitted to the Congress with the foregoing message made a survey of existing conditions in the public school system, examined the extent of inequality of educational opportunity, and reviewed the various efforts of the federal government to provide a better balance.

It was noted principally that, because of the decentralized nature of the educational system, the poor communities of the nation could not afford to provide adequate educational facilities and salaries. The uneven development of education was most noticeable in the contrast between the various geographical sections of the country. The rural areas of the South were found to be the most deficient in financial ability to provide for education.

In a speech before the National Education Association on June 30, 1938, I discussed this general problem, and the necessity of trying first to lift the educational system of those communities at the bottom, rather than merely giving assistance to those at the top (see Item 86, this volume).

In making its recommendations, the committee tried to keep in mind the twin objectives of strength through local control of education, plus adequate financial aid to these local units. It was stressed that unless additional financial aid were extended, millions of children would continue to be denied adequate educational opportunities.

In order to extend the opportunities for education, a six year program of federal grants was recommended, to start in 1939, and to increase annually. The following kinds of assistance for education were to be covered by these grants-in-aid:

a. General aid to elementary and secondary education
b. Improved preparation of teachers
c. Construction of school buildings
d. Administration of state departments of education
e. Educational services for adults
f. Library services for rural areas
g. Cooperative educational research

The committee recommended that these grants be distributed according to plans jointly approved by the department of education in each state and by the United States Office of Education, in order that there be equitable distribution among the neediest areas. To preserve control over the way in which these funds were to be spent, a uniform basis of reporting was outlined, along with provision for auditing the accounts of state and local agencies employing federal funds.

The largest expenditures were recommended for general aid to public elementary and secondary schools, commencing with $40,000,-000 in 1939-1940, and increasing by $20,000,000 annually until $140,-000,000 for the fiscal year 1944-45.

The Committee reported that local resources for competent personnel were often too limited, and that low salaries and insecure tenure should be remedied. An increase in practice teaching and a broader training for teachers were urged, and a federal-aid program for this purpose, starting at $2,000,-000 annually, was suggested.

A program of consolidation of school districts and rehousing of schools, particularly in rural areas, was included in the report. The committee indicated that safe, sanitary, and well-located public school buildings were needed, and that it would be wise to encourage the construction of facilities for public libraries and community center activities. For this program, the committee recommended an expenditure of $20,000,000 at first, which amount should be graduated up to $30,000,000 in 1945.

In order to make the state departments of education adequate to administer the new federal-aid funds, it was suggested that $1,000,-000 annually be expended for this purpose, with $2,000,000 eventually contemplated.

The above grants were to be allocated among the states in proportion to their relative financial needs, as estimated by such agencies as the Bureau of the Census, the Treasury Department, the Office of Education, and the Department of the Interior.

Certain changes were recommended in the program of federal aid for vocational education. The report stressed that there had been an excessive amount of federal control over this phase of the educational system, and that there were disorganization and lack of cooperation among the various agencies administering vocational education plans. It was suggested that control over vocational education be decentralized, and that federal aid to vocational education be consolidated into one fund.

The report commended the student-aid program of the National Youth Administration, and stated that student aid for those aged over eighteen should generally be authorized on a work basis. To enable a better placement of students and a clearer conception of career opportunities, it was recommended that the Bureau of Labor Statistics establish an Occupational Outlook Service, and that a counseling agency be permanently established in the National Youth Administration and the United States Employment Service. The committee also favored the expansion of vocational training in industry through an increase in the budget of the Federal Committee on Apprentice Training, and the expansion of cooperative work camps and work projects along educational

lines under a new National Youth Service Administration.

For educational services to adults, it was recommended that $5,000,-000 be appropriated during 1939-1940, and that this amount be graduated upward to reach $15,000,000 by 1944-1945. These funds were to be used for civic and vocational part-time adult educational activities, including workers' education, citizenship classes for aliens, and the teaching of illiterates.

The report noted that library service in rural areas was particularly inadequate, and recommended that $2,000,000 be spent during 1939-1940, and that this amount be raised annually until it reached $6,000,000 in 1944-1945.

The committee recommended that a special survey be made of the needs for vocational rehabilitation of the physically disabled, of the best methods of meeting those needs, and the costs of an adequate program. It was also suggested that more effective cooperation be instituted between the Federal Vocational Rehabilitation Service and the various federal and state agencies concerned with related problems of health, social welfare, and employment.

Several recommendations were made regarding education in special federal jurisdictions. The report suggested that a comprehensive code of basic general legislation be enacted for the public school system of the District of Columbia, conferring authority to maintain a unified system, and placing the District of Columbia and the territories upon the same basis as the states for the purpose of allotment of funds. It was recommended that the United States Office of Education be responsible for the allocation of sufficient funds for the education of children living on government reservations or at foreign stations. A continuation of the policy of the Office of Indian Affairs to educate the Indians to develop their own social and economic resources was recommended, as well as an extension of higher education for Indian youth.

The committee favored the establishment of a special federal fund for cooperative educational research, demonstrations and planning, with $1,250,000 to be appropriated during the fiscal year 1938-1939, this amount to be increased annually to $3,000,000 in 1944-1945. In order to facilitate coordination and aid in long-range planning, it was suggested that there be increased cooperation among the various state and local planning and educational agencies, and that an interdepartmental committee be set up to coordinate the educational activities of the various agencies of the federal government.

The principal result, so far, of this report has been the increased public discussion and attention given to the general problem of federal relations to education. The document will undoubtedly serve for many years to come to influence thought and action on the subject among educational groups and public bodies.

Administrative steps have been taken to carry out some of the recommendations of the report. Legislation to put into practice the major features of increased federal aid — which is the foundation of the report — has been introduced and widely debated in and out of the Houses of the Congress. It has not yet been passed, however, as of June 1, 1941.

Two important points of policy should be: (1) to continue state and local control over education in each state, and not to federalize such control in any way; (2) to make federal grants for education, not on a merely matching basis with the states, because such a basis does not adequately help those regions or localities where tax values are low and funds for education are inadequate.

28 ⟨ A Letter to the Governors of Several States Urging the Adoption of Housing Legislation in Their States. March 1, 1938

My dear Governor Stanford:

IT IS urgent that action should be taken now to stimulate the construction industry, particularly in the field of residential building which has lagged far behind other forms of business activity. An extensive housing program would provide direct and indirect employment at the very point in our economic structure where re-employment seems to have been most retarded.

Both public and private housing construction should be accelerated. In addition to relieving unemployment, a public low-rent housing and slum-clearance program would provide decent homes for which there is a distressing need among the one-third of our population which is ill-housed. Millions today are living in urban and rural habitations which fail to comply with minimum standards of health, safety and decency. The continued existence of these conditions breeds disease and crime and impairs the health and vitality of our present and future generations.

There is a serious obstacle to public housing construction in your State and it is for this reason that I am writing to you. The United States Housing Act of 1937 provides for a program of Federal loans and subsidies to public agencies to aid in the development of a low-rent housing and slum-clearance program. Before any state can participate in this program, it must have legislation authorizing public agencies to undertake low-rent housing projects. Thirty states have already enacted such legislation, but none has been passed in the State of Arizona. The $500,000,000 available for expenditure by the United States Housing Authority could be spent in the states that now have adequate housing legislation. However, I would like to see the

State of Arizona participate in this program and I am sure that you, too, desire your State to obtain its share of these funds. This will not be possible unless legislation is enacted at an early date enabling the development of housing projects by local public agencies in Arizona.

If you will write me that, in connection with any contemplated special session of your Legislature, you are interested in public housing legislation under which your State can qualify for Federal aid, I shall be glad to request the United States Housing Authority to make suggestions to you regarding the type of legislation which appears desirable. The proposed legislation would permit the creation of a public housing authority in a municipality or county, with power to construct low-rent housing projects and to isssue bonds payable only from the revenues of such projects without any recourse to the taxing power. This legislation would also authorize these municipalities and counties to cooperate with their housing authorities in the undertaking of such projects. However, the legislation would be purely of an enabling character, so that it would not become effective in any community until its governing body so elected. Of course, the public housing projects constructed under this state legislation would not be competitive with private business, since these projects would not be open to families who could afford to live in decent privately-owned dwellings.

I hope that you will give serious consideration to the early enactment of public housing legislation in your State. Such legislation would make it possible for Arizona to join the other states in a nation-wide public program to relieve unemployment through the eradication of unsafe or insanitary housing and the provision of decent housing for families in the lowest income group.

Very sincerely yours,

Honorable R. C. Stanford,
Governor of Arizona,
Phoenix, Arizona

28. State Housing Legislation

(Identical letters also sent to the Governors of the following States: California, Idaho, Iowa, Kansas, Maine, Minnesota, Mississippi, Missouri, Nevada, New Hampshire, New Mexico, Oklahoma, South Dakota, Utah, Virginia, Washington, and Wyoming.)

NOTE: In order to provide employment and also to start building decent homes for people of low income, direct federal construction of housing projects had been undertaken by the Public Works Administration in 1933 (see Item 117 and note, 1933 volume). However, the administration has always recognized that the responsibility for planning, constructing, and managing low-cost housing should ultimately rest with state and local authorities, and that the initial program of direct construction and management by a central federal agency was only a temporary expedient to make a beginning in the general program.

By the passage of the United States Housing Act of 1937 (Public No. 412, 75th Congress, 50 Stat. 888) emphasis was placed upon the work of local housing authorities, which have the duty and responsibility to initiate, own, and manage low-cost housing projects. The machinery for the housing program in this way has been largely decentralized. The participation of the Federal Government now consists principally of loans, capital grants, or annual contributions to the local housing authorities for low-cost housing developments and slum clearance work, together with general supervision

and fixing of standards. Thus, the Federal Government under the statute acts primarily as banker for these local housing agencies; and, although advice, standards, and technical assistance are provided by the United States Housing Authority, the initiative rests with the local authorities.

It was necessary, therefore, after the United States Housing Act was passed, that the states should themselves enact adequate legislation which would enable the program to be carried forward in the states in coordination with the federal system. For that reason, the foregoing letter was written in identical form to the governors of eighteen states, which, as of March 1, 1938, had not yet passed legislation authorizing local public housing agencies to undertake housing projects and use Federal funds for purposes of loans and subsidies for slum clearance and decent low-cost housing.

In addition to the letters written to the governors of these eighteen states having no enabling legislation, I wrote at the same time to the governors of ten other states in which the housing laws were so inadequate that it was very difficult for the United States Housing Authority to proceed speedily and efficiently with its program in those particular states. In four of these latter ten states, which permitted no tax-exemption for housing projects, I suggested that they adopt tax-exemption legislation, so that the rents could be made reasonable enough for families in the lowest income group. Without such tax-exemption it was impossible, in the absence of other forms of local grants, for the United States Housing Authority to fix rentals low enough to carry out the social and economic benefits of the statute.

As of the end of 1940, eight of the eighteen states to which I sent the foregoing letter of March 1, 1938, had passed the necessary legislation to set up local housing authorities to cooperate with the United States Housing Authority. Additional legislation has also been passed in each of the ten other states which formerly had inadequate housing statutes.

For a discussion of the work and accomplishments of the United States Housing Authority, and its method of operation, see note to Item 143, 1937 volume.

29 ⟨ Greetings on the Twenty-fifth Anniversary of the United States Department of Labor. March 3, 1938

My dear Madam Secretary:

Will you please extend my warm greetings to the many friends of labor who are joining tonight and tomorrow in the celebration of the twenty-fifth anniversary of the establishment of the United States Department of Labor.

The quarter of a century that has passed since it came into being has been marked by significant changes in our conceptions of the rights of wage earners. Today there is general recognition that there should be a floor to wages and a ceiling to hours, that there should be adequate annual income, that working conditions should be safe and healthy and that child labor should be eliminated from industry.

There is ample and concrete evidence over these years, and particularly since 1933, of honest effort to promote the welfare of our wage earners, through the adoption of a progressive, humane and far sighted program. Included in it are the Social Security Act intended to safeguard workers against the major hazards of life and the National Labor Relations Act which defines the right of workers to organize and bargain collectively.

Out of this program upon which we are now embarked will come far reaching benefits, not only to wage earners but to all our people in the years to come. In helping to carry it out the Department of Labor will continue its great service in the interest of the men and women who work for a living and thus discharge its duty. The wage earners of the United States may well be proud of what the Department of Labor has done for them in its quarter century of existence and what it is destined to do for them in the future.

Very truly yours,

Hon. Frances Perkins,
Secretary of Labor,
Washington, D. C.

30 (The Four Hundred and Thirty-ninth Press Conference (Excerpts). March 4, 1938

(Publication of salaries of corporation executives — The objectives and policies of the New Deal — Fiscal policy — Purchasing power — Wage and hour legislation — Ending special privilege.)

Q. Mr. President, I suppose some of these gentlemen will ask you about the tax bill. I was talking to Bumgardner [Clerk of House Ways & Means Committee] and he told me that something had been left out of that bill which was in the former bill, and that is the publication of the salaries of corporation executives. That is not in the bill. Do you approve of that?

THE PRESIDENT: I did not know that, until I read it in the paper yesterday morning and I am very, very sorry that that has been left out. I think it is a question of simple morality. I think I stated, once upon a time, that in addition to public office being a public trust, private office is also a public trust.

There are two types of corporation executives. One is the executive of a company that has a large number of public shareholders. Its stock is owned by thousands and tens of thousands of people. It is traded in, and new people buy it from day to day.

Theoretically, a stockholder has the right to go to a meeting of the corporation in some small town in Kentucky or in Wilmington, Delaware, and say, "How much did the President and the Vice President, et cetera, get last year by way of salary and bonus?" Practically, he does not. Practically, the purchaser of the stock of that company does not know and has no way of finding out, unless he goes to particular pains to find out, what the corporation's salaries are.

Again, private office is a public trust. Why should not the public know what the executives of these corporations get? Let us use some examples: Did the public know for years, until it was brought out in an investigation, what Mr. Grace of Bethlehem Steel was getting by way of salary and bonus? They did not; and there was a wave of public indignation that went over the country when it was discovered that one man was getting a million dollars a year.

Why should not the public know the salaries of the executives of General Motors Corporation? There is no reason why they should not know it. It is a private office with a public trust.

Take the other type of corporation, the closely held, family-owned corporation. There it is a slightly different matter because it is owned by one man or one family. But we know of not just a few sporadic cases but of a great many cases where the family-owned company has, on the public record, made at the end of the year no profit at all. That is, the published record — the books — show no profit, show the company barely in the black or perhaps even with a loss. At the same time, it is perfectly possible for the owners, the members of the family, to be paying themselves the profits of the company by way of very large salaries. Actually, the company may be making a large profit which, because of the hidden character of the proceedings, is not known to the general public.

A corporation of that kind is able to say, "No, we cannot afford to improve the conditions of the people who work for us because we are not making any money. See our books." Actually the family may be drawing down the kind of salary that is so large that the public as a whole, the Government and competing companies have a right to know about it. That is another phase of it.

In other words, private office is a public trust. And there is absolutely no valid reason why, in my judgment, that clause, the present clause for publicity with respect to corporation executives' salaries, should be repealed. It is a question of morals, public morals.

Q. Mr. President, you said there was no other way. The S.E.C. does have these figures. These are for the tax bill. Is there any reason for the duplication?

THE PRESIDENT: I don't care, as long as the public knows all about it. How it is done is perfectly immaterial. As long as every newspaper in the United States, in pursuance of the policy of freedom of the press, has the right to publish them.

Q. Mr. President, would you make any distinction between corporations whose stock is on the market and those that are not?

THE PRESIDENT: No. . . .

Q. This being the anniversary season, perhaps you have an anniversary message of some sort for us?

THE PRESIDENT: That is pretty difficult. Of course it has so many ramifications.

I think possibly the significant thing is that, after five years, the old Ship of State is on the same course. It is a course which is aimed at the same things which I described, offhand, one day in a press conference when my friend from the Vancouver *Sun* asked a question. You might get that out.

It was not very long, about two paragraphs. We have the same objectives and the same ideals.

Along that line, I think again it is worth while to draw the distinction between objectives and policies towards those objectives, as the broad subject on one side, and what we call methods on the other side. I was talking yesterday, to illustrate, about the fiscal policy of the Government, which includes a great many things. It includes the problem of foreign exchange. It includes the problem of the price level. It includes the problem of public finance. A great many people are prone to mix methods with objectives. If you will remember a year ago, April, we were afraid that the objective of the Government towards the stabilization of the price level, or values, which is a better word, would be threatened by inflation, a boom, and therefore we put the helm of the ship hard a-starboard to prevent the ship, because of the fluctuation of the wind, from leaving her course. A year later, less than a year later, last autumn, the wind shifted and we were threatened with deflation. Therefore, we shifted the helm of the ship hard a-port, in order to keep the ship on the course. Well, that is illustrative of maintaining an objective and it is illustrative also of the fact that so many people, when you shift the helm in order to maintain the same course, call it a change in policy. Most of you good people are guilty of it, and a lot of other people are, too. You do not see the big thing. You see the thing of immediate moment.

This is not a complaint, because it is a perfectly natural, human thing to do. It makes a story. But on the general objective we have gone a long way and of course we are going further.

One of the objectives is increased purchasing power for the people. I can illustrate that by a story I have told to a number of people. Some of my friends, who are in special lines of business, fine people, honest people, have come in to me and talked to me. They are people I have known by their first names for years, and I say to them, "By the way, what is your thought on the problem of the sharecropper and the tenant-farmer? I am sort of stumped by that but I think we ought to do something. What do you think we ought to do?" Well, I have tried that on a good many people and the invariable answer from these perfectly fine business men I have talked to has been this: "What do you mean, Mr. President? What do you mean by the sharecropper problem?"

Well, I have explained it to them, and repeated, "What do you think we ought to do?" The invariable answer has been, "I don't know anything about it. I have never thought of it." And then I have said to them, "We have fifteen or twenty million Americans in this country who today have no purchasing power. There are fifteen or twenty million Americans falling into that category. They are farm tenants, sharecroppers. You fellows are making things, all kinds of things, automobiles, hardware, clothing, all the things that you see in a country store. Aren't you interested in giving those prospective, possible customers some purchasing power for the things you make?" And then they have said to me, "Why, Mr. President, I have never thought of that. I never thought of that."

Today people are beginning to think of that. And that is the most hopeful thing at the present time. The most hopeful thing at the present time is that we are getting people to think about the rounded problem of Government and of all the people of the country, instead of just thinking along their own special line of business.

In that way, also, I am encouraged to think that we will get away, more and more, from what we call the pressure groups in the country, small groups coming down here with great vociferation, and very often putting through legislation which is beneficial only to one particular group.

Just to explain it a little bit further, on the question of the big objectives we have accomplished an enormous amount. There are some things we have failed to accomplish. We think, for instance, that through a system of the control of crop surpluses we are going to maintain to a great extent the purchasing power of the fifty million people who are directly or indirectly dependent on agricultural prices. Of course, that is all to the good for the industrial side of things, not only for the owners of industrial corporations but for the workers in industrial corporations. And it has only been lately that I have been able to get business men to say to me, "Why, sure we are in favor of that policy, that crop policy, Mr. President." And I have said to so many of them — I think I told you this before — "Will you come out and say that out loud?" And I think some of them will, as the days go by, say, "Yes, we are in favor of that sort of thing."

On the question of wages and hours, we are working still — in fact, that was your question — we are working still to try to put a floor under wages in the United States and a ceiling over hours. Well, maybe we won't get it at this session of the Congress — I hope we will — but it is one of those things which is related to national economy. People have different ideas about it. Some people say that the minimum wage phase of it is the most important. Other people say that the maximum hour part of it is the most important. But the general objective is just the same on wages and hours as it is with crops and as it is with finance. The whole thing is a rounded picture, and, taking it by and large, we have gone a long way on that.

And then the final phase is that we are not discontinuing our efforts to end — Oh, I suppose the simplest term to be understood is "special privilege." We still believe that it is for the good of the country, for the economic good of the country, for the value of stocks and bonds and everything else, to end special privilege. There is still a great deal of special privilege. The tax bill of two years ago was intended to end certain forms of special privilege. The bill of last year was intended to end other forms of special privilege, such as incorporating yachts and starting insurance companies in the Bahamas. Taking it by and large, the country sympathizes with the point of view of ending special privileges.

I do not know that there is anything more. These things occur to me out of my mind at the present moment. I have not prepared anything on this. We are going along toward the same objectives; we have gone a long way on the road and we are going further. . . .

(See Item 70, 1935 volume, for the press conference at which, in reply to the request of the editor of the Vancouver *Sun*, I discussed the social objectives of the New Deal.)

31 ⟨ The Four Hundred and Fortieth Press Conference (Excerpts). March 8, 1938

(Background of the dispute which resulted in the removal of Arthur E. Morgan, Chairman of the Tennessee Valley Authority.)

Q. Have you asked the three TVA directors in for a conference next week?

THE PRESIDENT: No, not next week; this week, Friday morning.

Q. All three?

THE PRESIDENT: All three.

Q. At the same time?

THE PRESIDENT: Right after I see you, at 11.00 o'clock.

Q. All three at the same time?

THE PRESIDENT: All three at the same time. If you want something for background, this goes back. It is a long, long story. There have been all of these disagreements and disputes for about a year. Finally, last September, this disagreement between the majority and the minority came to a head in this way: There was an article in the *Atlantic Monthly*, the September number, if you remember. The majority of the Directors passed a resolution in regard to the article by the minority member, in effect asking that the allegations impugning the integrity of the majority should either be made good or be withdrawn.

That was sent to me and I sent a letter to Dr. Arthur Morgan on the third of September. There is no use in cluttering up the record and giving you the whole letter, but I called his attention to the resolution disavowing such methods in the discussion of TVA problems as injurious to the project and the public interest. Then I went on and I said this to Dr. Arthur Morgan:

> "Naturally, I am concerned by this and do not think that the matter can properly rest where it is. May I suggest, therefore, that there is a very definite obligation on you either to withdraw what your colleagues believe to be an impugning of their integrity or that you present whatever specific facts you may have, if any, to justify your statements.
>
> "After all, no great constructive work can be carried out if those in charge of the administration of the work feel that their integrity and motives have been challenged by a fellow member. I know that you will agree with me in this."

Well, in reply to that letter I got no reply, but Dr. Morgan came to see me about two weeks later on and I said, "It is a pretty serious thing to impugn the motives of your fellow members, their integrity." "Well," he said, "I did not mean it that way. I did not mean to impugn their motives. I have no question as to their personal integrity."

"Well," I said, "for Heaven's sake don't do it again. Go back and see if you cannot work in harmony with your two fellow members."

Well, that is about all that happened in the fall, but evidently conflict was going on underneath. Now it has come to a head in these statements to the public and to the press and on Friday all three members are going to appear before me. I am going to ask that the statements by all of them be justified, if they can justify them, but that I want facts and not opinions. I want nothing but facts.

To give you an illustration of the true awkwardness of the situation, I got two telegrams today. One was from New Jersey. It says — mind you, this is from a person who had absolutely no access to anything except the newspapers — "Please, Mr. President, you must vindicate Dr. Arthur Morgan." The other one, from Illinois, said, "Please, you must vindicate the majority and not surrender to the power interests."

Now, of course, that kind of public opinion is worth nothing at all because it is not based on any facts. There isn't one of you that has any facts. I haven't either. Let us stick to the facts. That is why we are having this meeting on Friday.

Q. What time is the meeting, Mr. President?

THE PRESIDENT: Eleven o'clock.

Q. If they cannot justify the statements they have been making, then what?

THE PRESIDENT: Now you are asking a question before the case has been heard by the court.

Q. Do you expect any of them to remain in office?

THE PRESIDENT: That is asking the decision of the court before I have any evidence.

There you are! Aren't those last two questions absolutely typical? Did you ever know anything to beat it? "What are you going to do before you get the testimony?"

Q. How are we going to find out what did go on?

THE PRESIDENT: I am going to ask questions.

Q. How will we find out?

THE PRESIDENT: I will tell you all about it.

Q. When?

THE PRESIDENT: After we get through.

Q. Do we have a press conference?

THE PRESIDENT: At half past ten. You will get it, don't worry. You will get the facts.

Q. Mr. President, do you know whether you have power under

the TVA Act to call for the resignation or require the resignation of a member of the Commission?

THE PRESIDENT: I have not the faintest idea, not the faintest. In other words, I have not investigated that end. I haven't the faintest idea. I am interested in the facts regarding these allegations, which are of a general nature, on both sides.

Q. Is Senator Norris going to sit in with you? Has he been invited to sit in with you?

THE PRESIDENT: He has not.

Q. Will you have anyone else there besides yourself and the three Commissioners?

THE PRESIDENT: I think Steve [Early] will be here so that he can give you a report on it. . . .

(See Item 36, this volume, for T.V.A. removal proceeding.)

32 ❨ The President Presents a National Plan to the Congress for the Conservation and Development of Our Water Resources. March 10, 1938

To the Congress:

IN ACCORDANCE with my message of August 13, 1937 (in returning without my approval Senate Joint Resolution 57), I am presenting herewith for your consideration a comprehensive national plan for the conservation and development of our water resources.

This report on Drainage Basin Problems and Programs has been prepared by the National Resources Committee in consultation with other Federal agencies. It suggests policies, investigations, and construction necessary to carry forward a broad national program for water conservation and utilization.

It is based upon the findings of 45 joint State-Federal basin committees, composed of more than 500 local, State, and Federal officials. These drainage basin committees have met in the field and have drafted plans for their local areas. Arrangements have been made to publish the detailed reports on individual drainage basins at a later date.

The proposals in the report provide a guide for authorizations of surveys and construction of irrigation, flood-control, navigation, rural water supply, wildlife conservation, beach erosion control, hydroelectric power, and other water projects. Because it was necessary to confine the program to projects that are primarily for water control and use, many related land-use projects are not included. Land policy has significant water implications, but it pertains to a large sphere of activities requiring separate though related treatment.

The preferred water projects have met the test of conformity to a general regional program, and, although they are set forth in terms of a six-year program, they are susceptible to completion during either a shorter or longer period, as fiscal policy may dictate. The total cost of the recommended work at both Federal and non-Federal levels is about equal to the average annual expenditures for these purposes during recent years. The six-year program suggested in the report should be read in the light of budgetary requirements and must, of course, be adjusted each year to correspond with budget recommendations and with action by the Congress.

Our knowledge of the Nation's water resources and our ideas on their best use and control change rapidly in the light of new investigations and of dynamic economic conditions. Water plans should be flexible. The history of flood-control plans for the alluvial valley of the Mississippi River affords many examples of plans, once considered comprehensive, which soon were replaced by others. Water plans should be revised annually.

Changing public interest, first in navigation, then in irrigation, and then in flood-control, water power or pollution, has produced a collection of unrelated water policies. The recommendations in this report define in broad strokes an integrated water policy for the country as a whole. Such a Federal water policy is needed.

Notwithstanding the small amount of time available for the revision of earlier Federal programs, the planning mechanism which was developed for this report seems to have given gratifying results. Starting with local and State groups, organized through the regional offices of the National Resources Committee, plans and programs have been prepared in the field and reviewed in Washington. The process has not interfered with the normal and established duties of the agencies charged by the Congress with construction and surveys of water conservation projects. Rather it has promoted cooperation among such agencies in Washington and with State and local interests as well.

I recommend careful study of these documents by the Congress because they present a frame of reference for legislative programs affecting water conservation, and because they illustrate an approach to the systematic husbandry of our natural resources on a democratic, regional basis.

NOTE: The foregoing report was a revision and extension of the program of water projects transmitted by me to the Congress on February 3, 1937 (see Item 9, 1937 volume).

The basic concept of conservation embodied in this report was two-fold:

1. That because of the interlocking relationships among water problems, plans for the wise use and control of water should be drawn up with due regard for all feasible uses and controls. The end to be sought is a unified plan of improvement for each drainage basin in the country, taking into account flood control, pollution abatement, power development, navigation, urban and rural water supply, irrigation, wildlife, recreation, and related questions of land management.

2. That in order to attain the end indicated above, it is necessary for all Federal and State agencies concerned to join in the preparation of unified programs, and to coordinate their efforts in carrying out individual units of those programs.

These principles have been accepted more and more widely by the Congress in contradistinction to prior action, which had frequently concerned limited, individual phases of water conservation, with slight regard for other phases. The successful experiment in the Tennessee Valley had done a great deal, however, to show the benefits of unified river basin development.

The programs for the different drainage basins of the nation which were included in this comprehensive report, which I transmitted on March 10, 1938, were based upon studies made by drainage basin committees composed of representatives of the chief Federal and State agencies interested in the water problems of the particular area under consideration. This method of cooperation is recommended in the report for all future programs and for all projects to carry out the programs.

Subsequent legislation and allotments of funds by me for purposes of water conservation have followed quite closely the program of projects included in this report. The need for multiple-purpose water development has now been fully recognized; and important advances toward that end have been made in the Reclamation Project Act of 1939 (53 Stat. 1187), and the Case–Wheeler Act of 1940 (Pub. No. 848, 76th Congress).

For other documents discussing the use and control of water resources, see Items 50, 52, and 103, 1937 volume; Item 31, 1939 volume, and references cited in the accompanying notes.

33 ❰ A Radio Address for the Mobilization for Human Needs. Washington, D.C. March 11, 1938

Chairman Taft, Community Chest Workers, Friends of Human Needs:

I AM happy again to greet the faithful workers assembled for their annual meeting in behalf of this national Mobilization for Human Needs. It is significant that this year marks the twenty-fifth anniversary of Community Chests and Councils — the rounding out of a full quarter of a century of united approach by the private social agencies to the problems which they face throughout the Nation.

Twenty-five years ago the proposal that an entire community should pool its efforts in a single drive to finance all welfare agencies, regardless of race or creed, was as radical as it was far-sighted. So I am glad to greet you descendants of that radical group. The birth of the Community Chest was an important milestone in the evolution of our present viewpoint regarding aid to the unfortunate.

A natural development of this evolution is this Mobilization for Human Needs in which leaders and organizations of nation-wide repute add their voices and influence to those of the local leaders. I have been glad to speak nationally in behalf of your local campaigns.

Let me state plainly that I do not feel any of our governmental efforts can ever be substituted for the distinctive, voluntary expression of personal interest in human suffering which manifests itself through the Community Chest.

The founders of the Community Chest did not — they could not — envision the problem of mass unemployment among able-bodied and willing men and women which has resulted from our complex industrial system. This evolution created an entirely new problem. Previous efforts had been made to make maladjusted individuals fit into society, and of course this broad field of effort still exists. But when, in 1933, we faced the fact that nearly one out of every three able-bodied workers in America had no job, we had to face the added fact that it was the system which was out of gear.

Here is one difference between direct relief and work relief. Direct relief is aimed at many problems of human misfortune — adjusting maladjusted families, taking care of the sick, tiding over a great number of kinds of crises in family life. Work relief is aimed at the problem of getting jobs for normal people who can give useful work to the country, and seeking adjustment of a maladjusted society rather than an adjustment of maladjusted individuals.

The importance of these employable millions may be more fully understood, perhaps, when it is realized that approximately one-third of them are under twenty-five years of age and will be either assets or liabilities for many years to come, depending upon public policies toward them. If we do not give them a chance at something like normal living, it is inevitable that they will become millions of individual problems. For these able-bodied unemployed, I am definitely committed to the giving of jobs instead of relief.

Except in supplementing certain Social Security laws as passed by the States, the Federal government has left the care of un-employables — the problem of maladjusted individuals — to the states and localities, the field which is the natural sphere of the Community Chests. The Federal government has chosen to con-fine itself to the normal victims of the maladjusted economy, to create work for the employable unemployed. It is true that the national economy does not today permit the Federal govern-ment to give useful work to all the employable needy unem-ployed, but the Federal government is doing so in the great ma-jority of cases.

The able-bodied unemployed need work and should have it. But equally the economic system needs that they should have it. A Federal works program not only serves the unemployed, it saves the jobs of those who have jobs. Our industrial production cannot progress, as it must, unless our masses have income with which to buy its products. That, in brief, is an aspect of the re-lief problem — and a most important aspect — which I commend to the thoughtful consideration of all who are enlisted in this splendid Mobilization for Human Needs. Only in jobs and more jobs, at good pay, shall we find national stability and individual security.

Meanwhile, encouraged and inspired by a quarter of a cen-tury of practical activity, which has seen the base of charitable giving steadily spread, I hope you will widen your appeal until every citizen with a competence — great or little — extends the helping hand to his less favored brother. That is an ambitious goal, but I believe it can be reached.

Here is a work in which diverse creeds and classes can unite for the common good. Let us strive to bring into every com-munity practical exemplification of the ideal of being a good neighbor. In that spirit I appeal to the American people to pre-sent a united front in the 1938 Mobilization for Human Needs.

34 ❲ The President Suggests a Comprehensive Congressional Study of the Forest Land Problem of the United States. March 14, 1938

To the Congress:

I FEEL impelled at this time to call to the attention of the Congress some aspects of our forest problem, and the need for a policy and plan of action with respect to it.

Forests are intimately tied into our whole social and economic life. They grow on more than one-third the land area of the continental United States. Wages from forest industries support five to six million people each year. Forests give us building materials and thousands of other things in everyday use. Forest lands furnish food and shelter for much of our remaining game, and heathful recreation for millions of our people. Forests help prevent erosion and floods. They conserve water and regulate its use for navigation, for power, for domestic use, and for irrigation. Woodlands occupy more acreage than any other crop on American farms, and help support two and one-half million farm families.

Our forest problem is essentially one of land use. It is a part of the broad problem of modern agriculture that is common to every part of the country. Forest lands total some six hundred and fifteen million acres.

One hundred and twenty odd million acres of these forest lands are rough and inaccessible — but they are valuable for the protection of our great watersheds. The greater proportion of these protective forests is in public ownership. Four hundred and ninety-five million acres of our forest lands can be classed as commercial. Both as to accessibility and quality the best four-fifths, or some three hundred and ninety-six million acres of these commercial forests, is in private ownership.

This privately owned forest land at present furnishes 96 per cent of all our forest products. It represents 90 per cent of the productive capacity of our forest soils. There is a continuing drain upon commercial forests in saw timber sizes far beyond the annual growth. Forest operations in them have not been, and are not now, conducive to maximum regrowth. An alarming proportion of our cut-over forest lands is tax-delinquent. Through neglect, much of it is rapidly forming a new but almost worthless no man's land.

Most of the commercial forest lands are in private ownership. Most of them are now only partially productive, and most of them are still subject to abuse. This abuse threatens the general welfare.

I have thus presented to you the facts. They are simple facts; but they are of a character to cause alarm to the people of the United States and to you, their chosen Representatives.

The forest problem is therefore a matter of vital national concern, and some way must be found to make forest lands and forest resources contribute their full share to the social and economic structures of this country, and to the security and stability of *all* our people.

When in 1933 I asked the Congress to provide for the Civilian Conservation Corps I was convinced that forest lands offered one source for worth-while work, non-competitive with industry, for large numbers of our unemployed. Events of the past five years have indicated that my earlier conviction was well founded. In rebuilding and managing those lands, and in the many uses of them and their resources, there exists a major opportunity for new employment and for increasing the national wealth.

Creation of the National Forest system, which now extends to thirty-eight States, has been a definite step toward constructive solution of our forest problem. From national forest lands comes domestic water for more than six million people. Forage, occurring largely in combination with timber, contributes stability to one-fourth the western range livestock industry. Through correlated and coordinated public management of timber and all other resources, these public properties already help support almost a million people and furnish healthful recreation to more

than thirty million each year. By means of exchanges and purchases, the Congress has for many years encouraged additions to
this system. These measures should very definitely be continued
as funds and facilities are available.

The Congress has also provided that the national government
shall cooperate with the various States in matters of fire protection on privately owned forest lands and farm woodlands. The
States are in turn cooperating with private owners. Among other
measures the Congress has also authorized an extensive program of forest research, which has been initiated and projected;
Federal cooperation in building up a system of State forests;
cooperative activities with farmers to integrate forest management with the general farm economy; the planting of trees in
the Prairie-Plains States — an activity which has heretofore been
carried on as an emergency unemployment relief measure with
outstanding success and material benefit; and — under the Om-
nibus Flood Control Bill — measures to retard run-off and erosion on forested and other watersheds.

Progress has been made — and such measures as these should
be continued. They are not adequate, however, to meet the present situation. We are still exploiting our forest lands. Forest communities are still being crippled; still being left desolate and
forlorn. Watersheds are still being denuded. Fertile valleys and
industrial cities below such watersheds still suffer from erosion
and floods. We are still liquidating our forest capital, still cutting our accessible forests faster than they are being replaced.

Our forest budget still needs balancing. This is true in relation to future as well as present national needs. We need and
shall continue to need large quantities of wood for housing, for
our railroads and our telephone and telegraph lines, for news-
print and other papers, for fiber containers, for furniture, and
the like. Wood is rich in chemicals. It is the major source of cel-
lulose products, such as rayon, movie films, cellophanes, sugars
of certain kinds, surgical absorbents, drugs, lacquers, phono-
graph records. Turpentines, rosins, acetone, acetic acid, and al-
cohols are derived from wood. Our forest budget should, there-

fore, be balanced in relation to present and future needs for such things as these. It should also be balanced in relation to the many public services that forests render, and to the need for stabilizing dependent industries and communities locally, regionally, and nationally.

I am informed, for example, that more than one hundred million dollars has recently gone into development of additional forest industries in the southeastern section of our country. This means still more drain from southern forests. Without forestry measures that will insure timber cropping there, existing and planned forest enterprises must inevitably suffer. The Pacific Northwest contains the greatest reserves of virgin merchantable timber in the continental United States. During recent years many private forest lands have been given better fire protection there, and there are more young trees on the ground. But the cutting drain in our virgin Douglas fir forests is about four times current growth, and unless existing practices are changed the old fir will be gone long before new growth is big enough for manufacture into lumber.

I recommend, therefore, study by a joint committee of the Congress of the forest land problem of the United States. As a nation we now have the accumulated experience of three centuries of use and abuse as guides in determining broad principles. The public has certain responsibilities and obligations with respect to private forest lands, but so also have private owners with respect to the broad public interests in those same lands. Particular consideration might therefore be given in these studies, which I hope will form the basis for essential legislation during the next session of Congress, to the situation with respect to private forest lands, and to consideration of such matters as:

1. The adequacy and effectiveness of present activities in protecting public and private forest lands from fire, insects, and diseases, and of cooperative efforts between the Federal government and the States.

2. Other measures, Federal and State, which may be necessary and advisable to insure that timber cropping on privately

owned forest lands may be conducted as continuous operations, with the productivity of the lands built up against future requirements.

3. The need for extension of Federal, State, and community ownership of forest lands, and of planned public management of them.

4. The need for such public regulatory controls as will adequately protect private as well as the broad public interests in all forest lands.

5. Methods and possibilities of employment in forestry work on private and public forest lands, and possibilities of liquidating such public expenditures as are or may be involved.

Facilities of those technical agencies that, in the executive branches of the government, deal with the many phases of our forest problem will of course be available to such committee as the Congress may appoint. These technical agencies will be glad to assist the Committee in assembling and interpreting facts, indicating what has been done, what still needs to be done, and in such other ways as the Committee may desire.

I make this suggestion for immediate study of our forest problem by the Congress in the belief that definite action should be taken by the Congress in 1939. States, communities and private capital can do much to help — but the fact remains that, with some outstanding exceptions, most of the states, communities and private companies have, on the whole, accomplished little to retard or check the continuing process of using up our forest resources without replacement. This being so, it seems obviously necessary to fall back on the last defensive line — Federal leadership and Federal action. Millions of Americans are today conscious of the threat. Public opinion asks that steps be taken to remove it.

If the preliminary action is taken at this session of the Congress, I propose to address letters to the Governors of those States in which the amount of state and privately owned forest land is substantial, enclosing to them a copy of this Message to the Congress and asking their full cooperation with the Congress and with the Executive Branch of the National Government.

NOTE: Pursuant to the foregoing message, the Congress by concurrent resolution established a Joint Committee on Forestry to investigate the condition, ownership and management of forest land "as it affects a balanced timber budget, watershed protection and flood control and the other commodities and social and economic benefits which may be derived from such lands" (52 Stat. 1452).

The resolution creating the Committee specified that it should study the five matters to which I referred in my message, as well as the need for additional legislation and other measures to implement the program.

Public hearings were conducted in eight centers throughout the country, and representatives of many organizations, groups and private individuals testified upon what should be done to protect and improve our forests. The Committee report was transmitted to the President of the Senate and the Speaker of the House of Representatives on March 24, 1941.

After summarizing the outstanding features of American forests, their uses and their needs, the Committee recommended a sixteen-point program for their protection and rehabilitation. The main note which the Committee struck was that federal appropriations should be increased for such measures as

forest fire and insect control, the furnishing of tree seed and seedlings to landowners; legislation providing credits and financial aid for the development of forests and their industries, research in forest products and management, extension of state and local ownership, development in farm forest cooperatives and federal forest land acquisition. The report also advocated a greater supervision over timber, forage, wildlife, recreation, and watershed resources on national forests, and an investigation of the monopolistic purchase of pulpwood.

The Joint Committee on Forestry brought to the attention of the public the need for additional protective measures, particularly on the vast tracts of privately-owned forest land. The Committee also pointed out the social and economic dangers which follow destructive exploitation, and showed clearly the need for some extension of public ownership.

However, many students of forestry believe that the actual recommendations of the Committee were not as strong as the situation would demand, and did not go to the root of the problem. The Joint Committee took the position that the states should administer and enforce the regulation of forests, with the federal government approving the standards and providing financial support. But the history of state regulatory legislation has demonstrated that private forest industries have often been able to regain control of the situation in their own interests. There must be some provision for positive federal action if state legislation proves inadequate.

The public interest should be safeguarded through the substantial acquisition of new tracts of forest land by federal, state and local public agencies. Although the Joint Committee felt that the present rate of acquisition should be maintained, it advocated nothing more definite than that this rate should be increased "when possible."

(For further discussion of measures taken and contemplated to protect our forests, see Item 80, 1937 volume; Item 98, 1939 volume; Items 5 and 88, 1940 volume.)

35 ⟨ In Celebration of the Birthday of Thomas Jefferson. Proclamation No. 2276. March 21, 1938

WHEREAS Thomas Jefferson, author of the Declaration of Independence and third President of the United States, was the advocate of great causes and high ideals of human freedom — principles adopted as fundamental by the American people; and

WHEREAS Thomas Jefferson as lawyer, statesman, philosopher, scientist, farmer, and architect lived a life of such rich diversity that it encompassed the full scope of the knowledge of his time, and — of happy significance to his country — knew how to carry theory into practice, and from youth to a fine old age exemplified in all of his work the principle that the true evidence of life is growth; and

WHEREAS Public Resolution No. 60, 75th Congress, approved August 16, 1937, provides:

That the President of the United States of America is authorized and directed to issue a proclamation calling upon officials of the Government to display the flag of the United States on all Government buildings on April 13 of each year, and inviting the people of the United States to observe the day in schools and churches, or other suitable places, with appropriate ceremonies in commemoration of the birth of Thomas Jefferson:

NOW, THEREFORE, I, FRANKLIN D. ROOSEVELT, President of the United States of America, do hereby call upon officials of the Government to display the flag of the United States on all Government buildings on April 13, 1938, and on April 13 of each succeeding year, and do invite the people of the United States to observe the day in schools, churches, and other suitable places, with appropriate ceremonies in commemoration of the birth of Thomas Jefferson.

36 ⟨ The President Transmits to the Congress the Record of the Removal of the Chairman of the Tennessee Valley Authority. March 23, 1938

To the Congress:

I TRANSMIT herewith for the information of the Congress my opinion setting forth the reasons which impelled me to remove Arthur E. Morgan, and my letter to him removing him, as a member and Chairman of the Board of the Tennessee Valley Authority. I further transmit the opinion of the Attorney General in regard to my power to remove for cause members of the Board of the Tennessee Valley Authority. I also append the transcript of the hearings which were had before me on March 11, 18 and 21, 1938, and which I think merit the serious consideration of all those interested in the T.V.A. I have filed my letter to Arthur E. Morgan and the transcript of the hearings, together with all exhibits marked for identification in the transcript, with the Secretary of State.

It is clearly the right of the Congress to undertake at any time any fair inquiry into the administration of the Tennessee Valley Authority or its policies which the Congress may deem in the public interest. But I cannot in the meanwhile abdicate my constitutional duty to take care that the laws be faithfully executed.

I call the attention of the Congress to the fact that on the evidence presented I was obliged to find that,

(a) Arthur E. Morgan publicly made grave and libelous charges of dishonesty and want of integrity against his fellow directors, and when called upon to sustain them repeatedly refused to do so;

(b) On the face of the record, charges of the other directors that Arthur E. Morgan has obstructed the work of the Tennessee Valley Authority were substantiated by proof, were not refuted, and therefore must be accepted as true;

(c) Arthur E. Morgan was contumacious in refusing to give the Chief Executive the facts, if any, upon which he based his charges of malfeasance against his fellow directors, and in refusing to respond to questions of the Chief Executive relating to charges of obstruction made against him by his fellow directors.

Arthur E. Morgan has repeated the assertion that he will answer questions only to a committee of the Congress. Obviously, there can be no objection to hearings before such a committee. But the Congress will, I am sure, realize that if any member of the Executive branch of the Government, of high degree or low degree, is given the right by precedent to refuse to substantiate general charges against other members of the Executive branch of Government and to insist on disclosing specifications only to a committee of the Congress, efficient administrative management of government would be destroyed in short order.

The letter of removal follows:

Dear Dr. Morgan:

As A result of the hearings had before me on March 11, 18, and 21, 1938, I regret to inform you that I feel obliged to remove, and do hereby remove, you as member and Chairman of the Board of the Tennessee Valley Authority. This removal is to become effective as and from March 23, 1938.

36. Removal of Chairman of Tennessee Valley Authority

As is more fully explained in the memorandum opinion which I read at the hearing on March 21, and by the record before me, I have been impelled to remove you for the following reasons:

(a) Openly making grave and libelous charges of dishonesty and want of integrity against your fellow directors without reasonable excuse or justification.

(b) Obstructing the work of the Tennessee Valley Authority.

(c) Refusing to submit to the demand of the Chief Executive for the facts upon which you relied in openly making grave and libelous charges of dishonesty and want of integrity against your fellow directors and refusing to respond to questions of the Chief Executive relating to charges of obstruction made against you by your fellow directors.

I have taken note of the fact that you have not presented to me in person or in writing any reason why I should not remove you other than the statement recorded in the transcript of the proceedings before me on March 21, 1938.

A duplicate of this letter is being filed with the Secretary of State.

Yours respectfully,

Dr. Arthur E. Morgan,
Knoxville, Tenn.

The Presidential memorandum on the facts requiring the removal is as follows:

Under the Constitution of the United States, the Chief Executive is directly charged to "take care that the laws be faithfully executed." I have been confronted for some time with a threat to the continued successful functioning of the Tennessee Valley Authority, a great executive agency. And let me say at this point that, on the whole — considering that this was a great experiment in Government, an experiment intended to help the lives and the social conditions under which millions of people live — as such an experiment it has been proved successful. I think we have accomplished great things for the people of the whole Tennessee watershed.

But of late we have all of us been confronted with certain conditions which threaten the continued successful operation of this great experiment. I go back fourteen months to January, 1937, when in a public speech and articles in the public press one of three members, the Chairman of the Board of Directors of the Authority, seemed to intimate — but without specifications or supporting evidence — that he doubted the integrity of his fellow members.

Largely as a result of questions raised at that time, questions relating primarily to the administrative setup of the Authority, I asked a committee of three, all of them experienced in administrative affairs, to go to the Tennessee Valley and report to me on some of the questions that had been raised, including the question of the appointment of a general manager, which I think in the first instance had been suggested by Arthur E. Morgan in a letter to me. A report of this committee approved the appointment of a general manager, and indeed one had already been appointed as acting general manager.

Historically, the next difficulty arose in the Board of Directors over the choice of a permanent general manager. Things dragged on through the summer of 1937.

At the end of August, again in the public press — but again without specifications or supporting evidence — Arthur E. Morgan used language intimating that he doubted the integrity of his fellow members. I wrote him at that time:

> "that there is a very definite obligation on you either to withdraw what your colleagues believe to be an impugning of their integrity or that you present whatever specific facts you may have, if any, to justify your statements."

In reply, Chairman Morgan informed me that while he was highly critical of the work of his colleagues, he had no intention of impugning their good faith or personal integrity. He complained about the internal organization of the Tennessee

Valley Authority and requested me to intervene in his behalf. I urged him to return and to try to complete the internal reorganization in harmony with his fellow directors. And on my calling their attention to his statement that he did not have access to records, his fellow directors denied this statement categorically and stated that all records were and would be open to the inspection of the chairman.

Things went on until December, 1937. The constitutionality of the TVA Act was at stake in a law suit that had been brought by eighteen utility companies. I think it was a matter of almost public record—the record of the time—for it was mentioned in the press and in the record that has been brought out last week and the week before—that during this litigation Chairman Morgan widely disseminated within the Authority's organization charges of unethical professional conduct against counsel for the TVA who were in charge of the litigation—again without specification or evidence.

On January 18th this year, the majority members submitted to me, without publicity—and it was, in fact, not published in any way—an official memorandum complaining of certain specific kinds of unpermissible conduct on the part of Arthur E. Morgan, including the making of unsupported charges, including an unwillingness to cooperate in carrying out decisions of a majority of the Board, and including serious interference with the work of key members of the Authority's staff in the performance of their duties. In contrast to Arthur E. Morgan's charges against them, the complaint of the majority against him did not charge him with dishonesty or lack of integrity. I think that is a fact that directly bears on the pro's and con's of this inquiry.

On March 3 and on March 5, 1938, Arthur E. Morgan made extensive and unequivocal charges of dishonesty and lack of integrity in public office on the part of the majority members— again in the public press—and again without specifications or evidence.

Despite my long personal friendship for Arthur E. Morgan

and my appreciation of his many public services in the past, this action by him compelled action by me.

As Chief Executive constitutionally responsible for the faithful execution of the Tennessee Valley Authority Act, I could not ignore charges of dishonesty, bad faith and conspiracy in its administration.

In fairness to Dr. Harcourt Morgan and Mr. David Lilienthal — in fairness to them as public officials and as American citizens — I had to make public their accusations of obstruction against Arthur E. Morgan because, without notice to me, he had made public his accusations of dishonesty against them. I could not wash my hands of these grave and libelous charges against men whose alleged guilt had not been proven, any more than I can today wash my hands of these charges because of the possibility or the probability that at some later date they may be investigated by another branch or branches of the Federal Government.

Therefore, I summoned the three members of the Board of the T.V.A. to appear before me on March 11, face to face with each other, to present such facts as they might have to support the serious charges which they had made. It was not a formal court proceeding, but a simple and fair way to get the truth — to let each confront the other and tell his story in straightforward non-technical words.

I informed the members that I was concerned at this particular inquiry, not with the pro's and con's of TVA policy, but with their charges of dishonesty on the one hand and misconduct on the other.

I first called on Arthur E. Morgan to substantiate with facts the several charges of dishonesty and want of integrity which he had made against his fellow directors. I called his attention to the fact that the gist of his complaint in regard to the handling of the Berry marble claims appeared in his own words to be that "the real difficulty has been in the effort to secure honesty, openness, decency, and fairness in Government." And I pointed

156

out to him that common decency toward his fellow directors called for utter frankness and candor on his part.

At the hearing on March 11th, Arthur E. Morgan flatly refused to submit to me any evidence in support of his charges. He read a prepared statement to the effect that the "meeting is not, and in the nature of the case cannot be, an effective or useful fact-finding occasion. To properly substantiate the charges is not the work of a morning." When asked whether he had any reason to believe that the hearing would be confined to a morning or whether he would be prepared to submit facts if given one week or two weeks to do so, he failed to reply.

The majority members explained the action which they had taken in the Berry marble claims case, as well as their action on the Arkansas Power and Light Company contract, and on the Aluminum Company contract, to which Arthur E. Morgan had referred in his public statements. I could not expect a more adequate explanation than that which they made, especially in view of the failure and refusal of Arthur E. Morgan to submit the facts on which he relied to support his charges.

I then asked the majority members to present the facts in support of their charges against Arthur E. Morgan.

The majority members first referred to a number of his published articles and speeches during 1937 which, they contended, contained unsupported and unsupportable statements impugning their honesty and integrity. Whether or not these articles or speeches were intended to impugn the motives of the Directors, it is, unfortunately, clear that the more recent public statements of Arthur E. Morgan, to which the majority members also referred, do without question assail the personal honesty and integrity of the majority members in unmistakable terms.

But Arthur E. Morgan refused, although I pleaded with him and gave him repeated opportunity, to present any facts in justification of his attacks upon the integrity of the majority of the Board.

The majority members also proffered facts tending to show

157

that in the course of delicate and important conversations between the Authority and private interests, Arthur E. Morgan had private conferences and communications with one or more utility executives, with a large prospective power purchaser, and with an electric equipment manufacturer, which conversations and conferences might well have hampered the Government in carrying out the decisions of the majority of the Board.

As a matter of law and common sense, when there is dissension within a multiple-headed executive agency, it is difficult to draw the line where dissent becomes obstruction. I have serious doubt as to the propriety of a number of things which Arthur E. Morgan did in an effort to create a situation in which he could force an acceptance of his own ideas. But just so long as we have multiple-headed administrative boards we ought to allow considerable latitude for human discretion and not frighten a minority into acquiescence. Therefore, I have sought to resolve every doubt in favor of Arthur E. Morgan. Nevertheless, significance does attach to the multiplying of these instances in which he trespassed into doubtful territory.

For example, the majority members proffered facts tending to show that Arthur E. Morgan did not send a telegram to me as directed by the Board. Although here in this case Arthur E. Morgan may have committed only a technical wrong, he having testified that he had changed his mind, an instance of this sort, standing alone, would have no significance; but, taken in the light of many other acts, the chain, the whole chain, must be given significance.

The majority members also offered facts tending to show — and I think I should say fairly show — on the face of them that Arthur E. Morgan interfered with and obstructed the Tennessee Valley Authority Counsel in vitally important constitutional litigation which affected the very life of the Authority, a litigation to which I have previously referred.

To the demands of the counsel under accusation that Arthur E. Morgan should give evidence and specifications the latter refused to make reply. The interference reached such a point that special counsel for the TVA, Honorable John L. O'Brian, formerly the Assistant to the Attorney General of the United States under the previous Administration, an independent lawyer of great experience and wide reputation, felt impelled to write to the Chairman as follows:

Dear Dr. Morgan:

I have your letter of December 30, 1937.

Prior to the trial and during the trial I have actively participated in and have closely observed the preparation and presentation of the testimony. Since receiving your recent letter, I have again gone over the file of material concerning the preparation and presentation of the engineers' testimony in the case now on trial, and have talked with the attorneys and also with a number of the witnesses. As a result, I am more than ever confirmed in the opinion which I previously expressed to you that the case has been handled with unusual ability and in accordance with the highest standards of integrity.

Your charges, coming while the case was actively on trial, have had a disrupting and demoralizing effect upon all the attorneys and upon the conduct of the Authority's case. After careful review of the matter I am convinced that the charges must have originated in some misunderstanding and have no real foundation in fact. The matter ought to be definitely cleared up in justice to the lawyers and also in justice to the Authority's case which needs the best efforts of all of the attorneys. As all the attorneys are now under great strain in the stages of this trial I am writing to ask whether you will not clear the record and set the members of the legal staff free from a very heavy and, I think, unwarranted burden of anxiety at this critical time.

It is a matter of record that the TVA had intrusted the conduct of this important litigation to highly competent counsel. Its unusually capable General Counsel had the assistance of an able, independent special counsel. Whatever differences there may have been within the Board as to the conduct of this litigation no evidence has been submitted to me which would have justified the minority member at a most critical stage of the proceedings in openly charging reputable counsel with unethical conduct, thereby, consciously or unconsciously, prejudicing the case of the government. In spite of all this Arthur E.

Morgan, when given the opportunity by me, has offered no explanation for this reckless and astounding conduct.

I concluded the first hearing on March 11 as follows:

"I have now heard the charges and countercharges of the T.V.A. Board. I have endeavored to give each side the opportunity of answering the complaints of the other side. Frankly, I am disappointed that Chairman Morgan has not answered by giving any factual answers to the questions which I have put, but I hope that in the course of the next week Chairman Morgan will realize that it is of the utmost importance to the continuation of the work that he should reply to very simple factual questions.

"He should have every opportunity so to do. And, therefore, if it is agreeable to him and to the other two members, who also may want to present additional facts, I will set a resumption of this hearing for a week from today, Friday morning, at eleven o'clock, and if you care to appear in person at that time it will be entirely agreeable to me. If you prefer to submit any factual report in writing without appearing, use your own judgment."

A second hearing was accordingly held on March 18th.

At this second hearing, Arthur E. Morgan persisted in his refusal to participate in any inquiry to ascertain facts regarding his charges of dishonesty and want of integrity, although in a prepared statement he referred "by way of illustration" to certain facts and circumstances tending to show that the Berry marble claims were worthless and that there was reason to suspect the bona fides of the claims. But there is absolutely no evidence before me that the majority members of the Board ever contended either that these marble deposits had any commercial value or that they themselves had no reason to suspect the bona fides of the claims.

The evidence shows on the contrary that claims aggregating millions had been filed against the Government; that the majority of the Board were as deeply concerned about them as was Arthur E. Morgan; and that the Board's counsel was endeavoring to obtain all available evidence to oppose the claims on the ground that the marble was commercially valueless and that the claims were not advanced in good faith.

The majority members, acting on the advice of TVA counsel, believed that it would tend to protect rather than hurt the Government's case if an independent expert under a conciliation agreement made a report on the value of the marble deposits without binding either the Authority or the claimants in any way.

When this procedure was proposed at a Board meeting, Arthur E. Morgan objected to it. As a member of the Board he had a right so to do. He believed, apparently, that, despite the express terms of the agreement, it would in some way adversely affect the rights of the Authority to contest the claims. The majority members, conscious of the hazards of any litigation and not having as yet unearthed any legal or direct evidence of the bad faith which they nevertheless suspected, were equally within their rights in voting to adopt the procedure that had been suggested by the Authority's counsel. There is not the slightest basis for Arthur E. Morgan's imputing bad faith to the majority members because they and the Authority's counsel differed with him on technical points of legal procedure. It seems strange and, I think, unwarranted for Arthur E. Morgan on the one hand to complain that as a layman he cannot adequately explain to me why his colleagues acted improperly and, on the other hand, as a layman to take it upon himself to accuse his colleagues of gross misconduct in the handling of a lawsuit.

Arthur E. Morgan's whole attitude toward this inquiry in itself gives credence to the charge that he has been unwilling to cooperate with his fellow directors in the administration of the Act and that he is temperamentally unfitted to exercise a divided authority. His fellow directors have responded as a matter of course and have given specifications to support their grievances. With the exception of a few fragmentary questions and answers on the Berry marble claims, Arthur E. Morgan has stood aloof and refused to cooperate in this proceeding or even to supply the simplest facts asked of him by his own administrative superior, the Chief Executive. The contrast is obvious. The contrast is disheartening.

I have tried to be mindful of the debt the public owes to Arthur E. Morgan for past services, of his sense of the righteousness of his own convictions, and of the patience with which the public interest demands that a situation of this kind be worked out if possible. I have therefore struggled with this problem for over a year, and, in its present acute form, for six months. I have been patient.

But, as I have said before, there is a limit to patience. I must greatly consider the position in which Dr. Harcourt Morgan and David Lilienthal find themselves. Some decision on this record is due to them, in all fairness. If there should be no decision after Arthur E. Morgan has refused to substantiate his grave and libelous charges against them, they would be definitely, seriously and permanently injured in their rights and standing as citizens and as public officials.

Furthermore, I must greatly consider the continuing operations of an important government agency. It would violate my constitutional duty to take care that the laws are faithfully executed if I should leave unsupported charges hanging indefinitely over the heads of two officials who have cooperated in the difficult task of divided authority and thereby permit a recalcitrant non-cooperative official further freedom to sabotage Government operations at a crucial time.

Finally, I must also consider the consequence of permitting the establishment of a precedent whereby any subordinate in the executive branch of the Government can refuse to give to his superior or to the Chief Executive himself facts sought in order to straighten out difficulties which he charges exist in his own departmental work; can refuse accountability to the Chief Executive for his actions as a member of the executive branch, even though he be charged with misconduct in office; and can insist that orderly executive functioning and discipline be maintained only through the processes of legislative committees. It is worth-while to consider what would happen to the efficiency of Government if this suggestion were made the general rule. Obviously the Congress has full power of investigation; but, obviously also, the Constitution of the United States declares that "the executive power shall be vested in a President of the United States." Under such circumstances indulgence of my personal wish to continue my patience with Arthur E. Morgan would be unfair to his colleagues, to his Government and to the public. I therefore feel obliged to act upon the evidence now before me.

On that evidence I am obliged to find that:

(a) Arthur E. Morgan has failed to sustain the grave and libelous charges of dishonesty and want of integrity which he has made against his fellow directors; his conduct in this respect is legally and morally unjustified;

(b) On the face of the record, the charges of the other directors that Arthur E. Morgan has obstructed the work and injured the morale of the organization of the Tennessee Valley Authority must be accepted as true; he has refused to offer testimony in denial of the charges;

(c) Arthur E. Morgan is guilty of insubordination and contumacy in refusing to submit to the Chief Executive's demand for any facts upon which he based charges of dishonesty and want of integrity on the part of his fellow directors, and in refusing to respond to questions of the Chief Executive relating to charges of obstruction made against him by his fellow directors.

Under these circumstances, I feel myself under the painful duty of requesting Arthur E. Morgan at once publicly to withdraw the charges that he has made impugning the honesty, good faith, integrity, and motives of his fellow directors, and to give to them and to the country assurances that he will, in the future, loyally cooperate with his fellow directors in carrying out the provisions of the Tennessee Valley Authority Act.

I make this request of him.

If he cannot accede, it is his duty to resign.

I hope—I deeply hope—that Arthur E. Morgan will not make it necessary for me to take further action. He has had ample time and ample opportunity to make his decision. If he determines to follow neither of these courses, I will give him until tomorrow, Tuesday, 2:30 P.M. on March 22, to present to me in person or in writing any reason why, as Chief Executive, I should not take further action in the case as a necessary result of the findings which I have just read to him.

NOTE: The history and issues involved in this controversy are adequately set forth in the memorandum of facts transmitted by me to the Congress with the foregoing message.

The removal by me of Arthur E. Morgan as Chairman of the Tennessee Valley Authority has been sustained by the courts. See Morgan v. Tennessee Valley Authority, 28 Fed. Supp. 732 (Dist. Ct., E.D. Tenn.—Aug. 11, 1939; affirmed 115 Fed. (2d) 990 (C.C.A. 6th Circuit—Dec. 6, 1940); No. 742 certiorari denied, 85 Law Ed. 663, which was issued by the United States Supreme Court on March 17, 1941.

37 ("The United States Is Rising and Is Rebuilding on Sounder Lines." Address at Gainesville, Georgia. March 23, 1938

THIS CELEBRATION, the outward and visible commemoration of the rebirth of Gainesville, is more than a symbol of the fine courage which has made it possible for this city to come back after it had been, in great part, destroyed by the tornado of 1936. These ceremonies touch the interest and life of the whole Nation because they typify citizenship which is latent in the American character but which too often remains quiescent and too seldom expresses itself. You were not content to clear away the debris which I, myself, saw as I passed through Gainesville a couple of days after the disaster. You were not content with rebuilding along the lines of the old community. You were not content with throwing yourselves on the help which could be given to you by your State and by the Federal Government.

On the contrary, you determined in the process of rebuilding to eliminate old conditions of which you were not proud; to build a better city; to replace congested areas with parks; to move human beings from slums to suburbs. For this you, the citizens of Gainesville, deserve all possible praise.

It is true that in the planned work of rebuilding you received Federal assistance.

Chairman Jesse Jones of the Reconstruction Finance Corporation tells me that they invested nearly one million dollars in Gainesville with the objective of helping to rebuild the city and that he knows of no similar sum which has been used to better advantage. The Public Works Administration aided in projects for schools, for an almshouse, for a courthouse, for water works and for a jail, and the Works Progress Administration assisted not only in cleaning up the wreck and taking care of destitute people but also in repairing sewers and sidewalks, street lighting, repaving, and parks and schools. But all of this would have been wholly insufficient if you had not provided far greater help from your own ranks in the form of money and in the form of unselfish cooperation.

In the task there has been an essential unanimity in the gift of personal interest and personal service. Few among your citizens have held back. You had needs — great needs. They were met in accordance with the democratic principle that those needs should be filled in proportion to the ability of each individual to help.

I tell you that this has a national significance and I want to give you a few illustrations of where and how the application of this principle to national problems would amply solve our national needs.

Today, national progress and national prosperity are being held back chiefly because of selfishness on the part of a few. If Gainesville had been faced with that type of minority selfishness your city would not stand rebuilt as it is today.

The type of selfishness to which I refer is definitely not to be applied to the overwhelming majority of the American public.

Most people, if they know both sides of a question and are appealed to, to support the public good, will gladly lay aside selfishness. But we must admit that there are some people who honestly believe in a wholly different theory of government than the one our Constitution provides.

You know their reasoning. They say that in the competition of life for the good things of life; "Some are successful because they have better brains or are more efficient; the wise, the swift and the strong are able to outstrip their fellowmen. That is nature itself, and it is just too bad if some get left behind."

It is that attitude which leads such people to give little thought to the one-third of our population which I have described as being ill-fed, ill-clad and ill-housed. They say, "I am not my brother's keeper" — and they "pass by on the other side." Most of them are honest people. Most of them consider themselves excellent citizens.

But this nation will never permanently get on the road to recovery if we leave the methods and the processes of recovery to those who owned the Government of the United States from 1921 to 1933.

They are the kind of people who, in 1936, were saying, "Oh, yes, we want nobody to starve"; but at the same time insisted that the balancing of the budget was more important than making appropriations for relief. And when I told them that I, too, wanted to balance the budget but that I put human lives ahead of dollars and handed them the government estimates and asked them just where they would cut the appropriations, inevitably they came back at me and said, "Mr. President, that is not my business, that is yours."

They have the same type of mind as those representatives of the people who vote against legislation to help social and economic conditions, proclaiming loudly that they are for the objectives but do not like the methods, and then fail utterly to offer a better method of their own.

I speak to you of conditions in this, my other State. The buying power of the people of Georgia and of the people of many other States is still so low today that the people of these states cannot purchase the products of industry. Therefore, industry itself is cut off from an outlet it otherwise would have. People cannot buy at stores unless they have cash or good credit. Stores cannot fill their shelves unless they have customers.

Mills and factories cannot sell to stores who have no customers.

I speak not only of the workers in the bottom third of our population — millions of them who cannot afford a suit of clothes. I speak also of millions of other workers who are so under-employed and so underpaid that the burden of their poverty affects the little business man and the big business man and the millionaire himself.

Georgia and the lower South may just as well face facts — simple facts presented in the lower South by the President of the United States. The purchasing power of the millions of Americans in this whole area is far too low. Most men and women who work for wages in this whole area get wages which are far too low. On the present scale of wages and therefore on the present scale of buying power, the South cannot and will not succeed in establishing successful new industries. Efficiency in operating industries goes hand-in-hand with good pay and the industries of the South cannot compete with industries in other parts of the country, the North, the Middle West and the Far West, unless the buying power of the South makes possible the highest kind of efficiency.

And let us well remember that buying power means many other kinds of better things — better schools, better health, better hospitals, better highways. These things will not come to us in the South if we oppose progress — if we believe in our hearts that the feudal system is still the best system.

When you come down to it, there is little difference between the feudal system and the Fascist system. If you believe in the one, you lean to the other.

With the overwhelming majority of the people of this State, I oppose feudalism. So do many among those who by virtue of their circumstances in life belong to the most prosperous 5 per cent of the population. Men and women in the professions, the overwhelming majority of the small storekeepers, a growing number of the bankers and business men — they are coming more and more to see that the continuation of the American system calls for the elimination of special privilege, the dissemination of the whole of the truth, and participation in prosperity by the people at the bottom of the ladder, as well as those in the middle and at the top.

One thing is certain — we are not going back to the old days. We are going forward to better days. We are calling for cooperation all along the line, and the cooperation is increasing because more and more people are coming to understand that abuses of the past which have been successfully eradicated are not going to be restored.

To those in and out of public office, who still believe in the feudal system — and believe in it honestly — the people of the United States and in every section of the United States are going to say "We are sorry, but we want people to represent us whose minds are cast in the 1938 mold and not in the 1898 mold."

To those who come forward, and they are coming in increasing numbers day by day, we say: "We, the Government of the United States, all of us in that Government, want to cooperate for the good of the whole people and the whole Nation. To you we extend the hand of welcome."

Gainesville suffered a great disaster. So did the Nation in those eight years of false prosperity followed by four years of collapse. Gainesville showed a united front for the good of its whole population, rich and poor alike. It rose to rebuild on sounder lines.

The United States is rising and is rebuilding on sounder lines. We propose to go forward and not back.

NOTE: This address was delivered on my way to Warm Springs, Georgia, for a holiday. I left Washington on March 22, 1938, and returned on April 3, 1938. In addition to this speech, I also made extemporaneous talks not printed in these volumes at Toccoa, Georgia, on March 23; Griffin, Georgia, on March 23; Columbus, Georgia, on March 30; Pine Mountain Valley Project, Georgia, on March 31; and at the Warm Springs Foundation Luncheon Party on April 1.

38 ⟨ The United States Moves to Help Refugees from Germany. State Department Release. March 24, 1938

THIS GOVERNMENT has become so impressed with the urgency of the problem of political refugees that it has inquired of a number of Governments in Europe and in this hemisphere whether they would be willing to cooperate in setting up a special committee for the purpose of facilitating the emigration from Austria and presumably from Germany of political refugees. Our idea is that whereas such representatives would be designated by the Governments concerned, any financing of the emergency emigration referred to would be undertaken by private organizations within the respective countries. Furthermore, it should be understood that no country would be expected or asked to receive a greater number of immigrants than is permitted by its existing legislation. In making this proposal the Government of the United States has emphasized that it in no sense intends to discourage or interfere with such work as is already being done on the refugee problem by any existing international agency. It has been prompted to make its proposal because of the urgency of the problem with which the world is faced and the necessity of speedy cooperative effort under governmental supervision if widespread human suffering is to be averted.

NOTE: The foregoing release of the Department of State was issued when the refugee problem had reached an acute stage in 1938. At that time it became apparent that some orderly plan for inter-governmental cooperation had to be formulated to deal with the mass emigrations which had become necessary, for the facilities of private organizations to find places of refuge had become overtaxed.

Beginning in 1933, the oppression of political, religious, and economic minorities, particularly in Germany and in the German-dominated countries, had caused hundreds of thousands of men, women, and children to seek escape from sheer brutality. Neighboring countries absorbed some of the emigrants at first; but when pressure at the source became intense, it became impossible for these countries to harbor the refugees for more than a temporary period.

On March 23, 1938, I took the initiative, and requested the Secretary of State to invite the cooperation of thirty-two governments which might assist in facilitating the orderly emigration of these persecuted people, and in providing refuge and settlement for them as emigrants. The response of some of the governments approached was heartening, and among the most cordial replies were those from France and the Dominican Republic. In marked contrast to the others, Italy tartly refused to collaborate in any scheme which would care for what she pleased to term her enemies. The Union of South Africa declined to participate actively; but she nevertheless sent an observer to the meeting.

All the other governments had answered favorably by May, 1938; and at that time I named the Honorable Myron C. Taylor, with the rank of Ambassador, as my representative at the projected meeting of the Committee mentioned in the foregoing statement. France extended her hospitality, and suggested that the Committee meet at Evian on the shores of Lake Leman.

Pending the meeting of this so-called Intergovernmental Committee at Evian in July, 1938, I set up two other bodies to lay the groundwork for the Evian meeting. In March, 1938, I named an Advisory Committee on Political Refugees, which consisted of a number of private individuals under the chairmanship of James G. McDonald, former High Commissioner for Refugees of the League of Nations. To cooperate with the Advisory Committee I named a special interdepartmental committee of government officials. These two bodies aided in formulating the instructions and the guiding principles for the conduct of the American delegation which went to Evian.

For centuries this country has always been the traditional haven of refuge for countless victims of religious and political persecution in other lands. These immigrants have made outstanding contributions to American music, art, literature, business, finance, philanthropy, and many other phases of our cultural, political, industrial, and commercial life. It was quite fitting, therefore, that the United States government should follow its traditional role and take the lead in calling and conducting the Evian meeting.

When the Evian meeting opened

in July, 1938, Ambassador Taylor was chosen chairman by the delegates. In his opening statement to the meeting, he reviewed the seriousness of the refugee problem and stressed the necessity for prompt formulation of a long-range, comprehensive program. He urged that the Intergovernmental Committee cooperate with the existing refugee agencies of the League of Nations and the International Labor Office, and set up permanent machinery for handling the situation. He pointed out that the problem was no longer one of private concern, but was one requiring intergovernmental action. Ambassador Taylor further suggested that accurate information should be compiled about the number and condition of refugees, the possibilities for resettling them, and the means of financing the emigrations. He concluded the statement, which had been agreed upon with me, by emphasizing that "discrimination and pressure against minority groups and the disregard of elementary human rights are contrary to the principles of what we have come to regard as the accepted standards of civilization."

During subsequent sessions of the Evian meeting, representatives of the other nations present outlined the position of their governments on the problem. Unfortunately, most of the governments seemed overly cautious in their attitude about receiving these refugees; and

while they were generally sympathetic, no constructive plans were submitted.

As this is written in June, 1941, it seems so tragically ironical to realize how many millions of the citizens of these various countries either are themselves now refugees, or pray for a chance to leave their native lands and seek some refuge from the cruel hand of the Nazi invader. Even the kings and queens and princes of some of them are now in the same position as these political and religious minorities were in 1938 — knocking on the doors of other lands for admittance.

The basis for the future work of the Intergovernmental Committee was laid in a resolution adopted on July 14, in which it was announced that thenceforth the committee would remain in permanent session. The resolution also suggested the appointment of a director to negotiate with the countries of exodus and refuge. Mr. George Rublee, an American international lawyer, was subsequently chosen as the first director of the committee, charged with this responsibility.

The second meeting was held in London on August 3, 1938. Mr. Taylor opened the London meeting by stating that its purpose was to set in motion the machinery established at Evian, to evaluate the information assembled, and to get more specific statements of what

171

each of the participating countries was willing to do.

On the second day of the London meeting, Mr. Taylor, in reviewing the situation, stated that approximately 660,900 persons in Germany were in search of opportunities for resettlement. He suggested that the director negotiate with Germany in an endeavor to make the emigration more orderly and to allow the refugees sufficient funds and property to take with them.

After the adjournment of the London meeting, the strategy of the approach to Germany was discussed at a meeting of the officers of the Intergovernmental Committee held in London on August 31, 1938. Although it was fully appreciated that the policy of the German government toward Jewish minorities was the prime cause of the entire problem, the Committee did not wish to incite any additional persecutions which would undoubtedly have come as an immediate consequence of criticizing Germany for its inhuman attitude. Instead, it was decided to approach the German government upon the question of lightening the heavy financial burdens which she had placed upon potential emigrants.

On October 5, 1938, through our Ambassador at London, I urged Prime Minister Chamberlain to intervene with the German government in behalf of the refugees. This message, hitherto unpublished, was as follows:

October 5, 1938
Noon

Embassy,
    London.

"Please call urgently upon the Prime Minister and convey to him orally the following personal message from the President:

'I fully share your hope and belief that there exists today the greatest opportunity in years for the establishment of a new order based on justice and on law. Now that you have established personal contact with Chancellor Hitler I know that you will be taking up with him from time to time many of the problems which must be resolved in order to bring about that new and better order. Among these is the present German policy of racial persecution, which has perhaps done more harm than any other to the estimate of Germany held by public opinion in America regardless of class, race or creed.

'The Intergovernmental Committee has scrupulously avoided any emotional or critical approach to the problem and is on the contrary seeking a solution along strictly practical lines. While it may be too much to expect an early change in the basic racial policy of the German Government, nevertheless it would seem reasonable to anticipate that the German Government will assist the other Governments upon which this problem has been forced by relaxing the pressure upon these people sufficiently to permit the arrangement of orderly emigration and by permitting them to take with them a reasonable percentage of their property. The German Government, in forcing these persons to leave its territory without funds and without property, cannot be unmindful of the fact that it is thereby imposing great burdens on her friendly neighbors and on other nations throughout the world who, for humanitarian considerations, are doing what they can to alleviate the lot of these people. All other countries represented in the Intergovernmental Committee are thereby given new and serious problems to solve.

'As time may be of the essence, I am sending you this message without further delay in the hope that you will be able to find an appropriate opportunity to lay these considerations before the Reich Chancellor. His acceptance in principle of these considerations would permit the Director of the Intergovernmental Committee to enter into useful conversations with the appropriate German authorities concerning details.'"

Ambassador Kennedy telegraphed that he delivered the foregoing message to Prime Minister Chamberlain on the morning of October 6. However, in reply, the Prime Minister indicated preference for an approach to Germany through the American and British Ambassadors at Berlin.

Meanwhile, Director Rublee, in making his report to the Committee, stressed the fact that the participating countries should give additional assurance that they would receive some of the emigrants. He recommended that steps be taken to re-train potential refugees, and outlined a five-year program for the absorption of 500,000 refugees at the rate of 100,000 annually. This proposal was outlined in order that a definite plan for absorption of emigrants could be presented to Germany.

On October 18, 1938, Ambassador Wilson called upon Herr Weizsaecker in Berlin. The Ambassador left a memorandum outlining the history of the Intergovernmental Committee and he urged that Director Rublee be received by the German Government. Apparently, however, in the German Government there was still a division over the extent to which cooperation should be carried on in such a scheme.

The officers of the Intergovernmental Committee held a second meeting in London, December 2, 1938, at a time when the outlook for refugees was becoming darker hourly. Most nations participating in the program of resettlement still seemed reluctant to commit themselves on the actual number of refugees that they would receive. Countries bordering upon Germany were finding it increasingly difficult to retain illegal entrants without turning them back to Germany. In the face of these difficulties, the officers' meeting could do little pending a move by Germany, and after reviewing the situation briefly, they adjourned.

Just when it seemed that Germany would refuse to take any cognizance of the problem, Dr. Hjalmar Schacht paid a visit to London on December 15, 1938, and presented to Mr. Rublee and British officials the German plan for the evacuation of refugees. The Schacht Plan was later modified after further conversations with Marshal Goering and his aide, Helmuth Wohlthat. In a confidential memorandum to Mr. Rublee, Herr Wohlthat set forth the conclusions of his Government following these conversations. This memorandum came to be known as the "Rublee Plan" (see Item 84, 1939 volume).

The memorandum outlined the projected emigration of 150,000 Jewish wage-earners out of the 600,000 Jews in Germany during a three to five year period. The rest were old people who would probably have to remain in Germany, and women and children. The memorandum mentioned that passports would be provided for refugees, that Jews in concentration camps were to be released when the program got under way, and the German Government would aid in retraining wage-earners awaiting emigration. Assurance was given that those unfit for emigration would be allowed to live in tranquillity.

Included in all the proposals of the German Government was a de-

vice by which the provision of adequate funds to the refugees was made contingent upon the purchase of German exports. To finance emigration, not less than 25 per cent of Jewish property in Germany was to be placed in a trust fund administered by one foreign and two German trustees, and a private corporate purchasing agency on the outside of Germany was to provide the funds for buying German exports which the refugees could take with them. The essence of this scheme was that transfer of Jewish resources to other countries would take the form of increased purchase of German goods.

When the Schacht Plan was originally proposed, this government informed Ambassador Taylor that it was opposed to a plan which was "asking the world to pay a ransom for the release of hostages in Germany and barter human misery for increased exports." Regarding the subsequent plans of the German Government, this government felt that they also were unsatisfactory; yet a blunt rejection was not stated lest this break off negotiations altogether.

Therefore, at a full meeting of the Intergovernmental Committee held in London on February 14, 1939, Ambassador Taylor stated that the latest German plan contained in the Wohlthat memorandum represented a slight improvement over existing conditions. He advised that the Committee take cognizance of the proposal, without definite approval. The recommendation of Ambassador Taylor was carried out in a resolution adopted by the Committee which took cognizance of the projected formation of an internal trust fund and an external corporation to finance the emigration of German refugees.

Conversations with the German Government on the details of the plan continued, with the Vice-Director of the Committee, Mr. Robert Pell, making several trips to Berlin for that purpose. The Committee continued its efforts to ascertain which areas were open for resettlement, in order to make some more definite arrangement with Germany. On April 5, 1939, Mr. Pell reported in a memorandum to Herr Wohlthat that several new areas were open for resettlement, notably in Australia, Canada, British Guiana, the Dominican Republic, the Philippine Islands, and Northern Rhodesia. Although the United States had a strict quota system in effect, figures were presented to show that this country was already receiving one-fourth of the annual emigration from Germany, or about 27,000 annually.

On the eve of the fourth meeting of the Intergovernmental Committee, held in London, July 20, 1939, some progress had been made toward arriving at a solution of the refugee problem. Through the initiative of this government, the machinery for intergovernmental cooperation had been set in motion. Although many of the governments of possible settlement and refuge were slow to follow the lead of the United States, and although the pressure in Germany became more intense as the months proceeded, we did succeed in opening several new areas and in impressing all countries concerned with the seriousness of the problem. (For a further discussion of the policy and actions of this government toward refugees, see Items 84 and 143, 1939 volume.)

39 ⟪ The President Transmits to the Congress a Proposed Hungarian Relief Debt Settlement. March 28, 1938

To the Congress:

I TRANSMIT herewith, for the consideration of the Congress, a communication from the Minister of Hungary on the relief indebtedness of Hungary to the United States, in which the Hungarian Government tentatively formulates for the consideration of the American Government a possible basis for a new debt arrangement between the two countries to replace completely the Debt Agreement of 1924 and accruals thereunder.

The indebtedness of the Government of Hungary to the Government of the United States is not a war debt, but is properly designated as a relief debt, having been contracted in May, 1920, under the authority of the Act of March 30, 1920, which authorized the United States Grain Corporation, with the approval of the Secretary of the Treasury, to sell or dispose of flour in its possession for cash or on credit at such prices and on such terms or conditions as considered necessary to relieve the populations in the countries of Europe or countries contiguous thereto suffering for the want of food. The American Relief Administration acted as the Fiscal Agent of the United States Grain Corporation in dispensing this relief.

The original indebtedness, the principal amount of which was $1,685,835.61, with interest accrued thereon from May, 1920, to December, 1923, at the rate of four and one-fourth per cent per annum, was funded as of the latter date, by agreement made in April, 1924, into bonds of Hungary in the aggregate principal amount of $1,939,000, maturing serially in the succeeding years for sixty-two years, bearing three per cent for the first ten years and thereafter at the rate of three and one-half per cent per annum. In approving this debt settlement, the Congress authorized the Secretary of the Treasury to subordinate the lien of the bonds taken under it to the lien of the Hungarian Reconstruction Loan, which was about to be issued and sold in numerous countries, including the United States. In May, 1924, the Secretary, acting upon this authorization, formally subordinated the American Government's lien to the lien of the Reconstruction bond issue.

On December 23, 1931, the Hungarian Government proclaimed a transfer moratorium suspending payment in foreign currencies of all Hungarian foreign obligations, public and private, except the aforesaid Reconstruction Loan of 1924. Payments on the latter loan were subsequently suspended in part. During 1937, the Hungarian Government began liquidating the transfer moratorium by negotiating agreements with the foreign holders of Hungarian obligations for the acceptance of reduced payments in full satisfaction of existing indebtedness. It is in this connection that the Hungarian Government has now come forward of its own initiative in an effort to reach an agreement with the United States Government under which the relief indebtedness can also be discharged in full.

No readjustment of the terms of payment of the Hungarian indebtedness to the United States can be made except pursuant to Act of Congress. The Hungarian Government is seeking a definitive readjustment of the terms of payment of this indebtedness on the basis of full payment over a period of years of the total original amount borrowed, without interest.

The Hungarian Government calls attention to the similarity between its suggested basis for payment and that accepted by the United States in the Austrian Debt Agreement of May 8, 1930, which provided that a sum very slightly in excess of the original Austrian indebtedness incurred in 1920 should be repaid without interest in forty annuities. The Congress of the United States, after full consideration of the nature of the Austrian indebtedness, voted by a large majority in the House of Representatives and by a unanimous procedure in the Senate, to authorize the signature of the draft agreement which had been prepared by the Treasury Department and the representatives of the Austrian Government. The Hungarian debt is a relief debt like the Austrian one.

The Hungarian Minister also suggests that the terms compare favorably with those in several other debt settlements, and that in announcing the signature of the Debt Agreement with Austria in 1930, the Secretary of the Treasury said:

The settlement compares favorably with the settlements made by the United States with the Governments of Greece, Italy and Yugoslavia.

It has of course been the consistent policy of the United

States to consider each debt in the light of the circumstances of the debtor government, and it is with this in view that the Hungarian communication is transmitted to the Congress.

I believe the proposals of the Hungarian Government should receive the most careful consideration of the Congress. They represent a noteworthy wish and effort of the Hungarian Government to meet its obligations to this Government.

In its simplest terms, the offer of the Hungarian Government is to repay to the United States the whole of the Relief Loan but without payment of any interest thereon.

NOTE: On December 23, 1931, the Hungarian Government had proclaimed a general transfer moratorium, which suspended payment of its foreign obligations, including its relief debt to the United States. In 1937 this general moratorium was terminated; and Hungary resumed payment on its debts at reduced rates.

In February, 1938, the Hungarian Government presented a proposal for a new arrangement on a permanent basis, which provided for payment of the original debt, without interest, in equal installments covering approximately thirty years. This was the first proposal for a permanent adjustment of debts which had been received by the United States since the general suspension of payments in 1932-1934 by European Governments on the so-called war debts to the United States.

The proposal to settle the Hungarian Debt, which I transmitted in the foregoing message, has not yet been acted upon by the Congress as of January 1, 1941.

40 ⟨ A Tribute to Colonel House by the President. March 28, 1938

A GREAT and unique figure has been lost to our national life in the death of Colonel House. The trusted friend and advisor in foreign affairs of a great war President, Colonel House possessed a sagacity, prudence, patriotism and integrity which made his counsels invaluable in one of the most critical periods of world history.

Few Americans have possessed in such degree the confidence

of statesmen at home and abroad as did this modest and self-effacing man who placed his country's good and the good of humanity above all personal considerations.

As one who had long enjoyed the privilege of his friendship I shall miss his wise counsel and unvarying loyalty.

41 ❮ The President Refutes Dictatorship Charges Connected with the Pending Reorganization Bill. March 29, 1938

My dear ――――:

M ANY THANKS for your letter telling me that you are concerned over the charges in several newspapers that the reorganization bill now before the Congress, would make me a Dictator.

1. As you well know I am as much opposed to American Dictatorship as you are, for three simple reasons.

A: I have no inclination to be a dictator.

B: I have none of the qualifications which would make me a successful dictator.

C: I have too much historical background and too much knowledge of existing dictatorships to make me desire any form of dictatorship for a democracy like the United States of America.

2. The reorganization bill now before the Congress is the culmination of an effort starting over forty years ago to make the business end, i.e., the Executive branch, of the Federal Government more business-like and more efficient. Seven or eight of my immediate predecessors in the Presidency have recommended similar reorganization measures.

There are two methods of effecting a business-like reorganization. It can be done by complex and detailed legislation by the Congress going into every one of the hundreds of bureaus in the executive departments and other agencies.

Or it can be done by giving to the President as Chief Executive authority to make certain adjustments and reorganizations by executive order, subject to overriding of these executive orders by the Congress itself.

I would have been wholly willing to go along with the first method, but attempts at detailed reorganization by the Congress itself have failed many times in the past, and every responsible member of the Senate or the House is in agreement that detailed reorganization by the Congress is a practicable impossibility.

We come then to the second alternative — reorganization by executive order subject to overriding by the Congress.

3. In any reorganization you will realize I am sure that if it changes existing administrative set-ups, consolidates jobs or makes other kinds of savings either from the point of view of cost or from the point of view of bureaucratic authority, such changes are bitterly fought by those who stand to lose some authority and by those who are so wedded to existing practices that they go to any length to prevent the slightest change which seeks greater efficiency.

Several states have put into effect reorganizations of their departments. The changes have resulted in some economy. But chiefly these reorganizations in state governments have increased the efficiency of these state governments to a very marked extent. That result is what we seek in the bill now before the Congress.

4. You know that when over a year ago I recommended a reorganization to the Congress all parties and all factions agreed on the need for such a measure. You know, too, that a year later a carefully manufactured partisan and political opposition to any reorganization has created a political issue — created it deliberately of whole cloth.

5. The opposition has planted bogies under every bed. It was said, for example, that the work of the army engineers was to be abolished in spite of the fact that the Congress, and the Congress alone, can determine who will do river and harbor dredging and build flood control levees. It is charged that the splendid work of the Forest Service is to be hamstrung — hamstrung, I suppose, by the best friend forestry ever had in the

United States. It is charged that the extremely efficient Veterans Bureau or the excellent Railroad Mediation Board is to be damaged beyond repair. I cite these merely as example of a score of equally silly nightmares conjured up at the instigation either of those who would restore the government to those who owned it between 1921 and 1933, or of those who for one reason or another seek deliberately to wreck the present administration of the government of the United States.

6. One point remains:

There are those who honestly believe that every minor change, every minor detail of conducting the business of the administrative branch of the government, should receive in effect a positive Congressional approval before such changes go into effect. The bill in its present form makes the executive orders relating to such changes — and most of them are minor — subject to disapproval by the Congress within sixty days by joint resolution. Let me state to you categorically that if such a joint resolution were passed by the Congress disapproving an order, I would, in the overwhelming majority of cases, go along with carefully considered Congressional action.

I can think of no cases where the President would not gladly yield to a clear expression of Congressional opinion.

But there are two cogent reasons why the bill should go through as it is now drawn. The first is the constitutional question involved in the passage of a concurrent resolution, which is only an expression of Congressional sentiment. Such a resolution cannot repeal executive action taken in pursuance of a law. The second is the very remote possibility that some legislative situation might possibly arise in the future where the President would feel obligated to veto a joint resolution of the Congress and properly require a two-thirds vote to override his veto. I repeat that I visualize no such possibility between now and 1940, when the authority given is to end. Thus you will see that charges of dictatorship are made out of whole-cloth — even if I wanted to be a dictator, which Heaven knows, I do not.

With every good wish, always sincerely,

NOTE: Modern democracies demand efficient tools. This generation has seen the rise of dictatorship in many countries, after periods of executive and administrative impotence. In a democracy we are constantly faced with the challenging problem of how to keep the organization of government abreast with social change.

The history of the efforts to provide a modern, businesslike set-up in the administration of our own government is a long one.

Prior to 1900, committees of Congress at various times made studies and recommendations concerning the administrative branch of the government. At first these studies were confined to the methods of expending public moneys and the possibilities for retrenchment. Later, studies were made of the organization of the executive branch, but none of the congressional committees formulated comprehensive plans for over-all reorganization.

Since Theodore Roosevelt's time, the initiative for administrative reform has come generally from the executive rather than from the Congress. As I pointed out in the foregoing letter, it is a practical impossibility for the Congress drastically and thoroughly to reorganize the administrative branch in a detailed fashion, because of the multitude of sectional and departmental pressures and personalities involved, with the resultant temptation to log-rolling.

In 1905, President Theodore Roosevelt established a committee to investigate the business methods of the executive departments; and many procedural reforms in the collection, disbursement, and accounting of funds were instituted as a result of the committee's researches.

President Taft's "Commission on Economy and Efficiency" also did a vast amount of spade-work in the field of budget control and accounting procedure, and made recommendations for the consolidation or abolition of certain agencies.

As a result of these recommendations, the Congress passed the Act of August 24, 1912 (37 Stat. 434), granting reorganization powers to President Taft similar to those contained in the Reorganization Bill of 1938, but making no requirement even for congressional approval of his action. Yet a great hue and cry of "dictatorship" was raised in 1938, while the Congress was considering passing a bill which granted similar reorganization powers but which reserved to Congress, however, the power to override any suggestions for administrative reorganization advanced by the President.

President Wilson was keenly interested in reorganizing the executive branch of the government, and the Overman Act (40 Stat. 556) gave the President authority, as a war measure, to coordinate and consolidate executive bureaus and agencies in the interest of economy and efficiency. In the debates upon this bill, the same cries of "dictatorship," and "abdication by Congress of its constitutional functions" were raised, as were raised in 1938. However, under the statute, President Wilson made many notable changes in the War Department before the Act expired in 1919.

None of these prior attempts had involved any comprehensive plans of reorganization.

In President Harding's administration, however, the Congress authorized the appointment of a Joint Committee on Reorganization, composed of representatives of the Congress and of the executive branch. The recommendations of this committee were similar in many respects to the provisions of the 1938 reorganization bill. A Department of Education and Welfare was contemplated, for example, to which were to be transferred the Public Health Service, the Bureau of Education, the Bureau of Pensions, the Veterans' Bureau, the Federal Board for Vocational Education and several other agencies. When a like proposal was included in the 1938 measure, it was attacked on the grounds that it would mean federal dictatorship over education (see Item 52, this volume). The plan submitted during the Harding administration stipulated that the General Accounting Office should be transferred to the Treasury Department; yet this was also one of the principal items in the 1938 bill which

roused great, irrational opposition.

Although President Coolidge urged the enactment of the above recommendations, the bill failed to pass.

From 1929 until 1933, a few agencies were consolidated by statute under President Hoover. Under the Economy Act of 1932 (47 Stat. 413), President Hoover, after a short study by an economy committee, was given wide powers to reorganize. Finally in December of 1932, having been defeated for re-election, the President did transmit, pursuant to this legislation, a far-reaching plan of reorganization to the Congress. It was rejected. A majority of the Congress felt that the responsibility for reorganization should rest upon the incoming President.

The next step in reorganization was a two-year power to transfer or abolish by executive order any executive agencies or functions, which was granted to the President in a rider to the Treasury-Post Office Appropriation Bill (47 Stat. 1517) of March 3, 1933. In a number of executive orders (see for examples, Items 63, 71 and 71A, 1933 volume), some progress was made in consolidating related functions.

By 1935 I became convinced, however, that it would take an overhauling of the entire administrative mechanism in order to make it run more efficiently and economically.

It had become apparent that the

government was becoming cluttered with a number of uncoordinated, independent units which did not fit into any organized plan. With the expansion of the fight for economic recovery and reform along many fronts, it was natural that many new agencies should be created. Aside from the Bureau of the Budget, I had no staff to assist in the managerial direction and control over the expanded governmental structure. It had become almost impossible for me to confer at sufficient length with so many department and commission heads; and it became quite obvious that some rearrangement of the system was essential.

Accordingly, in October, 1935, I started preliminary conversations regarding a broad administrative survey, which I felt should cover such things as over-all administrative activities, and the elimination of conflicts in authority among the various agencies. In December, the National Resources Committee outlined a proposal for such a study.

During February and March, 1936, I discussed these problems further with Secretary of the Interior Ickes, Mr. Louis Brownlow, and the staff of the National Resources Committee. I decided that a small committee of administrative experts should be set up to study and report upon the general scheme of organization and the managerial functions of the Chief Executive.

On March 20, 1936, I appointed a Committee on Administrative Management consisting of Mr. Brownlow, Chairman; Dr. Charles E. Merriam and Dr. Luther Gulick (see Item 43, 1936 volume). I also sent letters on the same date to the Vice-President and to the Speaker of the House of Representatives, requesting that the two Houses of Congress cooperate through special committee, lest there be duplication of the work of the Committee on Administrative Management (see Item 43A, 1936 volume). The House and Senate Committees, headed by Representative Buchanan of Texas and Senator Robinson of Arkansas, were set up as suggested.

Under the Deficiency Appropriation Act of 1936, the Congress authorized me in June, 1936, to allocate $100,000 to this Committee on Administrative Management; and with the use of this sum the Committee commenced its work.

Many were the problems to be reviewed and analyzed.

First was the question of coordinating the administrative activities of the executive branch as a whole. Although the National Emergency Council had been established to aid in the coordination of emergency activities, it had been largely concerned with federal-state cooperation. A more effective mechanism was necessary, such as had been employed during the World War.

Another task of the Committee was to examine the possibility of coordinating and directing the activities of the various planning agencies of government. The National Resources Committee had already started the interrelated planning of natural and human resources, and the question of how such plans could implement the executive program was studied.

Next, in connection with the whole problem of financial management, the Committee studied ways and means of developing the Bureau of the Budget to help the President direct the financial and administrative activities of the government. This was to be done through continuous surveys of the internal organization and practices of governmental agencies in order to bring about improved financial methods, eliminate duplication and overlapping.

The Committee also investigated the extent to which the Comptroller-General, who acted in the dual role of comptroller and auditor, interfered with the day to day administration of the government through controlling spending policy. It studied the advisability of setting up an independent auditor who would report directly to the Congress.

The question of how to develop a positive and aggressive personnel administration to attract men and women of high capacity and character to the governmental service was also a matter studied by the Committee. Because of the President's responsibility in this regard,

it was felt that he should be given more adequate tools for raising the caliber and efficiency of the personnel.

The Committee's inquiries covered a multitude of other subjects:

For many years there had been a need, for example, for some coordination in the issuance of executive orders governing the administrative operations of departments and agencies. The Committee carefully analyzed the possibilities of achieving such coordination, and also the extent to which machinery could be set up to integrate the various rules and regulations which were issued by the administrative agencies themselves.

The practice of submitting legislative proposals by the various administrative agencies without reference to general policies of the executive branch of the government was also studied with an aim to eliminating conflicts in policy. Under the Budget and Accounting Act of 1921, it had been mandatory to clear through the Bureau of the Budget all financial legislative proposals suggested by the various departments; and a similar procedure for other legislative measures had been developed to some extent by the National Emergency Council under my administration. The Committee analyzed these procedures with a view to determining the most effective staff machinery required for coordination of all proposals for legislation.

One of the most striking phenomena of modern government is the rapid growth of independent regulatory agencies since the Interstate Commerce Commission was created in 1887. With the onset of the economic depression, many new agencies were established outside of the regular executive departments, creating serious problems of supervision and direction. At my suggestion, the Committee attempted to determine how these independent bodies could be fitted into the general executive framework.

Closely linked to this was the question of how best to organize the newly created government corporations, which had been established to aid flexibility, business efficiency, opportunity for experimentation and freedom of operation. They would have to be coordinated with other governmental activities to be utilized most efficiently in the public interest. A further area demanding coordination was the federal field service. Here there was a great amount of duplicating work carried on by different departments operating in the same geographical localities outside of Washington.

The Senate and House Committees which were set up at my suggestion (see Items 43 and 43A, 1936 volume) engaged the Brookings Institution to make a detailed study of the functions of the hundred or more independent agencies in our government, in order to discover the extent of overlapping and duplication, and to see what specific changes should be made. The Committee on Administrative Management confined itself, under a division of work agreed upon, to studying how the independent agencies might best be grouped into a more coordinated operating structure of over-all management.

Early in January, 1937, the Committee on Administrative Management presented its report to me. On January 9, I discussed the report at a conference with the Vice-President and the Congressional leaders. In my message of January 12, 1937, I transmitted the Committee's report to the Congress, along with a summary of the proposals advanced therein (see Items 241 and 241A, 1936 volume).

The report recommended a five-point program of reorganization of the executive branch of the government, including the following:

1. Expansion of the White House staff to deal with its greatly increased duties, and to speed the clearance of information needed for Executive decisions.

2. Strengthening of the managerial agencies, particularly those dealing with budget and efficiency research, personnel and planning.

3. Extension of the merit system in all directions, and reorganization of the civil service under a single administrator, aided by a citizen board to serve as

"watch-dog" of the merit system.

4. Addition of cabinet departments of Social Welfare and Public Works, and placement of the independent agencies, boards and commissions within these and the other ten major executive departments.

5. Establishment of Executive accountability to the Congress through provision of an independent post-audit of all fiscal transactions by an auditor-general, and the restoration of complete responsibility for accounts and current transactions to the Executive.

As I pointed out in my message to the Congress, this program contained no recommendations for any increase of presidential power. The recommendations were designed only to enable the President to discharge his constitutional duties with effective tools of management.

Precise recommendations as to the way in which the bureaus could be regrouped were omitted from the report, which in the main limited itself to general principles which the Committee proposed to carry out the general objectives of efficient administrative management.

It did, however, make definite suggestions for a number of specific reforms:

It recommended, for example, that the President be given six executive assistants to enable him to maintain contact with the departments and facilitate the upward flow of information to the President and the downward flow of Executive decisions.

With respect to the activities of the Bureau of the Budget, the report called for an expansion of the staff, which had been decreased by years of over-economizing at the expense of efficiency. It was suggested that the Director of the Bureau of the Budget be relieved of routine administrative duties so that he would be free to develop the Bureau into a more effective controlling agency. The Committee recommended that the execution, as well as the preparation, of the budget should be supervised by the Bureau of the Budget. Further, the Committee stated that a special research division should be created within the Bureau in order to investigate questions of organization and to encourage the various departments and bureaus to study their own procedural problems.

Having studied the problems arising in connection with executive orders, the Committee suggested that the preparation, consideration and clearance of executive orders be undertaken by the Bureau of the Budget, and that wider use be made of such orders to establish uniform codes to cover such matters as budgetary controls, personnel, supplies and coordination.

Since the passage of the Budget and Accounting Act of 1921, the administrative departments had been required to clear their fiscal proposals through the Bureau of the Budget. Now, to aid the President in reviewing the various legislative recommendations proposed by the administrative departments, and in order to avoid conflicts in policy and legislative trends, it was suggested that the Bureau of the Budget expand its clearance to include non-fiscal legislative proposals of the departments.

The Committee also recommended that a division of information for all government agencies be established within the Bureau, which might also aid in sponsoring interdepartmental associations of officials to help the coordination of field service activities.

In regard to the other managerial aids to the President, it was recommended that the National Resources Committee be established as a permanent board to act as a central planning agency and to coordinate the activities of departmental, state and local planning agencies in investigating problems dealing with natural and human resources.

A number of suggestions were made for the revamping of personnel management. With an aim to creating a real career service the Committee suggested that all but policy-determining positions should be included within the merit system, and that salaries should be raised all along the line. It was felt that more effective and responsible personnel management would be achieved through the abolition of the board form of organization in the Civil Service Commission, and by the establishment of a new central personnel agency under a single Civil Service Administrator. A Civil Service Board of seven non-salaried private citizens was recommended to act in an advisory capacity.

The Committee stressed the fact that the growth of independent commissions had created a "headless fourth branch" of the government, which hampered coordination of governmental policies. The Committee had to face the problem of how to achieve better supervision of all policy-determining activities, and at the same time preserve the impartiality of the independent commissions in their quasi-judicial functions. The Committee concluded that each regulatory commission should be put within the executive departments; and that each one should be divided into two sections: an administrative section and a judicial section. The administrative section was to be directly responsible to the department head; whereas the judicial section was to be completely independent, except for the purposes of budget, general personnel administration and the procurement of supplies.

In order to bring the independent regulatory commissions within the executive departments, and to achieve a more logical grouping of all governmental agencies, the Committee suggested the creation of two new cabinet departments. The first was to be the Department of Social Welfare. It was designed to advise the President with regard to social welfare; to administer federal public health, education and social activities; to protect the consumer; to conduct the federal aspects of federal-state programs of social security; to administer all federal elee-mosynary, corrective and penal institutions; and to administer probation and parole.

The second was to be the Department of Public Works. It was designed to advise the President with regard to public works; to design, construct, and maintain large-scale public works which are not incidental to the normal work of other departments; to administer federal grants to state or local governments or other agencies for construction purposes; and to gather information with regard to public works standards throughout the nation.

It was further suggested that the name of the Department of the Interior should be changed to the Department of Conservation.

The Committee gave intensive consideration to the problems of accounting and auditing, and the necessity of strengthening the accountability of the executive branch to the Congress.

If the executive branch is to direct the fiscal affairs of government satisfactorily, it must possess adequate accounting machinery in order to obtain reliable information on the status of governmental revenues and expenditures. The Committee therefore felt that the authority to prescribe and supervise accounting systems, forms, and procedures in the federal establishments, should be transferred from the Comptroller General to the Secretary of the Treasury. This was not a new proposal. It had been suggested to the Congress by President Hoover in 1932; and in 1934 a special committee on federal expenditures of the United States Chamber of Commerce recommended that a satisfactory accounting system be put directly under executive control.

More important, however, was the question of the combination of the inconsistent functions of control of expenditures, and the audit thereof. Both were within the General Accounting Office, headed by the Comptroller General. Under this system, the Comptroller General has the power to settle all claims against the United States, and, in that way, exercise current control over expenditures by making the final decisions as to the legality of administrative action involving expenditures. On the other hand, the Comptroller General is charged with auditing functions. This means that he later audits his own accounts or financial acts and decisions reached by himself beforehand. Thus the Congress is deprived of a complete, detailed, critical, independent post-audit of national expenditures.

The Committee sought to remedy this by retaining the General Accounting Office as an agent of Congress, but changing its name to describe its new functions as the "General Auditing Office," and that of the Comptroller General to "Auditor General," and reserving to them the power to make a comprehensive audit of all the accounts of fiscal officers. The Committee also recommended that the Attorney General be empowered to decide disputes as to jurisdiction between the Treasury Department and department heads in the settlement of accounts and claims.

During February, March and April of 1937, after I had transmitted the report of the Committee on Administrative Management to the Congress, the House and Senate Committees on Government Organization held joint hearings in executive sessions. Four bills were introduced in the House of Representatives and one bill in the Senate, embodying between them almost all the principles of the program recommended by the President's Committee. The only important departures from the Committee recommendations were: (1) the exemption of the regulatory commissions from the President's reorganization power; (2) the failure to provide for an increase in salaries in the higher brackets of civil service; and (3) the dropping

of the proposal to create a new Department of Public Works.

However, very little was accomplished with these bills during the first session of the Seventy-fifth Congress in 1937, because the Congress and the country were mostly preoccupied with the Supreme Court fight, the struggle for reform of the judiciary (see Introduction to 1937 volume).

In the remaining months of 1937, the reorganization program was widely discussed. In my "fireside chat" of October 12, 1937 (see Item 135, 1937 volume), I pointed out the necessity of giving the executive branch of the government some twentieth century machinery with which to carry out a twentieth century program. In my message to the extraordinary session of the Congress on November 15, 1937 (see Item 152, 1937 volume), I restated the five paramount objectives of administrative reorganization, and recommended that the Congress take steps to carry out the proposals.

During the special session of 1937, and for some time after the convening of the regular session in 1938, action was delayed while the Senate filibustered on the anti-lynching bill. Finally, in February, 1938, reorganization became the order of business in the Senate.

Almost immediately, minority groups began to agitate and propagandize against this reorganization program — a program which in principle had been recommended in part by nearly every President, Republican and Democrat, since Theodore Roosevelt. The press, or a great portion of it, was enlisted to trumpet the assertion that this was a "dictator bill"; and many reactionary newspapers attempted to arouse the people by dire predictions that passage of the bill meant the end of our freedom. Of course, thinking persons everywhere realized the simple fact that administrative reorganization was only a necessary move in the strengthening of the machinery of our democracy and in equipping it better to combat the threat of totalitarianism.

The most irrational arguments imaginable were advanced against the bill, the most frequently stated of which was the bland assertion that the proposals were unprecedented and dictatorial, and involved an abdication by the Congress of its constitutional legislative functions.

Few of the opponents of reorganization knew, or were willing to admit, that practically all the proposals of the President's Committee had been either recommended or put into effect for brief periods under previous administrations. Recognizing that reorganization can best be accomplished by the executive, the Congress in 1903, 1912, 1917, 1919, and 1932 had vested power in the President to transfer governmental agencies by executive order. President Hoover had even gone so far as to recommend that these executive orders be made effective without any opportunity for the Congress to approve or disapprove of them.

Many critics of reorganization charged that the creation of a single Civil Service Administrator was a partisan move to enable the President to corrupt the merit system. Yet in a message to the Congress on February 17, 1932, President Hoover had endorsed a similar proposal; and as early as 1789 the first Congress had concluded that single-headed responsibility was a sound principle in the exercise of executive functions.

Likewise, under previous Republican administrations, there had been similar proposals that the function of "controlling" expenditures be vested in an officer responsible to the President; and that a new executive department be created to have jurisdiction over federal functions relating to education and public welfare.

A barrage of telegrams descended upon the members of the Senate and the House of Representatives. The charge of "dictator" which at first seemed such a flagrant distortion of the facts as not to justify recognition, soon was conjured into a real fear in the minds of many people. Some radio orators, demagogues, a large part of press and many of the pernicious Congressional lobbies served to deluge Congressmen with telegrams. What these people were really seeking to accomplish was not so much to block this particular legislation, as to try to discredit the administration so as to block any further thought of social reform, and, incidentally, reduce the effectiveness of its reform program by preventing efficiency generally in government.

Under these circumstances I felt that a simple restatement of the purposes of the bill would clear the air; and I sent the letter printed as Item 41 above.

The Senate passed the reorganization bill in March, 1938, by a vote of 49-42. In the House, however, the fight against the bill was led by Representative O'Connor, a constant obstructionist of progressive legislation (see Item 104, this volume). The pressure of propaganda was too great for the House of Representatives; and a motion to send the bill back to committee carried by a vote of 204-196 on April 8, 1938.

As soon as the House took this action, I addressed a letter to Representative Sam Rayburn, the majority leader of the House of Representatives, thanking him for his efforts and stating that there was no occasion for personal recrimination (see Item 44, this volume).

After the tumult and the shouting of the 1938 fight had died, the reactionary opponents of administrative reorganization apparently felt that their purpose had been accomplished. When a very similar reorganization bill was proposed in 1939, it passed with little opposition (see note to Item 44, this volume). During 1939 and 1940, I presented five plans for administrative reorganization, all of which became effective under the terms of the Act (see Items 66 and 77, 1939 volume; Items 24, 29, and 51, 1940 volume).

Although two years have since elapsed, the United States, in spite of all the dire predictions of the reactionaries, is still a democracy; and the witch-hunt for a dictatorship lurking in the reorganization bill now seems even more stupid and ridiculous than it did in 1938.

42 ❧ A Special Press Conference with Editors and Publishers of Trade Papers. Washington, D.C. April 8, 1938

(Government spending — Flood control — Checking soil erosion — Stabilization of farm prices — Need for wage and hour legislation — Tax evasion — Administrative reorganization.)

MR. RAY BILLS: The first thing that we would like to ask you is, while it has been deemed necessary to do a lot of direct pump priming, we would like to know, nevertheless, what other methods there are and in what ways we can help that would tend to increase private employment and make more prosperous times.

THE PRESIDENT: That is a pretty large order.

Q. If you have any specific suggestions on that phase, we would like to know them.

THE PRESIDENT: Well, let us take up one thing you mentioned: priming the pump. I think that is a pretty narrow view to take because, after all, your industries, and trades will be going after we are all dead. We hope they will be going in a private capitalistic system. That is what we are working for, to avoid having happen in this country what has happened in so many other countries. That is the long range. Therefore, I do not look at this just from the point of view of priming the 1938 pump. I am thinking about it in the terms of 1948, 1958 and 1968.

Money spent by the Government during the past few years and money that will be spent in the next few years is not merely money to put people to work at that particular moment with merely the result of adding to the national debt. It is also, in large part, money spent to do things that ought to have been done in the past and never were done.

Take our natural resources: We spent a lot of money there. Why? Of course it has put people to work, but, at the same time, it has greatly benefited this country from the standpoint of the year of 1968. It had to be done. The soil was running away.

On flood control, I will give you a very simple example from the point of view of dollars and cents. Take the old Tennessee River: The Tennessee River was destroying actual physical property—not counting only the soil but bridges, buildings, factories, homes, roads and highways, things of that kind—at an average rate prior to 1933 of between twenty-five and thirty million dollars a year. That was capital being destroyed, just absolutely removed. Of course that was insured against flood, and the insurance companies paid up, but that is destruction of capital just the same. It does not make much difference whether the owner pays or the insurance companies pay. We figured at that time that at a total ultimate cost of between three and four hundred million dollars we would eliminate, in toto, that annual cost of twenty-five or thirty million dollars. Well, that of course created a debt. Those particular public works have been paid for out of current appropriations, current taxes. It was not bonded.

Flood control on the Mississippi, on the Ohio, on the Connecticut, on the Susquehanna and Delaware—they all fall under the same category. In other words, by spending money for five or six or seven years, you get rid of a loss, an annual loss, running between 20 per cent—15 per cent to 20 per cent of the total expenditure. From the business point of view, that is pretty good financing.

Soil erosion comes under the same classification. We have soil erosion in the Northeast; we have it all over the country. If you can stop soil erosion, you are preventing the loss of capital. We are doing it on two bases.

As I said, this is for background. What I miss in the trade papers, as I do in 85 per cent of the daily press, is any positive approval of any of these things that are intended to save the Nation's capital.

I find in what might be called "the opposition press" of all kinds, the "Yes, but—" attitude. They will say, "Oh, yes, we are in favor of flood control, but we do not like this way of doing it." Or, "We do not like this party doing it, or this President doing it. We would rather have someone else doing it." "Soil erosion? Oh, yes, it is a fine thing to have in this country, but we object to the use of money for it."

With soil erosion goes the whole agricultural business, in which thirty or forty million people are engaged. One of the things that we have all felt—I think everybody believes in the principle—we want to cure is the wide cycle of swings that we have had in the past—two-dollar wheat up, and thirty-cent wheat down. In the farming business you cannot have any permanent purchasing power for the things that your industries produce, if the farmers have two-dollar wheat one time and thirty-cent wheat another time. You cannot have real purchasing power in the South if they have thirty-cent cotton one year, and four or five years after that they have four- or five-cent cotton. It just does not make any sense.

It throws people out of work in the industries of the nation if the farming population cannot buy their goods. It means unemployment, and that the Government has to spend a lot of money for relief. If that sort of thing continues in this country, it is going to make for radicalism. The people affected by those swings, going out of work or going broke on the farm, will stand it just so far. Education is spreading all through the country; and the farmers of the country who have been rather inarticulate on the whole in the past will not continue to be. The cotton farmer in the South, for example, is beginning to understand more about it, and if he is faced with the prospect of four- or five-cent cotton he is not going to lie down and calmly take it, as he has in the past. It makes for radicalism. We know some of our radical people out in the Northwest. It will encourage a recurrence of that radical movement in the Northwest, and it will spread through the corn belt.

That is why we have tried to get some kind of control over the big swings of crop prices. They are caused by the same sort of thing that happens in automobiles—excess production. There is too much wheat in storage and too much cotton carry-over. It is a business just like any other business, and when you get a carry-over that is very, very large, what do you do? You close the factory, you cut prices, you have to get rid of the unwieldy surplus. It is the same old story.

But what happens when you do propose a crop bill to meet that dangerous condition? Oh, I am not saying it is the ideal crop bill. No. But at least it is an effort. I don't begin to get from industry any kind of active, two-fisted support for such legislation. That is my complaint: I do not get two-fisted support. If they had a better idea as to what should be done, it would be fine; but the people who oppose a crop control bill do not propose any alternative. It is like a typical editorial in The New York Times: "Oh, yes, we are in favor of maintaining good prices for crops but this bill is terrible. It is regimentation on the farmer." Period, end of the paragraph, end of the story! (*Laughter*)

Come to some of the other things — wages and hours legislation, for example. Take any one of four or five dozen big papers. "Oh, yes, we are in favor of good wages, but the Wages and Hours Bill, that is unthinkable."

All right, I had one in the other day and I said, "I just read your editorial and that is just what you said. Now, I will give you three examples, one a little factory in New England, paying girls four and a half or five dollars a week." He said, "Well, conditions compel it."

I said, "When we had NRA, those girls were getting eleven dollars a week and the industry seemed to survive and the girls had purchasing power."

"Yes," he said, "that is right."

Well, was it bad when everybody was paying eleven dollars a week to those girls? No, it worked pretty well.

Number two: Down in the South there is a little old cotton factory that has spindles that date back to 1880, something like that. A little group of people in the South found a mill in New England which had been closed for a couple of years during the period when most of the cotton mills in New England closed — it was in the 1929 panic. This little group bought all of these New England spindles that were already fifty years old and they moved them down to Georgia. They got an old factory and started up. Well, of course it is highly, completely inefficient. That type of factory ought not to be in existence.

Well, they have managed to hang on by their eyelids since then, by paying four and five dollars a week to the operators in the mill. That is not their average, taking in consideration those who are paid at a higher rate; but a great many, I think the majority of their operators, are getting less than seven dollars a week. They are going on, competing with properly equipped, modern mills that pay good wages.

Now, out West, in one or two factories that we know of, they are working people sixty hours a week since the NRA went out. I call that unfair competition. Whenever you start to get a wages and hours bill, the Congressman for that particular district gets a piteous plea, "For God's sake don't do anything or you won't go back to Congress." So, he tries to get an amendment to take care of his district. That is pure selfishness.

Now, on the wages and hours bill, we have two simple objectives and both will put more people back to work. One is a floor under wages — I don't care what it is, so long as it is a reasonable floor; and the other is a ceiling for hours, so as to put industry on a fair basis.

But, do I get support from industry for a wages and hours bill along that line? No, I don't want a drastic thing at once that says it cannot be over forty hours a week, under any circumstances even with overtime. That is a thing we have to work up toward gradually over a period of years. I would just as soon start with the present average scale. In the South the average wage of people working in lumber mills is 22½ cents an hour and out on the Coast the same type of work in lumber mills calls for 79 cents an hour. "And," says one editorial, "wouldn't it be certainly crazy suddenly to jump these people in the South from 22½ cents to 79 cents an hour?" Well, of course nobody ever suggested it.

The bulk of industry, I honestly believe, wants a floor and a ceiling; and it does not want anything drastic done that will throw everything out.

Let us take your lumber people in the South: Here is the

lumber trade. They spend, the Southern Pine Association, thousands of dollars advertising all through the South, and what does the advertisement say? It says, "Farmers to arms!" Now, that is a nice thing for industry to advertise in the paper, "Farmers to arms!" They then say, "If this terrible Wages and Hours Bill goes through, you farmers will have to pay for your field labor a minimum of three dollars a day." Of course, the fact is that there has never been any thought of including field labor in the Wages and Hours Bill.

And then, in the women's magazines and papers, they have full-page ads, "Housewives beware! If the Wages and Hours Bill goes through, you will have to pay your Negro girl eleven dollars a week." Of course, you know if you come from the South, you can employ lots of excellent domestic help in the South for board and lodging and three or four dollars a week.

No law ever suggested intended a minimum wages and hours bill to apply to domestic help.

Now, why can't industry come out as a whole and furnish positive help in getting a reasonable floor and a reasonable roof. I don't get any positive help. I can go on with a dozen different subjects — desirable objectives on which I am not getting positive help. It is always holding back. They say, "Yes, I am in favor of the principle but —" How many people really mean that, that they are in favor of the principle?

Take the question of taxes, for example. I will give you a couple of very simple propositions to think over: Today it is the national policy, whether we like it or not — it is generally accepted by the people and you will never be able to change it — to maintain a graduated tax upon personal incomes.

Now, that being so, have I had any help from industry when I have sought to eliminate abuses of that principle? How many of your papers supported me last year when I tried to eliminate the Bahamas corporations, the incorporation of yachts, the incorporation of farms, et cetera and so on? Did any of you people come out and say, "By gosh, the President is dead right on that." These fellows who are using that kind of expedients to avoid taxation are evading the law, perhaps not the letter of the law because it is awfully hard to draw a law without any legal loopholes. But did you give me any support in regard to evasion of the spirit of the law? I ask you that question very seriously.

A great lawyer in New York — I don't give a rap about names, names have nothing to do with it — a big lawyer in New York discovered what looked like a legal way, and probably was, strictly speaking. He goes down to the Bahamas and for two hundred and fifty dollars incorporates a life insurance company in the Bahamas. He is in the upper brackets. He and four or five other people in the upper brackets go to the president of the new company, who is a law clerk in this man's office, and say, "I want to insure myself for a million dollars." The president says, "Fine, here is your policy. Please pay us a premium." Of course the amount of the premium was high — $100,000. "Here is my check. Now, Mr. President, my managing clerk, I want to borrow a million dollars on that policy." So he is given another check, and borrows a million dollars, and he pays interest on that at a high rate, and deducts that from his personal income tax.

Another big man has a wife who happens to be extremely wealthy. This is legal, mind you, perfectly legal, and they have a lot of children, seven or eight children. His wife makes him trustee for, I don't know what, five or six million dollars for the children, but it is a revocable trust. She can end it tomorrow and get all the securities back. She turns these securities over to her husband, and then proceeds to borrow the whole amount back on the securities and deducts the interest on that loan from her net income, which means that instead of paying, roughly, on four or five hundred thousand dollars a year net, her net is only eighty or a hundred thousand dollars.

Now, there is no moral indignation among you business men, among you people who represent them, when you hear about these things.

There are not only those evasions. You have today the capital gains tax. I take it that most of us in this room are fixed about the same way, financially. Occasionally we can make a capital gain, through an investment or the purchase and later sale of a piece of property, we can make a capital gain of five or ten thousand dollars. A good many of you have done it; I have done it. The rate under this proposed Senate bill is 15 per cent. I have a very good friend of mine that has a profit on 10,000 shares of a certain stock, which he has held more than a year, of $500,000. He is pretty good; we are none of us in that class, I take it. Now, under the theory of taxation, he ought to pay more than 15 per cent, under the Senate bill, he does not.

On undistributed profits, I know two brothers who inherited a business and ran it together, jointly, for quite a while. It is a good business and its actual value is about $10,000,000.

One of these brothers got to be fifty years old and, with a good deal of common sense, he said, "I am getting $250,000 a year out of this business. I am not a high liver. I only spend about $50,000. I guess I will get out. I want to retire, see the world and have a quiet time." So his brother, in a perfectly friendly way, buys him out and now owns the business. Of course he still owes the $5,000,000 he borrowed to pay to the brother who got out.

The brother who got out went to Scudder, Stevens and Clark and said, "I have got $5,000,000 in cash. Give me a recommended list of investments." They did, a good sound list, which contained some Governments, and municipals, and first mortgage real estate, and first mortgage railroads, and some preferred and common stock. It was a perfectly sound distribution of a five million dollar investment.

He, of course, had no way of escaping any of his personal income tax. They were all corporations, a hundred different

corporations. His net was $200,000 a year from these invest-
ments. On that he had to pay about — what is it on $200,000.
It is up to about 50 per cent — he had to pay $100,000 in in-
come taxes.

His brother is still engaged in the business. His business
made $200,000 over and above the proper amount that
should be applied to depreciation and put into surplus. He
had $200,000 as his profit. But he did not declare it. He only
wanted to use $50,000, so he left $150,000 in the treasury of
his company, and declared a dividend of $50,000 to himself.
The net result that his tax was only $10,000.

Now, is that equitable? The money of both those fellows
was working, there is no question about that. In one case it
was working in one mill, and in the other case it was working through one hundred different corporations.

Now, do I find, among business men, any effort to help me
to equalize that sort of thing?

Taking the case of a very rich man whom you all know —
we won't mention any names — he had a corporation that was
worth about $15,000,000. He knew he was going to die. He
got to be — oh, I don't know — sixty-five years old and he
knew that his expectancy of life was another five or ten years.
His corporation had an absolutely adequate surplus to carry
on the business. Everybody knew that, and he admitted it.

He said to himself, "By gosh, I might die and then my
estate will have to pay a pretty heavy inheritance tax." So he
started in, and out of the earnings of his corporation, he accumulated for the next eight or nine years $3,000,000 of ad-
ditional surplus, unnecessary surplus. He died and his heirs
have, let us say, ten certificates of stock representing the entire ownership of this corporation, a fifteen million dollar
corporation. They have to find $3,000,000 in cash; so they
take two of these certificates and sell them to the corporation for $3,000,000, taking the $3,000,000 to pay the inheritance tax. Now, the surplus is decreased by that amount, but

they still own eight certificates which represent 100 per cent of the ownership of the corporation.

In other words, that accumulation for the purpose of paying an inheritance tax was accumulated not on the personal income tax rate but on the 12½ per cent corporation tax which was the rate at that time. Is that fair?

Now, that is the kind of thing that we are trying to eliminate, and that is all. It is merely equalization. It is fair trade practice in taxation. But do I get any help on it?

Well, I have said a lot of things and have covered a lot of ground. But I want to emphasize that from industry itself, this Government is getting lip service and that is about all, in trying to correct unfair trade practices. That is where you people, if you leave out politics entirely — for it is not a question of politics, but a question of Government — if you get in behind us and help up and down the line, would be rendering a fine public service.

Have you got any more thoughts?

Q. You have supplied the text for a number of editorials, Mr. President.

THE PRESIDENT: You can be of perfectly tremendous help. Of course you people have not taken any part in this question of reorganization. The Reorganization Bill is absolutely nothing new in my young life. We have had the problem for forty or more years. You could not run your business the way the United States Government is set up, largely because of politics. Let us call it that, because it is perfectly true.

I have been getting along with a perfectly inefficient machine for five years, and I can do it for the next three and one-quarter years. But people have been talking about the grant of powers involved.

I don't care — let Congress reorganize. But when Congress starts to reorganize what happens?

We have, for example, in this Government today six or seven different agencies that are engaged in making maps. I don't mean field work, I mean printing maps. We have six or seven map-printing establishments right here in Washington, and some through the country. Do you think that Congress can ever be induced to consolidate them? Oh, no, the pressure from those six or seven bureaus would be too strong. They would say, "Leave us alone, we want these six or seven map-making plants in the District of Columbia." Congress won't do it.

Yet they have all agreed that somebody ought to do it. Well, there isn't anybody to do it, unfortunately, except the President. A year ago they thought that the idea was perfectly grand, but today they find that it is giving him certain powers. I don't want the powers, God knows. If the thing does not go through, I will rock along all right.

As far as powers go, I figured out the other day that there is not a single power I have that Hoover and Coolidge did not have. Can anyone name any power I have today that Hoover and Coolidge did not have? . . .

You spoke this morning about priming the pump again. We are going to spend more money if we can get it out quickly. It is going to help this immediate situation; but it is not that alone, it is the long range end of it that is important. In using that money along that line, somebody has to spend it. If Congress wants to earmark every dollar of it, that is all right. But again, you cannot get Congress to earmark every project. It is impossible. You cannot turn it over to the courts, it would be unconstitutional.

You have to turn it over to the Executive Department under the Constitution. Earmark all you want, as far as you can, but somebody has to spend the money. It is not a power which I desire. It means setting up machinery overnight. I would much rather Congress earmark it, but you know what you would get if they did. You would get a "You scratch my back, I will scratch yours." You would get a pork barrel bill.

I am glad you do not have to talk in your trade papers on the immediate political things of the moment. You are free agents. You are working for business, and so am I. I think you are in a very, very fortunate position. I have absolutely no sympathy for you, as I have for the daily newspaper people. (*Laughter*)

You are going strong, keep it up.

(See note to Item 24, this volume, for discussion of the stabilization of farm prices; see Item 57 and note, 1937 volume, for an account of wages and hours legislation; see Item 65 and note, 1937 volume, for tax evasion and measures taken to check it; see note to Item 41, this volume, for a discussion of administrative reorganization.)

43 ⟨ The President Again Recommends a New Airport for Washington, D.C. April 9, 1938

My dear Mr. Chairman:

I AM writing you again in regard to the serious, long-standing failure to get an adequate airport or airports for the Nation's Capital.

The situation is such that if a serious accident takes place the blame will fall, I fear, on the Congress itself.

If you do not mind my offering unsolicited but, I believe, practical advice, here it is:

(a) The present Washington–Hoover field can never be made of permanent service for commercial planes entering or leaving the Capital — because of its low altitude and the impossibility of providing long enough runways in all directions. Until a better field or fields can be provided, we shall have to continue the use of the Washington–Hoover airport, and I am entirely willing, as a temporary matter, to have the Military Road closed and any other slight temporary improvements made. This, however, is, of course, not a final solution.

(b) We need to get a full-sized, all-weather airport as quickly as possible. I have surveyed all available sites and conclude that the Camp Springs site is the only one which can be bought at a reasonable figure and put into actual operation inside of a year and a half. It requires little grading and the work can be done in large part by WPA labor. At the Camp Springs site we should buy at least two thousand acres of land, and on this land we can get runways of any required length in all directions.

Objection has been raised by the Navy Department because of the Radio Receiving Station five miles away. This matter, I think, we can work out in conference between your Committee and the Naval Affairs Committee, and it should not prohibit us from using what is, by all odds, the best all-weather airport for planes of every size.

(c) The only objection to Camp Springs is its distance from the center of the hotel and shopping district. The Capital of the United States need not, and should not, be limited to one airport. For commercial and military reasons we should have two.

I, therefore, recommend that the Gravelly Point site be also developed. This is primarily a pumping proposition. It is infinitely better than the Washington–Hoover field but is not a 100 per cent site for long-distance flying or flying when there is a river fog. It would take four or five years to complete the Gravelly Point airport, as the fill would have to be high and require a long time to settle. Nevertheless, I think that if the work is spread over four or five years, the annual cost will not be heavy and the Capital will have another airport which could be used under good weather conditions, which, incidentally, occur over 75 per cent of the time. Also, the Gravelly Point site is only ten or twelve minutes from the center of things, as against thirty minutes to the Camp Springs site.

It is because I visualize this subject not only as one of immediate emergency to prevent serious accidents, but also as one which looks to greatly increased air traffic in the future, that I hope quick action can be taken at this session.

Very sincerely yours,

Honorable Morris Sheppard,
Chairman, Military Affairs Committee,
United States Senate,
Washington, D.C.

(An identical letter was sent to Honorable Andrew J. May, Chairman, Military Affairs Committee, House of Representatives.)

(For further discussion of the Washington airport, see Items 127 and 139, this volume; and Item 103, 1940 volume.)

44 ❮ A Message on the Defeat of the Reorganization Bill. April 9, 1938

Dear Sam:

THANKS for the fine fight. Will you also thank the Speaker and the others.

The reorganization bill is intended to simplify and improve the public service. With this single objective in view, I have given it my earnest approval.

The question presented is solely one of policy. Therefore, the legislative developments of yesterday offer no occasion for personal recrimination, and there should be none.

Very sincerely yours,

Honorable Sam Rayburn,
House of Representatives,
Washington, D.C.

NOTE: The proposals of the President's Committee on Administrative Management (see Items 241, 241A, 1936 volume) were for the most part embodied in bills which were introduced in the Congress during 1937 and 1938.

During the third session of the Seventy-fifth Congress, a reorganization bill passed the Senate, but because of the pressure of manufactured propaganda it failed of passage in the House of Representatives (see note to Item 41, this volume).

The foregoing letter was written to Majority Leader Rayburn immediately after the reorganization bill had been defeated.

The Reorganization Act of 1939, however, received little opposition during the first session of the Seventy-sixth Congress, and was approved by me on April 3, 1939 (Public No. 19, Seventy-sixth Congress, 53 Stat. 561).

According to the terms of the Reorganization Act of 1939, the President is directed to investigate the organization of all executive agencies of the government and to determine the changes necessary to accomplish the following purposes:

"1. To reduce expenditures to the fullest extent consistent with the efficient operation of the Government;

"2. To increase the efficiency of the operations of the Government to the fullest extent practicable within the revenues;

"3. To group, coordinate, and consolidate agencies of the Government, as nearly as may be, according to major purposes;

"4. To reduce the number of agencies by consolidating those having similar functions under a single head, and to abolish such agencies as may not be necessary for the efficient conduct of the Government; and

"5. To eliminate overlapping and duplication of effort."

It was provided that when the President, after investigation, finds that transfer, consolidation, or abolition of functions is necessary to accomplish one of the above objectives, he should transmit to the Congress a reorganization plan embodying his specific proposals. The plan becomes effective if Congress does not within sixty days pass a concurrent resolution disapproving the plan.

The Act did not embody several of the original recommendations of the Committee on Administrative Management. It failed to include any provisions for developing the general Accounting Office and the Comptroller General into an independent postauditing agency. It exempted a number of independent boards and commissions from the terms of the Act. It did not touch upon the suggestion that a single-headed administrator be established to direct the Civil Service Administration. (The recommendations of the Committee regarding civil service were later carried out, however, through the establishment of the Liaison Office for Personnel Management; see note to Item 125, 1939 volume.) Finally, it made no provision for the addition of Departments of Public Works and Social Welfare to the ten major executive departments. However, the Act did authorize the appointment of six administrative assistants to the President, as recommended by the Committee on Administrative Management.

During 1939 and 1940, I submitted five reorganization plans to the Congress, all of which became effective when the Congress defeated moves to vote them down (see Items 66 and 77, 1939 volume; Items 24, 29 and 51, 1940 volume).

45 ❧ The President Transmits to the Congress Recommendations on the Railroad Problem. April 11, 1938

To the Congress:

DURING the past month I have consulted with a large number of individuals on the increasingly difficult problem of our railroad transportation. As the Congress is aware, the relationship of the Federal Government to the railroads has been for fifty years through the medium of the Interstate Commerce Commission. This distinguished body was originally set up with the primary purpose of ending serious abuses on the part of the carriers, such as rebating and cutthroat competition.

As the years went by the Congress, from time to time, has extended the authority of the Interstate Commerce Commission, vesting in it other quasi-legislative and quasi-judicial powers and giving to it also a number of purely executive functions. While the latter powers are, in all probability, unconstitutional in that they create executive authority in a fourth branch of the Government instead of in the President, I do not at this time raise that issue because for the present it is more important for all of us to cooperate in preventing serious bankruptcies among a large number of railroad companies, great and small.

I invited Chairman Splawn of the Interstate Commerce Commission, and Commissioners Eastman and Mahaffie to present somewhat hurriedly and informally, recommendations relating to this serious situation—and I have kept the chairmen of the appropriate committees of the Senate and House of Representatives informed of the report.

Summarized, the three members of the Interstate Commerce Commission recommend as a means of immediate relief the following:

1. That approximately $300,000,000 be made available from Gov-

ernment funds for the purchase of railroad equipment, the equipment to be the security for the advance.

2. That for twelve months the Reconstruction Finance Corporation be empowered to make loans without certification by the Interstate Commerce Commission that the railroad can meet its fixed charges.

3. That other forms of Government credit be considered from the point of view of public policy.

4. That Government traffic pay the full rate by eliminating land grant reductions.

5. That the Commission does not feel justified in expressing an opinion for or against reduction of railroad wages.

6. That reorganization procedure under section 77 of the Bankruptcy Act receive the attention of the Congress, and they suggest consideration of the establishment of a single court in charge of reorganizations.

The long-term program suggested by the Commissioners includes:

1. That a Federal Transportation Authority be created for two years to plan and promote action by railroad companies to eliminate waste, aid consolidation and coordination.

2. That the Interstate Commerce Act be amended to broaden the powers of the Commission with respect to pooling of earnings or traffic, to eliminate "the consolidation plan," and to approve unifications; that the Authority be permitted to intervene in such proceedings before the Commission, and make recommendations through the Commission to the President and the Congress.

3. That the Authority investigate economy and all types of transportation, encourage special fitness, and abate destructive competition.

4. That attention be given to railroad financial abuses now under investigation.

The full report of the three members of the Interstate Commerce Commission is transmitted herewith, and I am transmitting also certain comments which have been made by others with whom I have talked:

(*a*) Letter to the President from the Secretary of the Treasury, March 25, 1938.

(*b*) Letter to the President from the Chairman of the Reconstruction Finance Corporation, March 28, 1938.

(*c*) Letter to the President from the Chairman of the Securities and Exchange Commission, March 28, 1938.

(*d*) Memorandum to the President from Assistant Secretary of Commerce Ernest G. Draper, March 29, 1938.

(*e*) Memorandum to the President from the Administrator of Farm Security, March 31, 1938.

(*f*) Memorandum to the President from Henry Bruere, president of the Bowery Savings Bank, New York City.

(*g*) Memorandum to the President from J. J. Pelley, president, Association of American Railroads, April 4, 1938.

(*h*) Letter to the President from George M. Harrison, president, Brotherhood of Railway and Steamship Clerks, April 2, 1938.

(*i*) Statistical data from the Interstate Commerce Commission relating to revenues and expenses of transportation in the United States in the year 1936, separated between types of transport.

Insofar as information in regard to the railroad problem is concerned, there is probably no other subject to which the Congress, year after year, has devoted more study or obtained more information. The troubles of the railroads are not new, but they have been getting, on the whole, steadily more difficult since before the World War. It is true that a general upturn in business would undoubtedly help to keep many railroads from actual receivership. But it is also true that resumption of traffic at last year's level would not solve their growing difficulties permanently.

Most of us have definite objection to Government subsidies to the railroads to enable them to meet the interest on their outstanding bonds or for any other purpose, and most of us also oppose Government ownership and operation of the railroads. I do.

The suggestions made by the three members of the Interstate Commerce Commission should, of course, be read in the light of the comments thereon made in the letters appended thereto.

I ask your special consideration of the fact that matters relating to transportation in its wider sense are now dealt with by the following departments or agencies of the Government:

1. The Bureau of Public Roads of the Department of Agriculture.

2. The Bureau of Air Commerce of the Department of Commerce.

3. The United States Maritime Commission.

4. The Division of Transportation of the Bureau of Foreign and Domestic Commerce of the Department of Commerce.

5. The Interstate Commerce Commission.

6. The Lighthouse Service of the Department of Commerce.

7. The Bureau of Navigation and Marine Inspection of the Department of Commerce.

These agencies deal with special phases of transportation rather than the transportation problem in its broader national aspect. Some of the functions are executive, some are legislative, and some are judicial.

From the point of view of business efficiency, such as a private corporation would seek, it would seem to be the part of common sense to place all executive functions relating to all transportation in one Federal department — such as the Department of Commerce, the Department of the Interior, or some other old or new department. At the same time all quasi-judicial and quasi-legislative matters relating to all transportation could properly be placed under an independent commission — a reorganized Interstate Commerce Commission. And such action would be highly constitutional.

I refer to this, not by way of recommendation, but only as one method which should receive congressional study.

In the meantime, and until it has been possible for the Congress to make any and all studies for permanent solution of the railroad problem, some immediate legislation is, I believe, necessary at this session, in order to prevent serious financial and operating difficulties between now and the convening of the next Congress.

NOTE: On March 15, 1938, I called together at the White House a group of men to consider the serious financial situation of the railroads of the country, and to suggest what action, if any, could and should be taken by the Federal Government for the relief or improvement of existing conditions. There were included in the group, representatives of the Senate and House Committees on Interstate Commerce, the Departments of Treasury, Agriculture, and Commerce, the Interstate Commerce Commission, the Reconstruction Finance Corporation, the Securities and Exchange Commission, and other citizens concerned with the railroad situation from the points of view of management, employees, and security holders.

The conference was continued on March 17, 1938; and I requested a committee, made up of the Chairman and two other members of the Interstate Commerce Commission, to confer and consult with the other members of the group, and to report specific recommendations.

This committee consulted representatives of the railroad, motor truck, and motor bus industries, as well as shippers and workers themselves. It collated much valuable information in regard to general economic conditions and the bearing of transportation on them.

The committee submitted its report to me on March 24, 1938; and I transmitted it to the Congress with the foregoing message.

In addition to this report of the three members of the Interstate Commerce Commission, I transmitted suggestions and recommendations which had been made to me by others with whom I had talked on the general subject. They are all enumerated in my message above.

The recommendations made by the three members of the Interstate Commerce Commission are listed by me in the message. Six of these recommendations were suggested as means of immediate relief; and four of them as part of a long term program.

All these reports, suggestions, and recommendations were transmitted by me to provide a basis for consideration by the Congress of the whole railroad problem.

Taking up separately the recommendations of the members of the Interstate Commerce Commission as summarized in my foregoing message:

Recommendation No. 1, proposed as a means of immediate relief, did not result in any Congressional legislation. However, since the date the message was submitted, the Interstate Commerce Commission has approved loans to railroads totaling $55,000,000, made by the Reconstruction Finance Corporation for the purchase of cars or locomotives, where such equipment was furnished as the security for the loan for the full purchase price thereof.

Recommendation No. 2 was adopted by legislation.

With respect to recommendation No. 3, the Reconstruction Finance Corporation has, since the time of the message, used its credit to assist the Boston & Maine Railroad in a voluntary reorganization of its capital structure. Furthermore, the Transportation Act of 1940 (Title III, Part III, Sec. 331) has increased the total amount which the Reconstruction Finance Corporation may devote to railroad loans.

Recommendation No. 4 was adopted, subject to some conditions, in the Transportation Act of 1940 (Title III, Part II, Sec. 321).

Recommendation No. 5 was really not a recommendation but a statement of conflicting views on the general question of reduction of wages and salaries. Subsequently the railroads sought to bring about a horizontal reduction of 15 per cent in the wages of their employees. Under the Railway Labor Act this resulted in the creation of an emergency fact-finding board. On October 29, 1938, this emergency board made its report, which was adverse to the railroads (see note to Item 14, 1937 volume).

As of January 1, 1941, no legislation embodying the sixth recommendation has been enacted, al-though a bill providing, among other things, for a single court to have charge of railroad bankruptcy proceedings has passed one house of the Congress.

With respect to the recommendations made as a long term program, the first, second, and third recommendations enumerated in my message have not been embodied, as of January 1, 1941, in any legislation. However, in conformity with this suggestion, the Transportation Act of 1940 (Title I, Sec. 7) amended the Interstate Commerce Act by eliminating the so-called "Consolidation Plan." At the same time it created a temporary board of investigation and research (Title III, Part I, Sec. 301) to continue, among other things, the investigations recommended in the said report.

With respect to recommendation No. 4, no legislation, except for one minor matter, has been enacted as of January 1, 1941.

46 ❬ A Tribute to Benjamin Franklin. April 12, 1938

My dear Mr. Staples:

I REGRET exceedingly that I shall be unable to be with you on May nineteenth for the dedication of the Benjamin Franklin Memorial at which time an heroic statue of Franklin to be placed in Franklin Hall of the Memorial will be unveiled.

One of the greatest and most useful of public men in our colonial and early national periods, Franklin with every generation looms ever larger in world history. Time, as we know, is a great leveler and shows little respect to any save those whose lives are linked with great achievements. But Franklin touched the life of his time at so many angles and his character showed so many and such diversified facets that he would be sure of remembrance on account of any one of several achievements.

Now, nearly a hundred and fifty years after his death, his accomplishments assume their due proportions. As statesman, diplomatist, economist, philosopher and scientist he would have a claim upon the respect of posterity even though he had not given us the immortal "Autobiography," reflecting in every page the true wisdom and sound common sense of which Franklin was the embodiment. It is in keeping with his strongly practical nature that the Memorial you are dedicating will serve a useful purpose.

Very sincerely yours,

Philip C. Staples, Esq.,
The Franklin Institute,
Philadelphia, Pennsylvania.

47 ❡ The President Discusses the Pending Tax Bill. April 13, 1938

Dear Mr. Chairman:

THE REVENUE BILL as it passed the House and the Revenue Bill just adopted by the Senate differ in many particulars. While differences in detail can, I am confident, be ironed out in conference committee without sacrifice of fundamental principles, in two major respects important principles of fairness in taxation are in issue. I wish to bring these two matters briefly to your attention at this time.

1. *Capital Gains.* — For many years the country has accepted without question the principle of taxation in accordance with ability to pay. This principle applies to all forms of additional

wealth accruing to individuals. There is no fairness in taxing the salaried man and the merchant upon their incomes and taxing at far lower rates the profits on the capital of the speculator. Nor is it fair to subject the salaried man and the merchant to progressive surtaxes upon their earnings and at the same time to tax capital gains, large or small, at the same flat rate, to the particular advantage of the taxpayer who otherwise would pay much higher surtax rates. In other words, as a matter of principle, if additional wealth in the form of earnings from business, such as dividends, interest, or wages, is taxed at progressive rates then capital gains should also be taxed at progressive rates.

The present law treats capital gains very favorably — more favorably than dividends, interest, or salaries earned over similar periods of time. The advantage given to capital gains under the present law, as compared to ordinary income, in many cases runs as high as 50 per cent. Under the Senate Bill this preferential advantage is further increased by reducing the tax to a flat rate, no matter how large are the taxpayer's capital gains or how large his other income. For example, a man who makes a capital gain in a given year amounting to $5000 would have to pay a tax of not more than 15 per cent; while at the same time the man who makes capital gains of $500,000 in a given year will also pay a tax of not more than 15 per cent. Desirable as it is to foster business recovery, we should not do so by creating injustices in the tax system, particularly injustices at the expense of the man who earns his income — injustices to the advantage of the man who does not.

2. *Corporation Taxes.* — For many years the Congress has sought to devise a fair system for taxing incomes from business, whether received by individual proprietors, by partnerships, or by corporations. Legally the corporation is a separate entity from the individuals who own it. Hence, while individual proprietors and partners are taxable at the usual normal tax and surtax rates upon the entire incomes of their businesses, whether taken out of the business or left in it, the corporate charter sets up a Chinese wall which prevents the earnings from being taxed to

the shareholders who really own them, unless those earnings are actually distributed to the shareholders in the form of dividends. Thus a wide and basically unfair disparity between the taxation of individual proprietors and partnerships on the one hand, and of corporations on the other is created, unless some provision for taxing undistributed corporation earnings appears in the law.

At present, corporations are taxable on their earnings at a normal rate of from 8 to 15 per cent, whether the earnings are paid out in dividends or not. If dividends are declared, the individual stockholders who get the earnings pay an additional normal personal income tax. If their incomes are large enough, they pay progressive surtaxes also. Consequently, the Treasury stands to lose where the corporation does not distribute earnings, whereas if earnings were distributed, the Treasury would collect additional taxes on the personal income tax returns of the stockholders. Moreover, with no undistributed profits tax, the partnership or individual proprietor is discriminated against as compared to the corporation. Finally, with no undistributed profits tax, the avoidance of surtaxes through the use of the corporation becomes a readily available device, for those persons in the higher surtax brackets, who seek legally to keep their net personal incomes down for taxpaying purposes, and to hide their actual profits by leaving them in the corporations they own.

For these reasons and others, I recommended the undistributed profits tax in 1936, and the Congress adopted it. Modifications shown by experience to be desirable, in particular the exemption of small corporations, should be made, but the principle of the tax is sound, and it should be retained in our tax system. Otherwise we grant a definite incentive to the avoidance of personal income tax payments through methods which are legal, but which are contrary to the spirit of the principle that every citizen should pay taxes in accordance with his means. It would be particularly undesirable to eliminate the undistributed profits tax at this time, in favor of a flat rate of tax, representing an increase in the tax burden on many small corporations, and on all corporations which follow established American practices of dividend distribution; and a decrease in the tax burden of many large corporations, which have hoarded their earnings in the past, and would be encouraged to resume the practice in the future.

The Bill as passed by the House gives a flat exemption from the undistributed profits tax to those smaller corporations which make net earnings up to $25,000 per year. Out of the total of 200,000 taxpaying corporations, approximately 176,000 are exempted from the undistributed profits tax under this provision. This means that any young and growing corporation earning up to $25,000 per year can in the discretion of its directors set aside all its earnings for growth and expansion. Moreover, under the House Bill, corporations with incomes in excess of $25,000 can also accumulate reserves for legitimate purposes by paying an additional tax of only from 1 to 4 per cent on undistributed earnings.

There are many other provisions in the two bills which will improve the equity of the tax system, and the efficiency of its administration. Some pending amendments grant unjustifiable exemptions from a fair general rule, complicate the law, and should be eliminated. It is most important, however, to hold fast to that which is good in the tax system. Equal taxation of incomes of similar size and equal taxation of corporations and individual taxpayers are axiomatic. The repeal of the undistributed profits tax and the reduction of the tax on capital gains to a fraction of the tax on other forms of income strike at the root of fundamental principles of taxation.

Business will be helped, not hurt, by these suggestions.

Faithfully,

Honorable Robert L. Doughton,
Chairman, Ways and Means Committee,
House of Representatives,
Washington, D.C.

(An identical letter was sent to Honorable Pat Harrison, Chairman, Finance Committee, United States Senate, Washington, D. C.)

NOTE: The foregoing letter was sent by me to the responsible chairmen of the House and Senate committees which were then considering the Revenue bill of 1938. As it had passed the House of Representatives, it differed in two important respects from the bill as it had passed the Senate. These two differences involved the treatment of capital gains and losses and the taxation of corporation income.

I pointed out that the existing law favored those who had made substantial capital gains as compared with other forms of income, in that it provided that only certain percentages of such gains should be taken into account in computing net income. I also indicated that under the pending Senate bill this advantage was proposed to be increased, since it provided a flat rate of tax on capital gains regardless of the amount of the taxpayer's income, instead of graduating it on the principle of ability to pay.

With respect to corporation taxes, I reaffirmed my conviction that an undistributed profits tax should be continued, with slight modifications to help smaller corporations. The principle of this tax is to prevent widespread evasion of taxes on what is really personal income through the accumulation of corporate earnings. (For further discussion of the taxation of undistributed corporate surplus profits, see Items 29, 1936 volume; Item 144, 1937 volume; Item 54 (pages 265-274), this volume.)

After my letter the Conference Committee of the two Houses deliberated for almost a month and submitted its report on May 11, 1938. The Conference bill was a compromise between the two, and was wholly unsatisfactory with respect to both objections raised by me. The bill was passed, however, on May 16, 1938; and for the first time, either as Governor of New York or President of the United States, I permitted a bill to become a law without my signature.

The reason for this is that I did not want to veto the bill because it contained many provisions which were not only desirable but essential, and I would have had to veto the entire bill in order to disapprove these unsatisfactory provisions. On the other hand, I wished emphatically to express executive disapproval of the unfair and discriminatory provisions relating to taxation of capital gains and corporation incomes.

I explained my action on this bill in a speech delivered at Arthurdale, West Virginia, on May 27, 1938, which is printed as Item 67, this volume.

48 ⟨ "Our Ideal Is Democratic Liberty . . . Our Method Is Increased Understanding . . . Our Basis Is Confidence." Address to Pan American Union. April 14, 1938

My friends of Pan America:

THERE could be no more fitting occasion than the present for me to greet my friends of the twenty other American Republics. We have learned in this Western Hemisphere what community of interest really means. We have worked for it, created it, and now we glory in it. Properly, therefore, Pan American Day is set aside as an annual testimony to the significance which the American family of nations has for the whole world.

Never was that significance greater than today. The twenty-one American Republics present proudly to the rest of the world a demonstration that the rule of justice and law can be substituted for the rule of force; that resort to war as an instrument of policy is not necessary; that international differences of all kinds can be solved through peaceful negotiation; that the sanctity of the pledged word faithfully observed and generously interpreted offers a system of security with freedom. The three hundred millions of people who live in the American Republics are not different from other human beings. We have the same problems, the same differences, even the same material, for controversy which exists on other continents. Yet, we have undertaken contractual obligations to solve these normal human differences by maintaining peace; and that peace we are firmly resolved to maintain. It shall not be endangered by controversies within our own family; and we will not permit it to be endangered from aggression coming from outside of our own hemisphere.

This, a common objective of all of us, forms a lasting foundation for the maintenance of an international understanding that is unique in the history of civilization.

The American peoples, who today fortunately live as good

neighbors, not only enjoy a privilege, but undertake a heavy responsibility. Fortunate in being remote from the tumult of conflicting doctrines and from the horrors of armed conflict — from the tragedies whose shadows lie heavy on the world, the American Republics, nevertheless, face a serious test. If our good fortune is to continue, our will must be strong.

All of us, in every Republic, gained our independence because our fathers were willing to sacrifice their lives and all that they possessed for a great ideal. Some part of that duty to sacrifice rests also on us, their children. We have progressed far along the path that leads to government by the people in the interest of all the people. Our democratic system has conferred on all of us an inestimable gift of individual liberty within the law. We are vitally concerned with preserving the high standards of international restraint, international culture and international morality, which the lesson of centuries has taught is the first requirement of peaceful relationships between nations.

Now, more than ever before, we of this American Hemisphere must make plain that these principles, upon which so great a civilization is founded, are vibrant, productive and dynamic. National and international law and morality are not the restraints of weaklings; they are signs of serene strength — confidence in our purpose, and in our ability to maintain independence and democracy.

Particularly I am glad that in December of this present year representatives of all of our governments will once more assemble. This time it will be in the great capital of Peru. During these turbulent years the Inter-American Conferences have come to be an instrument for bringing ever closer the relationships between our several nations. In Lima we have a renewed opportunity to counsel together. I assure you that we in the United States have found peculiarly welcome the views, the opinions and the friendly advice of the statesmen of our sister republics. Public opinion in all of our countries benefits from learning with greater frequency and in greater extent the thoughts, the desires and the needs of the peoples of the other American nations.

In constant testimony of our mutual friendship and trust is the increasing progress in communications. The North, Central and South American voices which reach us through the air are the voices of friends. Only a short time ago the people of the United States were enabled to hear a gracious message broadcast to them by my friend, the President of Argentina, and a few days later they listened to the address delivered to them by the Minister of Foreign Affairs of Brazil, whom we here had been privileged to have in Washington as Brazil's Ambassador during the past three years. His significant words were applauded in every American home.

Our ideal is democratic liberty. Our instrument is honor and friendship. Our method is increased understanding. Our basis is confidence. So and not otherwise, in common effort we safeguard in this new world the great rights of our liberties and build our civilization for the advancement of humanity throughout the world.

(For other addresses to the Pan-American Union, see Item 37, 1933 volume; Item 42, 1937 volume; Item 56, 1939 volume; Item 33, 1940 volume.)

49 ⟮ Recommendations to the Congress Designed to Stimulate Further Recovery. April 14, 1938

To the Congress:

THE PROSPERITY of the United States is of necessity a primary concern of Government. Current events, if allowed to run undisturbed, will continue to threaten the security of our people and the stability of our economic life. The National Administration has promised never to stand idly by and watch its people, its business system and its national life disintegrate. It is because the course of our economics has run adversely for half a year that we owe it to ourselves to turn it in the other direction before the situation becomes more definitely serious.

When this Administration took office it found business, credit and agriculture in collapse. The collapse had followed on the heels of overspeculation in and overproduction of practically every article or instrument used by man. During the processes of overspeculation and overproduction — in the twenties — millions of people had been put to work, but the products of their hands had exceeded the purchasing power of their pocketbooks, with the result that huge surpluses, not only of crops but also of buildings and goods of every kind, overhung the market. Under the inexorable law of supply and demand, supplies so overran demand which would pay that production was compelled to stop. Unemployment and closed factories resulted. Hence the tragic years from 1929 to 1933.

Starting in March, 1933, the Congress and the Administration devoted themselves unceasingly, not only to reestablishing reservoirs of credit, but to putting purchasing power in the hands of the consuming public and actually securing a more equitable distribution of the national income. Thus the downward spiral was stopped — and not merely stopped, but started on an upward course — a trend lasting through four years and a half.

In 1928 the national income was eighty billion dollars; in 1932 it had fallen to less than forty billion dollars.

Since the low point of 1932, each year, including 1937, has shown a steady increase in the income which the Nation produced, reflected in increased wages and salaries, in increased dividends, interest and individual's income. In 1937, the total of our citizens' income had risen to sixty-eight billion dollars.

At the end of 1936 the efforts of the Government to aid in increasing the Nation's purchasing power and in stimulating business had become so well recognized that both the business community and the Government felt that a large measure of the Government's spending activities could be materially reduced.

But the very vigor of the recovery in both durable goods and consumers' goods brought into the picture early in 1937 certain highly undesirable practices, which were in large part responsible for the economic decline which began in the later months of that year. Again production outran the ability to buy.

There were many reasons for this overproduction. One was fear — fear of war abroad, fear of inflation, fear of nation-wide strikes. None of these fears has been borne out. There were other causes of overproduction, and these causes differed in each industry.

The net result of these causes and ill-advised practices was a repetition, on a small scale, of what had happened in 1927, 1928 and 1929 on a much larger scale. In other words, production in many important lines of goods outran the ability of the public to purchase them. For example, through the winter and spring of 1937 cotton factories in hundreds of cases were running on a three-shift basis, piling up cotton goods in the factory and in the hands of middle men and retailers. For example, also, automobile manufacturers not only turned out a normal increase of finished cars, but encouraged the normal increase to run into abnormal figures, using every known method to push their sales. This meant, of course, that the steel mills of the Nation ran on a twenty-four hour basis, and the tire companies and cotton factories speeded up to meet the same type of abnormally stimulated demand. The buying power of the Nation lagged behind.

Thus by the autumn of 1937 the Nation again had stocks on hand which the consuming public could not buy because the purchasing power of the consuming public had not kept pace with the production.

During the same period prior to last autumn, the prices of many vital products had risen faster than was warranted. For example, copper — which undoubtedly can be produced at a profit in this country for from ten to twelve cents a pound — was pushed up and up to seventeen cents a pound. The price of steel products of many kinds was increased far more than was justified by the increased wages of steel workers. In the case of many commodities the price to the consumer was raised well above the inflationary boom prices of 1929. In many lines of goods and materials, prices got so high that buyers and builders ceased to buy or to build.

Once more, as in 1929, the economic process of getting out the raw materials, putting them through the manufacturing and finishing processes, selling them to the retailers, selling them to the consumer, and finally using them, got completely out of balance. The Government of the United States, fearing just such an event, had issued warnings in April, 1937, against these practices of overproduction and high prices. The Federal Reserve System curtailed banking credit, and the Treasury commenced to "sterilize" gold as a further brake on what it was feared might turn into a runaway inflation.

The simple fact is that the laying off of workers came upon us last autumn and has been continuing at such a pace ever since that all of us, Government and banking and business and workers, and those faced with destitution, recognize the need for action.

It should be noted in fairness that since January 1, 1937, the President has recommended to the Congress only four measures of major importance to the business of the country:

1. Legislation to stabilize agriculture. A comprehensive law was approved by me two months ago.
2. Legislation to end serious loopholes in our personal income tax laws. This was enacted last summer.
3. Legislation to put a floor under wages and a ceiling over hours of labor in industry, and
4. Tax legislation to remove inequities from the undistributed profits tax, especially as they affect the smaller type of business. Both this measure and the third are still under consideration by the Congress:

The record speaks for itself. No other measures affecting business have been proposed.

All the energies of Government and business must be directed to increasing the national income; to putting more people into private jobs; to giving security and the feeling of security to all people in all walks of life.

I believe that improvement in Government and business practices must go hand in hand with recovery—that they should be, and will be, a definite aid to recovery. While I do not wish in this message to overemphasize some of the needs, I do want to say that I believe that we must be definitely aware of certain of them—the elimination of future tax-exempt bonds of all kinds of Government agencies; the subjecting of Government salaries and wages of all kinds to Federal and State income taxes; a serious undertaking to solve the railroad problem and the problems of monopolistic practices and price fixing. These are no new subjects; nor have I anything to add to them except the statement that their solution will help and not hurt business.

At the same time, I must repeat what I believe the overwhelming majority of both Houses of the Congress will agree to—that the Congress and the Chief Executive can ill afford to weaken or destroy great reforms which, during the past five years, have been effected on behalf of the American people. In our rehabilitation of the banking structure and of agriculture, in our provisions for adequate and cheaper credit for all types of business, in our acceptance of national responsibility for unemployment relief, in our strengthening of the credit of state and local government, in our encouragement of housing, slum clearance and home ownership, in our supervision of stock exchanges and public utility holding companies and the issuance of new securities, in our provision for social security, the electorate of America wants no backward steps taken.

We have recognized the right of labor to free organization, to collective bargaining; and machinery for the handling of labor relations is now in existence. The principles are established even though we can all admit that through the evolution of time administration and practices can be improved. Such improvement can come about most quickly and most peacefully through sincere efforts to understand and assist on the part of labor leaders and employers alike.

The never-ceasing evolution of human society will doubtless bring forth new problems which will require new adjustments. Our immediate task is to consolidate and maintain the gains achieved.

In this situation there is no reason and no occasion for any American to allow his fears to be aroused or his energy and enterprise to be paralyzed by doubt or uncertainty.

Our situation is vastly different from that which we faced five years ago. Let us use the tools already forged and laid out on the bench.

At this immediate time we suffer from a failure of consumer demand. The hoped for reemployment of this spring is not proceeding fast enough to create an economic upturn.

Therefore the problem calls for action both by the government and by the people.

It cannot be disputed that the national income which was thirty-eight billions in 1932, sixty-eight billions in 1937, is now running at the lesser rate of about fifty-six billions. If it can be increased to eighty billion dollars in the course of the next year or two the whole economic picture will be different. Hundreds of thousands more people will be employed in private industry, hundreds of thousands fewer will be in need of relief, and consumer demand for goods will be greatly stimulated. I do not set eighty billion dollars as the national income goal. It ought to rise in the next decade to more than one hundred billions. I want to make it clear that we do not believe that we can get an adequate rise in national income merely by investing, lending or spending public funds. It is essential in our economy that private funds be put to work and all of us recognize that such funds are entitled to a fair profit.

As citizen income rises, let us not forget that government expenditures will go down and government tax receipts will go up.

How and where can and should the Government help to start an upward spiral?

I propose to the Congress three groups of measures:

1. In the first category I place additional appropriations for

the fiscal year beginning July, 1938. These will not put more money in the hands of the consuming public than we are spending in the current fiscal year, but they will prevent men and women from being thrown out of work on July 1. They will stop the spiral from continuing its downward course:

(a) I recommend an appropriation of one billion two hundred and fifty million dollars for the Works Progress Administration, to be used during the first seven months of the next fiscal year. Such a grant is ammunition of the highest grade for attack on recession. It will not greatly increase the present rate of expenditure, but ought to be sufficient to care for the additional men and women who have come or are coming to an end of their unemployment insurance payments.

(b) For the Farm Security Administration an appropriation of one hundred and seventy-five million dollars for the next fiscal year.

(c) For the National Youth Administration the sum of seventy-five million dollars to cover the full fiscal year.

(d) For the Civilian Conservation Corps the sum of fifty million dollars additional to maintain the existing number of camps now in operation.

I call your attention to the fact that these appropriations will avert the laying off of people now receiving assistance from the Federal Government.

In this same category of stopping the downward spiral, I also place the authorization recently given for the lending of money to business enterprises by the Reconstruction Finance Corporation. I do so because the greater part of such loans will go to businesses which are in grave danger of shutting down and throwing people out of employment. Some of the money, but, in all probability, only the smaller part of the loans, will enable businesses to employ more people or start new enterprises.

2. In the second category, the Administration proposes immediately to make additional bank resources available for the credit needs of the country. This can be done without legisla-

tion. It will be done through the de-sterilization of approximately one billion four hundred million dollars of Treasury gold, accompanied by action on the part of the Federal Reserve Board to reduce reserve requirements by about three-quarters of a billion dollars. The Federal Reserve Board informs me that it is willing to do so. These measures will make more abundant the supply of funds for commerce, industry and agriculture. By themselves, however, monetary measures are insufficient to start us on a sustained upward movement.

As a part of better administration I hope that federal banking supervision can be better coordinated. In addition, I am requesting that the Securities and Exchange Commission consider such simplification of regulations as will assist and expedite the financing, particularly, of small business enterprises.

3. I come, therefore, to the third category which I consider to be vital. The first two categories — maintenance of relief and the expansion of credit — might prove sufficient, but in my judgment other measures are essential. You and I cannot afford to equip ourselves with two rounds of ammunition where three rounds are necessary. If we stop at relief and credit, we may find ourselves without ammunition before the enemy is routed. If we are fully equipped with the third round of ammunition, we stand to win the battle against adversity.

This third proposal relates solely to definite additions to the purchasing power of the Nation by providing new work:

(a) I ask for certain amendments to the United States Housing Authority Act to permit the undertaking of the immediate construction of about $300,000,000 of additional projects. The Federal Housing Administration is prepared to increase the already mounting volume of home and apartment construction.

(b) I ask for a renewal of Public Works projects. I believe that by the expenditure of $450,000,000, and the granting of authority to loan up to $1,000,000,000 to states and their sub-divisions, a vast number of well thought out, needed and permanent public improvements can be undertaken this summer and autumn. I believe that the aid of the Federal Government should be put in optional form — either the existing method of 45 per cent grant and 55 per cent loan, or the advancing of the whole sum as loans to states and their subdivisions without interest. Under such a plan the Federal Government would assume the payment of interest and the borrowing authority would assume the payment of the principal by amortization or rental.

Under either method the ultimate cost to the Federal Government and to the states and their sub-divisions is approximately the same.

It is my thought that the total ultimate out-of-pocket cost to the Federal Government by either or both methods should be limited to one billion dollars, and furthermore that no loans or grants should be made on any state or local projects which cannot be started within six months of the date of the enabling legislation, and completed within a year or a year and a half from the commencement of work.

(c) I recommend the appropriation of $100,000,000 to the Bureau of Public Roads for highways in excess of the amount I have previously recommended in the budget for the fiscal year 1939, but I request that this additional amount be used only for projects which can be definitely started this calendar year.

(d) I recommend an appropriation of $37,000,000 over and above estimates for the immediate undertaking of flood control and reclamation works to be expended on projects already authorized by this or former Congresses.

(e) I recommend the appropriation of $25,000,000 additional for Federal buildings.

A summary of these recommendations falls into two categories:

1. Expenditures from the Treasury for work:

Works Progress Administration $1,250,000,000
Farm Security Administration   75,000,000

National Youth Administration ....$ 75,000,000
Civilian Conservation Corps 50,000,000
Public Works Administration 450,000,000
Highways 100,000,000
Flood Control 37,000,000
Federal Buildings 25,000,000

$2,062,000,000

2. Loans from the Treasury for work:

Farm Security Administration 100,000,000
Public Works Administration 550,000,000
United States Housing Authority 300,000,000

$950,000,000

It should be noted that state and local public works under-taken on a loan basis, instead of a loan and grant basis, will reduce the item in the first classification and increase the item in the second classification.

Let us unanimously recognize the fact that the Federal debt, whether it be twenty-five billions or forty billions, can only be paid if the Nation obtains a vastly increased citizen income. I repeat that if this citizen income can be raised to eighty billion dollars a year the national government and the overwhelming majority of state and local governments will be "out of the red." The higher the national income goes the faster shall we be able to reduce the total of Federal and state and local debts. Viewed from every angle, today's purchasing power—the citizens' income of today—is not sufficient to drive the economic system at higher speed. Responsibility of government requires us at this time to supplement the normal processes and in so supplementing them to make sure that the addition is adequate. We must start again on a long steady upward incline in national income.

I have set my hope, my aim on stabilized recovery through a steady mounting of our citizens' income and our citizens' wealth. And in that process, which I believe is ready to start, let us avoid the pitfalls of the past — the overproduction, the overspeculation and indeed all the extremes — which we did not succeed in avoiding in 1929. In all of this, government cannot and should not act alone. Business must help. I am sure business will help.

We need more than the materials of recovery. We need a united national will.

We need to recognize nationally that the demands of no group, however just, can be satisfied unless that group is prepared to share in finding a way to produce the income from which it and all other groups can be paid. Unjust claims defeat themselves. You, as the Congress, I, as the President, must, by virtue of our offices, seek the national good by preserving the balance between all groups and all sections.

We have at our disposal the national resources, the money, the skill of hand and head to raise our economic level — our citizens' income. Our capacity is limited only by our ability to work together. What is needed is the will.

The time has come to bring that will into action with every driving force at our command. And I am determined to do my share.

The responsibility for making this national will effective rests on every individual whether in the government or in industry, or in finance, or in labor, or in the professional fields. Every man and woman in the United States has the great privilege of making this will productive. And the beneficiary will be the whole of the American people.

Certain positive requirements seem to me to accompany the will — if we have that will.

There is placed on all of us the duty of self-restraint. We still rely on personal responsibility — a responsibility guided by a common conscience. That is the discipline of a democracy. Every patriotic citizen must say to himself or herself, that immoderate statement, appeals to prejudice, the creation of unkindness, are offenses not against an individual or individuals, but offenses against the whole population of the United States.

Use of power by any group, however situated, to force its interest or to use its strategic position in order to receive more from the common fund than its contribution to the common fund justifies, is an attack against, and not an aid to, our national life.

Self-restraint implies restraint by articulate public opinion, trained to distinguish fact from falsehood, trained to believe that bitterness is never a useful instrument in public affairs. There can be no dictatorship by an individual or by a group in this Nation, save through division fostered by hate. Such division there must never be.

Amid the voices which now seek to divide group from group, occupation from occupation, section from section, thinking Americans must insist on common effort in a common endeavor and a common faith in each other. Let every business man set out to use his strength of mind and heart and his confidence in his fellow man and his country. Let every labor leader find not how work can be stopped but how it can be made to proceed smoothly, continuously and fairly. Let every public official consider that his task is to use his authority so that the service he renders is adapted to curbing abuses and helping honest effort. Let every one of us work together to move the life of the Nation forward.

We, a successful democracy, face a troubled world. Elsewhere schools of thought contend that democracy is doomed to failure. They tell us that free speech and the free exchange of views will destroy democracies. My conviction, on the contrary, is that the United States retaining free speech and a free exchange of views can furnish a dynamic example of successful government, provided the Nation can unite in practical measures when the times call for united action. The driving force of a Nation lies in its spiritual purpose, made effective by free, tolerant but unremitting national will.

In the Western Hemisphere the good neighbor policy has so strengthened the American Republics that a spiritual unity in our relations now prevails. Can that good neighbor message be accepted and practised in our national life?

49. Recommendations to Stimulate Recovery

If we accept that high and splendid road this free democracy will give successful answer to the fears and questionings which today trouble the minds and souls of men and women the world over.

NOTE: The foregoing message and the following so-called "fireside chat" on the same evening were delivered during the acute recession in business activity which had taken place between the early summer of 1937 and March of 1938. Industrial production both in the heavy industries and in the consumers' goods industries had fallen drastically. This decline was reflected in varying degrees throughout the entire field of American business — in distribution, in transportation, and in the service industries. And with it, of course, had come a progressive decline in employment, and in prices of farm products, raw materials, wholesale commodities, and common stocks.

The reasons for this severe recession were, as I pointed out in my message, overproduction of materials of all kinds, which outran the buying power of the consuming public, resulting in large inventories which could not be moved. Together with this overproduction had come an unwarranted rise in prices, going beyond the ability or willingness of buyers to buy. The economic processes had gotten completely out of balance, in spite of warnings issued by the government in April, 1937, against these practices of overproduction and high prices. See Item 35, pages 140-143, 1937 volume.

There had been an unduly rapid acceleration of activity in the latter part of 1936 and the early months of 1937. In each year from 1933 through 1936, there had been a gradual but substantial increase in employment, industrial activity, and national income. From the low point of 38 billion dollars of national income in 1932, a steady increase year by year had taken place, so that for 1936 the national income was 65 billion, and in 1937 it had risen to 68 billion. During the early stages of this recovery, the greatest industrial activity had taken place in plants manufacturing consumers' goods. In 1936 and in the early part of 1937, the heavy manufacturing industries and the construction industries, which had lagged behind the consumer goods industries, showed substantial advances.

In 1936 there came the artificial stimulus of the veterans' bonus. There was also the very extensive program of public works, as well as the governmental expenditures for social purposes.

By the spring of 1937 the financial markets were reflecting not only the increased activity but the anticipation of continued high earnings. Speculative activities and the belief of a continued increasing demand led to an overproduction and accumulation of inventories dangerously in excess of the actual volume of sales, and of the normal buying demands. With this came a continual advancement of the prices of basic commodities, a rising production, and continued speculation in the securities markets.

In the late spring of 1937, the public works program began to taper off too quickly. The new social security taxes were beginning to withdraw some of the funds from private sources. The net Federal contribution to national buying power declined from 4.3 billion dollars in 1936 to 1.1 billion dollars in 1937.

The recommendations which I made to meet the situation are detailed in the foregoing message.

By the middle of the year 1938, things began to improve. Inventories had declined in a marked degree, and there came an increased activity in the production of textiles, shoes, and residential construction. By the late summer of 1938 the same upward turn came in heavy industries, such as steel. By the spring of 1939 there was a decided business up-swing. By August, 1939, just prior to the outbreak of the war in Europe, economic conditions had completely changed:

1. Production had increased 28 per cent from its low of the summer of 1938, although it was still 13 per cent below the peak level of 1937.

2. August, 1939, showed an increase of employment of nearly two million above the level of the summer of 1938, the greatest increases being in the heavy industries.

3. Factory payrolls had increased by 26 per cent.

4. The production of steel had risen by 127 per cent.

5. Cotton production had risen by 41 per cent.

6. Freight car loadings had advanced by 21 per cent.

7. Residential construction was 60 per cent greater.

This up-turn was due to a number of factors. Among the more important was the fact that government expenditures in providing employment and purchasing power had been greatly increased. In 1939, the net contribution of government to buying power was over 3.6 billion dollars, or more than three times as much as in 1937. During this time there came the rebuilding of inventories in more or less normal proportions; and, of course, the foreign orders for war materials and other supplies had begun to have their effect.

The following tables show the economic changes between July, 1937, and the spring of 1938, when the foregoing message was sent; and also the changes between June, 1938 and August, 1939.

49. Recommendations to Stimulate Recovery

INDEXES OF INCOME, EMPLOYMENT, PRODUCTION, AND OTHER BUSINESS ACTIVITY

(Adjusted for seasonal variation, except as noted)

	Base Period	1937 July	1938 Mar.	1938 June	1939 Aug.	Per cent Change July '37 to June '38	Per cent Change June '38 to Aug. '39	Per cent Change July '37 to Aug. '39
Income payments.....	1929	89	81	79	85	−12	+ 8	− 4
Factory employment* .	1923–25	111	91	84	96	−24	+ 14	−13
Factory payrolls*......	"	105	78	71	90	−32	+ 26	−15
Industrial Prod. Total	1935–39	120	84	81	104	−33	+ 28	−13
Steel..............	"	142	53	49	111	−65	+127	−22
Automobiles........	"	144	57	49	84	−66	+ 71	−42
Cotton.............	"	118	81	81	114	−31	+ 41	− 3
Wool..............	"	97	53	68	106	−30	+ 56	+ 9
Shoes.............	"	108	93	88	107	−19	+ 22	− 1
Freight carloadings....	1923–25	80	60	58	70	−28	+ 21	−13
Construction conts. ...	"	67	46	54	73	−19	+ 35	+ 9
Residential........	"	44	33	42	67	− 5	+ 60	+52
Other.............	"	86	56	64	78	−26	+ 22	− 9
Dept. store sales.......	1923–25	92	86	82	89	−11	+ 9	− 3
Wholesale prices*.....	1926	87.9	79.7	78.3	75.0	−11	− 4	−15

* Not adjusted for seasonal variation.
Sources: Income payments—Bureau of Foreign and Domestic Commerce.
    Factory Employment & Payrolls—Bureau of Labor Statistics.
    Industrial production, Freight carloadings, Construction contracts, and Department store sales—Federal Reserve Board.
    Wholesale prices—Bureau of Labor Statistics.

NONAGRICULTURAL EMPLOYMENT
(In thousands)

	1937 July	1938 March	1938 June	1939 Aug.	Absolute change Jul. '37 to Jun. '38	Absolute change Jun. '38 to Aug. '39	Absolute change Jul. '37 to Aug. '39
Total...........	36,076	33,108	32,881	34,882	−3,195	+2,001	−1,194
Total employees[1].	29,951	26,977	26,749	28,739	−3,202	+1,990	−1,212
Manufacturing .	10,467	8,890	8,376	9,515	−2,091	+1,139	− 952
Mining........	938	883	812	807	− 126	− 5	− 131
Construction...	1,337	839	1,044	1,440	− 293	+ 396	+ 103
Trans. & utilities	3,187	2,823	2,796	2,977	− 391	+ 181	− 210
Trade........	6,174	5,932	5,937	6,065	− 237	+ 128	− 109
Finance, service, & misc.	4,221	4,010	4,099	4,183	− 122	+ 84	− 38
Government[2]...	3,627	3,600	3,685	3,752	+ 58	+ 67	+ 125

[1] Excludes self-employed, casuals and domestic servants.
[2] Excludes military and naval personnel.
Source: Bureau of Labor Statistics, Revised figures.

(See also, on the same subject, the following Item.)

50 ❲ "Dictatorships Do Not Grow Out of Strong and Successful Governments, but Out of Weak and Helpless Ones." Fireside Chat on Present Economic Conditions and Measures Being Taken to Improve Them. April 14, 1938

FIVE months have gone by since I last spoke to the people of the Nation about the state of the Nation.

I had hoped to be able to defer this talk until next week because, as we all know, this is Holy Week. But what I want to say to you, the people of the country, is of such immediate need and relates so closely to the lives of human beings and the prevention of human suffering that I have felt that there should be no delay. In this decision I have been strengthened by the thought that by speaking tonight there may be greater peace of mind and the hope of Easter may be more real at firesides everywhere, and that it is not inappropriate to encourage peace when so many of us are thinking of the Prince of Peace.

Five years ago we faced a very serious problem of economic and social recovery. For four and a half years that recovery proceeded apace. It is only in the past seven months that it has received a visible setback.

And it is only within the past two months, as we have waited patiently to see whether the forces of business itself would counteract it, that it has become apparent that government itself can no longer safely fail to take aggressive government steps to meet it.

This recession has not returned us to the disasters and suffering of the beginning of 1933. Your money in the bank is safe; farmers are no longer in deep distress and have greater purchasing power; dangers of security speculation have been minimized; national income is almost 50 per cent higher than in 1932; and government has an established and accepted responsibility for relief.

But I know that many of you have lost your jobs or have seen your friends or members of your families lose their jobs, and I do not propose that the government shall pretend not to see these things. I know that the effect of our present difficulties has been uneven; that they have affected some groups and some localities seriously, but that they have been scarcely felt in others. But I conceive the first duty of government is to protect the economic welfare of all the people in all sections and in all groups. I said in my message opening the last session of Congress that if private enterprise did not provide jobs this spring, government would take up the slack—that I would not let the people down. We have all learned the lesson that government cannot afford to wait until it has lost the power to act.

Therefore, I have sent a message of far-reaching importance to the Congress. I want to read to you tonight certain passages from that message, and to talk with you about them.

In that message I analyzed the causes of the collapse of 1929 in these words: "overspeculation in and overproduction of practically every article or instrument used by man . . . millions of people had been put to work, but the products of their hands had exceeded the purchasing power of their pocketbooks. . . . Under the inexorable law of supply and demand, supplies so overran demand which would pay that production was compelled to stop. Unemployment and closed factories resulted. Hence the tragic years from 1929 to 1933."

I pointed out to the Congress that the national income—not the Government's income, but the total of the income of all the individual citizens and families of the United States—every farmer, every worker, every banker, every professional man and every person who lived on income derived from investments— that national income amounted, in the year 1929, to eighty-one billion dollars. By 1932 this had fallen to thirty-eight billion dollars. Gradually, and up to a few months ago, it had risen to a total of sixty-eight billion dollars — a pretty good come-back from the low point.

I then said this to the Congress:

"But the very vigor of the recovery in both durable goods and consumers' goods brought into the picture early in 1937 certain highly undesirable practices, which were in large part responsible for the economic decline which began in the later months of that year. Again production outran the ability to buy.

"There were many reasons for this overproduction. One was fear — fear of war abroad, fear of inflation, fear of nationwide strikes. None of these fears has been borne out.

". . . Production in many important lines of goods outran the ability of the public to purchase them. For example, through the winter and spring of 1937 cotton factories in hundreds of cases were running on a three-shift basis, piling up cotton goods in the factory and in the hands of middle men and retailers. For example, also, automobile manufacturers not only turned out a normal increase of finished cars, but encouraged the normal increase to run into abnormal figures, using every known method to push their sales. This meant, of course, that the steel mills of the Nation ran on a twenty-four hour basis, and the tire companies and cotton factories speeded up to meet the same type of abnormally stimulated demand. The buying power of the Nation lagged behind.

"Thus by the autumn of 1937 the Nation again had stocks on hand which the consuming public could not buy because the purchasing power of the consuming public had not kept pace with the production.

"During the same period . . . the prices of many vital products had risen faster than was warranted. . . . In the case of many commodities the price to the consumer was raised well above the inflationary boom prices of 1929. In many lines of goods and materials, prices got so high that buyers and builders ceased to buy or to build.

". . . The economic process of getting out the raw materials, putting them through the manufacturing and finishing processes, selling them to the retailers, selling them to the consumer, and finally using them got completely out of balance.

". . . The laying off of workers came upon us last autumn and has been continuing at such a pace ever since that all of us, Government and banking and business and workers, and those faced with destitution, recognize the need for action."

All of this I said to the Congress today and I repeat it to you, the people of the country tonight.

I went on to point out to the Senate and the House of Representatives that all the energies of government and business must be directed to increasing the national income, to putting more people into private jobs, to giving security and a feeling of security to all people in all walks of life.

I am constantly thinking of all our people — unemployed and employed alike — of their human problems of food and clothing and homes and education and health and old age. You and I agree that security is our greatest need; the chance to work, the opportunity of making a reasonable profit in our business — whether it be a very small business or a larger one — the possibility of selling our farm products for enough money for our families to live on decently. I know these are the things that decide the well-being of all our people.

Therefore, I am determined to do all in my power to help you attain that security, and because I know that the people themselves have a deep conviction that secure prosperity of that kind cannot be a lasting one except on a basis of business fair dealing and a basis where all from top to bottom share in prosperity, I repeated to the Congress today that neither it nor the Chief Executive can afford "to weaken or destroy great reforms which, during the past five years, have been effected on behalf of the American people. In our rehabilitation of the banking structure and of agriculture, in our provisions for adequate and cheaper credit for all types of business, in our acceptance of national responsibility for unemployment relief, in our strengthening of the credit of state and local government, in our encouragement of housing, slum clearance and home ownership, in our supervision of stock exchanges and public utility holding companies and the issuance of new securities, in our provision for social security, the electorate of America wants no backward steps taken.

"We have recognized the right of labor to free organization, to collective bargaining; and machinery for the handling of labor relations is now in existence. The principles are established even though we can all admit that, through the evolution of time, administration and practices can be improved. Such improvement can come about most quickly and most peacefully through sincere efforts to understand and assist on the part of labor leaders and employers alike.

"The never-ceasing evolution of human society will doubtless bring forth new problems which will require new adjustments. Our immediate task is to consolidate and maintain the gains achieved.

"In this situation there is no reason and no occasion for any American to allow his fears to be aroused or his energy and enterprise to be paralyzed by doubt or uncertainty."

I came to the conclusion that the present-day problem calls for action both by the Government and by the people, that we suffer primarily from a failure of consumer demand because of lack of buying power. It is up to us to create an economic upturn.

"How and where can and should the Government help to start an upward spiral?"

I went on to propose three groups of measures and I will summarize the recommendations.

First, I asked for certain appropriations which are intended to keep the Government expenditures for work relief and similar purposes during the coming fiscal year at the same rate of expenditure as at present. That includes additional money for the Works Progress Administration; additional funds for the Farm Security Administration; additional allotments for the National Youth Administration, and more money for the Civilian Conservation Corps, in order that it can maintain the existing number of camps now in operation.

These appropriations, made necessary by increased unemployment, will cost about a billion and a quarter more than the estimates which I sent to the Congress on the third of January.

Second, I told the Congress that the Administration proposes to make additional bank reserves available for the credit needs of the country. About one billion four hundred million dollars of gold now in the Treasury will be used to pay these additional expenses of the Government, and three-quarters of a billion dollars of additional credit will be made available to the banks by reducing the reserves now required by the Federal Reserve Board.

These two steps, taking care of relief needs and adding to bank credits, are in our judgment insufficient by themselves to start the Nation on a sustained upward movement.

Therefore, I came to the third kind of Government action which I consider to be vital. I said to the Congress:

"You and I cannot afford to equip ourselves with two rounds of ammunition where three rounds are necessary. If we stop at relief and credit, we may find ourselves without ammunition before the enemy is routed. If we are fully equipped with the third round of ammunition, we stand to win the battle against adversity."

The third proposal is to make definite additions to the purchasing power of the Nation by providing new work over and above the continuing of the old work.

First, to enable the United States Housing Authority to undertake the immediate construction of about three hundred million dollars of additional slum clearance projects.

Second, to renew a public works program by starting as quickly as possible about one billion dollars worth of needed permanent public improvements in states, counties and cities.

Third, to add one hundred million dollars to the estimate for federal aid highways in excess of the amount I recommended in January.

Fourth, to add thirty-seven million dollars over and above the former estimate of sixty-three million dollars for flood control and reclamation.

Fifth, to add twenty-five million dollars additional for federal buildings in various parts of the country.

In recommending this program I am thinking not only of the immediate economic needs of the people of the Nation, but also of their personal liberties — the most precious possession of all Americans. I am thinking of our democracy and of the recent trend in other parts of the world away from the democratic ideal.

Democracy has disappeared in several other great nations — not because the people of those nations disliked democracy, but because they had grown tired of unemployment and insecurity, of seeing their children hungry while they sat helpless in the face of government confusion and government weakness through lack of leadership in government. Finally, in desperation, they chose to sacrifice liberty in the hope of getting something to eat. We in America know that our own democratic institutions can be preserved and made to work. But in order to preserve them we need to act together, to meet the problems of the Nation boldly, and to prove that the practical operation of democratic government is equal to the task of protecting the security of the people.

Not only our future economic soundness but the very soundness of our democratic institutions depends on the determination of our Government to give employment to idle men. The people of America are in agreement in defending their liberties at any cost, and the first line of that defense lies in the protection of economic security. Your Government, seeking to protect democracy, must prove that Government is stronger than the forces of business depression.

History proves that dictatorships do not grow out of strong and successful governments, but out of weak and helpless ones. If by democratic methods people get a government strong enough to protect them from fear and starvation, their democ-

racy succeeds; but if they do not, they grow impatient. Therefore, the only sure bulwark of continuing liberty is a government strong enough to protect the interests of the people, and
a people strong enough and well enough informed to maintain
its sovereign control over its government.

We are a rich Nation; we can afford to pay for security and
prosperity without having to sacrifice our liberties in the bargain.

In the first century of our republic we were short of capital,
short of workers and short of industrial production; but we
were rich in free land, free timber and free mineral wealth.
The Federal Government rightly assumed the duty of promot-
ing business and relieving depression by giving subsidies of
land and other resources.

Thus, from our earliest days we have had a tradition of substantial government help to our system of private enterprise.
But today the government no longer has vast tracts of rich land
to give away and we have discovered that we must spend large
sums to conserve our land from further erosion and our forests
from further depletion. The situation is also very different from
the old days, because now we have plenty of capital, banks
and insurance companies loaded with idle money; plenty of
industrial productive capacity and several millions of workers
looking for jobs. It is following tradition as well as necessity, if
Government strives to put idle money and idle men to work, to
increase our public wealth and to build up the health and
strength of the people — and to help our system of private enterprise to function.

It is going to cost something to get out of this recession this
way, but the profit of getting out of it will pay for the cost
several times over. Lost working time is lost money. Every
day that a workman is unemployed, or a machine is unused, or
a business organization is marking time, is a loss to the Nation.
Because of idle men and idle machines this Nation lost one
hundred billion dollars between 1929 and the spring of 1933.
This year you, the people of this country, are making about
twelve billion dollars less than last year.

If you think back to the experiences of the early years of this Administration you will remember the doubts and fears expressed about the rising expenses of Government. But to the surprise of the doubters, as we proceeded to carry on the program which included Public Works and Work Relief, the country grew richer instead of poorer.

It is worthwhile to remember that the annual national people's income was thirty billion dollars more in 1937 than in 1932. It is true that the national debt increased sixteen billion dollars, but remember that in this increase must be included several billion dollars worth of assets which eventually will reduce that debt and that many billion dollars of permanent public improvements — schools, roads, bridges, tunnels, public buildings, parks and a host of other things — meet your eye in every one of the thirty one hundred counties in the United States.

No doubt you will be told that the Government spending program of the past five years did not cause the increase in our national income. They will tell you that business revived because of private spending and investment. That is true in part, for the Government spent only a small part of the total. But Government spending acted as a trigger to set off private activity. That is why the total addition to our national production and national income has been so much greater than the contribution of the Government itself.

In pursuance of that thought I said to the Congress today: "I want to make it clear that we do not believe that we can get an adequate rise in national income merely by investing, lending or spending public funds. It is essential in our economy that private funds be put to work and all of us recognize that such funds are entitled to a fair profit."

As national income rises, "let us not forget that Government expenditures will go down and Government tax receipts will go up."

The Government contribution of land that we once made to business was the land of all the people. And the Government contribution of money which we now make to business ultimately comes out of the labor of all the people. It is, therefore, only sound morality, as well as a sound distribution of buying power, that the benefits of the prosperity coming from this use of the money of all the people should be distributed among all the people — at the bottom as well as at the top. Consequently I am again expressing my hope that the Congress will enact at this session a wage and hour bill putting a floor under industrial wages and a limit on working hours — to ensure a better distribution of our prosperity, a better distribution of available work, and a sounder distribution of buying power.

You may get all kinds of impressions in regard to the total cost of this new program, or in regard to the amount that will be added to the net national debt.

It is a big program. Last autumn in a sincere effort to bring Government expenditures and Government income into closer balance, the Budget I worked out called for sharp decreases in Government spending.

In the light of present conditions those estimates were far too low. This new program adds two billion and sixty-two million dollars to direct Treasury expenditures and another nine hundred and fifty million dollars to Government loans — and the latter sum, because they are loans, will come back to the Treasury in the future.

The net effect on the debt of the Government is this: between now and July 1, 1939 — fifteen months away — the Treasury will have to raise less than a billion and a half dollars of new money.

Such an addition to the net debt of the United States need not give concern to any citizen, for it will return to the people of the United States many times over in increased buying power and eventually in much greater Government tax receipts because of the increase in the citizen income.

What I said to the Congress in the close of my message I repeat to you.

"Let us unanimously recognize the fact that the Federal debt, whether it be twenty-five billions or forty billions, can only be paid if the Nation obtains a vastly increased citizen income. I repeat that if this citizen income can be raised to eighty billion dollars a year the national Government and the overwhelming majority of State and local governments will be 'out of the red.' The higher the national income goes the faster shall we be able to reduce the total of Federal and state and local debts. Viewed from every angle, today's purchasing power — the citizens' income of today — is not sufficient to drive the economic system at higher speed. Responsibility of Government requires us at this time to supplement the normal processes and in so supplementing them to make sure that the addition is adequate. We must start again on a long steady upward incline in national income.

"... And in that process, which I believe is ready to start, let us avoid the pitfalls of the past — the overproduction, the overspeculation, and indeed all the extremes which we did not succeed in avoiding in 1929. In all of this, Government cannot and should not act alone. Business must help. I am sure business will help.

"We need more than the materials of recovery. We need a united national will.

"We need to recognize nationally that the demands of no group, however just, can be satisfied unless that group is prepared to share in finding a way to produce the income from which it and all other groups can be paid. . . . You, as the Congress, I, as the President, must, by virtue of our offices, seek the national good by preserving the balance between all groups and all sections.

"We have at our disposal the national resources, the money, the skill of hand and head to raise our economic level — our citizens' income. Our capacity is limited only by our ability to work together. What is needed is the will.

"The time has come to bring that will into action with every driving force at our command. And I am determined to do my share.

". . . Certain positive requirements seem to me to accompany the will — if we have that will.

"There is placed on all of us the duty of self-restraint. . . . That is the discipline of a democracy. Every patriotic citizen must say to himself or herself, that immoderate statement, appeals to prejudice, the creation of unkindness, are offenses not against an individual or individuals, but offenses against the whole population of the United States. . . .

"Self-restraint implies restraint by articulate public opinion, trained to distinguish fact from falsehood, trained to believe that bitterness is never a useful instrument in public affairs. There can be no dictatorship by an individual or by a group in this Nation, save through division fostered by hate. Such division there must never be."

Finally I should like to say a personal word to you.

I never forget that I live in a house owned by all the American people and that I have been given their trust.

I try always to remember that their deepest problems are human. I constantly talk with those who come to tell me their own points of view; with those who manage the great industries and financial institutions of the country; with those who represent the farmer and the worker; and often with average citizens without high position who come to this house. And constantly I seek to look beyond the doors of the White House, beyond the officialdom of the National Capital, into the hopes and fears of men and women in their homes. I have traveled the country over many times. My friends, my enemies, my daily mail, bring to me reports of what you are thinking and hoping. I want to be sure that neither battles nor burdens of office shall ever blind me to an intimate knowledge of the way the American people want to live and the simple purposes for which they put me here.

In these great problems of government I try not to forget that what really counts at the bottom of it all, is that the men and women willing to work can have a decent job to take care of themselves and their homes and their children adequately; that the farmer, the factory worker, the storekeeper, the gas station man, the manufacturer, the merchant—big and small—the banker who takes pride in the help he gives to the building of his community, that all these can be sure of a reasonable profit and safety for the savings they earn—not today nor tomorrow alone, but as far ahead as they can see.

I can hear your unspoken wonder as to where we are headed in this troubled world. I cannot expect all of the people to understand all of the people's problems; but it is my job to try to understand those problems.

I always try to remember that reconciling differences cannot satisfy everyone completely. Because I do not expect too much, I am not disappointed. But I know that I must never give up—that I must never let the greater interest of all the people down, merely because that might be for the moment the easiest personal way out.

I believe we have been right in the course we have charted. To abandon our purpose of building a greater, a more stable and a more tolerant America, would be to miss the tide and perhaps to miss the port. I propose to sail ahead. I feel sure that your hopes and your help are with me. For to reach a port, we must sail—sail, not tie at anchor—sail, not drift.

(See also on the same subject, Item 49, this volume.)

51 ⟨ Presidential Statement on Accord Reached Between Great Britain and Italy. April 19, 1938

As THIS Government has on frequent occasions made it clear, the United States, in advocating the maintenance of international law and order, believes in the promotion of world peace through the friendly solution by peaceful negotiation between nations of controversies which may arise between them. It has also urged the promotion of peace through the finding of means for economic appeasement. It does not attempt to pass upon the political features of accords such as that recently reached between Great Britain and Italy, but this Government has seen the conclusion of an agreement with sympathetic interest because it is proof of the value of peaceful negotiations.

NOTE: The foregoing statement by me followed the announcement that Great Britain and Italy had concluded a series of accords relating primarily to the Mediterranean Sea and to a settlement of the Abyssinian problem which was still an issue between the two governments.

My statement made it clear that this government in no sense attempted "to pass upon the political features" of the agreement. The agreement involved the *de jure* recognition by Great Britain of the Italian conquest of Ethiopia.

The foregoing statement in no way implied any change in the position of the American Government with respect to recognition of the Ethiopian conquest. This government has consistently refused, in so far as possible, to recognize the seizure of territory by force.

The statement merely expressed the gratification that a solution of the controversial questions between the two nations had been arrived at through peaceful negotiations, especially at a time when other nations in the world had decided upon the use of force alone as a method of solving political differences.

In other words, it was the method of solution and not the substance thereof which prompted the statement.

52 ⟨ A Special Press Conference with Members of the Associated Church Press. Washington, D.C. April 20, 1938

(The fight for progressivism — The type of opposition to the reorganization bill — Effect of the arms embargo on Spain — Civil liberties — The danger of fascism — Naval defense and its uses.)

DR. JOHN VAN SCHAICK: [after introducing the individual members] Well, the first man that has something burning in his soul to ask the President should speak up or forever hold his peace. (*Laughter*)

Q. I would like to ask, if you feel at liberty to answer, if there is truth in what Paul Anderson and Irving Brant and even Colonel McCormick have indicated, that from here on it is going to be a fight for the New Deal, that you are definitely lined up with the Progressives and that it is going to be a fight?

THE PRESIDENT: I would not say from here on because it has been going on all of my lifetime. It has been going on with a good deal of vigor for the past five years and I think it will continue as long as I live and as long as most of us live. I think it is a matter of principle.

Q. The reason I ask the question is that Colonel McCormick has indicated that we have won two victories — we have killed the Court Bill and the Reorganization Bill and it is a question of repealing some of the other Acts, such as the TVA Act. (*Laughter*)

THE PRESIDENT: I guess so. (*Laughter*) But they are not going to do it, so that is all right. (*Laughter*)

Of course, on the Reorganization Bill — As you know, the Reorganization Bill was originally suggested by President Benjamin Harrison, and every President ever since, because we have a machinery here, administrative machinery, that is awfully old-fashioned, that sort of grew up like Topsy. What we want to do is to put it on the same kind of an efficient basis that we would run an industrial plant, or a private charity, or even the financial end of a church. We want to make it efficient.

One of the suggestions that the three people who drew up the original bill, Louis Brownlow and Professor Merriam and Luther Gulick, made was that certain functions that are in the wrong place at the present time should be put in a better place.

For example, the Office of Education, which has certain specific powers given it by the Congress and certain specific sums of money given to it each year by the Congress, is today in the department which happens to have as its main functions the building of irrigation ditches, the running of national parks, and taking care of Indians. Now, why the Federal Office of Education should have been put into that department, I don't know; I guess it just got stuck there, put in there because there was no other place to put it. So, in their proposal, they proposed setting up a new department of the Government that would handle what might be called the humanities, the problem of relief, the problem of public health, handle the Office of Education, handle the art projects of the Government, handle the cultural end of Government and the health and educational ends of Government. But, all of a sudden, there broke out — I don't know who started it, but I do know who carried it on; and one was the gentleman from near Detroit who talks on the air. He claimed that this was an attack on the educational system of the Nation, whereupon, immediately, the Members of the Congress, the House and the Senate, were flooded with telegrams that this bill would give the President of the United States a chance to grab all the church schools of the Nation, the Protestant church schools and the Parochial schools, although I don't know what the President of the United States was going to do with them when he did grab them. (*Laughter*)

Of course, they entirely overlooked the fact that it does not make much difference whether it is in the Interior Department or the Welfare Department or the Navy Department, for that matter. All he can do is to carry out the laws that have been on the statute books for a great many years, and do it inside of a definite sum of money that has been given to carry it out. I have nothing to say about it.

That is just an illustration of the kind of false information that this country is up against all the time, engendered by political motives. I hope it is engendered by that and not by hard feeling.

DR. VAN SCHAICK: Well, you have a group of people here that are a little out of that. The Church Press is a little more independent. There were two or three matters that came up in our meetings. One was that we felt, as Protestants, a very keen desire not to have public money come to us, as Protestants, and we thought the same thing ought to apply in any democratic country to any church school. We say that with a good deal of feeling. But that was merely one of the subjects. The other was neutrality. We hope that you have been thinking of the way our neutrality laws have been operating, have been working out. For example, in Spain, they have worked out against the Loyalists.

THE PRESIDENT: They have not, as a matter of fact, in that particular case; but the neutrality law — I am talking off the record — but the neutrality law at the present time is so rigid that, acting on it in accordance with its rigidity, may mean a complete lack of neutrality. . . .

In the case of Spain, that is a thing that is very, very little understood. If I were, tomorrow, or if I had last month or the month before declared that war was not going on in Spain — mind you, I have to find the fact one way or the other — what would have happened? It would have meant that the Franco forces, which are in control of the ocean, completely in control, would have been able to get direct shipments of munitions from this country, right into the revolutionary camp because they have complete control of the seas. By the same token, if last week or the month before I had said that there isn't any war in Spain — I have to find that fact — the Barcelona government could not have gotten anything from this country direct because it would have been captured by the Franco people who control the ocean. That would not have been neutrality; I would have been playing into the hands of Franco.

As the situation is today, undoubtedly there are bombs and munitions of various kinds going from here via Germany or Holland or Belgium or even England, going out from here to there and being reshipped, without our knowledge, but of course we have a pretty good guess that they are going from there to Franco. It is a long, rather arduous route around. At the same time, there is also a good deal of American munitions going to France, consigned to France, and we know pretty well that it is going from France into the Barcelona government.

So, actually, as a matter of fact, we are maintaining neutrality in the highest sense, which is not to help one fellow more than the other.

Does that explain something new? It is a new point of view from what most people are getting.

Q. If the embargo on arms to Spain was lifted, it would not help the Loyalists, in your judgment?

THE PRESIDENT: No, it would not; it would help Franco because the Loyalists could not get them except through France.

Q. There is a concerted movement, we have been led to believe, to try to have you lift the embargo?

THE PRESIDENT: I know it. It is by the people who sympathize with the Government of Spain and of course they have never thought the thing through.

Q. We are a little keen to have the Civil Liberties Union get a little more money to find out some more facts.

THE PRESIDENT: I am a hundred per cent with you. I think it ought to be a continuing proposition of the Civil Liberties Union presenting cases year in and year out, not only the type of case that has been investigated so well but a lot of other things. As you know, there are subversive forces in this country. I suppose the easiest term to apply is to call them the Fascist element in the United States, who are able to get very large sums of money quickly into their possession and sweep the country off its feet with some kind of a great publicity move before the country has an opportunity to think about it one way or the other. The people get this tremendous mass of stuff thrown at them, one way or the other, through newspapers and by letters, and it sweeps them off their feet. They can either rush a thing through or block something which, in their mature judgment, they would not be for at all. That is where it affects the civil liberties of the country. I think Beebe is doing a fine piece of work on that.

Q. [Dr. Van Schaick] I saw him this morning. It is very fine of you to say so.

THE PRESIDENT: Any other thought?

Q. I would like to ask you, how great is the danger of Fascism in this country? We hear about Fascism-baiting in the United States.

THE PRESIDENT: I think there is danger because every time you have the breaking down or failure of some process we have been accustomed to for a long time, the tendency is for that process, because of the breakdown, to get into the hands of a very small group. I am not going to repeat anything about sixty or eighty families, but (*laughter*) you come down to where — the Vice President himself has kept harping on it all the time — any large movement does ultimately have to be financed or taken care of through New York City, whether we like it or not. I will give you an example:

One of our southern states that I spend a lot of time in, has a very large power company, the Georgia Power Company. There are a lot of people in Georgia that want to own and run Georgia power, but it is owned by Commonwealth and Southern in New York. They need some money. Georgia has plenty of money with which to extend electric light lines to the rural communities, and the officers of Georgia Power Company themselves want it Georgia owned or Georgia run. But they have to go to New York for the money. If it were not for that, we would not have any utility problem, and all of them would be owned in the districts which they serve, and they would get rid of this financial control.

You take the new lumber companies that want to start on this wonderful process of making print paper out of yellow pine. One reason for the low wages of the workers in the pulp mills of Mississippi, Georgia, North Carolina and South Carolina is that practically all profits go north, they do not stay south. If the profits stayed south, the whole scale of living would go up.

I am greatly in favor of decentralization and yet the tendency is, every time we have trouble in private industry, to concentrate it all the more in New York. Now that is, ultimately, fascism.

Q. Mr. President, we are very much interested in the amount of territory that will be taken in by this expanded Navy or the enlarged Naval program. How far would you extend a defense program, say, with an enlarged Navy?

THE PRESIDENT: I would have to get you to give me two definitions first.

Q. I am for it. (*Laughter*)

THE PRESIDENT: What would you do at the present moment — I am not talking about 1945 — in the case of an attack on the Philippines by some nation? The American flag is flying there. What would you do if they were attacked?

Q. As long as we had them and they were attacked, I would protect them.

THE PRESIDENT: Then that shows you the limit of the American Navy in the Pacific. That is No. 1, so that answered that end. If the flag was flying there we would protect them, even though we want to get out just as soon as we possibly can. As long as the flag is flying we cannot let another nation walk in there and say, "Get out tomorrow."

Now, another thing; this is a threefold question: Suppose certain foreign governments, European governments, were to do in Mexico what they did in Spain. Suppose they would organize a revolution, a Fascist revolution in Mexico. Mexico is awfully close to us. Suppose they were to send planes and officers and guns and were to equip the revolutionists and get control of the whole of Mexico and thereupon run the Mexican Government, run the Mexican Army and build it up with hundreds of planes. Do you think that the United States could stand idly by and have this European menace right on our own borders? Of course not. You could not stand for it.

That means we would have to have a big enough Navy to keep them from getting into Mexico. Mind you, the Mexican flag is still flying. Mind you, it is not the Spanish flag; it is not the Italian flag or the German flag. We probably all agree that we could not stand for a foreign nation doing that under the guise of a Mexican flag.

Q. Isn't the three thousand miles sufficient?

THE PRESIDENT: Yes, it is a long distance across the ocean. We would not be attacked from across the ocean, however, if they came from Mexico.

Q. Yes, but there isn't any reason now for any European nation to come across and establish such a conflict in Mexico.

THE PRESIDENT: They did it in Spain.

Q. I know, but that is across the Atlantic.

THE PRESIDENT: It is three days from Germany, and Mexico is only seven days from Germany.

Q. Would you feel — this is a hypothetical question — would you feel at the beginning of such activity that the Monroe Doctrine would be operative so they could be checked at their inception rather than later?

THE PRESIDENT: Absolutely, and I will give you an illustration: In 1861 we were engaged in a war between the states. Certain European nations, the French and the Austrians, combined; and they sent an army into Mexico and they sent an Emperor into Mexico. We were awfully busy. We did not do anything about the Monroe Doctrine, we had too many troubles of our own. It went on for four years and finally, at the end of the War Between the States, the Administration turned its face towards Mexico and said to France and Austria and Maximilian: "I am awfully sorry, you people have to get these French troops out of here in a hurry." We sent Sherman's army, or an army commanded by Sherman, down to Texas. But they had four years to get control of that country and they would be there yet if we had not done something.

Venezuela is a good deal closer to Europe. How far is Venezuela away from the United States? It is further than Mexico. As to Cuba, we would obviously do as we did in the case of Mexico. Venezuela is South America. It is only four hundred miles; it is an hour and a half by some of these modern planes, an hour and a half further than Cuba. We ought to agree that we ought to enforce the Monroe Doctrine in Venezuela. Cleveland did.

How about Brazil? It is half way to Europe. Brazil — Would we do it in the case of Brazil? Well, you have a principle established. Does the principle only apply near by and not to the rest of the Americas? We are trying to keep an independent continent, north and south.

Let me tell you about Iowa: I have a Chinese friend who was in college with me. He is a merchant in Canton, but I hear from him once a year. I got a letter from him the other day. "Do you remember me telling you about my brother away in the interior, about three hundred miles southwest of Hankow? He was very prosperous, with an awfully nice home and a fine family. He had always been a pacifist. He has opposed a Chinese Army to protect the Nation of China. He said, 'We are so big, there is nobody that would dare to trouble us.' I have never agreed with my brother."

It is a Christian family. And the other day he said, "I am very sorry to tell you that my brother and his wife and four children were killed." They lived in the Iowa of China. Those planes came over and dropped a bomb on the house where they were cooling off. They killed three hundred people in the near-by village, and two minutes later they were gone. They had wiped out one of the rural communities of the Iowa of China. He never thought it could happen, I never thought it would happen, and his brother in Canton never thought it would happen.

We know today — it was in the papers — that in 1918, before the war ended, the Germans were building a Zeppelin with the perfectly definite objective of sending her out in the spring of 1919 by way of the Great Circle Route, over Iceland, Greenland and down to New York, to drop a cargo of bombs on New York City. We have known that from the documents we picked up afterwards.

Q. How can we ever defend a territory going down from Maine, through the Virgin Islands, and all the territory embraced by the Monroe Doctrine and around toward the Philippine Islands and coming back to the United States?

THE PRESIDENT: Well, of course if you have one enemy, we are all right. But suppose you have two enemies in two different places, then you have to be a bit shifty on your feet. You have to lick one of them first and then bring them around and then lick the other. That is about the only chance.

DR. VAN SCHAICK: Thank you very much, Mr. President.

(See note to Item 51, 1937 volume, for a discussion of the embargo upon arms shipments to Spain.)

53 ⟨ "All of Us, and You and I Especially, Are Descended from Immigrants and Revolutionists." Extemporaneous Remarks Before the Daughters of the American Revolution. Washington, D.C. April 21, 1938

Daughters of the American Revolution:

I COULDN'T let a fifth year go by without coming to see you. I must ask you to take me just as I am, in a business suit [exploding flashlight bulb] — and I see you are still in favor of national defense — take me as I am, with no prepared remarks. You know, as a matter of fact, I would have been here to one of your conventions in prior years — one or more — but it is not the time that it takes to come before you and speak for half an hour, it is the preparation for that half-hour. And I suppose that for every half-hour speech that I make before a convention or over the radio, I put in ten hours preparing it.

So I have to ask you to bear with me, to let me just come here without preparation to tell you how glad I am to avail myself of this opportunity, to tell you how proud I am, as a Revolutionary descendant, to greet you.

I thought of preaching on a text, but I shall not. I shall only give you the text and I shall not preach on it. I think I can afford to give you the text because it so happens, through no fault of my own, that I am descended from a number of people who came over in the *Mayflower*. More than that, every one of my ancestors on both sides — and when you go back four generations or five generations it means thirty-two or sixty-four of them — every single one of them, without exception, was in this land in 1776. And there was only one Tory among them.

The text is this: Remember, remember always that all of us, and you and I especially, are descended from immigrants and revolutionists.

I am particularly glad to know that today you are making this fine appeal to the youth of America. To these rising generations, to our sons and grandsons and great-grandsons, we cannot overestimate the importance of what we are doing in this year, in our own generation, to keep alive the spirit of American democracy. The spirit of opportunity is the kind of spirit that has led us as a nation — not as a small group but as a nation — to meet the very great problems of the past.

We look for a younger generation that is going to be more American than we are. We are doing the best that we can and yet we can do better than that, we can do more than that, by inculcating in the boys and girls of this country today some of the underlying fundamentals, the reasons that brought our immigrant ancestors to this country, the reasons that impelled our Revolutionary ancestors to throw off a fascist yoke.

We have a great many things to do. Among other things in this world is the need of being very, very certain, no matter what happens, that the sovereignty of the United States will never be impaired.

There have been former occasions, conventions of the Daughters of the American Revolution, when voices were raised, needed to be raised, for better national defense. This year, you are raising those same voices and I am glad of it. But I am glad also that the Government of the United States can assure you today that it is taking definite, practical steps for the defense of the Nation. . . .

54 ❧ A Special Press Conference with the Members of the American Society of Newspaper Editors. Washington, D.C. April 21, 1938

(*Text of remarks addressed to D.A.R. — An editorial on vindictive criticism — Racial intolerance — The solid South and intelligent Democracy — C.I.O.-A.F. of L. dispute — Undistributed profits tax — Moral principle in taxation — One-sidedness in newspaper stories — Responsibilities of the press — Neutrality law and the Spanish and Sino-Japanese conflicts — National Labor Relations Board.*)

THE PRESIDENT: I can hardly realize that another year has gone by since we had a gathering in this room. I think this is a little larger one. My impression of last year is that I asked questions and you fellows got into the most awful row among yourselves. (*Laughter*)

I am not going to ask any questions but I am going to tell you what I said to the D.A.R. today. (*Laughter*) I am going to preach the same sermon to you that I preached to them. It is a perfectly good text. I said that I probably had a more American ancestry than nine out of ten of the D.A.R. I had various ancestors who came over in the *Mayflower* and similar ships — one that carried the cargo of furniture —

and furthermore that I did not have a single ancestor who came to this country after the Revolutionary War; they were all here before the Revolution. And, out of the whole thirty-two or sixty-four of them, whichever it was, there was only one Tory. (*Laughter*) Well, they began to wonder if they ought to applaud that or not. And, I said, now I will come down to the text. It is just as good for you people as it was for the D.A.R. I am putting you in the same category. (*Laughter*) I said, Here is the text: Keep in the front of your heads all of the time, dear ladies, first, that you are the descendants of immigrants. And they did not know whether to applaud that or not. Secondly, that you are the descendants of revolutionists. They did not know whether to applaud that or not. So there is the text and I won't expound on it any further.

Now shoot. (*Laughter*) [There was no response from the audience.]

Perhaps if nobody wants to shoot, I will read an editorial to you. (*Laughter*) Probably none of you has read it. It is from a magazine called "Editor and Publisher." And it is based on something that Bill White said. Where is Bill?

Q. He is here. (*Laughter*)

THE PRESIDENT: It is entitled "Our Business Clinic." It says:

"For a clear-headed diagnosis of current business troubles, we commend among the many appearing in this issue that of William Allen White, the Sage of Emporia. The famous editor of the *Gazette*, who said a few weeks ago that he had seen yesterday and today and was not afraid of tomorrow, cuts with keen words through the hysteria which has bedevilled the land for ten years.

"Mr. White is correct when he says —

I won't forgive him for this — the connotation of it —

"— that Roosevelt, Stalin, Mussolini, and Hitler —"

Now, Bill! (*Laughter*) . . . Anyway, these four famous gentlemen, including Roosevelt,

"— can all pass from the scene and that the fundamental world problems would not be changed."

Amen.

"It is a problem as ancient as recorded history and it has sharpened its business edge in the age of steam, electricity and machines. It is the problem of giving to each his share of the world's production. It cannot be solved by any single panacea. It cannot be solved in a year, a decade, or possibly a century, and, human nature being what it is, we sometimes believe it may not be capable of any solution.

"Meanwhile, we've all got to live. We want comfort, according to our lights, and our ideal of comfort may range all the way from a soft mattress to a Diesel yacht."

Not an incorporated yacht. (*Laughter*)

"No one of us can write what he thinks is his fair share of the nation's produce; none knows how he wants his share paid. But we all want, and keep on wanting, and eventually we can hope to arrive at a compromise with Utopia that will be better than what we have.

"History may appraise Mr. Roosevelt's collision —

I am glad he did not say "collusion."

"— collision with the established order as an over-idealistic and impractical attempt to hasten that happy day, but it may also damn those who followed their selfish (and wholly) normal instinct of self-preservation in opposing him. And long before the historians begin tossing their dry bones around, the strange animal that is *homo americanus* may reach the conclusion that his savage assaults against the President of the United States of the past few weeks were unreasoning and largely unreasonable.

"It is as futile to expect an armistice in politics this year as it is to look for a solution of the problem Mr. White states — but why not let us have an abatement of hatred and vilification? They have not affected the business decline, except possibly to deepen it and to delay the rebound. They will not keep us from dictatorship, if we are bent on that nitwit experiment. They may hasten dictatorship, if political frenzy is carried to the extent of libeling a President, defeating a bill that had only superficial faults, and then calling the defeat a vote of 'no confidence' in a man who received seventy per cent of the popular vote seventeen months ago. Dictators goosestep into power on the heels of governments which lose public confidence, and Mr. Roosevelt, despite his self-admitted lack of qualifications, may be forced to the job by his foes. If not he, someone far less qualified.

"Let us chuck politics and alibis out the window, and get down to business again."

And so we are down to business again.

Well, last year I asked all the questions and I decided this year I would not ask any of them except by way of reply to questions that could only be answered by counter-questions. That is fair. Now, don't all shoot at once but here I am.

Q. Mr. President, do you sense any growth of racial intolerance in the United States?

THE PRESIDENT: I should say less than there was ten or twenty years ago. I think, in other words, it would be harder to start a movement based on racial intolerance today than it would have been ten or twenty years ago. I still think it can be done. It is always a possibility, but I think we are wiser and there is less sectionalism. I think we have learned a lot.

Q. Mr. President, do you think the South — what we call the solid South — will stay Democratic very long?

THE PRESIDENT: Will the solid South be Democratic very long? The South is a funny place, I have lived there a long time.

Q. I have just come through the South and I lived there fifteen years every winter. That is why I asked the question.

THE PRESIDENT: I am glad you asked the question. You and I remember things that have happened in the South in our lifetime, before you and I went down there. We remember the days of Tom Watson in Georgia. That was an appeal to prejudice. It was an appeal addressed to a very, very ignorant vote. We have to recognize that fact, because the average boy or girl in my State of Georgia — I am talking about the average in the days of Tom Watson — had had no high school and, as far as the grade school was concerned, had had an average school year of three or four months. That was the condition. They did not read the daily paper, they did not read a magazine. They were getting the lowest form of pay in

the entire nation, and they were therefore completely susceptible to the demagogue. And, in Georgia, we have had
our demagogues, as we all know. You can still have demagogues in Georgia. . . .

The South, because it is still educationally behind the rest
of the nation, is peculiarly susceptible to the demagogue.
Fair? Fair statement?

Q. Yes.

THE PRESIDENT: I think it is a pretty fair statement to make.

Q. May I offer a comment on the general question of whether
the South will be Democratic again or not? Some months
ago a friend of mine — I am from Montgomery, Alabama —
was in the State of Ohio. Somebody asked him if the solid
South is still voting Democratic and he replied, "No damn
Yankee is going to stop us; it is going to be the ruin of this
country."

THE PRESIDENT: Let me put it this way: I think the South is
going to remain Democratic, but I think it is going to be
a more intelligent form of democracy than has kept the
South, for other reasons, in the Democratic column all these
years. It will be intelligent thinking; and, in my judgment,
because the South is learning, it is going to be a liberal
democracy. The South cannot be fooled any more by the
kind of things that were published in southern magazines this
past winter.

The Southern Pine Association, aided and abetted by a
large number of newspapers in the South, editorially and in
their news columns, on the question of the Wages and Hours
Bill, carried a full page ad and some of you people ran them
and got paid for them. The ads were entitled, "Farmers! To
Arms!" And you ran them. They were paid for by the Southern Pine Association. That was a definite, deliberate inciting
of the farmers of the South to take up arms. It was wholly
indefensible; it was an unpatriotic act for any newspaper to
publish that headline. Now you are getting it straight from
the shoulder. "Farmers! To Arms!" How did you dare pub-

lish an advertisement of that kind in your paper? How did you dare to do it?

And then, what did it say? It went on to tell lie after lie. The chief feature of the ad was this: "If a wages and hours bill, putting a floor under wages and a ceiling over hours, goes through, you farmers of Georgia and Alabama, you will have to pay $3.00 a day to your field labor." That is a lie and every editor who ran that ad knew it was a lie. Go on.

Q. Mr. President, where in your opinion is this strife between the two major labor organizations tending from a social and economic standpoint?

THE PRESIDENT: Where is what?

Q. Where is it leading, the strife between the two major labor organizations?

THE PRESIDENT: Oh, I don't know. When you get that kind of a very personal row, it will end in two wings of labor that will become fairly well established and become fairly permanent, or it may end in their working out some kind of a compromise and agreement between the two. In other words, as I said to you last year, this is in the evolutionary process, similar to that which organized labor was going through in other countries twenty and thirty years ago. It is evolutionary. Probably five years from now we shall not recognize or shall have forgotten the existing situation.

Q. We all want to see renewed confidence and renewed investment on the part of private enterprise and the consequent absorption of unemployment. Do you not think that the repeal of the undistributed profits tax will help a lot?

THE PRESIDENT: I will ask you a question. (*Laughter*)

Q. I do not think that is fair, Mr. President. (*Laughter*)

THE PRESIDENT: This is an actual case and I am going to ask you what you think of it: Here are two brothers and they both inherited, each of them, $5,000,000. One brother bought the other brother out. So the brother that was bought out from the cotton mill, which they jointly owned, went up to New York. He went up to New York about ten or twelve

years ago and put his $5,000,000 into investments. He got
Scudder, Stevens and Clark to tell him how he ought to
invest his $5,000,000. They gave him a list of a certain per-
centage of Government bonds and municipals, State bonds,
public utilities, some real estate mortgages, some preferred
stock and some common stock, in accordance with the best
advice that an investing firm can give you. He received on
his $5,000,000 investment about $200,000 a year income
by way of coupons and dividend checks, and, on the whole,
his investment has turned out pretty well. He has been getting his income and he has been living, because he is a
simple man, on about $50,000 of it. But because he had an
income of $200,000, he had to pay in State and Federal
income taxes about half of it. He had about $100,000 left and,
as I say, he only spent $50,000 of it, and he put the other back
into what you and I would call "savings." But the taxes he
paid were about $100,000 a year and he figured that he did
not want to engage in active work. He was very much interested, as a matter of fact, this particular fellow, in art
and literature. He never kicked, he paid his $100,000 in
taxes year after year.

He came down to see me. Of course, he was in the upper
brackets all right. He came down to see me about two years
ago and said, "I am going to ask a question. My $5,000,000
is working. I own mortgages, stocks, bonds that are actually
producing goods, building buildings, maintaining places for
people to live in, building new buildings, starting new enterprises. I am paying half of my total income to the Government every year." He said, "Do not ever mention this to my
brother. His $5,000,000 is in that old family cotton factory
and he has made, since we parted company, about $200,000
a year profit. Like myself, he is a man of comparatively simple
tastes and he spends about $50,000 a year. He only declares
a dividend to himself of $50,000 a year or perhaps $60,000
a year. His tax that he pays to the Government is about
$10,000. His property, his ownership in business, is the

same as mine and his property earns the same return. But, because he owns this cotton mill, he only declares enough in the way of dividends to keep himself going and he leaves all the rest there to accumulate. The net result is that he is accumulating and putting to work $140,000 or $150,000 a year, but that is capital rolling up. All it costs him is $10,000 a year. I have a diversified list of investments and my tax is $100,000 a year. Mr. President, do you think that is equitable?"

I pass that question on to you.

Q. Mr. President, don't you have a section in the Revenue Act to take care of cases like that?

THE PRESIDENT: No.

Q. It is there in the law.

THE PRESIDENT: You have had, since 1913, a Section 102. Cordell Hull introduced it when he was a Member of the House in that year and that section says that the Treasury Department shall have the right to tax any undistributed earnings which, in the judgment of the Treasury Department, are not necessary for the surplus of the business. For twenty-five years, or not that long—for about fifteen years—the Treasury Department took cases of that kind to the courts and they lost in about 99 per cent of the cases that they brought, because the Court said, "Who is the best judge as to what the surplus should be? Why, obviously, the owner of the business. Therefore, we are not going to take the plea of the Treasury. We are going to take the statement of the owner of the business." In other words, it was a completely unenforceable section.

The present Senate Bill attempts to strengthen it by saying that the burden of proof should be on the private company.

Now, you have a choice to make: The Treasury Department, that knows probably more about collecting taxes than any editor in the United States, or the President, says that that change in the law is utter rubbish. You won't be able to prevent the thing you are trying to avoid by putting the bur-

267

den of proof on the owner of the business. It is utterly absurd. Now, you and I may think it is beautiful language, but the experts who have to collect the taxes, they tell the people of the United States and the papers of the United States that they cannot collect under it. There is your answer.

Q. Mr. President, do you think that the incident which you have elaborated is typical?

THE PRESIDENT: I am glad you asked that question. Every person who admits the principle comes down to me, and I cite an instance or two, or five, or ten, or twenty, and their answer is, "That is the exception." Now, those exceptions in terms of dollars in our lifetime are not exceptions in terms of dollars; they are the rule. In terms of the percentage of corporations that do that, yes, they are exceptions, but they are not exceptions when it comes down to the amount of money involved.

Q. If there is a rat in the hayloft, why burn down the whole barn to get the rat out?

THE PRESIDENT: The treasurer of a company came in to see me the other day. He raised that question, both on the undistributed earnings tax and on the capital gains tax. I said, "You admit the principle?" He said, "Certainly." I said, "The principle ought to be the principle of nondiscrimination. It ought to mean the principle that by the use of the corporate method you ought not to be able to do things that you could not do if you were in business as an individual or a partnership; that you ought not to avoid the payment of taxes through a perfectly legal tax avoidance method." He admitted the whole thing; and then I said, "Well, do you think that I ought, because there is a tremendous agitation at the present time, to say, 'Don't burn down the barn to catch the rats'?" as you say. He said, "Certainly, there come times when you have got to forget principle."

I pointed out another case to him and he said, "That is an exception." This a case of a man who owned a newspaper, a very successful newspaper. The paper had built up a large surplus, what was supposed to be a wholly adequate surplus. Now, let us assume that it was an adequate surplus, and that the paper ought to have had that surplus in order to make sure that for a lean year or two it would be able to keep going. The assumption is that the surplus was an adequate one. He died, and because most of his money was in the newspaper, when it came to paying the State and Federal inheritance taxes, his family, his executors and trustees did not have the cash to pay it with. Well, that often happens because we Americans do not look forward to what they call "death duties" in England. The average rich man in England makes provision in various ways for death duties. But does your American, like most of us that you know, make provision for paying inheritance taxes when he dies?

Well, the trustees did not have the cash to pay it. So they said to themselves, because, after all, they were trustees not only for the estate but essentially for the paper itself, they said, "Buy some of our preferred stock that we own in the paper out of your surplus." And then, transforming themselves into the owners of the paper, they said, "All right, we will pay you such and such a sum out of our surplus for that preferred stock." As the owners of the paper, they paid to the trustees, who were themselves, enough cash out of the surplus to pay the inheritance tax. As trustees, they delivered to themselves as the owners of the paper, a certificate for X number of shares of preferred stock, which they then proceeded to tear up and put into the wastepaper basket.

The estate owned essentially all of the newspaper before that transaction, and after it was all over, it still owned essentially the same proportion of the newspaper. In other words, while this particular owner of the paper, in my judgment, had never anticipated anything like that being done, he had, in fact, used that surplus, built it up year after year at a price of 12½ per cent tax on earnings, whereas, if it had been distributed to him, he would have paid about 55 per cent on the earnings of the paper.

That is principle, just plain common or garden variety of principle. A newspaper pointed that out, one which has demanded the entire repeal of the tax on undistributed earnings.

Q. In the specific case, that would have thrown that newspaper into borrowing money in Wall Street or from the banks and would have destroyed the—you would have put it right in the hands of Wall Street. We do not want them to control the American press.

THE PRESIDENT: If this man, knowing that some day he was going to die, had done one or two things—if, out of his annual income, he had taken out insurance on his life, which is one of the English methods, and built up a policy to take care of his inheritance tax when he died—

Q. [interposing] Which would have been taxed—

THE PRESIDENT: —the paper would not have had to dip into this surplus and would not have had to go and borrow the money in Wall Street. Or the other English method, if he had set up a special trust fund out of his income and paid the inheritance tax out of that, the trustees would not have had to borrow money or sell preferred stock to the paper.

Q. In the specific case you are mentioning there, under the income tax rates it would have been utterly impossible to set up a fund which would amount to a sufficient—

THE PRESIDENT: [interposing] He could have taken out insurance. The British manage to do it.

Q. Who can do it?

THE PRESIDENT: The British.

Q. Do the British have the undistributed profits tax?

THE PRESIDENT: They have something that is the equivalent of it. They do not call it that.

Q. Mr. President, in the matter of a surplus tax: In my town we have an industry which started out with eight hands and a boss. He is dead now. He had a million when he died. From year to year he put the surplus which he had into the business and one year he had $220,000. So he conceived the idea of building a nice building in our town. He wanted a building in our town — you know I live in a little town in Wisconsin — and he built this nice building out of the surplus. He had to borrow some money and paid 8 per cent on it, but in two years more his surplus amounted to a sufficient amount so that he took it over and owned it in fee simple; he had a warranty deed for it.

Now, under this surplus taxation, it would not have been possible, comfortably for him, with a tax on this surplus, to do those things, because the tax would have taken such a proportion of the savings out of that business that he would not have been able to do those things. And whatever things they want to do now in the expansion of this business, they are held back by this tax. Now, I do not say that this is wrong; I do not discuss it from the standpoint of its being a tax which is a robber tax. Of course I think it is, but then that is a difficult matter to prove. (*Laughter*)

You and I disagree and we can disagree normally. But he can't do that [referring to the putting up of new buildings]. The president of this organization spoke to me a few days ago and he said, "I would like to build a new building but I am damned if I can do it under the new tax system because it takes away from me —" . . .

THE PRESIDENT: The man who owned that paper, he made $220,000 a year. What was that? That was a profit on his money, wasn't it?

Q. I wish I could do that.

THE PRESIDENT: So do I. It was a profit on his money. If he did not happen to have it in this one thing, a newspaper, on this $220,000 he would have had to pay about $120,000, as, for example, if he had had that income from fifty different newspapers. In this case he happened to own one newspaper and therefore he asks that that $220,000 pay only a 12½ per cent tax instead of a 55 per cent tax. Principle?

Q. Yes, but he might have had some expansion. I am going through, right now, all of this agony of a man who died and owned a newspaper and I happen to be the fall guy and right now I am trying to straighten this inheritance tax out and God knows what we will have when we get through. We might have enough to pay one man, one in the Newspaper Guild, one salary for one week. But what I am trying to impress upon you, Mr. President, from your place here in Washington, where you look over this country, where you see my State with all of those small industries, who have to build up little things —

THE PRESIDENT: [interposing] Right.

Q. — from time to time must have to build up a little surplus for expansion and to make more people work in those places. We have 2,721 factories gone out of business since March 4, 1933, Mr. President, in my State.

THE PRESIDENT: How many went out between 1929 and 1933?

Q. No, I have got them all dated from cheese factories down and we need this surplus so that we can build up there, without extraordinary taxes to take it away from people who want to use it for expansion.

THE PRESIDENT: Has anybody called your attention to the House Bill?

Q. Yes, I am sorry I have, too.

THE PRESIDENT: It says this: It says that the average standard corporation tax is to be greatly increased over what it is now. It is to go as high as 16 per cent. Now, you are a corporation. You are making $25,000 a year. You can soak the whole of the $25,000. You are talking about these stories, about the little corporation that is just getting by. With the little corporation, under the House Bill up to $25,000 a year profit, which is not to be sneezed at, you can put all your earnings back into the property. You do not have to distribute any of them. You pay the normal corporation tax of 16 per cent and then from there on, up to the corporation that makes

$75,000 a year, you get a special preference because you are a little fellow.

Let me go on the air sometime and talk about these little fellows, little corporations, the little "small fry" that are only making up to $75,000 a year. Why, they are poverty-stricken, just paying $75,000 a year. And, because they are so small in their profits, they get a special exemption, too. They can distribute almost all of their profits without any penalty whatsoever.

And then when you get to the corporations that make over $75,000 a year, of course the average citizen in this country figures out that that is a pretty successful corporation. Then what happens? If they don't distribute all their earnings, mind you, they get a 30 per cent exemption right away to start with, and if they do not distribute the other 20 per cent, they are subject to a 4 per cent penalty, which raises their tax to the enormous sum of 20 per cent a year instead of 16 per cent. Now, has that been brought out? It has not.

Q. I want to say, Mr. President, that out of a report of the earnings of some 6400 industries in the State of Wisconsin, only eleven earned in excess of $75,000 a year. You see, the rest of them are poverty-stricken.

THE PRESIDENT: Then the House Bill only affects eleven out of 6400 in the State of Wisconsin?

Q. We would like to make more, Mr. President.

THE PRESIDENT: It affects only eleven.

Let us go one step further. The Senate Bill eliminates that 4 per cent for withholding dividends from distribution, eliminates that tax entirely, and substitutes for it an additional 2 per cent on all of your 6,000 corporations in the State of Wisconsin, making a flat 18 per cent corporation tax instead of 16. With this net result — that I have only seen mentioned in about half a dozen major papers in the United States — that your 5,989 corporations in Wisconsin will have to pay 18 per cent on their earnings instead of 16 per cent and, by the Senate Bill, you are helping eleven on the condition that they do not want to distribute 70 per cent of their earnings.

Q. Mr. President, I might say that I am opposed to both bills.

THE PRESIDENT: Yes, all right. But we are talking about a practical proposition. Under the Senate Bill you will obtain $30,000,000 more revenue from corporations as a whole than you will under the House Bill. Did you ever print that? In other words, corporate industry in the United States is soaked $30,000,000 more by the Federal Government under the Senate Bill than it is under the House Bill. Now, that is an interesting fact. You are soaked $90,000,000 more to the smaller corporations and $60,000,000 less to the larger corporations, or a net increase in the burden on industry under the Senate Bill of $30,000,000 more than under the House Bill.

Q. Mr. President, do you see any hope of the House and Senate conferees getting together on the tax bill?

THE PRESIDENT: I hope they will, very much. If you were sitting here in my place, as President of the United States, what would you do? Would you say, like my friend of this corporation, in this kind of a situation, "Forget principle"? Would you say that?

Now, we can work this thing out if we approach it from the point of view of giving to the public both sides of the case. I want principle in this country maintained.

Now, coming to the second phase, if you don't mind, capital gains: Back in — some of you people are a little bit older than I am; I think Bill [William White] is a little bit older than I am — wasn't it in 1888 that the Democratic platform contained a recommendation for income taxes?

Q. [Mr. White] I do not remember. I have had such hard work earning a living that I never looked into the philosophy of taxation. (*Laughter*)

THE PRESIDENT: Well, anyway, it became one of the major party items. The main thought was an income tax based on the ability to pay. It was in 1894, in one of the Cleveland administrations, they passed an income tax on the graduated basis. That is to say, the more you made, the higher you paid. It was declared unconstitutional by the Supreme Court and it was reintroduced into practically every Democratic platform, and finally in 1913 a Constitutional amendment was ratified levying a tax on income from whatever source derived.

The Congress in 1914 passed an income tax law and a capital gains law. Both of them were based on the theory that there are a great many people in this country who increase their income by different means, some from rents and royalties, some from dividends, some from the interest on bank accounts or bonds, and some of them from trading operations in real estate, in stocks or in bonds. The first income tax law that was held valid incorporated the principle of a graduated capital gains tax as well as a graduated income tax on the theory that both of them were taxation of increases in wealth. That, I take it, has been a fairly consistent principle of the American people from that date to this. It happens to be a quarter of a century.

The House Bill recognized what was probably the fact, that the existing capital gains tax was too high. They therefore reduced it, and they reduced it to what was considered a fair differential, a fair graduation of rates to be paid on capital gains. I was entirely willing to go along with it as long as they maintained the principle. That is the principle and it is the American principle. The Senate, however, abandoned the American principle, adopted and held for a quarter of a century, and said this — and I will give you an illustration: The other day I had two men come to visit me, both of them old friends. One of them has got — he is about as rich as I am, which does not mean much. Last year, a few year ago, he bought a couple of hundred shares of stock and he has a nice little profit, even today. He thinks the company is doing well, but he does not want to hold it. He has a $5,000 capital gain in it and he is willing to pay his 15 per cent. The other man who came in has a block of 10,000 shares of a certain stock that he bought at 20 and can sell to-morrow for 70. He has a net profit in that of $500,000. He is all for the Senate Bill because the Senate Bill would only tax him 15 per cent on a half million dollar profit, just like the little fellow, who has a $5,000 profit. Therefore the Senate Bill is a complete negation and abandonment of what has become an established American policy.

Now, what do I do? Do I say again, "Oh, well, let us encourage business, to hell with principle?" And a lot of you are asking me to do it.

Q. What you refer to as principle is not principle in a moral sense; it is just a theory on one sort of taxation.

THE PRESIDENT: Well, I don't know. I think it goes a little deeper than that.

Q. Is it a moral principle?

THE PRESIDENT: I do think so.

Q. That is what is meant by principle.

THE PRESIDENT: I think it is a moral principle. In other words, I think that the man with an income, whether it is from capital gains, or stock, or bonds, or a newspaper, who is making a million dollars a year — and we know a good many people in this country who are doing it; there are somewhere around fifty or sixty at the present time who are making a million dollars a year or more — I think he ought to pay a larger percentage of his income to his Government than the man who is making a salary, as a managing editor, of $10,000 a year.

Q. Well, I do not think anybody disputes that.

THE PRESIDENT: I think that is principle; I do not think it is a theory of taxation.

Q. Isn't the argument for the abolition of capital gains the general benefit the country would have from increased transactions rather than the benefit of saving taxes for the comparatively few taxpayers who actually sell things at a profit?

THE PRESIDENT: "The hands of Esau!" Now, this same fellow who has got a profit of fifty points on 10,000 shares of stock —

I have known him for a great many years — I said, "You want to sell it and keep your profit? What will you do with it?" He said, "I have two or three pretty good lines." I said, "What do you mean 'lines'?" He said, "I have watched two or three things that I can go into, things that I think have a big future ahead of them where I can get in on what you and I would call the ground floor."

"Well," I said, "they are going concerns?" "Yes."

And I said, "You want to put your money to work?" "Yes."

"So you would put your money in as new capital in these firms, this half million?" He said, "I will go out and buy my stock on the Stock Exchange, as I did before."

I said, "Is that putting new capital into these companies? No, you are only transferring ownership from A to B. That is not putting new money to work."

Now, half the people, when you come down to it and analyze it, fall into that category. You are not putting your money into new business, you are going and buying something from somebody else.

Q. Can you tell us about your expectations on private spending and private investment?

THE PRESIDENT: Let me put it this way: Somebody at the Press Conference the day before yesterday asked me what was new about this new program. I said it was a new phase. It is going to work, provided the country gets the truth told about it, provided we get all angles presented to the public, provided the element of fear is eliminated with the help of everybody in the United States.

In other words, if we work together on this thing, it is going to work. If we do not work together on it, it may fail. At the present time, the responsibility for that rests more essentially on the Press of the country than it does on the business of the country.

Q. What would you suggest that the Press tell business?

THE PRESIDENT: I would not tell business anything.

Q. Treat them rough. (*Laughter*)

Q. Mr. President, do you think the American Press—we are newspapermen here and not stock market speculators and not anything like that—do you think the American newspapers have been unfair?

THE PRESIDENT: I do not think they have been unfair, but I think they have been more responsible for the inciting of fear in the community than any other factor.

Q. I would like to ask you, Mr. President, in what particular?

THE PRESIDENT: I will give you, if you want, examples. I can multiply them about a thousand times.

As my old friend up the river says, I broke out of the papers the other day some clippings. Here is an example: The other night, oh, three nights ago, two nights ago, there was an A.P. story. Well, I never expect an A.P. story to give my side the lead. I have not for years and I have always managed to survive.

Q. Do you think the A.P. is unfair to you?

THE PRESIDENT: I am not saying it is unfair. Listen, let me finish: Every time, for example, that there is a debate in the Senate—well, you have got, what is it, 11, 12, 13, 14 Republican Senators, 3 or 4 Progressives like George Norris and La Follette, and you have got, oh, a half dozen, 6 or 8, old-line Democratic Senators who, if they lived in the North, would not be Democrats anyway. All the rest are Democrats.

Now, what happens? You have got a very small minority, less than a third who are not Democrats. Arthur Vandenberg gets up, or somebody else gets up, Carter Glass gets up, and makes a speech. Then the majority of the Senate hops all over him and makes some speeches on the other side.

Now, what is your lead? I know the mechanics of the thing. Your lead is based on speeches coming from less than a third of the Senators every time.

Now, your Press associations, especially the A.P., will, in their second or third paragraph, mention the fact that Alben Barkley or somebody else replied, and they will give them space, but your lead and the headlines of 85 per cent of the larger papers of the country will feature the speech of the Minority Member of the House or the Senate.

The other day, there was a party on the air. There was Vandenberg, and on the Democratic side there was Senator Hill of Alabama. Well they each, I think, had — whatever it was — half an hour on the air. The first I knew about this fact — I very rarely listen on the radio and I had not arranged it in any way — was the next afternoon when I got the first edition of the New York *Sun*. I read the headline, "Huge Recovery Plan Attacked by Republicans; Vandenberg Denounces Roosevelt Relief Program; Says Pump Priming Means Bigger Debts, Bigger Deficits." Then there is the Washington headline, A.P., and it goes on. This is the main story, right-hand column. And it goes on, "continued on page 7," and talks all about what Vandenberg said. And then it goes on and talks about what John Hamilton gave out.

"Well," I said to myself, "that is funny for the A.P. I do not believe it left out what Mr. Hill said, but there is not a peep, there is not a mention of Lister Hill in the *Sun*."

So — it happened to be on my bed that night — I happened to pick up another New York paper and this story carried the whole of the A.P. story. Now, this A.P. story in its lead mentions the anti-New Deal attacks of the Republicans, it mentions Hamilton in the second paragraph and eventually, in the third paragraph, it talks about the feeling in the Congress. In the fourth paragraph it talks about the Administration side. That was left out of the *Sun* story. In the fifth paragraph, it talks about my weekly conference with the Congressional people — that was left out in the *Sun*. The sixth paragraph [reading] "The Vandenberg speech was made during a broadcast with Senator Hill of Alabama. Hill said —" And then Hill's remarks were carried in the seventh, eighth and ninth paragraphs. In other words, outside of the lead, the A.P. did give you a truthful newspaper story. It did not mention Hill in the lead but, further down in the story, it said what Hill said. And the New York *Sun* deliberately cut out what the A.P. had said to them. If you people think that is fair newspaper editing, I do not. Now, you find hundreds of cases of that kind.

Then, there are papers that have their special bureaus in Washington. You know perfectly well that the special bureau chiefs down here write what the owner of the newspaper tells them to write, and they leave out half of the truth. They give a one-sided picture to the American people.

Q. In the *Sun* of the previous day, did they not carry, in full, your Address to the Congress and your radio remarks of the same day?

THE PRESIDENT: Oh, they have to do that. That is not what I am talking about.

Q. Can you name an instance in the history of the world where continuous borrowing has led to anything less than a great catastrophe?

THE PRESIDENT: Yes. Read the history of England during and after the Napoleonic War. Read the editorials and get the figures and facts. You can get them from the London *Times*. It is an amazing story.

Q. William Allen White said, "Treat the businessmen rough."

Perhaps he means from the Kansas point of view. I am from the New England industrial region. I have never seen industrialists in our section more down in the mouth over the troubles they are facing, and it comes primarily from the taxation, from the things that we have been discussing here. They have surpluses which they have been in the habit of keeping through generations, in looking out for the rainy day. May I ask, under this load of taxes, who is going to hold the umbrella over those corporations in the rainy season that seems bound to come? Is the Government to hold the umbrella or who is to hold it?

THE PRESIDENT: That is what I would call an extremely unfair question because they are allowed to put 30 per cent back and any amount up to 100 per cent at a 4 per cent tax. That is not going to prevent them.

Q. If the going is good; but unfortunately the people up there are not like people, your friends, who are buying stock at twenty and selling it at seventy.

THE PRESIDENT: Your corporations in New England are, unfortunately, not earning the $75,000 which would be exempt.

Q. I think there are a good many Washington correspondents who are accredited from Washington papers. I have never got an order from my publisher, in all the fifteen or sixteen years, to write a story one way or the other. I might have written your story wrong, but I never got an order. I think it is true of the bulk of them.

THE PRESIDENT: It is true of a great many. But, do you know the number of people who have resigned all over the country because they could not go along with the orders they have got? We get them every week. I have got a letter here from an exceedingly good editor who was fired for writing a pro-Administration editorial — two of them. However, he is now asking for a job. He says he will take a hundred dollars a week.

Q. He will get it, too, won't he? (*Laughter*)

Q. [Mr. William Allen White] I think I have a little comfort for you. Seven years ago I was down here on another visit, and a man tapped me on the shoulder and said that the President wanted to talk to me, and here, in this hall, walking up and down, was the President. And he was talking about conditions and grumbling with his hands behind his back. He said, "Look here, here is the New York *World*; here is the New York *Sun.*"

Now, what is the difference between a Republican paper abusing a Democrat and the Democratic paper abusing a Republican? I would forget it. That is the way they make their money and that is the way they want to run their paper. It cannot hurt you, and it gives them some comfort. (*Laughter*)

THE PRESIDENT: Well, there are two points I would like to make on that:

You never saw me walking up and down with a long face because of anything I ever read in any newspaper. There is a difference from the incumbent of seven years ago.

Q. It was the same intestinal disturbance. (*Laughter*)

THE PRESIDENT: Number two, I do not think, taking it by and large and speaking seriously, that the New York *World* at that time, and other papers that brought out unfair attacks on Mr. Hoover, did the Nation very much good. I do not think it is to be condoned because of the fact that editors and papers and candidates — and candidates — did it in the past and that, therefore, it is all right to do it again.

Q. [Mr. William Allen White] I don't either; I did not think so then and I do not now.

THE PRESIDENT: I do not think it helps the country. The point that I get back to, the point that I made before, is that the Press can be largely responsible for cutting out the petty stuff and getting their shoulders in behind national recovery, if they want to do it.

They won't hurt me. Oh, no! It is a much bigger thing than any individual. But they may hurt about 125,000,000 people. They have a very great responsibility.

The responsibility is based on a very simple effort that I hope the Press will make, and that is to tell the whole story, both sides, evenly, equally and fairly, without recriminations, without the kind of petty stuff that we have been so accustomed to, both from the New York *World* of the old days and the Chicago *Tribune*, let us say, of these days. It does not do the country any real good. As I have said, now for the fifth year, you are only hurting the Press.

People like to read the Walter Winchells and the Paul Mallons and the other columns; they like to read the amusing stories, the Pearson and Allen stuff, and so forth and so on. But, in the long run, they are getting to the point of saying, "Oh, it is funny, it is grand; I love to read it every morning but what can I believe? I have read so much of this sort of stuff now for years and years."

And I want to tell you, with due solemnity, that we are beginning to get a phrase in this country that is not good for this country; it is bad for this country and it is bad for the newspapers: "Oh, that is one of those newspaper stories."

Now, that is an actual fact, and, mind you, I am more closely in touch with public opinion in the United States than any individual in this room. I have a closer contact with more people than any man in this room. I get a better cross-section of opinion.

Do not fool yourselves about "yes men." I have had them ever since I have been in public life. I have paid more attention to the "no men" than I have to the "yes men." I can tell a "yes man" inside of a couple of weeks of association with him. I do not get fooled.

You, all of you — it is an essential thing — it is not a derogatory statement on my part — you cannot get a national picture the way I can. You cannot understand, no matter how hard you study the thing, the rounded aspect of the national problems the way a man right here in Washington can.

In the first place, your business is a local one. Some of you are connected with chain papers; you rely to a certain extent on the judgment of people who, again, are in the local field. There is not a newspaperman that comes into my office that understands the ramifications of the national problems. They try awfully hard and they are a grand crowd. I am for them — I won't say a hundred per cent — but I am for them ninety-five per cent.

Among any group — lawyers, doctors, clergy and editors and politicians — there is a certain percentage of people out of a hundred that you cannot trust. In the newspaper game those boys down here in Washington have as high a standard of ethics and morals and fair play as any profession in the United States. I take off my hat to them. But a lot of them labor under a very big handicap. It does not trace back, of necessity, to their editors. It traces back to the owner of the paper, essentially.

Q. Are these charges that you lay at the door of the newspapers — do you find that true of the majority of the newspapers? When you say, "the Press as a whole," we would like to know of how many you find that true.

THE PRESIDENT: It is awfully hard to give figures. In the first place, I would eliminate practically all the country newspapers because that is a different story. But take the newspapers that subscribe to A.P. or U.P. I would say that eighty-five per cent of them have been inculcating fear in this country during the past year.

Q. Mr. President, do you think that has been intentional on the part of the owners of the papers? Do you think eighty-five per cent of the owners of the papers —

THE PRESIDENT: Yes, intentional in a perfectly natural human way. The owner of the paper has seen the thing from his own personal view and, if I were the owner of the paper, I might do the same thing.

Q. There has been interest in Congress on the matter of American neutrality. I wonder if you would comment, possibly on the Scott Resolution and also on the broader question of achieving neutrality through legislation?

THE PRESIDENT: This being off the record, I think I can tell you the story the way I told it to Bill Borah [Senator Borah] today.

Senator Borah came down to lunch with me and he has been a good deal disturbed — a good many of us have — by the fact that this country has split up and become so emotional over the Spanish situation. Well, we had an extremely satisfactory talk and when I had explained the Spanish thing, he said, "I think you are a hundred per cent right and, if you get a chance, I hope that you will tell the public the story you told me."

Well, I hesitate to do it. I have not had a chance to talk to Steve [Mr. Early]. I thought of doing it tomorrow morning

284

at the Press Conference, but I do not know whether, in Press Conference, in formal conversation, the idea can be got across.

Now, as he and I both agreed, the object of neutrality is to prevent the United States from doing two things: first, from becoming involved in a foreign war. The second is, in the event of a foreign war, to put the United States in a position where it won't help one side or hurt the other side. In other words, where we will be fair to both sides in the conflict.

Then I went back and I pointed out that, when the Spanish Revolution broke out, and after it had been going for a comparatively short time, they began to kill a lot of people. In other words, from that point of view, it was war. It was generally recognized by the world as a civil war, which came under the Act.

The Act, however, to my sorrow and to Senator Borah's sorrow, attempted to lay down a mandatory rule. As he said to me today, it is impossible in English language, in the form of a statute, to anticipate every future foreign trouble that may happen because every one is apart from every one that happened before.

Well, we had undoubtedly a Spanish civil war with apparently two equal sides. Both sides, both the Spanish Government and Franco, had navies of approximately the same size; they were about equal. Therefore, we figured, that by declaring that there was a war, therefore the Neutrality Act applied, and therefore there would be an embargo placed by us on the shipment of planes or munitions or guns or anything else. In that way, we would not be favoring either side. For several months that resulted in a fairly strict neutrality. We did not help one side more than the other. Very few shipments of planes or munitions or guns went out of this country and got into Spain on either side.

Then the advent of war brought about a situation where Franco got complete control of the sea. This meant immediately—and he has had it ever since—that if, by some hook or crook, I could determine that there wasn't any war in Spain and thereby allow the shipment of arms to both sides, both to Franco and to Barcelona, the effect would be that Franco, controlling the sea, could send his ships directly to the United States and load them up with bombs and airplanes and anything else that he could buy and take them over right to his own army.

The Spanish Government, the Barcelona Government, because it did not control the sea, would not be able to buy anything by direct shipment to Barcelona or Valencia. Therefore, to have changed the neutrality proclamation in the last few months would have been definitely aiding and abetting the Franco Government.

Now, as a matter of fact, the situation is this: We have also read about this terrible, inhuman bombing of the civilian population in Barcelona. We have also read—and while I have no information on the subject, it probably is true— that American-made bombs have been dropped on Barcelona by Franco airplanes. That is possible. If those bombs were of American manufacture, they were bombs that were sold by American manufacturers to Germany, that is to say, either to the German Government, which is a perfectly legal thing to do, or to German companies, which is also perfectly legal, and they were shipped to Germany and reshipped down to Franco's forces.

At the same time, we also know that there have been munitions which have left this country and have been sold in France. That is a perfectly bona fide sale. These sales, either to the French Government, or to French agents, or French companies—being entirely legal—in all probability, a good many of these shipments have all gone to the Barcelona Government, so the net effect of what we have been doing in the past year and a half has been as close to carrying out an actual neutrality—not helping one side against the other—as we can possibly do under the existing law.

Now, the same thing applies to the Japanese–Chinese situation. In that case we have not put into effect the neutrality proclamation, for the very simple reason that if we could find a way of not doing it, we would be more neutral than if we did.

Now, if we declared neutrality, what would happen? Japan could not buy any munitions from us, but they are not buying them anyway. China is buying munitions from us via England, via Singapore, via Hong Kong — not direct — through English purchases and, undoubtedly, American munitions are going into China today. But, on the other hand, Japan has complete, free access to all of our raw material markets because they dominate the ocean. They are buying their copper, their oil, their cotton — they are buying all kinds of things, scrap metal by the shiploads, which is going into munitions, and they would be able, under the Neutrality Act, to continue to buy oil and copper and scrap metal.

Therefore, by virtue of this excuse that they are not at war — it is only an excuse — we are maintaining, in fact, a neutral position.

Q. We are achieving that, despite the neutrality?

THE PRESIDENT: Despite the neutrality law; and that is the trouble with a neutrality law that attempts to tie the hands of an administration for future events and circumstances that no human being can possibly guess.

Q. Would you mind saying what your thought is on the Scott Resolution?

THE PRESIDENT: The Scott Resolution is a perfectly simple thing. It asks the State Department, in effect, to repeat to the Congress what is already known to everybody. That, in the case of Ethiopia, we took such and such a position. That, in the case of China and Japan, we took such and such a position. And, I think it will be answered in that way. We shall simply lay the records before Congress of what we have said and done in the last two years.

Q. There is something that I do not quite understand; perhaps you would be willing to explain. I think, in your last Fireside Chat, you spoke about certain legislation this Administration got through, the T.V.A., the Wagner Act, the Utility Act, and others. I think you admitted they were not perfect. Why has not legislation started so that they would not be one-sided?

THE PRESIDENT: For this very simple reason: The Wagner Act ought to have various amendments made to it, but we are a funny people over here. We at once go to the extremes, both on the side of labor and on the side of the employer. We all get upset and excited, and we say things we do not mean, and we make overstatements.

Now, in England, when they put social legislation on the statute books, they do it with the knowledge that every year or so they will amend it. Social security over there went into effect in 1911 and I think, without exception, every Parliament has amended it. Now, how do they amend it? They have a Royal Commission that looks it over. The Commission is nonpartisan, there are business men on it, and there are labor people on it. They decide that the thing needs certain improvements. The Royal Commission makes a report to the Parliament, and the thing goes through, almost automatically, without fuss or feathers.

If we had that temperament over here, we would have improved the Wagner Act this year and improved the Social Security Act this year, keeping them out of politics.

Q. Perhaps that is what Congress needs?

THE PRESIDENT: I think you are right.

Q. Why does the National Labor Relations Board regard itself as a bunch of prosecutors instead of a fact-finding body?

THE PRESIDENT: Well, that is a statement, and I do not know that it is wholly justified. I think it is in some cases, but on the other hand, there is another side to the picture.

Let me tell you a story that is known to four or five of you who are here tonight. There is a certain cotton mill in the

South. The conditions of wages in that cotton mill are good; the conditions of housing are good. They are well above the average. As long as ten or twelve years ago, the owners of this mill abandoned the company-owned house. Pretty nearly every operative in that mill owns or rents his own house. The cotton mill does not own or rent any houses at all. Taking it by and large, the conditions of employment are good. They have had very little labor trouble.

Not long ago, the Cotton Textile Workers' Union, in pursuance of organization provided for in fact by the law — it is perfectly legal — sent down to this town two organizers. Well, I happened to know one of them; and that particular man is just as good an American as anybody in this room. He is a labor organizer but he is a very good citizen. He took with him another man; I do not know him but his reputation is exceedingly good. They went down to this town with the specific purpose of seeking to create a union among the textile workers.

They got in town about ten o'clock in the morning. They had a list of eight or ten of the operators. They were going to see them at the noon hour.

So they went to the factory and they asked, "Where is so and so? Where can I find so and so?"

They were engaged in asking questions, when one of the mill police tapped him on the shoulder and showed his badge and said, "Come with me."

He said, "We have not done anything; we are outside and on the street and just asking to see some fellows."

"Oh, we know; come with me."

They were taken to the police station and locked up in a cell on the charge of vagrancy. Both of them had, oh, fifteen or twenty dollars apiece in their clothes.

They said, "We are not vagrants; we came down here from such and such a city."

"But you are organizers."

"Of course we are organizers."

"Well, you are in a bad place."

They were kept in jail until five o'clock, just before dark, and the judge came in and said, "What are you doing here?"

"We are down here to try to start an organization of the textile workers of this mill."

"That is what you think," he said. "Ten dollars fine and out of town before six o'clock, and do not come back."

They did not know what they were fined for, but they paid the fine, and as they went out of the courtroom, one of the marshals, or policemen, went up to them and said, "Which way are you boys going?" They said, "We have got to get out of town and we thought we would go to such and such a town, ten miles away."

"Well," said the policeman, "I will give you a lift; I turn off two miles short."

They rode with him and he said, "This is where I turn off." They got out and started to hike down the road. They went about a quarter of a mile and out of a clump of bushes came some men with blackjacks and they got the worst beating up that any two people could get without getting killed. They spent a week in the hospital, and they were served notice by a man who brought the message, "Do not go into that town." Now, those were authorities of that government, town and county.

Now, you do not get those facts, and that is one reason why the National Labor Relations Board sometimes tries to bring out facts of that kind. It is their duty to do it. They have a perfect right to go into that town. It is their duty.

Q. Mr. President, what would you do in a case like this: There came into Tupelo, from Baltimore, a C.I.O. organizer. He did not know a blessed thing about conditions in that community. There was a cotton mill. The workers were satisfied with the working conditions. They had good houses and all of their children were in school.

Those organizers proceeded to organize a C.I.O. body. Well, the owners of the mill said, "We cannot meet your terms and conditions. We are just barely keeping our heads above water and so, therefore, we will close down the mill. We will simply liquidate." As a result, 400 workers were thrown on charity.

Well, the people who took the load became tired of supporting those 400 idle workers; and a few nights ago they took the C.I.O. organizer out and gave him a fairly good strafing, although not as good as he should have had. They had a woman and they gave her a little beating up, too.

Now, there are 400 people destitute because they came down here and disturbed the conditions.

THE PRESIDENT: Were they a majority of the mill?

Q. There were none of them keen about it. There were just a few in there. The majority of them did not want it.

THE PRESIDENT: Did the majority join?

Q. No, the majority did not.

THE PRESIDENT: What did the National Labor Relations Board do?

Q. The National Labor Relations Board apparently got a man down there to hold a hearing at the mill and he started the hearing after the mill closed.

There you have a case of force, and that ought not to be allowed to close the mill. That was the will of ten per cent; and they had no right to close the mill.

THE PRESIDENT: The answer is not in beating up. The answer is going to the courts about it. Now the machinery — heavens above! — the machinery needs improving, of course it does, but do it the English way. Do not damn everybody about it. Try to get the thing improved.

Q. Is it true that the press is taking an unfair advantage of the National Labor Relations Board when it prints that defendants before the Board were absolutely prohibited from presenting their testimony as they chose to present it? Is that another evidence of the unfairness of the press?

THE PRESIDENT: You will have to give me a specific case on that. I was once a lawyer; and I know that by the presentation of testimony you can tie up a case for weeks, if you want to. It is a very simple thing. It depends on the judge. Again, you may be before a court that shoves off too fast.

Q. There was an important decision last week. I confess I have forgotten the title. It was a steel concern. They were denied the right to testify.

THE PRESIDENT: Now, you talk about the press. Every month, on the average, since that particular Board has been going, they have handled approximately 200 cases. At the end of the month they give a report on what happens. Out of the 200 cases, you will find on the average that 185 have been settled by some local arbitrator and they never turned up in Washington. That is about 185 out of 200. You will find that another ten, out of the fifteen, are still pending, without any proceeding whatsoever and that, out of 200 cases, there will be five that are not settled or are in the process of being settled. Well, 195 cases out of 200 is a pretty good average.

Now, those figures are given to the newspapers every month. I will put it this way: For the first month after the Board made its report, it was printed in the papers that they had settled 195 out of 200 without fuss or feathers. From that time, there never was a word about that monthly report.

About a month ago, I told the Press about it in a Press Conference and it was printed only because the President of the United States called their attention to it, and pretty nearly everybody sent a story to their papers about it. Half the papers did not print the story. It was not on any first page. Most of the stories were cut from half a column down to a clip on the fourteenth page.

Q. Do you think it would do any good for the Government to conduct elections in a great many towns, where there seems to be uncertainty, so that no one knows which side is in the majority; and they sit around, not knowing what will happen, because the C.I.O. doesn't work, and the other side can't work. Couldn't the Government go in and have an election?

THE PRESIDENT: My opinion is Yes, and that we ought to do it.

Do you remember the Detroit case in 1934, when that automobile strike threatened? Do you remember, I appointed a board of three, that they went out to Detroit and this board of three ran the election themselves? I think it is a good thing to do.

Q. I am from Canton, Ohio, and a couple of weeks ago, the National Labor Relations Board decided in a steel case that the company should deal with the C.I.O. if they are in the majority. A couple of weeks ago they decided that the company union should disband itself, yet there is a feeling that it is in the majority. Should the Government go in and decide?

THE PRESIDENT: I think they should do it. When either side raises a question on the actual representation, I think the Government should have a vote under its jurisdiction.

MR. ALFRED H. KIRCHHOFER: It is with reluctance that we will have to take our leave.

THE PRESIDENT: It is grand to see you. But I do want to repeat, in the utmost friendliness, that this situation is very largely in your hands. And do not worry, it is nothing in your own lives. Not a bit. That part of it is easy. I am thinking about the American public and I am thinking about the newspapers of this country. I do not want them to lose their influence as newspapers giving all the news. I feel very, very strongly about it for the sake of the public and even for the sake of the Press; and if, from now on, we can have a presentation from the Press of both sides of the news, it will be a perfectly magnificent thing.

I will tell you a story: A year and a half ago, when John Boettiger went out to take charge of the Seattle *Post-Intelligencer*, we all knew he had a hot potato. In the first place, he had a paper that ran between three and four hundred thousand dollars a year in the red. That is no joke. In the second place, he had old man Hearst as a boss, which is no joke either. (*Laughter*)

However, he had got a pretty good understanding out of the old man, Hearst, that he would not have to run those box editorials that Hearst wrote. Well, that was something. (*Laughter*) That was a gain. Then, in addition to that, he was going to a city that has had more violent labor troubles than almost any other city in this country.

He said, "What would you do?" I said, "Two pieces of advice from a student of publicity. Eliminate your editorial page altogether. Nobody reads it."

Now, that is horrid for me to say that to you. Mr. Ochs told me a great many years ago — not so many, about four or five years ago — that in his judgment only eight per cent of the readers of The New York *Times* read any of the editorials, and less than half of one per cent read one editorial all the way through. Now, that is Mr. Ochs.

So, I said, "John, cut out your editorial page entirely. Run some features on it, run some cartoons on it, run letters to the editor on it and clip editorials that appeal to you from other papers or weeklies or monthly magazines." (*Laughter*)

I said, "Number 2: On your news stories. You are a newspaper. You are in a labor dispute town. The next time you have a strike down on the water front, take two of your best men and say to Mr. A, 'You go down and you cover the water-front story for tomorrow's papers and you get in your story, the story of the strikers from their point of view, and write your lead that the strikers claimed yesterday that so and so and so and so, and that the leader of the strikers, Bridges' man, said so and so and so and so.'

And then say to Mr. B, 'You go down there and you write your story from the point of view of the shippers, the owners of the freight that is tied up, the point of view of the steamship owners whose ships are tied up, and you write your lead that yesterday on the water front the shippers and the shipowners claimed the following.' You run those two stories in parallel columns on the front page, and do not make them too long, so that the reading public will get both sides at the same time."

Q. Did he follow your suggestion, sir?

THE PRESIDENT: He did not. (*Laughter*)

Q. Has he made a big success of his paper?

THE PRESIDENT: He is in the black, probably because he did not take my advice. But I will say this, that he did honest reporting.

Q. That was good advice, Mr. President.

THE PRESIDENT: You think it was good advice? Well, anyway he got in the black and that is the main thing.

MR. KIRCHHOFER: We are very grateful to you. We hope we can come next year.

THE PRESIDENT: I enjoyed all the shafts and I think I returned them with interest, so it is all right. (*Applause*)

(For the address to the D.A.R., see Item 53, this volume; for further discussion of the undistributed profits tax, see Items 47 and 67, this volume; for an account of the work of the National Labor Relations Board, see Item 90, 1935 volume, Item 71, this volume, and accompanying notes.)

55 ⟨A Recommendation to the Congress to Terminate Tax Exemptions for the Future. April 25, 1938

To the Congress:

THE SIXTEENTH AMENDMENT to the Constitution of the United States, approved in 1913, expressly authorized the Congress "to lay and collect taxes on incomes, from whatever source derived." That is plain language. Fairly construed, this language would seem to authorize taxation of income derived from state and municipal, as well as federal bonds, and also income derived from state and municipal as well as federal offices.

This seemingly obvious construction of the Sixteenth Amendment, however, was not followed in judicial decisions by the courts. Instead, a policy of reciprocal tax immunity was read into the Sixteenth Amendment. This resulted in exempting the income from federal bonds from state taxation and exempting the income from State bonds from federal taxation.

Whatever advantages this reciprocal immunity may have had in the early days of this nation have long ago disappeared. Today it has created a vast reservoir of tax exempt securities in the hands of the very persons who equitably should not be relieved of taxes on their income. This reservoir now constitutes a serious menace to the fiscal systems of both the states and the nation because for years both the federal government and the states have come to rely increasingly upon graduated income taxes for their revenues.

Both the states and the nation are deprived of revenues which could be raised from those best able to supply them. Neither the federal government nor the states receive any adequate, compensating advantage for the reciprocal tax-immunity accorded to income derived from their respective obligations and offices.

A similar problem is created by the exemption from state or federal taxation of a great army of state and federal officers and employees. The number of persons on the pay rolls of both state and federal government has increased in recent years. Tax exemptions claimed by such officers and employees — once an inequity of relatively slight importance — has become a most serious defect in the fiscal systems of the States and the nation, for they rely increasingly upon graduated income taxes for their revenues.

It is difficult to defend today the continuation of either of these rapidly expanding areas of tax exemption. Fundamentally our tax laws are intended to apply to all citizens equally. That does not mean that the same rate of income tax should apply to the very rich man and to the very poor man. Long ago the United States, through the Congress, accepted the principle that citizens should pay in accordance with their ability to pay, and that identical tax rates on the rich and on the poor actually worked an injustice to the poor. Hence the origin of progressive surtaxes on personal income as the individual personal income increases.

Tax exemptions through the ownership of government securities of many kinds — federal, state and local — have operated against the fair or effective collection of progressive surtaxes. Indeed, I think it is fair to say that these exemptions have violated the spirit of the tax law itself by actually giving a greater advantage to those with large incomes than to those with small incomes.

Men with great means best able to assume business risks have been encouraged to lock up substantial portions of their funds in tax-exempt securities. Men with little means who should be encouraged to hold the secure obligations of the federal and state governments have been obliged to pay a relatively higher price for those securities than the very rich because the tax-immunity is of much less value to them than to those whose incomes fall in the higher brackets.

For more than twenty years Secretaries of the Treasury have reported to the Congress the growing evils of these tax exemptions. Economists generally have regarded them as wholly inconsistent with any rational system of progressive taxation.

Therefore, I lay before the Congress the statement that a fair and effective progressive income tax and a huge perpetual reserve of tax-exempt bonds cannot exist side by side.

The desirability of this recommendation has been apparent for some time but heretofore it has been assumed that the Congress was obliged to wait upon that cumbersome and uncertain remedy — a constitutional amendment — before taking action. Today, however, expressions in recent judicial opinions lead us to hope that the assumptions underlying these doctrines are being questioned by the court itself and that these tax immunities are not inexorable requirements under the Constitution itself but are the result of judicial decision. Therefore, it is not unreasonable to hope that judicial decision may find it possible to correct it. The doctrine was originally evolved out of a totally different set of economic circumstances from those which now exist. It is a familiar principle of law that decisions lose their binding force when the reasons supporting them no longer are pertinent.

I, therefore, recommend to the Congress that effective action be promptly taken to terminate these tax-exemptions for the future. The legislation should confer the same powers on the states with respect to the taxation of federal bonds hereafter issued as is granted to the federal government with respect to state and municipal bonds hereafter issued.

The same principles of just taxation apply to tax exemptions of official salaries. The federal government does not now levy income taxes on the hundreds of thousands of state, county and municipal employees. Nor do the states, under existing decisions, levy income taxes on the salaries of the hundreds of thousands of federal employees. Justice in a great democracy should treat those who earn their livelihood from government in the same way as it treats those who earn their livelihood in private employ.

I recommend, therefore, that the Congress enact legislation ending tax exemption on government salaries of all kinds, conferring powers on the states with respect to federal salaries and powers to the federal government with respect to state and local government salaries.

Such legislation can, I believe, be enacted by a short and simple statute. It would subject all future state and local bonds to existing federal taxes; and it would confer similar powers on states in relation to future federal issues.

At the same time, such a statute would subject state and local employees to existing federal income taxes; and confer on the states the equivalent power to tax the salaries of federal employees.

55. Termination of Tax Exemptions

The ending of tax exemption, be it of government securities or of government salaries, is a matter, not of politics, but of principle.

NOTE: In the foregoing message I indicated the reasons for my recommendation that steps be taken promptly by the Congress to eliminate for the future the exemption which the employees of the various States had enjoyed from federal income tax, and also the exemption which federal employees had enjoyed from the income taxes of their respective states.

The Income Tax Amendment of the Constitution, which provided for "taxes on incomes, from whatever source derived," certainly made it as clear as the English language could, that this reciprocal exemption of taxation was in conflict with the Constitution.

This granting of exemption was typical, however, of how the courts can read into clear language, interpretations which often frustrate the will of the Congress, and even the will of the people as it had been expressed, for example, in the Sixteenth Amendment. This is one of the instances I had in mind when I decided to reject the method of constitutional amendment with respect to the Supreme Court fight of 1937, realizing that no matter how clearly expressed the intention might be in such amendment, there was always the danger of some unwarranted judicial interpretation influenced by intangible economic theories and "personal economic predilections."

In the same message I also recommended that the Congress remove from future issues of Federal obligations the exemption from federal income tax, so as to put an end gradually to tax exempt government bonds, which had been the means by which men with large incomes were able unfairly to avoid taxation.

The message also contained the recommendation that the reciprocal tax exemptions between state bonds and federal bonds be removed. Federal bonds had been exempt from state taxation, and state and municipal bonds had been exempt from federal taxation; and this reciprocal tax immunity had deprived both the federal and the state governments of much needed tax revenue.

I also expressed the hope that the courts themselves would review the reciprocal exemptions which had been made in the past so that immunity should no longer attach to this income from salaries and interest derived from state and federal obligations.

Shortly after this message it became clear that the Supreme Court of the United States was ready to reconsider the old unjust doctrine of reciprocal immunity of governmental salaries from taxation. The case of Helvering vs. Gerhardt, 304 U. S. 405, decided on May 16, 1938, held that the salary of an employee of the Port of New York Authority was subject to the federal income tax. That decision gave impetus to the movement to remove the tax immunity of public employees.

A special committee was set up by the Senate on June 16, 1938, to study the question of tax exemptions given to governmental securities and salaries, and to report thereon not later than March 1, 1939.

On January 19, 1939, I sent another message on this subject, which is printed as Item 15, 1939 volume.

56 ❨A Recommendation for Liberalizing the Old-age Insurance System. April 28, 1938

My dear Mr. Chairman:

I AM very anxious that in the press of administrative duties the Social Security Board will not lose sight of the necessity of studying ways and means of improving and extending the provisions of the Social Security Act.

The enactment of the Social Security Act marked a great advance in affording more equitable and effective protection to the people of this country against widespread and growing economic hazards. The successful operation of the Act is the best proof that it was soundly conceived. However, it would be unfortunate if we assumed that it was complete and final. Rather, we should be constantly seeking to perfect and strengthen it in the light of our accumulating experience and growing appreciation of social needs.

I am particularly anxious that the Board give attention to the development of a sound plan for liberalizing the old-age insurance system. In the development of such a plan I should like to have the Board give consideration to the feasibility of extending its coverage, commencing the payment of old-age insurance annuities at an earlier date than January 1, 1942, paying larger benefits than now provided in the Act for those retiring during the earlier years of the system, providing benefits for aged wives and widows, and providing benefits for young children of insured persons dying before reaching retirement age. It is my hope that the Board will be prepared to submit its recommendations before Congress reconvenes in January.

Very truly yours,

Mr. Arthur J. Altmeyer,
Chairman,
Social Security Board,
Washington, D. C.

NOTE: The Social Security Act (Public No. 271, 74th Congress; 49 Stat. 620) expressly provides that the Social Security Board shall conduct studies and make recommendations related to the most effective methods of providing economic security through social insurance.

Pursuant to the foregoing request, the Board made a thorough survey of those proposals which I suggested in my letter to Chairman Altmeyer, along with various other changes which it appeared advisable to make. The Board submitted its report and recommendations; and I transmitted it to the Congress on January 16, 1939 (see Item 11, 1939 volume).

The report of the Board advocated the adoption of all the suggestions which I had asked in the above letter to be considered. Subsequently, these recommendations were written into law when the amendments to the Social Security Act were adopted on August 11, 1939 (see Item 109, 1939 volume).

For example: 1. *Extending the coverage of the old-age insurance*

system. Under the 1939 amendments, the old-age insurance provisions of the Social Security Act were extended to include about 1,100,000 additional persons. The additional groups covered were seamen, bank employees, and employed persons, age sixty-five and over.

2. *Commencing the payment of old-age insurance annuities at an earlier date than January 1, 1942.* The 1939 amendments advanced the date for beginning monthly old-age insurance benefit payments to January 1, 1940.

3. *Paying larger benefits than now provided in the Act for those retiring during the earlier years of the system.* Under the original Act, the basic amount paid in old-age retirement benefits was computed from the total accumulated wages of the person retiring. Thus, an individual who reached sixty-five within a short time after the passage of the Act would not have a very large annuity because the wages accumulated would be small. Under the amendments adopted

in 1939, the basis for paying benefits was changed from *accumulated* wages to *average* wages. In this way, a person retiring in the early years of the system would receive more than a paltry amount.

4. *Providing benefits for aged wives and widows.* The 1939 amendments to the Act granted supplemental benefits to the wife, age sixty-five or over, of an insured individual. The total amount of the wife's benefit equals one half of the husband's.

Additional provision was made for widows' old-age insurance benefits. Since the adoption of the 1939 amendments, when the widow of a fully insured individual reaches 65 she is eligible for a total benefit of three-fourths of that of her late husband. Regardless of age, a widow with one or more children now also receives a total benefit equal to three-fourths of that of her late husband.

5. *Providing benefits for young children of insured persons dying before reaching retirement age.* Under the 1939 amendments, monthly insurance benefits equal to one-half of the amount due to the parent are made available to unmarried dependent orphans who have not yet reached eighteen years of age.

57 ❴ Proclamation No. 2092 on the Coinage of Silver Is Revoked. Proclamation No. 2282. April 28, 1938

WHEREAS by Proclamation No. 2092 of August 9, 1934, the United States mints were directed to receive for coinage or for addition to the monetary stocks of the United States silver situated on August 9, 1934, in the continental United States, including the Territory of Alaska; and

WHEREAS such proclamation provides, in part:

"Notice is hereby given that I reserve the right by virtue of the authority vested in me to revoke or modify this Proclamation as the interest of the United States may seem to require."

AND WHEREAS I find that the interest of the United States requires the revocation, except as herein provided, of the said proclamation:

NOW, THEREFORE, I, FRANKLIN D. ROOSEVELT, President of the United States of America, under and by virtue of the authority vested in me by section 43 (b) (2), Title III of the act of May 12, 1933, 48 Stat. 52, as amended, and the Silver Purchase Act of 1934 (48 Stat. 1178), and by virtue of all other authority in me vested, do hereby revoke the said Proclamation No. 2092 of August 9, 1934, except as to the provisions thereof relating to settlement for silver received by the United States coinage mints pursuant to Proclamation No. 2067 of December 21, 1933, which provisions shall not be affected by this proclamation.

Notice is hereby given that I reserve the right by virtue of the authority vested in me to revoke or modify this proclamation as the interest of the United States may seem to require.

NOTE: Proclamation No. 2092, of August 9, 1934, printed as Item 145, 1934 volume, and Executive Order No. 6814, printed as Item 146, 1934 volume, required the delivery of silver to the United States mints at fifty cents per fine ounce (see note to Item 146, 1934 volume).

The foregoing Proclamation of April 28, 1938, revoked Proclamation No. 2092. It was accompanied by Executive Order No. 7877 of the same date, which revoked the Executive Order No. 6814.

These revocations did not, however, revoke the provisions of the Proclamation of December 21, 1933 (see Item 187A and note, 1933 volume), as modified by subsequent proclamations, directing the coinage mints of the United States to receive for coinage any United States silver offered to it which had been mined subsequently to December 21, 1933, from natural deposits within the borders of the United States.

58 ⟨ A Statement on the Use of Army Officers in the Civilian Conservation Corps. April 29, 1938

My dear Senator Bulkley:

ACKNOWLEDGMENT is made of your letter of April twenty-sixth, calling attention to the Executive Order issued in 1935 relative to field officers of the organized Reserve Corps with the rank of Major, Lieutenant-Colonel and Colonel who were in command of Civilian Conservation Corps Districts.

When the Civilian Conservation Corps was organized in the

spring of 1933 all Army officers assigned to active duty with the Corps were drawn from the Regular Army personnel. This continued during the first six months, but when it was realized that the Corps would continue in operation for some time the War Department informed me that it would seriously interfere with the routine operation of the Regular Army and would be detrimental to the best interests of the Nation for such a large number of Army personnel to be assigned to Civilian Conservation Corps duty.

Therefore, on or about October 1, 1933, I authorized the Director of the Civilian Conservation Corps to advise the War Department to substitute Reserve officers with the grade of Captain, First Lieutenant and Second Lieutenant in place of Regular Army officers on active duty with the Corps. A substantial number of Regular Army officers holding the rank of Major, Lieutenant-Colonel and Colonel continued to give their services to the Corps in command of Districts. This continued until the expansion program in the spring of 1935 when, due to the tremendous increase that was authorized in the enrolled strength of the Corps, the War Department notified the Director of the Civilian Conservation Corps that the Department would not have a sufficient number of officers of field-grade rank to supply the needs of the Corps. I, therefore, authorized the calling of Reserve Officers holding the field-grade rank for active duty with the Corps. They continued on active duty until the reduction program had brought about the closing of a large number of camps which made it necessary materially to reduce the number of officers needed to supervise the work of the Corps.

Under this reduced program the War Department advised the Director of the Civilian Conservation Corps that they could furnish a sufficient number of Regular Army officers of field-grade rank to carry on the necessary supervisory work. This work is now performed by Regular Army personnel who, of course, are permanently on the Federal pay roll. Reserve officers of field-grade rank are not called to active duty because of the expense. The Corps must be operated as economically as possible. We try to utilize wherever possible the personnel of the existing regular governmental agencies.

Very sincerely yours,

Honorable Robert J. Bulkley,
United States Senate,
Washington, D. C.

NOTE: At the time of writing the foregoing letter, there had been a certain amount of protest on the part of reserve officers above the grade of captain, against the policy of the Civilian Conservation Corps in refusing to employ such officers in their camps.

As I explained in the letter, this policy had been adopted because the CCC did not need the services of higher ranking officers in the reserve. For at that time regular army officers above the rank of captain were available for such duties with the CCC. The regular army officers were on the federal payroll already, and would not have to be paid extra for their services for the CCC; whereas officers taken from the reserve duty would have to be paid when called for active duty.

This policy has saved the government substantial amounts of money.

59 ⦅ Recommendations to the Congress to Curb Monopolies and the Concentration of Economic Power. April 29, 1938

To the Congress:

UNHAPPY events abroad have retaught us two simple truths about the liberty of a democratic people.

The first truth is that the liberty of a democracy is not safe if the people tolerate the growth of private power to a point where it becomes stronger than their democratic state itself. That, in its essence, is Fascism — ownership of Government by an individual, by a group, or by any other controlling private power.

The second truth is that the liberty of a democracy is not safe if its business system does not provide employment and produce and distribute goods in such a way as to sustain an acceptable standard of living.

Both lessons hit home.

Among us today a concentration of private power without equal in history is growing.

This concentration is seriously impairing the economic effectiveness of private enterprise as a way of providing employment for labor and capital and as a way of assuring a more equitable distribution of income and earnings among the people of the nation as a whole.

THE GROWING CONCENTRATION OF ECONOMIC POWER

Statistics of the Bureau of Internal Revenue reveal the following amazing figures for 1935:

Ownership of corporate assets:

Of all corporations reporting from every part of the nation, one-tenth of 1 per cent of them owned 52 per cent of the assets of all of them;

and to clinch the point:

Of all corporations reporting, less than 5 per cent of them owned 87 per cent of all the assets of all of them.

Income and profits of corporations:

Of all the corporations reporting from every part of the country, one-tenth of 1 per cent of them earned 50 per cent of the net income of all of them;

and to clinch the point:

Of all the manufacturing corporations reporting, less than 4 per cent of them earned 84 per cent of all the net profits of all of them.

The statistical history of modern times proves that in times of depression concentration of business speeds up. Bigger business then has larger opportunity to grow still bigger at the expense of smaller competitors who are weakened by financial adversity.

The danger of this centralization in a handful of huge corporations is not reduced or eliminated, as is sometimes urged, by the wide public distribution of their securities. The mere number of security-holders gives little clue to the size of their individual holdings or to their actual ability to have a voice in the management. In fact the concentration of stock ownership of corporations in the hands of a tiny minority of the population matches the concentration of corporate assets.

1929 was a banner year for distribution of stock ownership. But in that year

three-tenths of 1 per cent of our population received 78 per cent of the dividends reported by individuals. This has roughly the same effect as if, out of every 300 persons in our population, one person received 78 cents out of every dollar of corporate dividends while the other 299 persons divided up the other 22 cents between them.

The effect of this concentration is reflected in the distribution of national income.

A recent study by the National Resources Committee shows that in 1935-36:

47 per cent of all American families and single individuals living alone had incomes of less than $1,000 for the year; and at the other end of the ladder a little less than 1½ per cent of the nation's families received incomes which in dollars and cents reached the same total as the incomes of the 47 per cent at the bottom;

Furthermore, to drive the point home, the Bureau of Internal Revenue reports that estate tax returns in 1936 show that:

33 per cent of the property which was passed by inheritance was found in only 4 per cent of all the reporting estates. (And the figures of concentration would be far more impressive, if we included all the smaller estates which, under the law, do not have to report.)

We believe in a way of living in which political democracy and free private enterprise for profit should serve and protect each other — to ensure a maximum of human liberty not for a few but for all.

It has been well said that "the freest government, if it could exist, would not be long acceptable, if the tendency of the laws were to create a rapid accumulation of property in few hands, and to render the great mass of the population dependent and penniless."

Today many Americans ask the uneasy question: Is the vociferation that our liberties are in danger justified by the facts?

Today's answer on the part of average men and women in every section of the country is far more accurate than it would have been in 1929 — for the very simple reason that during the past nine years we have been doing a lot of common sense thinking. Their answer is that if there is that danger it comes from that concentrated private economic power which is struggling so hard to master our democratic government. It will not come as some (by no means all) of the possessors of that private power would make the people believe — from our democratic government itself.

FINANCIAL CONTROL OVER INDUSTRY

Even these statistics I have cited do not measure the actual degree of concentration of control over American industry.

Close financial control, through interlocking spheres of influence over channels of investment, and through the use of financial devices like holding companies and strategic minority interests, creates close control of the business policies of enterprises which masquerade as independent units.

That heavy hand of integrated financial and management control lies upon large and strategic areas of American industry. The small business man is unfortunately being driven into a less and less independent position in American life. You and I must admit that.

Private enterprise is ceasing to be free enterprise and is becoming a cluster of private collectivisms: masking itself as a system of free enterprise after the American model, it is in fact becoming a concealed cartel system after the European model.

We all want efficient industrial growth and the advantages of mass production. No one suggests that we return to the hand loom or hand forge. A series of processes involved in turning out a given manufactured product may well require one or more huge mass production plants. Modern efficiency may call for this. But modern efficient mass production is not furthered by a central control which destroys competition among industrial plants each capable of efficient mass production while operating as separate units. Industrial efficiency does not have to mean industrial empire building.

And industrial empire building, unfortunately, has evolved into banker control of industry. We oppose that.

Such control does not offer safety for the investing public. Investment judgment requires the disinterested appraisal of other people's management. It becomes blurred and distorted if it is combined with the conflicting duty of controlling the management it is supposed to judge.

Interlocking financial controls have taken from American business much of its traditional virility, independence, adaptability and daring—without compensating advantages. They have not given the stability they promised.

Business enterprise needs new vitality and the flexibility that comes from the diversified efforts, independent judgments and vibrant energies of thousands upon thousands of independent business men.

The individual must be encouraged to exercise his own judgment and to venture his own small savings, not in stock gambling but in new enterprise investment. Men will dare to compete against men but not against giants.

THE DECLINE OF COMPETITION AND ITS EFFECTS ON EMPLOYMENT

In output per man or machine, we are the most efficient industrial nation on earth.

In the matter of complete mutual employment of capital and labor we are among the least efficient.

Our difficulties of employing labor and capital are not new. We have had them since good free land gave out in the West at the turn of the century. They were old before we undertook changes in our tax policy or in our labor and social legislation. They were caused not by this legislation but by the same forces which caused the legislation. The problem of bringing idle men and idle money together will not be solved by abandoning the forward steps we have taken to adjust the burdens of taxation more fairly and to attain social justice and security.

If you believe with me in private initiative, you must acknowledge the right of well-managed small business to expect to make reasonable profits. You must admit that the destruction of this opportunity follows concentration of control of any given industry into a small number of dominating corporations.

One of the primary causes of our present difficulties lies in the disappearance of price competition in many industrial fields, particularly in basic manufacture where concentrated economic power is most evident — and where rigid prices and fluctuating payrolls are general.

Managed industrial prices mean fewer jobs. It is no accident that in industries, like cement and steel, where prices have remained firm in the face of a falling demand, payrolls have shrunk as much as 40 and 50 per cent in recent months. Nor is it mere chance that in most competitive industries where prices adjust themselves quickly to falling demand, payrolls and employment have been far better maintained. By prices we mean, of course, the prices of the finished articles and not the wages paid to workers.

When prices are privately managed at levels above those which would be determined by free competition, everybody pays.

The contractor pays more for materials; the homebuilder pays more for his house; the tenant pays more rent; and the worker pays in lost work.

Even the Government itself is unable, in a large range of materials, to obtain competitive bids. It is repeatedly confronted with bids identical to the last cent.

Our housing shortage is a perfect example of how ability to control prices interferes with the ability of private enterprise to fill the needs of the community and provide employment for capital and labor.

On the other hand we have some lines of business, large and small, which are genuinely competitive. Often these competitive industries must buy their basic products from monopolistic industry, thus losing, and causing the public to lose, a large part of the benefit of their own competitive policy. Furthermore, in times of recession, the practices of monopolistic industries make it difficult for business or agriculture which is competitive and which does not curtail production below normal needs, to find a market for its goods even at reduced prices. For at such times a large number of customers of agriculture and competitive industry are being thrown out of work by those non-competitive industries which choose to hold their prices rather than to move their goods and to employ their workers.

If private enterprise left to its own devices becomes half-regimented and half-competitive, half-slave and half-free, as it is today, it obviously cannot adjust itself to meet the needs and the demands of the country.

Most complaints for violations of the anti-trust laws are made by business men against other business men. Even the most monopolistic business man disapproves of all monopolies but his own. We may smile at this as being just an example of human nature, but we cannot laugh away the fact that the combined effect of the monopolistic controls which each business group imposes for its own benefit, inevitably destroys the buying power of the nation as a whole.

COMPETITION DOES NOT MEAN EXPLOITATION

Competition, of course, like all other good things, can be carried to excess. Competition should not extend to fields where it has demonstrably bad social and economic consequences. The exploitation of child labor, the chiseling of workers' wages, the stretching of workers' hours, are not necessary, fair or proper methods of competition. I have consistently urged a federal wages and hours bill to take the minimum decencies of life for the working man and woman out of the field of competition.

It is of course necessary to operate the competitive system of free enterprise intelligently. In gauging the market for their wares, business men, like the farmers, should be given all possible information by government and by their own associations so that they may act with knowledge and not on impulse. Serious problems of temporary overproduction can and should be avoided by disseminating information that will discourage the production of more goods than the current markets can possibly absorb or the accumulation of dangerously large inventories for which there is no obvious need.

It is, of course, necessary to encourage rises in the level of those competitive prices, such as agricultural prices, which must rise to put our price structure into more workable balance and make the debt burden more tolerable. Many such competitive prices are now too low.

It may at times be necessary to give special treatment to chronically sick industries which have deteriorated too far for natural revival, especially those which have a public or quasi-public character.

But generally over the field of industry and finance we must revive and strengthen competition if we wish to preserve and make workable our traditional system of free private enterprise.

The justification of private profit is private risk. We cannot safely make America safe for the businessman who does not want to take the burdens and risks of being a businessman.

THE CHOICE BEFORE US

Examination of methods of conducting and controlling private enterprise which keep it from furnishing jobs or income or opportunity for one-third of the population is long overdue on the part of those who sincerely want to preserve the system of private enterprise for profit.

No people, least of all a democratic people, will be content to go without work or to accept some standard of living which obviously and woefully falls short of their capacity to produce. No people, least of all a people with our traditions of personal liberty, will endure the slow erosion of opportunity for the common man, the oppressive sense of helplessness under the domination of a few, which are overshadowing our whole economic life.

A discerning magazine of business has editorially pointed out that big business collectivism in industry compels an ultimate collectivism in government.

The power of a few to manage the economic life of the nation must be diffused among the many or be transferred to the public and its democratically responsible government. If prices are to be managed and administered, if the nation's business is to be allotted by plan and not by competition, that power should not be vested in any private group or cartel, however benevolent its professions profess to be.

Those people, in and out of the halls of government, who encourage the growing restriction of competition either by active efforts or by passive resistance to sincere attempts to change the trend, are shouldering a terrific responsibility. Consciously, or unconsciously, they are working for centralized business and financial control. Consciously or unconsciously, they are therefore either working for control of the government itself by business and finance or the other alternative — a growing concentration of public power in the government to cope with such concentration of private power.

The enforcement of free competition is the least regulation business can expect.

A PROGRAM

The traditional approach to the problems I have discussed has been through the anti-trust laws. That approach we do not propose to abandon. On the contrary, although we must recognize the inadequacies of the existing laws, we seek to enforce them so that the public shall not be deprived of such protection as they afford. To enforce them properly requires thorough investigation not only to discover such violations as may exist but to avoid hit-and-miss prosecutions harmful to business and goverment alike. To provide for the proper and fair enforcement of the existing anti-trust laws I shall submit, through the budget, recommendations for a deficiency appropriation of $200,000 for the Department of Justice.

But the existing anti-trust laws are inadequate — most importantly because of new financial economic conditions with which they are powerless to cope.

The Sherman Act was passed nearly forty years ago. The Clayton and Federal Trade Commission Acts were passed over twenty years ago. We have had considerable experience under those acts. In the meantime we have had a chance to observe the practical operation of large-scale industry and to learn many things about the competitive system which we did not know in those days.

We have witnessed the merging-out of effective competition in many fields of enterprise. We have learned that the so-called competitive system works differently in an industry where there are many independent units, from the way it works in an industry where a few large producers dominate the market.

We have also learned that a realistic system of business regulation has to reach more than consciously immoral acts. The community is interested in economic results. It must be protected from economic as well as moral wrongs. We must find practical controls over blind economic forces as well as over blindly selfish men.

Government can deal and should deal with blindly selfish men. But that is a comparatively small part — the easier part — of our problem. The larger, more important and more difficult part of our problem is to deal with men who are not selfish and who are good citizens, but who cannot see the social and economic consequences of their actions in a modern economically interdependent community. They fail to grasp the significance of some of our most vital social and economic problems

314

because they see them only in the light of their own personal experience and not in perspective with the experience of other men and other industries. They, therefore, fail to see these problems for the nation as a whole.

To meet the situation I have described, there should be a thorough study of the concentration of economic power in American industry and the effect of that concentration upon the decline of competition. There should be an examination of the existing price system and the price policies of industry to determine their effect upon the general level of trade, upon employment, upon long-term profits and upon consumption. The study should not be confined to the traditional anti-trust field. The effects of tax, patent and other government policies cannot be ignored.

The study should be comprehensive and adequately financed. I recommend an appropriation of not less than $500,000 for the conduct of such comprehensive study by the Federal Trade Commission, the Department of Justice, the Securities and Exchange Commission, and such other agencies of government as have special experience in various phases of the inquiry.

I enumerate some of the items that should be embraced in the proposed study. The items are not intended to be all inclusive. One or two of the items, such as bank holding companies and investment trusts, have already been the subject of special study, and legislation concerning these need not be delayed.

(1) *Improvement of Anti-Trust Procedure.* A revision of the existing anti-trust laws should make them susceptible of practical enforcement by casting upon those charged with violations the burden of proving facts peculiarly within their knowledge. Proof by the Government of identical bids, uniform price increases, price leadership, higher domestic than export prices, or other specified price rigidities might be accepted as *prima facie* evidence of unlawful actions.

The Department of Justice and the Federal Trade Commission should be given more adequate and effective power to investigate whenever there is reason to believe that conditions exist or practices prevail which violate the provisions or defeat the objectives of the anti-trust laws. If investigation reveals border-line cases where legitimate cooperative efforts to eliminate socially and economically harmful methods of competition in particular industries are thwarted by fear of possible technical violations of the anti-trust laws, remedial legislation should be considered.

As a really effective deterrent to personal wrong-doing, I would suggest that where a corporation is enjoined from violating the law, the court might be empowered to enjoin the corporation for a specified period of time from giving any remunerative employment or any official position to any person who has been found to bear a responsibility for the wrongful corporate action.

As a further deterrent to corporate wrong-doing the Government might well be authorized to withhold government purchases from companies guilty of unfair or monopolistic practice.

(2) *Mergers and interlocking relationships.* More rigid scrutiny through the Federal Trade Commission and the Securities and Exchange Commission of corporate mergers, consolidations and acquisitions than that now provided by the Clayton Act to prevent their consummation when not clearly in the public interest; more effective methods for breaking up interlocking relationships and like devices for bestowing business by favor.

(3) *Financial controls.* The operations of financial institutions should be directed to serve the interests of independent business and restricted against abuses which promote concentrations of power over American industry.

(a) *Investment trusts.* Investment trusts should be brought under strict control to insure their operations in the interests of their investors rather than their managers. The Securities and Exchange Commission is to make a report to Congress on the results of a comprehensive study of investment trusts and their operations which it has carried on for nearly two years.

The investment trust, like the holding company, puts huge aggregations of the capital of the public at the direction of a few managers. Unless properly restricted, it has potentialities of abuse second only to the holding company as a device for the further centralization of control over American industry and American finance.

The tremendous investment funds controlled by our great insurance companies have a certain kinship to investment trusts, in that these companies invest as trustees the savings of millions of our people. The Securities and Exchange Commission should be authorized to make an investigation of the facts relating to these investments with particular relation to their use as an instrument of economic power.

(b) *Bank Holding Companies.* It is hardly necessary to point out the great economic power that might be wielded by a group which may succeed in acquiring domination over banking resources in any considerable area of the country. That power becomes particularly dangerous when it is exercised from a distance and notably so when effective control is maintained without the responsibilities of complete ownership.

We have seen the multiplied evils which have arisen from the holding company system in the case of public utilities, where a small minority ownership has been able to dominate a far-flung system.

We do not want those evils repeated in the banking field, and we should take steps now to see that they are not.

It is not a sufficient assurance against the future to say that no great evil has yet resulted from holding company operations in this field. The possibilities of great harm are inherent in the situation.

I recommend that the Congress enact at this session legislation that will effectively control the operation of bank holding companies; prevent holding companies from acquiring control of any more banks, directly or indirectly; prevent banks controlled by holding companies from establishing any more branches; and make it illegal for a holding company, or any corporation or enterprise in which it is financially interested, to borrow from or sell securities to a bank in which it holds stock.

I recommend that this bank legislation make provision for the gradual separation of banks from holding company control or ownership, allowing a reasonable time for this accomplishment — time enough for it to be done in an orderly manner and without causing inconvenience to communities served by holding company banks.

(4) *Trade associations.* Supervision and effective publicity of the activities of trade associations, and a clarification and delineation of their legitimate spheres of activity which will enable them to combat unfair methods of competition but which will guard against their interference with legitimate competitive practices.

(5) *Patent laws.* Amendment of the patent laws to prevent their use to suppress inventions, and to create industrial monopolies. Of course such amendment should not deprive the inventor of his royalty rights, but generally speaking, future patents might be made available for use by any one upon payment of appropriate royalties. Open patent pools have voluntarily been put into effect in a number of important industries with wholesome results.

(6) *Tax correctives.* Tax policies should be devised to give affirmative encouragement to competitive enterprise.

Attention might be directed to increasing the intercorporate dividend tax to discourage holding companies and to further graduating the corporation income tax according to size. The graduated tax need not be so high as to make bigness impracticable, but might be high enough to make bigness demonstrate its alleged superior efficiency.

We have heard much about the undistributed profits tax. When it was enacted two years ago, its objective was known to be closely related to the problem of concentrated economic power and a free capital market.

Its purpose was not only to prevent individuals whose incomes were taxable in the higher surtax brackets from escaping personal income taxes by letting their profits be accumulated as corporate surplus. Its purpose was also to encourage the distribution of corporate profits so that the individual recipients could freely determine where they would reinvest in a free capital market.

It is true that the form of the 1936 tax worked a hardship on many of the smaller corporations. Many months ago I recommended that these inequities be removed.

But in the process of the removal of inequities, we must not lose sight of original objectives. Obviously the nation must have some deterrent against special privileges enjoyed by an exceedingly small group of individuals under the form of the laws prior to 1936, whether such deterrent take the form of an undistributed profits tax or some other equally or more efficient method. And obviously an undistributed profits tax has a real value in working against a further concentration of economic power and in favor of a freer capital market.

(7) *Bureau of Industrial Economics.* Creation of a Bureau of Industrial Economics which should be endowed with adequate powers to supplement and supervise the collection of industrial statistics by trade associations. Such a Bureau should perform for business men functions similar to those performed for the farmers by the Bureau of Agricultural Economics.

It should disseminate current statistical and other information regarding market conditions and be in a position to warn against the dangers of temporary overproduction and excessive inventories as well as against the dangers of shortages and bottleneck conditions, and to encourage the maintenance of orderly markets. It should study trade fluctuations, credit facilities and other conditions which affect the welfare of the average business man. It should be able to help small business men keep themselves as well-informed about trade conditions as their big competitors.

No man of good faith will misinterpret these proposals. They derive from the oldest American traditions. Concentration of economic power in the few and the resulting unemployment of labor and capital are inescapable problems for a modern "private enterprise" democracy. I do not believe that we are so lacking in stability that we shall lose faith in our own way of living just because we seek to find out how to make that way of living work more effectively.

This program should appeal to the honest common sense of every independent business man interested primarily in running his own business at a profit rather than in controlling the business of other men.

It is not intended as the beginning of any ill-considered "trust-busting" activity which lacks proper consideration for economic results.

It is a program to preserve private enterprise for profit by keeping it free enough to be able to utilize all our resources of capital and labor at a profit.

It is a program whose basic purpose is to stop the progress of collectivism in business and turn business back to the democratic competitive order.

It is a program whose basic thesis is not that the system of free private enterprise for profit has failed in this generation, but that it has not yet been tried.

Once it is realized that business monopoly in America paralyzes the system of free enterprise on which it is grafted, and is as fatal to those who manipulate it as to the people who suffer beneath its impositions, action by the government to eliminate these artificial restraints will be welcomed by industry throughout the nation.

For idle factories and idle workers profit no man.

NOTE: In the foregoing message, I called attention to the growing threat to democracy which was in- herent in the ever-increasing concentration of economic power in the hands of a comparatively small group of corporations and individuals; and that allied with that threat was the danger which comes from a business system which does not provide employment, and produce and distribute goods in a way which provides an acceptable standard of living.

I called attention to statistics of the Bureau of Internal Revenue, showing the growing concentration of economic power as revealed in the ownership of corporate assets, in the income and profits of corporations, and in the income and property of individuals. I also pointed out the financial control which had developed over all forms of American industry. There was also included a statement showing the effects of the decline of competition on employment and general living standards. General suggestions were made for a program of action involving: improvement of anti-trust procedure; more rigid scrutiny of mergers and interlocking relationships; restriction of abuses involved in concentrated financial controls, including investment trusts, and bank holding companies; supervision of trade associations; amendment of patent laws, to prevent the suppression of inventions and the creation of industrial monopolies; adoption of tax policies to give encouragement to competitive enterprise; and the creation of a Bureau of Industrial Economics to supplement and supervise the collection of industrial statistics by trade associations, to disseminate current statistical and market information, and to perform generally for business men functions similar to those performed for the farmers by the Bureau of Agriculture Economics.

In response to the foregoing message, the Congress adopted Public Resolution No. 113, 75th Congress, approved June 16, 1938 (52 Stat. 705), creating the Temporary National Economic Committee. This was a joint legislative-executive committee, and its duties were:

"(a) To make a full and complete study and investigation with respect to the matters referred to in my message of April 29, 1938, on monopoly and the concentration of economic power in, and financial control over, production and distribution of goods and services; and to hear and receive evidence thereon, with a view to determining, but without limitation, (1) the causes of such concentration and control and their effect upon competition; (2) the effect of the existing price system and the price policies of industry upon the general level of trade, upon employment, upon long-term profits, and upon consumption; and (3) the effect of existing tax, patent, and other Government policies upon competition, price levels, unemployment, profits, and consumption; and to investigate the subject of governmental adjustment of the purchasing power of the dollar so as to attain 1926 commodity price levels; and

"(b) To make recommendation

to Congress with respect to legislation upon the foregoing subjects, including the improvement of antitrust policy and procedure and the establishment of national standards for corporations engaged in commerce among the states and with foreign nations."

The committee was composed of three members of the Senate, appointed by the President of the Senate; three members of the House of Representatives, appointed by the Speaker of the House of Representatives; and one representative from each of the following departments and agencies, designated by the respective heads thereof: Department of Justice, Department of the Treasury, Department of Labor, Department of Commerce, the Securities and Exchange Commission, and the Federal Trade Commission.

The final report of the Temporary National Economic Committee pointed out that its unique character, made up, as it was, of equal numbers of legislative and administrative members of the federal government, gave it unusual opportunity for thorough study of the concentration of economic power. The close relationship which was thus provided with federal agencies served to make available well-developed research, vast collections of statistics, and much data which customarily do not become public information, and which are not systematically made available to congressional committees.

The Temporary National Economic Committee began its public hearings on December 1, 1938, with an economic prologue presented by Isador Lubin, Commissioner of Labor Statistics, Department of Labor; Willard L. Thorp, adviser on economic studies, Department of Commerce; and Leon Henderson, executive secretary of the committee. Their testimony dealt with the amount of employment, salaries and wages, national and gross farm income, and dividends which had been lost during the depression; the extent of concentration in various industries by number of employees, assets, and amount of production controlled; the amount of unemployment and the size of the labor supply; the basic assumptions of the American competitive capitalistic system; and the problems confronting the Temporary National Economic Committee.

The hearings, which continued intermittently until April 26, 1940, covered a wide range of subjects including, among others: patents, monopolistic practices in industries, consumer problems, savings and investment, problems of small business, cartels, the effect of wars on prices, interstate trade barriers, the impact of technology upon the worker, and detailed studies of certain industries, including construction, petroleum, iron and steel, copper, life insurance, and investment banking.

More than thirty-one volumes of hearings were published by the Temporary National Economic Committee. Only a few of the outstanding facts elicited in some of the more important hearings can be set forth within the space limitations of this volume.

PATENTS

Hearings on patents demonstrated the various kinds of uses — good and bad — to which patents may be put by various industries. The automobile industry, for example, is an industry in which there has been no substantial restriction achieved through patent monopolies. Since the first cross-licensing agreement in 1915, practically all automobile patents have been readily accessible to any manufacturer, though some of them have been on a royalty basis. In sharp contrast is the use made of patents in the glass container industry in which only two firms, closely bound by cross-licensing contracts, controlled 96.6 per cent of the glass containers produced in 1937 through licensing manufacturers and leasing machinery to them.

LIFE INSURANCE

The enormity of the life insurance business is indicated by the fact that in 1937 there was $109,-600,000,000 of life insurance in force, and the total income of life insurance companies was 7.5 per cent of the entire national income. The high degree of concentration in life insurance business is demonstrated by the fact that in 1937, 5 companies controlled 54.4 per cent, 16 companies controlled 80.6 per cent, and 25 companies controlled 87.2 per cent of all assets of the 308 life insurance companies. In 1937, there were $20,600,000,000 of industrial insurance in force, and of this amount ten companies had 92.04 per cent, with the two largest having 73.26 per cent between them.

HOUSING

The failure of the private construction industry in the United States to build homes in price ranges proportionate to the various income groups is demonstrated by the fact that in 1930-37 only 10.5 per cent of homes built were within the reach of those with annual incomes of $1,000 and less, while 36.5 per cent of our population is in this income group. At the other extreme, 51.3 per cent of homes built in the same period were within the reach of those with incomes of $3,000 and more, but only 8.0 per cent of the population is in this income group.

The concentration of control in the building materials industry is revealed in the attached exhibit (No. 910 before the committee), which shows the percentage of production controlled by the four leading companies.

SAVINGS AND INVESTMENT

From 1923 to 1929 business enterprise financed more than 75 per cent of their annual average expenditure of $8,500,000,000 for plant and equipment from internal sources; from 1935 to 1937 they financed 92 per cent of their annual average expenditure of $5,800,000,000 from internal sources. Total savings in the twenty years, 1910-30, increased 382 per cent, while in the same period the population of continental United States showed a growth of only 33½ per cent.

The concentration of control over this vast fund of savings in the principal reservoirs of the nation is shown by the attached exhibit (No. 611 before the committee).

PETROLEUM

Between $11,000,000,000 and $15,000,000,000 are invested in the petroleum industry in the United States. Of this total amount, only twenty of the major integrated companies had assets totaling about $8,000,000,000 in 1938; and the five largest companies alone had over 60 per cent of this amount. Other evidence of concentration in the industry was: the ownership of 94.2 per cent of the stocks of crude petroleum and six selected petroleum products by the twenty major companies in 1937 (see attached committee Chart X); the fact that 71.8 per cent of crude oil pipeline mileage (trunk and gathering) and 96.1 per cent of gasoline pipeline mileage in 1938 was owned by the twenty major companies; while fifteen major companies alone owned 87.2 per cent of all the dead-weight tonnage of oil tankers under American registry.

Chart X is particularly significant in showing how the concentration had grown in the period 1926-1937.

COPPER AND STEEL

Three companies alone in 1937 mined 77.6 per cent of all the copper produced in the United States. Their increasing share in the total production of copper from 1915 to 1937 is shown by the fact that the same three companies in 1915 had mined only about 27 per cent of such copper.

In the steel industry, concentration of capacity for making pig iron, ingots and selected steel products varies from 66.2 to 100 per cent controlled by the ten largest producers.

SECURITY UNDERWRITING

The concentration in this field is overwhelming. For example, from September, 1935, to June, 1939, one investment banking house managed 32 per cent of all the registered bond issues managed by thirty-eight leading firms. It managed all the first-grade registered bond issues of manufacturing companies; 71 per cent of all the first-grade registered bond issues of electric light and power, gas, and water companies; all the first-grade registered bond issues of transportation and communication companies, principally telephone issues; and 74 per cent of all the first-grade registered bond issues of all other issuers.

During the same period the same investment banking houses managed four-fifths of all the first-grade registered bond issues managed by the thirty-eight leading firms in the United States.

WAR AND PRICES

The hearing before the committee on war and prices compared the rise of prices during the first World War, and during the four months following the outbreak of war in September, 1939. It was shown that by the time the United States had entered the war in 1917, there had been a 25 per cent increase in the cost of living. By 1920 the average of all items in the cost of living had increased by 108 per cent; food 118 per cent, and clothing 212 per cent.

In comparison, it was shown that after the Second World War had started and by December, 1939, the all-commodity index had increased about 5 per cent, but that twenty-eight basic commodities that enter into the industrial picture had gone up 19 per cent. Competent witnesses testified to their opinion that a repetition of the World War extreme pattern was unlikely and unnecessary, because industry today generally has much greater capacity to produce, and is also much better geared to the use of substitute products in case individual prices get too high.

TNEC MONOGRAPHS

The committee designated certain agencies to conduct special studies and prepare the technical aspects of hearings. In order to obtain a well-rounded analysis and treatment of the broad subject of the concentration of economic power and its effects, not only direct testimony was elicited at the hearings, but economists and experts in particular fields made studies of problems raised in the hearings and prepared separate reports upon them.

This resulted in the publication of forty-three separate monographs, which were regarded by the committee as expert testimony presented at its hearings, and solely as the responsibility of their authors.

Some of the more outstanding monographs are listed below, and can be obtained at the Government Printing Office:

No. 1, Price Behavior and Business Policy

No. 3, Who pays the Taxes?

No. 8, Toward More Housing

No. 9, Taxation of Corporate Enterprise

No. 10, Industrial Concentration and Tariffs

No. 12, Profits, Productive Activities and New Investment

No. 16, Anti-trust in Action

No. 18, Trade Association Survey

No. 19, Government Purchasing — an Economic Commentary

No. 20, Taxation, Recovery, and Defense

No. 21, Competition and Monopoly in American Industry

No. 22, Technology in Our Economy

No. 26, Economic Power and Political Pressures

No. 27, The Structure of Industry

No. 28, Study of Legal Reserve Life Insurance Companies

No. 29, The Distribution of Ownership in the Two Hundred Largest Non-financial Corporations

No. 31, Patents and Free Enterprise

No. 32, Economic Standards of Government Price Control

No. 37, Saving, Investment, and National Income

No. 38, A Study of the Construction and Enforcement of the Federal Antitrust Laws

No. 39, Control of the Petroleum Industry by Major Oil Companies

PRELIMINARY REPORT

On July 17, 1939, a Preliminary Report of the Temporary National Economic Committee was presented to the President of the Senate. Some, but not all the recommendations contained therein, were:

1. A series of amendments to the patent laws and to the procedure in the Patent Office designed to reduce the delay in the Patent Office and to reduce the life of a patent; and to require filing of any assignment of a patent or any interest therein.

2. Provisions forbidding any person to assign a patent, or to grant any right or license under a patent, on any condition which restricts the assignee in respect of the amount which he may produce under the patent, the price at which he may sell any such article, the purpose for which or manner in which he may use the patent or any article produced thereunder, or the geographical area within which he may produce or sell such article; and subjecting violators to forfeiture of their patents, which would thereupon become part of the public domain.

3. New civil remedies, which would treat a violation of the antitrust laws as a kind of tort against the general public interest; which would provide for remedies in the nature of actions for damages brought by the United States against offending companies and against the responsible officers and directors thereof; and would permit actions to suspend or terminate employment by an offending company of the officers and directors responsible for the violation.

4. Amendments to section 7 of the Clayton Act, to prohibit a corporation from acquiring the assets as well as the stock or other share capital of another corporation or corporations engaged in interstate

commerce under the conditions therein stated.

A great many separate recommendations were made by the different agencies having representation on the committee. Public sessions for the consideration of these recommendations were begun on January 15, 1941, and continued until March 11, 1941. Recommendations, for example, had been made by the antitrust division of the Department of Justice, by the Federal Trade Commission, by Commissioner Pike of the Securities and Exchange Commission, by Senator Mead, by the Department of Labor, by Senator O'Mahoney, the chairman of the committee, and by others. These separate recommendations have all been included as such in the report of the committee.

On March 31, 1941, the Final Report of the Temporary National Economic Committee was submitted to the Senate; and it has been printed as Senate Document 35, 77th Congress, 1st Session.

In this report, the committee reiterated the recommendations which it had made concerning patents in its preliminary report; and also called attention to the fact that some of its prior patent recommendations, contained in that preliminary report, and relating to delay in the Patent Office and the life of a patent, had been enacted into law by the Congress as Public Acts Nos. 286, 287, 288, 341, and 358 (76th Congress, 1st Session).

In addition, the majority of the committee recommended among other things:

1. Legislation making available any future patent to anyone who is willing and able to pay a fair price for the privilege.

2. Legislation requiring trade associations (whose members are engaged in interstate commerce) to register and file periodical reports of their activities.

3. Prohibition of certain specific activities of trade associations which tend to violate the antitrust laws.

4. Legislation authorizing the Federal Trade Commission to forbid corporations from acquiring the assets of competing corporations over a certain size, unless it be shown (a) that such acquisition is in the public interest and that it will promote greater efficiency and economy; (b) that it will not substantially decrease competition, or restrict trade or tend to a monopoly either in a particular section of the country or in the country as a whole; (c) that no more than certain proportions of the industry, as fixed by the Congress, may be controlled by such corporations; and (d) that the acquiring company has not been engaged in any unlawful methods of competition or any violations of the Federal Trade Com-

mission Act in order to bring about the merger.

5. Legislation prohibiting the acquisition of stock or control of competing companies, with proper exceptions for bona fide investments and for the control of true subsidiaries by parent corporations.

6. Commendation and approval of "such efforts as the food stamp plan, slum clearance, and low-cost housing, the extension of hospital and medical facilities, and the development of vocational and cultural programs for the less privileged of our people . . ."

7. Recommendations "to all public and private bodies responsible for industry location" of "the desirability of decentralizing industry to the end that the maximum economic benefits can be secured from plants operated at their most efficient size, the depressing aspects of the factory system be prevented, and the American way of life be preserved."

8. Legislation to deal with the control now exercised by foreign governments and their industry over American concerns through patent laws.

9. Repeal of the Miller–Tydings Act legalizing resale price maintenance contracts (see Items 48, 99 and notes, 1937 volume).

10. Legislation establishing a committee on federal-state relationships, charged with the responsibility of collecting current information as to trade practices among the states, and with the duty of devising ways and means of preventing uneconomic barriers to trade.

11. Centralization of purchasing in one agency as much as possible; with purchasing planned so as to obtain the needed goods without dislocating the general economy.

12. Various recommendations to the respective states where insurance companies are domiciled, with respect to the supervision and control of such insurance companies; so as to make supervision by state officials more adequate, require better equipped agents and agency practices, bring about more frequent and thorough examinations of insurance companies, standardize policies, prevent the wiping out of competition, and bring about a fundamental change in the conduct of industrial insurance.

13. Although stating that, for the present, federal regulation of the life insurance business is not required, the committee recommended (a) a federal statute preventing life insurance companies from using the mails or the radio to sell insurance in any state where they have not been lawfully admitted to do business; (b) permitting state insurance commissioners to apply under the National Bankruptcy Act to the appropriate United States Court for liquidation or reorganization of any life insurance company; (c) prohibiting officers and directors of insurance companies operating in more than one state from using their positions for improper personal gain directly or indirectly; (d) federal legislation making life insurance officials legal

trustees to be bound by customary fiduciary standards; and (e) a thorough investigation of all forms of fire, casualty, and marine insurance.

14. Allocation of defense funds in such a way as to eliminate monopoly control of basic products.

15. Various measures designed to stimulate the investment of capital in new enterprise.

16. Expansion and development of research by the Department of Labor and the Federal Trade Commission dealing with the current functioning of our economy.

17. Legislation prohibiting the use of "basing point" and other industrial pricing systems which result in uneconomic location of plant equipment, and the elimination of price competition.

18. Additional appropriations to strengthen the machinery for enforcing the anti-trust laws by the Department of Justice and the Federal Trade Commission.

All the items mentioned in my foregoing message of April 29, 1938, were covered by the TNEC either in its hearings or in the monographs above mentioned, except the subject of financial controls.

The reason for this exception was that in my message I had mentioned the fact that the Securities and Exchange Commission had been conducting a comprehensive study of investment trusts and their operations for nearly two years, and that it was going to make its own report thereon. The subject of bank holding companies was included in this study of investment trusts.

The Securities and Exchange Commission has already transmitted to the Congress, Part One, Part Two, and Chapters I and II of Part Three of its over-all report on investment trusts.

Part One, which was transmitted by the Commission to the 75th Congress on June 10, 1938, consists of a discussion of the nature, classification, and origins of investment trusts and investment companies.

Part Two, the transmission of which to the 76th Congress was completed on March 10, 1939, consists of a statistical survey of investment trusts and investment companies.

Part Three, the transmission of which to the 76th Congress was begun on April 29, 1939, deals with the abuses and deficiencies in the organization and operation of investment trusts and investment companies.

The Commission has also transmitted to the Congress the following six supplemental reports:

Investment Trusts in Great Britain; Investment Counsel, Investment Management, Investment Supervisory, and Investment Advisory Services; Commingled and Common Trust Funds Administered by Banks and Trust Companies; Companies Sponsoring Installment Investment Plans; Fixed and Semifixed Investment Trusts; and Companies Issuing Face Amount Installment Certificates.

Many bills have been introduced in the Congress to carry out these various recommendations. The hearings and monographs and reports will form the basis of future thinking and action with respect to this great industrial and social problem of the day — monopolies and concentration of economic power.

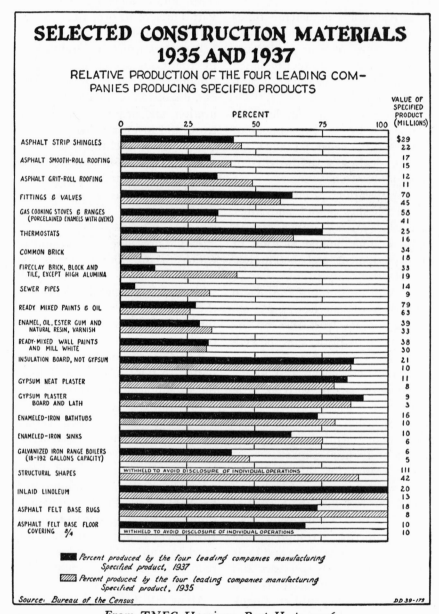

SELECTED CONSTRUCTION MATERIALS 1935 AND 1937

RELATIVE PRODUCTION OF THE FOUR LEADING COMPANIES PRODUCING SPECIFIED PRODUCTS

Source: Bureau of the Census

From TNEC Hearings, Part II, p. 5526

CONCENTRATION OF ASSETS
IN PRINCIPAL RESERVOIRS
OF SAVINGS*
1937

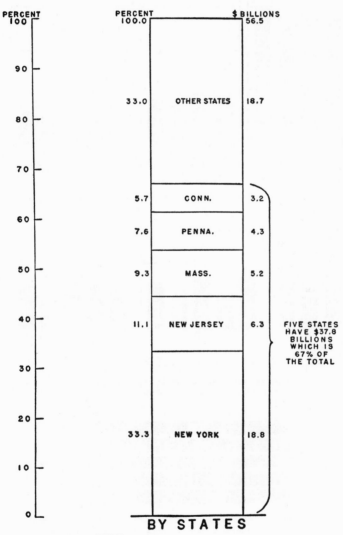

PERCENT
100

90

80

70

60

50

40

30

20

10

0

PERCENT
100.0

		$ BILLIONS 56.5
33.0	OTHER STATES	18.7
5.7	CONN.	3.2
7.6	PENNA.	4.3
9.3	MASS.	5.2
11.1	NEW JERSEY	6.3
33.3	NEW YORK	18.8

FIVE STATES
HAVE $37.8
BILLIONS
WHICH IS
67% OF
THE TOTAL

BY STATES

\# LIFE INS COS, SAVINGS DEPOSITS
IN ALL BANKS, & BLDG & LOAN ASSOCIATIONS

DS-1213 PREPARED BY SEC. & EXCH COMMR

Source: TNEC Hearings, Part 9, p. 3765

331

YEAR-END STOCKS OF CRUDE OIL AND PRINCIPAL PRODUCTS IN THE UNITED STATES

20 MAJOR COMPANIES AND "ALL OTHER" COMPANIES
1926, 1931, 1935-37

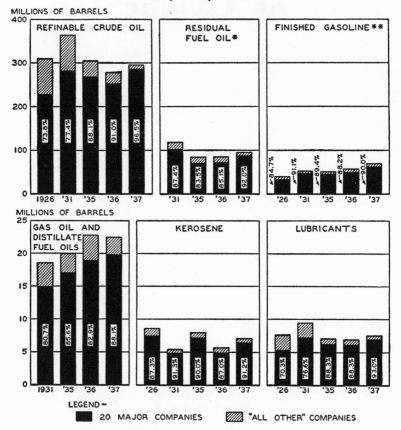

MILLIONS OF BARRELS

REFINABLE CRUDE OIL

RESIDUAL FUEL OIL*

FINISHED GASOLINE**

GAS OIL AND DISTILLATE FUEL OILS

KEROSENE

LUBRICANTS

LEGEND —
■ 20 MAJOR COMPANIES   ▧ "ALL OTHER" COMPANIES

PERCENTAGES OF AGGREGATES OF THE SIX SELECTED STOCKS HELD BY:

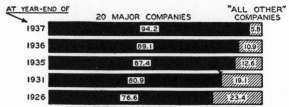

AT YEAR-END OF	20 MAJOR COMPANIES	"ALL OTHER" COMPANIES
1937	94.2	5.8
1936	89.1	10.9
1935	87.4	12.6
1931	80.9	19.1
1926	76.6	23.4

* INCLUDING HEAVY CRUDE OIL FOR CALIFORNIA. COMPARABLE DATA NOT AVAILABLE FOR 1926

** FOR 1926, INCLUDES STOCKS AT REFINERIES ONLY; FOR OTHER YEARS, INCLUDES STOCKS AT REFINERIES, BULK TERMINALS, AND IN PIPE LINES.

SOURCE: U. S. BUREAU OF MINES

From TNEC Hearings, Part 14-A, p. 7717

60 ⦅ Urging That the Congress Be Permitted to Vote on the Wages and Hours Bill. April 30, 1938

Hon. Mary T. Norton,
Chairman, Labor Committee,
House of Representatives,
Washington, D. C.

Your letter telling me that as a result of the action of eight members of the Rules Committee a wage and hour bill has again been prevented from reaching the floor of the House was given to me last night just as I took the train.

I want to make it wholly clear that the rules under which the House of Representatives acts are properly not the concern of the Executive Branch of the Government — nor have I any right whatsoever as President to criticize the rules.

Nevertheless, because you and I are old friends and because I myself have been a member of a legislative body, I feel free to give you my personal view of a difficult situation which has arisen because of yesterday's action and the similar preceding action of the Rules Committee several months ago.

Because of my personal experience, both in legislative and executive capacities, I have a profound respect for and devotion to the democratic legislative process. The continuing fairness of that legislative process is the foundation of enduring democracy.

It must always be the right of a legislative body to reject a bill if it is not satisfactory to a majority of its members. And it is equally the right of a legislative body, through committees, to sift out the hundreds of bills which are introduced each year, to hold hearings on them, and to produce orderly calendars for the consideration of the whole membership. That is the democratic process.

There are, however, certain types of measures in each session which are of undoubted national importance because they relate to major policies of government and affect the lives of millions of people.

60. Congressional Vote on Wages and Hours Bill

It has always seemed to me that in the case of these measures — few in number in any one session — the whole membership of the legislative body should be given full and free opportunity to discuss them. This discussion may end in drastic amendment, or in recommittal, or even in complete rejection.

In the case of wage and hour legislation, the majority party of the House is committed to legislation by its national platform — and I have no personal doubt that a large majority of the membership of the House believes that the House as a whole should pass its judgment on such legislation.

You have the situation, however, where a bill was held up by a majority vote of a small committee, was then reported by the petition system, was debated and recommitted to the Labor Committee for further consideration.

A new bill has been reported by the Labor Committee. I do not pass judgment on its merits or demerits. The fact remains that the subject should once more be properly before the House.

The Rules Committee, by a narrow vote, has declined to grant a rule and the full membership of the House — four hundred and thirty-five members — is thereby prevented from discussing, amending, recommitting, defeating or passing some kind of a bill to put a floor under wages and a ceiling over hours.

I still hope that the House as a whole can vote on a wage and hour bill — either by reconsideration of its action by the Rules Committee itself or by the petition route.

As I have suggested before, I hope that the democratic processes of legislation will continue. That is my personal view.

(For a discussion of the wages and hours bill, see note to Item 57, 1937 volume.)

61 ⟨ White House Statement on the Sale of Helium for Export. May 11, 1938

THE PRESIDENT is without legal power to override the judgment of Secretary Ickes and to direct the sale of helium for export.

The Congress has prohibited export sale of helium unless it is found that the quantity, under the circumstances, is not of military importance. The sale is so guarded that it requires the approval of the Secretary of the Interior and also unanimous approval of the National Munitions Control Board, which consists of the Secretaries of State, War, Navy, Treasury, and Commerce. Congress has in effect required unanimous agreement of six Cabinet officers that a proposed sale is not of military importance in order to authorize sale.

This is a discretion which each such Cabinet officer may exercise for himself.

(See also Item 58, pages 218-222, and Item 60, 1937 volume; Item 62, pages 339-340, this volume.)

62 ⟨ The Four Hundred and Fifty-eighth Press Conference (Excerpts). May 13, 1938

(Unemployment census — Study of industrial prices and inventories — Export of helium.)

THE PRESIDENT: I think the only thing I have today is a letter from Mr. [John] Biggers, making his semi-final report on the unemployment census. He points out that the cost of the census, including everything, will not exceed $1,986,000 out of the $5,000,000 that was authorized for the census. In other words, $3,000,000 will be turned back to the Treasury. The printed report will be submitted shortly and made public.

He points out that the saving in cost and in speed with which the whole thing was done was due primarily to the utilization of the facilities of other governmental agencies, the Post Office Department and others. In the short time that the census was concluded, he has tabulations for 3,070 counties and special tabulations for 952 cities, cities with a population of 10,000 or more, broken down in such form that each state, county and city can use this information as a valuable aid in solving its own unemployment problem.

The staff of the organization is now substantially disbanded, only a few people being left to check the final reports and the liquidation of accounts.

85,000,000 unemployment report cards were distributed to every home in the country in one day.

The voluntary educational campaign in which the press, the radio, and the motion pictures all played important parts had so well acquainted the people with the purpose and importance of the census that over 11,000,000 people voluntarily filled out registration cards. 5,833,401 reported as totally unemployed—

Q. May I have that figure again?

THE PRESIDENT: 5,833,401 reported as totally unemployed; 2,011,615 as unemployed, except for emergency work; and 3,219,502 as partially unemployed.

Fifteen tons of postal cards came into Washington.

The census demonstrated the possibility of quick action and cooperation among the branches of the Government to undertake emergency tasks.

Regardless of fluctuating totals, the data showing characteristics and composition of unemployment have permanent value. These facts developed include a study of ages and sex; dependent workers; geographical distribution; industries and occupations — Steve [Early] will make this available for you — all of which will be necessary as a basis for any comprehensive reemployment plan. Since this information is available by counties and cities of 10,000 and more population, an opportunity and a challenge are presented to local communities to assist in solving our principal economic problem.

An interesting revelation is the fact that as the main bread-winner of a family is thrown out of work, additional members of the family seek work which accentuates the number of unemployed in depression times. Likewise, it proves the fact that to bring about recovery, it is not necessary to provide jobs equal in number to the unemployed, because, as breadwinners are restored to work, other potential workers vanish from the labor market.

That seems to be fairly well established. In other words, the unemployment census has real value; and makes it much more easy for the Government to conduct the next unemployment census in conjunction with the decennial census of 1940.

Q. Mr. President, do you think this unemployment census should be a continuing function so that fortnight by fortnight or month by month the Nation should know accurately the changing figures of unemployment?

THE PRESIDENT: I think we are, in general, working toward a system of that kind. In other words, it may be called a voluntary registration system.

Q. If I recall correctly, before John Biggers started that I got the impression, both from you and Mr. Hopkins, that such a census would be of no practical value, or words to that effect. Has it turned out —

THE PRESIDENT: [interposing] It has turned out to be of real value, not only for the bringing together of definite figures for the time that it was taken, which was the first week in December, but it also ended all kinds of perfectly crazy stories, stories that were put out by all kinds of people, where the figures varied by millions, and gave us a perfectly definite point of departure. Also, it is very useful for the future.

Q. Will the machinery used in that poll and the method of this poll be studied with a view to national defense or possible mobilization of machinery?

THE PRESIDENT: I had not thought of it; it is a new one on me.

Q. While we are on the subject of recovery; the Administration speakers, including yourself, said that the causes of the present depression, the primary causes, were the unabsorbed inventories and unwarranted increases in prices.

THE PRESIDENT: Those were the factors, yes.

Q. Prime factors?

THE PRESIDENT: Not the only factors.

Q. But now that the spending and lending program is on its way, have you a program to meet these two points —

THE PRESIDENT: [interposing] No —

Q. — the unwarranted increase in prices and unabsorbed inventories?

THE PRESIDENT: Unfortunately, not. We did — we were working towards it, as we all know, in an experimental way under NRA, really, honestly, in an experimental way. However, we had to desist from those experiments when NRA was declared unconstitutional. And at the present time the whole thing is being started anew, not with any thought, as I have said so often, of reconstituting NRA. It is being started anew through the study of what was really misnamed the monopoly problem — because it is a far wider problem than the mere discussion of certain definite monopolies — and the study of them will go hand in hand with this investigation I hope the Congress will authorize before they adjourn.

Q. The reason I asked is because they say that the other spending program failed. I am just wondering if there is an answer.

THE PRESIDENT: Of course the other spending program did not fail, but it got to such a point that certain other economic and business methods ran away with the ball.

Q. I was wondering whether there was some way of regulating running away with the ball?

THE PRESIDENT: That is right.

Q. Have you any plan in mind?

THE PRESIDENT: No.

Q. Mr. Murray, of the Steel Workers' Organization Committee, proposed and Mr. Lewis later endorsed the proposal, that you seek a conference of business, industry, finance, labor and agriculture to work out with you what each might do.

THE PRESIDENT: Well, those conferences are going on every day.

Q. He meant where representatives of all the groups would be together with you.

THE PRESIDENT: Well, they are, every day.

Q. Mr. President, regarding the helium question, which you took up with members of various departments the other day and afterwards indicated that the matter was for decision of the National Munitions Control Board, that Board had already approved the export. Did you intend that they should reopen the question?

THE PRESIDENT: I think probably there will be another meeting of the Board very soon.

Q. When?

THE PRESIDENT: Very soon; I don't know when.

Q. Who has the power to call that meeting?

THE PRESIDENT: The Chairman.

Q. The Chairman yesterday said it would depend on you.

THE PRESIDENT: Perfectly true; I have not asked him yet because I have not seen him.

Q. Do you understand that the Board acted illegally when it approved the export of helium?

THE PRESIDENT: I don't know; it is a question of law, I suppose. The statute is very definite in setting up the National Munitions Board. It says, "The Secretaries" of these different Departments—"The heads" of these Departments. Well, by Government custom, as you know, these interdepartmental boards meet with the membership composed of Assistant Secretaries and, in order that the record may be perfectly clear, we want to have a meeting with the Secretaries present. Legally, whether the action of the Board when it is constituted by Assistant Secretaries may be all right, nobody knows.

Q. In weighing the laws governing the export of helium, does the Board take into consideration the intent of the Congress, the intent of the time when it was passed, which was immediately after the *Hindenburg* disaster?

THE PRESIDENT: They take into consideration the language of the statute primarily. When any question comes up as to the construction of the language, they are at full liberty to look into the debates on the floor or the hearings of the committee prior to the passage of the statute. . . .

(For an account of the unemployment census, see note to Item 114, 1937 volume; see Item 61, this volume, for the statement on the sale of helium for export.)

63 ⟨A Step Toward Reducing Duplication in Governmental Statistical Reports. May 16, 1938

My dear Mr. Chairman:

I AM concerned over the large number of statistical reports which Federal agencies are requiring from business and industry. In view of comments that come into this office, I desire to know the extent of such reports and how far there is duplication among them. Accordingly, I am requesting the Central Statistical Board, under the authority of Section 1 of the Act creating the Board, to report to me on the statistical work of the Federal agencies, with recommendations looking toward consolidations and changes which are consistent with efficiency and economy, both to the government and to private industry.

Specifically, I am interested in the approximate number of financial and other statistical reports and returns regularly required from business and industry and from private individuals by agencies of the Federal government under existing law, and the authority under which each is collected; specific indications of the extent and kinds of duplication existing among them, and the diversity of accounts and records which they necessitate. I assume that exhibits of the questionnaires and report forms are already available in large part in the Board's files, and I am sure that all of the Federal agencies will cooperate in providing any additional information that is relevant.

With a view to reducing the amount of duplication in statistical reports, will you indicate the principal points at which the enactment of legislation by the Congress appears to be necessary in order to effect consolidations or changes, with the recommendations of the Board regarding them?

I should like to have the complete report of the Board by January 1, 1939.

Very sincerely,

Honorable Stuart A. Rice,
Chairman, Central Statistical Board,
Washington, D. C.

NOTE: In recent years there have been complaints from business men and from other sources concerning the great number and duplication of various reports and returns which have to be made by business men and farmers to the federal government. These complaints became particularly numerous after the business recession of 1937.

I had several conferences with the Chairman of the Central Statistical Board, which had been established in 1933 (see Item 104, 1933 volume) to act as a coordinating agency for the federal statistical and reporting services.

On May 16, 1938, I sent him the foregoing letter requesting the Central Statistical Board to make a study of the situation and to submit its recommendations looking toward consolidations, elimination of duplication, and other changes "consistent with efficiency and econ- omy, both to the government and to private industry."

The final report of the board was submitted to me on December 31, 1938, and was transmitted by me to the Congress on January 10, 1939.

The report was the first comprehensive survey ever made of the various questionnaires, returns, and reports made to the federal government by the general public.

The report has been printed as House Document No. 27 of the 76th Congress, 1st Session. It points out that most of the data collected by the government is necessary to the performance of governmental functions, or is used in connection with the performance of government services for the firms and individuals making the reports. These are known as administrative returns; and for the year ending June 30, 1938, there were approximately 97,500,000 of such returns of various kinds filed.

Non-administrative returns are made for the purpose of furnishing information which is not directly concerned with administrative questions, but which is used for the formulation of public policy. During the fiscal year ending June 30, 1938, there were about 38,000,000 of these filed, including 12,000,000 collected by the census of unemployment.

The board reported a substantial amount of unnecessary duplication in existing reporting requirements. Some of this duplication arises from the fact that identical returns have to be submitted to both state and federal governments. There is also duplication in connection with furnishing financial statements which may be required for a number of different governmental purposes. Such duplications, for example, would occur in reports to the Bureau of Internal Revenue in income tax returns, to the Securities and Exchange Commission, to the Interstate Commerce Commission, and to the Federal Power Commission. Similar duplication often occurs in furnishing the payroll of a concern or its sales revenues.

The conclusion was reached that "much of this duplication may be unavoidable and may impose no serious hardship on respondents. It is nevertheless certain that in some cases an unnecessary number of separate reports are required from the same respondent."

The board made nine separate recommendations aimed at eliminating unnecessary duplication, and coordinating the report requirements of the various federal agencies.

These recommendations are as follows:

1. That it be recognized as sound in principle and necessary in practice that the various statistical and report-collecting services of the federal government be for the most part attached to agencies having administrative or other responsibilities relating to the subjects of the reports; and that, because of this decentralization of the statistical and reporting services, it is essential that there be a statistical coordinating agency with adequate powers.

2. That provisions in law be made to relieve any federal agency or officer of any requirement under existing law directing the collection of reports from the public, if substantially equivalent information which will meet the needs of such agency or officer is available from other reports to any federal agency.

3. That provision in law be made to promote and encourage federal agencies collecting information on a confidential basis to make such information available for the use of other federal agencies under rules designed to afford proper protection for the in-

terests of individual respondents, these rules to be promulgated by the President upon recommendations of the statistical coordinating agency.

4. That in cases where the statistical coordinating agency is unable to reduce or eliminate unnecessary duplication in reports to federal agencies, it be required to hold a hearing on the nature and reasons for such duplication and to report its findings to the President; and that the President be given power to eliminate such duplication.

5. That provision in law be made that, notwithstanding any previous provision of law to the contrary, no respondent shall be required to report information to a federal agency when such information is obtainable from reports previously made to the same agency, unless the collecting agency shall have established before the statistical coordinating agency that the duplicate request is necessary.

6. That provision in law be made as follows: (a) that when the needs of two or more federal agencies for reports pertaining to a given field of interest or from a given group of respondents can satisfactorily be met by the collection of such reports through a single agency serving as the agent of both or all such agencies; and when the statistical coordinating agency after due investigation shall have found such an arrangement to be in the public interest, it shall, subject to approval of the President, provide

for the collection of the reports involved by a single agency which it shall designate; (b) that after such a designation such arrangement shall apply to any new collection service within the field of interest or involving the group of respondents in question, unless the need for other arrangements is established before the statistical coordinating agency; and (c) that such arrangement shall be extended to reports now being collected, as soon as found practicable and in the public interest; provided that such arrangement shall not be allowed to hamper any agency in obtaining information needed in the performance of its duties.

7. That further consideration be given to technical changes in the federal tax laws and procedures which provide, in so far as is consistent with fiscal policy, for: (a) the consolidation of tax returns in cases in which any considerable group of persons is required to file two or more types of such returns in any one year; (b) acceptance by the Bureau of Internal Revenue, in lieu of all or part of any tax return, of any sworn report made to a regulatory agency which provides the required information; and (c) such other modifications in tax returns as would lighten the burden of making reports either to the tax authorities or to other federal agencies.

8. That the statistical coordinating agency be directed to arrange

for the establishment and maintenance of classified address lists of respondents so that for each important group of respondents there may be a standard list available to all Federal statistical and report-collecting agencies.

9. That federal agencies be required by law to keep uniform records of all questionnaires and report forms adopted and used to collect information from the public and to make reports on their adoption and use to the statistical coordinating agency; and that responsibility in each agency for authorizing the use of such forms and for the maintenance of such records be centralized.

Although no legislation has as yet resulted from the report, there have been several positive results obtained. Firstly, it seems to have put an end to proposals in some quarters that federal statistical activities be all centralized in a single agency. Secondly, it has brought general recognition that some of the requirements for filing returns, and some of the information called for, are unnecessary and can be eliminated.

Pursuant to Reorganization Plan No. I submitted by me on April 25, 1939 (see Item 66, 1939 volume), the functions of the Central Statistical Board were transferred to the Division of Statistical Standards of the Bureau of the Budget. That Division is now effectuating some of the recommendations contained in the report of the Central Statistical Board by means of inconspicuous and detailed adjustments in federal service.

As of May 1, 1941, it may be said that of the board's nine recommendations mentioned above, the first has been generally accepted as a statement of principle. The second, fourth, and fifth may become unnecessary if the Bureau of the Budget is able to adopt the appropriate procedures to attain the objectives of these recommendations, as it is now trying to do. The sixth recommendation represents a general objective toward which the Bureau of the Budget is constantly exerting its efforts. The seventh is the subject of current negotiations. The eighth is in process of accomplishment with the aid of two WPA projects. The ninth has been put into effect through a Budget circular.

64 ⁅ A Recommendation to the Congress on the Production and Conservation of Phosphates to Rebuild Soil Fertility. May 20, 1938

To the Congress:

THE SOIL of the United States faces a continuing loss of its productive capacity.

That is a challenging statement. It would seem, therefore, to be the part of wisdom for the Government and the people of the United States to adopt every possible method to stop this loss and begin to rebuild soil fertility.

We give the name of "soil conservation" to the problem as a whole; and we are already active in our efforts to retard and prevent soil erosion, and by the more intelligent use of land to build up its crop, its pasturage and its tree producing capacity.

As a result of the studies and tests of modern science it has come to be recognized that phosphorus is a necessary element in human, in animal and in plant nutrition. The phosphorus content of our land, following generations of cultivation, has greatly diminished. It needs replenishing. The necessity for wider use of phosphates and the conservation of our supplies of phosphates for future generations is, therefore, a matter of great public concern. We cannot place our agriculture upon a permanent basis unless we give it heed.

I cannot overemphasize the importance of phosphorus not only to agriculture and soil conservation but also to the physical health and economic security of the people of the Nation. Many of our soil types are deficient in phosphorus, thus causing low yields and poor quality of crops and pastures.

Indeed, much of the present accelerated soil erosion in the United States has taken place, and is still taking place, on land that has either been abandoned or is ready to be abandoned because of a low productivity brought about by failure to maintain the fertilizing elements in the soil. In many cases the re-

345

claiming of eroded land is largely a matter of stimulating plant growth, such as legumes and grasses; but hand in hand with this we must also replenish the actual phosphorus content of the soil.

Recent estimates indicate that the removal of phosphorus from the soils of the United States by harvested crops, grazing, erosion, and leaching, greatly exceeds the addition of phosphorus to the soil through the means of fertilizers, animal manures and bedding, rainfall, irrigation and seeds.

It appears that even with a complete control of erosion, which obviously is impossible, a high level of productivity will not be maintained unless phosphorus is returned to the soil at a greater rate than is being done at present. Increases by the addition of phosphorus to the soil must be made largely, if not entirely, in the form of fertilizers which are derived principally from phosphate rock.

Therefore, the question of continuous and adequate supplies of phosphate rock directly concerns the national welfare.

The total known world supply of phosphate rock is estimated at 17.2 billion tons, of which 7.2 billion tons is located in the United States. Nearly all the remainder is controlled by Great Britain, France and Russia. The supply in the United States is distributed as follows: Florida 7.4 per cent, Tennessee 1.4 per cent, Western States (Idaho, Montana, Utah and Wyoming) 90.8 per cent, and other States (Arkansas, Kentucky, South Carolina, and Virginia) 0.4 per cent. The domestic production of phosphate rock amounted to 3,351,857 tons in 1936, drawn from Florida (78.3 per cent), Tennessee (19.2 per cent), and Idaho and Montana (2.5 per cent). Exports of phosphate rock amounted to 1,208,951 tons, almost entirely from Florida, and consumption of phosphate rock for non-agricultural purposes totaled 352,275 tons.

Thus, it appears that of the total domestic production of phosphate rock only 53 per cent was used for domestic agricultural purposes.

Owing to their location in relation to the principal fertilizer-consuming districts, the Florida and Tennessee deposits, which contain less than 10 per cent of the nation's supply, are furnishing more than 97 per cent of all the phosphate rock used for domestic agricultural purposes. Under present conditions, by far the greater portion of our phosphate requirements will continue to be drawn from the Florida and Tennessee deposits so long as these deposits last. When it is realized that the consumption of phosphatic fertilizer must be increased considerably if our soils are to be maintained reasonably near their present levels of fertility, which in many cases are far below the levels necessary for an efficient agriculture, it becomes apparent that the deposits of Florida and Tennessee will last but a comparatively short period.

It is hardly necessary to emphasize the desirability of conserving these deposits to the fullest extent for the benefit of agriculture in the East, the South and a considerable portion of the Middle West.

At the same time, serious attention should be given to the development of the Western phosphate deposits in order that they may be made to serve economically the widest possible territory. It is evident that our main reliance for an adequate supply of phosphate must eventually be placed on our Western deposits.

As of December 1, 1936, the Government owned 2,124,904 acres of proven and potential phosphate lands in Idaho, Montana, Utah and Wyoming, and 66,916 acres in Florida. The Government owns no extensive areas of phosphate land in other States. Although an exact estimate of the tonnage of phosphate rock on Government land is not available, the quantity in the Western reserve no doubt exceeds 5 billion tons. It appears that only a small portion of the Florida supply is on Government land.

I call your special attention to the interesting and valuable work of the Tennessee Valley Authority and the Department of Agriculture in devising new processes for treating phosphate rock and for using the new types of phosphate products. This

347

work promises to make the great Western deposits available to a large area of America.

These developments by themselves, however, will not lessen the drain on the comparatively small deposits in Tennessee and Florida because the methods of treatment can be used as well on these deposits as on those in the West. Inasmuch as the deposits in Tennessee and Florida are, and will continue to be, of vital importance to American agriculture, it is to the national interest that they be conserved to the fullest extent.

The disposition of our phosphate deposits should be regarded as a national concern. The situation appears to offer an opportunity for this nation to exercise foresight in the use of a great national resource heretofore almost unknown in our plans for the development of the nation.

I invite the especial attention of the Congress to the very large percentage of known phosphate rock which is on government owned land—probably three-quarters of the whole supply—and to the fact that the Eastern supply, while in private ownership, is today being exported in such quantities that when and if it is wholly depleted, Eastern farms will have to depend for their phosphate supply on the Far Western lands.

It is, therefore, high time for the Nation to adopt a national policy for the production and conservation of phosphates for the benefit of this and coming generations.

To the end that continuous and adequate supplies be insured, and that efficient forms of this key element, phosphorus, be available at the lowest cost throughout the country, I recommend that a joint committee of the Senate and of the House of Representatives be named to give study to the entire subject of phosphate resources, their use and service to American agriculture, and to make report to the next Congress.

NOTE: The foregoing message was sent to call attention to the apparently heavy drain being made on the phosphate reserves of Florida and Tennessee, and to recommend that the Congress, through a committee, study the "entire subject of phosphate resources, their use and service to American agriculture." At this time there had been disturbing information concerning the large export of phosphate rock from this country, especially from Florida deposits. The importance of the subject had become manifest by the renewed interest in the conservation of soil and soil resources as a national policy, and by the interest in the work of the Tennessee Valley Authority in the production and use of phosphate fertilizers.

As a result of the foregoing message, Public Resolution No. 112, 75th Congress, 3rd Session, approved June 16, 1938, created a joint committee of Senators and Representatives to make a thorough study and investigation of the subject, with particular reference to the following: (1) The use of phosphates in American agriculture. (2) The domestic consumption and export of phosphates. (3) The adequacy of the supply of phosphates in the United States. (4) The development of phosphate deposits in the United States. (5) Methods of conservation of phosphates in the United States.

Many hearings were held; and a first report was submitted to the Congress on January 17, 1939, printed as Senate Document No. 21, 76th Congress, 1st Session.

The specific recommendations of the committee were the following:

1. That the Congress consider the advisability of appointing a committee for the study of the amount, ownership, and method of utilizing potash, borax, and such other mineral resources of the United States as may appear advisable.

2. That the United States Geological Survey be given the means of making a thorough study and survey of the reserves of phosphates in the United States, and that, due to the interrelation of phosphate and potash in fertilization, potash be included in such survey and study.

3. That the experimental and demonstration work and facilities of the Tennessee Valley Authority as to fertilization be continued.

4. That the program of the Agricultural Adjustment Administration in furnishing concentrated phosphate fertilizers to farmers in lieu of benefit payments be continued, with provision made for meeting the increased demands of farmers for this product.

5. That a plant for experimental, educational and demonstration purposes be established in the vicinity of the vast Western deposits of phosphate, in order that those resources which are mainly located on public lands be conserved and wisely used for the benefit of American agriculture.

6. That when government agencies, such as the Forest Service, Biological Survey, or the Farm Security Administration, or others, desire to purchase lands to increase national forests, bird or game refuges, or to acquire tracts for resettlement, or for other purposes,

where feasible such purchase be made in lands where phosphate deposits are present. The committee suggested that state agencies adopt a similar policy, and wherever practicable cooperate with federal agencies in this respect. These recommendations were made because the committee investigation of phosphate in Florida showed that large blocks of phosphate land owned by private companies or individuals were in a non-productive state, not likely to be mined for generations. This land was, however, blocked out in tonnage, grade, and location, suitable for mining when commercial conditions warranted. The committee felt that such land could probably be purchased at a very low rate.

7. That adequate legislation be enacted to protect American process patents.

The life of the committee was extended by Public Resolution No. 48, 76th Congress, 1st Session, approved August 10, 1939, and the time for making its final report was extended to January 15, 1940. A further report was submitted on January 15, 1940, and the life of the committee was extended to January 15, 1941, by Public Resolution No. 68, 76th Congress, 3rd Session, approved May 3, 1940.

65 ❨ A Statement on the Observance of Foreign Trade Week. May 20, 1938

My dear Mr. Secretary:

THIS ANNUAL observance throughout the country of Foreign Trade Week is an altogether fitting recognition of the vital role of foreign commerce in the economic life of the nation. Our own experience, no less than that of other nations, is living testimony to the fact that a healthy and vigorous flow of trade between nations is an indispensable requirement for general and lasting prosperity.

We have profited by that experience. For four years our Government has been engaged in a major effort to reopen the channels of trade. The trade agreements that we have concluded with seventeen foreign countries during this period attest to the progress that has been made. With patient persistence we are thus gradually building more secure foundations for our own national economic well-being. At the same time we are strengthening the foundations of enduring world peace, which is so essential to the continued progress of civilization and to the well-being of the people of every land.

Very sincerely yours,

The Honorable,
The Secretary of State,
Washington, D. C.

(See Item 33, 1934 volume, Item 31, 1940 volume, and accompanying notes, for an account of the trade agreements program.)

66 (The President Urges Acceptance of the Settlement of the Chaco Controversy. May 25, 1938

His Excellency:
Dr. Felix Paiva,
Provisional President of Paraguay,
Asunción, Paraguay

THE PEACE CONFERENCE which has been in session at Buenos Aires for almost three years in an effort to assist the Governments of Paraguay and Bolivia to reach a settlement of the Chaco controversy now presents a final proposal for a direct agreement between the two countries. That proposal represents the impartial and informed conclusions of a group of distinguished and able delegates who have participated in the negotiations over a period of three years.

There has been an exhaustive exchange of views between members of the Governments of Paraguay and Bolivia and delegates of the Conference. The proposal is based upon the results of these long negotiations, upon the inter-American principle of the settlement of international differences by peaceful means, and upon the Protocol of June 12, 1935, which was ratified by Paraguay and Bolivia under the auspices of the six mediatory governments.

In the opinion of the Government of the United States, the

proposal should be acceptable to Paraguay and Bolivia because it assures peace and security to both parties, because it is just and equitable, and because it takes into consideration the national interests of both countries.

Armed conflict in the Chaco was terminated almost three years ago through the voluntary agreement between Paraguay and Bolivia as embodied in the provisions of the Protocol of June 12, 1935. There was no victor and no vanquished, although the peoples of the two countries still suffer from the inevitable misery and destruction of war. The six mediatory governments are convinced that the people of Paraguay and Bolivia want no renewal of war and are strongly in favor of a definitive settlement of the Chaco controversy. I am sure that Your Excellency is in entire accord with this will for peace, and that your Government will spare no effort to bring to bear every influence in favor of the opportunity now presented by the Conference proposal.

The Governments of Argentina, Brazil, Chile, Peru, Uruguay and the United States have worked together energetically and loyally for three years in an effort to assist Paraguay and Bolivia to reach a direct settlement of their differences. They stand together now in unqualified support of a proposal which they believe is equitable, is in the best interests of the two parties, and, as a safeguard to peace on this hemisphere, is of vital concern to each and every one of the American republics. Under these circumstances, the Government of the United States considers it an obligation of friendship and of duty strongly to urge acceptance of the Conference proposal by the Governments of Paraguay and Bolivia.

Accept, Excellency, the assurances of my highest consideration and the expression of my sincere wishes for the well-being and happiness of the Paraguayan people.

FRANKLIN D. ROOSEVELT

His Excellency:
Colonel Germán Busch,
President of the Junta of Government of Bolivia,
La Paz, Bolivia

THE PROPOSAL which the Peace Conference presents to the Governments of Bolivia and Paraguay for the definitive settlement of the Chaco controversy is, in the opinion of the Government of the United States, an equitable one which offers every possibility for lasting peace, security and the national interests of the two parties. It is the result of the most careful study and impartial deliberation on the part of the delegates of the mediatory countries. It is in keeping with the pledge of the American republics to settle by peaceful means the international differences that may arise among them. It was formulated after full and frank exchanges of views between Conference delegates and members of the Governments of Bolivia and Paraguay at La Paz and Asunción. It represents a final effort to fulfill one of the obligations assumed under the Protocol of June 12, 1935, signed by the two parties under the auspices of the six mediatory governments.

Almost three years have elapsed since hostilities ceased in the Chaco, as a result of the voluntary agreement between Bolivia and Paraguay. That agreement put an end to the death and destruction of armed conflict, but the burden of suffering and loss must still weigh heavily upon the two peoples. I am confident that Your Excellency shares my deep conviction that the peoples of the two countries want peace and should have peace. The Peace Conference at Buenos Aires has been striving for three years to assist the Governments of Bolivia and Paraguay to make peace secure. An opportunity to crown these long negotiations with success now presents itself. There exists for all of those participating, directly or indirectly, in the work of the Peace Conference a solemn obligation to seize that opportunity.

The Government of the United States has cooperated loyally and actively with the Governments of Bolivia and Paraguay and with the governments of the other mediatory nations in seeking a just and definitive settlement of the Chaco controversy. It has a vital interest, in common with its sister republics of the Americas, in preserving peace in our hemisphere. In the present instance, the Government of the United States records its complete solidarity with the Governments of Argentina, Brazil, Chile, Peru and Uruguay in urging in the strongest and most friendly manner the acceptance by the Governments of Bolivia and Paraguay of the proposal referred to.

Accept, Excellency, the assurances of my highest consideration and the expression of my best wishes for the welfare and prosperity of the Bolivian people.

FRANKLIN D. ROOSEVELT

NOTE: For a general statement of the Chaco dispute and the efforts to mediate it, see Item 95 of 1934 volume, and note attached.

The Chaco Peace Conference was called in Buenos Aires on July 1, 1935 (see Item 163, 1935 volume). It was a difficult task to reconcile the conflicting interests and bitter feelings which had been created on both sides during the war. There were the pressing questions of boundary delimitation, demobilization, release of prisoners, fixing of war responsibilities, and measures of security.

After lengthy negotiations, even by May, 1938, the atmosphere was still far from clear. The foreign ministers of both Bolivia and Paraguay had been finally persuaded to come to Buenos Aires to discuss proposals. There were still mutual fears and suspicions, and there had been repeated incidents in the Chaco.

It was arranged to have the Presidents of the countries which had acted as mediatories in the Chaco dispute — Brazil, Chile, Peru, Argentina, the United States, and Uruguay — send messages to the two countries involved in the dispute, urging a final settlement of this controversy.

The foregoing telegrams were sent by me, and messages of the same general purport were sent by the Presidents of the other mediatory countries. Unless the settlement was adopted by the two countries, it seemed that the probable alternative was a resumption of the war.

My letter of May 25, 1938, was acknowledged by the Presidents of Bolivia and Paraguay, both of whom indicated a desire for a peaceful settlement.

Finally a treaty was signed by the two Republics at Buenos Aires, July 21, 1938. By it peace was reestablished; and the boundaries were to be fixed by the Presidents of the Republics of Argentina, Brazil, Chile, the United States, Peru, and Uruguay as arbitrators.

Once again, the nations of the Western Hemisphere provided an example of how international disputes could be settled without resort to force and bloodshed.

67 ⟨ "We . . . Are Getting More Practical Results in . . . Bettering the Social Conditions of the Nation out of Our Taxes than Ever Before in Our History." Address at Arthurdale, West Virginia. May 27, 1938

My friends of Arthurdale:

AT LAST after many attempts dating back through several years, I have succeeded in coming to Arthurdale — and I can greet you as old friends because you are Mrs. Roosevelt's old friends and also because I have heard so much about you.

Much has been written all over the country about you good people, about the conditions of life in certain towns in this part of the world and about what the United States has done here at Arthurdale. The Nation has heard about Scott's Run, with its very poor conditions of life, and the Nation has heard about Arthurdale with its vastly improved conditions of life. But I think I voice the thoughts of you who live here when I say to the country over the radio that about the last thing that you would want would be to be publicized as some rare and special type of Americans.

I think you will agree with me if I put history this way:

Back in 1933 the whole Nation knew that it faced a crisis in economic conditions but the Nation did not realize that it also faced a crisis in its social conditions. If anyone were to ask me what is the outstanding contribution that has been made to American life in the past five years, I would say without hesitation that it is the awakening of the social conscience of America.

As one part, and only one part, of the effort of your government to improve social conditions, we undertook, as you remember, in dozens of places scattered over almost every part of the country, to set up, with the cooperation of the local people themselves, projects to provide better homes, a better chance to raise foodstuffs, and a better chance to make both ends meet in maintaining a reasonably decent standard of living through the passing years.

Many different types of projects were undertaken—some of them in wholly rural sections, some in cities, some in suburbs, some for industrial workers, some for miners, some, like Arthurdale, a combination of industry and farming. These projects represent something new, and because we in America had little or no experience along these lines, there were some failures—not a complete failure in the case of any given project, but partial failures due to bad guesses on economic subjects like new industries or lack of markets.

On the whole, however, the percentage of good guesses in the average of these projects has been extraordinarily high, and for this success the principal part of the credit properly should go to the individual families who, themselves, have come to live in these new communities, people like you here in Arthurdale.

The lessons that we have all learned are going to save a hundred times their cost in dollars just as fast as government or private capital—or as I hope, both of them—go on with the inevitable task of improving living conditions throughout the country and helping Americans to live as modern science has made it possible for them to live. This extra cost of pioneering ventures, such as this, represents development cost which we justifiably charge off as the inevitable cost of all progress—just as we have in the past charged off the huge government share in the development costs of the railroads, the cables, the airplanes, and the hundreds of millions of dollars in improved highways that have made the automobile possible. But what is equally important to me, the lessons learned from this first bold government venture will save human lives and human happiness as well as dollars in this march of progress that lies ahead of us.

This is a high school graduation and I am speaking just as much to you who graduate today as I am to your parents and your grown-up friends. You are the citizens of tomorrow — not just this graduating class, but thousands of other high school graduating classes in every state of the Union.

Last night a very old and dear friend of mine gave me a little clipping out of a North Carolina paper. He is with me today, my old Chief, former Secretary of the Navy under Woodrow Wilson, Josephus Daniels, now the United States Ambassador to Mexico. This clipping goes back a quarter of a century. It is headed May 26, 1913. It says that Franklin Roosevelt, Assistant Secretary of the Navy, delivered the Commencement Address at A. & M. College in North Carolina. "The economics of a life of a people," he said, "often seem like academic questions when we study them out of textbooks, but they seem like life or death when we try to feed a hungry family. The question of production of food supply was an academic question twenty years ago; today it is becoming a question of bread and butter." So you see, as my old Chief said, the Assistant Secretary of the Navy has not changed very much in twenty-five years.

Now, I will carry you back a shorter distance.

When you, today's graduates, were of grade school age we, your elders in the United States, were asleep at the switch and your government also was asleep at the switch. For many years, other nations of the world were giving serious attention to and taking definite action on many social problems while we in the United States were pushing them aside with the idea that perhaps some day we might get around to meeting them.

We had heard ten years ago of the ideals of ending child labor, of initiating a five-day week, of shortening working hours, of putting a floor under wages, of clearing slums, of bringing electricity into the homes, and of giving families the chance to build or buy a home on easy terms, of starting old-age pensions and unemployment insurance. But, my friends, all those things were in the greater part just a beautiful dream — a dream until your government, five years ago, got tired of waiting, stepped in and started to make the dreams come true.

Government has done little more than to start the ball rolling. Government knows how much more remains to be done. But Government hopes, now that it has taken the first risks and shown the way, that private capital and business men will see how much it is to their own advantage — and profit — to keep the ball rolling, and keep it rolling so well that the inevitable wider improvement in American social conditions will come about in normal course of private enterprise without compelling the Government to use large amounts of taxpayers' money to keep America up to date.

A great many sincere people — good citizens with influence and money — have been coming to West Virgina mining towns in the past two or three years, to see the conditions under which American families lived, conditions under which, unfortunately, many American families still live. Many of these people have come to see me after their visit to Scott's Run or similar places, and have expressed to me their surprise and their horror at things they have seen. They have said to me: "I did not imagine that such conditions could exist in the United States."

They have wanted to help at the particular spot they have seen, but the lesson that I have found it difficult to get across to them has been the fact that they have seen only one spot or two spots — tiny, single spots on the great map of the United States, a map that is covered over with hundreds and even thousands of similar spots. Un-American standards exist by no means in a few coal towns only. They exist in almost every industrial community and they exist in very many of the farming counties of the country.

Now, of course, pending the time that private capital and private enterprise will take up the burden, the money your Government is spending to encourage the Nation to live better — especially that part of the Nation which most needs it — is taxpayers' money.

Two questions therefore, arise: "Is that spending of taxpayers' money justified from the point of view of the individual taxpayer?" and "How should the money be raised?"

So far as the taxpayer's individual interest is concerned, I always look at it this way:

Taxes — and I am talking about taxes to you who are graduating today just as much as your parents for the very good reason that very soon you will be taxpayers yourselves — taxes, local and state and federal combined, are nowhere near as high in this country as they are in any other great nation that pretends to be up-to-date. If I were a business man making and hoping to continue to make good profits, I would remind myself as I paid my income tax, moderate by the standards of other nations, that the most important factor in the kind of an active economic life in which profits can be made is people — able, alert, competent, up-to-date people — people to produce and people with ability to consume. Money invested to make and keep the people of this Nation that kind of people is therefore a good business investment.

And if I were the same man thinking about inheritance taxes, of what I was going to leave, of what I could leave to my children, I would say to myself that to leave them a living in a nation of strong and able men and women is to leave them a better heritage of security than a few thousand dollars saved on an inheritance tax.

Now, how should taxes be paid?

For a great many years the Nation as a whole has accepted the principle that taxes ought to be paid by individuals and families in accordance with their capacity to pay. To put it another way, it has meant a graduated tax on a man's increase in wealth. For instance, a poor man or poor family whose increase in wealth in a given year is below a certain figure pays no direct Federal taxes at all; he pays some indirect taxes but no direct taxes; when the family gains more than $2,500 in a year, he gets into the income tax group, and that type of family starts in by paying a small percentage on the year's gains.

As the gains get still larger, the percentage of the tax goes up so that, for example, when a family's wealth increases to let us say a gain of $100,000 a year, they have to pay a third of it to the Federal Government. In the case of still richer people, with half a million dollars a year income or a million dollars a year income, they may have to pay more than half of their large incomes to the State and Federal governments.

Last week, the Congress passed a new tax bill. It contained many good features — improvements in tax administration, the elimination of a number of nuisance taxes on articles in common use, the lightening of the tax burden on small corporations in accordance with what I recommended to the Congress last fall. I hope that these changes made by this tax bill may be helpful to business and that this belief may, in itself, be a factor in the revival of business enterprise.

But, when the President of the United States has a bill sent to him from Congress, he has to read the whole bill; and on the other side of the ledger, I cannot help but regret that two very fundamental principles of government must once more be called to the attention of the American public.

Both of these matters of principle, stripped of every attempt to confuse, are extraordinarily simple and can be understood by every citizen.

In 1936, many large corporations, and especially those big corporations that were owned or controlled by a comparatively small number of very rich stockholders, were in the habit of failing to declare the dividends, the profits that they had earned. In that way these stockholders, small in number, large stockholders, were in a position to leave the profits their money had made in the controlled corporation — paying the Government on these profits only the normal corporation tax of from ten to fifteen per cent. By this method, these stockholders were able to avoid paying a personal income tax at a much higher rate, at a rate which in many cases would have involved a tax payment of fifty per cent, or sixty per cent, or even higher because the stockholders were in what are known as the upper brackets of the personal income tax.

The Treasury Department found many instances of closely held corporations which, starting with the comparatively modest capital of several million dollars — and that is considered modest capital by a lot of people — had, over a period of years, grown into corporations worth several hundreds of millions of dollars without ever declaring a dividend to their stockholders. That meant a definite, though of course a strictly legal, device by which these stockholders greatly increased their wealth year after year without having to pay to the Government more than a normal corporation tax, thus escaping very large sums of personal income tax payments.

The Revenue Act of 1936 sought to end this serious loophole.

In principle our objective was right, but in practice, probably because it was a new thing, the Act as finally worked out in the Senate undoubtedly did prevent many small corporations from normal and reasonable business expansion, from building up adequate surpluses, or from paying off old debts.

The tax bill this year sought to get rid of these inequitable features, quite properly, but to retain at the same time the principle of stopping the tax avoidance that I have described. As finally passed, the bill retains the principle but the penalty for these large corporations for withholding dividends to their stockholders has been made so small — only two and a half per cent at the most — that it is doubtful, very doubtful, whether it will wholly eliminate the old tax avoidance practices of the past.

It is true that the bill seeks to strengthen the authority of the Government to act against companies that clearly seek to avoid these surtaxes for their stockholders by failing to declare dividends out of their profits; and I hope that this new provision, together with the recent favorable decision by the Supreme Court in interpreting the prior law, will retard the revival of the old evil. It seems to me that it is the definite duty and interest of the public — and you are the public — the interest of the Legislative and Executive branches of the Government, to watch very closely to see what happens during the coming year, as a result of these new provisions.

361

We must always remember that this old method of greatly increasing private fortunes through the withholding of corporate dividends was open and useful only to those citizens who already had wealth large enough to control these large corporations — people whose personal income was already large enough to put them in the higher surtax brackets.

The position of this Administration is this:

We are delighted to remove any existing barriers against every little business in the Nation which is seeking to set itself squarely on its own feet, seeking to pay off its debts and seeking to make a reasonable profit; but the Administration does not want large closely-held corporations making large profits to be used as a vehicle by the small number of their owners to avoid legitimate income taxes. And I think the people of this country are squarely behind the Administration in this belief.

It is also true that for a number of years it has been recognized that this progressive taxation of wealth realistically ought to apply not only to salaries and to dividends and to bond coupons but also to other forms of wealth, such as increases in one's capital by selling any form of property at a profit, that are known as capital gains.

This new bill, that is still before me at this moment, wholly eliminates the progressive tax principle with respect to these capital gains: it taxes small capital profits and large capital profits at exactly the same tax rate. That, my friends, is not right.

In other words, if you or I were to sell stocks that we have held for a few years, at a profit of, let us say, five thousand dollars, we would have to pay a tax of fifteen per cent on that profit under this new bill; whereas the man who has made a profit of five hundred thousand dollars on stocks that he has owned is required, under this new bill, to pay a tax of only fifteen per cent, just as you and I would. Nobody, by any stretch of the imagination, can say that this new provision maintains the principle of payment in proportion to ability to pay.

Some people who have favored this abandonment of principle have justified their position on the ground that one has to abandon principles once in a while when there is an emergency, and that the abandonment of this particular principle will encourage many rich men to take a new risk with their capital and invest it in new enterprises.

But this school of thought finds it very difficult to answer the fact that almost all — over eighty per cent of all capital gains that are reported — are profits made in the stock market — profits made not by developing new companies, not by starting new industries the way they are being started at Arthurdale, oh, no, but profits made by buying stocks of old companies, buying them low and selling them high, or by the still possible method of selling stocks short — selling stocks you do not own — and then buying them in at a lower price.

The abandonment of the principle of progressive tax payments in accordance with capacity to pay may encourage a small amount of capital to go into new productive enterprises, but, chiefly, it will help those who make large profits in buying and selling existing stocks.

New productive enterprise, and you here in this community know what that term means, is not created by the buying of stocks of established companies when they are low and selling them when they are high. I should like to see a revision of our tax laws which would really encourage new enterprise and new investment and the undertaking by private capital of projects like this, that the Government has undertaken here in Arthurdale. But there is no assurance that untaxed savings will go into such new investment or new enterprise. They may be hoarded or they may be lost in the inflation or the deflation that occurs in the shuffling about of existing investments.

We, as a nation, ought to adopt tax policies that will encourage men to venture, and to build new productive wealth. Unless something is added to the combined wealth of the nation, one man's capital gain may be nothing more than another man's capital loss.

In this analysis of this abandonment of what I believe is a basic principle, I have attacked no person. I have merely called the attention of the country to certain clear-cut inescapable facts — and especially to the fact that this tax bill which, in many respects, is a good one, actually abandons the accepted principle of progressive taxation at a point which is very important in our economic life.

Here again is an example of a provision of law which actually, and in plain English, gives an infinitely greater tax concession to the man who makes a very great profit than to the man who makes a comparatively small profit. It helps the very few, therefore, at the expense of the many. To carry on government, you and I know that some definite total sum has to be raised, whether it is county government or a state government or a federal government. If the many who make small capital gains have to pay the same rate as the few who make large capital gains, it means that the tax rate for the little fellow must be higher than if we had stuck to the accepted principle of a graduated tax.

In accordance with recommendations that I have made during several years past, I hope that the Congress, when the new Congress comes back next January, will undertake a broader program of improving the Federal tax system as a whole, in the light of accepted principles of fairness in American taxation, and of the necessary incentives in our economic life.

You will see the difficulty in which your President has been placed. This tax bill contains features that ought to become law, but it contains several undesirable features, especially the ones I have just been talking about.

Here is the problem: If I sign the bill — and I have until midnight tonight to sign it — many people, with some justification, will think that I approve the abandonment of an important principle of American taxation. If I veto the bill, it will prevent many of the desirable features of it from going into effect.

I am choosing this occasion, when old and young are gathered together, when people are listening in every state of the Union — I am taking this occasion to make an announcement: For the first time since I have been President, I am going to take the third course which is open to me under the Constitution.

67. *Address at Arthurdale, W. Va.*

At midnight tonight, this new tax bill automatically will become law; but it will become law without my signature or my approval. By taking that course, I am calling the definite attention of the American people to those unwise parts of the bill that I have been talking to you about today — one of them which may restore in the future certain forms of tax avoidance of the past, and of continued concentrated investment power, which we in Washington had begun to end; and the other feature, a definite abandonment of a principle of tax policy long ago accepted as part of our American system.

Two things we can well remember.

The first is that our whole tax system, state, local and federal, can and must be greatly improved in the coming year.

The second is that we in this country are getting more practical results in the way of bettering the social conditions of the nation out of our taxes than ever before in our history. That is why it is a pretty good idea to talk taxes not only to parents of America but also to the younger generation of America.

I have been thrilled today by all I have seen. I have been made happy in meeting so many people that I have heard a lot about, by seeing them in their own homes, by seeing the splendid work that has been going on. I want to tell you, my friends of Arthurdale, that I am proud of what I have seen today and I am proud of all of you, old and young alike, who are helping so greatly to make this community an American success.

(See also Item 47 and note, this volume, for discussion of the tax bill.)

68 ❦ Graduation Address at the United States Naval Academy, Annapolis, Maryland.

June 2, 1938

A QUARTER of a century ago I began coming to Graduation Exercises at the United States Naval Academy. I find it a good custom and I hope to be following it occasionally when I have reached the age of the oldest Admiral on the retired list. As a retired Commander-in-Chief of the Navy I could do nothing else.

The only time I disgraced myself was, I think, during the World War. Because of the strenuous work in the Navy Department, I was a bit in arrears on sleep. On that occasion the temperature in Bancroft Hall was in the neighborhood of a little over a hundred. There I was sitting on the right of the Superintendent of the Naval Academy. The speaker of the occasion began his address. My eyes slowly but firmly closed. I think indeed that my mouth fell open. I slept ungracefully but soundly directly in front of the eyes of the entire graduating class. Could anything be more un-military, more humiliating and, at the same time, more completely satisfactory?

You who are about to become officers of the Navy of the United States have had four years of advice — kindly advice but very firm advice. I do not propose to add to it, except to make one friendly suggestion which is not addressed to you as officers but is intended to apply to you just as much as to this year's graduates in any other college or school in the country.

No matter whether your specialty be naval science, or medicine, or the law, or teaching, or the church, or civil service, or business, or public service — remember that you will never reach the top and stay at the top unless you are well-rounded in your knowledge of all the other factors in modern civilization that lie outside of your own special profession.

That applies to all of world thought and world problems, but it applies, of course, with special emphasis to the thought and the problems of our own Nation.

Let me illustrate by quoting what Theodore Roosevelt once said to me when he was in the White House. A bill for the conservation of natural resources, a nation-wide measure which he had strongly recommended, had been defeated in the Congress by a coalition of votes of members who saw in the bill no special advantage to their own individual Congressional districts. And when he learned of the defeat of this pet measure, he said what almost every President has said, first or last: "I wish we could have a Constitutional Amendment requiring that no person could run for Congress unless he had filed a certificate that he had visited every one of the forty-eight states in the Union."

You who graduate today will fill many important Government posts during many intervals of shore duty. In these posts you will need national knowledge — knowledge of the problems of industry, knowledge of the problems of farming, knowledge of the problems of labor and knowledge of the problems of capital. You will need to know intimately the geography and the natural and human resources of the United States. You will need to know the current operations of federal and state and local governments. You will be called on for decisions in your line of duty where such knowledge will be of at least daily desirability — daily help to you in coming to your own conclusions and carrying out your own assigned tasks.

Preliminary knowledge of that kind you have; but the best of it, the most important part of it, will come to you through the passing years.

It will come to you in two ways. Firstly, by the experiences of your daily life. Those experiences can be profitable to you or not in proportion to your ability to relate each experience to the whole field of experiences. Secondly, you will have the opportunity constantly to widen your knowledge by your own individual efforts. You can confine your field of thought to your professional work or you can widen your field of thought to include a current interest in every current event.

Today you are graduating with the certification by the Government of the United States that you are gentlemen — and the fact that you have been able to graduate at all from the Naval Academy proves that you are scholars. In all of the years to come I want you, and I expect you, to prove that you have another qualification — that you are also thorough-going, up-to-date, intelligent American citizens.

And now we have a very pleasant surprise. A number of years ago our close neighbor on the north, the Government of our sister nation, Canada, sent back to the United States some flags which had been captured by Canadian and British soldiers in the War of 1812. Shortly after that, the Government of the United States sent back to Canada the mace of the Canadian Parliament which American soldiers and sailors had taken during the War of 1812.

Today I am glad to say that we are honored by the presence of Sir Herbert Marler, the Canadian Minister to the United States. He is with us as another token of the very close bonds that link our two sister nations together.

There is with us today another Canadian, the Mayor of a neighboring city, Saint John, New Brunswick. Mayor MacLaren has had in his family, for many years, a very precious relic, a relic connected with the first and most famous officer of the American Navy, John Paul Jones, whose body lies in the crypt of our Chapel.

Now, I am going to ask Mayor MacLaren, of Saint John, to come forward and do his bit.

————

(Mayor MacLaren's address follows):

Mr. President:

IT is my great privilege and high honor to stand here today in such illustrious company, and complete the mission that has brought me from my home in Saint John, New Brunswick.

The object of that mission is to present to you, Sir, and through you to the great American Nation, the quadrant used by that famed officer of your early life as a nation and as a power upon the waters

68. Graduation Address at U.S. Naval Academy

— Commodore John Paul Jones, the Father of the American Navy.

In making this presentation, I am but performing a filial duty, for the quadrant had rested for many years in the possession of my late father, Mr. J. S. MacLaren, and it had been his wish that it should some day become the property of the American people.

Mr. President, I pay tribute to the gallantry that made John Paul Jones one of your outstanding heroic figures. It is fitting that his mortal remains should rest at this hallowed shrine of the American Navy. It is appropriate also that you should preserve those possessions of his that the years have permitted to remain. To add to those already in your keeping it is my great pleasure to place in your hands the quadrant that so well served its gallant owner.

In closing, Mr. President, may I add a personal word. The people of the City of Saint John, of which I have the honour to be Mayor, and of the Province of New Brunswick, are happy and proud to greet you as one of ourselves on the occasions when you visit your summer residence on Campobello Island. That these occasions may be many more in number is our earnest wish.

(The President continued as follows:)

On behalf of the Government and especially on behalf of all the graduates of the United States Naval Academy, I extend our very deep thanks to my neighbor, Mayor MacLaren, of Saint John, for this token that fits in so well in this historic spot.

And now there will be no more speaking, there will be something more important. Before you actually become Bachelors of Science, let me stress that in the days to come you do not place too much emphasis on the word "Bachelor."

And so, I congratulate you on your graduation. Your Commander-in-Chief is proud of you. Good luck and happy voyage.

69 ⟨A Denial of Any Shift in Policy of Providing Relief Through a Work Program.

June 7, 1938

My dear Mr. Mayor:

IN REPLY to your telegram regarding federal relief program, there is no intention of shifting from present policy of providing relief for able-bodied unemployed through a work program. The states and municipalities must continue to provide for direct relief as their fair share of the total program and cannot expect assistance from the federal government in meeting this responsibility.

Any confusion regarding the respective responsibilities of federal, state and local governments which results in a weakening of the efforts of states and municipalities in the field of direct relief or of the federal work program will prove disastrous and should at all costs be avoided. I will appreciate very much your cooperation in making this clear to mayors.

Very sincerely yours,

Honorable F. H. LaGuardia,
United States Conference of Mayors,
New York, N. Y.

NOTE: In May, 1938, when the WPA appropriations for the fiscal year 1939, commencing July 1, 1938, were under consideration, an amendment was inserted by the Senate Appropriations Committee authorizing WPA to set aside a fund of $50,000,000 to be used in emergencies for providing direct relief rather than work relief.

Of course, by that time the policy and practice had become firmly established that the Federal Government should provide only work relief, leaving home relief and direct relief to the respective states and municipalities.

The purpose of this proposed Senate amendment was explained in debate to be two-fold: first, to provide some direct relief when it would not be feasible to provide work relief promptly enough during the drastic business recession then in progress; secondly, to permit direct relief in the event of the recurrence of flood or drought or similar disaster.

However, the amendment was also supported by some Senators who were in favor of abandoning the work program altogether and of returning to a system of using federal funds for direct relief.

Later, this amendment was amended to provide for $125,000,-000, and was passed by the Senate in that form. Many newspapers in their headlines featured the passage of this amendment by the Senate as the beginning of the return to the dole.

On June 2, 1938, Mayor La-Guardia of New York City, as the President of the United States Conference of Mayors wired me, expressing the view that if the federal government went into the field of direct relief, it would reduce the chances of the states and municipalities of the nation appropriating sufficient money to fulfill their responsibility for home relief.

Accordingly, I restated the policy of the federal government in the foregoing telegram of reply, dated June 7, 1938.

After the Senate had passed the bill and it had gone to conference, the amount authorized for direct relief was reduced to $25,000,000; and the language of the amendment was modified considerably to leave the method of disbursement, if any, to the discretion of the President.

Of this amount $15,700,000 was used; but it was used only to purchase surplus stocks of clothing which were at that time a glut on the clothing market and an obstacle to reemployment in the clothing industry. This clothing was distributed to needy families. No other direct relief was extended either directly or indirectly as a result of this provision.

For a further discussion of the advantages of work relief over cash relief, see Item 75 (page 242), 1933 volume; Item 31, 1934 volume; Item 173 (pages 474-475), 1935 volume; Item 178 (pages 492-493), 1936 volume; Item 83 (pages 405-406), this volume; Item 71, 1939 volume; and accompanying notes.

70 ❡ Transmitting to the Congress, Conventions and Recommendations of the International Labor Conference. June 9, 1938

To the Congress:

THE CONGRESS, by a Joint Resolution approved June 19, 1934, authorized me to accept membership for the Government of the United States in the International Labor Organization.

Pursuant to that authorization I accepted such membership on behalf of the Government of the United States.

Representatives of this Government and of American employers and American labor attended the Twenty-third Session of the International Labor Conference held at Geneva, June 3 to 23, 1937.

That Conference adopted four drafted conventions and seven recommendations, to wit:

The Recommendation (No. 50) concerning international cooperation in respect of public works;

The Recommendation (No. 51) concerning the national planning of public works;

The draft Convention (No. 59) fixing the minimum age for admission of children to industrial employment (revised 1927);

The draft Convention (No. 60) concerning the age for admission of children to non-industrial employment (revised 1937);

The Recommendation (No. 52) concerning the minimum age for admission of children to employment in family undertakings;

The draft Convention (No. 61) concerning the reduction of hours of work in the textile industry;

The draft Convention (No. 62) concerning safety provisions in the building industry;

The Recommendation (No. 53) concerning safety provisions in the building industry;

The Recommendation (No. 54) concerning inspection in the building industry;

The Recommendation (No. 55) concerning cooperation in accident prevention in the building industry;

The Recommendation (No. 56) concerning vocational education for the building industry.

No action by the Congress appears necessary in connection with the Recommendation (No. 50) concerning international cooperation in respect of public works. The United States Government already has indicated its readiness to cooperate in the work of an international committee and a representative of the Government will be appointed to attend its first sitting. The various branches of the Government will be prepared to communicate annually to such a committee statistical and other information concerning public works already undertaken or planned.

The United States Government has already endorsed the principle of stabilizing public works, contained in the Recommendation (No. 51) concerning the national planning of public works, and is endeavoring to put that principle into practice. The terms of the Recommendation embrace many proposals which the United States is already applying.

The standards stipulated in the draft Convention (No. 59) fixing the minimum age for admission of children to industrial employment (revised 1937), the draft Convention (No. 60) concerning the age for admission of children to non-industrial employment, and the Recommendation (No. 52) concerning the minimum age for admission of children to industrial employment in family undertakings are considerably below those generally prevailing in the United States.

The draft Convention (No. 61) concerning the reduction of hours of work in the textile industry is the subject of a separate message which I am addressing to the Senate.

The principles set forth in the draft Convention (No. 62) concerning safety provisions in the building industry, the Recommendation (No. 53) concerning safety provisions in the building industry, the Recommendation (No. 54) concerning inspection in the building industry, the Recommendation (No. 55) concerning cooperation in accident prevention in the building industry, and the Recommendation (No. 56) concerning vocational education for the building industry are presented for the consideration of the Congress in connection with its consideration of legislation now before it designed to promote safety in the building industry.

In becoming a member of the International Labor Organization and subscribing to its constitution this Government accepted the following undertaking in regard to such draft conventions and recommendations:

Each of the Members undertakes that it will, within the period of one year at most from the closing of the session of the Conference, or if it is impossible owing to exceptional circumstances to do so within the period of one year, then at the earliest practicable moment and in no case later than eighteen months from the closing of the session of the Conference bring the recommendation or draft convention before the authority or authorities within whose competence the matter lies, for the enactment of legislation or other action. (*Article 19 (405), paragraph 5, Constitution of the International Labor Organization.*)

In the case of a federal State, the power of which to enter into conventions on labor matters is subject to limitations, it shall be in the discretion of that Government to treat a draft convention to which such limitations apply as a recommendation only, and the provisions of this Article with respect to recommendations shall apply in such case. (*Article 19 (405), paragraph 9, Constitution of the International Labor Organization.*)

In accordance with the foregoing undertaking the above named four draft conventions and seven recommendations are herewith submitted to the Congress with the accompanying report of the Secretary of State, and its enclosures, to which the attention of the Congress is invited.

NOTE: Of the conventions and recommendations transmitted to the Congress in the foregoing message, the only one which I actually recommended for adoption was Draft Convention 61, which dealt with the reduction of hours of work in the textile industry. With respect to the others, I pointed out either that no action was necessary by the Congress, or that some of the conventions were considerably below standards generally prevailing already in the United States. As to the others, I merely submitted them to the Congress for consideration. As of January 1, 1941, no action has been taken by the Congress.

(For a further account of the participation of this government in the International Labor Organization, see Item 61, 1935 volume; Item 74, 1936 volume; Item 75, 1937 volume; and Item 61, 1940 volume.)

71 ⟨A Denial of Intention to Revise the National Labor Relations Act. June 10, 1938

My dear Hatton:

THERE has just come to my attention the minority report of the Committee on Judiciary relative to H.R. 6449 "Amending the Walsh-Healy Act."

I note this minority report states: "The President of the United States has recognized the disastrous effects of industrial strife now prevalent in the country and the unsatisfactory operation of the National Labor Relations Act, and has announced that a special commission will be appointed by him to study the entire problem, looking to recommendations for labor legislation in the Seventy-sixth Congress."

I wish to call to your attention the fact that I have no intention of appointing any commission to study the operation of the National Labor Relations Act. I assume that the signers of the minority report have reference to the proposed study of industrial relations in Great Britain. As I publicly stated on June 3, I am solely interested in securing a report on the status of industrial relations in Great Britain with particular emphasis on the functioning of collective agreements, in order that certain current misconceptions may be clarified.

I am taking the liberty of bringing these facts to your attention so that the House of Representatives may be correctly informed of the purpose of the proposed survey of British industrial relations.

Very sincerely yours,

Honorable Hatton W. Sumners,
House of Representatives,
Washington, D. C.

NOTE: For a description of the National Labor Relations Act (49 Stat. 449), and the early work of the National Labor Relations Board, see Item 90 and note, 1935 volume.

In the 64 months ending January 31, 1941, the National Labor

Relations Board handled 32,942 cases covering approximately 6,900,-000 workers. These figures include 21,693 charges of unfair labor practice involving 3,700,000 workers and 11,249 petitions involving 3,200,000 workers for the determination of collective bargaining representatives.

More than 90 per cent of all cases received during the given period were disposed of, leaving 3,061 cases pending on January 31, 1941. Of the 29,881 cases closed, 14,316, involving approximately 2,200,000 workers, were settled by agreement of both parties. 5,024 cases involving 1,200,000 workers were dismissed by the board and regional directors before any formal action was taken. 8,043 cases involving 1,500,000 workers were withdrawn by the complainant or petitioner before formal action. 2,498 cases involving 800,000 workers were closed in some other way, including compliance with board decision, certification after election, refusal by the board to certify, intermediate report finding no violation, and transfer to other agencies such as Conciliation Service of the Department of Labor and the State Labor Relations Boards.

A total of 3,166 strike cases involving 400,000 workers were handled by the board; 2,383 of these cases were settled. The number of strikes averted through board action was 938, involving 200,000 workers. More than 300,000 workers were reinstated after strikes or lockouts; an additional 22,000 workers were reinstated after discriminatory discharge.

More than 1,400,000 valid votes were cast in the 3,837 elections held during the given period.

72 (The President Transmits to the Congress the Proposed Codification of the Nationality Laws. June 13, 1938

To the Congress:

I TRANSMIT herewith a Report concerning the Revision and Codification of the Nationality Laws of the United States, submitted upon my request, by the Secretary of State, the Attorney General, and the Secretary of Labor. The Report is accompanied by a draft Code with three appendices containing explanatory matter, prepared by officials of the three interested Departments who are engaged in the handling of cases relating to nationality.

376

72. Codification of Nationality Laws

The Report indicates the desirability from the administrative standpoint, of having the existing nationality laws, now scattered among a large number of separate statutes, embodied in a single, logically arranged and understandable Code. Certain changes in substance are likewise recommended.

In the enclosed letter forwarding the Report to me the Secretary of State calls attention to a single question on which there is a difference of opinion between the Departments of Justice and Labor on the one hand and the Department of State on the other hand. If the committees of Congress decide to consider this question, the views of the three Departments may be presented directly to them.

I commend this matter to the Congress for the attentive consideration which its wide scope and great importance demand.

NOTE: Provisions governing the general subject of nationality had been passed from time to time in the United States in a somewhat haphazard manner. As a result, they were spread through a large number of unconnected and unrelated statutes. There had always been, therefore, considerable uncertainty and confusion in the state of the laws; and there was indeed difficulty at times in finding the rule governing questions arising from time to time in connection with the general subject.

By Executive Order No. 6115 dated April 25, 1933, I designated a committee consisting of the Secretary of State, the Attorney General, and the Secretary of Labor, to make a study of all the nationality laws of the United States, to recommend revisions therein, and to present a codification of those laws into one comprehensive nationality statute, which could be presented for action to the Congress.

This committee, after considerable research, drafted a proposed Nationality Code which they submitted to me.

In the foregoing message to the Congress I transmitted this proposed code, recommending its enactment into law. With very few changes, it was passed by the Congress and approved by me on October 14, 1940.

There are now combined in this single code all the many statutes which had been previously passed governing nationality, including, however, necessary changes and adjustments governing certain aspects of the subject.

73 ❨ A Letter Stating Our Policy on Arming for Defense. June 14, 1938

My dear Mr. O'Laughlin:

I CONGRATULATE you upon the completion by the Army and Navy Journal of seventy-five years of publication.

Now, even as in the stirring days when your paper was established, the Federal Government has the inescapable obligation laid upon it by the Constitution to "provide for the common defense." That means not only the development of adequate military forces but the vigorous use of our good offices in the promotion of world peace.

In pursuance of this constitutional duty, it has been our effort to place the Army and the Navy in a position to protect our territory and our vital interests. It has been our effort through treaties designed to remove trade barriers and irritations, through mediation, through disarmament negotiations, and through proper representations at critical moments, to lessen, and if possible, eliminate the factors that make for war.

None of the things we have done contemplates aggression. None goes beyond what is essential to set up proper safeguards against aggression. As others decrease their armaments we will gladly join them by reducing those which present world conditions force us to provide for our own protection.

Very sincerely yours,

Mr. John Callan O'Laughlin,
Army and Navy Journal,
Washington, D. C.

74 ❨ Veto of Legislation Involving Interest Rates on Farm Loans. June 15, 1938

To the House of Representatives:

I RETURN herewith, without my approval, H.R. 10530, entitled "An act to extend for two additional years the 3½-per-centum interest rate on certain Federal land-bank loans, and to provide for a 4-per-centum interest rate on Land Bank Commissioner's loans until July 1, 1940."

Section 1 of the bill extends for two additional years beginning July 1, 1938, the 3½ per cent interest rate on certain federal land bank loans.

Section 2 of the bill extends for approximately one year, that is, from July 22, 1939, to June 30, 1940, the 4 per cent interest rate on Land Bank Commissioner loans.

SECTION I. FEDERAL LAND BANK LOANS

The question presented by the proposed legislation is not whether Federal land bank borrowers will be required during the coming year to pay interest on their Federal land bank loans at the full rates specified in their mortgage contracts; the question is the amount of reduction that will be effected. Since the average contract rate of interest on outstanding Federal land bank loans is approximately 5 per cent, the emergency 4 per cent rate provided for under present law would mean an average interest reduction of 20 per cent to Federal land bank borrowers during the fiscal year 1939. It amounts to an average reduction of approximately 28 per cent in the case of those borrowers whose contract rates of interest exceed 5 per cent. Thus if this bill does not become law there will still be savings to borrowers amounting to from 20 per cent to 28 per cent.

The interest reductions granted to Federal land bank borrowers will have involved upon the expiration of the present provisions of law in July, 1939, a total cost to the Treasury estimated at approximately $143,500,000. If H.R. 10530 becomes law, the total cost to the Treasury to June 30, 1940, is estimated at $183,900,000.

The burden of interest charges on a typical farmer who refinanced his 6 per cent private loan with a Federal land bank in 1933 would appear to be less on the basis of present prices, and the emergency Federal land bank interest rate of 4 per cent provided for under present law less than the burden which was carried by the same farmer on his old loan during the period 1910-14 or during the period 1921-30.

As of March 31, 1938, approximately 86 per cent of all loans of the Federal land banks were in good standing as opposed to approximately 50 per cent delinquency when the emergency legislation was first passed.

SECTION 2. LAND BANK COMMISSIONER LOANS

A reduced rate of interest on Land Bank Commissioner loans was first provided for by the Act of July 22, 1937, which fixed the rate at 4 per cent for a period of two years from the date of its enactment. Under the provisions of H.R. 10530 the emergency 4 per cent rate would be continued from July 22, 1939, to June 30, 1940. There would appear to be no substantial reason for establishing at this time a policy with respect to the interest rate on Land Bank Commissioner loans for the period beginning July 22, 1939.

The total cost to the Treasury of interest reductions on Land Bank Commissioner loans to the expiration of the date of the existing Act, July 21, 1939, is estimated at $16,500,000. If the 4 per cent rate is extended to June 30, 1940, an additional expense of $8,300,000 is estimated.

Adding the expense of interest reductions on Land Bank Commissioner loans to the estimated cost of such reductions on Federal land bank loans, the total cost to the Treasury upon the expiration of the provisions of existing law in July, 1939 would approximate $160,000,000. If H.R. 10530 becomes law, the total cost to the Treasury to June 30, 1940, on both Federal land bank and Land Bank Commissioner loans is estimated at $208,700,000.

For all these reasons, I am constrained to withhold my approval of the bill, H.R. 10530.

NOTE: The reasons for my veto of this legislation are sufficiently stated in the memorandum above (see Item 84, 1937 volume, for similar veto in the preceding year; and Item 54, 1933 volume, for a discussion of these loans as a means of reducing the farmer's debt burden).

The bill was passed by the Congress over my veto, as Public No. 643, 75th Congress, 3rd Session (52 Stat. 709).

75 ❨ A Greeting to the Tenth World's Christian Endeavor Convention in Melbourne, Australia. June 15, 1938

Dear Dr. Poling:

THERE is something inspiring and soul-stirring about the very scope of the Tenth World's Christian Endeavor Convention to be held in Melbourne, Australia. The fact that Christians from all parts of the world are to make a far journey to Melbourne demonstrates that the message of the Nazarene is a vital and compelling force in the lives of millions of men and women.

This is most reassuring in a world in which the forces of greed and avarice and a disregard of fundamental human rights have brought disaster and despair where peace and plenty and true happiness should reign supreme. We regret that sorrow and heavy burdens are the possession of many; but we do not abandon hope.

I have said, and I desire to reiterate it to this body of Christians gathered from many lands, that what this weary world most needs is a revival of the spirit of religion. Would that such a revival could sweep the nations today and stir the hearts of men and women of all faiths to a reassertion of their belief in the Providence of God and the brotherhood of man. I doubt if there is in the world a single problem, whether social, political, or economic, which would not find ready solution if men and nations would rule their lives according to the plain teaching of the Sermon on the Mount.

In sending my greetings to the Tenth World's Christian Endeavor Convention may I express the hope that its deliberations will turn the hearts and minds of men and women everywhere toward this great but simple truth.

Very sincerely yours,

Reverend Daniel A. Poling, D.D.,
President, The World's Christian Endeavor Union,
Philadelphia, Pennsylvania.

76 ⟪A Letter of Greeting on the Close of the Congressional Session. June 16, 1938

My dear Mr. Speaker:

IN THESE closing hours of the 1938 Session of the 75th Congress I want to extend through you to the members of the House of Representatives of the United States my sincere good wishes.

I am confident that the country joins with me in the belief that this session of the Congress has resulted in much constructive legislation for the benefit of the people. Definitely, we are making progress in meeting the many new problems which confront us.

With appreciation of all that you have done,

Faithfully yours,

Hon. William B. Bankhead,
Speaker of the House of Representatives,
Washington, D. C.

(A similar letter was sent to the presiding officer of the Senate.)

(For a summary of the accomplishments of the Seventy-fifth Congress, see Item 80, pages 391-394, this volume.)

77 ❢ A Letter to the Members of the Committee to Study Industrial Relations in Great Britain. June 21, 1938

My dear Miss Dickerman:

It is with great pleasure that I have learned that you have accepted the invitation of the Secretary of Labor to cooperate in the preparation of a report on industrial relations in Great Britain.

In view of the many comments that have come to my attention relative to industrial relations in Great Britain, I feel that there is a definite need for an impartial report which will adequately portray the real situation that prevails in British industry. I trust that, through conferring with British Government officials, industrial leaders, and labor officials, you will be in a position to report to the Secretary of Labor not only on the exact status of labor-employer relations in England, but also on the evolution of the established and accepted procedures that account for the current state of industrial relations in that country.

Very cordially yours,

Miss Marion Dickerman,
Hyde Park, N. Y.

(Identical letters were sent to William Ellison Chalmers, Lloyd K. Garrison, Gerard Swope, Anna M. Rosenberg, William Davis, Robert Watt, and Henry I. Harriman.)

NOTE: By the foregoing letter of June 21, 1938, I appointed a committee of nine people, consisting of employers, labor experts, and other citizens, to visit Great Britain in order to study their system of industrial relations between capital and labor. They were later requested to study the same subject in Sweden.

Our country had recently passed through a short epidemic of sit-down strikes, and the Congress of Industrial Organizations (CIO) had been growing in strength and numbers, and had been engaged in many widespread labor stoppages as a result of these strikes (see Item 72 and note, 1937 volume).

There were many newspapers and many representatives of large employers of labor, and other persons, who were continually urging that certain drastic steps be taken by the Congress and the President based on English and Swedish experience and laws. The assumption was that the English and Swedish trade unions at that time were showing a larger measure of response to the needs of the general community, and that this attitude was a result of statutes which had been enacted for the purpose of controlling them. The general contention of these newspapers and employer-representatives was that

statutes should be enacted in this country requiring all unions to incorporate; prohibiting all sympathetic strikes; and outlawing contributions by trade unions to political parties.

The committee which I appointed went to England and Sweden; and conducted its study and investigations. Its report on the industrial relations in Great Britain was submitted on August 25, 1938, and was released to the press with a statement by me on August 31, 1938 (see Item 109, this volume). Its report on industrial relations in Sweden was submitted on September 19, 1938, and was released to the press with a statement by me on September 22, 1938 (see Item 118, this volume).

78 ⟨A Request for a Report by the National Emergency Council on the Problems and Needs of the South. June 22, 1938

My dear Mr. Mellett:

Discussions in Congress and elsewhere in connection with legislation affecting the economic welfare of the Nation have served to point out the differences in the problems and needs of the different sections of the Country and have indicated the advisability of a clear and concise statement of these needs and problems in a form readily available, not only to the members of Congress, but to the public generally.

Attention has recently been focused particularly upon the South in connection with the Wages and Hours Bill, and I should like the National Emergency Council to undertake the preparation of such a statement of the problems and needs of the South. In preparing this statement I suggest that you call freely upon the various governmental departments and administrative agencies for information as to matters with which they are especially acquainted, and also that you request the assistance of Southerners well known for their interest in the South and familiarity with its problems.

The outcome of this undertaking may indicate the advisability of similar studies with reference to other sections of the country.

Very sincerely,

Honorable Lowell Mellett,
Executive Director,
National Emergency Council

NOTE: Pursuant to the foregoing letter, the Conference on Economic Conditions in the South was called to meet in Washington to discuss the economic and social problems of the South, and the difficulties which it faces.

Leading southern educators, publishers and editors, bankers, business men, farmers and laborers participated in the Conference, and assisted the National Emergency Council in an advisory capacity.

A report summarizing the conclusions of this group and of the National Emergency Council was presented to me following the adjournment of the Conference. These conclusions are discussed in the note to Item 88, this volume.

79 ❨ The Competitive Classified Civil Service is Extended. Executive Order No. 7916.

June 24, 1938

By virtue of and pursuant to the authority vested in me by the Constitution, by Section 1753 of the Revised Statutes (U.S.C., Title 5, Section 631), by the Civil Service Act of January 16, 1883 (22 Stat. 403), and as President of the United States, it is hereby ordered as follows:

Section 1. Effective February 1, 1939, all positions in the Executive civil service, including positions in corporations wholly owned or controlled by the United States, which are not now in the competitive classified civil service and which are not exempted therefrom by statute, except (1) policy-determining positions and (2) other positions which special circumstances require should be exempted, are covered into the competitive classified civil service: *Provided,* That this section shall not be deemed to apply to positions filled by appointment by and with the advice and consent of the Senate: *And provided further,* That no positions shall be exempted from the competitive classified civil service under clauses (1) and (2) above except such as shall be designated in subsequent Executive orders issued after investigation showing the necessity and justification for such exemptions. This section shall also apply to positions affected by statutes which exempt them from the competitive classified civil service but authorize the President in his discretion to cover them into such service.

Section 2. Within ninety days from the date of this order the heads of all departments and independent establishments, including corporations wholly owned or controlled by the United States, whose personnel or any part thereof is affected by Section 1 of this order, shall certify to the Civil Service Commission for transmission by it with its recommendations to the President the positions in their respective departments or agencies which in their opinion should be excepted from the provisions of Section 1 of this order as policy-determining or for other reasons.

Section 3. The incumbent of any position which is covered into the competitive classified civil service by Section 1 of this order shall acquire a classified civil service status (1) upon recommendation by the head of the agency concerned and certification by such head to the Civil Service Commission that such incumbent was in the service on the date of this order and has rendered satisfactory service for not less than six months, and (2) upon passing a suitable noncompetitive examination prescribed by the Civil Service Commission under the civil service rules: *Provided,* That he is a citizen of the United States and is not disqualified by any provision of law or civil service rule. Any such incumbent who fails to meet the foregoing requirements of this section shall be separated from the service within thirty days (exclusive of leave to which he is entitled) after the Commission reports that he is ineligible for classification unless the head of the agency concerned certifies to the Commission that such incumbent has rendered satisfactory service and that he should be retained although without acquiring a competitive classified status.

Section 4. New appointments to any positions covered into the competitive classified civil service by Section 1 of this order shall not be affected by the provisions of said section until the Civil Service Commission shall have established registers of eligibles for such positions as a result of examinations held in accordance with the civil service rules and regulations and with this order.

Section 5. The Civil Service Commission shall, subject to the Civil Service Act, the rules thereunder, and the Classification Act of 1923, as amended, initiate, supervise, and enforce a system as uniform as practicable, for the recruitment, examination, certification, promotion from grade to grade, transfer, and reinstatement of employees in the classified civil service, other than employees therein excepted by Executive orders, issued pursuant to clauses (1) and (2) of Section 1 hereof, which system shall, so far as practicable, be competitive, with due regard to prior experience and service.

Section 6. Effective not later than February 1, 1939, the heads of the Executive departments and the heads of such independent establishments and agencies subject to the civil service laws and rules as the President shall designate, shall establish in their respective departments or establishments a division of personnel supervision and management, at the head of which shall be appointed a director of personnel qualified by training and experience, from among those whose names are certified for such appointment by the Civil Service Commission pursuant to such competitive tests and requirements as the Civil Service Commission shall prescribe: *Provided,* however, that if the head of a department or establishment requests authority to appoint a presently acting personnel or appointment director, officer, or clerk, as such director of personnel, such personnel or appointment director, officer, or clerk may be appointed upon certification by the Civil Service Commission that he is qualified therefor after passing such tests as the Civil Service Commission shall prescribe. It shall be the duty of each director of personnel to act as liaison officer in personnel matters between his department or establishment and the Civil Service Commission, and to make recommendations to the departmental budget officer with respect to estimates and expenditures for personnel. He shall supervise the functions of appointment, assignment, service rating, and training of employees in his department or establishment, under direction of the head thereof, and shall initiate and supervise such programs of personnel training and management as the head thereof after consultation with the Civil Service Commission shall approve, including the establishment of a system of service ratings for departmental and field forces outside of the Classification Act of 1923, as amended, which shall conform as nearly as practicable with the system established under the said Act. Subject to the approval of the head of such department or establishment and of the Civil Service Commission he shall establish means for the hearing of grievances of employees and present appropriate recommendations for the settlement thereof to the head of his department or establishment. He shall serve as a member of the Council of Personnel Administration hereinafter established, and perform such other functions as the head of the department or agency after consultation with the Civil Service Commission shall prescribe. A director of personnel may be transferred from one department or establishment to another from time to time, subject to the provisions of the civil service rules and with the approval of the head of the agency to which transfer is proposed.

Section 7. Effective February 1, 1939, there is established a Council of Personnel Administration consisting of the directors of personnel of the several departments and independent establishments, one additional representative of the Bureau of the Budget, one additional representative of the Civil Service Commission, and such additional members as the President shall designate. The President shall designate one of the members of the Council to act as chairman thereof, and the Council may designate an executive director. The Council shall advise and assist the President and the Commission in the protection and improvement of the merit system, and recommend from time to time to the President or the Commission needed changes in procedure, rules, or regulations. When directed so to do by the President or the Commission, the Council shall hold hearings and conduct investigations with respect to alleged abuses and proposed changes. The Council shall carry on programs of study to coordinate and perfect the executive personnel service in all its branches, and shall report upon the progress of personnel administration throughout the service. The Council shall have an executive committee of five members: one representing the ten executive departments to be chosen by the Directors of Personnel thereof; one representing the independent establishments and agencies to be chosen by the Directors of Personnel thereof; one representing the Bureau of the Budget to be chosen by the Director thereof; one representing the Civil Service Commission to be chosen by it; and one to be designated by the President. Executive Order No. 5612 of April 25, 1931, is hereby revoked.

Section 8. The Civil Service Commission shall, in cooperation with operating departments and establishments, the Office of Education, and public and private institutions of learning, establish practical training courses for employees in the departmental and field services of the classified civil service, and may by regulations provide credits in transfer and promotion examinations for satisfactory completion of one or more of such training courses.

Section 9. Schedules A and B of the Civil Service Rules, as presently existing, relating to positions excepted from examination and positions which may be filled upon non-competitive examination, will be superseded by schedules designating policy-determining positions and other positions which special circumstances require should be exempted, which schedules will be set forth in subsequent Executive orders as provided in section 1 hereof.

NOTE: The primary purpose of this executive order was to extend the competitive classified service to cover positions which up to that time had been exempt from the civil service system either by reason of statute or executive order, or by provisions of the civil service rules. There were a few exceptions made, which are included in Section I of the order.

The order also directed each of the executive departments and independent agencies to establish a division of personnel supervision and management, at the head of which should be a Director of Personnel.

The order then provided that these various directors of personnel should, together with other designated persons, form a Council of Personnel Administration, to advise and assist the President and the Civil Service Commission in the protection and improvement of the merit system, and to recommend from time to time needed changes. This Council has since served as a valuable clearing house in personnel matters of general interest.

The order also directed the Civil Service Commission to establish practical training courses for employees in the classified civil service.

When the foregoing executive order was issued, it was believed that approximately 81,000 positions would be brought within the jurisdiction of the merit system on the effective date of the order, viz., February 1, 1939.

However, this number was reduced by several statutes which were subsequently passed by the Congress, withdrawing many thousand positions from the effect of the order. The result was that when the order took effect on February 1, 1939, approximately only 24,000 employees were brought into the classified Civil Service by it.

After the promulgation of this order, and during the consideration given to it by various agencies in the period up to the time of its effective date, the question was raised by a number of agencies as to the inclusion of attorney positions. On January 31, 1939, immediately before the taking effect of this order, I issued a new Executive Order No. 8044, which suspended the foregoing Executive Order No. 7916, with respect to certain positions, including professional and scientific positions. This action was taken in order to have further consideration of the problems involved in the legal and other professional and scientific positions. Most of the employees involved were attorneys. By the same order, I appointed a committee to make a comprehensive study of the positions included in the new executive order, and to report to me with respect thereto (see Item 24, 1939 volume).

80 ❨ "I Have Every Right to Speak . . . Where There May Be a Clear Issue Between Candidates for a Democratic Nomination Involving . . . Principles, or . . . a Clear Misuse of My Own Name." Fireside Chat. June 24, 1938

OUR GOVERNMENT, happily, is a democracy. As part of the democratic process, your President is again taking an opportunity to report on the progress of national affairs to the real rulers of this country — the voting public.

The Seventy-fifth Congress, elected in November, 1936, on a platform uncompromisingly liberal, has adjourned. Barring unforeseen events, there will be no session until the new Congress, to be elected in November, assembles next January.

On the one hand, the Seventy-fifth Congress has left many things undone.

For example, it refused to provide more businesslike machinery for running the Executive Branch of the Government. The Congress also failed to meet my suggestion that it take the far-reaching steps necessary to put the railroads of the country back on their feet.

But, on the other hand, the Congress, striving to carry out the Platform on which most of its members were elected achieved more for the future good of the country than any Congress between the end of the World War and the spring of 1933.

I mention tonight only the more important of these achievements.

1. It improved still further our agricultural laws to give the farmer a fairer share of the national income, to preserve our soil, to provide an all-weather granary, to help the farm tenant toward independence, to find new uses for farm products, and to begin crop insurance.

2. After many requests on my part the Congress passed a

Fair Labor Standards Act, commonly called the Wages and Hours Bill. That Act — applying to products in interstate commerce — ends child labor, sets a floor below wages and a ceiling over hours of labor.

Except perhaps for the Social Security Act, it is the most far-reaching, far-sighted program for the benefit of workers ever adopted here or in any other country. Without question it starts us toward a better standard of living and increases purchasing power to buy the products of farm and factory.

Do not let any calamity-howling executive with an income of $1,000 a day, who has been turning his employees over to the Government relief rolls in order to preserve his company's undistributed reserves, tell you — using his stockholders' money to pay the postage for his personal opinions — that a wage of $11 a week is going to have a disastrous effect on all American industry. Fortunately for business as a whole, and therefore for the Nation, that type of executive is a rarity with whom most business executives heartily disagree.

3. The Congress has provided a fact-finding Commission to find a path through the jungle of contradictory theories about wise business practices — to find the necessary facts for any intelligent legislation on monopoly, on price-fixing and on the relationship between big business and medium-sized business and little business. Different from a great part of the world, we in America persist in our belief in individual enterprise and in the profit motive; but we realize we must continually seek improved practices to insure the continuance of reasonable profits, together with scientific progress, individual initiative, opportunities for the little fellow, fair prices, decent wages and continuing employment.

4. The Congress has coordinated the supervision of commercial aviation and air mail by establishing a new Civil Aeronautics Authority; and it has placed all postmasters under the civil service for the first time in our history.

5. The Congress set up the United States Housing Authority to help finance large-scale slum clearance and provide low rent

housing for the low income groups in our cities. And by improving the Federal Housing Act, the Congress made it easier for private capital to build modest homes and low rental dwellings.

6. The Congress has properly reduced taxes on small corporate enterprises, and has made it easier for the Reconstruction Finance Corporation to make credit available to all business. I think the bankers of the country can fairly be expected to participate in loans where the Government, through the Reconstruction Finance Corporation, offers to take a fair portion of the risk.

7. The Congress has provided additional funds for the Works Progress Administration, the Public Works Administration, the Rural Electrification Administration, the Civilian Conservation Corps and other agencies, in order to take care of what we hope is a temporary additional number of unemployed and to encourage production of every kind by private enterprise.

All these things together I call our program for the national defense of our economic system. It is a program of balanced action — of moving on all fronts at once in intelligent recognition that all our economic problems, of every group, of every section, are essentially one.

8. Because of increasing armaments in other nations and an international situation which is definitely disturbing to all of us, the Congress has authorized important additions to the national armed defense of our shores and our people.

On another important subject the net result of a struggle in the Congress has been an important victory for the people of the United States — a lost battle which won a war.

You will remember that on February 5, 1937, I sent a message to the Congress dealing with the real need of Federal Court reforms of several kinds. In one way or another, during the sessions of this Congress, the ends — the real objectives — sought in that message, have been substantially attained.

The attitude of the Supreme Court toward constitutional questions is entirely changed. Its recent decisions are eloquent testimony of a willingness to collaborate with the two other branches of Government to make democracy work. The Government has been granted the right to protect its interests in litigation between private parties involving the constitutionality of Federal statutes, and to appeal directly to the Supreme Court in all cases involving the constitutionality of Federal statutes; and no single judge is any longer empowered to suspend a Federal statute on his sole judgment as to its constitutionality. Justices of the Supreme Court may now retire at the age of seventy after ten years service; a substantial number of additional judgeships have been created in order to expedite the trial of cases; and greater flexibility has been added to the Federal judicial system by allowing judges to be assigned to congested districts.

Another indirect accomplishment of this Congress has been its response to the devotion of the American people to a course of sane consistent liberalism. The Congress has understood that under modern conditions government has a continuing responsibility to meet continuing problems, and that Government cannot take a holiday of a year, a month, or even a day just because a few people are tired or frightened by the inescapable pace of this modern world in which we live.

Some of my opponents and some of my associates have considered that I have a mistakenly sentimental judgment as to the tenacity of purpose and the general level of intelligence of the American people.

I am still convinced that the American people, since 1932, continue to insist on two requisites of private enterprise, and the relationship of Government to it. The first is complete honesty at the top in looking after the use of other people's money, and in apportioning and paying individual and corporate taxes according to ability to pay. The second is sincere respect for the need of all at the bottom to get work — and through work to get a really fair share of the good things of life, and a chance to save and rise.

After the election of 1936 I was told, and the Congress was told, by an increasing number of politically — and worldly —

wise people that I should coast along, enjoy an easy Presidency for four years, and not take the Democratic platform too seriously. They told me that people were getting weary of reform through political effort and would no longer oppose that small minority which, in spite of its own disastrous leadership in 1929, is always eager to resume its control over the Government of the United States.

Never in our lifetime has such a concerted campaign of defeatism been thrown at the heads of the President and Senators and Congressmen as in the case of this Seventy-fifth Congress. Never before have we had so many Copperheads — and you will remember that it was the Copperheads who, in the days of the War Between the States, tried their best to make Lincoln and his Congress give up the fight, let the Nation remain split in two and return to peace — peace at any price.

This Congress has ended on the side of the people. My faith in the American people — and their faith in themselves — have been justified. I congratulate the Congress and the leadership thereof and I congratulate the American people on their own staying power.

One word about our economic situation. It makes no difference to me whether you call it a recession or a depression. In 1932 the total national income of all the people in the country had reached the low point of thirty-eight billion dollars in that year. With each succeeding year it rose. Last year, 1937, it had risen to seventy billion dollars — despite definitely worse business and agricultural prices in the last four months of last year. This year, 1938, while it is too early to do more than give an estimate, we hope that the national income will not fall below sixty billion dollars. We remember also that banking and business and farming are not falling apart like the one-hoss shay, as they did in the terrible winter of 1932-1933.

Last year mistakes were made by the leaders of private enterprise, by the leaders of labor and by the leaders of Government — all three.

Last year the leaders of private enterprise pleaded for a sudden curtailment of public spending, and said they would take up the slack. But they made the mistake of increasing their inventories too fast and setting many of their prices too high for their goods to sell.

Some labor leaders, goaded by decades of oppression of labor, made the mistake of going too far. They were not wise in using methods which frightened many well-wishing people. They asked employers not only to bargain with them but to put up with jurisdictional disputes at the same time.

Government, too, made mistakes — mistakes of optimism in assuming that industry and labor would themselves make no mistakes — and Government made a mistake of timing, in not passing a farm bill or a wage and hour bill last year.

As a result of the lessons of all these mistakes we hope that in the future private enterprise — capital and labor alike — will operate more intelligently together, and in greater cooperation with their own Government than they have in the past. Such cooperation on the part of both of them will be very welcome to me. Certainly at this stage there should be a united stand on the part of both of them to resist wage cuts which would further reduce purchasing power.

Today a great steel company announced a reduction in prices with a view to stimulating business recovery, and I was gratified to know that this reduction involved no wage cut. Every encouragement should be given to industry which accepts a large volume of high wage policy.

If this is done, it ought to result in conditions which will replace a great part of the Government spending which the failure of cooperation made necessary this year.

From March 4, 1933, down, not a single week has passed without a cry from the opposition "to do something, to say something, to restore confidence." There is a very articulate group of people in this country, with plenty of ability to procure publicity for their views, who have consistently refused to cooperate with the mass of the people, whether things were going well or going badly, on the ground that they required more concessions to their point of view before they would admit having what they called "confidence."

These people demanded "restoration of confidence" when the banks were closed—and again when the banks were reopened.

They demanded "restoration of confidence" when hungry people were thronging the streets—and again when the hungry people were fed and put to work.

They demanded "restoration of confidence" when droughts hit the country—again now when our fields are laden with bounteous yields and excessive crops.

They demanded "restoration of confidence" last year when the automobile industry was running three shifts and turning out more cars than the country could buy—and again this year when the industry is trying to get rid of an automobile surplus and has shut down its factories as a result.

It is my belief that many of these people who have been crying aloud for "confidence" are beginning today to realize that that hand has been overplayed, and that they are now willing to talk cooperation instead. It is my belief that the mass of the American people do have confidence in themselves—have confidence in their ability, with the aid of Government, to solve their own problems.

It is because you are not satisfied, and I am not satisfied, with the progress we have made in finally solving our business and agricultural and social problems that I believe the great majority of you want your own Government to keep on trying to solve them. In simple frankness and in simple honesty, I need all the help I can get—and I see signs of getting more help in the future from many who have fought against progress with tooth and nail.

And now, following out this line of thought, I want to say a few words about the coming political primaries.

Fifty years ago party nominations were generally made in conventions—a system typified in the public imagination by a little group in a smoke-filled room who made out the party slates.

The direct primary was invented to make the nominating process a more democratic one — to give the party voters themselves a chance to pick their party candidates.

What I am going to say to you tonight does not relate to the primaries of any particular political party, but to matters of principle in all parties — Democratic, Republican, Farmer-Labor, Progressive, Socialist, or any other. Let that be clearly understood.

It is my hope that everybody affiliated with any party will vote in the primaries, and that every such voter will consider the fundamental principles for which his party is on record. That makes for a healthy choice between the candidates of the opposing parties on Election Day in November.

An election cannot give a country a firm sense of direction if it has two or more national parties which merely have different names but are as alike in their principles and aims as peas in the same pod.

In the coming primaries in all parties, there will be many clashes between two schools of thought, generally classified as liberal and conservative. Roughly speaking, the liberal school of thought recognizes that the new conditions throughout the world call for new remedies.

Those of us in America who hold to this school of thought, insist that these new remedies can be adopted and successfully maintained in this country under our present form of government if we use government as an instrument of cooperation to provide these remedies. We believe that we can solve our problems through continuing effort, through democratic processes instead of Fascism or Communism. We are opposed to the kind of moratorium on reform which, in effect, is reaction itself.

Be it clearly understood, however, that when I use the word "liberal," I mean the believer in progressive principles of democratic, representative government and not the wild man who, in effect, leans in the direction of Communism, for that is just as dangerous as Fascism.

The opposing or conservative school of thought, as a general proposition, does not recognize the need for Government itself to step in and take action to meet these new problems. It believes that individual initiative and private philanthropy will solve them — that we ought to repeal many of the things we have done and go back, for instance, to the old gold standard, or stop all this business of old age pensions and unemployment insurance, or repeal the Securities and Exchange Act, or let monopolies thrive unchecked — return, in effect, to the kind of Government we had in the twenties.

Assuming the mental capacity of all the candidates, the important question which it seems to me the primary voter must ask is this: "To which of these general schools of thought does the candidate belong?"

As President of the United States, I am not asking the voters of the country to vote for Democrats next November as opposed to Republicans or members of any other party. Nor am I, as President, taking part in Democratic primaries.

As the head of the Democratic Party, however, charged with the responsibility of carrying out the definitely liberal declaration of principles set forth in the 1936 Democratic platform, I feel that I have every right to speak in those few instances where there may be a clear issue between candidates for a Democratic nomination involving these principles, or involving a clear misuse of my own name.

Do not misunderstand me. I certainly would not indicate a preference in a State primary merely because a candidate, otherwise liberal in outlook, had conscientiously differed with me on any single issue. I should be far more concerned about the general attitude of a candidate toward present day problems and his own inward desire to get practical needs attended to in a practical way. We all know that progress may be blocked by outspoken reactionaries and also by those who say "yes" to a progressive objective, but who always find some reason to oppose any specific proposal to gain that objective. I call that type of candidate a "yes, but" fellow.

And I am concerned about the attitude of a candidate or his sponsors with respect to the rights of American citizens to assemble peaceably and to express publicly their views and opinions on important social and economic issues. There can be no constitutional democracy in any community which denies to the individual his freedom to speak and worship as he wishes. The American people will not be deceived by anyone who attempts to suppress individual liberty under the pretense of patriotism.

This being a free country with freedom of expression — especially with freedom of the press — there will be a lot of mean blows struck between now and Election Day. By "blows" I mean misrepresentation, personal attack and appeals to prejudice. It would be a lot better, of course, if campaigns everywhere could be waged with arguments instead of blows.

I hope the liberal candidates will confine themselves to argument and not resort to blows. In nine cases out of ten the speaker or writer who, seeking to influence public opinion, descends from calm argument to unfair blows hurts himself more than his opponent.

The Chinese have a story on this — a story based on three or four thousand years of civilization: Two Chinese coolies were arguing heatedly in the midst of a crowd. A stranger expressed surprise that no blows were being struck. His Chinese friend replied: "The man who strikes first admits that his ideas have given out."

I know that neither in the summer primaries nor in the November elections will the American voters fail to spot the candidate whose ideas have given out.

(For a discussion of the struggle to maintain liberalism, see also **Introduction** to this volume and references cited therein.)

81 ❲ A Greeting to the National Association for the Advancement of Colored People.

June 25, 1938

Dear Mr. White:

I AM happy to extend to the Twenty-ninth Annual Conference of the National Association for the Advancement of Colored People cordial greetings and best wishes for the success of its efforts in advancing the interests of the Negro race and bringing about that cooperation and understanding between the races so essential to the maintenance of a vital democracy.

I have watched with interest the constructive efforts of your organization, not only in behalf of the Negro people in our nation, but also in behalf of the democratic ideals and principles so dear to our entire nation. For it is evident that no democracy can long survive which does not accept as fundamental to its very existence the recognition of the rights of its minorities.

I wish you a most successful meeting.

Very sincerely yours,

Mr. Walter White,
National Association for the Advancement of Colored People,
Columbus, Ohio.

82 ❲ Address at the Tercentenary Celebration, Wilmington, Delaware. June 27, 1938

Your Royal Highnesses:

THIS IS a day of happy significance to three nations. I welcome you, for you represent a true friendship under which we have lived from the earliest times unmarred by any rift, unbroken by any misunderstanding. You are thrice welcome to our shores.

It is a matter of keen sorrow and regret to me that His Royal Highness the Crown Prince is unable to be at this historic spot today, but all of us pray that his recovery will be speedy and complete — and I personally look forward to welcoming him and his family at Hyde Park or at Washington the end of this week.

And I am grateful to Prince Berchel for the message that he has given to us from his distinguished grandfather. When he returns to Stockholm, I hope that he will give to His Majesty King Gustavus V my affectionate regards and the affectionate regards of all the American people.

I accept with profound gratitude, in behalf of the people of the United States, this noble monument placed here through the generosity of the people of Sweden. I am confident that to generations yet unborn in Sweden and in the United States it will typify close association and continued good will between our two nations.

It is therefore with much pleasure and sincere appreciation, that I turn over to the Governor of the State of Delaware this monument to hold in perpetuity in custody for the American people.

I am fortunate in having personal association with the Colony of New Sweden, for one of my ancestors, Wilhelm Beekman, served as Vice Governor of the Colony of New Sweden on the Delaware River from 1658 to 1663. And I am also proud that Swedish blood runs in my veins, for another of my ancestors, old Martinus Hoffman, was an early Swedish settler in New Amsterdam.

My friend, the Governor of Delaware, holds office in direct official succession from the old Governors of New Sweden — which reminds me of a recent rhyme descriptive of that famous Swedish Governor, Johan Printz, that doughty pioneer who is said to have tipped the scales at more than three hundred pounds.

> "No Gov. of Del.
> Before or since
> Has weighed as much
> As Johan Printz."

Your Royal Highnesses, it is a privilege to make grateful acknowledgment of the outstanding contributions made to our national life by men and women of Swedish blood. To this spot came the pioneers. But in the succeeding centuries tens of thousands of others have come to our shores and added their strength and their fine qualities of good citizenship to the American nation. In every phase of our history, in every endeavor — in commerce and industry, in science and art, in agriculture, in education and religion, in statecraft and government, they have well played their part.

Nor have we as Americans forgotten that after the War of the Revolution, Sweden was the first neutral European power to negotiate a treaty of amity and trade with our young and struggling nation. All these things we Americans recall today with grateful hearts.

And to you who are here as representatives of the people of Finland, I extend an equally hearty welcome. Men and women from Finland through the generations have also contributed greatly to our American civilization. Finland, small in size but mighty in honor, occupies an especially warm place in the American heart.

Sweden, Finland and the United States will continue their service in the days to come in the cause of friendship and in the cause of peace among the nations of the world.

83 ❮ The Four Hundred and Seventieth Press Conference (Excerpts). Hyde Park, New York. June 28, 1938

(Fair Labor Standards Act — Appointments — The aim of work relief — Public works — Economic results of rearmament — Ambassador to Russia — Architectural plans for Hyde Park cottage.)

THE PRESIDENT: Doris [Miss Fleeson], how are you? I am glad the big boy lets you sit down.

Q. [Miss Fleeson] Better than at the Nelson House.

THE PRESIDENT: It must be overrun.

Q. [Miss Fleeson] Yes, it is.

THE PRESIDENT: Here is the oldest [indicating Mr. Joseph Early, of the *Brooklyn Eagle*]. I think you and I started together almost at the first session.

Q. [Mr. Early] It was my first assignment and you gave me a good many stories for the first page of the Senatorial fight.

THE PRESIDENT: January, 1911. You would never know it to look at him.

Q. [Mr. Early] Thank you — gray hair and things of that sort.

Q. What can you do in the way of stories in 1938?

THE PRESIDENT: I don't know. George [Durno] had a pretty good idea. He was going to come in here and say, "Thank you, Mr. President," and let it go at that. (*Laughter*)

Q. Mr. Aubrey Williams made the front page this morning with some interesting statements.

THE PRESIDENT: Did he? I haven't seen any papers except the *Poughkeepsie Eagle News*. I wanted to read about the boat race and that is all I have done. It was wicked we did not get to see it.

Q. Terrible.

THE PRESIDENT: It did two things, it proved the supremacy of the Navy and —

Q. [interposing] And Harvard. (*Laughter*)

THE PRESIDENT: And Harvard.

Q. Have you signed any bills that we ought to know about?

THE PRESIDENT: I have signed twenty-two this morning. I guess Mac and Kannee will have a release on it.

Q. Any comment on the Wage and Hour Bill?

THE PRESIDENT: I don't think so. I mentioned it in my speech Friday night. I think that covered it all right. I do think that next to the Social Security Act it is the most important Act that has been passed in the last two or three years.

Q. Have you thought about appointing the Administrator yet?

THE PRESIDENT: Not yet. I hope to appoint an Administrator

before I leave, but that is one appointment I am not dead sure about. The bill does not go into effect for sixty days, you know, so I have time to turn around.

Q. How about the Civil Aeronautics Authority?

THE PRESIDENT: I am working on that. It is up to 550 applications now.

Q. How many are politicians?

THE PRESIDENT: Oh, I would say about a third.

Q. How about our Judges?

THE PRESIDENT: They will come along in driblets.

MR. MC INTYRE: I am not convinced as to what "politicians" covers.

THE PRESIDENT: Work it out with Doris [Miss Fleeson]. (*Laughter*)

Q. In the morning papers there is a story from Washington in which it says that WPA is going to boost its rolls from 2,700,000 to 3,150,000, thereby adding 400,000. Those figures are approximate. Is there going to be any concerted start of the spending lending money?

THE PRESIDENT: With WPA? Yes.

Q. Are the other agencies going to tie in?

THE PRESIDENT: Of course you know about PWA. They are going as fast as they possibly can and those are the two major things. CCC will be up to its new number on the first of July — the new enrollees. . . .

Q. Is it correct to say that July first is the start of this, and that they will all shove off together?

THE PRESIDENT: As far as it is humanly possible.

Q. On that relief picture, if it does not seem too naive, how should our relief policy be stated? Many people are asking, "Does the Government owe them —"

THE PRESIDENT: [interposing] I should say this, that the object of work relief as distinguished from the dole is to give wages for work instead of just enough money to keep body and soul together without work. During the past six months there has been an increase — perhaps that is not fair because it brings it down a little bit late, the increase took place between last October and this April — an increase of unemployed to such numbers that existing funds did not make it possible to take care of every able-bodied person who was able to work, to take care of them with work.

Now, this addition will take care of a large part of that additional number of able-bodied citizens who can work, and for whom we did not have enough money before.

Q. I had in mind a more fundamental thing. There used to be a favorite statement with some people that the Government has no obligation to any of these people.

THE PRESIDENT: It is a continuing policy and there are two perfectly definite schools of thought. One is to give them wages for work to a sufficient extent to keep them going, in as decent a way as we can afford to do. The other school of thought is merely to give them enough money for food and clothing, without asking them to work for it.

Q. Might it not be called a sort of continuing emergency proposition? I mean, you will probably always have them with you, and they will probably always have to be taken care of.

THE PRESIDENT: I would not put it that way because you are only stating a third of the problem — a quarter of the problem. It is far deeper than that. Technology, economics, or whatever you choose to call it — some people say it is the result of the World War, other people say it is the result of new needs of civilization, other people stress the new machinery by which you can turn out, with the same amount of labor, twice as much goods as you did eighteen or twenty years ago — they are causes, and all are contributing factors. In every civilized country there is more unemployment than ever before in history — world history.

Now, that is the simple fact, and no country has devised a permanent way, a permanent solution, of giving work to people in the depression periods as well as in the boom periods. The only method devised so far that seemed to give 100 per cent of relief, or nearly so, is the method of going in for armaments, putting the unemployed to work manufacturing goods which have no permanent capital value — goods which do not reproduce wealth. Of course, everybody knows that while that may work for a year or two years or a few years, it is by no means the permanent solution of the problem. We are all groping and trying to find a way of doing it without the use of armaments.

Q. What do you think of the recommendation made, I believe, by the National Resources Committee for a reservoir public works program, with the projects all set up and approved, which you could let out almost immediately?

THE PRESIDENT: That is one of the answers but not the only permanent answer. That particular answer has been used with very great effect in Sweden which, however, is a very small compact country.

Q. It worked to a certain extent on this program, did it not?

THE PRESIDENT: We are, to a certain extent, using it here at the present time. The difference over here has been that we did apply that method in 1933, 1934 and 1935, but in the process, when it was working in 1935, 1936 and 1937, we did not pay off the cost of it, but the Swedes did.

Q. How did they do that?

THE PRESIDENT: In other words, in time of prosperity the Swedes laid aside enough in Government revenue to pay for the things they did in the period of depression.

Q. Do you think that experience is worth emulating in this country?

THE PRESIDENT: Well, it is being studied.

Q. To go back to the statement you made a little bit ago regarding armaments, can it be said or thought that our new armament program has something to do with rehabilitation?

THE PRESIDENT: Relatively very little, Claude [Mahoney] because, if you will remember the figures I used three or four months ago about the armament figures in some of the countries of Europe, they ran as high as 45 or 50 per cent of the national income. Well, at that time, our armament figures were about 12 per cent. With the new program I should say, as a guess — I have not checked — the armament percentage of our Government expenditures may run as high as 15 or 16 per cent. Therefore, it is not to be compared with the economic result in those countries where they are spending 45 or 50 per cent. . . .

Q. A few weeks ago fifty-five members of a college faculty sent a petition to you calling for an administrative policy with respect to Spain. Have you made any reply to them?

THE PRESIDENT: I can only tell you in the utmost secrecy, if you promise not to use it. I did not know that I got it. (*Laughter*)

MR. MC INTYRE: You got it.

THE PRESIDENT: What did you do with it?

MR. MC INTYRE: It was one of six hundred.

THE PRESIDENT: I think it was mislaid in the mails.

Q. [Mr. Durno] Thank you, Mr. President. I am a little late on that.

Q. Mr. President, can we look for the appointment of an Ambassador to Moscow within the next —

THE PRESIDENT: [interposing] That is one of the things I am going to talk to the Secretary of State about next Monday. I have not done a thing about it and if I get time before I leave, I will look over these [indicating] — look over the bids for this little cottage on top of the hill and maybe I can give you a story — I hope so.

And maybe on Thursday or Friday — what day is today? — maybe on Thursday or Friday I can take you up to the top of the hill and show you where it is going up.

Q. Did you sketch the plans yourself?

THE PRESIDENT: Yes. What I did was to draw the plan and Henry Toombs did the real job. I have to be careful about that because I haven't the license to practice architecture in this State.

Q. There are a lot of us here who are glad to hear you ask what date it is because we are having the same trouble. (*Laughter*)

Q. [Mr. Storm] We assume, Claude [Mr. Mahoney], you were speaking for yourself. (*Laughter*)

(For a further discussion of work relief, see Item 71 and note, 1939 volume, and references cited.)

84 ⟨ Veto of Legislation Authorizing Coins Commemorating Events of Only Local Significance. June 30, 1938

I FIND it necessary to withhold my approval of enrolled bill, H.R. 2734, "An Act to authorize the coinage of 50-cent pieces in commemoration of the four-hundredth anniversary of the journey and explorations of Francisco Vasquez de Coronado."

This enrolled bill would provide for the coinage at a mint of the United States to be designated by the Director of the Mint of not to exceed 100,000 silver 50-cent pieces in commemoration of the four-hundredth anniversary of the journey and explorations of Francisco Vasquez de Coronado, such coins to be of standard size, weight, and composition, and of a special appropriate single design to be fixed by the Director of the Mint, with the approval of the Secretary of the Treasury.

Bills are being introduced in Congress with increasing frequency authorizing the minting of coins commemorating events, many of which are of no more than local significance. During the ten-year period from 1920 to 1930 fifteen issues of 50-cent pieces of special design were authorized to be coined to commemorate historical events, an average of one issue every eight months. The aggregate amount of the coins authorized to be struck was over 13,000,000.

On April 20, 1930, the President, at the instance of the Treasury Department, which has long been opposed to the issuance of commemorative coins, vetoed H.R. 2029, "An Act to authorize the coinage of silver 50-cent pieces in commemoration of the seventy-fifth anniversary of the Gadsden Purchase." The veto of this measure had the effect of discouraging for a time the enactment of legislation of this nature, and no new commemorative coins were authorized until 1933. Since that date twenty-eight issues of such coins have been authorized, an average of one issue every two and a fraction months, notwithstanding the fact that the Treasury has consistently during this period expressed its disapproval of this type of legislation. The aggregate amount of the coins authorized to be struck was approximately 3,800,000 pieces. At the end of the last session of the Congress there were pending, I am advised, at least sixty-six bills to provide for the coinage of as many different issues of commemorative coins.

The rate at which new issues of commemorative coins have been authorized since 1932 has increased three-fold over the ten-year period between 1920 and 1930. These coins do not have a wide circulation as a medium of exchange, and, because of the multiplicity of designs arising from the issuance of such coins, they jeopardize the integrity of our coins and cause confusion.

The Congress recognized the wisdom of maintaining uniformity in the designs of the various coins of the United States by providing in section 3510 of the Revised Statutes, as amended, that:

. . . no change in the design or die of any coin shall be made oftener than once in twenty-five years from and including the year of the first adoption of the design, model, die, or hub for the same coin. . . .

Recognizing that the practice of striking special coins in commemoration of historical events and of permitting the sponsoring organization to sell them at a profit was a misuse of our coinage system, which was assuming increasingly dangerous proportions, I sent to the Chairman of the Committee on Coinage, Weights and Measures of the House of Representatives, and to the Chairman of the Senate Committee on Banking and Currency, in June, 1935, a proposed bill which was designed to terminate the practice of striking commemorative coins and to authorize, in substitution, the striking of appropriate com-memorative medals. In January, 1937, I again wrote to the chairmen of such committees with respect to this matter. Bill S. 3086 of the 74th Congress, and Bill S. 1895 of the 75th Congress embodied those suggestions.

For the foregoing reasons I find it necessary to withhold my approval of this enrolled bill.

I have informed those interested in the celebration of this anniversary that the Mint of the United States will be glad to strike off a commemorative medal in place of the 50-cent coin.

85 ⟨ Address at Laying of Cornerstone of Federal Building at New York World's Fair. June 30, 1938

Governor Lehman, Mayor LaGuardia, Commissioner Flynn, Commissioner Whalen, Distinguished Guests:

THE MASTER MASON certifies that the cornerstone is well and truly laid and, in turn, I have assured him that I hold a union card.

I am glad that Mr. Whalen has spoken of his visits to Washington. He has never left Washington empty-handed. He is the most persuasive salesman in all the world.

On this occasion we formally commence the construction of the building of the Government of the United States at the New York World's Fair of 1939. I gladly express the appreciation of that Government to the representatives of sixty-two other nations who have graciously decided to take part in the Fair.

Already the plans for their participation are drawn, and to them I want to stress my hope that many of their countrymen will come to the Fair next year. To those countrymen a hearty welcome will be given. I emphasize this on the ground of reciprocity, because for many years the visiting balance has been somewhat uneven. Far more Americans have been traveling to the shores of other continents, especially Europe, than visitors from the other nations to our shores. I encourage all of my compatriots to learn all that they can at first hand about other nations and to make friends there, but I wish that more of the citizens of other nations would visit us and make friends here.

All of us realize, of course, that the affairs of many parts of the world are, to put it politely, somewhat distraught at this time. Such a condition necessarily accompanies wars and rumors of wars.

We in this Hemisphere are happily removed, in large measure, both from fear and from the controversies which breed it. In a larger sense, however, we cannot remain unconcerned, especially because it is our fortune to enjoy friendship and good relations with all nations.

You who represent the other nations here today have heard of what is known as the policy of the Good Neighbor. To that policy we have steadily adhered, and it may well be said that it is the definite policy of all the American Republics.

It is a policy which can never be merely unilateral. In stressing it the American Republics appreciate, I am confident, that it is a bilateral, a multilateral policy, and that the fair dealing which it implies must be reciprocated.

It is a policy which was not in its inception, or subsequently, limited to one hemisphere. It has proven so successful in the Western Hemisphere that the American Republics believe that it could succeed in all the rest of the world if the spirit which lies behind it were better understood and more actively striven for in the other parts of the world.

Furthermore, the policy of the Good Neighbor is, as we know, not limited to those problems of international relations which may result in war. We are against war and have agreed among ourselves quietly to discuss difficulties in such a way that the possibility of war has become remote. But the policy involves also matters of trade and matters affecting the interchange of culture between nations.

In these modern days when so many new economic and social

problems call for the revision of many old economic and social tenets, closer personal contacts are an essential to the well-being of nations of the world.

That is why the New York World's Fair and the San Francisco Fair are well-timed for 1939. They will encourage that interchange of thought, of culture, and of trade which is so vital today. They will give to the opposite ends of our country an opportunity to see the exhibits and the visitors from all the rest of the world — and they will give to those visitors a splendid chance to see something of the length and breadth of the United States.

All of us who are here today are looking forward to April, 1939, when this great Exposition will be formally opened. Although the plans were made some time ago, I do not think that it has yet been announced that the United States Fleet this coming winter will come to the Atlantic Ocean and will be present at the opening of the World's Fair. Yes, we are looking forward to that day, a day of meeting and of greeting. It has been well said that you cannot hate a man you know. Therefore, this Exposition will stand as a symbol of world peace for, without doubt, it is a useful advance on the patient road to peace that America treads.

86 ⟨ "If the Fires of Freedom and Civil Liberties Burn Low in Other Lands, They Must be Made Brighter in Our Own." Address Before the National Education Association. New York City. June 30, 1938

Dr. Woodruff, Members of the National Education Association:

IF YOU have followed the arguments of financial experts over the last few years, you have guessed that they have as many theories of keeping books as there are ends to serve. They do not always agree on the definition of capital, and they even disagree on what is an asset and what is a liability. That is true both in private business and in government.

But whatever differences bookkeepers and financiers may have over the rules of their professions, no man or woman of common sense can forget, or allow government to forget, what are the true and ultimate assets and liabilities of a nation.

The only real capital of a nation is its natural resources and its human beings. So long as we take care of and make the most of both of them, we shall survive as a strong nation, a successful nation and a progressive nation — whether or not the bookkeepers say other kinds of budgets are from time to time out of balance.

This capital structure — natural resources and human beings — has to be maintained at all times. The plant has to be kept up and new capital put in year by year to meet increasing needs. If we skimp on that capital, if we exhaust our natural resources and weaken the capacity of our human beings, then we shall go the way of all weak nations.

Before we can think straight as a nation we have to consider, in addition to the old kind, a new kind of government balance sheet — a long-range sheet which shows survival values for our population and for our democratic way of living, balanced against what we have paid for them. Judged by that test — history's test — I venture to say that the long-range budget of the present Administration of our government has been in the black and not in the red.

For many years I, like you, have been a pedagogue, striving to inculcate in the youth of America a greater knowledge of and interest in the problems which, with such force, strike the whole world in the face today. In these recent years we have taught the prudent husbandry of our national estate — our rivers, our soil, our forests, our phosphates, our oils, our minerals and our wild life. Along these lines we have made mighty strides — come further than in all the years before in knowledge of how to grapple with the problems of maintaining the estate that our forefathers handed down to us.

With the dissemination of this knowledge, we have taken action. Few men begrudge what that action has cost, because it has been based on operations physically large and spectacular, dramatic and easy to see. I am thankful that I live in an age of building, for it is far easier to dramatize to one's self the importance of the object if you see it while it is going up, than if you come along later and see it only in its completed stage. We are fortunate today in seeing the New York World's Fair of 1939 in the construction stage. This glimpse will make it mean more to us when we see it completed next year.

The other half of the preservation of our national capital is likewise a problem of husbandry — the conserving of health, energy, skill and morale of our population, and especially of that part of our population which will be the America of tomorrow.

This also is a problem of the fullest use and development of precious resources of ability which cannot be stored and will be lost if they remain unused. No nation can meet this changing world unless its people, individually and collectively, grow in ability to understand and handle the new knowledge as applied to increasingly intricate human relationships. That is why the teachers of America are the ultimate guardians of the human capital of America, the assets which must be made to pay social dividends if democracy is to survive.

We have believed wholeheartedly in investing the money of all the people on the education of the people. That conviction, backed up by taxes and dollars, is no accident, for it is the logical application of our faith in democracy.

Man's present day control of the affairs of nature is the direct result of investment in education. And the democratization of education has made it possible for outstanding ability, which would otherwise be completely lost, to make its outstanding contribution to the commonweal. We cannot afford to overlook any source of human raw material. Genius flowers in most unexpected places; "it is the impetus of the undistinguished host that hurls forth a Diomed or a Hector."

No government can create the human touch and self-sacrifice which the individual teacher gives to the process of education. But what Government can do is to provide financial support and to protect from interference the freedom to learn.

No one wants the Federal Government to subsidize education any more than is absolutely necessary. It has been and will be the traditional policy of the United States to leave the actual management of schools and their curricula to state and local control.

But we know that in many places local government unfortunately cannot adequately finance either the freedom or the facilities to learn. And there the Federal Government can properly supplement local resources.

Here is where the whole problem of education ties in definitely with natural resources and the economic picture of the individual community or state. We all know that the best schools are, in most cases, located in those communities which can afford to spend the most money on them — the most money for adequate teachers' salaries, for modern buildings and for modern equipment of all kinds. We know that the weakest educational link in the system lies in those communities which have the lowest taxable values, therefore, the smallest per capita tax receipts, and, therefore, the lowest teachers' salaries and most inadequate buildings and equipment. We do not blame these latter communities. They want better educational facilities, but simply have not enough money to pay the cost.

There is probably a wider divergence today in the standard of education between the richest communities and the poorest communities than there was one hundred years ago; and it is, therefore, our immediate task to seek to close that gap — not in any way by decreasing the facilities of the richer communities but by extending aid to those less fortunate. We all know that if we do not close this gap it will continue to widen, for the best brains in the poor communities will either have no chance to develop or will migrate to those places where their ability will stand a better chance.

To continue the parallel between natural and human resources, it is well to remember that our poorest communities exist where the land is most greatly eroded, where farming does not pay, where industries have moved out, where flood and drought have done their work, where transportation facilities are of the poorest and where cheap electricity is unavailable for the home.

All of this leads me to ask you not to demand that the Federal Government provide financial assistance to all communities. Our aid for many reasons, financial and otherwise, must be confined to lifting the level at the bottom rather than to giving assistance at the top. Today we cannot do both, and we must therefore confine ourselves to the greater need.

In line with this policy, the Federal Government during the past five years has given relatively far more assistance to the poorer communities than to the rich. We have done it through direct relief and through work relief, through the Resettlement Administration and the Farm Security Administration, the National Youth Administration, and through the rehabilitation of flooded, stranded or dust-blown areas. We have provided school houses, colleges, libraries, educational equipment and sanitation in every state of the Union. I include "sanitation" because it has always seemed to me that good health and good education must go hand in hand. We have placed many millions of dollars in the field of adult education through the Works Progress Administration, and here, again, most of the money has been expended in the poorer communities of the land.

I have spoken of the twin interlocking assets of national and human resources and of the need of developing them hand in hand. But with this goes the equally important and equally difficult problem of keeping education intellectually free. For freedom to learn is the first necessity of guaranteeing that man himself shall be self-reliant enough to be free.

Such things did not need as much emphasis a generation ago; but when the clock of civilization can be turned back by burning libraries, by exiling scientists, artists, musicians, writers and teachers, by dispersing universities, and by censoring news and literature and art, an added burden is placed upon those countries where the torch of free thought and free learning still burns bright.

If the fires of freedom and civil liberties burn low in other lands, they must be made brighter in our own.

If in other lands the press and books and literature of all kinds are censored, we must redouble our efforts here to keep them free.

If in other lands the eternal truths of the past are threatened by intolerance we must provide a safe place for their perpetuation.

There may be times when men and women in the turmoil of change lose touch with the civilized gains of centuries of education: but the gains of education are never really lost. Books may be burned and cities sacked, but truth, like the yearning for freedom, lives in the hearts of humble men and women. The ultimate victory of tomorrow is with democracy, and through democracy with education, for no people in all the world can be kept eternally ignorant or eternally enslaved.

87 ⟨ "Avoiding War, We Seek Our Ends Through the Peaceful Processes of Popular Government Under the Constitution." Address at the Dedication of the Memorial on the Gettysburg Battlefield, Gettysburg, Pennsylvania. July 3, 1938

Governor Earle, Veterans of the Blue and the Gray:

ON BEHALF of the people of the United States I accept this monument in the spirit of brotherhood and peace.

Immortal deeds and immortal words have created here at Gettysburg a shrine of American patriotism. We are encompassed by "The last full measure of devotion" of many men and by the words in which Abraham Lincoln expressed the simple faith for which they died.

It seldom helps to wonder how a statesman of one generation would surmount the crisis of another. A statesman deals with concrete difficulties — with things which must be done from day to day. Not often can he frame conscious patterns for the far off future.

But the fullness of the stature of Lincoln's nature and the fundamental conflict which events forced upon his Presidency invite us ever to turn to him for help.

For the issue which he restated here at Gettysburg seventy-five years ago will be the continuing issue before this Nation so long as we cling to the purposes for which the Nation was founded — to preserve under the changing conditions of each generation a people's government for the people's good.

The task assumes different shapes at different times. Sometimes the threat to popular government comes from political interests, sometimes from economic interests, sometimes we have to beat off all of them together.

But the challenge is always the same — whether each generation facing its own circumstances can summon the practical devotion to attain and retain that greatest good for the greatest number which this government of the people was created to ensure.

Lincoln spoke in solace for all who fought upon this field; and the years have laid their balm upon their wounds. Men who wore the blue and men who wore the gray are here together, a fragment spared by time. They are brought here by the memories of old divided loyalties, but they meet here in united loyalty to a united cause which the unfolding years have made it easier to see.

All of them we honor, not asking under which flag they fought then — thankful that they stand together under one flag now.

Lincoln was commander-in-chief in this old battle; he wanted above all things to be commander-in-chief of the new peace. He understood that battle there must be; that when a challenge to constituted government is thrown down, the people must in self-defense take it up; that the fight must be fought through to a decision so clear that it is accepted as being beyond recall.

But Lincoln also understood that after such a decision, a democracy should seek peace through a new unity. For a democracy can keep alive only if the settlement of old difficulties clears the ground and transfers energies to face new responsibilities. Never can it have as much ability and purpose as it needs in that striving; the end of battle does not end the infinity of those needs.

That is why Lincoln — commander of a people as well as of an army — asked that his battle end "with malice toward none, with charity for all."

To the hurt of those who came after him, Lincoln's plea was long denied. A generation passed before the new unity became accepted fact.

In later years new needs arose, and with them new tasks, worldwide in their perplexities, their bitterness and their modes of strife. Here in our land we give thanks that, avoiding war, we seek our ends through the peaceful processes of popular government under the Constitution.

It is another conflict, a conflict as fundamental as Lincoln's, fought not with glint of steel, but with appeals to reason and justice on a thousand fronts — seeking to save for our common country opportunity and security for citizens in a free society.

We are near to winning this battle. In its winning and through the years may we live by the wisdom and the humanity of the heart of Abraham Lincoln.

88 ❧ A Message to the Conference on Economic Conditions of the South. July 4, 1938

To the Conference on Economic Conditions of the South:

No PURPOSE is closer to my heart at this moment than that which caused me to call you to Washington. That purpose is to obtain a statement — or, perhaps, I should say a re-statement as of today — of the economic conditions of the South, a picture of the South in relation to the rest of the country, in order that we may do something about it: in order that we may not only carry forward the work that has been begun toward the rehabilitation of the South, but that the program of such work may be expanded in the directions that this new presentation will indicate.

My intimate interest in all that concerns the South is, I believe, known to all of you, but this interest is far more than a sentimental attachment born of a considerable residence in your section and of close personal friendship with so many of your people. It proceeds even more from my feeling of responsibility toward the whole nation. It is my conviction that the South presents right now the nation's No. 1 economic problem — the nation's problem, not merely the South's. For we have an economic unbalance in the nation as a whole, due to this very condition of the South.

It is an unbalance that can and must be righted, for the sake of the South and of the nation.

Without going into the long history of how this situation came to be — the long and ironic history of the despoiling of this truly American section of the country's population — suffice it for the immediate purpose to get a clear perspective of the task that is presented to us. That task embraces the wasted or neglected resources of land and water, the abuses suffered by the soil, the need for cheap fertilizer and cheap power; the problems presented by the population itself — a population still holding the great heritages of King's Mountain and Shiloh — the problems presented by the South's capital resources and the absentee ownership of those resources, and problems growing out of the new industrial era and, again, of absentee ownership of the new industries. There is the problem of labor and employment in the South and the related problem of protecting women and children in this field. There is the problem of farm ownership, of which farm tenancy is a part, and of farm income. There are questions of taxation, of education, of housing, and of health.

More and more definitely in recent years those in the South who have sought selflessly to evaluate the elements constituting the general problem have come to agree on certain basic factors. I have asked Mr. Mellett to present for your consideration a statement of these factors as prepared by various departments of the Government. I ask you to consider this statement critically, in the light of your own general or specific knowledge, in order that it may be made representative of the South's own best thought and that it may be presented to Congress and the public as such.

I had hoped to attend your meeting and listen to your discussions. Unhappily, other pressing work makes this impossible. Please accept my sincere regret that I cannot be with you and be assured that I anticipate with deep interest the result of your labors.

Cordially yours,

NOTE: On June 22, 1938, I requested the National Emergency Council to prepare a statement upon the problems and needs of the South, in order to have a clear and concise summary readily available for the members of Congress and the public at large (see Item 78, this volume). I suggested that the National Emergency Council seek the advice and assistance of outstanding southerners familiar with these problems. As a result of this suggestion, the Conference on Economic Conditions in the South was called to meet in Washington; and the foregoing message was sent to them by me on July 4, 1938.

Fifteen topics were discussed at this conference, and, although the conclusions did not attempt to be exhaustive in nature, they indicated clearly that the South is the Nation's No. 1 economic problem, and pointed out some of the reasons. The following is a summary of the findings of the Conference as embodied in their *Report on Economic Conditions of the South:*

1. *Economic Resources.* The South is blessed with rich mineral resources, crude oil, natural gas, fine climate, varied soils, soft coal, water-power, forests, and fisheries. Transportation and navigation facilities are excellent. Yet the South is handicapped by lack of factories, machines and tools; and it has been forced to make poor bargains in trading its rich physical resources for manufactured products. Its people as a whole are the poorest in the country.

2. *Soil.* Although the South has more than its share of good farm acreage and rich soil, its fertility has been, and is being, rapidly depleted. There are several reasons. Cotton, tobacco, and corn, the chief southern crops, are ploughed between the rows, encouraging the washing away of top-soil through gullies. The small farmers and the tenant farmers, typical of the South, are interested in immediate cash rather than soil-restoring crops. Training in methods of conserving the soil has not progressed very far. Forests, which act as natural guardians of the soil, have been cut over. Soil erosion has brought floods, which, in turn, have washed away soil. It is estimated that over $300,000,000 worth of fertile top-soil is eroded away annually — all irreplaceable capital.

3. *Water.* A substantial percentage of the Nation's installed hydroelectric generating capacity is possessed by the South, and the potential output is estimated at five times the power actually produced in 1937. Rainfall is in most sections abundant, and is so plentiful that some areas have to be drained before crops can be planted. Navigation facilities are excellent. At the present time, the South is occupied with controlling the huge damage inflicted by floods, malarial swamps, and water pollution.

4. *Population.* Although the birth rate is high in the South,

there has been a steady migration of skilled and educated workers to other sections of the country because of the presence of greater opportunities elsewhere. In recent years, further problems have been raised by the small number of workers proportioned to dependents; by the tendency of white workers to seek employment in traditionally Negro occupations; and the steady displacement of agricultural workers by machines.

5. *Private and Public Income.* The South is the poorest section of the country. The average per capita income in 1937 was $314 as compared with $604 in the rest of the country. The income of farmers and industrial workers is pitifully low in comparison with other sections. Too large a portion of the profits of southern industries goes to financiers in the North. Public income is proportionately lower in the South. This condition has not been alleviated by the unfortunate competition indulged in by local communities to induce industries to enter their towns and pay less than a fair share of the costs of government. Such industries also feel that they need not pay fair wages.

6. *Education.* There is a wide disparity between the number of children to be educated and the means for financing their education. With one-third of the Nation's children and only one-sixth of the Nation's school revenues, the educational system of the South has always been under a severe handicap. Teachers' salaries are low, schools are overcrowded; and illiteracy is higher in the South than in any other region. Higher educational institutions and medical schools are also inadequately endowed. It is impossible for the South to raise the money by taxation to provide the necessary educational facilities.

7. *Health.* Poverty and lower living conditions have contributed to unusually high sickness and death rates in the South. Malaria, syphilis, pneumonia, tuberculosis, and pellagra are widespread among the lower-income groups. The South does not have enough doctors, hospitals and clinics to combat these diseases.

8. *Housing.* According to conservative estimates, conditions of overcrowding, slums, and generally poor rural and urban living conditions indicate the necessity for the rebuilding of houses for four million, or one-half, of the families of the South, in order to provide decent housing. Excessive land valuations do not hamper this section as much as other more industrialized parts of the country; but the general poverty of the South has been a constant block to a thoroughgoing attack on the housing problem in that region.

9. *Labor.* Labor in the South is most poorly paid. On the farm and in industry, workers are constantly subjected to the competition and insecurity provided by migratory employees. Labor organization

has been slow and difficult; and collective bargaining power is small. Both industrial and agricultural laborers find it difficult to obtain sufficient work to tide them over slack seasons.

10. *Women and Children.* Low wages for the male members of the family often force southern women and children to work a great deal more than in other sections. This in turn depresses all wages. Child labor is more prevalent in the South than anywhere else. It affects both health and education. Only two southern states have minimum wage laws for women. There is an increasing amount of "home work" farmed out by factories for women to do at low pay.

11. *Ownership and Use of Land.* More than half of the southern farmers depend upon cotton as their sole means of livelihood; and their success or failure is bound up with a gamble upon the price and crop of cotton. Many mortgaged farms have been foreclosed and are now in the hands of banks and insurance companies. This process has made half of the southern farmers tenants rather than owners. These share-croppers and tenants move constantly from section to section, without any stable community life and with no desire to conserve the soil they farm.

While concentrating upon the production of cotton and tobacco, the South is failing to raise an adequate supply of the things it eats and wears. Poverty-stricken conditions have prevented proper nutrition.

12. *Credit.* Without very much native capital, the South has been forced to lean upon outside financiers, who have exacted their toll in interest rates and dividends. Bank deposits in the South are $150 per capita as compared with $471 in the rest of the United States. Investment banking firms and insurance companies do a comparatively small business in this section.

High interest rates have resulted from the scarcity of credit sources, and municipal bonds draw a much higher rate of interest than elsewhere. The stringent financial situation has been relieved somewhat, however, by the establishment of federal credit unions, and the extension of credit to farmers and business men by the various New Deal agencies.

13. *Use of Natural Resources.* Forests, coal, natural gas, bauxite, sulphur, zinc-ore and other natural resources have at times been despoiled and wasted in the South by unscrupulous operations, largely because outside capital has been used to such an extent. Inasmuch as these absentee owners are interested solely in exploiting the South purely for their own interests, rather than in developing it properly for the future, the rich natural resources of the South are constantly in danger of depletion.

14. *Industry.* An outstanding development in the South recently has been the rise of the cotton

manufacturing industry. Other industries which have recently developed and expanded are cottonseed products, cigarettes, and pulp mills. However, southern industry has been handicapped by discriminations in interterritorial freight rates, and in tariffs; and has therefore lagged far behind the rest of the Nation.

15. *Purchasing Power.* "The South is the Nation's greatest untapped market and the market in which American business can expand most easily," concludes the report on the question of the potential purchasing power of the South. The needs of the South are great, and its natural resources are still abundant. Southerners, however, are deficient in food, clothes, houses and household improvements, and farming equipment; and if the South continues to remain poverty-stricken, it is the northern producer, distributor, and worker who will lose in the long run by losing a great potential customer for their wares.

————

This report is the first concise, adequate statement of the problems of the South. They are, indeed, the problems of the whole Nation. For only with a prosperous South can there be full national prosperity.

As was stated in the letter transmitting the report to me:

"One thing appears to be made clear when the principal difficulties faced by the South are brought into perspective and when what the South has to offer the Nation is laid alongside what the South needs for its own people; that is, that the economic problems of the South are not beyond the power of men to solve.

"Another thing made clear, however, is that there is no simple solution. The solution must be part political, with the federal government participating along with state, county, city, town, and township government. But there must be participation also by industry, business and schools — and by citizens, South and North."

For further discussion of the South and its problems, see Item 54 (pages 263-265), Item 100, and Item 101, this volume.

89 ❦ "On a Thousand Fronts, Government . . . Is Playing the . . . Role of the Insurer of Security for the Average Man, Woman, and Child . . ." Address at Marietta, Ohio. July 8, 1938

*Governor Davey, Senator Bulkley, Chairman White and You,
the People of the Northwest Territory:*

LONG before 1788 there were white men here, "spying out this land of Canaan." An intrepid outpost breed they were — the scouts and the skirmishers of the great American migration. The sight of smoke from neighbors' chimneys might have worried them. But Indians and redcoats did not.

Long before 1788, at Kaskaskia and Vincennes, with scant help from the Seaboard, they had held their beloved wilderness for themselves — and for us — with their own bare hands and their own long rifles. But their symbol is Vincennes, not Marietta.

Here, with all honor to the scouts and the skirmishers, we celebrate the coming of a different type of men and women — the first battalions of that organized army of occupation which transplanted from over the Alleghenies whole little civilizations that took root and grew. They were giving expression to a genius for organized colonization, carefully planned and ordered under law.

The men who came here before 1788 came as Leif Ericson's men to Vineland, in a spirit all of adventure. But the men and women of the Ohio Company who came to Marietta came rather like the men and women of the Massachusetts Bay Company to Boston, an organized society, unafraid to meet temporary adventure, but serious in seeking permanent security for men and women and children and homes. Many of them were destined to push on; but most came intending to stay. Such people may

427

not be the first to conquer the earth, but they will always be the last to possess it.

Right behind the men and women who established Marietta one hundred and fifty years ago moved that instrument of law and order and cooperation — government. A representative of the national government entered Marietta to administer the Northwest Territory under the famous Northwest Ordinance. And what we are celebrating today is this establishment of the first civil government west of the original thirteen states.

Three provisions of the Northwest Ordinance I always like to remember.

It provided that "no person demeaning himself in a peaceable and orderly manner shall ever be molested on account of his mode of worship or for religious sentiment in the said territory."

It provided that "religion, morality and knowledge being necessary to good government and the happiness of mankind, schools and means of education shall forever be encouraged."

And it provided for the perpetual prohibition of slavery in the Territory.

Free, educated, God-fearing men and women — that is what the thirteen states hoped the new West would exemplify. It has well fulfilled that hope.

Every generation meets substantially the same problems under its own different set of circumstances. Anyone speculating on our great migration westward is struck with the human parallel between the driving force behind that migration and the driving force behind the great social exploration we are carrying on today.

Most of the people who went out to Ohio in 1788 and who followed wave on wave for another hundred years went to improve their economic lot. In other words, they were following the same yearning for security which is driving us forward today.

At the end of the wagon ruts there was something worth the physical risks. The standard of life in a log cabin amid fields still blackened with half-burned stumps was not high, but it was certain. A family, or at most a township, could be a whole self-sufficing economic system — plenty of food to eat if a man would but reach out and shoot or cultivate it; plenty of warm clothes if the women of the family were willing to spin; always a tight roof over the family's head if the little community would respond to the call for a roof-raising.

Whatever he used was a man's own; he had the solid joy of possession — of owning his home and his means of livelihood. And if things did not pan out there was always an infinite self-sufficiency beckoning further westward — to new land, new game, new opportunity.

Under such conditions there was so much to get done which men could not get done alone, that the frontiersmen naturally reached out to government as their greatest single instrument of cooperative self-help with the aid of which they could get things done. To them the use of government was but another form of the cooperation of good neighbors.

Government was an indispensable instrument of their daily lives, of the security of their women and their children and their homes and their opportunities. They looked on government not as a thing apart — as a power over our people. They regarded it as a power of the people, as a democratic expression of organized self-help like a frontier husking bee.

There were worried legalists back in the seaboard towns who were sure it was unconstitutional for the Federal Government to help to put roads and railroads and canals through these new territories — who were sure that the nation would never get back the money it was plowing into development of the natural and human resources of the Northwest.

But Abraham Lincoln, who incarnated the spirit of the people who were actually living in the Northwest Territory, summed up their attitude when he said: "The legitimate object of government is to do for a community of people whatever they need to have done, but cannot do at all, or cannot do so well, for themselves, in their separate and individual capacities."

Today, under new conditions, a whole nation, the critical thirteen states and all the West and South that has grown out of them, is on a mental migration, dissatisfied with old conditions, seeking like the little band that came to Marietta to create new conditions of security. And again the people see an ally in their own government.

Many a man does not own his cabin any more; his possessions are a bank deposit.

Scarcely any man can call his neighbors to raise his roof any more — he pays a contractor cash and has to have mortgage financing to find the cash. And if that financing is of the wrong kind or goes bad — he may need help to save his home from foreclosure.

Once old age was safe because there was always something useful which men and women, no matter how old, could do to earn an honorable maintenance. That time is gone; and some new kind of organized old-age insurance has to be provided.

In these perplexities the individual turns, as he has always turned, to the collective security of the willingness of his fellows to cooperate through the use of government to help him and each other. The spirit of the frontier husking bee is found today in carefully-drafted statutes — statutes insuring bank deposits; statutes providing mortgage money for homes through F.H.A.; statutes providing help through H.O.L.C. for those in danger of foreclosure. The cavalry captain who protected the log cabins of the Northwest is now supplanted by legislators, like Senator Bulkley, toiling over the drafting of such statutes and over the efficiency of government machinery to administer them so that such protection and help of government can be extended to the full.

On a thousand fronts, government — state and municipal as well as federal — is playing the same role of the insurer of security for the average man, woman and child that the Army detachments played in the early days of the old Northwest Territory. When you think it through, at the bottom most of the great protective statutes of today are in essence mutual insurance companies, and our recent legislation is not a departure from but a return to the healthy practices of mutual self-help of the early settlers of the Northwest.

Let us not be afraid to help each other — let us never forget that government is *ourselves* and not an alien power over us. The ultimate rulers of our democracy are not a President and Senators and Congressmen and Government officials but the voters of this country.

I believe that the American people, not afraid of their own capacity to choose forward-looking representatives to run their government, want the same cooperative security and have the same courage to achieve it, in 1938, as in 1788. I am sure they know that we shall always have a frontier — of social and economic problems — and that we must always move in to bring law and order to it. In that confidence I am pushing on. I am sure that the people of the Nation will push on with me.

NOTE: This was the first speech on a long trip which took me across the continent to the Pacific Coast via Texas. At San Diego, California, I boarded the U.S.S. *Houston* for a sea cruise down through the Panama Canal to Pensacola, Florida. From there I returned to Washington via Warm Springs, Georgia. I had left Washington on July 7, and I returned on August 12, 1938.

Several of the speeches and extemporaneous talks delivered by me on this trip are printed in this volume as Items 90, 91, 92, 93, 94, 95, 96, 97, 98, 100, 101, and 102.

In addition to these, I also made short, extemporaneous speeches at the following places, which have not been printed in these volumes because of limitations of space: Bowling Green, Kentucky, and Russellville, Kentucky, on July 8; Booneville, Arkansas, Wister, Oklahoma, McAlester, Oklahoma, Shawnee, Oklahoma, and Purcell, Oklahoma, on July 9; Bowie, Texas, Wichita Falls, Texas, Chillicothe, Texas, and Clarendon, Texas, on July 11; Salida, Colorado, on July 12; Carlin, Nevada, Imlay, Nevada, Sparks, Nevada, and Reno, Nevada, on July 13; Los Angeles, California, and San Diego, California, on July 16; Pensacola, Florida, on August 9; and Warm Springs, Georgia, on August 10.

I was accompanied on this trip by Dr. Waldo S. Schmitt of the United States National Museum, with the objective of making a survey of the fishes, marine invertebrates, flora, and other biological specimens in the many out-of-the-way places visited. To assist him in this work, Dr. Schmitt received the enthusiastic aid of a large number of the crew of the USS *Houston*. At almost every remote island a collecting expedition proceeded to the beach and, as a result, Dr. Schmitt was greatly aided in the collecting and preserving of a very large amount of natural history specimens. See also Item 108, this volume.

On our return to Washington these specimens were distributed among members of the Smithsonian staff and others for detailed study.

As a result, the Smithsonian Institution has already published, up to February 4, 1941, nineteen separate pamphlets in a field not hitherto adequately covered. Many new species and sub-species have been listed including, for example, a new palm from Cocos Island, which is not only a new species but constitutes a new genus. It has been given the name of "Rooseveltia Frankliniana."

90 ❰ The President Recounts Some of the Accomplishments of the New Deal to Date and Urges Continuance of the Same Policies. Address at Covington, Kentucky. July 8, 1938

Senator Barkley, Governor Chandler, my friends of Kentucky:

I AM glad to be back in Kentucky.

Some Republicans have suggested that I have come to Kentucky on a political mission. But I assure you the only reason is that I cannot get to Oklahoma without crossing Kentucky.

Every time that I have come into this State in the past few years, I have not been able to forget a certain trip which I made across a large part of Kentucky in the early autumn of 1932 — six years ago, though it seems a whole lot longer. And on that occasion, though I had been traveling in many states, what I saw in Kentucky stirred me more deeply than I had ever been stirred in my life — except perhaps in the days during the World War when I saw the misery and the suffering on the fields of France.

On my visit to Kentucky in 1932 my train moved slowly from Covington to Louisville and thence in a southeasterly direction, through villages and farming sections and mining districts. As we stopped at small stations the crowds congregated. Hunger, stark hunger, stared out at me from the faces of men and women and little children. There was scarcely a new dress or a new suit of clothes in the crowd. It was a chill day, very different from this day, and for the actual want of clothes people stood there shivering.

They were looking up at two men. One of them was a candidate for the Presidency, going about the country telling people that the national situation was grave — so deeply serious that the time for promises had come to an end and the time for action was at hand.

The other man on that train platform was a Senator from Kentucky — a man of experience in the affairs of his State and of his Nation — a man who had fought valiantly as a member of the then Democratic minority in Washington, voting against doing nothing, voting in favor of action to meet the growing needs of the Nation.

On that day's trip, I know that Senator Barkley and I were thinking little in terms of partisan politics. We were thinking in terms of American needs — not just Kentucky's needs but the deep-seated wants that had come into the lives of the people of every state, the lives of millions of people scattered throughout the Nation. Yes, tears were in our eyes that day. We were affected not alone by misery but by the fortitude we saw, because we realized that these people still had faith — faith in the institutions of the United States — faith in the Government of the United States — faith that their Government would, before it was too late, come through.

On that trip, too, between stops, your Senator and I talked of many things. We talked of economic conditions and social conditions — of the thousands of things that had to be done, in the East, and in the Middle West, and in the border states, and in the South and in the Far West, if America as a Nation was to carry on.

I shall never forget that day because I saw things with my own eyes that made me think more deeply about the fundamentals of life than I had ever thought before, and because I had an opportunity that day to talk of those things with a great American who had been on the "firing line" for years, and had striven to avert the disaster, and was willing and able to give practical advice for the cure of it.

I shall not recount the progress of the intervening years. You know the story of them as well as I do. I wish that I could follow that same railroad route today. I wish that I could look into the faces of the same men and women and children that I saw then. And if I could, I know very well that the facts of today would give the lie to those who seek to overthrow this Administration by telling you, as they have been telling you for six months or more, that conditions in the United States today can be compared with the conditions of 1932. You and I have the intelligence and the first-hand knowledge to laugh at that kind of political ballyhoo.

I shall not go into the story of those six years. You know today that your bank deposits are safe; that the problem of unemployment is far less serious; that more wheels of industry are turning; that the farmers are better off in a hundred ways; and most important of all, that our people are not half-clothed or half-starving.

But I do want to speak to you briefly of one part of the broad policy of your Government during these six years — only a part, mind you, but an essential part of a very big whole.

In that winter of 1932–1933, because of inaction on the part of the Federal Government, thousands of communities everywhere and many of the states of the Nation were facing bankruptcy. And as Governor of New York for four years, because I could get no assistance from Washington, I had been compelled, with the approval of my State Legislature — which, by the way, was Republican in both its branches — to care for the human needs of tens of thousands of the citizens of that State. Because I could get no assistance from Washington, I was compelled to create state deficits — to put the State Treasury into the "red." Why? In order to feed the destitute; to give work to the unemployed; to care for the thousands of people who had become dependent on the State for food and shelter. And, when I left Albany, the deficit of the State of New York was nearly a hundred million dollars.

If I were to go back there under similar circumstances, I would do the same thing I did then for the sake of human lives.

That was the experience of most states. They could get no help from the National Government to meet national problems. They were in debt and their borrowing capacity was close to an end. That was also the experience of hundreds of cities and counties. Taxes were not being paid to them, and if they had had to liquidate they would have been insolvent.

Your Federal Government — the one that started on March 4, 1933 — recognized this situation and promptly sought to restore the credit and the finances of the states, the cities and the counties. We put a national shoulder under national problems. We undertook a great program of work — work relief paid for by the Federal Government, thus helping every community to do a thousand necessary jobs which individual communities could not afford to do by themselves — public works on a matching basis, thus enabling states and cities and school districts and counties to build bridges and buildings and roads and flood control works which they could not afford to do alone; work which took the support of men, women and children off the backs of local communities.

In the six years that have intervened, many of our states, because of that help from the National Government, are now back in the "black" again — my own State of New York, and your own State of Kentucky among them. And I am heartily glad of it. Your Governor, my Governor, and a good many other Governors of other states are able to go before their people and announce proudly that they have balanced their budgets. More power to their arms!

I am happy and proud of how much the Federal Government has been able to help Kentucky and the other states. It would surprise many people to know how much that help has been. Take Kentucky for example:

1—In these six years, the Federal Government has allotted to Kentucky in new kinds of Federal expenditures for relief, work relief, public works, the education of youth, farm rehabilitation and crop benefits—approximately $280,000,000.

2—In these six years the Federal Government has spent in more traditional forms of Federal expenditure, such as matching funds for state highways on a fifty-fifty basis, aid to the state for the building of state institutions, flood control and river work, Federal public buildings and the maintenance of the regular agricultural services, at least another fifty million dollars.

3—In these six years Federal loans, through the R.F.C., the H.O.L.C., the Farm Credit Administration and other lending agencies—by extending the due date of obligations, by scaling the interest on obligations, giving financial institutions and borrowers alike a chance to reorganize and turn around—have averted from the taxable wealth and the taxable citizens of Kentucky the cost of bearing the liquidation of the 1929-33 depression. That, I conservatively estimate, has saved the financial resources of the State of Kentucky several hundred millions of dollars.

4—And finally, in these six years the prompt willingness of the Federal Government to take care of flood damage, to begin the prevention of soil erosion, to invest in the protection of Kentucky's natural capital and property while Kentucky had to save on those items—all that is worth incalculable millions of dollars more.

Add all that up when next you wonder why the National Government has not balanced its budget over the last six years.

If the Federal Government, your Government, had not done at least some of these things, the state governments would probably not have done them at all out of their own resources, because they could not. By assistance like this, not only in Kentucky, but in other states, state treasuries have been enabled to get out of the "red" and into the "black"—and that holds true for the credit of almost every municipality and town and school district and county throughout the Union.

It has taken courage for the Federal Government to go into the "red" to help state and local governments, to help them get out of the "red" or stay out of the "red." But, my friends, nationally it has been worth it.

Your Governor deserves due credit for getting this State on a sound financial basis. He never came to Washington and went away empty-handed. I say to him, and I say to you that I have considered him and do consider him a friend of mine, and that I think he has done a good job as the Chief Executive of his State.

At the same time, I am glad that Senator Barkley is here too. I have no hesitation in saying certain things in the presence of Alben Barkley.

I read in the papers that you are having a primary campaign in Kentucky, a primary campaign for the choice of the Democratic candidate for the United States Senate. Both candidates I know. Both are men of ability. Both are representative Kentuckians.

I want to make it definite and clear to you that I am not interfering in any shape, manner or form in the primary campaign in Kentucky. I do not live here—you do. You have the absolute right to vote for any candidate in accordance with the dictates of your conscience. No outside source ought to dragoon you.

Nevertheless, I have a clear right to tell you certain facts relating to the National Government, to national problems, facts which I believe to be true. The people of Kentucky have a vital part, a vital stake in these national facts and problems. As one of the great states of the Union, Kentucky is interested in national affairs and is therefore entitled to know every angle of national affairs.

At this stage of world and domestic issues, a serious time for the people of America, a serious time for the people of the whole world, leadership is important to the people of the United States as well as to the people of the individual states.

We in this country operate principally through what we call the party system. We so operate because we believe that party responsibility eliminates a large part of the confusion which would result from a complete lack of party leadership. That leadership, as you will readily realize, is necessary not only in the Executive Branch of the National Government but equally necessary in the two Houses of the Congress.

In the upper House, the leadership of the majority party has been entrusted by the votes of his colleagues to Senator Barkley, the senior Senator from Kentucky. I do not need to tell you of his long experience in all of our national problems. By virtue of that experience, by virtue of his ability, by virtue of his seniority, he serves on major committees, which deal with major legislation and, in addition to this, he speaks with the voice of the majority leader of the Democratic Party in the Senate of the United States.

His outlook on affairs of Government is a liberal outlook. He has taken a major part in shaping not only the legislation but the actual policies of the past six years.

I have no doubt whatsoever that Governor Chandler would make a good Senator from Kentucky — but I think that my friend, the Governor, would be the first to acknowledge that as a very junior member of the United States Senate, it would take him many, many years to match the national knowledge, the experience and the acknowledged leadership in the affairs of the Nation of that son of Kentucky, of whom the whole Nation is proud, Alben Barkley.

One word more. You have heard charges and the country has heard charges, and counter charges of the use of political influence exerted on primary voters. Charges have been bandied back and forth that employees of the Federal Government and workers on relief are being directed how to vote. And we have all heard charges that state employees, people on the state payroll and their friends are being directed how to vote. Let me assure you that it is contrary to direct and forceful orders from Washington, for any Federal Government employee to tell those under them how to vote and I trust that the same rule applies to those who work for or under the State of Kentucky.

Personally, I am not greatly disturbed by these stories because I have an old-fashioned idea, an old-fashioned faith, that the voters of Kentucky, no matter whom they employ or by whom they are employed, are going to vote their own personal convictions on Primary Day. That is as it should be.

I am glad to come to this beautiful spot today. I know about Latonia by reading the sporting pages of the papers. You live on a great river, the Ohio. And, by the way, the first steamboat that ever navigated this river was built and run by old Nicholas Roosevelt, my great grandfather's cousin. Slowly but surely, we, the new generation, are getting the old river under control, and I am equally certain that the people of America are slowly but surely getting their social and economic problems under control too. Let us keep up the good work.

91 ⟪ Informal, Extemporaneous Remarks at Louisville, Kentucky. July 8, 1938

Mr. Mayor, Senator Barkley, friends of Louisville:

THIS IS the first chance I have had to come to Louisville since the great flood of last year.

First of all, I want to congratulate you and also the citizens of other communities who suffered so greatly from that flood on the firm courage and the fine spirit with which you met that disaster.

Your Mayor told me a few minutes ago that every cloud seems to have its silver lining. Very certainly, in the case of Louisville, the flood reestablished human nature and made you all better neighbors to each other.

Not only in the crisis of a great flood but also in the long process of rebuilding, you have exemplified the spirit of self-help and cooperation between citizens and with the agencies of government.

I want to tell you in a very few words of another gain from that disaster. When I went to Washington, nearly six years ago, I found there were many different agencies of the Government concerned with disasters, and each one of them worked hard in its own line of work. But, there was no coordination among them.

That flood last year on the Ohio and the Mississippi gave me an opportunity to test out the new machinery I had created to meet national disasters. Last year, when the rain began to fall on the furthest creeks, in the upper reaches of the upper tributaries of the Ohio, all of the Federal agencies, working with the State agencies, were able to meet in cooperative efforts to combat the flood as it worked its way down toward the sea.

Through that leadership of coordination and especially through the leadership of a great American who unfortunately has passed on — Admiral Cary Grayson of the American Red Cross — all of the agencies; the Red Cross itself, the Army Engineers, the Corps Area Commanders, the Public Health Service, the Army and Navy Medical Corps, the lifeboats of the Navy and their crews, the Works Progress Administration, and the U.S. Coast Guard — all worked under a united leadership and threw all the resources of the Federal Government to the assistance of life and the salvaging of property.

Also as a result of that flood, we, in Washington, have worked out a definite national policy. The Ohio Basin and other great river basins subject to floods can and are going to be made safe for our American civilization.

Of course we are not going to pay for it all. We are proceeding on the definite policy that every community will gladly do as much of its share of the work of flood prevention as the community can properly afford, and that over and above those contributions your Federal Government is assuming responsibility. That is another proof of the necessity of planning. A lot of people laugh about all the planning we are doing in Washington.

But, in the long run, taking just flood prevention as one of the many examples, we shall save hundreds of millions of dollars by planning for the future.

Flood prevention pays. It pays even if the Federal Government has to create a temporary deficit by borrowing money for flood prevention works at this time.

In one of our great national watersheds — before the Federal Government stepped in with planning and with work — the average loss of property in a given year ran as high as twenty-five million dollars. That was just property alone — twenty-five million dollars a year without counting the toll of human lives — twenty-five millions of property damage to crops, to homes, to industrial plants, to highways and railways. It seems to me that, as a matter of practical business sense, it is well worth our while to spend, yes, two or three hundred million dollars on a watershed of that kind if thereby and for all time we can eliminate an annual loss of twenty-five million dollars.

On another watershed, the Missouri, the figures relating to the destruction of buildings and highways and industrial plants are not as great in annual loss as they are in other places but, in the case of the Missouri River and its tributaries, a careful checkup shows that thousands and thousands of acres of rich bottom land are being carried every year down to the Gulf of Mexico. Those lands are worth millions of dollars even as they are today. Think of their worth to the generations to come. Think of what they are worth, in terms of dollars, for the production of foodstuffs for future generations.

Here again, I think it is a mighty good business proposition to spend money now to save vast sums in future years.

Flood prevention is a national problem. The people of the Ohio Valley understand this and, I am sure, approve our intentions — under a well coordinated plan — to make the Ohio Basin flood proof; flood proof for our children and for their children.

In this work of planning and coordinating work on a vast scale, I want to acknowledge the splendid assistance I have received from the senior Senator from Kentucky. This is a national problem. We need people of national experience with a national point of view to carry it out.

I wish I could stay here longer and see all of the work that you have done. I have been tremendously interested in it. From many sources, not Louisville sources alone but people who have visited here from every part of the Union, I have been given reports of the splendid work of rehabilitation you have carried out. Some day I hope to be able to come back here and stay a little longer.

There is only one advantage I have over you good people: I am going to get bigger fish in the Pacific than you can get in the Ohio.

(See note to Item 4, 1937 volume, for an account of flood relief in the Ohio and Mississippi valleys in 1937.)

92 ⟨ "America Needs a Government of Constant Progress Along Liberal Lines." Address at Oklahoma City, Oklahoma. July 9, 1938

Senator Thomas, Governor Marland, Mr. Mayor, friends of Oklahoma:

I AM glad at last, after many years of wishing and trying, to come to Oklahoma City.

Your great State will always have a certain distinction in my memory, because it is the only part of the forty-eight states which bore a different name when, as a small boy, I started to study Geography. I am fortunate in being old enough to be able to remember it as Indian Territory and to remember also the enormous interest in every part of the country when the prospective settlers lined up at the borders and, at the sound of a bugle, rushed forward to establish new homes and new communities in this delightful part of the earth.

Since those days you good people have gone far. A splendid

future lies before you, and you can rest assured that your National Government knows very definitely that you are on the map.

During the past ten or fifteen years, when I was Governor of New York, and even before that, I have specialized on the subject of natural resources. Therefore, I am particularly glad that Oklahoma is natural-resources conscious, and I am glad that it appreciates so well that natural resources are national resources and that in their conserving and development, all of us, far and near, have to make our plans from the national point of view.

Slowly but surely we are developing a national policy, for example, in regard to the oil resources of the Nation, and your Governor has given great assistance toward that end.

Probably the most important long-range problem is something that affects all of us, whether we live in the city or the country—the use of land and water. I was sorry this morning that I could not have stopped to view the Grand River Dam Project. It was due to the persistent effort of my old friend, Senator Thomas, and Senator Lee, that that particular project is definitely under way, and I might say the same thing about other projects on other watersheds of this State.

I think the Grand River project is a good illustration of the national aspect of water control, because it is a vital link in the still larger problem of the whole valley of the Arkansas—a planning task that starts far west in the Rocky Mountains, west of the Royal Gorge, and runs on down through Colorado and Kansas and Oklahoma and Arkansas to the Mississippi River itself and thence to the sea. The day will come, I hope, when every drop of water that flows into that great watershed, through all those states, will be controlled for the benefit of mankind, controlled for the growing of forests, for the prevention of soil erosion, for the irrigation of land, for the development of water power, for the ending of floods and for the improvement of navigation.

A vision like that, my friends, will be of direct benefit to millions of our people, not only to the people of the territory

443

through which that river flows but indirectly to the people on the Pacific Coast, on the Atlantic Seaboard, and in the deep South. The price, the dollars and cents, we pay for a great development of that kind, will return to the pocketbooks of the State manyfold. The same thing applies to the Red River and to the tributaries that flow into the other streams.

In the same way, the Federal Government is using the fact, the unfortunate fact, of unemployment and the necessity for giving help to many of our people, in order to assist communities in the erection of much-needed public improvements. This is true, as you know, of the work of many agencies of the Federal Government, especially the Public Works Administration and the Works Progress Administration.

Senator Thomas has been of enormous help to me and to the Administration in keeping me advised as to the needs of your State, and as to how we, in Washington, could help meet them. I am told by him that the Works Progress program in Oklahoma is leaving permanent monuments all over the State, monuments that will last to the time of our great grandchildren; and that in the matter of new and improved schoolhouses in cooperation with WPA, this State has made a greater record than any other state in the Union.

I have to think along national lines and, in the last analysis, you do too. It is essential, of course, that if the national policies of the National Administration are to be carried forward there must be a general agreement on those policies among those who are responsible for the legislation which makes them possible.

Two weeks ago, in speaking over a national hookup, I referred to that fact — to the fact that the Nation is living today, and has been since March 4, 1933, under a government which is essentially liberal and nationally thinking in its outlook — a government which is progressively bettering our economic and social conditions.

I explained why, if the people want that kind of government to continue, they should choose officials to represent that point of view — and why, on the other hand, if the people want to go

And I suggested also that it is always a good thing to look beyond the surface of things and into men's hearts.

Do they really mean what they say -- or are they the kind that profess great devotion to the cause of bettering the lot of their fellowmen, and, when the time for action comes, find all kinds of reasons why they should not support the action proposed. ~~Sometimes~~ I refer~~red~~ to such people as - "Yes, but - people".

In the same way we find others who seek office, sincerely or otherwise, on impossible pledges and platforms -- people with panaceas for reforming the world overnight -- people who are not practical in an age which must be both practical and progressive. Theodore Roosevelt was perhaps a bit rough when he referred to such people as "the lunatic fringe". Strictly speaking they are not lunatics but in many cases a little push would shove them over the line.

During these past six years the people of this Nation have definitely said "yes" to the old biblical question - "Am I my brother's keeper"? In these six years I sense a growing

FACSIMILE OF A PAGE OF A DRAFT OF THE ADDRESS AT OKLAHOMA CITY, OKLA., JULY 9, 1938 back to the school of thought of the unfortunate twenties of this century, they should choose people with a conservative outlook.

And I suggested also that it is always a good thing to look beneath the surface of things, to look into men's hearts. Do they really mean what they say — or are they the kind that profess great devotion to the cause of bettering the lot of their fellow countrymen, and, when the time for action comes, find all kinds of reasons why they cannot support the action proposed. I have referred to people of that kind as "Yes, but" — people.

Of course, some are not even "Yes, but" — people, for I note that one of the candidates for a place on the Democratic State ticket in Oklahoma this year is nationally known as a Republican.

In the same way we find others who seek office, sincerely or otherwise, on perfectly impossible pledges and platforms — people with panaceas for reforming the world overnight — people who are not practical in an age that must be and can be both practical and progressive. Theodore Roosevelt was perhaps a bit rough in his language when he referred to such people as "the lunatic fringe." Of course, strictly speaking, they are not lunatics, but in many cases a little push would shove them over the line.

During these past six years the people of this Nation have definitely said "yes" — with no "but" about it — to the old Biblical question, "Am I my brother's keeper?" In these six years I sense a growing devotion to the teachings of the Scriptures, to the quickening of religion, to a greater willingness on the part of the individual to help his neighbor and to live less unto and for himself alone.

It is in that spirit, my friends, that your National Government seeks to carry on its task. It is in that spirit that, in the consideration of every new problem, our first question is this: "What makes for the greatest good of the greatest number?"

America needs a government of constant progress along liberal lines. America requires that this progress be sane and that this progress be honest. America calls for government with a soul.

445

93 (Informal, Extemporaneous Remarks. Fort Worth, Texas. July 10, 1938

My friends of Texas:

I AM glad to be back in Texas—and especially to have a nice quiet family day at my son Elliott's ranch. I always remember that when he first decided to build a house here on top of the hill, he was attracted by the fact that the wide view from here is a little like the view from our old home, far up the Hudson River.

This is a grand part of the country and I am glad indeed to have such a close family connection with it. Tomorrow, on my way to Colorado, I shall pass through a part of Texas I have never been to—Wichita Falls and Amarillo—and I am glad to know that this year the rainfall has greatly improved conditions in the Panhandle.

That makes me remember one of the objectives of the national administration—better land use and an all-weather crop program. Nine years ago, when I was Governor of the State of New York, I started my interest and efforts in the better use of land. People are apt to think of New York State as a vast metropolis; but outside of the city at the southern end of the State, more than six million people live on farms and in villages and small cities. Indeed, New York State ranks in the value of its agricultural products as the fifth or sixth state in the Union. A survey showed us that much of the farming land was being used in an uneconomical way, that thousands of acres were being badly eroded, that reforestation was a great need, that we had to plan for the help of stranded communities, for improving rural schools, bringing in electricity and good roads, and stopping the waste and the poverty that so often attended the older methods of doing business.

When I was working on these problems in Albany, I was struck by the fact that agriculture cannot be thought of or worked for just on state lines. Every crop on every farm in every county and every state has a definite tie-in — a relationship with similar crops in other states. That is why, since I have been in Washington, I have been working on the agricultural and cattle program from a national angle. For example, not only does cotton in Texas have a definite relationship to cotton in Georgia, but cotton in the South and Southwest is clearly connected with the economics of the wheat grower in the Dakotas, the cattleman of Wyoming and the potato grower of Maine. When one has a poor year, his lack of prosperity hits all of the others. When one is prosperous, all the others are helped.

In one sense, Texas is a great empire in itself — you can produce almost everything needed by man. But what gratifies me most of all is that the people of the Lone Star State are co-operating so well with all the other states of the Union in working out our mutual national problems. In this way we will get away from spotty prosperity, and work toward universal prosperity.

You need more industries in Texas, but I know you realize the importance of not trying to get industries by the route of cheap wages for industrial workers. Cheap wages mean low buying power. Low buying power means low standards of living; and that means low taxable values, and, therefore, difficulty in maintaining good schools, highways, sanitation and other public improvements.

I know from all that I have seen that new industries can and will be developed in this state because of your access to raw materials, because of the efficiency of your labor, because of the growing purchasing power, and because of the spirit of the people.

Yes, I am proud of the spirit of Texas, the spirit of all of its people. I have fished your coasts, I have seen your fields, your oil wells, your cattle, your waterways, your schools and colleges.

And now, as I sit here in a garden on top of a hill, with a breeze blowing and a sunset coming, surrounded by a very delightful gathering of Texans, all I can think of is that I want to come back again many, many times in the days to come.

94 (Informal, Extemporaneous Remarks. Childress, Texas. July 11, 1938

My friends:

I AM glad to come out to West Texas. I am glad to come out to Marvin Jones' district. Tom Connally and I have been "kidding" him on this train, wondering whether when we came into the home district of the Chairman of the Committee on Agriculture of the House of Representatives, whether we should find agriculture was a whole lot better here than in any other place in the country.

Marvin says that you are doing pretty well.

I have been very much interested in coming through this end of Texas. I have never been through here before. But I have been fairly familiar with it in a good many ways because, in the last six years, I have had to get a good deal of first-hand knowledge about the problems of every part of the country.

I am very glad to know that you are all water conscious. I hope the day will come — it will take a long time to do it — when every drop of water that falls out of the heavens will serve the highest use, the best use possible for mankind before it gets down into the Gulf of Mexico.

We are learning a lot; we know more about all these problems today than we did ten years or twenty years ago. Back in the East there are a good many people who laugh about the Dust Bowl, they laugh about the efforts on the part of man to change nature. I wish they could come out and see the people who live in this country and who are making good in this country.

That is why we in Washington, thinking in national terms, are doing everything that we possibly can to make every area of the United States a better place to live in, to give a greater security not only to this generation but to the children who are going to follow us in the days to come.

95 ⟨ Address at Ellwood Park, Amarillo, Texas. July 11, 1938

My friends of the Panhandle and you from neighboring cities who have been good enough to come here today:

IF I HAD asked the newspapermen on the train what the odds were, they would have given me 100 to 1 that it wouldn't be raining in Amarillo. But it is!

Even if Marvin Jones had not kept on telling me about Amarillo once a week for the past five and a half years, I would have known all about it because this is the spot where my wife was presented with the biggest bunch of flowers in all the world.

Before I left home Mrs. Roosevelt asked me especially to convey her greetings to Amarillo and to tell you how much she enjoyed every minute of her visit with you.

The biggest bouquet in the world — and here you are greeting me with the biggest band in the world. Back in the East enterprising communities have thought they were creating world records by assembling bands with five hundred instruments but out here you think nothing of a band with 2,500 instruments.

All this shows what you can do in the Panhandle if you put your minds to it; and that is why I am very happy that you are putting your minds on the subject of land and water use. Everywhere you go in the United States you find the problem of land and water use, and the same thing is true within any given state. For instance, in Texas, here in Marvin Jones' district, most of the time the problem is to get water to the land and to keep the land from blowing away. Down in Austin the problem of my friend, Congressman Lyndon Johnson, is to keep his land from washing away down the rivers and into the sea. And further down at San Antonio, where my friend, Congressman Maury

449

Maverick, represents a great city and its surrounding territory, the problem of land use there is tied up with better housing and the needs of a great municipality.

I wish that more people from the South and the East and the Middle West could visit this Plains country. If they did you would hear less talk about the great American desert, you would hear less ridicule of our efforts to conserve water, to restore grazing lands and to plant trees.

Back in the East, in Washington and on the Hudson River I have seen the top soil of the Panhandle and of Western Kansas and Nebraska borne by the wind high in the air eastward to the Atlantic Ocean itself. I want that sight to come to an end.

It can be ended only by a united national effort, backed up one hundred per cent by you who live in this area. You are giving us that backing.

Money spent for the building of ponds and small lakes, for the damming of rivers, for planting shelterbelts, for other forms of afforestation, for putting plough land back into grass, that is money well spent. It pays to do it, not only for this generation but for the children who will succeed to the land a few years hence.

People who are ignorant and people who think only in terms of the moment scoff at our efforts and say: "Oh, let the next generation take care of itself — if people out in the dry parts of the country cannot live there let them move out and hand the land back to the Indians." That is not your idea nor mine. We seek permanently to establish this part of the Nation as a fine and safe place which a large number of Americans can call home.

Every year that passes, we are learning more and more about the best use of land, about the conserving of our soil and the improvement of it, by getting everything we can out of every drop of water that falls from the heavens. Back in the Allegheny Mountains many of the rivers are called "flash streams" — dry beds or rivulets most of the year, but raging torrents sweeping all before them when a cloudburst or heavy rain occurs. And you have flash streams here.

We are fortunate in Washington in having as Chairman of the Agricultural Committee of the House of Representatives a man who has a well-rounded knowledge of the agricultural programs in every part of the United States. He and I have discussed many times the great objective of putting agriculture and cattle raising on a safe basis—giving assurances to those who engage in those pursuits, that they will not be "broke" one year and "flush" the next. We need a greater permanency, a greater annual security for all who use the soil.

The farming and cattle-raising population of the United States has no desire to be paid a subsidy or to be given a handout from the Federal Treasury. They have come to understand, and the rest of the country is learning, too, that the agricultural program of this Administration is not a subsidy. It is divided into three simple parts.

The first part represents government assistance to help the individual farmer to use his land for those products for which it is best fitted, and to maintain and improve its fertility.

The second objective is, with the approval of those who raise crops, to prevent overproduction and low prices, and at the same time to provide against any shortage—in other words, to apply common sense business principles to the business of farming and cattle raising. As a part of that second objective, we seek to give to the farmers throughout the country as high a purchasing power for their labor as those who work in industry and other occupations.

The third effort of your Government is directed toward a great decrease in farm tenancy and toward the increase in farm ownership by those who till the soil. This includes the encouragement of small farms and of even smaller acreages for those who live near the cities and work in the cities, and who should by all the rules of common sense grow on a few acres around their homes a substantial part of their own family food supply.

You have given me a wonderful reception today in Amarillo, not counting the rain, and I am happy, I am happy indeed, to have been able to see this extraordinarily interesting and progressive part of the United States. I am grateful to you for your cooperation with your National Government, and your understanding of all that we are trying to do in the National Administration to help those who are willing to help themselves.

96 ❡ Informal, Extemporaneous Remarks at Pueblo, Colorado. July 12, 1938

Governor Ammons, my friends of Pueblo:

IT IS GOOD to be back here. I was not quite sure this morning whether I was going to be back here or not, because I read in a Denver paper that this was the first time in twenty years that a President had come to Pueblo. I must have been dreaming about my 1936 trip to Pueblo, or else I was not President at that time.

I have been having a very delightful trip across the country. It is a very big country, and there are a great many parts of it that I cannot possibly see on a given trip. But what has impressed me on this trip are two things. The first is that we seem to have had a pretty good agricultural year, even down in the dust bowl. When I got to the last place in the world I thought I could possibly find rain — Amarillo — I got soaking wet.

And the other thing that impressed me was the growing understanding that everybody seems to have of our national problems.

The example that I used back East is one that directly affects this part of the State of Colorado, the Arkansas River. The average person on the Eastern Seaboard thinks of the Arkansas as some kind of a little creek that grows in Arkansas and drops down with a lot of floods into the Mississippi. And when I tell them that the Arkansas River starts way west of Pueblo, Colorado, back of the trans-continental divide, and that you here were once upon a time nearly wiped out by a flood on that river — that it wanders on down through this state and

Kansas and Oklahoma and Arkansas before it even reaches the Mississippi—then they go and get their geography books to verify what I said.

It is a pretty good illustration, because that river isn't just the problem of one state or one community. It calls for national planning; and national planning for the Arkansas River involves a great many different angles that you and I know—not only flood prevention but irrigation, reclamation, reforestation, power development and all the things that go with the development of an entire watershed.

The same thing applies of course to practically every other watershed in the state. You people in this State have a pretty well-rounded picture of what that means because you are on two watersheds, one running into the Gulf of Mexico and the other into the Pacific Ocean. You have certain problems—your Governor and I have talked about them—over the use of the water of the Colorado River and some of our friends down in lower Arizona and California, perhaps, have different ideas about the use of that water.

That illustrates why we have to have the Federal Government not running everything but acting as a focal meeting place for all kinds of national problems, so our states can resolve the difficulties they may have between each other. We are getting over the selfish point of view; we are thinking of all of our problems in national terms.

We have been trying—I think all of us sincerely—to make this nation conscious of the fact that it is a nation. If we succeed in that, it means we can make our democracy work, and that is our big objective.

We don't want and we are not going to copy other forms of government—ours is good enough for us.

Today I am going for the third or fourth time up through the Royal Gorge—one of the finest scenic spots in the whole of the United States. More and more this scenery of ours in the Rocky Mountains is being recognized as a national asset by people all over the country, and they are coming here for their vacation time. I believe that also is a good thing. If we could get everybody in the United States to travel all around the United States, we would eliminate in large part our political differences. We would get to know each other better.

It is in that spirit of the traveler, the man who wants to go around the country to take a look-see, to find out more about the problems of every section, that I am passing through Pueblo today. I wish I could stay longer. This trip is helping me to get a re-orientation of what is going on in the United States.

97 ⟨ Informal, Extemporaneous Remarks at Grand Junction, Colorado. July 12, 1938

My friends:

I AM glad to come back here. I have not been here for a number of years; but I know this route across the continent very well. I am glad to see what look like real signs of prosperity throughout the State of Colorado.

You know, this method of traveling is a very wonderful thing. The reason I delayed coming out on the platform was because I have been talking on the long-distance telephone right here, from the end of the car, to Washington, D. C., talking with Harry Hopkins, the Administrator of Works Progress; and before I leave here I am probably going to talk to a couple more Government officials in the National Capital. It shows how closely every part of the country is in touch with every other part.

On this trip, I have been paying special attention to the subject of water. You know what water means; you know the need of it. In Washington we believe that it is not only cotton and wheat and corn and hogs that are major crops in the United States, but that there are a lot of other crops — such as fruit; and that a lot of other things, like mining, are really in the position of being major industries. That is why we are trying to include them in the picture of national prosperity, not just a spotty prosperity that hits only certain areas of the country but the kind of prosperity that is felt in every single spot and every section of every state. That is why we are doing what we call "national planning."

There are a good many people that take a nearsighted point of view that there should not be any such thing as national planning, that every man ought to be for himself, that we ought to go back to the "good old days." But, since the fourth of March, 1933, your National Administration in every state of the Union has been trying to give help that will be well-rounded help, tying the prosperity of one section in with the prosperity of another.

It is a very interesting thing to me that if I had made a speech in the City of New York, five or six years ago, and told them that their prosperity in New York was definitely tied in with, let us say, the mines of Colorado, or with the fruit or beets or other crops of Colorado, they would have expressed only a mild interest, but very mild. They would not have seen the connection. In the same way, if I had gone out through this territory and had told you, five or six years ago, that your prosperity here was pretty closely tied up with some of the great industrial centers of the country, you would have expressed only mild interest, but it would not have meant very much to you. However, in these later years we have come to realize, all over the country, I think, that agricultural prosperity is definitely affected by industrial prosperity. In other words, if the workers in the great industrial plants in Pittsburgh and New York and Cleveland and Chicago and other places, have purchasing power, if the plants are running and paying them good wages, they can buy more of the things that you produce on the farm and in the mines. In the same way, if you are prosperous and have purchasing power, you out here can buy more of the things that are produced in the great industrial centers. That is what I call the successful working out of the processes of democracy; and, as you know, we are trying to make democratic government work.

We are not only delighted to have the Governor of Colorado and the Senators and the Congressmen with us today, but I am glad also that my old friend, the Governor of Utah, has joined the train.

On this trip I have to pass through most of Utah by night; but I know the State pretty well and when I wake up in the morning, my daughter and her husband from Seattle will be aboard. So, you see, this is a very happy family trip.

It has been good to see you all. I did not come out here for political reasons, but to take my annual "look-see" around the country. I hope to be back and see you good people in the western part of the State of Colorado again very soon.

98 ❡ "We Fervently Hope for the Day When the Other Leading Nations of the World Will Realize That Their Present Course Must Inevitably Lead to Disaster." Address at Treasure Island, San Francisco, California. July 14, 1938

Governor Merriam, ladies and gentlemen:

RARELY, perhaps never, in my life have I been as thrilled as I have today, starting with the visit to my old friends of nearly a quarter of a century ago at the Mare Island Navy Yard, and then taking that trip by motor over wonderful highways to that view of your two new bridges that I had never seen before. And that wonderful reception all along the line of march! And then, coming down from what I used to call Goat Island in the old days — although I believe it had a more official and more beautiful name — to this Island with its wonderful buildings that already prove what the Exposition is going to look like next year — all I can tell you is that I impatiently await the passage of months before I come back here to see it all.

Confidence that in the year 1939 the United States and all

the Western Hemisphere will be at peace is shown by the fact that in this Nation two great international expositions are about to be held.

It is our hope and our expectation that that confidence is well placed — and that the very fact of holding these two expositions means an added impetus to the cause of world peace. Great gatherings of such a nature make for trade, for better understanding and for renewed good will between the Nations of the world.

It has been suggested that it was a mistake to hold two expositions in one year — but I cannot agree with that because it seems to me that each is a supplement to the other. Thousands of Americans are already planning to visit both of the expositions next year — to see both ends of our wide Nation and perhaps to travel one way by the all-American route via the Panama Canal.

Furthermore, those who visit us from other countries will be stimulated to cross our country, the way I try to do every year that passes. Too often we are judged by those from other lands who spend a few hurried weeks or even days on one seaboard and think they know America.

At New York the other day I suggested, furthermore, that we Americans wish that many more people from other nations would come to visit us. We Americans have the travel habit and we wish that other people would acquire it. The more of them who visit us next year, the happier we shall be.

In the construction of the Golden Gate International Exposition, the Federal Government has been glad to be of material assistance to your plans.

In addition to the allotment by the Congress of a million and a half dollars, I am told that you have received nearly five million dollars in the form of useful work paid for by WPA funds, and nearly another two million dollars in equally useful work paid for from Public Works funds — in other words, total Federal assistance of more than eight and a quarter million dollars.

I am glad that the Federal Government has been able so greatly to help the fine spirit which throughout the western states encouraged and is encouraging this undertaking. And I am glad, too, that we have been able to help the State of California and the municipalities around San Francisco Bay in the construction of the two great bridges which I saw today for the first time. Those bridges form a magnificent illustration of the new saying that "what nature has put asunder, man can join together."

In another two hours I hope to review the United States Fleet, now at anchor in this great American harbor. That Fleet is not merely a symbol — it is a potent, every-ready fact in the national defense of the United States.

Every right-thinking man and woman in our country wishes that it were safe for the Nation to spend less of our national budget on our armed forces. All know that we are faced with a condition and not a theory — and that that condition is not of our own choosing. Money spent on armaments does not create permanent income-producing wealth, and about the only satisfaction we can take out of the present world situation is that the proportion of our national income that we spend on armaments is only a quarter or a third of the proportion that most of the other great nations of the world are spending at this time.

We fervently hope for the day when the other leading nations of the world will realize that their present course must inevitably lead to disaster. We stand ready to meet them, and to encourage them in any efforts they may make toward a definite reduction in world armament.

The year 1939 would go down in history not only as the year of the two great American World's Fairs, but would be a year of world-wide rejoicing if it could also mark definite steps toward permanent world peace. That is the hope and the prayer of the overwhelming number of men and women and children in all the earth today.

99 ❨A Call for a Coordinated National Health Program. July 15, 1938

My dear Miss Roche:

I AM glad that your Committee has had such an excellent response to its invitations to representatives of the public and of the medical and other professions to participate in the National Health Conference. I regret that because I shall be on a cruise I shall be unable to speak to the Conference.

I am glad that the Conference includes so many representatives of the general public. The professional experts can and, I feel sure, will, do their part. But the problems before you are in a real sense public problems. The ways and means of dealing with them must be determined with a view to the best interests of all our citizens.

I hope that your technical committee's report on the need for a national health program and its tentative proposals will be read and studied not only by the participants in the Conference but by every citizen. Nothing is more important to a nation than the health of its people. Medical science has made remarkable strides, and in cooperation with government and voluntary agencies it has made substantial progress in the control of various diseases. During the last few years we have taken several additional steps forward through the extension of public health and maternal and child welfare services under the Social Security Act, the launching of a special campaign to control syphilis, the establishment of the National Cancer Institute, and the use of Federal emergency funds for the expansion of hospital and sanitation facilities, the control of malaria, and many related purposes.

But when we see what we know how to do, yet have not done, it is clear that there is need for a coordinated national program of action. Such a program necessarily must take account of the fact that millions of citizens lack the individual means to pay for adequate medical care. The economic loss due to sickness is a very serious matter not only for many families with and without incomes but for the nation as a whole.

We cannot do all at once everything that we should do. But we can advance more surely if we have before us a comprehensive, long-range program, providing for the most efficient co-operation of Federal, state, and local governments, voluntary agencies, professional groups, media of public information, and individual citizens. I hope that at the National Health Conference a chart for continuing concerted action will begin to take form.

Very sincerely yours,

Miss Josephine Roche, Chairman,
Interdepartmental Committee to Coordinate Health and
Welfare Activities of the Federal Government,
Washington, D. C.

NOTE: In 1934, I appointed the Committee on Economic Security (see Item 117, 1934 volume), whose research and recommendations formed the basis of the Social Security Act. In an address to the Advisory Council of the Committee on Economic Security a few months after its appointment, I called attention to the need for study of plans which would minimize the economic loss due to sickness (see Item 179, 1934 volume).

The Social Security Act of 1935 (Public No. 71, 74th Congress, 49 Stat. 620) authorized an annual appropriation of $8,000,000 to enable the Public Health Service to assist states and their local subdivisions in training personnel and maintaining public health services. Under the 1939 amendments to the Act, this authorization was increased to $11,000,000 (see Items 11 and 109 and notes, 1939 volume).

With the passage of the Social Security Act, it was important that the health activities of the various federal agencies be coordinated, and that the problem of adequate protection of health receive additional study. Therefore, on August 15, 1935, I appointed the Interdepartmental Committee to Coordinate Health and Welfare Activities (see Item 108, 1935 volume). I instructed this Committee to appoint special subcommittees of physicians and other technical experts to study and make recommendations on health problems.

As a result, there was created the subcommittee called the Technical Committee on Medical Care, consisting of representatives of the Children's Bureau, the Social Security Board, and the Public Health Service. The Technical

Committee was headed by Dr. Martha M. Eliot of the Children's Bureau.

In the fall of 1937, it commenced a comprehensive survey of the health and medical work of the federal government.

The Technical Committee reviewed the existing health, hospital and medical services, and assembled the recent surveys of private and public agencies. It concluded that there were many deficiencies in the present facilities available, and that without federal assistance the states and local communities could not meet the demands of adequate protection against sickness.

The recommendations of the Technical Committee were embodied in a five-point program which was designed to expand gradually until full-scale operation was reached within ten years. The immediate necessity for increased public health, maternal and child health, and hospital facilities was emphasized. The Committee recommended, for example, that the federal government should undertake additional annual expenditures of $100,000,000 to be matched by a like amount in states and localities, for the eradication of tuberculosis, venereal diseases and malaria, the control of pneumonia and cancer, and for mental and industrial hygiene. Up to $165,000,000 was recommended for maternity care and care of newborn infants, medical care and services for crippled children — also to be divided equally between the federal government and the states and their subdivisions. The Committee further suggested that an average annual expenditure of $147,400,000 be divided between the federal government and states and localities on a 50-50 basis, for the construction and maintenance of additional hospitals and diagnostic centers.

The balance of the Committee report dealt with the need for medical care for the underprivileged and for a system of health insurance. It was advised that the federal government meet half the costs of an expenditure which would in ten years reach $400,000,000 annually for the medical care of lower income groups. Insurance plans to distribute the costs of sickness and disability among wage earners and the general population were also recommended.

It should be emphasized that this plan contemplated no centralized and bureaucratic control or form of "socialized medicine," as frequently charged by some critics. Rather, it was simply a proposal to work out the problem of giving some assurance to wage earners of continuity of income through periods of disability due to sickness, and accomplishing this within the federal system, with the responsibility of administration being placed upon the various states and localities.

After discussing the report of the

461

Technical Committee, the Interdepartmental Committee to Coordinate Health and Welfare Activities adopted it and submitted it to me in February, 1938. On March 8, 1938, feeling that this report should receive more intensive consideration by the public at large as well as medical experts, I wrote to Miss Josephine Roche, Chairman of the Interdepartmental Committee, as follows:

"I suggest that your Committee give consideration to the desirability of inviting at some appropriate time representatives of the interested public and of the medical and other professions, to examine the health problems in all their major aspects and to discuss ways and means of dealing with these problems."

Accordingly, the National Health Conference was called for the purpose, among others, of studying, criticizing and discussing the report. Over two hundred men and women representing labor, agriculture, the public and the medical profession assembled in Washington, D.C., for the three-day conference commencing July 18, 1938.

The foregoing letter of July 15, 1938, was addressed to the chairman of the conference and read by her to the conference.

Many divergent points of view were expressed at the conference during the presentation of prepared statements and in the open discussions. However, the conference agreed upon the fundamental need for more adequate medical care to avert disease and poverty. Difference of opinion arose over the relative tempo of a federal-state effort to meet that need. Above all, the conference was a success in highlighting to the public the proposals of the Interdepartment Committee and aiding in the crystallization of the policies to be pursued.

After the proceedings of the National Health Conference had been printed and transmitted to me, I sent a message to the Congress asking for the consideration of the recommendations of the Interdepartmental Committee (see Item 17 and note, 1939 volume).

100 ❡ The President Discusses Political Principles, Social Objectives, and Party Candidates with his Fellow-Georgians. Address at Barnesville, Georgia. August 11, 1938

Governor Rivers, Senator George, Senator Russell, and
my neighbors of Georgia:

FOURTEEN years ago a democratic Yankee, a comparatively young man, came to a neighboring county in the State of Georgia, in search of a pool of warm water wherein he might swim his way back to health; and he found it. The place — Warm Springs — was at that time a rather dilapidated small summer resort. His new neighbors there extended to him the hand of genuine hospitality, welcomed him to their firesides and made him feel so much at home that he built himself a house, bought himself a farm, and has been coming back ever since. And he proposes to keep to that good custom. I intend coming back very often.

There was only one discordant note in that first stay of mine at Warm Springs. When the first of the month bill came in for electric light for my little cottage, I found that the charge was eighteen cents per kilowatt hour — about four times as much as I was paying in another community, Hyde Park, New York. That light bill started my long study of proper public utility charges for electric current, started in my mind the whole subject of getting electricity into farm homes throughout the United States.

So, my friends, it can be said with a good deal of truth that a little cottage at Warm Springs, Georgia, was the birthplace of the Rural Electrification Administration. Six years ago, in 1932, there was much talk about the more widespread and cheaper use of electricity; but it is only since March 4, 1933, that your Government has reduced that talk to practical results. Electricity is a modern necessity of life, not a luxury. That necessity ought to be found in every village, in every home and on every farm in every part of the United States. The dedication of this Rural Electrification Administration project in Georgia today is a symbol of the progress we are making—and we are not going to stop.

As you know, when I want to go somewhere I generally try to choose the most direct route, but I slipped up this time. I wanted to come to Georgia, but I had to come via California, the Galapagos Islands, the Equator, the Panama Canal and Pensacola. But, before I left on that trip about a month ago, I invited a group of distinguished, broad-minded Southerners to meet in Washington to discuss the economic conditions and problems of the South. When they met, I said to them:

"My intimate interest in all that concerns the South is, I believe, known to all of you; but this interest is far more than a sentimental attachment born of a considerable residence in your section and of close personal friendship with so many of your people. It proceeds even more from my feeling of responsibility toward the whole Nation. It is my conviction that the South presents right now the Nation's No. 1 economic problem—the Nation's problem, not merely the South's. For we have an economic unbalance in the Nation as a whole, due to this very condition in the South itself.

"It is an unbalance that can and must be righted for the sake of the South and of the Nation."

The day before yesterday when I landed in Florida I received the report and the recommendations based on the advice of this distinguished commission. This report and the recommendations will be made public in the course of the next day or two; and I hope you will read it.

It is well said that this report "presents in only a small degree the manifold assets and advantages possessed by the South" because the report is concerned primarily not with boasting about what the South has, but in telling what the South needs. It is a short report divided into fifteen short sections; and it covers in a broad way subjects of vital importance, such as economic resources, soil, water, population, private and public income,

464

education, health, housing, labor, ownership and use of land, credit, use of natural resources, industry and purchasing power.

I am listing those fifteen headings with a definite purpose in mind. The very fact that it is necessary to divide the economic needs of the South into fifteen important groups—each one a problem in itself—proves to you and to me that if you and I are to cover the ground effectively, there is no one single simple answer. It is true that many obvious needs ought to be attained quickly—such as the reduction of discriminatory freight rates, such as putting a definite floor under industrial wages, such as continuing to raise the purchasing power of the farm population. But no one of these things alone, no combination of a few of them, will meet the whole of the problem. Talking in fighting terms, we cannot capture one hill and claim to have won the battle, because the battlefront extends over thousands of miles and we must push forward along the whole front at the same time.

That is why the longer I live, the more am I convinced that there are two types of political leadership which are dangerous to the continuation of broad economic and social progress all along that long battlefront. The first type of political leadership which is dangerous to progress is represented by the man who harps on one or two remedies or proposals and claims that these one or two remedies will cure all our ills. The other type of dangerous leadership is represented by the man who says that he is in favor of progress but whose record shows that he hinders or hampers or tries to kill new measures of progress. He is that type of political leader who tells his friends that he does not like this or that or the other detail; and, at the same time, he utterly fails to offer a substitute that is practical or worthwhile.

The task of meeting the economic and social needs of the South, on the broad front that is absolutely necessary, calls for public servants whose hearts are sound, whose heads are sane—whose hands are strong, striving everlastingly to better the lot of their fellowmen.

The report to which I referred is a synopsis—a clear listing of the economic and social problems of the Southland. It suggests the many steps that must be taken to solve the problems.

Some of these steps, it is true, can be taken by state governments, but you will readily realize that action by the states alone, even if such action on the part of many neighboring states could be simultaneous and immediate, would be wholly inadequate. The very good reason for that is that most of these problems involve interstate relationships, relationships not only among the states of this region but also between each and all of these states and the rest of the Nation.

It is not an attack on state sovereignty to point out that this national aspect of all these problems requires action by the Federal Government in Washington. I do not hesitate to say from long experience that during the past five years there has been a closer and more effective peacetime cooperation between the Governors of the forty-eight states and the President of the United States than at any other time in our whole national history.

You are familiar enough with the processes of Government to know that the Chief Executive cannot take action on national or regional problems, unless they have been first translated into Acts of Congress passed by the Senate and the House of Representatives of the United States.

Such action by the Congress, it is equally clear, must be vigorously supported by the Senators and Representatives whose constituents are directly concerned with Southern economics and Southern social needs. Senators and Congressmen who are not wholeheartedly in sympathy with these needs cannot be expected to give them vigorous support.

Translating that into more intimate terms, it means that if the people of the State of Georgia want definite action in the Congress of the United States, they must send to that Congress Senators and Representatives who are willing to stand up and fight night and day for Federal statutes drawn to meet actual needs — not something that serves merely to gloss over the evils of the moment for the time being — but laws with teeth in them which go to the root of the problems; which remove the inequities, raise the standards and, over a period of years, give constant improvement to the conditions of human life in this State.

You, the people of Georgia, in the coming Senatorial primary, for example, have a perfect right to choose any candidate you wish. I do not seek to impair that right, and I am not going to impair that right of the people of this State; but because Georgia has been good enough to call me her adopted son and because for many long years I have regarded Georgia as my "other state," I feel no hesitation in telling you what I would do if I could vote here next month. I am strengthened in that decision to give you my personal opinion of the coming Senatorial primary by the fact that during the past few weeks I have had many requests from distinguished citizens of Georgia — from people high and low — from the Chief Justice of the highest court of Georgia and many others.

Let me preface my statement by saying that I have personally known three of the candidates for the United States Senate for many years. All of them have had legislative or executive experience as Government servants. We may therefore justly consider their records and their public utterances — and we can justly, also, seek to determine for ourselves what is their inward point of view in relationship to present and future problems of government.

It has been pointed out by writers and speakers who do not analyze public questions very deeply that in passing through the State of Kentucky a month ago I gave as a reason for the reelection of Senator Barkley that he had had very long and successful service in the Congress of the United States and that his opponent did not have that experience. In Kentucky, there was no clear-cut issue between a liberal on the one side and a dyed-in-the-wool conservative on the other. Neither of the two principals on his record could be classified as a reactionary; therefore, the criterion of experience, especially that of the

Majority Leadership of the Senate of the United States, weighed heavily, and properly, in favor of Senator Barkley.

Here in Georgia, however, my old friend, the senior Senator from this State, cannot possibly in my judgment be classified as belonging to the liberal school of thought — and, therefore, the argument that he has long served in the Senate falls by the wayside. Here in Georgia the issue is a different one from that in Kentucky.

I speak seriously and in the most friendly way in terms of liberal and conservative for the very simple fact that on my shoulders rests a responsibility to the people of the United States. In 1932 and again in 1936 I was chosen Chief Executive with the mandate to seek by definite action to correct many evils of the past and of the present; to work for a wider distribution of national income, to improve the conditions of life, especially among those who need it most and, above all, to use every honest effort to keep America in the van of social and economic progress.

To the Congress of the United States I make recommendations — that is all — in most cases recommendations relating to objectives, leaving it to the Congress to translate the recommendations into law. The majority of the Senate and House have agreed with those objectives, and have worked with me; and I have worked with them to translate those objectives into action. Some have given "lip service" to some of the objectives but have not raised their little fingers actively to attain the objectives themselves. Too often these few have listened to the dictatorship of a small minority of individuals and corporations who oppose the objectives themselves. That is a real dictatorship and one which we have been getting away from slowly but surely during the past five years. As long as I live, you will find me fighting against any kind of dictatorship — especially the kind of dictatorship which has enslaved many of our fellow citizens for more than half a century.

What I am about to say will be no news, to my old friend — and I say it with the utmost sincerity — Senator Walter George.

It will be no surprise to him because I have recently had personal correspondence with him; and, as a result of it, he fully knows what my views are.

Let me make it clear that he is, and I hope always will be, my personal friend. He is beyond question, beyond any possible question, a gentleman and a scholar; but there are other gentlemen in the Senate and in the House for whom I have a real affectionate regard, but with whom I differ heartily and sincerely on the principles and policies of how the Government of the United States ought to be run.

For example, I have had an almost lifelong acquaintance and great personal friendship for people like Senator Hale from the State of Maine, for Representative James Wadsworth of New York and for the Minority Leader, Representative Snell. All of these lifelong conservative Republicans are gentlemen and scholars; but they and I learned long ago that our views on public questions were just as wide apart as the North Pole and the South.

Therefore, I repeat that I trust, and am confident, that Senator George and I shall always be good personal friends even though I am impelled to make it clear that on most public questions he and I do not speak the same language.

To carry out my responsibility as President, it is clear that if there is to be success in our Government there ought to be cooperation between members of my own party and myself — cooperation, in other words, within the majority party, between one branch of Government, the Legislative branch, and the head of the other branch, the Executive. That is one of the essentials of a party form of government. It has been going on in this country for nearly a century and a half. The test is not measured, in the case of an individual, by his every vote on every bill — of course not. The test lies rather in the answer to two questions: first, has the record of the candidate shown, while differing perhaps in details, a constant active fighting attitude in favor of the broad objectives of the party and of the Government as they are constituted today; and, secondly, does the candidate really, in his heart, deep down in his heart, believe in those objectives? I regret that in the case of my friend, Senator George, I cannot honestly answer either of these questions in the affirmative.

In the case of another candidate in the State of Georgia for the United States Senate — former Governor Talmadge — I have known him for many years. His attitude toward me and toward other members of the Government in 1935 and in 1936 concerns me not at all. But, in those years and in this year I have read so many of his proposals, so many of his promises, so many of his panaceas, that I am very certain in my own mind that his election would contribute very little to practical progress in government. That is all I can say about him.

The third candidate that I would speak of, United States Attorney Lawrence Camp, I have also known for many years. He has had experience in the State Legislature; he has served as Attorney General of Georgia and for four years; he has made a distinguished record in the United States District Court, his office ranking among the first two in the whole of the United States in the expedition of Federal cases in that Court. I regard him not only as a public servant with successful experience but as a man who honestly believes that many things must be done and done now to improve the economic and social conditions of the country, a man who is willing to fight for these objectives. Fighting ability is of the utmost importance.

Therefore, answering the requests that have come to me from many leading citizens of Georgia that I make my position clear, I have no hesitation in saying that if I were able to vote in the September primaries in this State, I most assuredly should cast my ballot for Lawrence Camp.

In dedicating this important project today, I want to express once more my abiding faith that we as a nation are moving steadily and surely toward a better way of living for all of our people. This electrification project is a symbol of our determination to attain that objective. But it is only one symbol; it is one hill out of ten thousand which must be captured. You and I will never be satisfied until all our economic inequalities are corrected, until every one of us, North, East, West and South has the opportunity so to live, that his education, his job and his home will be secure.

In many countries democracy is under attack by those who charge that democracy fails to provide its people with the needs of modern civilization. I do not, you do not, subscribe to that charge. You and I, we, the people of this State and the people of all the states, believe that democracy today is succeeding, but that an absolute necessity for its future success is the fighting spirit of the American people — their insistence that we go forward and not back.

(See Item 88 and note, this volume, for a summary of the Report on Economic Conditions of the South.)

101 ⟨ "In These Past Six Years, the South Has Made Greater Economic and Social Progress up the Scale than at Any Other Period in Her Long History." Address at University of Georgia, Athens, Georgia. August 11, 1938

Governor Rivers, Chancellor Sanford, President Caldwell, and you, the Members of the Faculty and friends of the University of Georgia:

IT IS with particular pride in and increased devotion to this State, that I find myself about to become an alumnus of the University of Georgia. During many years I have had important contacts with your Board of Regents, with your Faculty and with many of your graduates; and I can therefore appreciate the splendid service which you are rendering to the cause of education not only in the State of Georgia but throughout the Nation.

Many years have gone by since I first came to Warm Springs and got to know and to love the State and its people. For years before that, I had heard much of Georgia from the lips of that old friend of mine, George Foster Peabody, who, reversing my process, was born in Georgia and became a citizen of the State of New York. Wherever he lived, wherever he went, there was one thing about Mr. Peabody that stood out, and that was his love for humanity. I am proud today to be receiving a degree that was put through by Mr. Peabody some time before his unfortunate death. I wonder if you, who live here in the State all the time, can realize as well as I, who have been coming here once or twice a year, the amazing progress that has been made here in a short decade and a half—and especially in the past five years. If you see a person intimately morning, noon and night, you do not note the changes of growth or of health of that friend as readily as if you see him only at intervals; and that is why I feel that I can speak of Georgia with true perspective.

In my earlier years here I saw a South in the larger sense forgotten, forgotten in the midst of an unhealthy national speculation—a boom era which thought in terms of paper profits instead of human lives. And for those days what has the South to show today? A few great fortunes perhaps, but most of the profits went north.

Then came the tragic years of the depression: closed banks in almost every community, ruinous crop prices, idle mills, no money for schools or roads—a picture of despair—I knew Georgia of those days, too.

Yet, through all those years the South was building a new school of thought—a group principally recruited from younger men and women who understood that the economy of the South was vitally and inexorably linked with that of the Nation, and that the national good was equally dependent on the improvement of the welfare of the South. They began asking searching questions: Why is our pay, in other words, our earning capacity so low? Why are our roads so bad? Why are our sanitation and our medical care so neglected? Why are our teachers so inadequately paid? Why are our local school buildings and equipment so antiquated?

I do not mince words because, first of all, I have a right, a nation-wide right, a State right and withal a sympathetic and understanding right, to speak them, and, secondly, because you as well as I know them to be true.

It may not be politic but it is good American idealism to recognize, to state boldly that in 1932, six short years ago, the conditions of human life in Georgia and in other states of the lower South were as a whole at the bottom of the national scale. At the same time let us rejoice and take pride in the undoubted fact that in these past six years the South has made greater economic and social progress up the scale than at any other period in her long history. It is my objective and yours to maintain that march and to accelerate its pace.

On the side of education a long experience teaches us that the improvement of educational facilities is inevitably bound up with economic conditions. Years ago, when I first came to Georgia, I was told by a distinguished citizen of the State that public school education was well provided for because there was a law — or perhaps it was in the State Constitution itself — providing that every child should have a full school year — and that attendance for each school year through all the years of grade school and into the high schools was compulsory. But I soon discovered — as I might have known that I should — that school after school in the rural districts of the State — and most of the districts are rural districts — was open only four months or five months a year — or was too small to hold all the children that wanted to go to it, or could not employ enough teachers — or that children, whose parents wanted them to work instead of going to school, could stay away from school with complete immunity. Apparently a law or a clause in the Constitution was not enough. What is law without enforcement? Apparently, the Biblical method, the divine method "Let there be light — and there was light" did not work as mere man's dictum.

Then I began to analyze: Was it due to lack of interest? No, not at all. It was due to lack of money. Every man and woman I talked with deplored the wretched school conditions, wanted better schools, better trained and better paid teachers, wanted more teachers, wanted a full school year. But — the answer was always the same — we cannot get more money from taxes.

And why not? The answer again is simple: The taxable values were not there. The tax rates were not too low, but the actual going values of property were so meagre, that when taxes on those values were collected the sum received could not pay for adequate teachers or proper equipment. Public education was therefore dependent on public wealth. Public wealth was too low to support good schools.

That analysis of mine — made even before I was elected Governor of New York — led my mind to many other questions. Why were land values and therefore taxable values in Georgia so low? With that question came a study of land use, of worn-out land, of cheaper fertilizer, of forestation, of erosion, of crop diversification, of crop prices, of marketing, and of freight rates. And all of these things bore directly on the problem of better schools.

Why were people getting such low pay for a day's work? That led to a study of purchasing power, of decent wages, of the cost of living, of taxable income, of sound banking, of small merchants. And these things, too, bore directly on the problem of better schools.

In other words, social conditions — schools and hospitals, medical care, and better sanitation, and those other matters that were dependent in a similar way, clothing and housing and food, all those other things that we call by the general name of better social conditions — were intimately dependent on economic conditions: higher wages, higher farm income and more profits for small businessmen.

So you will see that my thoughts for the South are no new thing. Long before I had any idea of reentering public life I was planning for better life for the people of Georgia. In these later years I have had some opportunity to practice what I have long preached.

Obviously the Federal Government cannot carry the load

alone. In education, for example, the Government in Washington has greatly assisted by using the labor of people who really need help to build schoolhouses, to give student aid, and to pay at least a part of the salaries to many teachers. And Washington will help in the days to come, I am confident, by giving some grants in aid to those communities which need them the most. But let us remember well that the Government in Washington should not and cannot rightly subsidize public education throughout the United States. That must remain wholly free, wholly independent. Education should be run by the states and their subdivisions and not by the Federal Government.

Therefore, in the long run, the best way for your national government to assist state and local educational objectives is to tackle the national aspects of economic problems, to eliminate discriminations between one part of the country and another, to raise purchasing power and thereby create wealth in those sections where it is far too low, to save the waste and the erosion of our natural resources, to encourage each section to become financially independent, to take the lead in establishing social security, and at the same time to explain to the people in every part that constant progressive action is better than following the lead of either those who want to slow up or those who promise they will hand you the moon on a silver platter a week after they are elected.

At heart Georgia shows devotion to the principles of democracy. Georgia, like other states, has occasional lapses; but it really does not believe either in demagoguery or feudalism, even though they are dressed up in democratic clothes. . . .

To be a part of you is a great honor and a great privilege. You of the University are greatly responsible for the manner of meeting the problems of the present. You will be greatly responsible for the future. Well are you doing your part. From today onward I share proudly, more fully, in that part.

(For a discussion of the problems of the South, see also Items 88 and 100, this volume.)

102 ❨ Informal, Extemporaneous Remarks at Greenville, South Carolina. August 11, 1938

Governor Johnston, my friends of Greenville:

IT IS a long way around to come from Washington to South Carolina by way of the Pacific, the Galapagos Islands, the Equator, the Panama Canal and Pensacola, Florida. But I got here.

As you people probably know, I have made two speeches today and there was not time nor opportunity to prepare a third speech. Some of you may have heard what I said down in Georgia, at Barnesville. Those of you who did not hear me, I hope will read in the newspapers what I said of some of the economic and social problems of the South and of the necessity of meeting those problems by a consolidation of the interests of all the southern states, and then by consolidating those interests with the interests of the whole Nation.

That, my friends, cannot be done without legislation. As President, I cannot do it alone. The Congress of the United States must pass the laws.

That is why, in any selection of candidates for members of the Senate or members of the House of Representatives — if you believe in the principles for which we are striving: a wider distribution of national income, better conservation of our natural resources, establishment of a floor under wages and the bringing of a larger buying power to the farmers of the Nation — then I hope you will send representatives to the national legislature who will work toward those ends.

We need not just teamwork but more teamwork in the National Capital — and I believe we are going to get it.

Before I stop — and I believe the train is pulling out in a minute or two — I want to suggest two things to you.

The first is that a long time ago I promised Governor Johnston that I would come down some time this year to visit the capital of the State of South Carolina. I have never been there but I am coming.

The other thing is that I don't believe any family or man can live on fifty cents a day.

103 ⦅ "A Social Security Program Must Include All Those Who Need Its Protection." Radio Address on the Third Anniversary of the Social Security Act. White House, Washington, D. C. August 15, 1938

You, my friends, in every walk of life and in every part of the Nation, who are active believers in Social Security:

THE SOCIAL SECURITY ACT is three years old today. This is a good vantage point from which to take a long look backward to its beginnings, to cast an appraising eye over what it has accomplished so far, and to survey its possibilities of future growth.

Five years ago the term "social security" was new to American ears. Today it has significance for more than forty million men and women workers whose applications for old-age insurance accounts have been received; this system is designed to assure them an income for life after old age retires them from their jobs.

It has significance for more than twenty-seven and a half million men and women wage earners who have earned credits under State unemployment insurance laws which provide half wages to help bridge the gap between jobs.

It has significance for the needy men, women and children receiving assistance and for their families — at least two million three hundred thousand all told; with this cash assistance one million seven hundred thousand old folks are spending their last years in surroundings they know and with people they love; more than six hundred thousand dependent children are being taken care of by their own families; and about forty thousand blind people are assured of peace and security among familiar voices.

It has significance for the families and communities to whom expanded public health and child welfare services have brought added protection. And it has significance for all of us who, as citizens, have at heart the security and the well-being of this great democracy.

These accomplishments of three years are impressive, yet we should not be unduly proud of them. Our Government in fulfilling an obvious obligation to the citizens of the country has been doing so only because the citizens require action from their Representatives. If the people, during these years, had chosen a reactionary Administration or a "do nothing" Congress, Social Security would still be in the conversational stage — a beautiful dream which might come true in the dim distant future.

But the underlying desire for personal and family security was nothing new. In the early days of colonization and through the long years following, the worker, the farmer, the merchant, the man of property, the preacher and the idealist came here to build, each for himself, a stronghold for the things he loved. The stronghold was his home; the things he loved and wished to protect were his family, his material and spiritual possessions.

His security, then as now, was bound to that of his friends and his neighbors.

But as the Nation has developed, as invention, industry and commerce have grown more complex, the hazards of life have become more complex. Among an increasing host of fellow citizens, among the often intangible forces of giant industry, man has discovered that his individual strength and wits were no longer enough. This was true not only of the worker at shop bench or ledger; it was true also of the merchant or manufacturer who employed him. Where heretofore men had turned to neighbors for help and advice, they now turned to Government.

Now this is interesting to consider. The first to turn to Government, the first to receive protection from Government, were not the poor and the lowly — those who had no resources other than their daily earnings — but the rich and the strong. Beginning in the nineteenth century, the United States passed protective laws designed, in the main, to give security to property owners, to industrialists, to merchants and to bankers. True, the little man often profited by this type of legislation; but that was a by-product rather than a motive.

Taking a generous view of the situation, I think it was not that Government deliberately ignored the working man but that the working man was not sufficiently articulate to make his needs and his problems known. The powerful in industry and commerce had powerful voices, both individually and as a group. And whenever they saw their possessions threatened, they raised their voices in appeals for government protection.

It was not until workers became more articulate through organization that protective labor legislation was passed. While such laws raised the standards of life, they still gave no assurance of economic security. Strength or skill of arm or brain did not guarantee a man a job; it did not guarantee him a roof; it did not guarantee him the ability to provide for those dependent upon him or to take care of himself when he was too old to work.

Long before the economic blight of the depression descended on the nation, millions of our people were living in wastelands of want and fear. Men and women too old and infirm to work either depended on those who had but little to share, or spent their remaining years within the walls of a poorhouse. Fatherless children early learned the meaning of being a burden to relatives or to the community. Men and women, still strong, still young, but discarded as gainful workers, were drained of self-confidence and self-respect.

The millions of today want, and have a right to, the same security their forefathers sought — the assurance that with health and the willingness to work they will find a place for themselves in the social and economic system of the time.

Because it has become increasingly difficult for individuals to build their own security single-handed, Government must now step in and help them lay the foundation stones, just as Government in the past has helped lay the foundation of business and industry. We must face the fact that in this country we have a rich man's security and a poor man's security and that the Government owes equal obligations to both. National security is not a half and half matter; it is all or none.

The Social Security Act offers to all our citizens a workable and working method of meeting urgent present needs and of forestalling future needs. It utilizes the familiar machinery of our Federal-State government to promote the common welfare and the economic stability of the nation.

The Act does not offer anyone, either individually or collectively, an easy life — nor was it ever intended so to do. None of the sums of money paid out to individuals in assistance or insurance will spell anything approaching abundance. But they will furnish that minimum necessary to keep a foothold; and that is the kind of protection Americans want.

What we are doing is good. But it is not good enough. To be truly national, a social security program must include all those who need its protection. Today many of our citizens are still excluded from old-age insurance and unemployment compensation because of the nature of their employment. This must be set aright; and it will be.

Some time ago I directed the Social Security Board to give attention to the development of a plan for liberalizing and extending the old-age insurance system to provide benefits for wives, widows and orphans. More recently, a National Health Conference was held at my suggestion to consider ways and means of extending to the people of this country more adequate health and medical services and also to afford the people of this country some protection against the economic losses arising out of ill health.

I am hopeful that on the basis of studies and investigations now under way, the Congress will improve and extend the law.

I am also confident that each year will bring further development in Federal and State social security legislation — and that is as it should be. One word of warning, however. In our efforts to provide security for all of the American people, let us not allow ourselves to be misled by those who advocate short cuts to Utopia or fantastic financial schemes.

We have come a long way. But we still have a long way to go. There is still today a frontier that remains unconquered — an America unreclaimed. This is the great, the nation-wide frontier of insecurity, of human want and fear. This is the frontier — the America — we have set ourselves to reclaim.

This Third Anniversary would not be complete if I did not express the gratitude of the Nation to those splendid citizens who so greatly helped me in making social security legislation possible and to those patriotic men and women, both employers and employees, who in their daily activities are today making social security work.

First of all, to the first woman who has ever sat in the Cabinet of the United States — Miss Frances Perkins — then and now the Secretary of Labor. Then to the unselfish Commission of men and women who, in 1934, devoted themselves to the almost superhuman task of studying all manner of American problems, of examining legislation already attempted in other nations, and of coordinating the whole into practical recommendations for legislative action.

Finally, I think publicly, as I have so often thanked them privately, four men who have had long and distinguished careers in the public service — Congressman David J. Lewis of Maryland, who is known as one of the American pioneers in the cause of Social Security; Senator Robert F. Wagner of New York, who also was long its advocate; Senator Harrison of Mississippi and Congressman Doughton of North Carolina, who carried the bill successfully through the Senate and the House of Representatives. They deserve and have the gratitude of all of us for this service to mankind!

NOTE: The idea of Social Security, which some reactionaries used to label as alien to the American tradition, has become so firmly rooted here in America that business, labor, finance, and all political parties now accept it as a permanent system. During the years since the passage of the original Social Security Act in 1935, we have been constantly studying the system in operation. As the result of many investigations and surveys, we have been able to strengthen the original act and to extend it to cover additional activities (see Item 163, 1937 volume; Item 56, this volume; Items 11 and 109, 1939 volume, and accompanying notes).

When I signed the Social Security Act, I stated what I conceived to be the basic purposes of the legislation (see Item 107 and note, 1935 volume, for a more detailed analysis of how the various phases of the Act actually operate). The program attempts to deal with many of the factors which make for economic insecurity among our people.

The first threat against security — that of spending one's aged years in the poor house is dispelled in two ways. In the first place, an old-age insurance system is established, enabling retirement at sixty-five on a pension. The amount of the pension depends upon wages received and taxes paid by both employers and employees. At present (1941), payrolls and wages are taxed 2 per cent in order to raise the funds to pay the statutory benefits to workers and their wives who are over sixty-five. Survivors' benefits are now also available for aged widows or aged dependent parents, young widows with dependent children, and unmarried dependent orphans under eighteen.

In the second place, an old-age assistance program has been established, independent of the old-age insurance system. The assistance is in the form of federal grants-in-aid to the states to provide funds for the pensioning and relief of old people. When the federal government has approved the assistance plan of a particular state, it contributes with the states on a 50-50 basis up to a total of $40 per month per individual, with a little extra for administrative purposes.

The other great threat to security is the spectre of unemployment. Unemployment insurance has been set up largely on a state-administered basis in cooperation with the federal government. The federal payroll tax for this purpose is merely nominal, employers being freed from 90 per cent of this tax if they contribute an equal amount to state unemployment insurance plans approved by the Social Security Board.

The United States Employment Service also maintains employment offices in the states to facilitate ready placement of job applicants where needed.

In addition to these forms of assistance, federal grants are made by the Social Security Board in varying amounts to assist the states in aiding dependent children, and needy blind persons. Under the Social Security Act, the Children's Bureau of the Department of Labor administers grants to states for maternal and child welfare and the aid of crippled children; the United States Public Health Service administers grants to states to develop state health programs; and the Office of Education administers grants to states for vocational rehabilitation.

With the exception of the Children's Bureau, all the above offices and bureaus have been placed within the Federal Security Agency since the adoption of Reorganization Plan No. I (see Item 66, 1939 volume). From the standpoint of effective coordination of the social security program, this is of great importance inasmuch as closer working relationships have been established among the Social Security Board, the United States Public Health Service, the Office of Education, the National Youth Administration, and the Civilian Conservation Corps.

Administratively, the Social Security Board is composed of three members, appointed by the President by and with the consent of the Senate. Not more than two of the members may be of one political party; and the President designates the chairman. Administrative and executive action is in the hands of the executive director, who also supervises and coordinates the work of the various bureaus. The actuary of the Board performs the important function of planning the various phases of the program on a long-range basis to determine the adequacy of funds available, benefits which can be paid, etc.

There are three operating bureaus and three service bureaus within the Social Security Board.

The operating bureaus are:

1. The Bureau of Old-Age and Survivors' Insurance, which administers the monthly benefits which are paid to aged workers, their wives, or survivors and dependent children, under the old-age insurance scheme.

2. The Bureau of Employment Security, which administers the unemployment compensation features of the Social Security Act; analyzes and certifies the adequacy of state unemployment compensation laws; furnishes technical aid to the states in drafting their legislation; assists the states in developing their administrative policies and specifications; supervises the functions of the former United States Employment Service; aids farmers, veterans and District of Columbia residents to obtain employment; and assists public employment offices throughout the country.

3. The Bureau of Public Assistance, which supervises federal grants for old-age assistance, aid to dependent children, and aid to the needy blind. It advises and assists the states in initiating or amending

state public assistance laws, consults with the states on technical problems, acts as a clearing house for information gathered from the various states, and analyzes and develops standards and procedures.

The service bureaus within the Social Security Board consist of the Bureau of Research and Statistics, the Bureau of Accounts and Audits, and the Informational Service. These three service bureaus work in close conjunction with the operating bureaus.

The Bureau of Research and Statistics investigates such problems as the factors causing insecurity, the adequacy of existing legislation, and the problems caused by the application of the program to various population groups. It plans and conducts the statistical service, and advises the states on the statistical reports required by the Board. The Bureau publishes a record of the volume and trend of general relief in the United States, in collaboration with other government and private agencies.

The Bureau of Accounts and Audits maintains the accounting and auditing records of the Board. It has charge of an administrative audit and also a field audit of states receiving federal grants. It examines financial insufficiency of state plans submitted, and assists the states in improving their accounting procedures. It also advises the Board on governmental fiscal programs.

The Informational Service keeps the public posted, and answers inquiries about rights, benefits and responsibilities under the Act. It also cooperates with the states in planning and conducting their informational programs.

In the fiscal year ending June 30, 1940, individuals participating in the Social Security Act and related state legislation received a total of $1,085,800,000 in comparison with $897,000,000 for the preceding year. The amount for 1939-40 was distributed as follows:

Public assistance......... $587,700,000
Unemployment benefits.... 482,500,000
Old-age and Survivors insur-
ance.................. 17,600,000

The above amounts do not include the funds allotted to the states to cover administrative expenses, nor do they include expenditures by other federal agencies for public health, welfare and vocational rehabilitation services under the Social Security Act.

Since the United States Employment Service has been consolidated into the Social Security Board, the employment security program of the Board has been expanded and strengthened. The state employment offices maintained by federal funds filled more than 3,500,000 jobs during the past year, and were instrumental in making 1,100,000 supplementary placements. By the end of the fiscal year 1940, there were close to 1,500 employment offices and more than 3,000 itinerant service facilities provided throughout the country. Having the information drawn from state unemployment compensation systems at its disposal, the Board is now in a strategic position to help to bring workers and jobs together.

By June, 1940, approximately 28 million workers had wage credits under state unemployment compensation laws. At the same date, more than 40 million had received wages counting toward old age benefits. During the fiscal year, benefits were advanced to more than 5 million different persons unemployed in that period, totaling nearly $500,000,000, and the weekly average of workers receiving such benefits exceeded 873,000. In addition, under the Railroad Unemployment Insurance Act, administered by the Railroad Retirement Board, 161,000 workers received benefits totaling $14,800,000.

In the brief period since January 1, 1940 that the old-age and survivors' insurance system has been in operation, nearly 109,000 persons have received monthly benefits. When this program reaches its peak level, it will involve a larger number of persons and a larger amount of funds than any phase of the social security scheme. Although the amount already made available is small in dollars, it has been invaluable in restoring faith in the future.

The amendments to the Social Security Act passed in 1939 stimulated the states to participate actively in the public assistance plans under the Act. About 2,200,000 needy aged persons, 55,000 blind persons, and 1 million children in over 400,000 families were assisted under the terms of the Act during the fiscal year 1939-1940. It is interesting to note that whereas during the fiscal year 1938-1939 public assistance to the needy aged, blind and children constituted 14.4 per cent of the aggregate expenditures for public aid, in the year ending June 30, 1940, similar assistance represented 18.3 per cent of the aggregate expenditures of $3,300,-000,000 by the federal government for public aid.

The Social Security Board and the machinery set up under the program have played an important role in meeting the requirements of national defense. In April, 1940, an inventory was made of the active file of those who had registered at public employment offices. With the work histories of 5 million job-seekers available, it was easier to determine what the existing labor reserves were and where they existed.

In June, 1940, the Social Security Board assembled the Federal Advisory Council for Employment Security to consider defense problems. This body, consisting of representatives of employers, employees and the public, was originally appointed to advise the Board on questions arising in connection with the public employment offices. After a two-day conference, the Advisory Council presented an eight-point program which was accepted on June 28, 1940, by the Advisory Commission to the Council of National Defense.

This plan urged employers and employees to communicate their immediate and prospective employment requirements promptly to the local public employment office, and to depend upon this machinery to fulfill their needs. The employment offices were directed to recatalog the skills available, and take steps to institute training programs where there was a shortage. It was further recommended that the decentralized features of this program be preserved, that preference be accorded to citizens, and that in the event of universal registration for defense an inventory of employment qualifications be made.

Under the Second Deficiency Appropriation Act, approved June 27, 1940, $2,000,000 was appropriated to assist and supervise state employment services in selecting and placing workers in national defense industries. Funds were also provided for the Office of Education to cooperate with the Social Security Board in providing vocational training for workers selected from public employment registers.

Since the speeding up of the defense program, there has been very close cooperation with the National Defense Advisory Commission and the Office of Production Management, the War and Navy Departments, the Selective Service System, and Civil Service Commission.

The public employment offices, as of October 31, 1940, have registered a total of 192,129 workers equipped with skill or experience in about 500 different industries, including such essential defense activities as aircraft, machine-shop work and machine-tool manufacturing, foundry work, construction, shipbuilding, metal working, electrical equipment, radio, telephone and telegraph.

The employment offices have aided measurably in furthering the defense program through placing men in these industries. There is special cooperation with the Civil Service Commission in the maintenance of an adequate supply of men for placement in arsenals and navy yards. In order to maintain adequate labor reserves and to guide the transfer of workers from point to point, thirteen regional clearance offices have been established.

The Board has aided the War Department in analyzing army jobs, and has helped local selective service boards in assembling information to be used for classification or deferment of workers. As the result of visits to 20,000 defense plants, the Board has compiled estimates of defense labor requirements to be supplied to all of the defense agencies. These estimates are very significant summaries of employment conditions, changes in labor demand and supply, and trends in hiring practices.

In my message to the Congress

on September 14, 1940, I called attention to the need for additional legislation to protect the social insurance of those called into military service (see Item 96, 1940 volume). The Board has participated actively in developing plans for taking care of those who joined the armed forces.

There is, of course, still room for improvement in our social security system. I have repeatedly recommended that it be extended to cover many of the occupations now specifically exempted under the Act (see Item 163, 1937 volume; Item 56, this volume; Items 11 and 109, 1939 volume). Also, the health provisions of the Social Security Act are now inadequate to cover the costs of medical care and provide for temporary or permanent disability. There are other changes which have been suggested from time to time by the Board, the most pressing of which concerns the plight of those states financially incapable of matching federal grants for public assistance. In 1939, the Board recommended that the grants be placed upon a different basis in order to take care of the varying economic capacities of the states; but the Congress failed to pass this proposal.

Yet the program has gone a long way toward eliminating one of the most fearsome evils of our economic system — insecurity. It has provided new life and hope for millions of our citizens, and has bolstered the mechanisms of our economy to help it withstand the dislocations of war as well as the shock of great economic cycles of disaster in peace-time.

104 ❨ The Four Hundred and Seventy-sixth Press Conference (Excerpts). August 16, 1938

(A statement of policy on Democratic Party primaries — Plans for trip.)

Q. Mr. President, have you anything to say about the forthcoming primaries in New York where Congressman O'Connor is running against Jim Fay?

THE PRESIDENT: Oh, I guess so. This is not collusive on the part of Fred and myself. (*Laughter*) I guessed that somebody —

MR. STORM: As a matter of fact, Mr. President, I had the dope last week down at Warm Springs that there was some movement on foot for you to sound off against Mr. O'Connor but I held it up too late and I was scooped in the Sunday morning papers.

THE PRESIDENT: I knew that somebody would ask the question so I have a perfectly good statement here. It is long. I shall read it to you and I shall give it to Steve and he will give you copies so you won't have to take it down.

Q. Will you read it slowly, sir?

THE PRESIDENT: Yes. It is entitled, "Why the President 'Interferes.'" (*Laughter*)

And the first sentence is in quotes — you will see why afterwards. The first sentence is this: (*reading*) "The President of the United States ought not to interfere in party primaries."

And then the second sentence is not in quotes. (*Reading*)

That statement, in one form or another, is appearing these days throughout the Tory Press.

The idea is that the President should be aloof from such sordid considerations as who wins the primaries in his own party. But actually these primaries will determine to a large extent the makeup of the next Congress. And that, in turn, will determine whether or not the President can keep his campaign promises to the people.

Campaign promises are supposed to be the responsibility of the whole party. At least that's the theory. But in practice the head of the party alone is held responsible for them.

In American politics any one can attach himself to a political party whether he believes in its program or not.

That is a hot one.

We hear the phrase "read out of the party," but it doesn't mean anything. No one is read out of the Democratic or the Republican Party. There are many prominent Democrats today who are heart and soul against everything the Democratic Party has stood for since 1932. And those men are still in the party.

What's worse, not one of them was candid enough to oppose the renomination of Franklin D. Roosevelt in 1936, although after four years there was no doubt whatever as to the program Franklin D. Roosevelt was pursuing.

The same hidden opposition, after giving the New Deal lip-service in 1936, turned around and knifed it in Congress in 1937 and 1938.

Now that election time has come around again, the hidden opposition hides the ax behind its back and prepares to give the President lip-service once more.

In those circumstances there is nothing for the President to do — as the responsible head of the New Deal — but to publicly repudiate those who have betrayed the New Deal in the past and will again.

If men like Senator Tydings of Maryland said frankly: "I no longer believe in the platform of the Democratic Party as expressed in the New Deal; I'm running for re-election as a member of the Republican opposition to the New Deal," then there would be no reason and no excuse for President Roosevelt to intervene against them.

The issue would be clear. The voter could take his choice between the New Deal and Tydings' record of consistent opposition to it. But Tydings tells the voters he supports the "bone and sinew" of the New Deal. He wants to run with the Roosevelt prestige and the money of his conservative Republican friends both on his side.

In that case it becomes the President's right and duty to tell the people what he thinks of Millard Tydings.

That's why we welcome the report that Roosevelt help is going to be given to Tydings' opponent, Representative David J. Lewis, and to James H. Fay, candidate for the nomination in the Sixteenth Congressional District of New York.

Fay is running against Representative John J. O'Connor, one of the most effective obstructionists in the lower house. Week in and week out O'Connor labors to tear down New Deal strength, pickle New Deal legislation.

Why shouldn't the responsible head of the New Deal tell the people just that?

Q. That is very mild. (*Laughter*)

Q. It reads as though it was an editorial.

THE PRESIDENT: Yes, it was an editorial, but it is my statement now.

Q. How do we use that? As an answer to the question?

THE PRESIDENT: Yes.

Q. Is it to be in quotes, then?

Q. Direct quotes?

THE PRESIDENT: Yes.

Q. Here is a rather torrid question: Referring to the statement regarding support for the Democratic platform, among the items in that class do you include your Court plan?

THE PRESIDENT: The Court plan was not in the platform, but the Court plan is no longer an issue because, in effect, we obtained ninety-eight per cent of all the objectives intended by the Court plan. I made that clear on many occasions.

Q. In other words, any disfavor you may hold to any member of the House or Senate is not based on the Court plan?

THE PRESIDENT: No. That is a perfectly fair statement. However, it won't prevent the continued use of the assertion, will it?

Q. I hate to bother you with so much state politics, but out in Kansas it looks like a pretty bitter fight between Clyde Reed and Senator McGill. Mr. Reed supported you in 1936 and did not support Governor Landon. I wondered if you were going out that way any time in the fall?

THE PRESIDENT: Frankly, I have not heard anything about the Kansas situation.

Q. Do you contemplate going into Wisconsin and Minnesota?

THE PRESIDENT: Really, it is honestly true that I have no plans and no dates after this coming trip. I suppose I have had invitations to go into forty-eight states, including Vermont and Maine. But I have no plans whatsoever.

Q. Who asked you to go into Maine?

THE PRESIDENT: If you must know, I will tell you, my mother. (*Laughter*) But she is in Campobello.

105 ❧ "We in the Americas are No Longer a Far Away Continent, to Which the Eddies of Controversies Beyond the Seas Could Bring No Interest or No Harm." Address at Queen's University, Kingston, Ontario, Canada. August 18, 1938

Mr. Chancellor, Mr. Principal, Lieutenant Governor,
Mr. Prime Minister, my new found Associates of
Queens University:

To THE pleasure of being once more on Canadian soil where I have passed so many happy hours of my life, there is added today a very warm sense of gratitude for being admitted to the fellowship of this ancient and famous University. I am glad to join the brotherhood which Queen's has contributed and is contributing not only to the spiritual leadership for which the college was established, but also to the social and public leadership in the civilized life of Canada.

An American President is precluded by our Constitution from accepting any title from a foreign Prince, potentate or power. Queen's University is not a Prince or a potentate but, assuredly, it is a power. Yet I can say, without constitutional reserve, that the acceptance of the title which you confer on me today would raise no qualms in the august breast of our own Supreme Court.

Civilization, after all, is not national — it is international — even though that observation, trite as it is to most of us, seems to be challenged in some parts of the world today. Ideas are not limited by territorial borders; they are the common inheritance of all free people. Thought is not anchored in any land; and the profit of education redounds to the equal benefit of the whole world. That is one form of free trade to which the leaders of every opposing political party can subscribe.

In a large sense we in the Americas stand charged today with the maintaining of that tradition. When, speaking a little over a year ago in a similar vein in the Republic of Brazil, I included the Dominion of Canada in the fellowship of the Americas, our South American neighbors gave hearty acclaim. We in all the Americas know the sorrow and the wreckage which may follow if the ability of men to understand each other is rooted out from among the nations.

Many of us here today know from experience that of all the devastations of war none is more tragic than the destruction which it brings to the processes of men's minds. Truth is denied because emotion pushes it aside. Forbearance is succeeded by bitterness. In that atmosphere human thought cannot advance.

It is impossible not to remember that for years when Canadians and Americans have met they have lightheartedly saluted as North American friends with little thought of dangers from overseas. Yet we are awake to the knowledge that the casual assumption of our greetings in earlier times, today must become a matter for serious thought.

A few days ago a whisper, fortunately untrue, raced 'round the world that armies standing over against each other in unhappy array were about to be set in motion. In a few short hours the effect of that whisper had been registered in Montreal and New York, in Ottawa and in Washington, in Toronto and in Chicago, in Vancouver and in San Francisco. Your business men and ours felt it alike; your farmers and ours heard it alike; your young men and ours wondered what effect this might have on their lives.

We in the Americas are no longer a far away continent, to which the eddies of controversies beyond the seas could bring no interest or no harm. Instead, we in the Americas have become a consideration to every propaganda office and to every general staff beyond the seas. The vast amount of our resources, the vigor of our commerce and the strength of our men have made us vital factors in world peace whether we choose it or not.

Happily, you and we, in friendship and in entire understanding, can look clear-eyed at these possibilities, resolving to leave no pathway unexplored, no technique undeveloped which may, if our hopes are realized, contribute to the peace of the world. Even if those hopes are disappointed, we can assure each other that this hemisphere at least shall remain a strong citadel wherein civilization can flourish unimpaired.

The Dominion of Canada is part of the sisterhood of the British Empire. I give to you assurance that the people of the United States will not stand idly by if domination of Canadian soil is threatened by any other Empire.

We as good neighbors are true friends because we maintain our own rights with frankness, because we refuse to accept the twists of secret diplomacy, because we settle our disputes by consultation and because we discuss our common problems in the spirit of the common good. We seek to be scrupulously fair and helpful, not only in our relations with each other, but each of us at home in our relations with our own people.

But there is one process which we certainly cannot change and probably ought not to change. This is the feeling which ordinary men and women have about events which they can understand. We cannot prevent our people on either side of the border from having an opinion in regard to wanton brutality, in regard to undemocratic regimentation, in regard to misery inflicted on helpless peoples, or in regard to violations of accepted individual rights. All that any government, constituted as is yours and mine, can possibly undertake is to help make sure that the facts are known and fairly stated. No country where thought is free can prevent every fireside and home within its borders from considering the evidence for itself and rendering its own verdict; and the sum total of these conclusions of educated men and women will, in the long run, rightly become the national verdict.

That is what we mean when we say that public opinion ultimately governs policy. It is right and just that this should be the case.

Many of our ancestors, your ancestors and mine, and, by the

way, I have loyalist blood in my veins too, came to Canada and the United States because they wished to break away from systems which forbade them to think freely, and their descendants have insisted on the right to know the truth — to argue their problems to a majority decision, and, if they remained unconvinced, to disagree in peace. As a tribute to our likeness in that respect, I note that the Bill of Rights in your country and in mine is substantially the same.

Mr. Chancellor, you of Canada who respect the educational tradition of our democratic continent will ever maintain good neighborship in ideas as we in the public service hope and propose to maintain it in the field of government and of foreign relations. My good friend, the Governor General of Canada, in receiving an honorary degree in June at that University at Cambridge, Massachusetts, to which Mackenzie King and I both belong, suggested that we cultivate three qualities to keep our foothold in the shifting sands of the present — humility, humanity and humor. I have been thinking in terms of a bridge which is to be dedicated this afternoon and so I could not help coming to the conclusion that all of these three qualities imbedded in education, build new spans to reestablish free intercourse throughout the world and bring forth an order in which free nations can live in peace.

106 ❡ "The Bridge Which We Here Dedicate Is a Tangible Proof That Administration by Two Neighbors of a Job to be Done in Common Offers No Difficulty." Address at Dedication of International Bridge, Clayton, New York. August 18, 1938

My fellow bridge builder, Mr. Mackenzie King, and you who are here today representing millions of other bridge builders on both sides of the international line:

IT HAS always seemed to me that the best symbol of common sense was a bridge. Common sense is sometimes slow in getting into action, and perhaps that is why we took so long to build this one.

It is a particular pleasure to me to meet you here, where a boundary is a gateway and not a wall. Between these islands an international gap, never wide, has been spanned, as gaps usually are, by the exercise of ability, guided by cooperative common sense. I hope that all my countrymen will use it freely. I know that they will find, as I have done today and on many other occasions, a happy welcome on the Canadian shore, and forthright fellowship with neighbors who are also friends.

The St. Lawrence River is more than a cartographic line between our two countries. God so formed North America that the waters of an inland empire drain into the Great Lakes Basin. The rain that falls in this vast area finds outlet through this single natural funnel, close to which we now stand.

Events of history have made that river a boundary, and as a result the flow of these waters can be used only by joint agreement between our two governments. Between us, therefore, we stand as trustees for two countries of one of the richest natural assets provided anywhere in the world. The water that runs underneath this bridge spells unlimited power; permits access to raw materials both from this continent and from beyond the seas, and enhances commerce and production.

When a resource of this kind is placed at our very doors, I think the plain people of both countries agree that it is ordinary common sense to make use of it. Yet up to now the liquid wealth, which flowing water is, has run in large part unused to the sea. I really think that this situation suggests that we can agree upon some better arrangement than merely letting this water contribute a microscopic fraction to the level of the North Atlantic Ocean. The bridge which we here dedicate is a tangible proof that administration by two neighbors of a job to be done in common offers no difficulty. Obviously the same process applied on the larger scale to the resource of full sea-going navigation and of complete power development offered by the St. Lawrence River can build and maintain the necessary facilities to employ its magnificent possibilities.

I suppose it is true, as it has been true of all natural resources, that a good many people would like to have the job—and the profits—of developing it for themselves. In this case, however, the river happens to be placed in the hands of our two governments, and the responsibility for getting the results lies plainly at our doors.

At various times both the people of Canada and the people of the United States have dreamed of the St. Lawrence and Great Lakes development. They have translated those ideas into plans which with modern engineering skill can easily be carried out. While there has been no difference between us as to the object itself, history compels me to say that we have not been able to arrange matters so that both peoples have had the same idea at the same time. I offer a suggestion. How would it do for a change, if, instead of each of us having the idea at alternate intervals, we should get the idea simultaneously? And I am very much inclined to believe that we are rapidly approaching that happy and desirable event.

There are many prophets of evil. There always have been before anything was done. I am very clear that prophets of trouble are wrong when they express the fear that the St. Lawrence Waterway will handicap our railroad systems on both sides of the border. We know now that the effect of a waterway in most cases is not to take traffic away from railroad lines. Actually, it creates new possibilities, new business and new activity. Such a waterway generates more railroad traffic than it takes away.

There is today, a fourteen foot channel carrying traffic from the Great Lakes through the St. Lawrence River into the Atlantic Ocean. If this channel were improved and deepened to twenty-seven or thirty feet, every city in both nations on the Great Lakes and on the whole course of navigation from the sea to the Lakes would become an ocean port. The banks of the St. Lawrence Valley would become one of the great gateways of the world and would benefit accordingly. Here all that is needed is cooperative exercise of technical skill by joint use of the imagination and the vision which we know both our countries have. Can anyone doubt that, when this is done, the interests of both countries will be greatly advanced? Do we need to delay, do we need to deprive our peoples of the immediate employment and profit, or prevent our generation from reaping the harvest that awaits us?

Now let me make an unusual statement. I am sure that on neither side of the line will you misunderstand me. I consider that I have, myself, a particular interest in the St. Lawrence, dating back to my earliest days in the Legislature of the State of New York in 1911. I have a particular duty as President in connection with the development of the St. Lawrence, both for navigation and for power. The almost unparalleled opportunity which the river affords has not gone unnoticed by some of my friends on the American side of the border. A conception has been emerging in the United States which is not without a certain magnificence. This is no less than the conviction that if a private group could control the outlet of the Great Lakes Basin on both sides of the border, that group would have a monopoly in the development of a territory larger than many of the great empires in history.

If you were to search the records with which my Government is familiar, you would discover that literally every development of electric power, save only the Ontario-Hydro, is allied to, if not controlled by, a single American group, with, of course, the usual surrounding penumbra of allies, affiliates, subsidiaries and satellites. In earlier stages of development of natural resources on this continent, this was normal and usual. In recent decades we have come to realize the implications to the public — to the individual men and women, to business men, big and little, and even to government itself, resulting from the ownership by any group of the right to dispose of wealth which was granted to us collectively by nature herself.

The development of natural resources, and the proper handling of their fruits, is a major problem of government. Naturally, no solution would be acceptable to either nation which does not leave its government entirely master in its own house.

To put it bluntly, a group of American interests is here gradually putting itself into a position where, unless caution is exercised, they may in time be able to determine the economic and the social fate of a large area, both in Canada and the United States.

Now it is axiomatic in Canadian-American relations that both of us scrupulously respect the right of each of us to determine its own affairs. For that reason, when I know that the operation of uncontrolled American economic forces is slowly producing a result on the Canadian side of the border, which I know very well must eventually give American groups a great influence over Canadian development, I consider it the part of a good neighbor to discuss the question frankly with my Canadian neighbors. The least I can do is to call attention to the situation as I see it.

Our mutual friendship suggests this course in a matter of development as great and as crucial as that of the St. Lawrence River and the basin tributary to it. Fortunately among friendly nations today this is increasingly being done. Frank discussion among friends and neighbors is useful and essential. It is obvious today that some economic problems are international, if only because of the sheer weight which the solutions have on the lives of people outside, as well as inside any one country. To my mind, the development of St. Lawrence navigation and power is such a problem.

I look forward to the day when a Canadian Prime Minister and an American President can meet to dedicate, not a bridge across this water, but the very water itself, to the lasting and productive use of their respective peoples. Until that day comes, and I hope it may be soon, this bridge stands as an open door. There will be no challenge at the border and no guard to ask a countersign. Where the boundary is crossed the only word must be, "Pass, friend."

(See note to Item 114, 1940 volume, for discussion of the St. Lawrence project.)

107 ❮ The Four Hundred and Seventy-eighth Press Conference (Excerpts). Hyde Park, New York. August 23, 1938

(Political morality in party primaries.)

Q. Can you tell us anything about your conference with Senator Pope over the weekend?

THE PRESIDENT: Well, I can tell you what is actually the fact, that the chief question of discussion was a matter that involves public morality. It is rather interesting to me because a quarter of a century ago, when I first went to the Legislature of this State — Heavens, more than that, it was 28 years ago that I was elected — the burning issue in this State was whether we should adopt direct primaries or not.

A great many states had already adopted direct primaries in order to get rid of the old-fashioned form of boss-controlled conventions. So I took a great interest in the whole objective of direct primaries. The objective was a very simple one, and has been subsequently carried out in very nearly every state of the Union. It was to give the actual voters within a party, in recognition of the party system under which we live, the right to choose their candidates for public office. In every case in those days that I ever heard of, some method was devised by which the primary within one party would be limited to the members of that party.

There were always certain restrictions and definitions to carry out that purpose, for the very simple reason that a party primary, which was participated in even by a handful of people who did not belong to that party, immediately became void and of no effect — a complete destruction of the objective.

If, for example, in a contest within a party, one group within that party had 49 per cent of the vote and the other group had 51 per cent of the vote, it was entirely proper for the 51 per cent to win. That was a fair expression of opinion. If, however, 2 per cent or 3 per cent of people from another party were to enter the primary of the party to which they did not belong, the will of the party voters could be completely overcome and destroyed.

Now, that is a question of simple political morality. The interesting thing to me is the fact that the Tory press in this country has overlooked a very interesting opportunity to work for decent political morality.

We have certain examples that we all know about. The figures in the State of Idaho, for example, show that whereas in 1936 the Republican primary vote was about 42,000 and the Democratic primary vote was about 55,000, this year the Republican primary vote was only 30,000 and the Democratic primary vote was about 85,000. No matter how much you might try to hem and haw them off, these figures are complete proof positive that the direct primary system was morally and completely violated by the entrance of fifteen or twenty thousand Republicans into the Democratic primary.

There are two other illustrations. One is the letter by the Republican State Chairman of Georgia, which is now becoming famous, calling on all Republicans in the State of Georgia to enter the Democratic primary. It is being credibly reported that in Maryland also, Republicans are being begged to enter the Democratic primary.

Now, this has nothing to do with candidates. I am not mentioning the name of a single candidate. I am talking about principle.

I think it is something that ought to be of interest to all people who believe in the primary system. Of course there are still a lot of people who would like to go back to the boss-ridden convention system, but I am talking about people who believe in direct primaries. I think it is of interest to them to know of the destruction of the principle that is being carried on now, without very much protest on the part of the Tory press.

Well, now, you have a good story. It is in your hands.

But you have to make it perfectly clear that this comment of mine has nothing to do with the question of candidates — individual candidates. I am talking about principles, and I would say the same thing if Republicans in any state were to enter the Democratic primary with the object and purpose of helping somebody that I considered a close friend of mine — it is exactly the same thing. . . .

Q. If a Democrat enters a Republican primary, as O'Connor has done, does that fall in the same category?

THE PRESIDENT: Certainly; Democrats ought not to enter Republican primaries. It certainly ruins the whole purpose of the primary. It is a question of A, B, C morality. . . .

108 ❪ Informal, Extemporaneous Remarks Before the Roosevelt Home Club. Hyde Park, New York. August 27, 1938

You look just the way you did a year ago. You have not changed at all. After being away for a couple of months it is amazing to come back here and find so little change. There is Spratty [Mayor Spratt], who won't admit it out loud but still hungering to be President. There is John E. Mack, still claiming to be a farmer. There is the old Board of Supervisors, still playing politics. There is old Doc Bowen still running for Congress. And there are the nine school districts in the town of Hyde Park — which haven't got together yet. So it feels entirely natural to be back.

Moses [Mr. Smith] of course had to refer to the fishing trip, because I told him I had to have a subject to talk about; and I told him on the peril of his life not to mention this year the Hyde Park Post Office. (*Laughter*) We are going to get a new Post Office but the only way we shall get it quickly is to buy more postage stamps. Jim Farley told me that, and he is in the business. Actually it is a fact. As we get new post offices in the United States, we try to put them in those places that have the largest volume of business, those places that do not have Government buildings in them. That is why Rhinebeck had theirs allotted last year, and Wappingers is getting one this year. I hope that Hyde Park will rate one within the next couple of years.

Now, to go back to fishing. You do not always need a hook to catch a fish. I got a 110-pound sailfish without a hook. It shows that the plea of Spratty [Mayor Spratt] that he did not have a fishing rod does not mean a thing. As a matter of fact, it was an interesting story. I have eleven men in the same boat and a moving picture camera and two other cameras to prove the story.

Way down at a place called Cocos Island, about five hundred miles west of the Panama Canal, we were out fishing, trolling for sailfish. One of them took my line which was out about two hundred feet beyond the boat with a hook and feather on the end. He jumped in the air and, apparently, while he was on the end, another sailfish came along and got his beak all snarled up in the line. The fish that got caught on the hook got away, but the fish that got caught on his nose was hauled in.

As a matter of fact, there had been so much discussion on previous trips, about the size and weight and length and species of fish, that this year I took a full-fledged scientist with me from the Smithsonian Institution in Washington, Dr. Waldo Schmitt, who was such a success that we decided to change the Smithsonian to "Schmittsonian." (*Laughter*)

When we started from San Diego out on the West Coast, we ran down the Coast to Lower California which, as you know, belongs to Mexico. In talking to Dr. Schmitt that first day, I said: "Is there any particular thing or animal that you would like to find?" He said: "Oh, yes, I am writing a monograph, I have been on it two years, and the one thing I am searching for in these waters of Mexico and the islands of the Pacific — I want to find a burrowing shrimp."

"Well," I said, "Dr. Schmitt, why leave Washington? Washington is overrun with them. I know that after five years." (*Laughter*)

However, he not only found a burrowing shrimp on an island called Socorro, two or three hundred miles off the coast of Mexico, but it also turned out to be a new species of burrowing shrimp, so we called it the Schmitty Shrimp.

Then we went down to the Galapagos Islands. You have read stories of German baronesses going down there and committing murders and finally being murdered. We supposed that going down on the Equator the weather would be warm. Actually, we nearly froze to death because down there, about five hundred miles from the coast of Ecuador, there is a cold current called the Humboldt Current, which is just the opposite of our warm Gulf Stream on the Atlantic Coast. That Humboldt Current comes up from the Antarctic regions and passes through the Galapagos Islands, bounces off them and disappears in the middle of the Pacific. The result was that we had to sleep under blankets every night.

However, it was a grand cruise, a real holiday, and notable for the fact that during the entire trip we, in the party, wrote our own newspaper stories. That is why they were so good. (*Laughter*) We included a great deal of fine historical and — what is the word? — piscatorial information which the press had never printed before.

Then, on the way back, of course we stopped at Panama and I had a chance to see the greatest, to my mind far and away, the greatest, engineering work in the world. I was very lucky because in 1912 when I was in the State Senate, at the close of the session I went down to Panama before they let the water into the Canal. On that trip I saw the famous Cut through the mountain, and from the top of it, the trains, great huge trains of dump cars, locomotives, steam shovels, looked like gnats in the middle of this great Cut. Today, of course, the water is in it, and you get no idea of the labor that it took to build that Canal.

Incidentally, I was very happy to note that the American defenses of the Canal had improved very much since I was there three years before. We are getting airplanes, and submarines, and anti-aircraft guns, and various other things, to try to make reasonably certain that in case of war — which we are all trying to avoid in every possible way — we shall still be able to maintain the link of the Panama Canal between the Atlantic and the Pacific.

Then when I got back to the Continental part of the United States, I went down to my old stamping ground in Georgia and again heard of what they call "politics." And I have been hearing about it ever since. That is one reason why that little foundation up there on top of the hill, that John Mack referred to, is gradually evolving into a house, the object being to have some place in the United States where they won't talk politics.

Incidentally, I got an admission out of the Mayor. He was

looking at those stone walls, permanent walls, going up, and he said, in a sort of reminiscent way, "You know that is the only building that I have inspected in all these years that had not been partly paid for by the Federal Government." However, as we all know, the contribution that the Federal Government is making through the W.P.A. and the P.W.A. is not only putting people to work, but it is helping every community in the United States to get things which they otherwise could not afford to have. It is true in the greatest city of the Nation, New York, and it is true in the greatest county of the Nation, Dutchess.

And right along that line — let me see, there are about five weeks to go — I hope very much that we taxpayers in Hyde Park are going to be saved about $300,000. If we do not decide to save that $300,000 within the next five weeks, by agreeing on some plan to take care of the four or five hundred school children in these districts for whom we have not adequate facilities — if we do not do it in the next five weeks — we shall be just out of pocket $300,000 as taxpayers; and, eventually, we taxpayers in the town of Hyde Park shall have to put up the whole $300,000. That is a very simple situation.

If the people in this township were made to realize that there are nine school districts affecting 2400 or 2500 children for whom we need accommodations, I am sure that the democratic processes will so work in the next five weeks, that we shall be able to get a school project for the township and save about $300,000 for our own pockets. Now that, I take it, is just what you and I would call common sense. I believe that the people — the people who run the school districts and the voters who have to pass on the proposition — will vote somehow to save us that money.

That, perhaps, is the old Dutch coming out in me or maybe it is the old Scotch Irish coming out in me; but, anyway, I think most people in this town agree that we have to do something to give the children of this town, from almost every part of the town, better educational facilities.

One thing I am glad of is that, from now until after election day, I expect to spend the greater part of my time here in Hyde Park. Of course I shall make occasional trips to Washington to see that the Government continues as it ought to continue, but I shall spend the rest of the time back here where we live.

It is fine to see you again. I greatly appreciate and all the family appreciates these meetings of the Club at Moses Smith's and, as it has been well said, I hope they will continue for many, many years to come.

I might add to the suggestion that has been made about the "Heaven" across the river, that I am very confident that the people in that heaven in Ulster County will be good neighbors to us in Dutchess County.

And so I echo the hope that all of us, without exception, will be back here again in the summer of 1939.

I might add one thing with respect to the Mayor of New York [Mayor LaGuardia] and his wife: I hope that some day they buy a farm in Dutchess County and become neighbors of ours, too.

109 ⟨ Presidential Statement on the Report of the Commission on Industrial Relations in Great Britain. August 31, 1938

THE SECRETARY OF LABOR has given me the factual report on industrial relations in Great Britain. This report, unanimously submitted by eminent Americans representing various interests and points of views within our national life, comes in response to the request I made of them for an impartial statement on labor-employer relations as they exist in Great Britain.

To the members of the Commission on Industrial Relations in Great Britain who, at great personal sacrifice, have spent weeks in an intensive study of these problems in Great Britain and in the preparation of an objective report, I express the thanks of the Government. I, personally, am most appreciative of the services they have rendered.

The adequacy of this report attests again the usefulness of cooperative endeavors on the part of those in Government and those whose labors and interests, diversified as they may be, are closely identified with the labor-employer relationships as they exist in our country.

This report ought to be read through. Unless this is done, discussions of the facts contained therein will be of little value. To me, the most salient feature of it is the cooperative spirit coupled with restraint which is shown by those who represent both employers and employees in Great Britain. Collective bargaining is an accepted fact and because of this the machinery which carries it out is functioning.

A second report is to be submitted in the near future and this will give us a parallel study of industrial relations in Sweden. Experiences of other countries, very naturally, have been different from our own but they should be considered and studied as we analyze our own problems.

NOTE: The foregoing statement was made by me on releasing the report of the committee which I had appointed on June 21, to go to Great Britain and Sweden to investigate the subject of industrial relations between capital and labor in those countries (see Item 77 and note, this volume). The report was printed in full in a great many newspapers of the country; and its general features were widely distributed throughout the entire country.

The report on Sweden was released by me, with a statement, on September 25, 1938 (see Item 118, this volume).

Both these reports were unani-mous in form; and I believe that their findings of fact were generally accepted, in our country, as unbiased and authoritative. They dealt with a great many factors involved in worker-employer relations, including: the organization of unions and employers, collective agreements, settlement of labor disputes without stoppage of work, adjustment of interunion disputes, legislation relating to the existence and activities of trade unions, and the procedure of governmental agencies concerned with the settlement of industrial disputes. The reports also discussed the history and development of the existing methods of settling disputes; and submitted illuminating statistics of union membership, strikes, collective bargaining agreements, and employer associations.

There is, unfortunately, not sufficient space in this volume to print these reports in full.

The reports, however, indicated very clearly that the English statutes were not as restrictive upon labor unions as many Americans had supposed; and also that such restrictive laws as did exist in Great Britain and in Sweden were not the reasons, and did not form the basis, for industrial peace in either country. The reports pointed out rather that the maintenance of greater industrial peace in those two countries rested on the willingness of both capital and labor to work for stable industrial relations through collective agreements. It was shown that collective agreements, negotiated by responsible national labor leaders sitting in conference with responsible national leaders of industry, were the real foundation upon which uninterrupted relationships were established and continued.

The chief effects of these reports were to point out the lack of necessity or desirability at that time for drastic legislative restriction on trade unions; and to promote the growing acceptance in America, by labor and capital alike, of the efficacy of voluntary collective labor agreements as the basis of satisfactory and peaceful industrial relations.

110 ❡ A Letter on the Opportunities and Responsibilities of a Strong and Free Press. September 2, 1938

My dear Mr. Schroth:

I CONGRATULATE you upon the great opportunity for constructive service which becomes yours as publisher of the Brooklyn *Daily Eagle*. It is an opportunity which carries with it a grave responsibility, for in these fateful times there is vital need for a strong, fearless and free press.

By a free press I mean a press which is untrammeled by prejudice and unfettered by selfish bias, which will serve no cause but that of truth and which will recognize no master but justice. I think you have in the Brooklyn *Eagle* a happy medium through which to exemplify the highest ideals of American journalism. The paper has had a long history and has commanded the services of men of character and insight and vision. It has chronicled great events in our national life which have been a part of the broader life of the world at large.

As it has its own history and has witnessed so many changes, the thought occurs to me that in the present transition it can and should play an important part. These times, it seems to me, demand above all else truth in the news, for it is corollary of our democracy that the public can be depended upon to assess problems and policies at their true value if facts are presented as facts, and opinion as opinion — each in its true light. We are governed by public opinion. We cannot lay too much stress on the importance of truth in news.

Once the public realizes that its newspaper serves no interest save that of truth it will give that paper an allegiance that neither depression nor ill-fortune nor any form of hard times can weaken. I have faith in the American press just as I have faith in the American people and in our democratic institutions. I venture the opinion that the straightforward pursuit of truth and justice points one way to prosperity and large influence of American newspapers both great and small.

To you falls the privilege of assuming direction of a paper with a great past, a living tradition. Times change but the essentials of life remain. Ours is the task of seeking a new approach to the solution of age old problems which present new phases to changing generations. In all this he who serves the cause of truth will best serve the national interest.

Very sincerely yours,

Mr. Frank D. Schroth,
Publisher,
Brooklyn *Daily Eagle,*
Brooklyn, New York.

111 ⟨ Informal, Extemporaneous Remarks at Morgantown, Maryland. September 4, 1938

My friends:

FOR ME this is no new visit to Southern Maryland. When I was in the Navy Department a great many years ago, I used to come down by water. In those days it was very difficult to get down here by land. Today things have changed very greatly.

I remember that more than ten years ago two old friends of mine became greatly interested in connecting Tidewater Virginia with Southern Maryland. One of them was Steve Gambrill; and the other one was Walton Moore, who is now Counselor of the State Department. I, too, became interested when I came to Washington again in 1933. I came down here today, on a Sunday morning, because I think that Sunday is a good day to try to do something for one's neighbors. You are neighbors of us in the National Capital.

For a long time I have been looking at maps, as you know. For a long time I have felt that, for the good not only of the people of Southern Maryland but also for the good of the people of the United States, there ought to be a through road from Baltimore to Richmond — a cut-off if you like. It would be a road which, at the same time, would open up to the general traveling public — and we are traveling more and more every year — this very wonderful section of our country, a section that is good to look at, that is peopled by good citizens.

I have been very much interested in it, not only because of the point of view of you good people who live down here, but also because, as President of the United States, my duty is to try to take care of things as far as I can that meet national needs.

There is one other phase of this proposed bridge across the Potomac, and of the other bridges that are proposed further up the Chesapeake; and that is the phase of national defense.

I suppose there is no nation in the world whose people are more peace-loving than the people of the United States. I suppose there is no nation in the world that is more sincerely desirous of keeping out of war. At the same time, you and I know what world conditions are; and we do have to think sometimes of national defense against some emergency that may come through no fault of our own in the days to come.

And it is very important in thinking of national defense to see to it that the borders of the United States, the portions of the United States that lie fairly close to the seaboard, shall have proper access, in the event of war, for the conduct of defensive operations. Therefore, the whole Chesapeake Bay area is a very vital link in our national defense. The more that we can do to improve communication in this area in peacetime, the more insurance we are taking in the event of some possible future invasion.

I am having a very wonderful day getting better acquainted with a portion of the country that I knew before. As you know, I very often go up and down the River on weekends — weekends when I try not only to rest but also to think things over quietly. And today I am getting a thrill out of this morning's ride.

I have been talking with your Representatives — with the Governor of the State — and I think we are all one in feeling that this proposed bridge is one of the things that has got to be done just as fast as we can possibly do it.

I hope to come back, perhaps before I leave Washington, to talk at the inauguration, the starting, of this bridge across the Potomac River in this neighborhood.

NOTE: On this trip through Maryland, in addition to the speeches printed as Items 111 and 113 of this volume, I also made short, extemporaneous talks at Berlin, Maryland; Sharptown, Maryland; Salisbury, Maryland; and Annapolis, Maryland.

112 ❨A Tribute on the Passing of Cardinal Hayes. September 4, 1938

I AM deeply sorry to hear of the passing of His Eminence, Cardinal Hayes. I had the privilege of his friendship for many long years. His great spiritual leadership has had a deep influence on our generation, and all of us who knew him, and had sincere affection for him, will feel his loss.

113 ❨"The Democratic Party Will . . . Continue to Receive the Support of the Majority of Americans Just So Long as It Remains a Liberal Party." Address at Denton, Maryland. September 5, 1938

Congressman Goldsborough, Congressman Lewis,
ladies and gentlemen:

THIS IS Labor Day. For two reasons, which I think you will approve, I have accepted the invitation of your Congressman to come to the Eastern Shore of Maryland today.

The first reason for coming here is to give you and me a chance to reestablish a fact which we thought was long ago thoroughly established by the Constitution of the United States even if it is denied by some of your newspapers and by some of your candidates for public office. That fact is that the Free State of Maryland, proud of itself and conscious of itself, is also proud and conscious of being a most important part of the United States of America; that what happens in and to the Free State of Maryland matters mightily in and to the United States of America and, under the Constitution, to the Chief Executive and to the Congress of the United States; and finally, that in the Free State of Maryland — happily a part of the Union —

the Flag, the Constitution and the President are still as welcome as in all of the other forty-seven States of the Union.

The second, and the original reason for my coming here is also related to the unity of this Nation.

Unthinking people may believe that the first Monday in September — Labor Day — is set aside in special honor of those who work at a trade in mills and factories and railroads and mines. But that is a narrow interpretation, for this day belongs just as much to those who work with head and hand on the farms. There is no distinction between those who run farms or work on farms and those who work in industry. For you and I well know that most of the people in cities have come there comparatively recently from farms all over the country, including the Eastern Shore of Maryland and from farms of the Old World from which originally we all came.

America has always had — and America still has — a small minority who assume that there are not enough good things to go around to give that minority all that it wants and at the same time to give the rest of America — the overwhelming majority of America — a humane and modern standard of living. Even today that minority is shortsightedly sure that its interests must lie in exploiting all who labor on the farm as well as in the mill and the mine.

But at the same time all over the country the unity of interest of all common men and women — warm-hearted, simple men and women, willing to live and let live, whether in factory or on farm — grows steadily more evident. Clearer every day is the one great lesson of history — the lesson taught by the Master of Galilee — that the only road to peace and the only road to a happier and better civilization is the road to unity — the road called the "Highway of Fellowship."

But as this community of interest becomes apparent to those who live on farm and in city, the strategy of the cold-blooded few to divide and conquer, to make common men blind to their common interests, becomes more active. Class conscious itself, just because it does conceive its interest to be opposed to the interest of all other people, that small minority is deliberately trying to create prejudice between this and that group of the common people of America — to create a new class feeling among people like ourselves, who instinctively are not class conscious.

You in the State of Maryland — and the people of other states — have in recent weeks been treated to a number of examples of this deliberate attempt to create prejudice and class feeling which can be charitably explained only as political hysteria. But it does not help the cause of Constitutional Government or effective democracy anywhere to laugh off such things in campaign time on the general theory that anything is fair in love and politics.

Today above all else that minority is trying to drive a wedge between the farmers on the one hand and their relatives and their logical partners in the cities on the other. It is trying to narrow the broad definition of "labor" in the mind of the farmer, who above all people has always known what it means to have to labor from sun-up to sun-down. It is trying to make the farmer forget that the people in the cities who, like him, labor for their daily bread are his own people, flesh of his flesh, and blood of his blood, Americans just like him.

This is my fourth visit to the Eastern Shore since 1933 — perhaps more visits than any other President has made; and I have been honored by being given an honorary degree by your own historic Washington University.

You have sent your sons and daughters by the thousands into the industrial world. Your products of farm and fishery go to the greatest city markets of the United States. And you have never lost the sense of the lasting spiritual values in life.

That is why I have wanted to come here on Labor Day and preach a sermon, if you will, on that ancient text "We are all members one of another."

In order to make that relationship a benefit rather than a curse, in order to keep all of our people abreast of each other and in line with the present, our democratic form of Government must move forward on many fronts at the same time.

For a dozen years or more prior to 1933, the Federal Government had not moved forward at all. Life was out of balance and Government had failed completely to recognize that important social needs call for action. In a nation-wide effort to catch up with lost time, to bring a distant past up to the present, a whole series of new undertakings had to be launched in 1933. But remember well that these undertakings were on a complete front that included American citizens in every occupation and in every part of the country.

During this process there were of course many people both in private and public life who did not like to do the things that had to be done. They admitted the existence of certain abuses. But in their hearts they wishfully believed that improvement should come from individual initiative or local initiative without the help of Government. If improvement could not come without Government action, then they wanted no improvement at all.

People who feel and think like that I call "conservatives," and even "reactionaries." And people who feel that the past should be brought up to the present by using every legitimate instrument to do the job, including Government, I call "liberals" or "progressives."

Any man—any political party—has a right to be honestly one or the other. But the Nation cannot stand for the confusion of having him pretend to be one and act like the other.

A few days ago a brilliant newspaper writer came to the White House and asked me to illustrate the difference between a liberal and a conservative. I will condense for you what I told her.

For example, I said, "Mr. A" is a composite conservative. "Mr. A" admitted that in 1933 interest rates charged by private banking to ordinary citizens who wanted to finance a farm or a home were altogether too high; he admitted that there were excesses, sharp practices and abuses in issuing securities and buying and selling stocks and bonds; he admitted that the hours of work in his factory and a great many other factories were too long; he admitted that old people, who became destitute through no fault of their own, were a problem; he admitted that national and international economic conditions and speculation had made farming and fishing extremely hazardous occupations; and he even admitted that the buying power of farmers and fishermen had not kept pace with the buying power of many other kinds of workers.

But, "Mr. A" not only declined to take any lead in solving these problems in cooperation with his Government, he even found fault with and opposed, openly or secretly, almost every suggestion that was put forward by those who belonged to the liberal school of thought.

"Mr. B," on the other hand, was the composite of a liberal. He not only agreed with "Mr. A" on the needs and the problems, but "Mr. B" put his shoulder under the load, he gave active study and active support to working out methods, in cooperation with his Government, for the solving of the problems and the filling of the needs. "Mr. B" did not claim that the remedies were perfect but he knew that we had to start with something less than perfect in this imperfect world of ours.

If we have a Government run by the "Mr. A's" of this life, it is obvious that the Nation will slip behind once more in the march of civilization — bump along from one 1929 crisis to another. Yours is the choice of what kind of a Government you want.

I ran across an interesting thing the other day. Lord Bryce, in the last edition of his great work on the American Commonwealth, had this to say: "An eminent journalist remarked to me in 1908 that the two great parties were like two bottles. Each bore a label denoting the kind of liquor it contained, but each was empty. This at any rate may be said, that the parties may seem to have erred . . . by neglecting to discover and work out any principles capable of solving the problems which now perplex the country. In a country so full of change and movement as America, new questions are always coming up and must be answered. New troubles surround a Government and a way must be found to escape from them; new diseases attack the nation, and have to be cured. The duty of a great party is to face these, to find answers and remedies, applying to the facts of the hour the doctrines it has lived by, so far as they are still applicable, and when they have ceased to be applicable, thinking out new doctrines conformable to the main principles and tendencies which it represents."

That has been my conception of the obligations and ideals of the Democratic Party, for the Democratic Party has always been a party of ideas rather than money, and it has always failed when it has only been one of two empty bottles.

Yes, why should not we be frank with each other? The Democratic Party will live and continue to receive the support of the majority of Americans just so long as it remains a liberal party. If it reverts to the situation of thirty or forty years ago, which Lord Bryce described, it will fail.

As the leader of that party, I propose to try to keep it liberal. As President of the United States, I conceive that course to be in the best interests not only of Democrats but also of those millions of American men and women who are affiliated with other parties or with no party at all. And I have the right, in sincerity and honesty, to make that statement in any state, in any county and in any community of the United States of America.

Increasingly during these past six years a common understanding of what unity means has grown throughout the land. People have continued to ask their representatives, their executive representatives, their representatives in Legislatures and the Congress, to be liberal, to take the initiative, to be positive forces in improving social and economic conditions. That applies to farmers just as much as to industrial workers.

You who live on the farm or near the farm know well how farmers were exploited by those who controlled Government from the end of the World War down to 1933 — and by the monopolies they fostered which still give us trouble. But I think you realize also that for many long years industrial labor was exploited too. Farmers have come to realize that unless industrial labor is prosperous it cannot buy the food and the materials for clothing which are produced from the soil. Industrial labor has come to understand that unless the farmers of the country are prosperous they cannot buy the product of the factories.

Economic lesson number one of the past twenty years is that men and women on farms, men and women in cities, are partners. America cannot prosper unless both groups prosper. That is the keystone in the arch of the economic and social policy of your Administration in Washington.

May I illustrate again by taking some high-spots?

Nearly thirty years ago people who were injured in factories through no fault of their own found it difficult, if not impossible, to get adequate compensation for their injuries. A very proper demand arose for workmen's compensation laws. Thanks to the pioneering of a young Maryland legislator, the first Workmen's Compensation Act ever to be passed in the United States was adopted by Maryland. Ten years later, I, following this man's lead, was helping to pass a workmen's compensation law through the Legislature of the State of New York.

But what I want to emphasize is that workmen's compensation laws are not for the sole benefit of workmen injured in industry. They confer a definite benefit on farmers because the injured industrial worker is able to get his compensation promptly and continue to buy food for himself and his family.

Later on in the halls of Washington a young Congressman pushed and pleaded until he got a parcel post law on the statute books of the United States. That parcel post law was of principal benefit to those who in every state lived on R.F.D. routes. But it was not for their benefit alone, for it helped their brothers and sisters who worked in the cities of the country.

And that young Congressman was the same Maryland legislator of earlier days.

Many years later it became clear that the problem of dependent old age was a trying one, that the states and the Federal Government, that employers and employees, should come together to pass a nationwide old-age pension and unemployment insurance act. Once again the Representative from the Free State of Maryland took the lead and, thanks to his pioneering, decent security of life is assured today to millions of our people.

I know that, speaking here to you citizens in Denton and to people who are listening in on the radio all over Maryland, I know that I do not have to name that young man. That man is now well along in mature middle age, and I do not have to tell you his name. But in forty-seven other states there are people, millions of them, who are listening to what I am saying on this Labor Day, and for their benefit the name of that man is Representative Lewis of Maryland. And millions of people in all the other states of the Union are very proud of him.

It is the privilege of some of us to dream dreams, and of some of us to carry out the dreams of others. But in Maryland you are fortunate in having a man who not only has seen visions but has lived to make his dreams come true.

He symbolizes, for the farm and the city alike, the inherent humanity of the man who rises from humble circumstances, and the inherent ability to grow in vision and effectiveness in the fertile soil of American opportunity and the American tradition of equality.

It is suggestive to me that he has never forgotten that he learned to read and write at the knee of a Christian minister in Sunday School. That is why perhaps he has lived the life of the Good Samaritan — and he has never passed by on the other side.

You in Maryland will shortly vote in a primary. The choice in all parties is solely yours — that goes without saying. But may I express the hope that the choice you make will be the choice of all who are entitled to vote in the primaries — not the choice of a group, an "organization" group or an "anti-organization" group, not the choice of only part of the voters either in city or in country districts, but the choice of all who have the right to make the choice.

At a time of grave international troubles in many parts of

the world, the best contribution that we at home can make to our own security is to eliminate quickly all feelings of injustice and insecurity throughout our land. For our own safety we cannot afford to follow those in public life who quote the Golden Rule and take no steps to bring it closer.

As President, I have willingly defended the interests of each of the Nation's great groups to the others, even if the others were critical. I have been just as glad to defend business to labor and agriculture, and to defend labor to business and agriculture, as I have been to defend agriculture to labor and business. That is part of my public duty.

When I became President I found a country demoralized, disorganized, with each of these groups seeking to survive by taking advantage of the others. As in the time of George Washington in 1787, when there was grave danger that the states would never become a Nation — as in the time of Abraham Lincoln, when a tragic division threatened to become lasting — our own time has brought a test of our American Union.

A great part of my duty as President has been to do what I could to bring our people together again. That has been my unchanging purpose since March 4, 1933. The great test for us in our time is whether all the groups of our people are willing to work together for continuing progress.

Such progress, I need hardly remind you, comes ultimately from the rank and file of our citizens, and through the representatives of their free choice — representatives willing to cooperate, to get things done in the true spirit of "give and take" — not representatives who seek every plausible excuse for blocking action.

What you do, what I do, what any man or woman may do, is of small moment compared with what the people do. In this effort to preserve our democracy and our Union, I am confident that all who labor in the field and factory will carry on the good work, carry it through to a just and successful end.

That is our high purpose on this Labor Day of 1938.

114 ❧ The President Appoints a Committee to Find Means of Supplying Electric Power in a National Emergency. September 6, 1938

Dear Mr. Johnson:

THE REPORTS regarding the supply of electric power in the event of a national emergency made to me by the War Department and the Federal Power Commission in response to my request of March 18, 1938, have given me much concern. These studies have disclosed a shortage of power to meet the needs of the nation's industry in the event of war, such as to constitute a serious threat to the national security.

In order to take immediate steps toward the solution of this pressing problem I am appointing a committee of representatives from the War and Navy Departments, the Federal Power Commission, the National Power Policy Committee, the National Resources Committee and the Securities & Exchange Commission.

It is my desire that this committee find and recommend to me definite ways and means of meeting this problem. This will include drafting enabling legislation, recommending necessary appropriations, and other measures which appear appropriate.

Yours sincerely,

Hon. Louis Johnson,
Asst. Secretary of War,
Washington, D. C.

(Identical letters were sent to the following members of said Committee: Frederic A. Delano, National Resources Committee; Basil Manly, Federal Power Commission; Harold L. Ickes, National Power Policy Committee; Charles Edison, Assistant Secretary of the Navy, and William O. Douglas, Securities & Exchange Commission.)

NOTE: In 1935, as the result of Executive Order No. 6251 (see Item 116, 1933 volume), the Federal Power Commission issued its first national power survey report. This was the first attempt in our history to determine from a national point of view the relationship between

our present and future requirements for electric power and the
capacity of public and private
power plants to meet such demand.

The report pointed out that such
a survey was an essential factor in
planning national defense, in order
to avoid the kind of shortage of
power facilities which had interfered with our rearmament efforts
in 1918.

In March, 1938, I asked the Federal Power Commission, in view
of the international storm warnings from across the seas, to bring
up to date the power survey of
1935, indicating that it would "constitute a valuable contribution to
the plans for the mobilization of
industry in the event of war."

The Federal Power Commission
proceeded to make the new survey
in cooperation with the War Department. In July, 1938, it submitted a preliminary report to me, indicating that unless steps were
taken immediately to plan and
build new power facilities, there
would be serious shortages of electricity in the principal areas producing munitions and war materials.

Further studies during August
confirmed this view. I thereupon
called together in Washington a
meeting of representatives of all
the government agencies concerned
with power production and with
the needs of national defense.

At this meeting I set up a special
National Defense Power Committee, and sent each of its members

the foregoing letter, in which I requested the committee to make a
study and recommend to me "definite ways and means of meeting this
problem."

Important results were obtained.
Early in 1939 the various public
utilities which sold power in the
principal war material centers undertook to add new generating
capacity to their plants of not less
than one million kilowatts. Gen-
erators were standardized so as to
increase the capacity of manufacturers to build them more cheaply
and more quickly. Studies were
made of possible interconnection
facilities, some of which have already been carried out so as to increase the dependability of the supply of power for the defense industries.

The work of this special committee has now been taken over by the
National Power Policy Committee
(see Item 142, 1939 volume).

The work of 1938 and 1939 has
brought home to the utilities, and
to all others concerned, the realization that an adequate defense program, in terms of modern war,
would require rapid expansion in
the construction program of the
utility systems. These programs
have begun to be carried out, so
that instead of the one million kilowatts of new capacity pledged in
early 1939, installations and orders
placed by private utilities for new
generating capacity will exceed five
and a half million kilowatts by the

end of 1942. In addition to this, there will be another two and a half million kilowatts of new generating capacity added by Federal and other public projects. It may therefore be said that since September, 1938, when the foregoing letter was written, and up to the end of 1942, there will be added approximately eight million kilowatts. Current Federal Power Commission estimates indicate that even this extraordinary increase is not quite sufficient, and that another one and a half million kilowatts should be provided. Plans for meeting this need are going forward.

This is an example of the importance of continued adequate planning in all fields. For further discussion of this subject see Item 55 and note, 1940 volume.

115 ❪ A Message to the Convention of the American Legion. September 7, 1938

My dear Commander Doherty:

I EXTEND to you and to our great organization my sincerest greetings on the occasion of the Twentieth Annual National Convention. I wish that it were possible for me to accept the cordial invitation, which you extended earlier this year, to attend the Convention and I regret exceedingly that I shall be unable to be present in person. I recall with pleasure the warmth of the welcome you accorded me when I attended the Convention in Chicago five years ago.

About this time twenty years ago, many of you had just participated in a great victory in France. You were preparing to engage in the great offensive which brought the war to a close. Your services in France and at home earned your membership in the American Legion.

You have devoted yourselves to the preservation of peace since then. You have emphasized the importance of good citizenship, love of country and national defense. Surely such service to one's country brings rewards as glorious as those in war. Your voluntary effort to place a limitation upon war profits which members or others might gain in time of future wars, which we pray shall never come, is an evidence of highest patriotism.

Each of you today is in a position to promote responsible American citizenship. In many communities there is a need of such education in citizenship. How better can you now serve than as missionaries in American democracy?

Your war services to your country have earned you the admiration and commendation of the nation. In turn the nation has not been unmindful or lacking in gratitude. It has made generous provision for veterans and their dependents who suffered during the war.

Happily, we are now at peace but there is work to be done. The American Legion will assist, as it always has done, in maintaining and defending those true American principles of freedom, tolerance, justice and humanity, which are part of our priceless heritage.

I congratulate you upon the great progress the organization has made and send my best wishes to all of you.

Very sincerely yours,

National Commander Daniel J. Doherty,
American Legion National Headquarters,
Indianapolis, Indiana.

116 ❨ Informal, Extemporaneous Remarks at Rochester, Minnesota. September 14, 1938

My friends of Rochester:

I KNOW that I can really call you friends for all that you have done in these past few days for my family and myself.

I am going away not only with a full realization that every care will be taken with my oldest boy, but also with a better knowledge of the very wonderful work that is being done for humanity as a whole here in Rochester.

I want to thank all of you for what I can best describe as an understanding heart on the part of the people of Rochester. You have understood that I have come here not as President but as a father; and you have treated me accordingly. I am going away knowing that you are still going to pull for that boy of mine, and that his wife and my wife are going to be in very good hands during the period of recovery.

I am going back now, not to my home on the Hudson River but straight through to Washington; because, as you know from the newspapers, the condition of affairs in other parts of the world is extremely serious. That is why, as President, I have to go back to the National Capital.

Again I want to thank you. I am leaving here with a light heart. I am leaving not only with a most kindly feeling but with a most affectionate feeling for all of you good people in Rochester.

117 ❡ "Greatest . . . Have Been the Men Who Have Sought to Make the Constitution Workable in the Face of the New Problems and Conditions That Have Faced the American Nation from Year to Year." Radio Address on Constitution Day, Washington, D.C. September 17, 1938

Governor Lehman, my fellow citizens of the State of New York:

IT IS with deep personal disappointment that I find the affairs of the world such that I cannot be with my neighbors in Poughkeepsie today.

That my great-great-grandfather, Isaac Roosevelt, sat in the little old Court House here one hundred and fifty years ago and cast his vote with the slim majority in favor of ratification of the Federal Constitution is a family tradition of which I am proud.

There are two words in the English language which in the heat of political controversy are often forgotten or abused — the words "faith" and "confidence." It is well for us to remember that a very large minority of the inhabitants of the original Thirteen States opposed the adoption of the Constitution. They had witnessed the complete failure of government under the Articles of Confederation — yet they were opposed to a real union because they believed those leaders who viewed with alarm any effort to think and act in national terms instead of state and local terms.

And, believe me, the viewers with alarm, the patrons of ghosts and hobgoblins in those days had little to learn from the professional fear-mongers of 1938.

I wish that all of you might read the dusty newspapers and pamphlets and handbills of a hundred and fifty years ago. Feelings ran high. Vituperation and invective were the rule. The State of New York would cease to exist and its people would be squeezed to death between the cold-blooded Yankees of New England on the one side and the passionate aristocracy of the South on the other — if you believed one type of publicity. The people of the State of New York would be ruined by interstate tariffs and as a weak independent nation would be reconquered by George the Third, if you read the publicity of the other party.

Washington, Adams, Hamilton and Clinton were labeled traitors and dictators.

In the midst of these diatribes this Constitutional Convention in Poughkeepsie was faced with the problem of saying "yes" or "no." Then, as now, there were men and women afraid of the future — distrustful of their own ability to meet changed conditions; shortsighted in their dog-in-the-manger conception of local and national needs. They were afraid of democracy; afraid of the trend toward unity; afraid of Thirteen States becoming one Nation.

As the weeks went on and an insufficient number of states had approved the Constitution to put it into effect, its opponents at this Convention, realizing more and more that the very existence of that paper organization known as the United States of America was at stake and that public opinion was swinging against them, narrowed their opposition to the fact that the Constitution contained no Bill of Rights.

They held a slim majority against ratification, but at that moment a small group of delegates, in which I am glad to say Dutchess County was well represented, came forward with an appeal to the "faith and the confidence" of the Convention. They agreed that a permanent Constitution for the United States should contain a Bill of Rights — and they proposed ratification by the State of New York "in full faith and confidence" that a Bill of Rights would be promptly submitted to the several States by the first Congress to meet under the Constitution.

You and I know today that it was this proposal which won final adherence to the Constitution by a small margin; and more than that — that this proposal of "full faith and confidence" was in fact carried out by the Congress of the United States when it assembled.

I do not know that it is necessary to elaborate on this parable, or text. It is perhaps sufficient for me to say that when in almost every generation between 1788 and 1938 the American people have been faced with similar decisions, they have in the long run expressed their "full faith and confidence" in the integrity and safety of the national concept.

It required great patience between 1783 and 1788 to bring home the realization that thirteen separate colonies, become thirteen separate states, could not survive as thirteen separate nationalities. Leadership toward the thought of a united Nation had to be patient, and it was. Perseverance of leadership combined with patience has always won.

Once the Constitution was ratified it presented the outline of a form of government. To become a workable instrument of government its words needed men in every succeeding generation to administer it, as great as the men who wrote it.

And the greatest of them have been the men who have sought to make the Constitution workable in the face of the new problems and conditions that have faced the American Nation from year to year.

Yes, the greatest of them have not been those who have said — "It will not work; it cannot be done; it must be changed" — but rather those who have applied to the Constitution of the United States the spirit of "full faith and confidence" which has come down to us today from the Convention which met here in the summer of 1788.

118 (Presidential Statement on the Report of the Commission on Industrial Relations in Sweden. September 25, 1938

THE FACTUAL report on industrial relations in Sweden has been given me by the Secretary of Labor. It parallels the statement on industrial relations in Great Britain, prepared and submitted by the same nine eminent representatives of different points of view and interests within our country.

It, like its predecessor, is a unanimous report. It comes to me in response to my request for an impartial statement on labor-employer relations in Sweden.

The widespread interest and praise which the report on conditions existing in Great Britain received warrants my adding to my own thanks, the appreciation of all Americans concerned with the adjustment of our own problems. This report deserves the same thoughtful and thorough reading which I recommended for the British study.

Although differences between the practices within the two countries are apparent, the striking fact emerging from a study of the two documents is the similarity of approach and the widespread satisfaction with the procedures adopted. In Sweden, as in Great Britain, employers generally have fully accepted a program of collective bargaining; there is extensive independent organization of both groups and all concerned live up to the rules of the game, participating with restraint and mutual respect in the processes of collective bargaining.

(See also Items 77 and 109, this volume, for discussion of report on industrial relations in Great Britain.)

119 ⟨A Message to the Annual Convention of the American Federation of Labor. September 26, 1938

My dear President Green:

WILL YOU be good enough to extend my warm greetings to those who attend the Fifty-eighth Annual Convention of the American Federation of Labor? I wish much that I could accept your very kind invitation to the Convention but in these critical days Houston is, for me, a little too far from Washington.

During your lifetime and mine a vast improvement in the conditions of labor and the pay of labor in many occupations in most parts of the country has been brought about. This has come about largely through the efforts of organized labor. But much still remains to be done.

Collective bargaining is one of the most useful devices for fair and constructive human relations and collective bargaining in the industrial field presupposes some kind of organization of employees to conduct their part of such bargaining.

I hope you will give attention to the matter which I am always concerned about, namely, finding ways for steady employment of labor and increasing the annual purchasing power. It is what a worker earns for himself and his family in the course of a year which is important, not only for his own economic plan for his life, but for the economic life of the nation. In many sections and in many occupations which fall under the general classification of labor, there are millions of Americans who suffer from inadequate pay or over-long hours, or both.

Because for more than a quarter of a century I have had so many associations and friendships with officers of the American Federation of Labor and of the International Unions which it represents, I venture to express the hope that the Convention will leave open every possible door of access to peace and progress in the affairs of organized labor in the United States. If leaders of organized labor can make and keep the peace among various opinions and factions within the labor group itself, it will vastly increase the prestige of labor with the country and prevent the reaction which otherwise is bound to injure the workers themselves.

I commend to all representatives of labor and management the reading of the report on relations between employers and employees in England and in Sweden, which has been made by a number of prominent Americans during the past summer. The outstanding feature of this report is that in both these countries cooperation, compromise and labor peace seem to be the rule rather than the exception.

I hope the Federation will have a highly successful Convention and that you will ever keep before you the American ideals of greater social and economic security.

Very sincerely yours,

Honorable William Green,
President,
American Federation of Labor,
Washington, D. C.

(Read at Convention of American Federation of Labor, Oct. 4, 1938.)

120 ❡ The President's Message to Czechoslovakia, Germany, Great Britain, and France Seeking a Peaceful Solution of the Threat of War, September 26, 1938, and Hitler's Reply thereto, September 27, 1938

THE FABRIC of peace on the continent of Europe, if not throughout the rest of the world, is in immediate danger. The consequences of its rupture are incalculable. Should hostilities break out the lives of millions of men, women and children in every country involved will most certainly be lost under circumstances of unspeakable horror.

The economic system of every country involved is certain to be shattered. The social structure of every country involved may well be completely wrecked.

The United States has no political entanglements. It is caught in no mesh of hatred. Elements of all Europe have formed its civilization.

The supreme desire of the American people is to live in peace. But in the event of a general war they face the fact that no nation can escape some measure of the consequences of such a world catastrophe.

The traditional policy of the United States has been the furtherance of the settlement of international disputes by pacific means. It is my conviction that all people under the threat of war today pray that peace may be made before, rather than after, war.

It is imperative that peoples everywhere recall that every civilized nation of the world voluntarily assumed the solemn obligations of the Kellogg-Briand Pact of 1928 to solve controversies only by pacific methods. In addition, most nations are parties to other binding treaties obligating them to preserve peace. Furthermore, all countries have today available for such peaceful solution of difficulties which may arise, treaties of arbitration and conciliation to which they are parties.

Whatever may be the differences in the controversies at issue and however difficult of pacific settlement they may be, I am persuaded that there is no problem so difficult or so pressing for solution that it cannot be justly solved by the resort to reason rather than by the resort to force.

During the present crisis the people of the United States and their Government have earnestly hoped that the negotiations for the adjustment of the controversy which has now arisen in Europe might reach a successful conclusion.

So long as these negotiations continue, so long will there remain the hope that reason and the spirit of equity may prevail and that the world may thereby escape the madness of a new resort to war.

On behalf of the 130 millions of people of the United States of America and for the sake of humanity everywhere I most earnestly appeal to you not to break off negotiations looking to a peaceful, fair, and constructive settlement of the questions at issue.

I earnestly repeat that so long as negotiations continue, differences may be reconciled. Once they are broken off reason is banished and force asserts itself.

And force produces no solution for the future good of humanity.

Adolf Hitler's reply follows:

His Excellency the President of the United States of America,
Mr. Franklin D. Roosevelt,
Washington.

In your telegram received by me on September 26th, Your Excellency addressed to me an appeal in the name of the American people, in the interest of the maintenance of peace not to break off the negotiations regarding the dispute which has arisen in Europe and to strive for a peaceful, honorable and constructive settlement of this question.

Be assured that I can fully appreciate the lofty intent on which your remarks are based, and that I share in every respect your opinion regarding the unforeseeable consequences of a European war. Precisely for this reason, however, I can and must refuse all responsibility of the German people and their leaders, if the further development, contrary to all my efforts up to the present should actually lead to the outbreak of hostilities. In order to arrive at a fair judgment regarding the Sudeten-German problem under discussion, it is indispensable to consider the incidents, in which, in the last analysis the origin of this problem and its dangers has its cause.

In 1918, the German people laid down their arms, in the firm confidence that by the conclusion of peace with their enemies at that time the principles and ideals would be realized which had been solemnly announced by President Wilson and had been just as solemnly accepted as binding by all the belligerent powers. Never in history has the confidence of a people been more shamefully betrayed, than it was then. The peace conditions imposed on the conquered nations in the Paris suburbs treaties have fulfilled nothing of the promises given. Rather have they created a political regime in Europe which made of the conquered nations world pariahs without rights and which must be recognized in advance by every discerning person as untenable.

One of the points, in which the character of the dictates of 1919 was the most openly revealed was the founding of the Czechoslovakian state, and the establishment of its boundaries without any consideration of history and nationality. The Sudeten land was also included therein, although this area had always been German, and although its inhabitants, after the destruction of the Hapsburg monarchy, had unanimously declared their desire for annexation to the German Reich. Thus the right of self-determination, which had been proclaimed by President Wilson as the most important basis of national life, was simply denied to the Sudeten Germans. But that was not enough. In the treaties of 1919, certain obligations, with regard to the German people, which, according to the text were far-reaching, were imposed on the Czechoslovakian state. These obligations also were disregarded from the first. The League of Nations has completely failed to guarantee the fulfillment of these obligations in connection with the task assigned to it.

Since then, the Sudeten land has been engaged in the severest struggle for the maintenance of its Germanism. It was a natural and inevitable development that after the recovery of strength by the German Reich and after the reunion of Austria with it, the urge of the German Sudetens for maintenance of their culture and for closer union with Germany increased. Despite the loyal attitude of the Sudeten German party and its leaders, the difference with the Czechs became ever stronger. From day to day it became ever clearer that the Government in Prague was not disposed really to consider seriously the most elementary rights of the Sudeten Germans. Rather did it attempt with ever more violent methods of the Czechization of the Sudeten land. It was inevitable that this procedure would lead to ever greater and more serious tensions.

The German Government, at first, did not intervene in any way in this development of things, and maintained its calm restraint, even when the Czechoslovakian Government, in May of this year, proceeded to a mobilization of its army, under the purely fictitious pretext of German troop concentrations. The renunciation of military counter-measures at that time in Germany, however, only served to strengthen the uncompromising attitude of the Government in Prague. This has been clearly shown by the course of the negotiations of the Sudeten German party with the government, regarding a peaceful adjustment. These negotiations produced the conclusive proof that the Czechoslovakian Government was far from thoroughly grasping the problem of the Sudeten Germans and bringing about an equitable solution. Consequently conditions in the Czechoslovakian state, as is generally known, have in the last few weeks become utterly intolerable.

Political persecution and economic oppression have plunged the Sudeten Germans into extreme misery. To characterize these circumstances it is enough to refer to the following. There are at present 214,000 Sudeten German refugees who had to leave their house and home in their ancestral country and flee across the German border, as they saw therein the last and only possibility to escape from the revolting Czechoslovakian régime of violence and bloodiest terror. Countless dead, thousands of injured, ten thousands of persons arrested and imprisoned, desolated villages are the accusing witnesses before world opinion of an outbreak of hostilities carried out for a long time by the Prague Government which you in your telegram rightly fear.

Entirely aside from the German economic life in the Sudeten German territory, for 20 years systematically destroyed by the Czech Government, which already shows all the signs of ruin, which you anticipate as the result of an outbreak of war these are the facts which compelled me in my Nuremberg speech of September 13th to state before the whole world that the deprivation of rights of the three and one-half millions of Germans in Czechoslovakia must be stopped and that these people if they of themselves cannot find justice and help, must receive both from the German Reich. However, to make a last attempt, to reach the goal in a peaceful way, I made concrete proposals for the solution of the problem in a memorandum delivered on September 23rd to the British Premier, which, in the meantime has been made public.

Since the Czechoslovakian Government had previously declared itself already to be in agreement with the British and French Governments that the Sudeten German settlement area would be separated from the Czechoslovakian state and joined to the German Reich, the proposals of the German memorandum contemplate nothing else than to bring about a prompt and equitable fulfillment of that Czechoslovakian promise.

It is my conviction that you, Mr. President, when you realize the whole development of the Sudeten German problem from its inception to the present day, will recognize that the German Government has truly not been lacking either in patience or a sincere desire for a peaceful understanding. It is not Germany who is to blame for the fact that there is any Sudeten German problem at all, and that the present unjustifiable circumstances have arisen from it. The terrible fate of the people affected by the problem no longer admits of a further postponement of its solution. The possibilities of arriving at a just settlement by agreement are therefore exhausted with the proposals of the German memorandum.

It does not rest with the German Government, but with the Czechoslovakian Government alone, to decide, whether it wants peace or war.

ADOLF HITLER

121 ❨ The President Again Seeks Peace. September 27, 1938

His Excellency
Adolf Hitler
Chancellor of the German Reich
Berlin, Germany.

I desire to acknowledge Your Excellency's reply to my telegram of September 26. I was confident that you would coincide in the opinion I expressed regarding the unforeseeable consequences and the incalculable disaster which would result to the entire world from the outbreak of a European war.

The question before the world today, Mr. Chancellor, is not the question of errors of judgment or of injustices committed in the past. It is the question of the fate of the world today and tomorrow. The world asks of us who at this moment are heads of nations the supreme capacity to achieve the destinies of nations without forcing upon them, as a price, the mutilation and death of millions of citizens.

Resort to force in the Great War failed to bring tranquillity. Victory and defeat were alike sterile. That lesson the world should have learned. For that reason above all others I addressed on September 26 my appeal to Your Excellency and to the President of Czechoslovakia and to the Prime Ministers of Great Britain and of France.

The two points I sought to emphasize were, first, that all matters of difference between the German Government and the Czechoslovak Government could and should be settled by pacific methods; and, second, that the threatened alternative of the use of force on a scale likely to result in a general war is as unnecessary as it is unjustifiable. It is, therefore, supremely important that negotiations should continue without interruption until a fair and constructive solution is reached.

My conviction on these two points is deepened because responsible statesmen have officially stated that an agreement in principle has already been reached between the Government of the German Reich and the Government of Czechoslovakia, although the precise time, method and detail of carrying out that agreement remain at issue.

Whatever existing differences may be, and whatever their merits may be—and upon them I do not and need not undertake to pass—my appeal was solely that negotiations be continued until a peaceful settlement is found, and that thereby a resort to force be avoided.

Present negotiations still stand open. They can be continued if you will give the word. Should the need for supplementing them become evident, nothing stands in the way of widening their scope into a conference of all the nations directly interested in the present controversy. Such a meeting to be held immediately—in some neutral spot in Europe—would offer the opportunity for this and correlated questions to be solved in a spirit of justice, of fair dealing, and, in all human probability, with greater permanence.

In my considered judgment, and in the light of the experience of this century, continued negotiations remain the only way by which the immediate problem can be disposed of upon any lasting basis.

Should you agree to a solution in this peaceful manner I am convinced that hundreds of millions throughout the world would recognize your action as an outstanding historic service to all humanity.

Allow me to state my unqualified conviction that history, and the souls of every man, woman, and child whose lives will be lost in the threatened war, will hold us and all of us accountable should we omit any appeal for its prevention.

The Government of the United States has no political involvements in Europe, and will assume no obligations in the conduct of the present negotiations. Yet in our own right we recognize our responsibilities as a part of a world of neighbors.

The conscience and the impelling desire of the people of my country demand that the voice of their government be raised again and yet again to avert and to avoid war.

122 ⟨A Message on Education for American Education Week. September 27, 1938

To the teachers and patrons of American schools:

As AMERICAN EDUCATION WEEK is once more observed throughout the schools of the United States opportunity again is afforded to evaluate the part which our schools play in the preservation and promotion of democratic life.

The conflict is still sharpening throughout the world between two political systems. The one system represents government by freedom of choice exercised by the individual citizens. In the other, and opposing system, individual freedom and initiative are all made subordinate to the totalitarian state. In this conflict the part which education plays in each ideology is crucial.

Democracy cannot succeed unless those who express their choice are prepared to choose wisely. The real safeguard of democracy, therefore, is education. It has been well said that no system of government gives so much to the individual or exacts so much as a democracy. Upon our educational system must largely depend the perpetuity of those institutions upon which our freedom and our security rest. To prepare each citizen to choose wisely and to enable him to choose freely are paramount functions of the schools in a democracy.

So I think it is of happy significance that one of the topics selected for emphasis in this year's observance of Education Week is: "Holding fast to our ideals of freedom." Upon the maintenance of those ideals depends all of our happiness.

123 ⟨ The President Reports on the Public Works Administration Program.
September 30, 1938

TODAY the Public Works Administration met the first of three dead lines fixed for its present program by Congress, and Administrator Ickes has given me a brief report on progress which shows:

1. In the 101 days since I signed the 1938 PWA Act on June 21, communities all over the country have filed close to 10,000 applications for PWA improvements, volunteering to assess themselves 55 per cent of the cost to become partners with the Federal Government in the program.

2. No more applications can be accepted after today under the law. Fears expressed early in the summer that cities and States would not volunteer sufficient funds to carry out

the program have been proven unfounded. The response has been so eager that we have received double the number of worth-while projects we can care for.

3. Close to 7,000 projects, both Federal and non-Federal, have received allotments with my approval and are proceeding. Virtually all funds have been already allotted to eligible projects and a comparatively small balance still is available for projects (less than $100,000,000 which is being allotted out).

4. The next deadline fixed by Congress is January 1, 1939, and by that date construction must start. Although that deadline is still three months away, the program has been expedited to such an extent that over 1,000 projects are already under construction with dirt flying and walls rising.

5. The third and last deadline fixed by Congress is July 1, 1940, when the projects of the present program are to be completed. Administrator Ickes has required each body to which an allotment was made to contract to finish the work undertaken by that date.

The report shows that although the present program is the largest undertaken in such a limited time by PWA, the program is now operating successfully on a fast timetable and the recovery effects of the program are already being registered, not only by permanent public improvements but also by construction and materials production employment.

NOTE: For a discussion of the Public Works Administration (popularly known as PWA) see Items 80, 89 and 117 and notes, 1933 volume. It should be distinguished from the WPA.

Since the report of September 30, 1938, which was made by me in the foregoing item, remarkably rapid progress has been made.

As of January 1, 1941, just two years from the deadline of December 31, 1938, for the starting of construction on PWA projects authorized under the 1938 PWA Act, only a handful of projects remain uncompleted.

This vast program, which got under way in the last six months of 1938, consisted of 6,149 non-Federal projects costing $1,458,157,025, and of 1,830 Federal projects costing $199,999,716.

These 6,149 non-Federal projects were allotted from a vast number of applications, including 12,814 submitted by various sponsors throughout the country within the deadline date of September 30, 1938. These applications called for a program costing over $4,000,000,-000, and inasmuch as PWA was unable to finance this entire program within the funds appropriated, the Administrator, on September 6, 1939, ordered the return of 5,043 of the applications (for projects costing $1,700,000,000), to their sponsors, in order to enable them to secure other means for carrying out the construction of their projects.

By December 31, 1938, the deadline for starting construction, as set out in the Act, all PWA projects had commenced with the exception of a few which were delayed by litigation proceedings. By July 1, 1940, only 12 per cent of the projects remained uncompleted, and 11 per cent of the construction work remained to be placed. The latter date, which was designated in the Act as the deadline for completion of the program, was extended by an Act of Congress to July 1, 1941. This was done to enable completion of construction on those projects delayed by litigation, and on other projects which were delayed by weather and other uncontrollable causes.

At this time (January 1, 1941) there remains less than $60,000,000 of construction work to be done on Federal and non-Federal projects allotted under the 1938 PWA program.

124 ⟨ A Greeting to the Eighth National Eucharistic Congress. October 1, 1938

My dear Archbishop Rummel:

I SEND hearty greetings to you and through you to all who gather within the hospitable borders of the Archdiocese of New Orleans on the occasion of the Eighth National Eucharistic Congress. I trust that the deliberations will quicken the spiritual life of all who participate and inspire them with new zeal for the work of the Master whom we all serve.

We have just celebrated the one hundred fiftieth anniversary of the adoption of our Federal Constitution, which guarantees freedom of conscience as the cornerstone of all our liberties. We in this country are upholders of the ideal of democracy in the government of man. We believe with heart and soul that in the long struggle of the human race to attain an orderly society the democratic form of government is the highest achievement. All of our hopes have their basis in the democratic ideal.

Even before the adoption of our Declaration of Independence George Mason, in the Virginia Declaration of Rights, voiced what has become one of the deepest convictions of the American people: "That religion, or the duty which we owe to our Creator, and the manner of discharging it, can be directed only by reason and conviction, not by force or violence, and therefore all men are equally entitled to the free exercise of religion, according to the dictates of conscience; and that it is the mutual duty of all to practice Christian forbearance, love, and charity towards each other."

We still remain true to the faith of our fathers who established religious liberty when the nation began. We must remember, too, that our forebears in every generation, and wherever they established their homes, made prompt and generous provision for the institutions of religion. We must continue their steadfast reliance upon the Providence of God.

I have said and I repeat to this solemn Eucharistic Congress that no greater blessing could come to our land today than a revival of the spirit of religion. I doubt if there is any problem in the world today — social, political or economic — that would not find happy solution if approached in the spirit of the Sermon on the Mount.

May your prayers hasten the day when both men and nations will bring their lives into conformity with the teaching of Him Who is the Way, the Light and the Truth.

Very sincerely yours,

His Excellency,
The Archbishop of New Orleans,
New Orleans, Louisiana

125 ❨ A Message on Navy Day. October 12, 1938

My dear Mr. Secretary:

I COMMEND again to our countrymen the annual observance of Navy Day in accordance with the established custom of setting apart the birthday of Theodore Roosevelt for that purpose. On this eightieth anniversary of the birth of that distinguished American, it seems particularly fitting to pay tribute to the vision and foresight of one who always urged: "The work of upbuilding the Navy must be steadily continued."

We should rejoice that on this day when the Navy is at home to our people that we are at peace with all the world. But within the past year unsettled world conditions have made it imperative that we take stock of our national defense and face the facts. This survey of defense requirements was brought to the attention of the Congress with the result that an increase in strength of the Navy was authorized in approximation of the needs and responsibilities of our country. I believe it entirely consistent with our continuing readiness to limit armaments by agreement, that we maintain an efficient Navy adequate in men and material to insure positive protection against any aggressor. The Fleet must be ready.

Navy Day brings vividly to mind my pleasant official and personal association with the Navy. The lasting impression that I received of the Navy's efficient work in the stress and strain of war, strengthens my faith in its capacity to meet emergencies. I wish again to express my thanks and that of my fellow countrymen for the Navy's past achievement. The competent leadership that directs our forces afloat and ashore is to be commended.

War will be avoided by all honorable means, but should it come, I feel assured that the efficiency and devotion to duty of officers and men of the Navy will more than justify the confidence of our citizens in their first line of defense.

Very sincerely yours,

The Honorable,
The Secretary of the Navy,
Washington, D. C.

126 ❡ "No Matter How Much the Government Does, the Private Agencies of America Still Have Much to Do Before Any of Us Can Rest on Our Oars or on Our Laurels." Radio Address for the Mobilization for Human Needs.
October 14, 1938

I WANT to say a few words tonight to you, my fellow Americans, who believe in social welfare and social justice:

In troubled days when the nerves of men and women have been strained almost to the breaking point we have been in danger of losing sight of one very important fact — the all-pervading human kindness of men and women. This human kindness cannot be created artificially out of speeches and appeals — it is part of life itself.

In accordance with this thought, I am not this year making a speech or an appeal in behalf of the 1938 Mobilization for Human Needs, but I am calling your attention to the past and present generosity of the people of America. That generosity never has failed and please God it never will fail. In full faith and confidence, therefore, I present to you the news that local Community Chest drives will shortly be undertaken in all parts of the country.

There are some persons who say that the need for voluntary private agencies has decreased. They say that the government — Federal, state and local — has moved in and taken over part of the jurisdiction of the private agencies. Such persons talk as if the scope of voluntary action and mutual aid had been limited, or even eliminated.

Private community effort is not contradictory in principle to government effort, whether local, state or national. All of these are needed to make up the partnership upon which our Nation is founded. The scope of voluntary action cannot be limited, because the very desire to help the less fortunate is a basic and spontaneous human urge that knows no boundary lines. It is an urge that advances civilization. I like to think that it is a national characteristic.

Let me give you an example of successful working-together. One section of our country, New England, has recently been devastated by hurricane and tidal wave. Hundreds of lives were lost and millions of dollars worth of property was destroyed. This was indeed a tragedy. But there was one consolation in this New England tragedy. Hardly had the hurricane subsided when all the forces of government, assisting and cooperating with private agencies, were rushed to the aid of the injured, the sick and the homeless. How many lives were saved because of these efforts no one can say. The extent to which human suffering was alleviated is beyond all estimate. And we can say that no effort was spared to aid the victims of this disaster.

The rehabilitation work is still going on and will for many months to come. The Red Cross, the WPA, the CCC, the NYA, the Army Engineers and other Federal agencies are working with the local agencies, both private and public, to rehabilitate those stricken areas and to assist those who are in need. Certainly, there has been no conflict between government and private agencies — there has been more than enough work for both. And there is more than enough work for both in our national effort to lift up the lower one-third of our Nation to a standard of living that will conform with decency and comfort and self-respect.

It is true that our Government has assumed increased responsibilities for social welfare. We are giving work to more than three million men and women, unemployed through no fault of their own, on our WPA program. Through our Social Security program we are aiding the states in caring for the aged, for widows and children and the blind. We are providing new opportunities for more than a half million boys and girls through our CCC and NYA programs; and in many other ways the Federal Government, in cooperation with the state and local governments, is aiding our underprivileged citizens.

But you may well ask if the need for community action is as great as it was before, now that your Government has provided a national program of social security, how far must you go? I would answer that the need is just as great as before because Government help was intended and is intended to improve the old conditions and if local help and private help decrease today, we shall nullify the improvement we have sought, and return to just where we were before. Very definitely we need the effort of the pioneer agencies, the local voluntary agencies, because it is expended on concrete problems that must be met if our whole program is to go forward with the coordination that is its basic aim.

Community leaders have met the challenge of changing conditions. They are not looking backward with resentment against the Government. They have welcomed the acts of their Government as a liberation of their own efforts, as an opportunity to move forward on a wider front of social progress.

It is these men and women whom I salute. They are the shock troops of the social conscience. I call upon the American people to fall in behind such leadership and to widen the social horizon. I am thoroughly convinced that no matter how much the Government does, the private agencies of America still have much to do before any of us can rest on our oars or on our laurels. I am thoroughly convinced that the American people want to participate on a voluntary and individual basis in the endeavor to make this country the best possible place in which to live. I feel confident that this year's Community Chest drive will be successful in every part of the Nation, as it has been successful in the past and as it will continue to be successful for long years to come.

127 ❨ The Four Hundred and Ninety-first Press Conference (Excerpts). October 14, 1938

(New Washington airport — Budget — Study of mass production of defense weapons — Cooperation of utility companies with the Public Utility Holding Company Act — Power of devaluation of the dollar.)

Q. You look snappy this morning. [Referring to the President's new suit.]

THE PRESIDENT: I am not feeling snappy. I sat up last night hearing the European side of things from Ambassador Bullitt.

I am not going up to Hyde Park until Sunday noon because I cannot get all the work straightened out until then. . . .

Q. Have you heard of the progress of the work on the Gravelly Point Airport?

THE PRESIDENT: Somebody told me yesterday that they hoped to get the first dirt flying in about ten days and I said that when I got back, a week from Monday, I shall drive down with the Commission and look it over. Nothing formal.

Q. Did anybody tell you it will take two years instead of one?

THE PRESIDENT: I don't know.

Q. Your driving down there will inaugurate the work?

THE PRESIDENT: No speech or anything like that.

Q. They wanted you to run a steam shovel.

THE PRESIDENT: No, just drive around.

Q. At the last Conference you told us you might have something to say on the budget at this one. Any comment you can make?

THE PRESIDENT: The only comment is that I cannot make any comment, for the reason that new developments in national defense require such a complete restudy of American national defense that it will defer, necessarily, any budget comments for some time.

Q. Mr. Baruch, when he left yesterday, said that it was his opinion that the Army was lacking in modern equipment. He said that there is definitely not a first-class organization because of lack of what he termed, "modern arms." Do you propose, Mr. President, to ask for additional funds to supply the Army with —

THE PRESIDENT: [interposing] In the first place, I did not read Mr. Baruch's statement, except the headline, so I cannot comment on that, but there are a good many people, not just Mr. Baruch but a good many others, who are very carefully checking up on certain new elements in defense preparedness that have gradually been coming in for the past three or four years, elements that relate, just for example, to the problem of mass production, which we have never yet adequately considered. They are new things, and therefore they require a good deal of study.

Q. That mass production, does that include airplanes?

THE PRESIDENT: Yes, and other things, too.

Q. Have you taken any definite steps toward standardization of certain weapons and plane manufactures, also with the idea of preparing for mass production? I understand there are several branches where standardization is needed, or some people studying it think it is needed, to set up mass production.

THE PRESIDENT: You have answered your own question. The words, "mass production" necessarily mean "standardization." You cannot have mass production unless you have standardization.

Q. Has your product reached a point of development where you feel you can standardize?

THE PRESIDENT: Other nations are doing it.

Q. Is any centralized or interdepartmental body studying this?

THE PRESIDENT: No, I am doing it.

Q. Is that study being conducted with civilian advice?

THE PRESIDENT: Every known kind.

Q. Is it the intent to create an organization similar to the wartime War Industries Board?

547

THE PRESIDENT: No, this has nothing to do with machinery for running it. It is a question of national defense.

Q. Is it contemplated to materially increase the size of the Army?

THE PRESIDENT: I cannot give you anything on that, because then you get down to a kind of merely partial report. We are then only taking up one small phase. If you ask me, "Are you going to have two more submarines?" or, "Are you going to give up the cavalry?" or, "Are you doing one thing or the other?" it becomes a very difficult matter because it takes away the whole rounded picture. What I want to do is to give to the country a complete picture, when we are ready, rather than in comparatively minor detail.

For instance, talking off the record, talking about $150,000,000 for two new battleships, of course you people had to write something. It was not a new story, really, because the authorizations had been made last year. Obviously they had to go in. But I don't want to confuse the public by talking about items of that kind. I am thinking in general terms of national defense.

Q. Does the power study enter into it?

THE PRESIDENT: Yes.

Q. Do you contemplate creating a unified Department of Defense?

THE PRESIDENT: That is a pure detail of later administration. What I am doing now is studying a plan to meet needs under rather new world conditions.

Q. When will the plans be ready? Can you tell us the time?

THE PRESIDENT: By the third of January.

Q. Can you throw any light on the reason which led to this decision to reorganize the whole national defense picture?

THE PRESIDENT: I should say, offhand, that it started about a year ago because of information that was coming in at that time. It has been in progress for about a year and it has, in a sense, been forced to a head by events, developments and information received within the past month.

Q. Will you say, are you referring to technical or political matters?

THE PRESIDENT: Defense matters, not political.

Q. I mean information that is coming in, is it technical?

THE PRESIDENT: Yes, technical.

Q. Any comment on the statement made yesterday by Groesbeck, of the Electric Bond and Share, in which he pledged cooperation to the Holding Company Act?

THE PRESIDENT: I asked some information on it yesterday afternoon, supposing that the question would be asked. It is fairly long, and I shall try to touch the high spots.

I am, of course, very glad to read the statement made by Mr. Groesbeck at his stockholders' meeting, I think it was. In trying to evaluate it, I think we can say that the announcement illustrates exactly what I meant in the past when I urged cooperation between business and government in concrete, and not in abstract terms; in other words, not merely by lip service but by getting down to brass tacks.

Secondly, it ought to be clear that the term, "death sentence," which was invented, not by the Government or by the Press but by the utility propagandists, three years and a half ago — that is a matter of record — that that term brought more harm than good to the utilities. We are now going to have the opportunity to prove what we have always contended — go back and read the debates in the hearings — that that Section 11 in the Utility Act was not a death sentence but should properly have been called a "health sentence."

Q. Did you call it a "life sentence"?

THE PRESIDENT: Health sentence. That, apparently, is being recognized by the owners of public utility securities. They are beginning to think that their securities are worth more money now that certain officers of the utilities have given up the old term.

Next, since Mr. Groesbeck is a good business man, the prospect is that private business will be helped by his action in sitting down with a business-minded commission to work things out in a businesslike way; and we hope that other companies will come in. His views will be reflected in the views and statements of other people in similar positions. A number of companies, of course, are in and are cooperating, such as the American Water Works and Electric Company and the Columbia Gas and Electric Company.

Finally, we all wish that this delay might have been avoided, and that the utility companies might have cooperated without the many legal steps they took preceding the Supreme Court's decision upholding the constitutionality of the legislative provisions. On the other hand, this being a democratic country, where democratic processes work, it is a perfectly normal thing to expect that kind of a delay.

Q. Mr. President, do you feel it essential to seek extension of your powers over the dollar after next June thirtieth?

THE PRESIDENT: I have not the faintest idea. I had not thought of it until I read it in this morning's paper. It comes up this time every year, does it not? It is one of the hardy annuals. (*Laughter*) . . .

(See Item 110, 1935 volume, for a discussion of the Public Utility Holding Company Act; for powers over devaluation of the dollar, see Item 16, 1934 volume, and Item 14, 1939 volume.)

128 ⟨A Letter on the Palestine Situation.

October 19, 1938

My dear Senator Tydings:

I FULLY appreciate the concern expressed by you in your letter of October 14, 1938, regarding the Palestine situation. I have on numerous occasions, as you know, expressed my sympathy in the establishment of a National Home for the Jews in Palestine and, despite the set-backs caused by the disorders there during the last few years, I have been heartened by the progress which has been made and by the remarkable accomplishments of the Jewish settlers in that country.

As I have had occasion to inform a number of Members of Congress within the past few days, we have kept constantly before the British Government, through our Ambassador in London, the interest which the American people have in Palestine and I have every reason to believe that that Government is fully cognizant of public opinion on the matter in this country. We were assured, in the discussions which took place in London a little more than a year ago, that the British Government would keep us fully informed of any proposals which it might make to the Council of the League of Nations for the modification of the Palestine Mandate. We expect, therefore, to have the opportunity afforded us of communicating to the British Government our views with respect to any changes in the Mandate which may be proposed as a result of the forthcoming report of the Palestine Partition Commission. I understand, however, that under the terms of our convention with Great Britain regarding the Palestine Mandate we are unable to prevent modifications in the Mandate. The most we can do is to decline to accept as applicable to American interest any modifications affecting such interests unless we have given our assent to them.

You may be sure that we shall continue to follow the situation with the closest attention.

Sincerely yours,

The Honorable
Millard E. Tydings,
United States Senate.

129 ❨ The President Recommends Carrying Out the Proposals of the Northern Great Plains Committee. October 19, 1938

My dear Governor Cochran:

I AM sending you herewith a copy of a preliminary report by the Northern Great Plains Committee, entitled "Rehabilitation in the Northern Great Plains." This Committee, which included in its membership representatives of both Federal and State agencies, was appointed at my request by the National Resources Committee to suggest measures, including specific changes in Federal procedure and policy affecting land and water conservation, which might be carried out promptly in order to promote the rehabilitation of the area.

The Committee's recommendations are of three classes from the standpoint of action necessary to effectuate them.

First, certain improvements in the activities of Federal agencies may be made under existing authorizations of the Congress. I approve the recommendations of the Committee in these particulars, and I have directed all executive departments and agencies to modify their procedures accordingly. The report outlines the character of rehabilitation work which will be undertaken by the Federal government during the fiscal year 1939.

Second, several proposed changes in policy may be made only under new authorization of the Congress. I hope that the suggestions of this nature may receive careful study by the Congress at its next session.

Third, the responsibility for a number of basic lines of constructive action rests largely or wholly with state and local agencies. I recommend that you review the proposals of this class, and I hope that you may carry out such of them as are appropriate to the conditions in your state. A large measure of responsibility for the success or failure of a rehabilitation program in the Northern Great Plains rests with the state and local governments.

Sincerely yours,

Hon. Roy L. Cochran,
Governor of Nebraska,
Lincoln, Nebraska.

(Identical letters were sent to Governors of North Dakota, South Dakota, Wyoming and Montana.)

NOTE: For a discussion of the objectives and contents of the report, see Item 16 and note, 1937 volume.

The Northern Great Plains Committee recommendations involved proposals for action by both the federal government and state and local agencies; therefore I sent the foregoing letter to the five state governors in that area.

130 ⟨ The Four Hundred and Ninety-third Press Conference (Excerpts). Hyde Park, New York. October 21, 1938

(Statistics on tourist travel in national parks — Reform of rules of judicial procedure — Compliance with Wage-Hour law — Voluntary application of Wage-Hour law standards to intrastate commerce.)

Q. Good morning, Mr. President.

THE PRESIDENT: Good morning, Frederic [Storm]. How is the boy? What did you do yesterday with all the rain going on? What kind of golf did you play?

Q. Indoor golf.

MR. MC INTYRE: The game they call galloping golf.

THE PRESIDENT: Oh, that is a very expensive game.

Q. [Mr. Belair] Yes, sir; it is.

THE PRESIDENT: Now, let us see what I have got. I have several things here, if you are short of stories.

Q. We certainly are, Mr. President.

THE PRESIDENT: I can give you lots of stuff.

No. 1: I have always checked up on the tourist travel in

553

the National Parks, in just the way I used to check up every year when I was Governor, on the tourist travel in the Adirondack Park and in the Catskill Park and in the various State Parks, as being something of an indication of the condition of the country.

Here is a memorandum that I got from Slattery, which I will give Mac [Mr. McIntyre] to show to you. It has the figures in it but it is not to be used in a statement. It was made out in the form of a statement by me, because there is a whole lot of material here that you need not use. (*Reading*)

"As I have repeatedly emphasized, it is my desire, and the purpose of this Administration, to raise the American standard of living so that all of the people may enjoy better economic security and good living. Public use of the national parks, which are created for the benefit and enjoyment of the people, shows how well we have succeeded."

You can put that in your own language. (*Reading*)

"In 1933, administrative responsibility for many of the historical parks and national monuments was scattered among several departments of the Federal Government. For economy and the maintenance of consistent standards of public service, I consolidated that responsibility in the National Park Service of the Department of the Interior.

"In 1934, the first year that travel statistics were recorded for the consolidated national park and monument system, 6,337,206 people visited those reservations. In 1935, the travel figure climbed to 7,676,490; in 1936, it increased to 11,989,793; in 1937, it mounted to 15,133,432; and in 1938, 16,233,688 people visited the areas in the national park and monument system."

In other words, in four years the number of people who are visiting National Parks and Monuments has increased more than two and a half times, which is a very interesting thing. . . .

It is a beautiful statement. You can take all kinds of beautiful things out of it as long as you do not take it as my statement.

Q. This does not include the National Forests?

THE PRESIDENT: Yes. Of course, in the National Forests they have not the same kind of a checkup on numbers, as they have in the National Parks and Monuments, because so many people go into the National Forests without going over a road.

Q. In line with these statistics as reflecting the condition of the country, have you any comment to make upon the widespread back-to-work movement in the automobile industry.

THE PRESIDENT: Of course the only comment is that it is a very delightful fact.

Q. And that, of course, will help in holding down WPA spending?

THE PRESIDENT: Yes.

Then, here is another thing: I have been digging these things up. Here is another thing I have had for about a week or ten days. I cannot give you very much in the way of details on it because I have not got them. It is the kind of a thing that is good, if you want to write a special story when you get back to Washington.

Back in 1937, the Congress at the suggestion of myself and the Attorney General — this was part of the Court objective — passed a bill setting up a board, commission or group of Federal Judges to reorganize and reform Federal Court practice and procedure.

Up to that time there were a great many complaints about Federal Court practice. It was slow, it was not uniform, it had a great many excrescences. It had grown up over a great many years. It required speeding up for better justice, and, especially, for quicker justice. This committee of Federal Judges met and, in accordance with the terms of the Act, made a report last spring, which I sent to the Congress.

That report laid down a whole new series of simplification and standardization rules. The Act provided that the Congress would have the right to veto these rules before it adjourned; but that if they did not veto the rules before they adjourned, they would go into effect on the first of October. The Congress did not take any action on the rules, one way or the other, and therefore they went into effect on the first day of October.

The result is one of the most important steps that we have taken for the reform of Federal judicial procedure.

And it is rather interesting as a sidelight on methods of Government, taking it in a broad way. If the Congress had attempted to formulate rules themselves, which they had a perfect right to do, what would have happened? In all human probability, nothing would have happened. It was a more or less technical problem. It had been discussed for twenty years, and nothing had happened.

Therefore, the Congress very wisely said, "We haven't got the time, in a body consisting of the House and Senate, to go into the details of Court rules; therefore we will delegate the legislative function to set up rules to a committee of experts composed of Judges and assisted by the Department of Justice. And we will provide that what they bring in, in the form of rules, will automatically go into effect, provided the Congress itself does not veto them."

The result is that we have taken one of the most important steps we have ever taken.

Now, I do not have to point out to you the analogy between that procedure and a good many other problems of Government, such as reorganization and a good many other problems of actual administration. Rules of a Court are essentially an administrative problem, and these new rules will improve the administration of justice. They are laid down by the people who run the Courts, the Judges and the Department of Justice; and the Congress gave to itself the right to veto them.

MR. MCINTYRE: Is there any precedent for that action that you know of?

THE PRESIDENT: That we do not know, but it is an interesting accomplishment, and a very sound way for getting more or less technical problems solved. Most people in this country do not know about it at all because it has had just a stick or two. But all the lawyers who practised in the Federal Courts are quite thrilled by what has been accomplished.

Q. For the purposes of our stories, are not those rather unimportant in themselves, as far as our story is concerned?

THE PRESIDENT: No, they are tremendously important from the point of view of the lawyer. They are very drastic. It is the most drastic thing that has ever happened in the practice and procedure before the Federal Courts.

Q. Stories have been printed on it.

THE PRESIDENT: You will probably find it in the files but it is the kind of thing that is not known to the general public at all.

Q. Mr. President, naturally you are cheered over the method by which this was accomplished?

THE PRESIDENT: Yes, it is a practical way of accomplishing Administrative reforms.

Q. Have you anything else in mind that you think might be carried out along this line, such as reorganization?

THE PRESIDENT: Yes. After all, that is the principle. It is the principle and the objective of what I have said all along about reorganization. In other words, give to the people who are responsible for administration in the Executive Branch of the Government, just as they did to people who were responsible in the Judicial Branch of the Government, the right to bring in new rules, new plans, to the Congress; and give to Congress the right to veto those plans within a given time. Exactly the same thing.

Then I have one other thing here. I have had reports from Administrator Andrews, of the Wage-Hour Administration, that are very gratifying in that there is a general disposition being shown by employers throughout the country to comply with the law.

The response has been such that the Administrator has some hope that many employers engaged in intrastate commerce may voluntarily accept the standards that are being set up for interstate commerce.

MR. MC INTYRE: Couldn't they use that as a direct statement, just as you gave it?

THE PRESIDENT: Yes, it is all right.

Q. Mr. Andrews —

THE PRESIDENT: [interposing] Yes. In other words, the Federal Government has the constitutional right only to regulate wages and hours in interstate commerce; but it has been our thought behind the exercise of that right that local industries, operating only in commerce within a given state, would voluntarily adopt the standards of the other people. And it seems to be working out. . . .

Q. Is there anything you can tell us about your conversation with Mr. Bullitt?

THE PRESIDENT: No; he has been up here having a holiday. We have had no conversation.

Q. Nothing on war debts?

THE PRESIDENT: No, certainly not. I am sorry to spoil that story which appeared in the papers, too. (*Laughter*)

Q. The picnic lunch was right? We had that right?

THE PRESIDENT: Yes, you had that right. That was all right. . . .

(See Item 102, 1937 volume, and Item 105, 1939 volume, for a further discussion of judicial reforms; see notes to Items 41 and 44, this volume, for an account of the Reorganization Act of 1939; see note to Item 57, 1937 volume, for an analysis of the wages and hours act.)

131 ❨ A Statement on the Sit-Down Strikes in Michigan and Governor Murphy.
October 25, 1938

At the press conference of Oct. 25, 1938, one of the newspaper men.present asked the President the following question:

"Mr. President: Are you concerned with the testimony that has been given before the Dies Committee, particularly in the case of Governor Murphy, of Michigan? Testimony last week charged him with treasonable activities in the settlement of the sit-down strikes in Michigan two years ago."

The following reply was made:

THE PRESIDENT:

"Yes, I certainly am concerned with that kind of testimony. I should like to say something about it, but I think it probably would be better if I wrote something out instead of trying to talk extemporaneously."

Later, the following statement was issued to the press by the President:

I was very much disturbed. I was disturbed not because of the absurdly false charges made by a coterie of disgruntled Republican officeholders against a profoundly religious, able and law-abiding Governor; but because a Congressional Committee charged with the responsibility of investigating un-American activities should have permitted itself to be used in a flagrantly unfair and un-American attempt to influence an election.

At this hearing the Dies Committee made no effort to get at the truth, either by calling for facts to support mere personal opinion or by allowing facts and personal opinion on the other side. On the threshold of a vitally important gubernatorial election, they permitted a disgruntled Republican judge, a discharged Republican City Manager and a couple of officious police officers to make lurid charges against Governor Frank Murphy, without attempting to elicit from them facts as to their undeniable bias and their charges and without attempting to obtain from the Governor or, for that matter, from any responsible motor manufacturer, his version of the events.

Governor Murphy's painstaking and statesmanlike efforts to bring about a settlement of the sit-down strikes and to avert bloodshed and riot were not shrouded in secrecy. Every important move he made was communicated to the motor manufacturers and the union leaders affected, and was reported fully in the daily press. I received almost daily reports on the situation from the Governor.

Governor Murphy never said a word in condonation of the sit-down strike or any illegal practice. But the Governor was informed by responsible officials of the National Guard that any attempt on the part of the National Guard forcibly to eject the sit-down strikers at Flint would result in bloodshed and riot. Knowing these facts, the Governor labored in the open, in the American way, to bring about a prompt settlement of the labor trouble without resort to force.

Governor Murphy always insisted that the lawful order of the court must be obeyed. But knowing that negotiations for settlement were proceeding and that precipitous efforts to enforce the court order would result in violence which would disrupt peaceful negotiations, he requested the sheriff to postpone the enforcement of the court order over the week end. For that act a few petty politicians accuse him of treason; for that act every peace-loving American should praise him.

By Wednesday of the week following Governor Murphy's request for a temporary postponement of the enforcement of the court order, the strike — which was probably the most alarming strike which ever occurred in this country — was brought to an end without the loss of a single human life. That was a great achievement of a Great American. Governor Frank Murphy's great accomplishment elicited the commendation of all the important motor manufacturers involved, of Mr. Sloan and Mr. Knudsen of General Motors, of Mr. Chrysler of Chrysler Motors, and of the Fisher Brothers of the Fisher Body Corporation, of Mr. Barrett of Hudson Motors and of Mr. Graham of Graham Motors.

In handling the dangerous labor situation in Michigan in the dark days of 1937, Governor Murphy, as a true American, was concerned not only with the letter but the spirit of the law. Governor Murphy accordingly strove, and strove successfully, to effectuate a settlement not by force but by reason — a settlement which would satisfy not merely the letter of the law, but the community's sense of right and of justice.

Most fair-minded Americans hope that the committee will abandon the practice of merely providing a forum to those who, for political purposes, or otherwise, seek headlines which they could not otherwise obtain. Mere opinion evidence has been barred in court since the American system of legislative and judicial procedure was started.

Three weeks ago, the civilized world was threatened by the immediate outbreak of a world war. Cool heads pleaded for the continuance of negotiations. People may properly differ as to the result of such negotiations but the fact remains that bloodshed was averted.

In the Winter of 1937, Governor Murphy was confronted with the same kind of situation on a smaller scale. He knew that if negotiations were broken off bloodshed was inevitable. He worked successfully for the continuation of the negotiations. As a result of his fine leadership, there is no doubt that hundreds and even thousands of human lives were saved. That is the American way of doing things.

(See note to Item 72, 1937 volume for further discussion of the strikes of 1937.)

132 ❨ The President Resents the Misuse of His Name in the Pennsylvania Political Campaign. October 26, 1938

My dear Mr. Doyle:

I APPRECIATE very much your calling my attention to the misuse of my name and the name of my Administration in the Pennsylvania campaign.

Many months ago, I made it clear that while I am not asking voters to vote for Democrats, next November, as opposed to Republicans or members of any other Party, nevertheless, I have the right to speak out in those instances where there has been a clear or deliberate misuse of my own name. That has happened in Pennsylvania.

I recognize that my name and the name of my Administration cannot wholly be eliminated from the campaign. Candidates for Congress ought to express their views on the vital national issues. Candidates for state offices ought to express their views on the vital issues respecting the cooperation of the state administration with the national administration.

But I also recognize that there are local and personal issues wholly distinct from the national issues. I have endeavored to the best of my ability to keep away from such local and personal issues. No one human being, particularly if he is occupied with numerous and important national problems, can be expected to be able to inform himself sufficiently to pass upon local and personal issues in many different states and districts.

But in my own relations with the Earle administration I can truthfully say that I have found it at all times willing and eager to help in carrying into effect a liberal program for social and economic justice. I therefore feel that I have every right to object to Judge James' saying in his speeches that I have deliberately refrained from meddling in local issues in Pennsylvania because I was unwilling "to put my hands in that muddy water." That deliberately misrepresents the facts.

As Judge James has misused my name in the Pennsylvania campaign I do not think it is amiss for me to point out that, to put it mildly, there is a clear inconsistency in his position in appealing for the votes of opponents of the New Deal on the ground that he is opposed to the New Deal and in appealing for the votes of liberals on the ground that I am not actively participating in the Pennsylvania campaign.

That does not make sense.

As against his inconsistency, it seems to me that liberals in Pennsylvania, irrespective of party, can scarcely place their trust in the liberalism or desire for social justice of any candidates who are sponsored by such obvious reactionaries as the well-known Messrs. Annenberg, Grundy and Pew.

So much for that.

Very sincerely yours,

Mr. Michael Francis Doyle,
1500 Girard Trust Building,
Philadelphia, Pennsylvania.

133 ⟨ "It Is Becoming Increasingly Clear That Peace by Fear Has no Higher or More Enduring Quality Than Peace by the Sword." Radio Address to the Herald-Tribune Forum. October 26, 1938

Mrs. Reid, ladies and gentlemen of the forum:

No ONE who lived through the grave hours of last month can doubt the longing of most of the peoples of the world for an enduring peace. Our business now is to utilize the desire for peace to build principles which are the only basis of permanent peace.

It is becoming increasingly clear that peace by fear has no higher or more enduring quality than peace by the sword.

There can be no peace if the reign of law is to be replaced by a recurrent sanctification of sheer force.

There can be no peace if national policy adopts as a deliberate instrument the threat of war.

There can be no peace if national policy adopts as a deliberate instrument the dispersion all over the world of millions of helpless and persecuted wanderers with no place to lay their heads.

There can be no peace if humble men and women are not free to think their own thoughts, to express their own feelings, to worship God.

There can be no peace if economic resources that ought to be devoted to social and economic reconstruction are to be diverted to an intensified competition in armaments which will merely heighten the suspicions and fears and threaten the economic prosperity of each and every nation.

At no time in modern history has the responsibility which rests upon governments been more obvious or more profound.

I speak for a United States which has no interest in war. We covet nothing save good relations with our neighbors; and we recognize that the world today has become our neighbor.

But in the principle of the good neighbor certain fundamental reciprocal obligations are involved. There must be a deliberate and conscious will that such political changes as changing needs require shall be made peacefully.

That means a due regard for the sanctity of treaties. It means deliberate avoidance of policies which arouse fear and distress. It means the self-restraint to refuse strident ambitions which are sure to breed insecurity and intolerance and thereby weaken the prospect of that economic and moral recovery the world so sadly needs.

You cannot organize civilization around the core of militarism and at the same time expect reason to control human destinies.

For more than twelve years, the United States has been steadily seeking disarmament.

Yet we have consistently pointed out that neither we, nor any nation, will accept disarmament while neighbor nations arm to the teeth. If there is not general disarmament, we ourselves must continue to arm. It is a step we do not like to take, and do not wish to take. But, until there is general abandonment of weapons capable of aggression, ordinary rules of national prudence and common sense require that we be prepared.

We still insist that an armament race among nations is absurd unless new territories or new controls are coveted. We are entitled, I think, to greater reassurance than can be given by words: the kind of proof which can be given, for example, by actual discussions, leading to actual disarmament. Not otherwise can we be relieved of the necessity of increasing our own military and naval establishments. For while we refuse to accept as a permanent necessity the idea of force, and reject it as an ideal of life, we must be prepared to meet with success any application of force against us.

We in the United States do not seek to impose on any other people either our way of life or our internal form of government. But we are determined to maintain and protect that way of life and that form of government for ourselves. And we are determined to use every endeavor in order that the Western Hemisphere may work out its own interrelated salvation in the light of its own interrelated experience.

And we affirm our faith that, whatever choice of way of life a people makes, that choice must not threaten the world with the disaster of war. The impact of such a disaster cannot be confined. It releases a flood-tide of evil emotions fatal to civilized living. That statement applies not to the Western Hemisphere alone but to the whole of Europe and Asia and Africa and the islands of the seas.

In all that I have said to you I have reaffirmed the faith of the American people in democracy. The way of democracy is free discussion — as exemplified by the objectives of the Forum to which I am speaking. Free discussion is most greatly useful when it is restrained and relates to facts. It is not useful to suggest either to the American people or to the peoples of other nations that the American Government, its policies, its practices and its servants are actuated by motives of dishonor or corruption. To do so is, of necessity, an attack on the American system of constitutional representative government itself.

Let us work with greater unity for peace among the nations of the world, for restraint, for negotiations and for community of effort. Let us work for the same ideals within our own borders in our relations with each other, so that we may, if the test ever comes, have that unity of will with which alone a democracy can successfully meet its enemies.

134 ⟨A Telegram about Governor Benson of Minnesota. October 29, 1938

George W. Kelley,
Chairman, Working Newspapermen's Benson
   Volunteer Committee,
St. Paul, Minn.

THIS is my reply to the telegram you and your associates sent me on October 26. Will you please advise them. I have read with great interest your telegram upon the character of the political campaign in Minnesota. Apart from every other consideration, it is encouraging to receive this further evidence that American newspaper men are taking an increasingly courageous and intelligent interest in the problems of government.

If the political writers of Minnesota newspapers are inferring that I have deliberately withheld approval from or disapproved the candidacy of your progressive governor for reelection, they are of course misinterpreting my attitude. I have repeatedly indicated the high esteem in which I hold Governor Benson, and the interest I take in his efforts to develop liberal governmental policies in Minnesota. There is no reason for the modification of that attitude.

As a matter of ultimate good for the nation there is every reason why liberals throughout the nation should be working this year in the closest of harmonious cooperation.

135 ⟨ An Interdepartmental Committee on Printing and Processing Is Established. Executive Order No. 7998. October 29, 1938

BY VIRTUE of the authority vested in me as President of the United States, it is ordered as follows:

1. There is hereby established the Interdepartmental Committee on Printing and Processing, to be composed of representatives of each of the following-named departments and agencies, and such other departments or agencies as the Committee itself may designate:

> Bureau of the Budget
> Government Printing Office
> Department of Agriculture
> Department of the Interior
> Treasury Department
> Department of Commerce
> Social Security Board
> United States Tariff Commission
> Post Office Department

2. Each department or agency represented on the Committee shall have one representative, who shall be designated by the head thereof.

3. Pending selection of a permanent chairman by the Com-

mittee the representative of the Bureau of the Budget shall serve as its temporary chairman.

4. The members of the Committee shall be officers or employees of the department, independent establishment, or agency which they represent and shall serve without additional compensation.

5. The Committee shall promulgate rules and regulations relating to the establishment, coordination, and maintenance of uniform policies and procedures, consistent with law, for the efficient and economical utilization of printing and processing in the executive branch of the Government.

NOTE: The foregoing executive order was initiated originally by a letter, July, 1937, from the Chairman of the Congressional Joint Committee on Printing to the Director of the Budget, suggesting that a study be made of the printing problems and procedures of the executive departments and agencies. A special committee was set up with a Bureau of the Budget representative acting as chairman thereof. It submitted a report suggesting a number of changes in the printing and processing procedure, some of which would require the enactment of legislation and others of which could be made effective by executive order.

One of the recommendations of this committee was that a permanent Interdepartmental Committee on Printing and Processing be established to advise in printing and processing functions. The foregoing executive order set up such an interdepartmental committee.

This committee has held numerous meetings, has assembled a great deal of information, and submitted its first report and recommendations on February 24, 1940.

The necessary executive orders and legislation to carry out the recommendations of the committee are now being considered; but as of January, 1941, no action has been taken.

136 ❧ A Message to the National Foreign Trade Council. October 29, 1938

My dear Mr. Farrell:

IT is with great pleasure that I avail myself of this opportunity to send a message to the National Foreign Trade Council, assembled in convention to celebrate its twenty-fifth anniversary.

I hope that you will kindly convey to the delegates my most cordial greetings and my sincere good wishes for a very successful meeting.

Conventions of the National Foreign Trade Council are unique in the attention which they focus on the importance of our economic relationships with the world outside our borders and in the opportunity which they provide for discussion of the problems created by these relationships. I need not assure you of my personal interest in your discussions on this occasion.

The Council meetings have long been recognized as an occasion when business and government sit down together to review the record of the past year in the field of our foreign trade and to consider the work that lies ahead. In the promotion of our foreign trade both business and government have a definite function and a specific responsibility. The elimination of excessive and economically unjustifiable barriers to world trade is a task that only government can perform. To this task the government has been devoting itself with all energy since 1934 through the trade-agreements program.

As the government makes progress in removing excessive and arbitrary trade restrictions, it becomes the responsibility of business to make the most of the increased opportunities which are thereby created for the carrying on of trade. The trade-agreements program thus provides an excellent illustration of what cooperation between business and government can and should be. The cooperation which government has received from business in its foreign trade work has been highly gratifying.

The nation may well be proud of the work of our exporters, who, in spite of the increasingly complex world situation, will probably succeed this year in selling some three billion dollars' worth of American products to foreign countries, or more than twice the value of our foreign sales five and six years ago. I am confident that our business men will not slacken their efforts in the coming year to increase both our imports and our exports in a well balanced exchange which will be of advantage to both our customers and producers.

On our part I assure you that we shall go forward with all energy with the trade-agreements program to the advancement of stable prosperity at home, and peace abroad.

Very sincerely yours,

Mr. James A. Farrell, Chairman,
National Foreign Trade Council, Inc.,
New York, New York.

137 ❨ A Letter on Liberalism vs. Reaction in the California Political Campaign. October 31, 1938

Dear George:

I SHOULD have written you sooner had I not been expecting you here. Since our last conversation I have been keeping in close touch with the political situation in your State. Doubtless you have seen my letter to Jerry Voorhis.

What I have learned from many sources checks with what you told me. Apparently an impression is being carefully propagandized through California that since I do not agree with the "$30.00 every Thursday" plan I am indifferent to the nominees of the Democratic Party on both the State and National tickets.

That is a flat misrepresentation of my position. It is not true. I wish you would make clear to every Democrat, Progressive and Liberal you can reach that it is not true.

It is of national importance, in my opinion, that a liberal like Olsen rather than a reactionary be in the State House at Sacramento and that a liberal like Downey rather than a reactionary speak the voice of California in the Senate of the United States.

California is one of the great States of the Union. Its courage in solving its own problems and the way in which the power of its government is employed are of great concern to the whole Union. Like three or four other localities in the United States it is facing our most complicated social problems years ahead of the rest of the country.

Working out those problems demands the closest cooperation of the State Government with the United States Government. It requires leadership with vision, patience and tolerance in meeting local conditions—the attributes of a liberal in the fullest sense of the word.

As for the "$30.00 every Thursday" plan I have never concealed the fact that I am against it. I hope it will not be tried—because on the one hand I feel quite sure it will not work and because on the other hand I feel quite sure that we can evolve from the present Social Security statute methods of obtaining security for old age which will work better and better each year. But the plan is wholly a State issue with a separate place on the California State ballot for November eighth.

However important "$30.00 every Thursday" may seem in the heat of the local campaign it is actually only a small item compared with other fundamental trends which will be determined by the results of that campaign.

Sheridan Downey should be judged not by his position on this exclusively State issue but on the temper of mind with which he will meet the really national issues of a totally different kind on which a Senator of the United States has to vote on an average of once a day. And what is important for the people of California, in choosing a Senator, is that the people of California be represented by a man whose fundamental principles lie along progressive and liberal lines rather than by a dyed-in-the-wool reactionary of the vintage of Mark Hanna.

I hope, too, that Culbert Olsen and the other liberal candidates will be elected. As between Olsen and Merriam there can be no doubt as to who is the liberal.

As Woodrow Wilson liked to point out, the reactionaries can always present a front because their program is wholly negative.

They want to obstruct all action: they are not concerned with a constructive program of any sort.

Very sincerely yours,

Honorable George Creel,
Commissioner, U. S. Golden Gate International Exposition,
San Francisco, California.

138 ⟨ Postage Rates on Books Are Reduced. Proclamation No. 2309. October 31, 1938

W HEREAS I find after survey that the interests of the public, in the promotion of the cultural growth, education, and development of the American people, require that the postage rates on books of the class hereinafter described be modified:

NOW, THEREFORE, I, Franklin D. Roosevelt, President of the United States, under and by virtue of the authority vested in me by section 2 of the act of June 16, 1933, 48 Stat. 254, as amended by section 515 of title III of the act of May 10, 1934, 48 Stat. 760, Public Resolution 36, approved June 28, 1935, 49 Stat. 431, and Public Resolution 48, approved June 29, 1937, 50 Stat. 358, do proclaim that the postage rate on books consisting wholly of reading matter and containing no advertising matter other than incidental announcements of books, when mailed under such regulations as the Postmaster General shall prescribe, shall be for the period commencing November 1, 1938, and ending June 30, 1939, one and one-half cents a pound or fraction thereof, irrespective of the zone of destination.

139 ❨ The Four Hundred and Ninety-sixth
Press Conference (Excerpts). November 1, 1938

(Washington airport — Caribbean naval base — Visits of Colonel Ba-
tista and ex-Premier van Zeeland — Rumor of foreign exchange control
by France — Housing for lower income groups.)

Q. Looks like you aren't going to get your little opportunity to
go down to Gravelly Point before you go away.

THE PRESIDENT: Not this time. I think it is better to wait, Russell
[Young], because we haven't got the dirt ready to fly, but we
will, I hope, have it ready to fly by the time we get back. . . .

Q. What has got to be done over there at Gravelly Point before
you start? Is there anything important holding it up?

THE PRESIDENT: I think it is the allocation of the work among
the different departments that will do it for the Authority
[Civil Aeronautics Authority].

Q. Will they have to wait until you go there before they can
start?

THE PRESIDENT: I think they are still working on the plans.

Q. They won't start until you go there?

THE PRESIDENT: I don't know, they may. This is not going to be
a formal opening. I shall drive down and look it over. . . .

Q. Are you in favor of a naval base in the Caribbean?

THE PRESIDENT: We have one.

Q. Are you in favor of expanding that one, sir?

THE PRESIDENT: I cannot answer that question. That is almost
like asking, "Are you going to establish any more aviation
bases on the West Coast?"

Q. Is it too early to say when you expect to get back from Hyde
Park?

THE PRESIDENT: Certainly in time for the eleventh of November,
Armistice Day.

Q. Can you comment on the approaching visit of Colonel Ba-
tista?

THE PRESIDENT: No, except that he has been invited to come

here for the last couple of years and now I am very glad he is coming.

I am having a visit at the present time from an old friend of mine and a good friend of many of you, the former Prime Minister of Belgium, Mr. van Zeeland, who is sitting here behind me. . . .

Q. Mr. President, have you and Mr. van Zeeland come to any conclusions on the state of the world?

THE PRESIDENT: We have always had for a good many years very similar conclusions. The similarity has not changed.

Q. Could you share any of those with us? (*Laughter*)

THE PRESIDENT: No.

Q. Mr. President, has the Treasury informed you of the proposed efforts of the Daladier Government to absorb all the gold held by private investors and have foreign exchange control?

THE PRESIDENT: No.

Q. With possibly a revision of the Tri-Partite Agreement?

THE PRESIDENT: No; that is a new one on me. I think, Fred [Storm], it was a UP story I read on the ticker.

Q. [Mr. Storm] It ought to be true, Mr. President. (*Laughter*) . . .

Q. Can you tell us about your conference with these housing officials this morning?

THE PRESIDENT: Well, that was a further exploration of a problem that we have had for the last three years. We started in with the HOLC, which saved a very large number of existing homes. The next step was the FHA, which has been very successful in creating homes, new homes, for an income group — to put it in a rather broad statement — that could afford to pay ten dollars or more per room per month. Those figures, of course, are for the more northern part of the country.

That did not do much good, however, for the poorest group of tenants and home owners in the country. So then we started what was at first the Housing Division of the Public Works Administration; and that graduated into the present U.S. Housing Authority. That has been very successful in providing a great many homes for people in the lowest income group. It seeks to take care of people who can afford to pay five dollars or less.

That still leaves in the nation a very large group of people who can afford to pay between five and ten dollars per room per month, who have not been taken care of by any of the existing agencies. This talk this morning was to discuss ways and means of getting cheaper financing for that particular group of the population, so that we could have, for example, in the north, individual homes at a cost of approximately $3,000 which would rent on the basis of between five and ten dollars per room per month.

Those studies are continuing. We have not found a definite way out yet. We are still working on that problem; but it is a very great national need.

Q. Would that involve private capital?

THE PRESIDENT: That is what we are trying to get, private capital.

Q. Did the method of cheaper or mass construction enter into that?

THE PRESIDENT: Yes.

Q. That is a part of it?

THE PRESIDENT: That is a part of it, too.

Q. Anything to say on that?

THE PRESIDENT: That part of it is probably a little more easy than the question of getting the money. The problem of getting the money is not that the money is not there. But where the money is put in by the very large investors, where it is put in in great blocks by individuals and corporations, they seek, of course, some additional privilege for the use of that money. For example, many suggestions along the lines of tax exemption have been made for the money — I mean tax exemption in the higher brackets — in order to encourage that money to go in for this type of safe investment.

What I am exploring is the fact that we have in this country an enormous pool of money belonging to small investors, who do not come in the upper brackets of the income tax, and who are seeking to find investments that will bring them in a net of somewhere around 3, 3¼ or 3½ per cent. The machinery for bringing this type of investment to the small, individual family has never been developed.

I have had studies made in half a dozen communities, which show a surprising amount of potential investments of $1,000, $2,000, $5,000, where the people do not know what to put the money into. They had their fingers burnt in putting it into stocks and debenture bonds and things like that in 1927, 1928 and 1929. They won't go to the brokerage houses any more, and they won't go to the bankers, and the banks won't give them any advice — they used to — where to put the money. They don't know how to get a 3, or 3½ per cent return.

But the actual total of all these families and individuals that have small amounts, leads me to believe that there is a pool waiting for a form of investment such as the particular housing investment would be. Now, that is our problem and we haven't the answer yet. . . .

Q. Has any consideration been given to the question whether the effect of the minimum wage law will diminish the need for rental subsidies for the lowest paid group?

THE PRESIDENT: No. I suppose the applications to go into new U.S.H.A. houses will be five and ten times the number of rooms that we have available; so it will take a long time before that demand is satisfied, in spite of the improvement of wages.

Q. There are 1800 applications for the Langston Housing Units in Washington, which can take care of some 350 families; and they are from $3 to $5 a room, I think.

THE PRESIDENT: Yes.

(See also notes to Items 143 and 157, 1937 volume, for discussion of the USHA and the FHA.)

140 ❨A Telegram on Political Candidates and Principles in Wisconsin. November 1, 1938

Honorable Charles Broughton,
Democratic National Committeeman,
Sheboygan, Wisconsin.

YOUR very interesting letter has come to my attention. As you know I have previously indicated my interest in the campaign of Senator Duffy. Ryan always has cooperated loyally. He is a real friend of liberal government. I sincerely hope that the great liberal State of Wisconsin will not diminish its strength in the Senate of the United States by entrusting to one who is neither liberal in heart nor in mind the vitally important duty of representing Wisconsin in the Senate.

141 ❨On Newspapers and Editors – A Letter of Congratulations to the St. Louis Post-Dispatch. November 2, 1938.

My dear Mr. Pulitzer:

IT IS not my purpose primarily to deliver a lecture on the ethics of journalism; but our newspapers are so essentially public institutions that they are subject to the closest scrutiny of their readers. Since it is the readers who make possible by their patronage the publication of all of our papers perhaps the readers are entitled to be heard on that age-old question of a free press. The ramifications of that question are so many that a book would be required if all were to be dealt with.

But more forcible than any criticism from without is the self-searching inquiry of those within editorial sanctums and newspaper counting rooms as to what constitutes their obligation to the readers of American newspapers. After all, if certain tendencies need to be reformed the reform will have greater force if it comes from within rather than through external pressure from readers.

Grover C. Hall, Editor of the Montgomery *Advertiser*, in a recent issue of The Bulletin of the American Society of Newspaper Editors, uttered some truths not only frank but brutal in their frankness.

"That newspaper that happens to come by an enlightened, spirited publisher," wrote Mr. Hall, "is fortunate; the one that inherits a stuffed shirt and a merchant can never again hold up its head." Continuing, he said, "You see, the timid money-seeking publisher is the heir and assign of the rowdy, blatant office-seeking editor, and American journalism is still young and immature. Its traditions are tender and delicate. Neither the old-time newspaper editor nor the current type of publisher represents the ideal of journalism."

Mr. Hall made it clear that he was not talking of the great editors of other days nor yet of the great publishers of today. He was talking, he said, of the run-of-the-mine stuff, those who "have no blood on their spurs, much less their swords."

"Most of them came," he said, "not from news room desks but from the counting room, otherwise they would not have the money necessary to buy even a country daily. Some of them are lawyers, bankers, manufacturers and many are former advertising managers — few of them are journalists at heart. Most of them do not know the difference between an objective news story and a free reader for a furniture store. It pains and annoys them for a trained editor to call their attention to the difference. Few of them are sub-Pulitzers or sub-Ochses. They remember only that Pulitzer and Ochs were financially successful."

Now bear in mind this is not the criticism of an outsider. It is the considered opinion of a representative American editor and the vehicle of his utterance is none other than The Bulletin of the American Society of Newspaper Editors. Not to make Mr. Hall end on too pessimistic a note let me allow him this additional quotation: "Our newspapers are better today than ever before, but they are not yet half good enough, taking them state by state."

In these past few years there has been so much resounding thunder about the freedom of the press that one sometimes wonders what it is all about. Is the freedom of the press endangered from without? I doubt it. I am inclined personally to think that Editor Hall was moving in the right direction when he pointed an accusing finger in the direction of the newspaper counting room. I have implicit confidence that Mr. Hall knows whereof he speaks when he says run-of-the-mine publishers "do not know the difference between an objective news story and a free reader for a furniture store."

I have always been firmly persuaded that our newspapers cannot be edited in the interests of the general public, from the counting room. And I wish we could have a national symposium on that question, particularly in its relation to the freedom of the press. How many bogies are conjured up by invoking that greatly overworked phrase.

I do not think that anyone would seriously argue that the freedom of the press to criticize the Administration in office has, in any manner, been curtailed since the spring of 1933. A casual reading of a representative digest would reveal the fallacy of allegations to the contrary. Praise be! And may that freedom ever prevail — throughout this Administration and throughout every administration in all the years to come.

This is a theme which is worthy of serious thought in connection with the commemoration of the sixtieth anniversary of a great journal like the St. Louis *Post-Dispatch*. Assuming, as I do, that complete liberty to criticize government is a paramount right under freedom of the press — as we know it and as it is guaranteed under the Constitution — I have found it enlightening to peruse some editorials selected at random from various American newspapers.

Let me give you this quotation:

"All the material interests of the country are undergoing a strain without example. Every branch of business is suffering.

Enterprise is arrested. Capital lies idle, and bankruptcy is common. Relief must come first through severe economy in the public service, such as individuals are forced to practice in their private households."

That has such a familiar ring that it might be offered as a current editorial. As a fact, it is from our old friend, the *Sun* (New York) and the editorial quoted appeared in that paper in 1878, the year the *Post-Dispatch* was founded.

Here is one so fresh one would expect to find dew on the petals: "The greatest measure of centralization and of paternalism in government ever undertaken in this country since the adoption of the Federal Constitution, is undoubtedly the Inter-State Commerce bill."

So spake the same New York *Sun*, not this week, but fifty-one years ago last February.

Something which brings the past right up to the present is found in this wail: "There is depression, distrust and gloom on every hand," from the New York *Herald* of April 30, 1893.

This is the way a very old friend reversed English on the approach of the millennium, December 9, 1893: "There has never been anything more closely approaching monarchy or autocracy than there is in this country today under a so-called Democratic government. . . . It may as well be admitted, as dictators go, (the) President would make a very fair specimen. . . . He is right sometimes, and then we all have occasion to compliment him on his resolution, his dogged persistency, and his utter disregard for what seems to be the prevalent public opinion. Also he is wrong sometimes, and then his partisans have to admit that he is the most mulish and most obstinately wrong-headed man who ever sat in the chair of Washington. . . . The struggle between the would-be dictator and the people of the United States is one which men of all parties may watch with much interest." New York *Daily Tribune*.

The same paper felt no better on the day before Christmas of the same year. The writer had prescience, almost the gift of prophecy. Exemplifying the truth of an oft-quoted passage from

Ecclesiastes the *Tribune* said: "Millions are in distress because hundreds of thousands were deluded into believing that a change of party control would give them a larger share of the common prosperity, or misled by an irrational inclination to take the chances of 'A New Deal.'"

I think I ought to add for the record that Ecclesiastes' exact words were: "There is no new thing under the sun."

But here is one that is even more up-to-date: "The old man made a bad mistake on the Supreme Court business."

That appeared in the Brooklyn *Daily Eagle* the year this writer was twelve years old.

I give these quotations as evidence that the freedom of the American press to criticize the Federal Administration has not been interfered with during the three score years since the *Post-Dispatch* first saw the light of day. Whether the criticisms of contemporary editorial writers have the spice of originality I leave to the newspapers themselves and to their readers.

Whenever thought of the press of the country as a fundamental institution comes to mind my memory goes back to the admonition that Melville E. Stone once gave an enthusiastic young "cub" who was about to begin his career in the news reporting field as a member of the Washington staff of the Associated Press.

And so the receipt of your request that I contribute to the sixtieth anniversary edition of the St. Louis *Post-Dispatch* caused me, as I do habitually when the subject of news reporting and news writing is mentioned, to think again of that sagacious and farseeing newspaperman, Mr. Stone, and of the advice he gave to the young man about to enter journalism.

Mr. Stone knew out of the wealth of his long experience that freedom of the press would take care of itself if the newspapers were faithful to the trust which they undertook to discharge for their readers. His chief concern, I like to think, had to do with freedom of news rather than freedom of the press. At any rate, to the youngster about to embark on a career as a newspaperman the then General Manager of the Associated Press said: "Write factually, truthfully and simply. The American people are sufficiently intelligent, if given the facts, to draw their own conclusions — to form their own opinions."

Mr. Stone knew that freedom of the press could never be lost, endangered or encroached upon so long as we preserve our American form of democratic government. In that knowledge, he was as secure in his day as we are in ours. A free press is essential to us as a people and to the maintenance of our form of government. That is an axiom from which no thoughtful person will dissent. On the other hand, however, our government, federal, state and municipal, has rightfully and necessarily an interest in freedom of the news as well as in the preservation of a free press.

There was another great American newspaperman who knew that freedom of the press would never be endangered so long as our newspapers, as living, virile forces, faithfully performed their duties to their readers. The sire whose honored name the editor of the *Post-Dispatch* bears — Joseph Pulitzer — in establishing *The World* (New York) on May 10, 1883, made a declaration of purpose and policy that may still be upheld as the ideal for which all American newspapers should strive — a declaration which the *Post-Dispatch* for many years past has carried daily at its masthead. Mr. Pulitzer announced, with never a reference to freedom of the press, that he was establishing *The World* as:

An institution that should always fight for progress and reform, never tolerate injustice or corruption, always fight demagogues of all parties, never belong to any party, always oppose privileged classes and public plunderers, never lack sympathy with the poor, always remain devoted to the public welfare, never be satisfied with merely printing news, always be drastically independent, never be afraid to attack wrong, whether by predatory plutocracy or predatory poverty.

My own feeling is that these great luminaries of American newspaperdom, each of whom in his own way put the stamp of his vital personality upon his work, still have much to teach us.

May I extend my congratulations upon the attainment of the three-score mark by the *Post-Dispatch*.

Very sincerely yours,

Joseph Pulitzer, Esq.,
Editor,
The St. Louis *Post-Dispatch*,
St. Louis, Missouri.

142 ❡ The President Dedicates by Radio the Will Rogers Memorial in Claremore, Oklahoma. Hyde Park, New York. November 4, 1938

THIS AFTERNOON we pay grateful homage to the memory of a man who helped the nation to smile. And after all, I doubt if there is among us a more useful citizen than the one who holds the secret of banishing gloom, of making tears give way to laughter, of supplanting desolation and despair with hope and courage. For hope and courage always go with a light heart.

There was something infectious about his humor. His appeal went straight to the heart of the nation. Above all things, in a time grown too solemn and somber he brought his countrymen back to a sense of proportion.

With it all his humor and his comments were always kind. His was no biting sarcasm that hurt the highest or the lowest of his fellow citizens. When he wanted people to laugh out loud he used the methods of pure fun. And when he wanted to make a point for the good of all mankind, he used the kind of gentle irony that left no scars behind it. That was an accomplishment well worthy of consideration by all of us.

From him we can learn anew the homely lesson that the way to make progress is to build on what we have, to believe that today is better than yesterday and that tomorrow will be better than either.

Will Rogers deserves the gratitude of the nation and so it is fitting that the dedication of this Memorial should be a national event, made so by the magic of radio. The American nation, to whose heart he brought gladness, will hold him in everlasting remembrance.

(See also Item 153, 1936 volume, and Item 101, 1937 volume.)

143 ⟨ "The Fight for Social Justice and Economic Democracy . . . Is a Long, Weary, Uphill Struggle." Radio Address on Electing Liberals to Public Office. November 4, 1938

My friends:

O N THE EVE of another election, I have come home to Hyde Park and am sitting at my own fireside in my own election district, my own County and my own State.

I have often expressed my feeling that the mere fact that I am President should not disqualify me from expressing as a citizen my views on candidates and issues in my own State.

I have changed my mind about the nature of some problems of democratic government over the past few years as I have had more and more experience with them. I had never realized how much my way of thinking had changed until the other day when I was watching the finishing touches being put on a simple cottage I have recently built — a little cottage which, by the way, is not in any sense of the word a "dream house." Just watching the building go up made me realize that there was a time not so long ago when I used to think about problems of government as if they were the same kind of problems as building a house — definite and compact and capable of completion within a given time.

Now I know well that the comparison is not a good one. Once

you build a house you always have it. On the other hand, a social or an economic gain is a different matter. A social or an economic gain made by one Administration, for instance, may, and often does, evaporate into thin air under the next Administration.

We all remember well known examples of what an ill-advised shift from liberal to conservative leadership can do to an incompleted liberal program. Theodore Roosevelt, for example, started a march of progress during his seven years in the Presidency but, after four years of President Taft, little was left of the progress that had been made. Think of the great liberal achievements of Woodrow Wilson's New Freedom and how quickly they were liquidated under President Harding. We have to have reasonable continuity in liberal government in order to get permanent results.

The whole United States concedes that we in the State of New York have carried out a magnificent liberal program through our State government during the past sixteen years. If the continuity of that liberal government had been broken in this State during that time, we would be nowhere near the point we have reached today.

The voters throughout the country should remember that need for continuous liberal government when they vote next Tuesday.

On that day in every state the oldest of modern democracies will hold an election. A free people will have a free choice to pick free leaders for free men.

In other lands across the water the flares of militarism and conquest, terrorism and intolerance, have vividly revealed to Americans for the first time since the Revolution how precious and extraordinary it is to be allowed this free choice of free leaders for free men.

No one next Tuesday will order us how to vote, and the only watchers we shall find at the polls are the watchers who guarantee that our ballot is secret. Think how few places are left where this can happen.

But we cannot carelessly assume that a nation is strong and great merely because it has a democratic form of government.

We have learned that a democracy weakened by internal dissension, by mutual suspicion born of social injustice, is no match for autocracies which are ruthless enough to repress internal dissension.

Democracy in order to live must become a positive force in the daily lives of its people. It must make men and women whose devotion it seeks, feel that it really cares for the security of every individual; that it is tolerant enough to inspire an essential unity among its citizens; and that it is militant enough to maintain liberty against social oppression at home and against military aggression abroad.

The rest of the world is far closer to us in every way than in the days of democracy's founders — Jefferson, Jackson and Lincoln. Comparisons in this world are unavoidable. To disprove the pretenses of rival systems, democracy must be an affirmative, up-to-date conception. It can no longer be negative — no longer adopt a defeatist attitude. In these tense and dangerous situations in the world, democracy will save itself with the average man and woman by proving itself worth saving.

Too many of those who prate about saving democracy are really only interested in saving things as they were. Democracy should concern itself also with things as they ought to be.

I am not talking mere idealism; I am expressing realistic necessity.

I reject the merely negative purposes proposed by old-line Republicans and Communists alike — for they are people whose only purpose is to survive against any other Fascist threat than their own.

As of today, Fascism and Communism — and old-line Tory Republicanism — are not threats to the continuation of our form of government. But I venture the challenging statement that if American democracy ceases to move forward as a living force, seeking day and night by peaceful means to better the lot of our citizens, then Fascism and Communism, aided, unconsciously perhaps, by old-line Tory Republicanism, will grow in strength in our land.

It will take cool judgment for our people to appraise the re-
percussions of change in other lands. And only a nation completely convinced — at the bottom as well as at the top — that their
system of government best serves their best interests, will have
such a cool judgment.

And while we are developing that coolness of judgment, we
need in public office, above all things, men wise enough to avoid
passing incidents where passion and force try to substitute themselves for judgment and negotiation.

During my four years as Governor of the State of New York
and during my nearly six years as President, I am proud of the
fact that I have never called out the armed forces of the State
or Nation except on errands of mercy. That type of democratic
wisdom was illustrated last year by the action of Governor Murphy of Michigan when he persuaded the negotiators of the employers and employees to sit around a table. Thus he got an
agreement, avoided bloodshed, and earned the praise of both
sides of a controversy that had frightened a whole nation.

With such an approach, the New Deal, keeping its feet on the
ground, is working out hundreds of current problems from day
to day as necessities arise and with whatever materials are at
hand. We are doing this without attempting to commit the
Nation to any ism or any ideology except democracy, humanity
and the civil liberties which form their foundations.

Our economic and social system cannot deny the paramount
right of the millions who toil and the millions who wish to toil,
to have it function smoothly and efficiently. After all, any such
system must provide efficiently for distributing national resources and serving the welfare and happiness of all who live
under it.

The modern interdependent industrial and agricultural society which we live in is like a large factory. Each member of the
organization has his own job to perform on the assembly line,
but if the conveyor belt breaks or gets tangled up, no one in
the factory, no matter how hard he tries, can do his own par-

ticular job. Each of us — farmer, business man or worker — suffers when anything goes wrong with the conveyor belt.

If our democracy is to survive it must give the average man reasonable assurance that the belt will be kept moving.

Dictators have recognized that problem. They keep the conveyor belt moving — but at a terrible price to the individual and to his civil liberty.

The New Deal has been trying to keep those belts moving without paying such a price. It does not wish to run or manage any part of our economic machine which private enterprise can run and keep running. That should be left to individuals, to corporations, to any other form of private management, with profit for those who manage well. But when an abuse interferes with the ability of private enterprise to keep the national conveyor belt moving, government has a responsibility to eliminate that abuse.

We do not assume for a minute that all we have done is right or all that we have done has been successful, but our economic and social program of the past five and a half years has definitely given to the United States of America a more stable and less artificial prosperity than any other nation in the world has enjoyed in that period.

The very fact that the business slump that began last fall and kept running into last summer did not become a major economic disaster, like the terrible slump that ran from 1929 all the way through to 1933, is the best kind of proof that fundamentally we have found the right track.

You have just heard the news about the automobile factories and many other industries that are opening up for full employment again. And during the month of October alone over-all employment has risen nearly 3½ per cent.

I have been very happy in the last six months to see how swiftly a large majority of businessmen have been coming around to accept the objectives of a more stable economy and of certain necessary supervision of private activities in order to prevent a return of the serious abuses and conditions of the past. But if there should be any weakening of the power of a liberal government next Tuesday, it would resurrect false hopes on the part of some businessmen who are now beginning to change antiquated ideas, hopes that if they can hold out just a little longer no adaptation to change will be necessary.

There is no doubt of the basic desires of the American people. And because these basic desires are well known you find all parties, all candidates, making the same general promises to satisfy these desires.

During the weeks before a general election, all parties are the friends of labor, all parties are against monopoly, all parties say that the unemployed must have work or be given government relief, and all parties love the farmer.

Let me warn you now, as I warned you two years ago in my address at Syracuse, against the type of smooth evasion which says:

> "Of course we believe all these things; we believe in social security; we believe in work for the unemployed; we believe in saving homes. Cross our hearts and hope to die, we believe in all these things; but we do not like the way the present Administration is doing them. Just turn them over to us. We will do all of them — we will do more of them — we will do them better; and, most important of all, the doing of them will not cost anybody anything."

But when democracy struggles for its very life, those same people obstruct our efforts to maintain it, while they fail to offer proof of their own will and their own plans to preserve it. They try to stop the only fire engine we have from rushing to the fire because they are sales agents for a different make of fire engine.

New ideas cannot be administered successfully by men with old ideas, for the first essential of doing a job well is the wish to see the job done at all.

Judge parties and candidates, not merely by what they promise, but by what they have done, by their records in office, by the kind of people they travel with, by the kind of people who finance and promote their campaigns. By their promoters ye shall know them.

No national administration, however much it may represent the genuine popular will of the people, can in the long run prove enduringly effective if that administration can be cut off from the people by state and local political machinery controlled by men who are hostile.

My own State of New York is to choose a Governor. Ours is the most complex state in the Union — thirteen million population, great farming areas, hundreds of small communities, one huge city of seven million people, and many other cities, great and small.

Governing the State of New York requires the skill that comes from long experience in public affairs.

In 1918, twenty years ago, when I was thirty-six years old, I was invited to run for the Governorship of this State. I was then Assistant Secretary of the Navy. I declined the offer, because my job required me at that time to sail on a destroyer for overseas service. I am glad I did, for, looking back on that time, I do not think that I had experience and knowledge of public affairs wide enough to qualify as Governor. Besides, I did not think it quite right to abandon in mid-stream an important public job that I had undertaken.

Governing the State of New York is more than being an Assistant Secretary of the Navy or a local District Attorney. The Governor of this State is called upon to administer eighteen great departments of government and to supervise state institutions that house over one hundred thousand wards of the State. He must be able to understand, and handle the vast and intricate problems of agriculture. He is charged with the supervision of State finance and the maintenance of the State credit. He is responsible for its widespread system of roads, parks, canals, bridges and schools. He has to maintain, preserve and improve the great body of social legislation already on the statute books of the State — unemployment insurance, workmen's compensation, social security, help for the needy and the underprivileged; and he must see to it that these recent reforms are made to keep pace with the broadening conception of social justice.

Equal protection of the law — criminal and civil — for human rights as well as property rights; prosecution of criminals in high financial places as well as in low places; the preservation of civil and religious liberties — all these precious essentials of civilization are entrusted to him.

New York has State laws matching every progressive Federal measure of the last five years. They were all enacted under the guiding hand and driving energy of Governor Herbert H. Lehman.

Recruits in the battle for economic democracy are always welcome irrespective of party; but at a critical moment in the world's history we cannot take the risk of supplanting seasoned leaders like Governor Lehman with men, no matter how sincere, who have yet to win their spurs or prove what they really know or where they really stand in the fight for social justice. Those who truly and sincerely join the struggle for social justice, economic democracy for its own sake, do not throw stones at veteran fighters in that cause.

No one can properly minimize the need of active law enforcement, whether it be in a great city or in the rural counties of this or any other state. Certainly Governor Lehman has never minimized it, and has never hesitated to call to his assistance in law enforcement, young and vigorous prosecutors, irrespective of politics. We need more active law enforcement, not only against the lords of the underworld, but also against the lords of the overworld.

It is right — wholly right — to prosecute criminals. But that is not enough, for there is the immense added task of working for the elimination of present and future crime by getting rid of evil social conditions which breed crime. Good government can prevent a thousand crimes for every one it punishes.

The fight for social justice and economic democracy has not the allure of a criminal jury trial; it is a long, weary, uphill struggle — and those who give themselves unsparingly to it are seldom acclaimed at my lady's tea or at my gentleman's club.

As a resident and voter in the State of New York I urge my fellow citizens and voters, who are interested in preserving good government and American democracy, to vote for Herbert H. Lehman.

Just as a Governor is required to be much more than a good prosecutor, so a United States Senator must be much more than a good lawyer. A Senator from New York must do more than merely vote on whatever bills happen to drift by. He must be able and willing to take the initiative — to keep the legislative wheels turning in the right direction.

If you were to list some of the newly recognized major responsibilities of government to meet the complexities of modern life — security in old age, unemployment insurance, protection of the rights of labor, low-cost housing, and slum clearance — you would have a virtual resumé of the Acts of the Congress that bear the name of Robert F. Wagner. So often since 1933 has new legislation been described as "The Wagner Act" that the phrase has become confusing because there have been so many Wagner Acts. For example, there is not only the Wagner Labor Relations Act; there are the Wagner Social Security Act and the Wagner Housing Act; and although you might feel uncertain as to which particular Act is meant by the phrase, you can feel no uncertainty as to this — that any one of the Wagner Acts was an Act intended for the benefit of those who need the help and support of government against oppression and against intolerable conditions of living. His name stands in our history for courageous and intelligent leadership, constructive statecraft and steadfast devotion to the common man and the cause of civil liberties.

With him I hope the voters of this State will send to the Senate in Washington an experienced Member of the House of Representatives — James M. Mead — known through many years for his expert knowledge of three fields whose intricate problems press heavily upon government today — railroads, aviation and Civil Service, and for his unflagging support of every liberal measure that has come before the Congress. We need that legislative experience, that temper of mind, that expert knowledge in the United States Senate.

Look over the rest of the names on the ballot next Tuesday. Pick those who are known for their experience and their liberalism. Pick them for what they have done, and not just for what they say they might do.

And one last but important word: Pick them without regard to race, color or creed. Some of them may have come of the earliest Colonial stock; some of them may have been brought here as children to escape the tyrannies of the Old World. But remember that all of them are good American citizens now.

Remember that the Fathers of the American Revolution represented many religions and came from many foreign lands.

Remember that no matter what their origin they all agreed with Benjamin Franklin in that crisis: "We must indeed all hang together or most assuredly we shall all hang separately."

Remember that in these grave days in the affairs of the world we need internal unity—national unity. For the sake of the Nation that is good advice—and it never grows old.

144 (Presidential Statement on Senator Wagner of New York. November 4, 1938

WHEN we were in the Legislature together more than a quarter of a century ago, Senator Wagner and I were called Communists and Socialists because we worked for a fifty-four hour a week law for women and children in industry; for a full crew law for railroad trains; for factory inspection and workmen's compensation. Today we are proud of that old record.

Today we are called Communists and Socialists because we are trying to provide old age pensions, unemployment insurance and slum clearance and peacefully and equitably to solve problems of labor and capital which have accumulated without treatment for over thirty years. Tomorrow we shall be proud of that record too.

145 ❮ Greetings to the Fifth National Conference on Labor Legislation. November 12, 1938

To the delegates to the Fifth National Congress on
Labor Legislation:

My dear friends:

I AM asking the Secretary of Labor to extend my hearty greetings and felicitations to the delegates to the National Conference on Labor Legislation and to express my regret that it will be impossible for me to attend your meeting.

Previous sessions, such as this, have resulted in the formulation of a progressive program for the raising of labor standards in the interest of wage earners, employers and the general public. Moreover, since these conferences were inaugurated in 1933, they have been instrumental in the passage of many forward looking laws of benefit to workers in the States and the Nation.

In a message to your conference last year, I stressed the need of Federal wage and hour legislation in behalf of workers. The delegates adopted a resolution calling for the administration of such a law "by the United States Department of Labor, with participation and cooperation of State labor departments." Your views were adopted by the Congress and you are deserving of thanks for the yeoman service you rendered in helping to make the people of your States conscious of the need and desirability of legislation to put a floor under wages, a ceiling over hours and to end child labor in interstate industry.

I congratulate you upon the constructive work accomplished and I wish you all the success you so richly deserve in your work for a sound and well-rounded program of forward looking State labor legislation.

Sincerely yours,

146 ⟨ Greetings to the C.I.O. Convention.
November 12, 1938

Dear Mr. Lewis:

WILL YOU please extend my greetings and best wishes to the delegates in attendance at the Convention of the Committee for Industrial Organization and my regrets at being unable to accept your kind invitation to be present.

The wage earners of the United States have made great progress in recent years in regard to wages, hours of labor, general working conditions and economic security. This has been made possible through their cooperation with other great groups of Americans in formulating and carrying out a progressive program to elevate labor standards in the public interest. If the great gains already made are to be consolidated for the benefit of workers as well as management, it is essential that there be cooperation among the wage earning groups and because of this, I venture to express the hope, as I did also to the American Federation of Labor convention delegates, that every possible door to access to peace and progress in the affairs of organized labor in the United States be left open.

Continued dissension can only lead to loss of influence and prestige to all labor. On the other hand, collective bargaining will be furthered by a united labor movement making for cooperation, and labor peace which will be in the interest of all Americans.

I hope the Committee will have a successful and constructive convention.

Very sincerely yours,

Mr. John L. Lewis,
Committee for Industrial Organization,
William Penn Hotel,
Pittsburgh, Pa.

147 ❨ The Five Hundredth Press Conference (Excerpts). November 15, 1938

(Washington airport — German persecutions — Summons to Ambassador Wilson to return to report — Refugees — National defense in relation to continental solidarity.)

Q. Mr. President, before you get down to the unimportant things, I would like to ask you a national question: Have you settled the matter of the Gravelly Point airport? (*Laughter*) It may sound funny, but it is important, sir.

THE PRESIDENT: I will tell you; last Friday at Cabinet meeting, it was discovered that there were three different opinions from three groups of lawyers. Of course that creates a very difficult situation! (*Laughter*) So I referred the matter to the Department of Justice with the request that they straighten it out and make it legal to go ahead with Gravelly Point. At six o'clock that same night, they telephoned they had done it, and it is now legal.

Q. Have you approved the allotment, sir?

THE PRESIDENT: I think I did that before it was made legal! (*Laughter*)

Q. Then they can get their money now?

THE PRESIDENT: They can get their money now, so I am told, and go ahead.

Q. Another important question: Mr. Delano said today during the discussion of the memorial you were going to say something about the cherry trees.

THE PRESIDENT: I was going to withhold that until Friday, because you have so many other things today. I would suggest that you hold in abeyance that about the cherry trees.

Q. I will surely do so. . . .

THE PRESIDENT: Now let us come down to more serious things than cherry tree campaigns. Here are several things you will ask me, so I might as well shoot first.

First, about the situation in Germany: I just dictated the

following; it is not very long, and I think you might as well take it down:

"The news of the past few days from Germany has deeply shocked public opinion in the United States. Such news from any part of the world would inevitably produce a similar profound reaction among American people in every part of the nation.

"I myself could scarcely believe that such things could occur in a twentieth century civilization.

"With a view to gaining a first-hand picture of the current situation in Germany I asked the Secretary of State to order our Ambassador in Berlin to return at once for report and consultation."

That is the end of the statement. I think you know this. He is leaving on Thursday on the *Manhattan*, day after tomorrow.

Q. Mr. President, will that be mimeographed to give out?

THE PRESIDENT: Yes.

Q. Would you elaborate on that, sir?

THE PRESIDENT: No, I think it speaks for itself.

Q. What about the talk or rumors or report that that is called a "recall"?

THE PRESIDENT: Technically speaking, in diplomatic parlance, it is not a recall; it is a summons to come home.

Q. Have you any estimate how long Mr. Wilson will stay here?

THE PRESIDENT: Nothing further than what the Secretary of State said today.

Q. Have you made any protest to Germany?

THE PRESIDENT: Nothing has gone that I know of.

Q. There are reports from London that Mr. Kennedy has made a suggestion to the British Government concerning a place wherein the Jewish refugees would be taken care of.

THE PRESIDENT: I cannot comment on the report, because I know nothing of what has been happening in London. We do know that the Intergovernmental Committee on refugees is at work trying to extend its help to take care of an increasingly difficult situation.

Q. Mr. President, can you tell us whether you feel that there is any place in the world where you could take care of mass emigration of the Jews from Germany—have you given thought to that?

THE PRESIDENT: I have given a great deal of thought to it.

Q. Can you tell us any place particularly desirable?

THE PRESIDENT: No, the time is not ripe for that.

Q. Have there been any comments or protests made to you concerning the destruction or damage of American property in Germany?

THE PRESIDENT: Nothing has come through on that; I imagine the Embassy is checking up on it.

Q. You said nothing as yet on a possible protest to Germany; is there anything on that?

THE PRESIDENT: I cannot say anything on that.

Q. Would you recommend a relaxation of our immigration restrictions so that the Jewish refugees could be received in this country?

THE PRESIDENT: That is not in contemplation; we have the quota system.

Q. Mr. President, has there been time for you to obtain any idea of German reaction to the temporary withdrawal of Mr. Wilson?

THE PRESIDENT: Only what I have read through the press.

Q. Mr. President, switching from the German situation to the national defense, is there anything you can say in addition to the piecemeal stories we have been getting recently?

THE PRESIDENT: Yes, I think so; you know that we had a very large conference in here yesterday; you saw them. I can tell you the status of things at the present time. As I suggested before, you should not try to anticipate things. No decision has been made at the present time; we are simply in the study stage.

As a result of world events in the last few years, and as a

result of scientific advancement in waging war, the whole orientation of this country in relation to the continent on which we live—in other words, from Canada to Terra del Fuego—has had to be—our conception of it—has had to be changed. There is today a continental solidarity among the twenty-one republics and Canada, which is more definite, more unanimous than ever before in the last one hundred and twenty years, since the Latin-American republics have been struggling for their independence.

Therefore, on this continent we are substantially unanimous in the belief that as a continental doctrine we must be prepared to carry out the outline of continental solidarity that was established at Buenos Aires. It is very important to get the conception that this is a continental solidarity into which we fit as one of the republics. We therefore have to check up and see what is necessary in order to maintain this continental solidarity against any possible threat from any other continent.

These particular discussions that we are having relate to that problem; and the first thing we realize is the fact that any possible attack has been brought infinitely closer than it was five years or twenty years or fifty years ago. There are a good many reasons for that, and there is no use to go into all of them, but one of the reasons is the development in aircraft.

We are therefore studying national defense and continental solidarity against possible attacks from other hemispheres, other continents, along these different lines, including the problem of aircraft. Yesterday's meeting was confined almost entirely to the problem of aircraft. We are not ready to go into figures of any kind.

If I were writing the story, I could not give figures at this time. But the fact remains that the continental safety today is far too low on that particular phase. That is about all I can tell you, except that we are going to take steps, first with resources which are already at the disposal of the Government, and, second, by asking for legislation so as to place the defense of the United States and the continent against any possible aggression from the outside on a safer basis. That is about as far as we can go. . . .

Q. Mr. President, that means that the problem of national defense has now become a problem of continental defense; is that correct?

THE PRESIDENT: In cooperation with other republics and Canada.

Q. That is, it has changed in that period to a problem of continental defense rather than national?

THE PRESIDENT: Yes, but continental defense which does not rest solely upon our shoulders; in other words, it is defense in cooperation with the other twenty republics and Canada.

Q. Does that take into account the possibility of defection from continental solidarity?

THE PRESIDENT: I don't anticipate any such defection from continental solidarity.

Q. Will you tell us how much reason you have for believing in that solidarity?

THE PRESIDENT: A good deal of reason.

Q. Do you refer to the hemisphere?

THE PRESIDENT: North, Central, and South America.

Q. Mr. President, are you considering the possibility of it being necessary to build a fleet large enough to defend both the Atlantic and Pacific Coast at the same time?

THE PRESIDENT: No.

Q. Mr. President, yesterday Mr. Johnson said that the program might mean a half billion dollars more on the appropriation, and we assume that that was the Navy; is that true?

THE PRESIDENT: No.

Q. Was that the Army or both?

THE PRESIDENT: In the first place, the figure is wrong, and in the second place the assumption is wrong. The way the question was put, it might assume an additional five hundred million dollars over and above present expenditures in the budget. That is not necessarily so. . . .

Q. Could you amplify the new danger which makes this continental defense necessary.

THE PRESIDENT: Read the newspapers for the past five years.

Q. Mr. President, are you discussing the position of the Philippines in the new plan?

THE PRESIDENT: The American flag floats over the Philippines. . . .

(For a discussion of national defense, see Introduction and note to Item 48, 1940 volume; for a discussion of refugees, see also Items 38, 148, and 150, this volume, Items 84, 141 (pages 542-543), and 143, 1939 volume.)

148 ❰ The Five Hundred and First Press Conference (Excerpts). November 18, 1938

(Appointment of fiscal and monetary advisory board — Extension of passports for refugees — Jefferson Memorial and misleading newspaper stories about cherry trees.)

Q. Mr. President, I want to apply for a White House job.

THE PRESIDENT: Good.

Q. I want to be Coordinator of White House Press Conferences. You have one at a quarter to eleven and Mrs. Roosevelt has one at eleven.

THE PRESIDENT: The trouble was the Canadian Prime Minister came in. What are you going to do about that?

Q. Haven't you any influence with Mrs. Roosevelt to get her to postpone hers? (*Laughter*)

THE PRESIDENT: Ask the Canadian Prime Minister.

Q. To ask Mrs. Roosevelt to have hers at a different time?

THE PRESIDENT: Yes.

I am appointing a temporary board which will — I don't know what a really good name is, but the name is the least important — which will be an advisory board, a temporary advisory board, on certain fiscal and monetary subjects. Their duties — first, I will tell you who they are: The

Secretary of the Treasury, Chairman, and the members will be the Chairman of the Board of Governors of the Federal Reserve System, the Director of the Budget, and the Chairman of the Advisory Committee of the National Resources Committee. Each member can name an alternate from his agency to serve with him in his place and in his absence.

The duties of this board will consist of canvassing, systematically, the broader problems of fiscal and monetary policies in relation to national production and the national income. In other words, they will study the whole range of a great many problems that relate to fiscal and monetary policies in respect to sound and orderly recovery, and conditions essential to avoiding the peaks and valleys of booms and depressions.

It is just another step in tying in all the different agencies of the Government, so that they will view any given broad problem as a whole, instead of merely in its component parts. They will report from time to time informally. Probably this is as much as you will hear about it for some time.

Q. Mr. President, have you any comment or any thoughts on the summons home of the German Ambassador?

THE PRESIDENT: Has he been summoned home?

Q. Yes, sir.

Q. An official dispatch said that he had been summoned home to report in detail on the queer attitude of the United States toward domestic questions of Germany. (*Laughter*)

THE PRESIDENT: I don't think any comment is necessary. . . .

Q. On Tuesday, Mr. President, you intimated that you did not propose, or would not consider, lowering the immigration barriers for the benefit of German refugees. Since that time a good deal has been said in print that you might do so after all. Have you changed your mind?

THE PRESIDENT: No. There is one other factor that was brought up, that is a brand new one, which I did not hear about until yesterday. There are in this country at the present time quite a large number — I think you had better check these figures through the Secretary of Labor but I am inclined to think that they run as high as twelve to fifteen thousand — refugees from, principally, Germany and Austria — what was Austria — who are in this country on what are called "Visitors' Permits," I think that is the word.

In other words, they are here, not on a quota, but as visitors with proper passports from their own governments. The situation apparently has arisen that, because of a recent decree, those visitors' passports will be canceled as of the thirtieth of December, this year.

Now, as a matter of practical fact, a great many of these people — who are not all Jews by any means, since other religions are included in very large numbers among them — if they were to get back to Germany before the thirtieth of December, a great many of them believe that their treatment on reaching home might be a very serious problem. In other words, it is a question of concentration camps, et cetera and so on. They are not here under a quota so we have a very definite problem as to what to do. I don't know, from the point of view of humanity, that we have a right to put them on a ship and send them back to Germany under the present conditions. We can legally — the Secretary of Labor can, legally — give six months extensions so that they can stay in this country under the six months extension provision. As I understand it, the law does not say how many six months extensions there can be — it does not limit the number. So what I told the Secretary of Labor yesterday was that it would be a cruel and inhuman thing to compel them to leave here in time to get back to Germany by the thirtieth of December. I have suggested to Miss Perkins that they be given six months extensions. Under those extensions they cannot, as I understand it, apply for American citizenship. They are only visitors. Therefore, there being no adequate law on the subject, we shall simply present the facts to the Congress. If the Congress takes no action, these unfortunate people will be allowed to stay in this country.

Q. Will you repeat that, Mr. President?

THE PRESIDENT: They will be allowed to stay in this country under the six months extension law, because I cannot, in any decent humanity, throw them out.

Q. Do you understand that you may at the end of the first six months, extend for another period of six months?

THE PRESIDENT: Yes.

Q. And on and on?

THE PRESIDENT: I think so, but I am not clear about it. Anyway, we are going to present the situation to the Congress when it meets. I have no doubt that the Congress will not compel us to send these twelve or fifteen thousand people back to Germany, any more than the Congress compelled us to send a large number of the refugees of the old Russian regime back to Russia after Russia was taken over.

Q. Are they permitted to work over here?

THE PRESIDENT: Oh, as visitors, a good many of them, for example, are teaching in the universities and colleges.

Q. Will more visitors be admitted?

THE PRESIDENT: Well, there won't be very many more because they are not being given passports.

Q. In presenting this to the Congress, will the situation cover any possible change in the quota laws?

THE PRESIDENT: I think not.

Q. Will there be any possibility of these people changing their status, so that when there is an opening under the quota law they can remain as prospective citizens?

THE PRESIDENT: I don't think they can; I think they have to go back to the place of origin in order to come in under the quota. I think that is the law. They cannot be here; and then come in under a later quota under the present law. They would have to go back. It is a very difficult problem. . . .

Q. Were you going to have something to say about this cherry tree uprising today? (*Laughter*)

THE PRESIDENT: I am afraid that I would have to say something about newspapers if I said that. I don't mean all newspapers, I mean a few newspapers.

Q. Can't you say it? There is a press waiting to flash this news to the world down here. (*Laughter*)

THE PRESIDENT: I don't know whether I should be polite as to what was done by Washington newspapers or not, especially two newspapers in Washington. I suppose it is one of the most interesting cases — luckily they are rare — of a flim-flam game being started by the owner of a paper. It is a complete deception of the public and all you have to do is to read — I shall give them back to Steve, Steve dug them up for me — the clippings from some of the Washington newspapers in the course of the last few weeks. The statement in one paper, "Six hundred trees must give way to the Memorial." Another one, "Many of six hundred trees involved in Memorial may be lost." That is tuning it down a bit.

"328 cherry trees at shrine doomed by secret move." "Public arises at finding new monument dooms 328 cherry trees in Basin. This ten million dollar project. . . ." And so it goes.

It is the worst case of flim-flamming that this dear old capital of ours has been subjected to for a long time.

Now, of course, the facts are very simple. For a long time, dating back to when I was in the Navy Department, I thought it was a sort of funny thing that one of our three greatest Presidents had no memorial in the National Capital — practically no memorial of any kind. In the Wilson Administration there were a good many attempts made to get a memorial to Thomas Jefferson. Every time that a memorial was suggested, it was a strange thing that while quite a lot of people backed some memorial — they would not admit they did not like a memorial to Thomas Jefferson — they did not like the particular one suggested. So the thing failed.

When the Democratic Administration came back in 1933, we all decided we ought to have a memorial for Thomas Jefferson. As you know, of course, the thing hung fire in

Congress, and there were a lot of reports and so on and so forth. Finally it came down to a question of site; and there were four different sites proposed for a straight memorial. Out of the four, finally, by action of the Legislature, this particular site was picked. It is too late to change that site. There is going to be a memorial to Thomas Jefferson in accordance with the action of Congress on that site.

Then, number two, there was the question of the type of memorial which divides itself in two parts: First, should it be utilitarian? Well, that was all discussed. Should it be a stadium or a municipal hall or a race track? — somebody suggested a race track (*laughter*) and it was decided again, after complete discussion lasting about four or five years, that it should be a non-utilitarian memorial. So that was all gone into.

That decision having been taken, it became a question of what kind of non-utilitarian memorial it should be. There were two or three plans suggested. The first cost too much; and of course there was no unanimity of opinion in regard to the design — there never is. But the constituted legal authorities decided on a design; and that design is about to be carried out at a cost of somewhere around three million dollars.

Then, all of a sudden, a newspaper campaign! We have seen them before, we know what they are, the public does. They thought it would be good advertising to talk about the cherry trees. Well, I don't suppose there is anybody in the world who loves trees quite as much as I do, but I recognize that a cherry tree does not live forever. It is what is called a short-lived tree; and there are forty or fifty cherry trees that die, or fall down, or get flooded out, or have to be replaced. It is a short-lived tree and we ought to have, in addition to the 1,700 trees we have today, I think another thousand cherry trees. There are lots of places to put another thousand trees. Let us plant 2,700 trees instead of 1,700.

Actually, according to the records, this particular operation will result in a net loss of eighty-eight of the present cherry trees; and of course that net loss will be made up, not only those eighty-eight, as I hope, but 912 others.

So you see what a flim-flam game this has been.

A Jefferson Memorial, so far as hotelkeepers are concerned — well, I am just a hick from Dutchess County, a Democratic hick, and when I go back to Dutchess County I think it would be quite a magnet to me to come back to Washington, as a tourist, to see this new Jefferson Memorial, with another thousand cherry trees down around that Basin.

Q. They are Japanese cherry trees. Can you get them?

THE PRESIDENT: Why, sure. We are putting in forty or fifty every year.

Q. [Mr. Durno] What year will you be coming back, Mr. President? (*Laughter*)

THE PRESIDENT: Well, let us see. Let us put it this way: Early and often. (*Laughter*)

Q. Of course this is serious to some of us newspaper men. Women are going down there to chain themselves to these trees —

THE PRESIDENT: [interposing] The action has been taken by Congress; and if anybody wants to chain herself to the tree and the tree is in the way, we will move the tree and the lady and the chains, and transplant them to some other place. (*Laughter*)

Q. How much of this can be used that you have said about the cherry trees and the Memorial?

THE PRESIDENT: You can use it all, as long as you do not quote me. . . .

(For an account of the refugee problem, see Items 38, 147, and 150, this volume; Items 84, 141, 143, 1939 volume; and accompanying notes.)

149 ❪ A Thanksgiving Day Proclamation. November 19, 1938

I, FRANKLIN D. ROOSEVELT, President of the United States of America, do hereby designate Thursday, the twenty-fourth of November, 1938, as a day of general thanksgiving.

Our Fathers set aside such a day as they hewed a nation from the primeval forest. The observance was consecrated when George Washington issued a Thanksgiving proclamation in the first year of his presidency. Abraham Lincoln set apart "a Day of Thanksgiving and Praise to our beneficent Father who dwelleth in the heavens."

Thus from our earliest recorded history, Americans have thanked God for their blessings. In our deepest natures, in our very souls, we, like all mankind since the earliest origin of mankind, turn to God in time of trouble and in time of happiness. "In God We Trust."

For the blessings which have been ours during the present year we have ample cause to be thankful.

Our lands have yielded a goodly harvest, and the toiler in shop and mill receives a more just return for his labor.

We have cherished and preserved our democracy.

We have lived in peace and understanding with our neighbors and have seen the world escape the impending disaster of a general war.

In the time of our fortune it is fitting that we offer prayers for unfortunate people in other lands who are in dire distress at this our Thanksgiving Season.

Let us remember them in our families and our churches when, on the day appointed, we offer our thanks to Almighty God. May we by our way of living merit the continuance of His goodness.

150 ❲ Presidential Statement on Refugees in Palestine. November 23, 1938

IT IS reported here that the number of refugees to be permitted entry into Palestine will be materially increased, and in particular that many children and young people will be given refuge there. I have no means of knowing the accuracy of this report but I hope that it is true.

(See also Item 148 (pages 602-604), this volume, and references cited.)

151 ❲ Address at Thanksgiving Dinner, Warm Springs Foundation, Warm Springs, Georgia. November 24, 1938

(Following is the address, which was broadcast over the radio:)

WE, THE several hundred members of the Warm Springs' family, old and young, are gathered here again for our annual Thanksgiving dinner.

But, before we attack the turkey, I want to say a few words, not only to you but to many other people in every part of the country — on this day of national thanksgiving.

First about Warm Springs itself. The physical picture draws nearer to completion each year. The ramshackle old buildings of twelve years ago have been either completely modernized or replaced by new fire proof structures; and when I got here the other day I was delighted to see the new schoolhouse and the new Medical Center rising above the ground.

I am glad we are to have a schoolhouse because we know that it is of the utmost importance to have the education of the mind keeping pace with the re-education of the muscles.

Then, too, medical science has made such great strides in the past ten or twelve years that the treatment of the after-effects of infantile paralysis calls for many new forms of hospital care in addition to the water exercises and swimming of the older days.

Today we have the tradition of work well done. We have also the same ideal of continuing progress, backed up by determination and courage, what we call the spirit of Warm Springs. We are looking forward to the time when we can take care of at least two hundred patients at all times — or, in other words, treatment for about four hundred patients in any given year.

Several years ago we expanded the work of Warm Springs by helping communities throughout the country to raise money for the care of their own infantile paralysis cases, and, through their generosity, to give financial help to the cause of research into the origin of the disease. Last year we took a further step by establishing the National Foundation for Infantile Paralysis; and after January 30, 1939, we hope to have permanent Chapters of this National Foundation in all of the more than three thousand counties that make up the United States.

At this time of the Birthday Celebration half of all the funds raised in each county will be retained in trust for the Chapters for local use and the other half of the fund raised will go to the National Foundation for the national fight against infantile paralysis.

This Thanksgiving Day we have much to be thankful for. I wish that all who hear my voice could be with us and see this gathering of old and young in the big dining room at Warm Springs. We are thinking not of ourselves alone but of tens of thousands of other children and grownups and wishing for them that they may be having an equally happy Thanksgiving — lots of turkey and lots of fixin's.

I have had many telegrams today — Thanksgiving telegrams — and there is one that I want to read to you from an old friend who has helped Warm Springs in the past very greatly, Eddie Cantor, the actor and comedian, and he gives me a thought that I think we all are thinking of:

151. Warm Springs Thanksgiving Dinner

May you and yours have a happy Thanksgiving. I am thankful that I can live in a country where our leaders sit down on Thanksgiving Day to carve up a turkey instead of a Nation.

Now we shall have the blessing said and after that we shall go to it.

(Following the broadcast address were these extemporaneous remarks:)

I am very glad that you are glad that I am here. You are not gladder than I am to be with you members of the Warm Springs family after a lapse of two previous Thanksgivings, when I could not be here.

I think these parties get better each year that goes by. I am always thinking about the future — all of us are. Tonight as I sat here I could not help but think — and I was talking to Bobbie about it [boy seated next to the President] — regarding our problem. When we get up to two hundred patients here at one time, this dining room, which is only a very few years old, will have to be enlarged. Just think of that! We were wondering just which way we would push it. Of course, it cannot go that way [pointing] because that will interfere with what is going to be in time the loveliest campus of any college in the land, and I like to think of this as sort of a college which we all, old and young, attend.

At the same time, when I come to these Thanksgiving parties I think of the past. I think of the early years at Warm Springs a long time ago — fourteen years ago, when I first came. Fourteen years to me seems a very short time, but think of the people in this room who were not born fourteen years ago.

When I came down this year I learned of the death of two very old friends of mine, Mr. Persons and Mr. Colbert. A great many of you did not know them, and yet I remember a September of 1924, when I turned up here and occupied the only cottage, with one exception, that was open. The hotel was closed. Everything was closed and most everything was falling to pieces. Most of the roofs leaked and when you went to bed at night it sounded like thunder, because the squirrels were rolling nuts overhead. In those days it was pretty hard foraging for food. We did not have any wonderful store to go to as you have now. It was hard to get wood and food, and sometimes you had to travel ten miles to get a chicken for supper.

There were two people who were neighbors of ours, Mr. Persons and Mr. Colbert, and almost every evening someone would knock on the door and then their heads would come around the door and say: "Do you need some kindling-wood? Can I get you some eggs tomorrow?"

They were that kind of neighbors, and we are going to miss them a good deal.

You know this place would not have been possible if it had not been for that kind of reception and hospitality that I received. I was all alone down here. Some of our neighbors had lived down here around Warm Springs all their lives. They were the kind of people who extended the kind of hospitality that made me want to come back, and that is why the following spring I came back, and the influx of people began to arrive.

That is when Fred Botts was carried off the train — yes, he was a man in those days! And we thought he was going to look like a skeleton, or die of tuberculosis before night. We did not have any doctor down here and I acted as doctor. I did not know what to do and so I fed him cream. It put flesh on him. We got him in the pool and he was scared to death, and in about a week he began to walk in the pool, and that is one of the things we discovered, that people can walk in water when they cannot walk along on land. And that, you all know, has been increasing year by year.

The following year two more people came down. You have all heard, and most of you have known, our dear Dr. Hubbard, who left us this year. He and Miss Mahoney — and I saw Miss Mahoney this past summer when I was out in Los Angeles, and she wanted me to give her affectionate regards to the Warm Springs family. . . .

I am not going to make any more speech. All I can tell you is that I hope to be back again at the end of March or beginning of April, 1939, and most assuredly, unless something unforeseen turns up, I shall be back with you a year from now.

It was been a wonderful evening, and each year I think that these parties get better and better, and now, carrying out a custom of twelve years, I am going over to the door and I hope you will all come by and shake hands.

NOTE: On this trip to Warm Springs and to Chattanooga, Tennessee, I left Washington on November 20 and returned on December 6, 1938. In addition to the speeches printed as Items 151 and 152 in this volume, I also made short talks, not included herein, at Chickamauga Dam near Chattanooga, Tennessee, on November 21; Pine Mountain Valley, Georgia, on November 25; and Columbia, South Carolina, on December 5, 1938.

152 ⟨ "We Are Not Only the Largest and Most Powerful Democracy in the Whole World, but Many Other Democracies Look to Us for Leadership That World Democracy May Survive." Address at University of North Carolina, Chapel Hill, North Carolina. December 5, 1938

Governor Hoey, President Graham, my hosts of the Carolina Political Union, my new found alumni of the University of North Carolina:

FROM THE bottom of my heart I am grateful to all of you today, and very happy to be a part of this great University.

A very old friend of mine, the late Justice Cardozo of the Supreme Court of the United States wrote a few years ago:

We live in a world of change. If a body of law were in existence adequate for the civilization of today, it could not meet the demands of tomorrow. Society is inconstant. So long as it is inconstant . . . there can be no constancy in law. . . . Law defines a relation not always between fixed points, but often between points of varying position. . . . There is change whether we will it or not.

It is recognition of this philosophy that has made the University of North Carolina representative of liberal teaching and liberal thought. And it is my recognition of your recognition of that philosophy that brings me so willingly to Chapel Hill today.

It is a far cry from the days of my first visit to the University, nearly a quarter of a century ago, and the splendid new buildings that I saw in the last five minutes of my drive prove it. I came here then because my old Chief — that consistent North Carolina liberal, Josephus Daniels — told me that I should see for myself a great institution of learning that was thinking and acting in terms of today and tomorrow and not merely in the tradition of yesterday.

In those days, 1913 and 1914, the leadership of the Nation was in the hands of a great President who was seeking to recover for our social system ground that had been lost under his conservative predecessor, and to restore something of the fighting liberal spirit which the Nation had gained under Theodore Roosevelt. It seemed one of our great national tragedies that just when Woodrow Wilson was beginning to accomplish definite improvements in the living standards of America, the World War not only interrupted his course, but laid the foundation for twelve years of retrogression. I say this advisedly because it is not progress, but the reverse, when a nation goes through the madness of the twenties, piling up paper profits, hatching all manner of speculations and coming inevitably to the day when the bubble bursts.

It is only the unthinking liberals in this world who see nothing but tragedy in the slowing up or temporary stopping of liberal progress.

It is only the unthinking conservatives who rejoice down in their hearts when a social or economic reform fails to be 100 per cent successful.

It is only the possessors of "headline" mentality that exaggerate or distort the true objectives of those in this Nation whether they be the president of the University of North Carolina or the President of the United States, who, with Mr. Justice Cardozo, admit the fact of change and seek to guide change into the right channels to the greater glory of God and the greater good of mankind.

You undergraduates who see me for the first time have read your newspapers and heard on the air that I am, at the very least, an ogre — a consorter with Communists, a destroyer of the rich, a breaker of our ancient traditions. Some of you think of me perhaps as the inventor of the economic royalist, of the wicked utilities, of the money changers of the Temple. You have heard for six years that I was about to plunge the Nation into war; that you and your little brothers would be sent to the bloody fields of battle in Europe; that I was driving the Nation into bankruptcy; and that I breakfasted every morning on a dish of "grilled millionaire." (*Laughter*)

Actually I am an exceedingly mild mannered person — a practitioner of peace, both domestic and foreign, a believer in the capitalistic system, and for my breakfast a devotee of scrambled eggs. (*Laughter*)

You have read that as a result of the balloting last November, the liberal forces in the United States are on their way to the cemetery — yet I ask you to remember that liberal forces in the United States have often been killed and buried, with the inevitable result that in short order they have come to life again with more strength than they had before.

It is also true that other men in public life have protested in the past against certain forms of economic control and that epithets far stronger than any I have ever used have been employed even by Presidents of the United States. Those of us who knew Woodrow Wilson and Theodore Roosevelt and Grover Cleveland could hardly call any of them mollycoddles.

I was reading a letter of Theodore Roosevelt the other day,

written to a friend in the spring of 1908, and it will, I think, interest and amuse you if I quote from it. He was writing to a man who was fighting for social and political decency on the Pacific Coast. Here is what he said:

Now and then you must feel downhearted when you see men guilty of the most atrocious crimes who, from some cause or other, succeed in escaping punishment, and especially when you see . . . men of wealth, of high business, and in a sense of high social standing, banded together against you. My dear sir, I want you to feel that your experience is simply the experience of all of us who are engaged in this fight. There is no form of slander and wicked falsehood in which the New York papers, not only those representing the lowest type of demagogy, but those representing the interests that call themselves preeminently conservative, preeminently cultured, have not indulged in as regards myself. From all I can gather the feeling against me, not only in Wall Street, not only in the business houses of the greatest financiers of New York, but also in most of the uptown clubs . . . it is just in these places that the feeling against me has been most bitter. As a matter of fact, I do not care a snap of my fingers about it. I do not care whether they think well of me or think ill of me. But I do care a very great deal to do this work without flinching, on the one hand, and on the other hand without becoming angered and irritated to a degree that will in any way cause me to lose my head.

Now, so it is with you and your associates. You must keep reasonably goodnatured; but above all things you must not lose heart; and you must battle on valiantly, no matter what the biggest business men may say, no matter what the mob may say, no matter what may be said by that element which chooses to regard itself as socially the highest element. You are in a fight for plain decency, for the plain democracy of the plain people who believe in honesty and in fair dealing between man and man. Do not get disheartened; and keep up the fight.

Theodore Roosevelt, born of an old New York family, Southern on his mother's side, trained as a young man on our Western frontiers, was perhaps the first American President in modern times who knew the whole Nation. In the letter which I have read, and with this national background, it seems to me what he said in effect was, first, that the American people have, and must have, a definite objective for the improvement of government, for the improvement of social and economic conditions; second, that these objectives must be carried out by definite action, and, third, that in the attaining of them, the President and the Government and the people as a whole must have two essential qualities — first, a sense of proportion and perspective, and, second, good will and a sense of humor.

Almost every crisis in the history of our Nation has become a crisis because of a lack on the part of leaders or on the part of the people themselves, a lack of some of these essentials.

The very birth of the Democratic Party, at a time when President Washington publicly expressed the hope that the Nation could be run without Parties, was due to the simple fact that the Government itself was dominated by the great commercial and shipping interests of the seaboard, and failed to give recognition to the needs and the desires of the masses of the inhabitants of the original Thirteen States who did not subscribe to their theory that birth, wealth or political position could give to the possessors of these qualifications the sole right to govern. Hence the Democratic Party.

A generation later a Government dominated by the other extreme — the plainer people from the back country, from the Piedmont and the slopes of the Alleghenies, the Upper Hudson, and the backwoods of New England — paying scant attention to the ship owners of the seaboard, drove our Nation into the second war against Great Britain. And here in the South it is worth remembering that the first suggestion of secession from the Union was proposed by delegates from the New England States in the Hartford Convention of 1814.

In both cases tolerance and the national point of view were absent. Another generation went by and it was the same lack of tolerance, the same lack of a national point of view which brought about a war which was not inevitable — the War Between the States.

The scene changed and the Nation was confronted not by a sectional difference but by a struggle for economic and social control—a period which saw the control of our National Government by groups of individuals, who, owning their Government, through owning vast financial power, used the plea of development of our national resources that they might feather their own nests.

In the lifetime of people who are still with us, there were men who we must admit had courage and vision, who pushed railroads across the plains, opened mines, dammed rivers, created vast aggregations of capital; and left in their wake vast aggregations of national and state and local political power.

In a sense those were glorious days because the wide-open spaces were open to those native Americans and those who were flocking hither from the centers of Europe to find work in new fields.

A current author has recently emphasized the perfection of life that surrounded our population half a century ago. He draws a picture of the complete lack of any restraints on any individual and infers that every American of those days, no matter in what part of the country he or she lived, lived in a Utopia of work and play to which we should seek an immediate return.

I do not believe it.

A few days ago in Georgia I talked with an old friend whom I have known for ten years. He was what might be called an old-fashioned Southern conservative. We got to "reminiscing" about the old days when I first lived in Georgia. He reminded me of the days when cotton was selling at five cents a pound, and, while he admitted that the ramifications of our Federal legislation, and especially of Court decisions during the past six years were somewhat beyond him, nevertheless he allowed that some principle of crop control—cotton and tobacco, for example—decided on by a majority of the farmers themselves, was the most democratic way to prevent the return of five-cent cotton in a few years.

He reminded me of two little banks in Warm Springs, Georgia—banks in which many thousand of dollars of local savings had been deposited — of the failure of both of these banks and the loss of the savings — and of the fact today that deposits in the banks of the United States are safe; and, he remarked, "I hope that that type of liberal legislation will not be repealed."

He reminded me of the white men and Negroes who never saw, as the heads of families, one hundred dollars in cash the whole year round. He reminded me of the days in 1932 when the States of the Union were going broke, losing their credit because the whole burden of the relief of the starving was placed on their shoulders without the contribution of one dollar from the Federal Government. He reminded me of the complete lack of any social security program — of the days when a home-builder was charged fifteen and twenty per cent to borrow the money to build his house — of the days when slum clearance was a beautiful ideal on paper and nowhere else.

And when he left me, he said — "Young man, I don't know the United States the way you do but I know this section of the Nation pretty well. I don't understand the working out of all these new-fangled things that the Government has been starting in these past six years. But I know this section of the country and I want to tell you that there is a new spirit abroad in the land. I am not talking just about the fact that there is more buying power, that houses are painted that were never painted before, that our banks are safe, that our roads and schools are infinitely better. What I am talking about is that all of our young people in my section of the country and in every other section think that we are "going places.""

Those two words "going places" seem to be an essential in modern civilization everywhere.

They represent the conviction on the part of the young people of America that life never remains static; that there are better days ahead than ever before; that an opportunity to find a way of life, to earn a living, to raise a family in comfort and security are better today and will be better tomorrow. There may be those in the world who believe that a regimented people, whose every thought and action is directed by one man, may give some people a type of security which is pleasing to them. But whatever convictions I have, none is stronger than my abiding belief that the security and well-being of the American people can best be served by the democratic processes that have made this country strong and great.

The future, however, rests not on chance alone, not on mere conservatism, mere smugness, mere fatalism, but on the affirmative action which we take in America. What America does or fails to do in the next few years has a far greater bearing and influence on the history of the whole human race for centuries to come than most of us who are here today can ever conceive.

We are not only the largest and most powerful democracy in the whole world, but many other democracies look to us for leadership in order that world democracy may survive.

I am speaking not of the external policies of the United States Government. They are exerted on the side of peace and they are exerted more strongly than ever before toward the self-preservation of democracies through the assurance of peace.

What I would emphasize is the maintenance of successful democracy at home. Necessarily democratic methods within a nation's life entail change — the kind of change through local processes described by Mr. Justice Cardozo — the kind of change to meet new social and economic needs through recognized processes of Government.

Because we live in an era of acceleration, we can no longer trust to the evolution of future decades to meet these new problems. They rise before us today and they must be met today.

That is why the younger generation means so much in our current affairs. They are part of the picture in their twenties without having to wait until they pass middle age.

That is why I myself associate myself so enthusiastically with the younger generation.

That is why I am happy and proud to become an alumnus

of the University of North Carolina, typifying as it does American liberal thought through American action.

153 ❮A Letter on Employment by WPA of Those Eligible to Benefits under the Social Security Act. December 6, 1938

My dear Governor:

I HAVE discussed with the Deputy Works Progress Administrator your wire of November thirtieth protesting the dismissal from the Works Program of persons eligible for public assistance benefits under the Social Security Act.

The question of employing on the Works Program, persons who are eligible under the Federal law for Social Security benefits, is one to which the Works Progress Administration has given consideration over a long period of time. It involves not only the immediate problem of necessity, but a serious question of Federal policy.

It is assumed that Congress in enacting the Social Security Act intended to make provisions of a comparatively permanent nature for persons whose need is primarily due to causes other than unemployment. Under the circumstances, the Works Progress Administration feels that their first responsibility, especially in view of the fact that the number of persons whom they can employ is limited, must necessarily be toward those unemployed persons who cannot qualify for assistance under other Federal programs.

Moreover, since the public assistance features of the Social Security Act involve the states assuming the primary responsibility for assistance to mothers of dependent children and to aged persons, both through the enactment of appropriate legislation and the appropriation of state funds, there is a serious question as to whether the Works Progress Administration would not delay the assumption of this long time responsibility by the states, if they continued to employ such persons on the Federal Works Program.

Very sincerely yours,

His Excellency
A. Harry Moore,
Governor of New Jersey,
Trenton, New Jersey.

NOTE: In the fall of 1938, when the drastic business recession, which had commenced in the fall of 1937, had terminated, it became necessary to try to make reductions in the number of persons on WPA projects. Otherwise the program would not have remained within the limits of available funds.

Several methods were followed; and one of them was to remove from the WPA rolls those persons who would be eligible anyway for public assistance benefits under the Federal Social Security Act.

Many protests were received as a result of this action. My foregoing letter to Governor Moore of New Jersey, December 6, 1938, was in reply to one of such protests, and stated the reasons for establishing this policy, namely: (1) that the Social Security Act was intended for comparatively permanent relief for persons whose need was based on old age or causes other than unemployment; (2) that the limited funds of WPA should be first used for those who could not qualify for assistance under other parts of the federal programs; and (3) that if relief funds were used for such persons it would discourage the states from taking care of them.

Opponents of this policy maintained that (1) social security assistance in most states was inadequate; (2) that it was unemployment and not old age which was primarily responsible for the plight of most persons.

As a result of these protests, the Congress in its next statute providing a deficiency appropriation for the works program (Public Resolution No. 1, 76th Congress, 1st Session, approved February 4, 1939) stipulated that persons eligible for social security assistance should not be barred from unemployment work relief. Thereafter, in compliance with that provision, separation of such persons from the work relief rolls ceased, and as long as such persons were not actually receiving public assistance benefits under the Social Security Act, they were made eligible for work relief.

This policy has continued even though subsequent emergency relief appropriation Acts have not contained the same prohibition as that imposed by the statute which was passed in 1939.

154 ❰ The Five Hundred and Sixth Press Conference (Excerpts). December 6, 1938

(Judicial appointments — Financing national defense — Pilot training program of Civil Aeronautics Authority — Acquisition of reserves of essential national defense materials.)

THE PRESIDENT: Glad to see you. How are you all? Well, Dean [Russell Young] the report on the life and works of those who accompanied us to Warm Springs is that they were one hundred per cent. Now, that is going some. They behaved better than they do in Washington. Now, that is my influence.

Q. [Miss Fleeson] I thought it was mine. (*Laughter*)

Q. [Mr. Storm] Thank you, Mr. President. Such a reputation must be deserved.

Q. [Mr. Godwin] Did you take that picture of Fred?

THE PRESIDENT: It was all right. That was not Fred's fault. You cannot blame him for that. Blame the lady that took it.

Q. [Mr. Godwin] Fred got off at Alexandria this morning. He got off and walked home in disguise.

THE PRESIDENT: He will be explaining that for a year.

Q. [Mr. Godwin] He will have to do a year's explaining in twenty-four hours.

THE PRESIDENT: They tell me I have told them everything down at Warm Springs. (*Laughter*)

Q. Mr. President, can you tell us anything about your conversation this afternoon with the Ambassadors?

THE PRESIDENT: No; just conducting conversations, no news.

Q. Since you got back have you had time to consider appointments?

THE PRESIDENT: Not one. . . .

Q. Did Secretary Morgenthau report anything today of the work of his new committee on fiscal and monetary problems?

THE PRESIDENT: Just talking things over, that is all. I don't think there will be any particular news from it ever. In other words, it is one of those informal committees that meets from time to time, that is talking it over with people outside of the committee, and then talking it over with me. I don't think there will be any formal report. . . .

Q. There are frequent rumors that you may go down to the Lima Conference at the end, or towards the end. Can you tell us anything about that?

THE PRESIDENT: I guess there is no further news on something on which there has never been any news. (*Laughter*) . . .

Q. Anything on the estimated cost of this new armaments program?

THE PRESIDENT: No.

Q. When do we start for Lima, Mr. President? (*Laughter*)

Q. Senator Guffey demands that you run for office again in 1940. Will you accede to his request? (*Laughter*)

THE PRESIDENT: I don't think there is any news on that either.

Q. Mr. President, do you contemplate making an address to the Lima Conference by radio?

THE PRESIDENT: No.

Q. Mr. President, would you care to comment on the Franco-German peace pact?

THE PRESIDENT: No. (*Laughter*) You are getting lots of chances today.

Q. Do you care to discuss your plans for receiving Anthony Eden?

THE PRESIDENT: I have no plan for receiving Mr. Eden.

Q. It was stated that the State Department had sent over a request.

THE PRESIDENT: I suppose when he gets here I shall receive him just as I have a great many other foreign parliamentary bodies. I assume he will be brought in by his Minister, and I shall be very glad to see him as I have seen a great many in the past.

Q. Can you tell us on what date Governor Murphy's appointment will be sent to the Senate for Attorney General? (*Laughter*)

THE PRESIDENT: Gosh, they are getting better and better all the time. I am going to have all these questions framed, because this particular time they are good.

Q. Will it be the same day that you send Bob Jackson's name to the Senate? (*Laughter*)

THE PRESIDENT: Yes, getting better and better. . . .

Q. In reference to your determination not to name anyone to the Federal Bench who has reached the age of sixty, will you ever take into consideration other factors, and waive that in some cases or is it an inflexible rule?

THE PRESIDENT: The only way I can answer that is on the basis of past performance. I have had a great many requests and a great deal of pressure, as you know, from a great many members of the Senate and House to put on people over sixty. So far, I think that we have only put on—what was it?—two people over sixty-nine. And those, I think, were both promotions from the District Court, and made on the understanding that they would retire when they got to be seventy. . . .

Q. In the matter of national defense, have you fixed in your own mind any proportion or any per cent of the new money needed, which should be raised by taxation on a sort of "pay as we go" basis?

THE PRESIDENT: No.

Q. Do you think we should raise part of it without a fixed percentage?

THE PRESIDENT: I don't know yet, Fred [Essary]; we haven't got to that.

Q. I seem to recall that you remarked here once that you thought some of that money ought to be raised by taxation as in the case of any other expensive project that Congress might provide for.

THE PRESIDENT: Certainly, as a general proposition national defense ought to be paid for on a pay as you go basis, because it is not a self-liquidating project in any way.

You see there are, according to the practice of some countries like, for instance, Sweden—do not imply from that that I am going to do anything like that—but in some other countries they have differentiated among three types of expenditure. The first is the actual cost of running the Government in its current work and they try to raise all of that by taxation. Then they have two other classifications of expenditures. One is the absolutely self-liquidating expenditure, such as — well, for example, Boulder Dam would be — where the dam is completed and the contracts for the sale of water and power are all signed and we know that over a period of years it is going to pay itself out.

And then they have a third classification — I have forgotten what the technical term is — but it is the type of expenditure which will so increase the national welfare or, putting it the other way around, the national income, that there will be a resulting return of the money through the increase in national income over a period of years. It is not actually self-sustaining in the sense that you have contracts out. But national defense, very clearly in my judgment, falls under the category of something that ought to be paid for from year to year.

Q. That is why I differentiated between the new money necessary to carry on the program and the usual budgetary sums to be set aside, the additional money for the Navy, as an example.

THE PRESIDENT: Well, it ought to be paid for as we go along.

Q. Even if it takes additional taxation?

THE PRESIDENT: Yes; but, of course, that might, on the other hand, as I suggested, leave out of consideration certain expenditures of the Government which are self-liquidating. Therefore, Q.E.D., it may *not* be necessary to increase the total amount of taxes coming in. However, it is a matter that is being studied; it is a long and difficult study; nothing has been determined upon and it is purely in the study stage.

Q. In connection with the national defense program, one of the War Department reports indicated the other day that we are far behind technically as far as airplane production is concerned. Have you had any reports indicating that that is so?

THE PRESIDENT: No, I have not had that. I don't believe there is anything in that — not technically.

Q. The program of the Civil Aeronautics Authority to promote civil flying, has that any connection with the defense program to train a lot of civilian pilots?

THE PRESIDENT: Of course the training of reserve pilots is all part of any program for an increase in the number of planes that the Government has available to go in the air.

Q. Instead of training them purely in military planes, is there any plan for a Civil Aeronautics program where they will be used as a sort of reserve in this announced plan?

THE PRESIDENT: Not that I know of. Of course you train pilots on the same kind of a plane for civil aviation as you do for military aviation, when you teach them to fly. There is no distinction. . . .

Q. When you make your recommendations on national defense, will they include the use and conservation of natural resources used in national defense, or will they deal strictly in the military aspect?

THE PRESIDENT: What sort of things do you have in mind?

Q. Energy sources and minerals.

THE PRESIDENT: No, I do not think so. No, the only thing that might be a part of any national defense program would be certain resources which we have not got in this country. You know that the Army has made several recommendations saying that the Navy should have certain stock piles of things we have not got, like manganese and nickel and a few other things of that kind, and that does enter into a national defense program. They are things we do not have here. . . .

(For further discussion of national defense, see Introduction, and note to Item 48, 1940 volume.)

155 ❰ Informal, Extemporaneous Remarks to a Committee of the National Seaway Council. December 9, 1938

I HAVE always appreciated the support of the National Seaway Council in my efforts to assure the early undertaking of the Great Lakes-St. Lawrence Project. History shows that it has been the grand persistence of such organizations as yours which has ultimately enabled the country's leaders to overcome selfish opposition to great undertakings.

For many years it has been my sincere conviction that the St. Lawrence Project would prove second to none in its direct contribution to the economic welfare of millions of people on both sides of the border. It has seemed to me a logical continuance of the cooperation between two peoples which has afforded an almost unique example of the possibility of achieving peace among nations.

In my message of January 10, 1934, requesting consideration of the earlier treaty, I expressed the belief that fears the St. Lawrence Project would work to the disadvantage of other transportation agencies were groundless. I am more than ever convinced of that fact today. In the vast system of interdependence of which we are all parts, selfishness works inevitably to the disadvantage of any group seeking to preserve its special position by blocking the opportunity of others to enjoy the full use of nature's resources.

The economic story of this continent is an extraordinary record of the extent to which stimulus to economic growth in one region reacts to the benefit of all. Any area which has grown in economic importance becomes a greater market for the products of other regions. More products are exchanged and all transportation agencies participate in the growing prosperity.

The two nations, Canada and the United States, share a great water resource which is today only partially used. Removal of the barriers to its full use for navigation will release millions of horsepower of cheap hydro-electric energy in sections in which the rapidly growing market for power will soon overtake present sources of supply. Failure to take advantage of this cheap power will not only tend to cramp industrial development but will force the substitution of more costly power with the resulting burden on consumers of electricity. In an age so dependent upon transportation and power, serious consequences will follow failure to anticipate future requirements.

In view of the importance of these considerations, I am hopeful of an early agreement between the Canadian Government and our own.

(See note to Item 114, 1940 volume, for discussion of this subject.)

156 (The Five Hundred and Eighth Press Conference. December 10, 1938

(Plans for preserving Presidential papers, correspondence, etc. — Franklin D. Roosevelt Library at Hyde Park, N. Y.)

THE PRESIDENT: Have you had a chance to read this? [Indicating mimeographed copies of Press Release.]

MR. EARLY: They have not, sir.

THE PRESIDENT: Now, I think possibly you might let me explain first, and then read it, and then get a complete picture.

For the last two years I have been considering more and more the final disposal of what amounts to probably the largest collection of original source material of almost anybody over the last quarter of a century. It is very voluminous. It includes all of my papers when I was in the State Senate, all of my personal papers when I was in the Navy Department, including the war period. It includes the Vice Presidential Campaign of 1920 and the Convention of 1924, the Convention of 1928, the four years as Governor. I have, up in Albany, sixty packing cases full of those papers of the Governorship. It includes the Campaigns of 1928 and 1930, the Presidential Campaigns of 1932 and 1936, plus all the Presidential papers and the file I operate.

I have been taking the advice of many historians and others. Their advice is that material of that kind ought not to be broken up, for the future. It ought to be kept intact. It ought not to be sold at auction; it ought not to be scattered among descendants. It should be kept in one place and kept in its original form, because, so often in the past, Presidential papers and other public papers have been culled over during the lifetime of the owner, and the owner has thrown out a great deal of material which he personally did not consider of any importance which, however, from the point of view of future history, may have been of the utmost importance.

Therefore, in looking around as to what to do with it, because this relates not just to the Federal Government but to a great many other activities, such as my service in Albany a quarter of a century ago, all the papers as Governor, a great many personal papers that have no relationship to the Federal Government, it became a question as to where they should ultimately be deposited, if deposited in toto, in one place.

Then came the question as to whether it would not be better to put them somewhere where I could personally help the ultimate owner of the papers in going over them, listing them and so forth, annotating them. That made it almost imperative that they should be placed at Hyde Park, and, at the same time, that the ownership and title of all the papers, books, et cetera, should be in the Federal Government itself.

Therefore this plan: (*Reading*)

"Since 1910 — or in other words for a period of twenty-eight years — I have carefully preserved all of my correspondence, public papers, pamphlets, books, etc. This includes all incoming material and copies of practically all outgoing material. These papers cover my service of nearly three years in the New York State Senate; seven and one-half years as Assistant Secretary of the Navy, including the World War period and two trips to Europe; my business and legal correspondence; much political material between 1920 and 1928, including my campaign for the Vice Presidency, the 1924 Convention, and the 1928 Convention; my campaigns for Governor in 1928 and 1930; all of my personal papers as Governor of New York, 1929-1933; the campaigns for the Presidency, 1932 and 1936; and all of my Presidential papers from March 4, 1933, to date.

"Because these papers relate to so many periods and activities which are not connected with my service in the Federal Government, I do not wish to break them up, leaving a portion of them to the National Archives and dividing the rest among the State of New York Archives, the New York State Historical Society, the Dutchess County Historical Society, the Harvard College Library."

And I might add to that the Naval Records Office here.

"In other words, it is my desire that they be kept as a whole and intact in their original condition, available to scholars of the future in one definite locality.

"I have carefully considered the choice of locality and for many reasons have decided that it would be best that they remain permanently on the grounds of my family home at Hyde Park, Dutchess County, New York.

"I realize that the Library of Congress, the National Archives, the New York State Library, Harvard University and the New York State Historical Society—"

and others

"—would probably be glad to have the whole collection intact. It is my thought, however, that an opportunity exists to set up for the first time in this country what might be called a source material collection relating to a specific period in our history."

That is a very important thing because, so far as we know, it has never been done before.

"That part of my family's country place at Hyde Park on which we live will, without doubt, eventually go to the Federal Government to be maintained for the benefit of the public by the Federal Government.

"It is, therefore, my thought that funds can be raised for the erection of a separate, modern, fireproof building to be built near my family's house at Hyde Park, so designed that it would hold all of my own collections and also such other source material relating to this period in our history as might be donated to the collection in the future by other members of the present Administration."

Well, of course, that would include also members of the Administration when I was in Albany. Fred Storm, for instance, could leave his papers as part of that Administration.

Q. [Mr. Storm] I have a lot of them, Mr. President.

Q. [Mr. Durno] Only after he is dead. (*Laughter*)

THE PRESIDENT: He would not part with them before that?

Q. [Mr. O'Donnell] It is a question of libel if published before that. (*Laughter*)

THE PRESIDENT: (*Reading*)

"I forgot to mention that in addition to the very voluminous correspondence, I have also two rather specialized collections which are of some definite historic value: a collection of paintings, drawings, prints, manuscript letters and documents, log-books, pamphlets and books relating to the American Navy from 1775 to date; and a smaller collection of similar material relating to the Hudson River, and especially Dutchess County and the town of Hyde Park. These collections would be placed in the proposed building, together with the public papers, etc.

"I have also a very large number of books and pamphlets — far more than my children could possibly use, many of them inscribed by their authors to me. The bulk of these books would also be added to the contents of the building and, incidentally, they form the nucleus of a library relating to this period which would be available to students in the future."

Well, for example, I was just talking to Ernest Lindley and he said, "Have you got all the books relating to this Administration?"

I said, "I checked and I have here in the House about three-quarters of all the books that have been written in the last six years about this Administration. That is a good nucleus to start with. Most of them have been given to me by the authors themselves and that would mean the adding only of what is missing, which is about twenty-five per cent."

"It is my thought that if a building such as I suggest is erected and the material — not only my own but that of others who would contribute their own material — is placed there, the title to the building and all the material would be vested in the United States Government and placed under the primary responsibility of the Archivist of the United States." (Dr. Connor.)

"This would insure permanent care and the provision of adequate facilities for its use. At the same time, being somewhat familiar with historical material, its preservation and its availability for students and scholars, I should much like to have the assistance of recognized scholars in American History and Government, past and present. That is why I believe that a collection of this kind should be under the supervision of a committee of historians working in cooperation with the Archivist and the Librarian of Congress.

"It is my hope that during my lifetime I shall continue to live in the family home at Hyde Park, and if a period collection of this kind is permanently domiciled on what is my own place, I shall be able to give assistance to the maintenance of the collection during my lifetime. As I have said before, it is my expectation that while the title to the collections would vest immediately in the Government, my family's house and that portion of the place on which we live would revert to the Government on my death.

"All of this has the approval and consent of my Mother who owns the property during her lifetime.

"I may mention that the place at Hyde Park is located on the New York–Albany Post Road — two hours from New York City by train or motor, and four and one-half miles from the City of Poughkeepsie, which has good hotel and other accommodations."

Now, don't be — (*laughter*) don't slam that last statement. (*Laughter*)

Q. Mr. President, I am not quite clear. Do you mean the entire Hyde Park estate eventually?

THE PRESIDENT: I mean that portion on which we live, that portion from the Post Road down to the foot of the hill. . . .

Q. What prompted your decision to do this at this particular time?

THE PRESIDENT: I have been thinking about it for the last three years, three or four years. I suppose the amount — you see, here is one thing about it: The amount of material that I have is so infinitely larger than that of any previous President that it creates a new problem.

As I remember it, when we came in here we were told that President Hoover's mail averaged about four hundred letters a day. My mail has averaged, as you know, about four thousand letters a day. Well, there is all the difference in the world. The result is that just my Presidential files alone are so big, that you couldn't possibly put them in any private house; and I do not want to put them just into storage.

Q. The cataloging of your books has progressed pretty well. Have you any idea, approximately, how many books you have?

THE PRESIDENT: Just on books alone I would estimate about

seven thousand here and about seven thousand at Hyde Park.

Q. How about the New York house?

THE PRESIDENT: Oh, very few, only a few hundred, perhaps a thousand. About fifteen thousand all told. And then, of course, in addition to that, if you get down to the question of pamphlets, I suppose just in my American Navy collection alone there must be, of old pamphlets, four or five thousand at least in addition, and, of course, in my files there are a great many other pamphlets and documents which have been going to files rather than into slip cases — book cases.

Q. Of course this has never been done before in the history of the Government on the collection of papers. We wonder if you took the immediate step because of the recent developments in the past years with respect to the Lincoln papers, and the concern felt with respect to those of other Presidents, where there has been a bewildering lack of facts.

THE PRESIDENT: I have been interested in the subject a great many years of what happens to the papers of public officials.

Q. We still haven't got Lincoln's papers. Didn't T. R. save his and build a special vault?

THE PRESIDENT: Yes. . . .

Q. Of course his collections are nowhere near as extensive as yours.

THE PRESIDENT: Yes, because people did not write as much in those days. Curiously enough it [referring to T. R.'s collection] covered approximately the same period of years, a little over a quarter of a century, as mine does.

Q. There is no reference to the filing of a diary?

THE PRESIDENT: There is not. I think you will find among the papers three diaries that started on the first of January in three different years, far apart. I think the most voluminous one ran to the fourth of January.

Q. That is like Mark Twain. He kept it up for a week, got up, washed and went to bed. (*Laughter*)

THE PRESIDENT: Yes. I tried it once and it went on for four days, I believe.

Now, I invited to lunch the list which you have here. You know them all or know about them all. There is Ambassador Dodd; President Graham of North Carolina University; Archie MacLeish, a writer, and I think he has been connected with "Fortune"; Randolph Adams, Librarian of the University of Michigan; Edmund E. Day; Dr. Connor, Dr. Flick, State Historian at Albany; Dr. Charles A. Beard; Professor Frankfurter; Stuart Chase; Samuel I. Rosenman, who knows more about my papers than anybody else; Ernest Lindley, who has written more about the Administration than anybody else; President Paxson of the American Historical Association; Dr. Boyd, of the Historical Society of Pennsylvania; Mrs. Helen Taft Manning, of Bryn Mawr; Miss Marguerite Wells, President of the League of Women Voters; Professor Morison, of Harvard University; and Frank Walker, of New York.

Q. Any idea of the amount of the fund to be raised?

THE PRESIDENT: Well, we don't know, but Frank Walker has kindly offered to take charge of that part of it. There will be public subscription. All of this general list, all of these ladies and gentlemen have been good enough to say that they are very keen about it and go along. I am going to ask Professor Morison, who is here, to say a few words about that because that is their business rather than mine.

PROFESSOR SAMUEL MORISON: I think I may say that the conference that the President called today was one hundred per cent favorable to his proposal; especially because we who work in American history know how difficult it is to get at the records of the Presidents, and know the lamentable mistakes which have been made in the past in disposing of and dealing with Presidents' records. It has been the custom for every President of the United States, starting with John Adams, the first who lived in this House, to take away all his papers with him. Some of them, for instance the records of the two Adamses, are shut in a vault in Boston where nobody can get at them.

THE PRESIDENT: Really? I did not know that.

PROFESSOR MORISON: Nobody allowed in except the family.

Others have generally gone back to the President's old home, where they have been subjected to a great deal of dilapidation. The Presidents have sometimes passed their declining years in trying to rearrange them, with unfortunate results because the order of the documents has been entirely spoiled. And their widows have given them away as souvenirs, and children have played with them, and the rats have eaten them up. After a lapse of years, sometimes two or three generations, they are turned over to the Library of Congress, which is where the Jefferson, the Madison, the Monroe, the Washington and the Grover Cleveland and Theodore Roosevelt papers are now.

But that is an unsatisfactory system because, in the meantime, a great many of the papers have been disposed of. The Lincoln papers, for instance, which somebody mentioned, are scattered in numerous repositories, since Mrs. Lincoln gave them away, and the historian does not know where to turn to find the information he wants.

A great deal of the important evidence has been destroyed, some purposely, some by mere neglect and accident.

Thus President Roosevelt has proposed, for the first time, to keep all of his files intact. Of his predecessors, I believe President Hoover was the first one who did not destroy a considerable part of the White House files at the time he left. President Roosevelt proposes not only to keep his files intact, but to place them immediately under the administration of the National Archivist so that from the time they leave the White House they will be under public control and will not be subject to dilapidation or destruction or anything else. The whole thing will come down in its entirety to the historians of the future.

THE PRESIDENT: Sam, do you want to say anything about the Executive Committee, what we propose to do?

PROFESSOR MORISON: The Advisory Committee today is going to appoint a small Executive Committee to act in collaboration with Mr. Frank Walker to raise the necessary money for the building.

Later I presume another committee will be appointed under the National Archivist to aid him in arranging the collections and the archives.

I have spoken especially of the archives; but, of course, equally important are those collections of naval prints and pictures, and the President's collection of naval books and pamphlets, which is much the best collection of United States naval history in private hands today. That is a very important collection in itself, and that will be in the building with the rest.

THE PRESIDENT: Sam, do you want to say anything about the Advisory Committee having other people besides pure historians, or in other words, the economists?

PROFESSOR MORISON: The Advisory Committee today was just the nucleus, to which are going to be added men and women who represent economics, sociology and the various social sciences, that will be interested in these papers equally with historians. The historian of the future will be interested in the economic trends of our day, the social movements in a large sense, just as much as he is in the political history, even more so.

Q. Who are the members of that Advisory Committee?

PROFESSOR MORISON: That was the list that the President gave you. Others, representing the social sciences, for example, will be added to it as it is rather overloaded on the historian side right now. . . .

Q. Have you thought of the physical aspect of this building? Will it be of colonial style, in keeping with Dutchess County?

THE PRESIDENT: That is a thing we have not got very far on, but the general thought on the part of several architects is that it should be in keeping with older buildings which are typical of the locality. It should be simple, not high, probably one story, and probably built of field stone, like the older buildings of Dutchess County.

Q. The Post Office?

THE PRESIDENT: Yes. Absolutely simple but, of course, absolutely modern, with fireproofing, and nowadays you have to have air conditioning, or you have to have the same temperature in the record room the year round.

[Mrs. Roosevelt entered the room at this point and spoke to the President.]

THE PRESIDENT: I have to dedicate a piano now.

Q. How many acres in that part of the estate which will eventually go to the Government?

THE PRESIDENT: A hundred acres.

Q. Which will leave how much which does not go?

THE PRESIDENT: I have a farm away over on the other side of the road, way back and that has five or six hundred acres in it.

Q. I thought your estate was more than a hundred acres where the family house is?

THE PRESIDENT: Oh, no. You see my sister-in-law's place is next door.

Q. This, of course, will be private during your lifetime?

THE PRESIDENT: No, no; Oh, my, no.

Q. The minute you leave here it goes to the public?

THE PRESIDENT: As soon as they can get it arranged.

NOTE: The general plan and purposes of the library are outlined in this press conference and in the statement which I read to the reporters and which was later released to the press. As of June 1, 1941, the library building has been completed with funds raised by private subscription; and the various pictures, papers, books, ship models, etc., have already started to be moved into it in large quantities. The building has been constructed on land donated by me to the United States.

The library was formally dedicated on June 30, 1941.

From the time of the first President of the United States, it has been the universal custom for each outgoing President to take with him, as his own personal property, all the correspondence, documents, and papers which had come to the White House during his term of office. Apparently the same practice has prevailed among the outgoing Prime Ministers of Great Britain.

President Washington, for example, sent all his papers to Mount Vernon; and it was not until 1832 that a substantial portion of them were obtained by the State Department through purchase. By dint of conscientious activity over many years, the Library of Congress now, at last, has about 95 per cent of the known surviving papers of the first President.

The public papers of President John Adams and President John Quincy Adams have been closed by deeds of trust against research purposes until 1955. They are owned by descendants of these Presidents.

The main collection of Jefferson papers was eventually purchased by the government for the Library of Congress; but many of his papers are still scattered in various libraries and historical societies.

The papers of President Madison, including all the notes on the Federal Convention, did not come into possession of the United States until they were bought in 1848. Even thereafter a great portion of his papers turned up at private auction in 1892, and only recently have been contributed to the Library of Congress.

Papers of President Monroe, although the bulk of them are preserved in the Library of Congress, can be found in large quantities in private collections, public libraries, and in the Capitals of Great Britain and Russia.

The Lincoln papers in the possession of the Library of Congress will not be accessible until 1947; two other large collections are owned by private citizens; and the Illinois State Historical Society Library has a substantial portion of them.

It is generally believed that many of the papers of Presidents William H. Harrison, Tyler, Fillmore, Lincoln, Grant, and Harding have been burned.

Until very recent times it has been necessary for the Library of Congress to go out and purchase, or obtain gifts, of the papers of the Presidents.

Research has shown that invaluable papers of Ex-Presidents have been destroyed by widows, servants, and executors for one reason or another; or distributed about to relatives, friends, admirers, and autograph collectors and purchasers. Even such collections as have been deposited in private historical societies or in memorial libraries have been privately owned and controlled, rather than dedicated to public ownership and research.

The fact is that, although the Library of Congress has done a magnificent job in building up its collections of Presidential papers, few of these collections are today intact. Although in recent times Ex-Presidents and their families have designated the Library of Congress as the depository for most of their papers, there have generally been important restrictions on their use.

President Herbert Hoover has constructed a private library building at Stanford University, California, known as the "Hoover Library on War, Revolution, and Peace," for his own collection of papers and correspondence.

Because of this sad history of the dissipation and destruction of the papers of former Presidents, I gave serious consideration to the problem of the best way of handling my own public papers and correspondence and documents.

I came to the conclusion that, as soon after I left the White House as possible, they should all be turned over to the United States, as public property rather than as a private collection. I determined that they should be located in a spot generally accessible to the general public, and to scholars and students; that they should be stored in a building large enough to accommodate not only my own papers, but also the papers of all the leading public officials of the United States during my Administration who are willing to donate them; that they should be under the ownership, care and management of the United States Government; and that they should be open

to scholars and historians as soon as practicable, with due concern for the interests of the United States and for the living personalities of our day.

I think that historians of the future will agree that commencing with March 4, 1933, a definitely new era in the history of our country was inaugurated. Whether these historians and future generations will approve or disapprove the philosophy and government action during this era, I do not think it will be disputed by any of them or by any one else that it has marked a new period in American social, economic, and political history.

Accordingly, after consulting with an advisory committee consisting of leading historians, statesmen, and scholars in the United States, I decided to try to create a central library, for study and research into the history of this particular period of time in American life. It is my hope that the leaders of government and political and economic thought, associated with me in the administration of government affairs during these years, will also contribute their own papers and documents to this central repository, to which future students of this period may come to carry on their research.

I decided to construct this public institution at Hyde Park, New York, because I believe that we should begin to decentralize the collection of original historical documents in America, instead of concentrating them all in the city of Washington. The danger from fire, war, and other calamities is thereby reduced. The problems of storage and administration militate against concentration of all source materials for American history in a few great repositories. Modern facilities for transportation and communication, and modern photographic methods of reproduction should encourage and stimulate an increase in the number of research centers in American history.

Furthermore, the location of the library near my own residence will enable me, in later years, to assist in the arrangement, maintenance, and development of the collection.

The Congress has adopted legislation accepting the gift of the land and building to the United States. It is now under the jurisdiction of the Archivist of the United States and is being at present administered by him.

Part of the material which is now gradually being moved into the library will include the following general classes:

1. Public and personal papers. These include practically all my incoming, and copies of practically all my outgoing, correspondence, as well as other material, covering the years of my services as New York State Senator, 1910-13; as Assistant Secretary of the Navy, 1913-20; as Governor of New York, 1929-33; and as President of the United States. They include also a large volume of political material, especially material relating to the Presidential campaigns of 1920, 1924, 1928, 1932, 1936, and 1940; and an accumulation of other material of a miscellaneous character. The amount of correspondence which has come into the White House has been all out of line with that of preceding Administrations. It has been coming in at a daily average of over 4,000 per day, and the number of communications now in the White House files total many million pieces.

2. Many historical manuscripts, maps, paintings, etc. These consist of material relating to American history, especially the history of the American Navy since 1775, which, over a period of many years, I have collected from various sources. They include letters, log books, and other manuscripts; and also paintings, drawings, prints, and models of many famous American naval vessels.

3. A large portion of the books and pamphlets, on general subjects, which are in my own library.

It will be seen that a great deal of this material does not relate, strictly speaking, to the so-called New Deal Administrations. That part of it which is composed of my earlier writings and correspondence, political as well as economic and governmental, however, may be of historical value to those seeking appraisal of the development of this period, and of the philosophy and social doctrines which prevailed in it.

The rest of the collection will form part of a sort of museum which some people, in the future, might want to come to see as constituting a part of the daily life of one who served as their President. There is some value in having these items, which are always the object of interest to people, all in one place, to be visited conveniently by those who care to do so. They will be under government ownership and care, instead of the private ownership which controls some of the homes and collections of other Presidents.

I hope that this project will serve as a precedent for future Presidents, so that the rich sources of our history will be preserved for future generations who will want to study our times and our manner of life (see also on this subject Item 158, 1939 volume).

157 ❡ Increasing the Amount of Authorizations for the Federal Housing Administration.
December 13, 1938

My dear Mr. McDonald:

I HAVE your letter of December 6, 1938, in which you state that the unobligated balance of the present limitation of $2,000,000,000 on the aggregate amount of principal obligations of all mortgages insured and outstanding at any one time was $415,000,000 on December 1, 1938, and in which you recommend that the present limitation be increased to $3,000,000,000.

It is obvious from the statements in your letter that the present limitation will soon be reached and, if you are to continue insuring all eligible applications presented to you for the remainder of this fiscal year and for the fiscal year 1940, it will be necessary for you to have an increase in the present authorization.

Therefore, in accordance with the authority contained in Section 203 (a) of the National Housing Act, as amended, I hereby approve an increase of $1,000,000,000 in the amount of outstanding principal of mortgages which may be insured by the Federal Housing Administration, making an aggregate of $3,000,000,000.

Sincerely yours,

Honorable Stewart McDonald,
Administrator, Federal Housing Administration,
Washington, D. C.

NOTE: The original terms of the National Housing Act of 1934 provided that the aggregate total amount of all mortgages insured by the Federal Housing Administration on existing and future houses should not exceed $2,000,-000,000. Feeling that this limit placed a ceiling upon the amount of construction loans which could be insured, I recommended the liberalization of this provision in 1937 (see Item 157, 1937 volume). Pursuant to my recommendation, the Congress amended Section 203 (a) of the National Housing Act of February 3, 1938, to provide that the total amount of principal obligations of all mortgages insured and outstanding *at any one time* should not exceed $2,000,000,000, except that with the President's approval this amount could be raised to $3,000,000,000.

On December 6, 1938, Mr. Stewart McDonald, the then Administrator of the Federal Housing Administration, wrote me that the amount of mortgages insured was approaching dangerously close to the $2,000,000,000 limit set in the law. He pointed out that whereas the unobligated balance of the $2,000,000,000 insurance authorization was $415,000,000, nevertheless applications for mortgage insurance were being received at the rate of more than $100,000,000 a month, and mortgages in the process of appraisal amounted to $115,-000,000.

With these considerations in mind, it became obviously necessary to raise the limit to $3,000,-000,000 if the program of the Federal Housing Administration was to proceed at the same pace.

It was again necessary to raise this limit on November 8, 1940, when, acting under the 1939 amendments to the National Housing Act, I approved a limit of $4,000,000,000 (see Item 131, 1940 volume).

158 ❧ Indorsing University Scholarships for Refugees from Germany. December 14, 1938

My dear Mr. Lane:

I HAVE received your letter of December 2, 1938, and am deeply interested to note the plans which the President and Corporation of Harvard University and the student body are making to provide for scholarships and support for refugees of all creeds from Germany.

This program appears to be in the best traditions of the University, and I sincerely hope that it will be taken up by other institutions throughout the country.

Very sincerely yours,

Mr. Robert E. Lane,
Harvard Committee
To Aid German Student Refugees,
Cambridge, Massachusetts.

159 ❧ Address at Groundbreaking for the Thomas Jefferson Memorial, Washington, D. C. December 15, 1938

Mr. Gibboney, Members of the Thomas Jefferson Memorial Commission:

NEARLY a hundred years ago, the Congress of the United States, in response to a general public demand, undertook to provide a memorial in the Nation's Capital to the first President of the United States, George Washington. There followed many years of controversy both as to the type of memorial and as to its location. The Washington Monument emerged as the result of Congressional action.

Half a century ago, again in response to public demand, the

Congress began the consideration of a monument to the memory of Abraham Lincoln, the preserver of the Union. Years went by and a distinguished committee, following the broad objectives of the original plan for the development of the National Capital, recommended the creation of two broad axes in the general form of a cross—one axis from the Capitol through the Mall past the Washington Monument to the river bank, and the other axis from the White House past the Washington Monument to another point near the river.

In line with this well considered plan, the Congress erected the Lincoln Memorial at the end of the longer axis and it was then the clear intention both of the Congress and of the many planning committees and commissions who studied the subject to complete the other axis from the White House to the river by the erection of a public monument at the fourth corner of the cross.

For far more than fifty years, Thomas Jefferson, the third President of the United States, has been recognized by our citizens not only for the outstanding part which he took in the drafting of the Declaration of Independence itself, not only for his authorship of the Virginia statute for religious freedom, but also for the services he rendered in establishing the practical operation of the American Government as a democracy and not as an autocracy.

For very many years, it has seemed appropriate that with Washington and Lincoln, his services should be held in memory by the erection of a monument of equal dignity. We are breaking ground, today, for such a memorial. The Congress of the United States, through a distinguished Commission, has, after long consideration, chosen this site and made the first appropriations for the creation of the Thomas Jefferson Memorial.

In the days to come, the millions of American citizens who each year visit the National Capital will have a sense of gratitude that at last an adequate permanent National Memorial to Thomas Jefferson has been placed at this beautiful spot because as the Joint Resolution of the Congress says: "The American people feel a deep debt of gratitude to Thomas Jefferson" and "honor the services rendered by him."

160 ❡ A Letter in Behalf of Giving Aid to the Spanish Sufferers. December 19, 1938

My dear Mr. McDonald:

FACTUAL REPORTS on conditions in Spain give me deep concern over the extreme hardships and sufferings there of millions of civilians and particularly of the women and children.

Since the outset of the war in Spain the American Red Cross has expended a considerable sum in emergency assistance to Americans stranded in that country and in humanitarian work in the territories of both factions through the International Red Cross Committee. In view, however, of the increased suffering in Spain, the American Red Cross recently contributed the funds necessary to secure 60,000 barrels of flour for impartial distribution among the women and children in proportion to need in order to prevent starvation.

For this purpose the Red Cross obtained wheat from the Federal Surplus Commodities Corporation at a nominal cost and the United States Maritime Commission provided free ocean transportation to France. The Red Cross paid the cost of processing the wheat into flour, the rail transportation and other incidental charges and thus by an expenditure of some $66,000 it was able to furnish flour to the value of about $250,000.

The flour thus furnished by the Red Cross was distributed under the supervision of the American Friends Service Committee which has been carrying on impartial relief activities in Spain. The aid thus far rendered by the American Red Cross and the American Friends Service Committee has been of inestimable value but wholly inadequate to meet the needs. The 60,000 barrels of flour which were shipped will be entirely consumed by the end of January. Every effort should, therefore, be made to supplement considerably what has been done in order to prevent starvation on a wide scale.

I am informed by the American Red Cross that in view of its many other activities and responsibilities in this country and its other fields of work, it is unable to devote additional funds to relief in Spain or to undertake a campaign for contributions for this purpose. It, nevertheless, desires to make its services available and to assist in every other possible way in coping with this distressing situation.

Other countries are also rendering impartial assistance to civilians in Spain but it is estimated that some 500,000 bushels of wheat, representing about 100,000 barrels of flour per month, will be required for the next six months to meet the minimum needs of the women and children for bread alone. The Federal Surplus Commodities Corporation has, accordingly, offered to make available to the Red Cross this quantity of wheat for the next six months to be processed into flour at the same advantageous terms. To the extent that the United States Maritime Commission has empty space, it will transport this flour to France free of charge.

To carry out such a program will require approximately $500,000 to cover the cash outlay for the processing of the flour and other incidental costs. It was therefore thought advisable to form a committee to act in cooperation with the American Friends Service Committee in raising the necessary funds. The funds raised by the Committee are to be applied to cover the cost of additional flour and other surplus commodities which will be secured and made available through the American Red Cross. Thus, for every dollar contributed, it will be possible to furnish food for relief to the value of some four dollars.

Mr. Norman H. Davis, Chairman of the American Red Cross, has informed me of his conversation with you, of your sympathetic interest and of your willingness to serve as Chairman of the proposed Committee. I understand that Mr. Clarence Pickett of the American Friends Service Committee will confer with you regarding the membership and work of your Committee.

This is a great humanitarian service and your acceptance of the Chairmanship of the Committee is deeply appreciated by me. I am sure that many of our people will wish to aid in helping to meet this pressing need.

Very sincerely yours,

George McDonald, Esq.,
149 Broadway,
New York, N. Y.

(See also Item 8, this volume, and Item 41, 1940 volume, for similar Red Cross aid to the Chinese and the peoples in the invaded Low Countries.)

161 ❲ Christmas Greetings to Disabled Veterans. December 19, 1938

To you, who in time of national peril, have defended your country with courage, fortitude and heroic self-sacrifice, I extend my heartfelt holiday greetings. It is my earnest wish and that of an ever grateful nation that for you and those dear to you this Christmas season will be one of happiness and hope, and that the New Year will see your restoration to comfort and health in a happy nation long destined, in the Providence of God, to remain at peace.

162 ❲ Christmas Greetings to the Army and Navy. December 24, 1938

It gives me great pleasure to send my most cordial and hearty Christmas greetings to the Army and the Navy. Events of the past twelve months have served to focus public attention on the national defense and to bring home to all of our people a greater appreciation of the protective missions of our land and sea forces. The nation is grateful to its democratic armed forces, volunteers to a man, for their whole-hearted devotion to duty. It is my sincere hope that this holiday season will bring happiness and good cheer to all who wear the uniform of our republic.

163 ❨ Address on Lighting the Community Christmas Tree, Washington, D. C. December 24, 1938

Tonight is Christmas Eve. We are gathered again around our Community Tree here in Lafayette Park, across the street from the White House. Darkness has fallen over the Capital but all about us shine a myriad of brilliant lights. All our hearts, warmed by the eternal fire of Christmas rejoice, because new life, new hope, new happiness are in them.

In this setting I wish my fellow countrymen everywhere a Merry Christmas with peace, content and friendly cheer to all. I wish also to thank the thousands who have remembered me and my family this Christmas with individual greetings. We shall always treasure these friendly messages.

At this time let us hope that the boon of peace which we in this country and in the whole Western Hemisphere enjoy under the Providence of God may likewise be vouchsafed to all nations and all peoples. We desire peace. We shall work for peace. We covet neither the lands nor the possessions of any other nation or people.

We of the Western World who have borne witness by works as well as words to our devotion to the cause of peace, ought to take heart tonight from the atmosphere of hope and promise in which representatives of twenty-one free republics are now assembled in the Pan-American Conference at Lima, Peru. I consider it a happy circumstance that these deliberations will be successfully concluded soon after the birthday of the Prince of Peace. It is indeed a holy season in which to work for good will among men. We derive new strength, new courage for our work from the spirit of Christmas.

We do not expect a new Heaven and a new Earth overnight, but in our own land, and other lands — wherever men of good will listen to our appeal — we shall work as best we can with the instruments at hand to banish hatred, greed and covetousness from the heart of mankind.

And so the pledge I have so often given to my own countrymen I renew before all the world on this glad Christmas Eve, that I shall do whatever lies within my own power to hasten the day foretold by Isaiah, when men "shall beat their swords into ploughshares and their spears into pruning hooks; nation shall not lift up sword against nation, neither shall they learn war any more."

Index

Index

Index

Index

670

Index

672

Index

674

675

Index

Index

Index by Dr. Kenneth W. Hechler of Columbia University